HUMAN RESOURCE
MANAGEMENT

WILEY SERIES IN MANAGEMENT

HUMAN RESOURCE MANAGEMENT

Fifth Edition

David A. De Cenzo
Towson State University

Stephen P. Robbins
San Diego State University

John Wiley & Sons, Inc.
New York • Chichester • Brisbane • Toronto • Singapore

ACQUISITIONS EDITOR	Petra Sellers
ASSISTANT EDITOR	Ellen Ford
MARKETING MANAGER	Leslie Hines
SENIOR PRODUCTION EDITORS	John Rousselle/Edward Winkleman
ASSISTANT MANUFACTURING MANAGER	Mark Cirillo
ASSOCIATE PHOTO EDITOR	Lisa Passmore
PHOTO RESEARCHER	Susan Christenson
SR. FREELANCE ILLUSTRATION COORDINATOR	Jaime Perea

This book was set in New Baskerville by Progressive Information Technologies and printed and bound by Donnelley/Willard. The cover was printed by Phoenix Color.

Library of Congress Cataloging-in-Publication Data
De Cenzo, David A.
   Human resource management/David A. De Cenzo, Stephen P. Robbins.
—5th ed.
       p.   cm.

   Includes indexes.
   ISBN 0-471-12420-6 (cloth: alk. paper)
   1. Personnel management. I. Robbins, Stephen P., 1943–   .
II. Title.

HF5549.D396   1996
658.3—dc20   95-35625
                                                                                              CIP

Printed in the United States of America

10 9 8 7 6 5 4 3 2 1

Preface

Welcome to the fifth edition of our Human Resource Management text. We're glad you're taking the time to read this preface so as to get a better overview of this book. We'll use this section to address three important things: what this book is about, the important in-text learning aids, and who, besides the authors named on the cover, were instrumental in the book's development.

ABOUT THE BOOK

When we began discussing how to revise the fourth edition, we set a number of goals for ourselves. Our primary goal was to write a text that addressed the most critical issues in Human Resource Management (HRM). Over the past decade, management practice has gone through some dramatic changes. Those include work force diversity, downsizing, reengineering, total quality manage- ment (TQM), outsourcing, and rediscovering the importance of satisfying the customer. These changes have implica- tions for HRM. For example, as more or- ganizations reengi- neer their processes, many have replaced fulltime employees with contingent work- ers. A contingent work force presents new HRM challenges in areas such as train- ing, career development, and motivation. Societal and organizational change means that traditional HRM practices need to also change accordingly. A text for the late 1990s must reflect these changes while simulta- neously presenting the basic concepts of HRM. We have tried to achieve this delicate balance, presenting the basic HRM functions of getting, training, moti- vating, and keeping people, while also discussing the new world of HRM.

This book meets all the content knowledge areas specified by the Human Resource Certification Institute.

Interestingly, some of the "cutting edge" issues we presented in the fourth edition have now become a basic part of HRM. For instance, TQM and continu- ous process improvements introduced in our last edition are now part of main- stream HRM operation. Reinforcing TQM philosophies and supporting this ef- fort has made HRM an even more vital component of the management team. Similarly, the strategic nature of HRM continues to gain acceptance as more or- ganizations look to ensure that they have the "right" people at the right time.

In a dynamic field like HRM, a completely updated research base is a must.

You want to know, after all, the current state of the field. We have undertaken an extensive literature review to include hundreds of 1993 and 1994 citations from business periodicals and academic journals in this text. For example, the following is a partial list of the new topics in this edition, with chapter locations where they are first introduced: contingent workers (Chapter 2); decentralized work sites (Chapter 2); employee involvement (Chapter 2); up-to-date coverage of laws and Supreme Court rulings affecting HRM, including the latest on sexual harassment (Chapter 3); sexual orientation rights (Chapter 4); the family-friendly organization (Chapter 5); selection for self-managed teams (Chapter 7); 360-degree performance appraisal (Chapter 12); workplace violence (Chapter 15); and domestic partner benefits (Chapter 16). To facilitate integration of important current issues, we've used three themes throughout the text: International HRM, Equal Employment Opportunity, and Ethical Decisions in HRM. These will be found either as sections in selected chapters or as highlighted vignettes.

We also recognize that in HRM, as in a number of other fields, job success requires practical skills. Therefore, we've included skills boxes in many of the chapters in the text. These presentations provide a step-by-step basis for handling a particular facet of HRM. For example, in Chapter 3, we describe the steps you should follow to protect your organization from sexual harassment charges. Furthermore, we have included three appendices that focus on specific students' needs: "Making a Good Impression—Writing the Resume"; "The Critical Meeting—Improving Interviewing Skills"; and "Research in HRM."

Although practical skills are important, so, too, is thinking about the future. One of the most far-reaching trends, at least from an HRM perspective, is that jobs are disappearing. Jobs are not only being transferred to low-cost-labor countries and reduced through downsizing, but the whole notion of jobs as we know it seems to be changing. Global competition, downsizing, restructuring, and contingent workers have all had an impact. What will HRM be like if the organization is "de-jobbed?" We've attempted to answer that question in a number of places in the text.

LEARNING AIDS

Material

Our experience has led us to conclude that a text becomes highly readable when the writing is straightforward and conversational, the topics flow logically, and the authors make extensive use of examples to illustrate concepts. These factors guided us in developing this text as a highly effective learning tool. Previous text users have regularly commented on how clearly our books present ideas. We think this one, too, is written in a clear, lively, concise, and conversational style. Furthermore, our classroom experience tells us that students remember and understand concepts and practices most clearly when they are illustrated through examples. So we've used a wealth of examples to clarify ideas.

Each chapter of this book was organized to provide clarity and continuity. Each begins with Learning Objectives, which identify specifically what the reader should gain after reading the chapter. At the end of each chapter is a Summary section, which relates chapter material specifically to the learning objectives. There is a Key Terms section at the end of each chapter; these terms are defined in the margins and also in the glossary of the book.

Have you had students tell you that they read the assignments and thought they understood the material, but still didn't do well on the exam? Well, we have both had this experience and know that many students have, too. We decided, therefore, to do something about it. That *something* is the Testing Your Understanding questions at the end of each chapter. These questions are designed to assist readers in determining if they understood the chapter material. In most cases, questions link directly to the learning objectives. We've answered each of these questions for readers, and have provided the corresponding page in the text where the question came from. These questions have been specifically written to challenge your critical thinking, and generally require some application from the chapter's content.

We close out each chapter with an experiential exercise and a case application. These exercises and cases were specifically selected to reinforce material included in the chapter. Furthermore, each case represents an actual HRM situation faced by an actual organization.

Supporting Material

This book is supported by a comprehensive learning package that helps instructors create a motivating environment and provides students with additional instruments for understanding and reviewing major concepts. The Instructor's Resource Guide developed by Vicki Kamen, Colorado State University, provides many useful items, including sample syllabi, learning objectives, key concepts, chapter overview, chapter outline, lecture suggestions, review and discussion questions, media resources, and the additional case per chapter.

The Test Bank, developed by Trudy Somers, Towson State University, consists of approximately 1800 multiple-choice, true/false, and completion questions categorized by level of difficulty, text-page reference, and learning objective being tested. The Test Bank is available in paper form and in a computerized version called MICROTEST.

A set of full-color transparency acetates visually highlights key concepts and figures found in the text.

New to this edition is the *Wiley/Nightly Business Report Business Video Series.* This exciting collection of timely news stories has been prepared and developed by the best known and most highly respected business news program on public TV. A variety of clips provide students and professors with up-to-date insights into what's making news in the field of human resource management in the 90s. Topics include employee diversity, teamwork, training, health care and other benefits, legal issues, labor management relations, among others.

ACKNOWLEDGMENTS

Getting a finished book into a reader's hands requires the work of many people. The authors do their part by developing an outline, researching topics, and keyboarding sentences into their computers. But that only starts the process. A lot of other people contribute to the making and marketing of a textbook. We'd like to recognize just a few of the people who contributed to this text.

First of all are our reviewers. The reviewers for the fifth edition were fantastic. They gave us great feedback and provided some insight to us. The book you have before you is a much better learning tool because of our reviewers' insights. We cannot thank them enough, and hope that they see the benefits of their work. Specifically, we wish to recognize Joel Neuman, SUNY—New Paltz; Nestor St. Charles, Dutchess Community College; Edwin C. Leonard, Indiana

University/Purdue University; Philip Adler, Jr., Georgia State University; Mary A. Gowan, University of Texas at El Paso; Kate Laskowitz, Purdue University; Jusanne M. Vest, University of Southern Mississippi;; and Janice M. Feldbauer, Austin Community College.

A book doesn't simply appear automatically on bookstore shelves. It gets there through the combined efforts of many people. For us, this is the outstanding publishing team at John Wiley & Sons. Our acquisitions editors, Whitney Blake and Petra Sellers and our assistant editor, Ellen Ford, worked very closely with us throughout this project. Thank you again for all you did to bring this text to completion. We would also like to recognize a number of other Wiley people who gave their time and energy to bring this text to you, including: Leslie Hines, Marketing Manager; John Rousselle and Edward Winkleman, Senior Production Editors; Pete Noa, Senior Designer; Lisa Passmore, Associate Photo Editor; Jaime Perea, Senior Freelance Illustration Coordinator; and Mark Cirillo, Assistant Manufacturing Manager. We'd also like to thank Trudy Somers for her work in the "Testing Your Understanding" questions.

Last, we want to acknowledge a few people individually. For Dave, once again I wish to thank my family. My wife, Terri, gives me the opportunity to write for long hours, and my lovely kids—Mark, Meredith, Gabriella, and (new to this edition) Natalie—put up with a Dad who constantly reminds them not to touch his computer. Guess they'll get their own computer and lower my blood pressure in preparation for the sixth edition!

Steve wants to thank those organizations that provided his support team. This includes Restaurant Express, Take-Out Taxi, Sound Cleaning, Performance Shoes, Smart Mercedes, Four-Seasons Dry Cleaning, Blockbuster Video, and the Management of Harbor Properties.

_____
David A. De Cenzo

_____
Stephen P. Robbins

Brief Contents

Contents

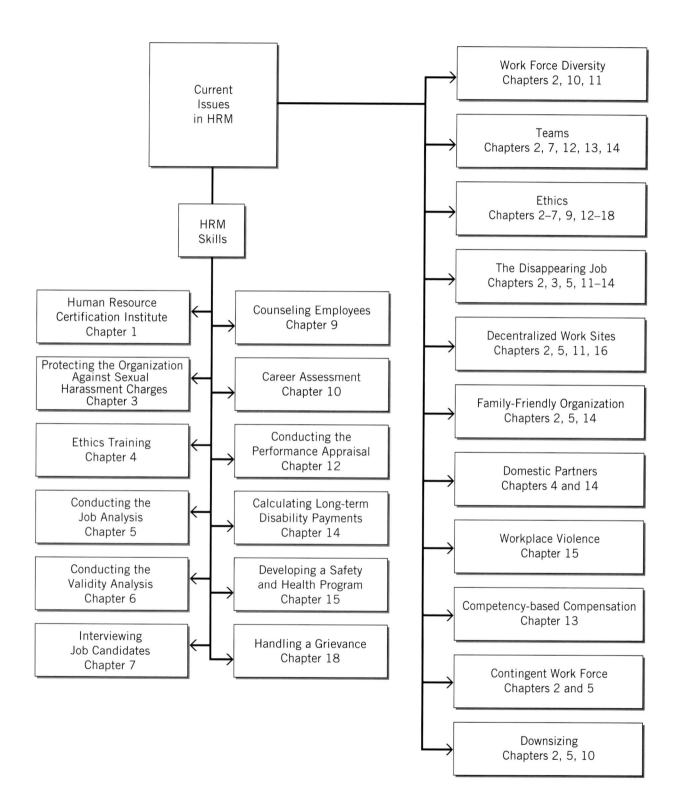

Current
Issues
in HRM

HRM
Skills

Work Force Diversity
Chapters 2, 10, 11

Teams
Chapters 2, 7, 12, 13, 14

Ethics
Chapters 2–7, 9, 12–18

The Disappearing Job
Chapters 2, 3, 5, 11–14

Decentralized Work Sites
Chapters 2, 5, 11, 16

Family-Friendly Organization
Chapters 2, 5, 14

Domestic Partners
Chapters 4 and 14

Workplace Violence
Chapter 15

Competency-based Compensation
Chapter 13

Contingent Work Force
Chapters 2 and 5

Downsizing
Chapters 2, 5, 10

**Human Resource
Certification Institute**
Chapter 1

**Protecting the Organization
Against Sexual
Harassment Charges**
Chapter 3

Ethics Training
Chapter 4

**Conducting the
Job Analysis**
Chapter 5

**Conducting the
Validity Analysis**
Chapter 6

**Interviewing
Job Candidates**
Chapter 7

Counseling Employees
Chapter 9

Career Assessment
Chapter 10

**Conducting the
Performance Appraisal**
Chapter 12

**Calculating Long-term
Disability Payments**
Chapter 14

**Developing a Safety
and Health Program**
Chapter 15

Handling a Grievance
Chapter 18

Chapter One

INTRODUCTION TO HUMAN RESOURCE MANAGEMENT

LEARNING OBJECTIVES

AFTER READING THIS CHAPTER, YOU WILL BE ABLE TO:

1. Define management and identify its primary functions.
2. Discuss the importance of human resources management.
3. Describe what is meant by the term *human resource management*.
4. Explain what environmental influences affect human resource management.
5. Describe how management practices affect human resource management.
6. Discuss the effect of labor unions on human resource management.
7. Outline the components and the goals of the staffing, training, and development functions.
8. List the components and goals of the motivation and the maintenance functions of human resource management.
9. Outline the major activities in the employment, training and development, compensation and benefits, and employee relations departments of human resource management.
10. Explain how human resource management practices differ in small businesses and in an international setting.

"Good morning, staff," said Austin Miller, vice-president of human resource management (HRM). "I'm glad you were able to clear your calendars for this important planning meeting. It's time once again for us to take a look at where we've been, and what issues need addressing as we continue to support this organization's strategic directions. Even though we meet regularly to discuss day-to-day activities, I feel it's prudent for us to have these planning sessions to reassess our value added to this corporation. So, now that you have settled in, let me start by giving you my 'state-of-HRM' recap.

"We have been providing a first-class service to our clients. Over the past couple of years, we have worked diligently to put in place many of the programs that have truly aided this company. For example, we now have our flexible benefits program fully functioning. In its first year alone, we were able to cut corporate benefit costs by 23 percent. We were also one of the first in the area to implement a detailed policy on sexual harassment. But a policy alone wouldn't suffice. We effectively enlightened each employee of this organization about the policy, and what is unacceptable behavior. We have helped design training programs that support senior management's total quality management (TQM) program. And let me remind you of these findings just released by our president. Through TQM efforts, productivity has improved more than 16 percent in the past twelve months. Much of this productivity increase has been attributable to our changing emphasis from specialized jobs to ones that have a more employee-involved, team approach. But as you know, doing this required management to restructure our work processes and the company. This meant that we had to support the corporation in its downsizing efforts. I'm proud of how we responded to this difficult task. We helped the affected workers by ensuring that open communications about the planned action was available to organizational members, and those that were laid off had all the necessary information a separating employee would need. Of course, our work in these areas must continue. While major layoffs appear to be over, we still have to be aware of the survivors' well-being. As you know, we lost one of our team members, and the critical work she performed is now being picked up by each of you. Accordingly, we will need to assist organizational members, and ourselves, in how to do more, with less.

"Although I could go on about our accomplishments, we cannot take the position that we've succeeded. On the contrary, there are new challenges ahead. Let me address some of the more important issues facing us over the next few years.[1]

"Organizations have evolved tremendously over the past decade. Change is no longer something that occurs in a controlled fashion. Rather, it is constantly before us, as we deal with the uncertainty brought about by a dynamic world. As such, we must train our managers to be more flexible in dealing with the changes that will arise. We must assist them in taking active roles in managing the change, as opposed to sitting back and helping them react to it. This means that we've got to retrain ourselves and other managers in terms of managerial competencies. Yet we cannot lose sight of the fact that all employees, not just managers, need this exposure. As we deal with the effects of changing the organizations's structure to one that is flatter and involves more work teams, we must be prepared to help those groups so that they can achieve their organizational goals.

"Closely aligned with these new job requirements will be our continued effort toward enhancing the skill levels of our workers. Today's jobs are more complex and require significant interaction with sophisticated technology. We must ensure that we have the right people for those jobs, which, in many cases, will require us to continuously train and upgrade our employees' skills. But keep in mind this will not be an easy task; all employees are not alike—either in skill level or in their backgrounds. Thus, we need to pay more attention to the diversity that exists in the work force.

"What do I mean by attention to diversity? By and large, I think that it means recognizing differences in people. We no longer have a homogeneous work force, but rather people from all walks of life. Accordingly, we need to be more sensitive to each person's background and their needs. In doing so, we can capitalize on the strengths that they bring to us. Consequently, we must advocate more acceptance of one another in the organization as we work toward achieving our common goals.

"In closing, let's not forget the continuing legislation that we face. Each day we make decisions that may be reviewed or questioned by people external to our organization. We must ensure that our HRM practices do not adversely affect any one group. We must give all employees an equal chance to realize their potential and fulfill their career dreams. When that happens, the organization can only benefit. But we can only do this by continuing to have in place effective HRM practices."

Introduction

When you reflect for a moment on Austin's comments, it is important to note that achieving organizational goals cannot be done without human resources. What is AT&T without its employees? A lot of buildings, expensive equipment, and some impressive bank balances. Similarly, if you removed the employees from such varied organizations as the Colorado Rockies baseball team, UPS, New York City government, or Motorola, what would you have left? Not much. It's people—not buildings, the equipment, or brand names—that make a company.[2]

This point is one that many of us take for granted. When you think about the millions of organizations that provide us with goods and services, any one or more of which will probably employ you during your lifetime, how often do you explicitly consider that these organizations depend on people to make them operate? Only under unusual circumstances, such as when you get put on hold for an hour on a company's toll-free customer-service line or when a major corporation is sued for a discriminatory HRM practice, that you recognize the important role that employees play in making organizations work. But how did these people come to be employees in their organizations? How were they selected? Why do they come to work on a regular basis? How do they know what to do on their jobs? How does management know if the employees are performing adequately? And if they are not, what can be done about it? Will today's employees

Austin Miller meets with her staff discussing HRM practices in the organization that must be designed to deal with such issues as globalization, downsizing, changing skill levels, corporate restructuring, and diversity.

be adequately prepared for the technologically advanced work the organization will require of them in the years ahead? What happens in an organization if a union is present?

These are some of the many questions whose answers lie in the subject of human resource management. Yet the field of HRM is not one that exists in isolation. Rather, it's part of the larger field of management. So, before we attempt to understand how an organization should manage its human resources, let's briefly review the essentials of management.

The Essentials of Management

Management is the process of efficiently achieving the objectives of the organization with and through people. To achieve its objective, management typically requires the coordination of several vital components that we call functions. The primary functions of management that are required are **planning**[3] (e.g., establishing goals), **organizing** (i.e., determining what tasks need to be completed to accomplish those goals), **leading** (i.e., ensuring that the right people are on the job with appropriate skills, and motivating them to levels of high productivity), and **controlling** (i.e., monitoring activities to ensure that goals are met). When these four functions operate in a coordinated fashion, we can say that the organization is heading in the correct direction toward achieving its objectives. Common to any effort to achieve objectives are three elements: goals, limited resources, and people.

In any discussion of management, one must recognize the importance of setting goals. Goals are necessary because activities undertaken in an organization must be directed toward some end. For instance, your goal in taking this class is to build a foundation of understanding HRM, and obviously, to pass the class (see the memo to students). There is considerable truth in the observation, "If you don't know where you are going, any road will take you there." The estab-

Management The process of efficiently getting activities completed with and through other people.

Planning A management function focusing on setting organizational goals and objectives.

Organizing A management function that deals with what jobs are to be done, by whom, where decisions are to be made, and the grouping of employees.

Leading A management function concerned with directing the work of others.

lished goals may not be explicit, but where there are no goals, there is no need for managers.

Limited resources are a fact of organizational life. Economic resources, by definition, are scarce; therefore, the manager is responsible for their allocation. This requires not only that managers be effective in achieving the established goals, but that they be efficient in doing so. Managers, then, are concerned with the attainment of goals, which makes them effective, and with the best allocation of scarce resources, which makes them efficient.

The need for two or more people is the third and last requisite for management. It is with and through people that managers perform their work. Daniel Defoe's legendary Robinson Crusoe could not become a manager until Friday's arrival.

In summary, managers are those who work with and through other people, allocating resources, in the effort to achieve goals. They perform their tasks through four critical activities—planning, organizing, leading, and controlling.

The Importance of Human Resource Management

Prior to the mid-1960s,[4] personnel departments in organizations were often perceived as the "health and happiness" crews.[5] Their primary job activities involved planning company picnics, scheduling vacations, enrolling workers for health-care coverage, and planning retirement parties. That has certainly changed during the past three decades.

Federal and state laws have placed many new requirements concerning hiring and employment practices on employers. Jobs have also changed. They have become more technical and require employees with greater skills. Furthermore, job boundaries are becoming blurred. In the past, a worker performed a job in a specific department, working on particular job tasks with others who did similar jobs. Today's workers are just as likely, however, to find themselves working on project teams with various people from across the organization. And, of course, global competition has increased the importance of organizations improving the productivity of their work force. This has resulted in the need for HRM specialists trained in psychology, sociology, organization and work design, and law. Federal legislation requires organizations to hire the best-qualified candidate without regard to race, religion, color, sex, or national origin—and someone has to ensure that this is done. Employees need to be trained to function effectively within the organization—and again, someone has to oversee this. Furthermore, once hired and trained, the organization has to provide for the continuing personal development of each employee. Practices are needed to ensure that these employees maintain their productive affiliation with the organizations. The work environment must be structured to induce workers to stay with the organization, while simultaneously attracting new applicants. Of course, the *someones* responsible for carrying out these activities are human resource professionals.

Today, professionals in the human resources area are vital elements in the success of any organization. Their jobs require a new level of sophistication that is unprecedented in human resources management.[6] Not surprisingly, their status in the organization has also been elevated.[7] Even the name has changed. Although the terms *personnel* and *human resource management* are frequently used interchangeably, it is important to note that the two connote quite different as-

●

Controlling A management function concerned with monitoring activities.

Memo

TO: Students reading this book

FROM: Dave DeCenzo and Steve Robbins

SUBJECT: How to get the most out of this text

All authors of a textbook generally include a preface section that describes why they wrote the book and what's unique about it, and then thank a lot of people for the role they played in getting the book completed. Well, we're no different; we did that, too. But it has become crystal-clear to us that two things are common about a book's preface. First, it's usually written for the professor, especially one who's considering selecting the book. Second, students don't read the preface. That's unfortunate, because it often includes information that students would find useful.

As authors, we listen to our customers. And many of ours have told us that they'd enjoy some input from us, but put where they can find it—not buried in the preface. So, we've written this memo. Our purpose is to provide you with our ideas about the book, how it was put together, and more importantly, how you can use it to better understand the field of HRM—and do better in this class!

This book was written to provide you with the foundations of HRM. Whether you intend to work in HRM or not, most of these elements will affect you at some point in your career. How? Take, for example, the performance appraisal. Although you might not currently be in a position to evaluate another individual's work performance, if you are working, you're more than likely to have your performance appraised. Consequently, it's important for you to have an understanding of how it should work, and the potential problems that may exist.

We began Part I of this book with the chapter you are now reading. The emphasis in Chapter 1 is to provide you with an overview of HRM, its approach, and its cast of characters. From there, we move to more global issues surrounding the HRM function. The environment in which HRM operates is changing rapidly, so we want you to get a feel for what is happening in the business world today and what implications it presents for HRM. Next, we need to turn our attention to the laws that affect HRM activities. Much of how HRM operates is guided by legislation and court decisions that prohibit practices that adversely affect certain groups of people. Without a good understanding of these laws, an organization's performance can suffer, and the organization can be vulnerable to costly lawsuits. Part I ends with a discussion of employee rights and a look at some ethical concerns influencing HRM.

Parts II through V provide coverage of the fundamental activities that exist in HRM. Part II explores the staffing function, with discussions on strategic human resource planning, recruiting, and selection. Part III addresses means for orienting, training, and developing employees. Part IV, the motivation function, reviews several areas designed to get the maximum effort from workers. Then, in Part V, we look at ways for management to keep high-performing employees.

Much of the discussion in Part II through V reflects typical activities in an organization that is not unionized. When a union is present, however, many of these practices might need modification to comply with another set of laws. As such, we reserved the final two chapters, Part VI, for dealing with labor–management relations.

While we are confident that completing six parts will provide the fundamentals of HRM, a book has to offer more. It should not only cover topics (we hope, in an interesting and lively way), it should also assist in the learning process. It should be written in such a way that you can understand it, it keeps your attention, and it provides you an opportunity for feedback. We think we've met each of these goals. Of course, only you can be the judge of our claim. But let's look at how we arrived at our conclusion.

To be understandable and lively means that we need to communicate with you. We make every attempt in this text to have it sound as if we were in front of your class speaking with you. Writing style is important to us. We use examples whenever possible—real companies, so you can see that what we talk about is happening in the "real world." In the past, people using our books have indicated that our writing style does help hold their attention. But the communication connection, albeit critical, is only half of the equation. The ultimate tests for you are: Does the book help you do well on exams? Does it help prepare you for a job?

We start every chapter with learning objectives. We view these as the critical learning points. They present a logic flow from which the material will be presented. If you can explain what is proposed in each learning objective, you'll be on the right track to understanding the material. But memory sometimes fools us. We read the material, think we understand it, see how the summaries directly tie the learning objectives together, then take the exam and receive a grade that is not reflective of "what we knew we knew." We have given a lot of thought to that issue, and think we've come up with something that will help—putting a feedback test in the book! Let's explain.

The typical textbook ends each chapter with a set of review questions. Unfortunately, your tests rarely look much like the review questions. Exams, for the most part, emphasize multiple-choice exams. So we've replaced the review questions with a set of test questions. These questions are actual questions that we've used to test our students' understanding of the material. If you can correctly answer these questions, then you're one step closer to enhancing your understanding of HRM. Recognize, of course, that these are only a learning aid. They help you to learn but don't replace careful reading or intensive studying. And don't assume that getting a question right means you fully understand the concept covered. Why? Because any set of multiple-choice questions can only test a limited range of information. So don't let correct answers lull you into a sense of false security. If you miss a question or don't fully understand why you got the correct response, go back to the corresponding pages in the chapter and reread the material. To help in this, the answer key we've provided will indicate the pages in the text from which each question was developed.

Learning, however, goes beyond just passing a test. It also means preparing yourself to perform successfully in tomorrow's organizations. You'll find that organizations today require their employees to work more closely together than at any time in the past. Call it teams, horizontal organizational structures, matrix management, or the like, the fact remains that your success will depend on how well you work closely with others. To help model this group concept for you, we have included a dozen class exercises in this text. Each of these experiential learning efforts is designed to highlight a particular topic in the text and give you an opportunity to work in groups to solve the issue at hand.

One last thing before we close: What can you take out of this course and use in the future? Many business leaders have complained about how business schools train their graduates. Although business schools have made many positive accomplishments, one critical component appears lacking—practical skills. The skills you need to succeed in today's business environment are increasing. You must be able to communicate, think creatively, make good and timely decisions, plan effectively, and deal with people. In HRM, we have an opportunity to build our skills bank. As you go through this text, you'll find a dozen or more practical skills that you can use on your job. We hope you give them special attention, practice them often, and add them to your repertoire.

If you'd like to tell us how we might improve the next edition of this book, we encourage you to write Dave DeCenzo at the Department of Management, Towson State University, Towson, Maryland 21204–7097; or e-mail him at DeCenzo-D@TowsonVX.Bitnet.

pects.[8] Once a solitary individual heading the personnel function, today the human resources department head may be a vice-president sitting on executive boards and participating in the development of the overall organizational strategy.[9] Companies today recognize the importance of people in meeting their goals. For instance, at Standard Chartered Bank and Sony Music Entertainment, people are "viewed as how each employee is important toward the organization achieving its strategic goals."[10] In return, these people have needs to be met. Consequently, when major decisions affecting the organization and its people are made by the company's executives, HR typically is present to represent the people side of the business (see "Meet Kathy McKee").

Many colleges and universities are also helping to prepare HRM professionals by offering concentrations and majors in the discipline. Additionally, there exists an accreditation process for HRM professionals. The Society for Human Resource Management offers opportunities for individuals to distinguish themselves in the field by achieving a level of proficiency that has been predetermined by the Human Resource Certification Institute as necessary for successful handling of human resources management affairs (see "HRM Skills").

Human Resource Management: A Closer Look

Human Resource Management Function in the organization concerned with the staffing, training, development, motivation, and maintenance of employees.

Human resource management is the part of the organization that is concerned with the "people" dimension. It is a staff, or support, function in the organization. Its role is to provide assistance in HRM matters to line employees, or those directly involved in producing the organization's goods and services. Every organization is comprised of people. Acquiring their services, developing their skills, motivating them to high levels of performance, and ensuring that they continue to maintain their commitment to the organization are essential to achieving organizational objectives. This is true regardless of the type of organization—government, business, education, health, recreation, or social action. Getting and keeping good people is critical to the success of every organization.

To look at HRM more specifically, we propose that it is an approach consisting of four functions—staffing, training and development, motivation, and maintenance. In less academic terms, we might say that HRM is made up of

Meet

Kathy McKee

Senior Vice-President of Human Resources,
Standard Chartered Bank

Kathy McKee is an individual with a vision. She intuitively knew that human resources played an integral role in helping an organization achieve its strategic goals. But is wasn't until 1993, about twenty years after her first human resources job, that she got the chance to prove her point.

Kathy McKee was an instrumental part of bringing about a successful blend of two companies. As vice-president of human resources at First Interstate Bank, Kathy was in the unenviable position of having to handle most of the HR activities associated with Standard Charter's acquisition of First Interstate. Interstate Bank had operations in Asia, Latin America, the United Kingdom, as well as the United States. Parts of these operations were being folded into Standard Charter, which at the time was 747 offices strong, located in sixty different countries, employing a diverse group of employees representing seventy different nationalities. With the acquisition came sweeping changes—layoffs, relocations, and the like. Expectedly, such actions were not always smoothly implemented. For example, in the Korean branch of First Interstate, workers were unhappy at the severance packages offered to them. And they reacted by taking the senior U.S. executive of the Bank hostage—until retention and bonus demands were met.

Chaotic as it appeared, McKee's skills in HR began to quickly shine. She worked closely with all the interested parties from both First Interstate and Standard Charter, focusing their attention to the value-addedness that could accrue when HR is viewed as a "strategic" partner. In this case, that meant showing Standard's management what HR could do for them in terms of "solving problems with good compensation packages and performance programs, putting in valuable retirement packages, and having a viable severance policy." Interestingly, she did this while not knowing if, once the dust settled in the acquisition, she would have a job.

The term *value added,* however, can often be viewed as a 1990s buzz word. McKee substantiates what is meant by the term. For instance, before the acquisition by Standard Charter, she developed corporate communications programs at First Interstate. These programs were designed to keep the 36,000-plus employees informed of their benefits programs. Additionally, through successful implementation of various benefit programs, she was able to reduce corporate pension costs and cut its long-term disability expenses by 50 percent. She also recognized that to provide excellent service to her customers, she needed an HRM function that did business differently. She reworked many of the function's work processes, centralizing specialized activities (like the long-term disability benefit), which led to significant cost savings for the company.

Today as senior vice-president of Standard Charter, Kathy McKee is responsible for all HR activities in the Bank's operations in the United States, Canada, and Central and South America. What she learned as she progressed in her career—as a recruiter, compensation and benefit management specialist, a trainer, labor-relations specialist, and affirmative action officer—has given her the skill base to make Standard Charter's HR division a critical cog in the Bank's success wheel.

Source: Story adapted from Linda Thornburg, "Moving HR to the Head Table," *HRMagazine* (August 1994), pp. 50–51.

HRM*Skills*

What skills and competencies are necessary for successful performance in HRM? Although it is extremely difficult to pinpoint exactly what competencies will serve you best when dealing with the uncertainties of human behavior, we can turn to the certifying body in HRM for answers. Specifically, the Human Resource Certification Institute (HRCI) suggests that certified HR practitioners must have exposure and an understanding in six specific areas of the field. These include management practices, selection and placement, training and development, compensation and benefits, employee and labor relations, and health, safety, and security. Let's briefly look at each one, and relate these specifically to the part of this book where they are addressed.

✔ Management Practices:

As a subset of management, HRM practitioners are required to have a general understanding of the field of management, its history and theories (especially those relating to the behavioral component), and the trends and their implications that exist today. Specific reference to text: Chapters 1, 2, and 11.

✔ Selection and Placement:

HRM practitioners require an understanding of how jobs are filled, the various methods of recruiting candidates, and the selection process. Emphasis in this area is on making good decisions about job candidates that use valid and reliable measures. Specific reference to text: The Staffing Function—Chapters 5, 6, and 7.

✔ Training and Development:

For employees to be successful in an organization, they must be trained and developed in the latest technologies and skills relevant to their current and future jobs. This means an understanding of adult learning methodologies, relating training efforts to organizational goals, and evaluating the effort. Specific reference to text: Chapters 8, 9, and 10.

✔ Compensation and Benefits:

One of the chief reasons people work is to fulfill needs. Intrinsic or extrinsic aside, one major need is compensation and benefits. Yet, these offerings are probably the most expensive offerings with respect to the employment relationship. As such, the HRM practitioner must understand the intricacies involved in establishing an effective, yet cost-effective compensation and benefits package. Specific reference to text: Chapters 12, 13, and 14.

✔ Employee and Labor Relations:

Working with employees requires an understanding of what makes employees function. Satisfying monetary needs alone will not have a lasting impact. Employees need to be kept informed and have an avenue in which to raise suggestions or complaints. When the case involves unionized workers, the HRM/Labor Relations practitioner must understand the various laws that affect the labor and management work relationship. Specific reference to text: Chapters 1, 16, 17, and 18.

✔ Health, Safety, and Security:

A basic need of individuals is the safety one must feel at the workplace. This means the freedom from physical and emotional harm. Mechanisms must be in place to provide a safe work environment for employees. Programs must permit the employee to seek assistance for those things affecting their happiness. Specific reference to text: Chapters 1, 4, and 15.

Source: Raymond B. Weinberg, Robert L. Mathis, and David C. Cherington, *Human Resource Certification Institute Certification Study Guide* (Alexandria, VA: Human Resource Certification Institute, 1991).

four activities: getting people, preparing them, stimulating them, and keeping them.

When one attempts to piece together an approach for human resource management, many variations and themes may exist. However, when we begin to focus on HRM activities as being subsets of the four functions, a clearer picture arises (see Figure 1-1). Let's take a closer look at each component.

The External Influences

The four HRM activities don't exist in isolation. Rather, they are highly affected by what is occurring outside the organization. It is important to recognize these **environmental influences** because any activity undertaken in each of the HRM processes is directly, or indirectly, affected by these external elements. For example, when a company downsizes its work force, does it lay off workers

Environmental Inflences Those factors outside the organization that directly affect HRM operations.

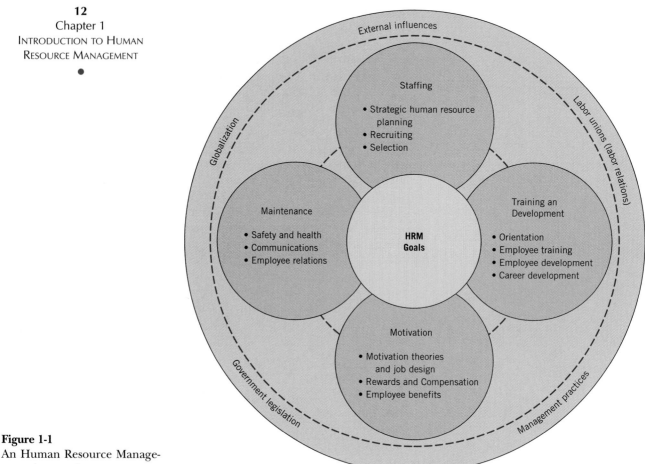

Figure 1-1
An Human Resource Management Approach

by seniority? If so, are an inordinate number of minority employees affected? Although any attempt to identify specific influences may prove insufficient, we can categorize them into four general areas—the dynamic environment, governmental legislation, labor unions, and current management practice.

The Dynamic Environment of HRM   It's been stated that the only thing that remains constant during our lifetimes is change (and paying taxes!). We must, therefore, prepare ourselves for events that have a significant effect on our lives. HRM is no different. Many events help shape our field. Some of the more obvious ones include globalization, work-force diversity, changing skill requirements, corporate downsizing, total quality management, reengineering work processes, decentralized work sites, and employee involvement. Although these topics are the focus of Chapter 2, let's briefly look at them now.

Globalization reflects the worldwide operations of many businesses today. We are no longer bound by continents or societal cultures. Work-force diversity includes the varied backgrounds of employees that are present in our companies today. Homogeneity of employees, and their needs, no longer exist. As Austin Millerson pointed out, our work today is more complex, requiring employees with sophisticated skills. Without them, many employees will lack the basic abilities to successfully perform in tomorrow's organizations.

How has Sears delt with the ever changing environment in which it faces? In part, to become more productive and to cut costs, they have eliminated thousands of jobs in the organization.

Corporate downsizing, total quality management, and reengineering all relate to one another. As the world changed, U.S. companies had to compete harder to maintain their leading industrial status. This meant doing things differently. In an effort to become more productive, organizations downsized to create greater efficiency by eliminating certain jobs. Of the jobs and work processes remaining, total quality management (TQM) looks at ways of improving job effectiveness. By continuously improving on methods, techniques, processes, and the like, companies made constant efforts to better what they produce. But what if what they produce, even if it's better, still doesn't satisfy the customer? In those cases, reengineering is necessary. Whereas TQM looks at new and improved ways of producing goods and services, reengineering looks at starting the processes over again from scratch. That is, instead of improving on an existing product, the organization would analyze what should be done and how they should do it. Searching for answers would not be constrained by current business practices.

Decentralized work sites are quickly becoming part of many organizations. With the technologies that are available (personal computers, fax machines, modems, etc.), work that was once done on the company premises may now be more cost-effectively handled at the employee's home. Lastly, employee involvement looks at how employees' work lives are changing. Involved employees now have more control over their jobs. Certain activities, like goal setting, were once the sole responsibility of managers. With employee involvement, such an action today permits participation.

Governmental Legislation Many employees today wishing to take several weeks of unpaid leave to be with their newborn children, and return to their previous job without any loss of seniority, have an easier time making the request. Although some employers may see such an application as negatively affecting the work flow, government legislation has given employees the right to take this leave. Laws supporting this and other employer actions are important to the HRM process. Listed in Figure 1-2 are a number of laws that have had a tremendous effect on HRM in organizations. We'll explore this critical area in depth in Chapter 3.

Labor Unions   Labor unions were founded and exist today to assist workers in dealing with the management of an organization. As the certified third-party representative, the union acts on behalf of its members to secure wages, hours, and other terms and conditions of employment. Another critical aspect of unions is that they promote and foster what is called a *grievance procedure,* or a specified process for the resolving of differences between workers and management. In many instances, this process alone constrains management from making unilateral decisions. For instance, a current HRM issue is the debate over employers' ability to terminate employees whenever they want. When a union is present and HRM practices are spelled out in a negotiated agreement, employ-

Figure 1-2
Some Laws Affecting HRM Practices

Year Enacted	Legislation	Focus of Legislation
1866	Civil Rights Act	prohibits discrimination based on race
1931	Davis–Bacon Act	paying prevailing wage rates
1935	Wagner Act	legitimized unions
1938	Fair Labor Standards Act	requires premium pay rates for overtime
1947	Taft–Hartley Act	balanced union power
1959	Landrum–Griffin Act	requires financial disclosure for unions
1963	Equal Pay Act	requires equal pay for equal jobs
1964	Civil Rights Act	prohibits discrimination
1967	Age Discrimination in Employment Act	adds age to protected group status
1970	Occupational Safety and Health Act	protects workers from workplace hazards
1974	Privacy Act	permits employees to review personnel files
1974	Employee Retirement Income and Security Act	protects employee retirement funds
1976	Health Maintenance Organization Act	requires alternative health insurance coverage
1978	Mandatory Retirement Act	raises mandatory retirement age from 65 to 70; uncapped in 1986
1986	Immigration Reform and Control Act	requires verification of citizenship or legal status in the United States
1986	Consolidated Omnibus Budget Reconciliation Act	provides for benefit continuation when laid off
1988	Employment Polygraph Protection Act	prohibits use of polygraphs in most HRM practices
1989	Plant Closing Bill	requires employers to give advance notice to affected employees
1990	Americans with Disabilities Act	prohibits discrimination against those with disabilities
1991	Civil Rights Act	overturns several Supreme Court cases concerning discrimination
1993	Family and Medical Leave Act	permits employees to take unpaid leave for family matters

ers cannot fire for unjustified reasons. Because of the complexities involved in operating under the realm of unionization and the special laws that pertain to it, we will defer that discussion until Chapters 17 and 18, when we will explore the unique world of labor relations and collective bargaining. However, although only about 12 percent of the work force is unionized, the effect unions have on other nonunion organizations, called the spillover effect, must be kept in perspective. That is, nonunion employees often look at what those in the unionized work force gain through contract negotiations. To maintain a nonunion status, then, HRM practices must be comparable to those where unions exist.

Management Thought   The last area of external influence is current **management thought.** Since the inception of the first personnel departments, management practices have played a major role in promoting today's HRM operations. Much of the emphasis has come from some of the early, and highly regarded, management theorists. Four individuals specifically are regarded as the forerunners of HRM support: Frederick Taylor, Hugo Munsterberg, Mary Parker Follet, and Elton Mayo.

Frederick Taylor, who is often regarded as the father of **scientific management,** developed a set of principles to enhance worker productivity. By systematically studying each job and detailing methods to attain higher productivity levels, Taylor's work was the first sense of today's human resource practices that we see. For instance, Taylor advocated that workers needed appropriate job training and should be screened according to their ability to do the job (a forerunner of skill-based hiring). Hugo Munsterberg and his associates made suggestions to improve methods of employment testing, training, performance evaluations, and job efficiency. Mary Parker Follet, a social philosopher, advocated people-oriented organizations. Her writings focused on groups as opposed to the individuals in the organization. Thus, Follet was one of the forerunners of today's teamwork concept and group cohesiveness. But probably the biggest advancement in HRM came from the works of Elton Mayo and his famous Hawthorne studies.

The **Hawthorne studies,** so named because they were conducted at the Hawthorne Plant of Western Electric just outside of Chicago, ran for nearly a decade beginning in the late 1920s. They gave rise to what today is called the *human relations movement.* The researchers found that informal work groups had a significant effect on worker performance. Group standards and sentiments were more important determinants of a worker's output than the wage incentive plan. Results of the Hawthorne studies justified many of the paternalistic programs that Human Resources managers have instituted in their organizations. We can point to the advent of employee benefit offerings, safe and healthy working conditions, and the concern by every manager for human relations as directly stemming from the work of Mayo and his associates at Hawthorne.[11]

In more modern times, we can see the influence of management practice affecting HRM in a variety of ways. Motivation techniques that have been cited in management literature, as well as W. Edwards Deming's influence on total quality management to enhance productivity, have made their way into HRM activities. Writers like Tom Peters and Peter Drucker emphasize employee involvement, teams, reengineering, total quality management, and the like. Implementing these will ultimately require the assistance of HRM professionals.

Now that you have a better picture of what affects this field, let's turn our attention to the functions and activities within HRM.

Management Thought Early theories of management that promoted today's HRM operations.

Scientific Management A set of principles designed to enhance worker productivity.

Hawthorne Studies A series of studies that provided new insights into group behavior.

The Staffing Function

Although recruiting is frequently perceived as the initial step in the staffing function, there are a number of prerequisites. Specifically, before the first job candidate is sought, the HR specialist must embark on strategic human resource planning (SHRP). This area alone has probably fostered the most change in human resources departments during the past fifteen years.

We can no longer hire individuals haphazardly. We must have a well-defined reason for needing individuals who possess specific skills, knowledge, and abilities that are directly likened to specific jobs required in the organization. The critical question then becomes, how do we know what jobs are critical? The answer to that question lies in the SHRP process. No longer does the HR manager exist in total darkness, or for that matter, in a reactive mode. Not until the mission and strategy of the organization have been fully developed can human resource managers begin to determine the human resource needs.

Specifically, when a company plans strategically, it determines its goals and objectives for a given period of time. These goals and objectives often result in structural changes being made in the organization; that is, these changes foster changes in job requirements, reporting relationships, how individuals are grouped, and the like. As such, these new or revised structures bring with them a host of pivotal jobs. It is these jobs that HRM must be prepared to fill.

As these jobs are analyzed, specific skills, knowledge, and abilities are identified that the job applicant must possess to be successful on the job. This aspect cannot be understated, for herein lies much of the responsibility and success of HRM. Through the job analysis process, HRM identifies the essential qualifications for a particular job. Not only is this sound business acumen, for these jobs are critically linked to the strategic direction of the company, but it is also well within the stated guidelines of major **employment legislation**. Additionally, almost all activities involved in HRM revolve around an accurate description of the job. One cannot recruit without knowledge of the critical skills required, nor can one appropriately set performance standards, pay rates, or invoke disciplinary procedures fairly without this understanding.

Once these critical competencies have been identified, the recruiting process begins. Armed with information from SHRP, we can begin to focus on our prospective candidates. When involved in recruiting, HR specialists should be attempting to achieve two goals. These goals are to obtain a large number of applicants, thereby giving human resources and line managers more choices, while simultaneously providing enough information about the job such that those who are unqualified will not apply. Recruiting, then, becomes an activity designed to locate potentially good applicants, conditioned by the recruiting effort's constraints, the job market, and the need to reach members of under-represented groups like minorities and women.

Once applications have come in, it is time to begin the selection phase. Selection, too, has a dual focus. It attempts to thin out the set of large applications that arrived during the recruiting phase and to select an applicant who will be successful on the job. To achieve this goal, many companies use a variety of steps to assess the applicants. The candidate who successfully completes all steps is typically offered the job, but that is only half of the equation. HRM must also ensure that the good prospects accept the job offer, if made. Accordingly, HRM must communicate a variety of information to the applicant, such as the organization culture, what is expected of employees, and any other information that is pertinent to the candidate's decision-making process.

Once the selection process is completed, the staffing function has come to an

Employment Legislation Laws that directly affect the hiring, firing, and promotion of individuals.

end.[12] The goals, then, of the staffing function are to locate competent employees and get them into the organization. When this goal has been reached, it is time for HRM to begin focusing its attention on the employee's training and development.

The Training and Development Function

Whenever HRM embarks on the hiring process, it attempts to search and secure a candidate whom we labeled as the "best" possible candidate. And while HRM professionals pride themselves on being able to determine those who are qualified versus those who are not, the fact remains that few, if any, new employees can truly come into an organization and immediately become fully functioning, 100 percent performers. First, employees need to adapt to their new surroundings. Orientation is a means of bringing this adaptation about. While it may begin informally in the late stages of the hiring process, the thrust of orientation continues for many months after the individual begins working. During this time, the focus is to orient the new employee to the rules, regulations, and goals of the organization, department, and work unit. Then, as the employee becomes more comfortable with his or her surroundings, more intense training can occur.

Reflection over the past few decades tells us that, depending on the job, employees often take a number of months to adjust to their new organizations and jobs. Does that imply that HRM has not hired properly, or the staffing function goals were not met? On the contrary, it indicates that intricacies and peculiarities involved in each organization's positions result in jobs being tailored to adequately meet organizational needs. Accordingly, HRM plays an important role in shaping this reformulation of new employees so that within a short period of time they, too, will be fully productive. To accomplish this, HRM embarks on four areas in the training and development phase: employee training, employee development, organization development, and career development. It is important to note that employee and career development are more employee centered, whereas employee training is designed to promote competency in the new job. Organization development, on the other hand, focuses on system-wide changes. While each area has a unique focus, all four are critical to the success of the training and development phase. We have summarized these four in Figure 1-3.

At the conclusion of the training and development function, HRM attempts to reach the goal of having competent, adapted employees who possess the up-to-date skills, knowledge, and abilities needed to perform their current jobs more successfully. If that is attained, HRM turns its attention to finding ways to motivate these individuals to exert high energy levels.

The Motivation Function

The motivation function is one of the most important, yet probably the least understood, aspects of the HRM process. Why? Because human behavior is complex. Trying to figure out what motivates various employees has long been a concern of behavioral scientists. However, research has given us some important insights into employee motivation.

First of all, one must begin to think of motivation as a multifaceted process—one that has individual, managerial, and organizational implications. Motivation is not just what the employee exhibits, but a compilation of environmental issues surrounding the job. It has been proposed that one's performance in an

Figure 1-3
Training and Development Phases

Employee Training:	Employee training is designed to assist employees in acquiring better skills for their current job. The focus of employee training is on current job-skill requirements.
Employee Development:	Employee development is designed to help the organization ensure that it has the necessary talent internally for meeting future human resource needs. The focus of employee development is on a future position within the organization for which the employee requires additional competencies.
Career Development:	Career development programs are designed to assist employees in advancing their work lives. The focus of career development is to provide the necessary information and assessment in helping employees realize their career goals. However, career development is the responsibility of the individual, not the organization.
Organization Development:	Organization development deals with facilitating system-wide changes in the organization. The focus of organization development is to change the attitudes and values of employees according to new organizational strategic directions.

organization is a function of two factors: ability and willingness to do the job.[13] Thus, from a performance perspective, employees need to have the appropriate skills and abilities to adequately do the job. This should have been accomplished in the first two phases of HRM, by correctly defining the requirements of the job, matching applicants to those requirements, and training the new employee on how to do the job. But there is also another concern, which is the job design itself. If jobs are poorly designed, poorly laid out, or improperly described, employees will perform below their capability. Consequently, HRM must look at the job. Has the latest technology been provided in order to permit maximum efficiency? Is the office setting appropriate (properly lit and adequately ventilated, for example) for the job? Are the necessary tools readily available for employee use? For example, if an employee prints on a laser printer throughout the day, and the printer is networked to a station two floors up, that employee is going to be less productive than one who has a printer on his desk. While not trying to belittle the problem with such an example, the point should be clear. Office automation and industrial engineering techniques must be incorporated into the job design. Without such planning, the best intentions of managers to motivate employees may be lost or significantly reduced.

Once the measures have been taken to ensure that jobs have been properly designed, the next step in the motivation process is to understand the implications of motivational theories. Some motivational theories are well-known by most practicing managers, but recent motivation research has given us new and more valid theories for understanding what motivates people at work. (We'll look at these issues in Chapter 11.) Performance standards for each employee must also be set. While no easy task, managers must be sure that the performance evaluation system is designed to provide feedback to employees regarding their past performance, while simultaneously addressing any performance weaknesses the employee may have.

A link must be established between employee compensation and performance: The compensation and benefit activity in the organization must be adapted to, and coordinated with, a pay-for-performance plan.

Throughout the activities required in the motivation function, the efforts all focus on one primary goal: to have those competent and adapted employees, with up-to-date skills, knowledge, and abilities, exerting high energy levels. Once that is achieved, it is time to turn the HRM focus to the maintenance function.

The Maintenance Function

The last phase of the HRM process is called the maintenance function. As the name implies, the objective of this phase is to put into place activities that will help retain productive employees. When one considers how job loyalty of employees has declined in the last decade—brought about in part by management responses to leveraged buyouts, mergers, acquisitions, downsizing, changing family requirements, and increased competition[14]—it is not difficult to see the importance of maintaining employee commitment. To do so requires some basic common sense and some creativity. HRM must work to ensure that the working environment is safe and healthy; caring for employees' well-being has a major effect on their commitment. HRM must also realize that any problem an employee faces in his or her personal life will ultimately be brought into the workplace. Employee assistance programs, such as programs that help individuals deal with stressful life situations, are needed. Such programs provide many benefits to the organization while simultaneously helping the affected employee.

In addition to protecting employees' welfare, it is necessary for HRM to operate appropriate **communications programs** in the organization. Included in such programs is the ability for employees to know what is occurring around them and to vent frustrations. Employee relations programs should be designed to ensure that employees are kept well informed, and to foster an environment where employee voices are heard. If time and effort are expended in this phase, HRM may be able to achieve its ultimate goal of having competent employees, who have adapted to the organization's culture, with up-to-date skills, knowledge, and abilities, who exert high energy levels, who are now willing to maintain their commitment and loyalty to the company. This process is difficult to implement and maintain, but the rewards should be such that the effort placed in such endeavors is warranted.

Communications Programs HRM programs designed to provide information to employees.

HRM Departments

In a typical nonunion HRM department, we generally find four distinct areas: employment, training and development, compensation/benefits, and employee relations. Typically reporting to a vice president of human resources, managers in these four areas have specific accountabilities. Figure 1-4 is a simplified organizational chart of an HRM department, with some typical job titles and a sampling of what these job incumbents earn.

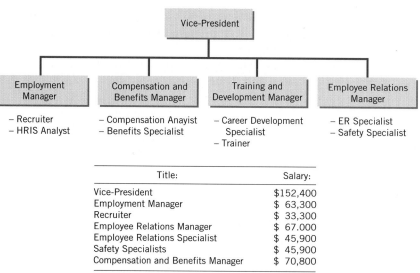

Figure 1-4
Sample HRM Organizational Chart (and average salaries of selected HRM positions in large firms.) [In small and medium sized firms, one individual may perform duties in several areas]

Title:	Salary:
Vice-President	$152,400
Employment Manager	$ 63,300
Recruiter	$ 33,300
Employee Relations Manager	$ 67.000
Employee Relations Specialist	$ 45,900
Safety Specialists	$ 45,900
Compensation and Benefits Manager	$ 70,800

Salary Figures Source: 1994 Human Resource Management Compensation Survey, William M. Mercer, Incorporated, as cited in Commerce Clearing House, Human Resources Management, *Ideas and Trends* (August 31, 1994), p. 141; 148; and "Human-Resources Manager", *Working Woman* (July 1994), p. 42.

The Employment Department

The main thrust of the employment function is to promote the activities of the staffing function. Working in conjunction with position control specialists (either in compensation, in benefits, or in a comptroller's office), the employment department embarks on the process of recruiting new employees.[15] This means correctly advertising the job to ensure that the appropriate skills, knowledge, and abilities are being sought. After sorting through resumes or applications, the employment specialist usually conducts the first weeding-out of candidates who applied but do not meet the job's requirements. The remaining applications are then typically forwarded to the line area for its review. After reviewing the resumes, the line manager may then instruct the employment specialist to interview the selected candidates. In many cases, this initial interview is another step in the hiring process. Understanding what the line manager desires in an employee, the employment specialist begins to further filter down the list of prospective candidates. During this phase, candidates who appear to "fit" the line area's need typically are scheduled to meet with the line manager for another interview.

It is important to note that the employment specialist's role is not to make the hiring decision, but to coordinate the effort with line management. Once the line area has selected its candidate, the employment specialist usually makes the job offer and handles the routine paperwork associated with hiring an employee.

The Training and Development Department

The training and development department of an organization is often responsible for a multitude of activities regarding training and developing employees. The training that occurs may be job-specific training or more developmental in nature (depending on whether or not line functions have their own trainers). Their focus, in either arena, is to enhance the personal qualities of

Training employees comes in many forms. In this seminar, the facilitator works with employees discussing the latest methods the company will employ in its redesigned work process. By helping employees learn the skills, the company helps itself in building a talented work force.

the employees such that the improvements made will manifest into greater organizational productivity. More importantly, the training and development members are often better known as the organization's internal change agents. The role of these change agents, or organizational development specialists, is to help the members of the organization cope with change. Changes that occur in an organization come in many forms. It can be a cultural change where the philosophy, values, and ways of operating are changed by top management. For instance, changing from a production focus of producing whatever the company wants and selling it to the public, to a marketing focus whereby what is produced and sold is contingent on consumer demand, requires a new organizational orientation.[16] A change may also occur in the organization's structure, which can result in layoffs, new job assignments, team involvement, and the like, and again requires new orientations by the organizational members. We may also see changes in procedures or policies where employees must be informed and taught to deal with such occurrences. For instance, a growing concern of companies has been to implement policies to stop sexual harassment from occurring in the organization. Not only must employees understand what constitutes sexual harassment, they must also become more sensitive to issues surrounding a diverse work force. Training and development often lead this charge.

In another area of training and development we find the activities surrounding career development. Training and development specialists are responsible for counseling employees, helping them to make better choices about their careers, and finding ways to achieve those desired goals.

The Compensation and Benefits Department

Work in a compensation and benefits department[17] is often described as dealing with the most objective areas of a subjective field. As the name implies, compensation and benefits is concerned with paying employees and administering their benefits package. These tasks are by no means easy ones. First of all, job salaries are not paid on a whim; rather, dollar values assigned to positions come from elaborate investigations and analyses. These investigations run the gamut of simple, logical job rankings (i.e., the position of president of a company should be paid more than the position of a maintenance engineer) to extensive analyses. Once these analyses are finished, job ratings are statistically compared to determine the relative worth of the job to the company. External factors, such as market conditions, limited supply, and the like, may affect the overall range of job worth. Additionally, analysis is conducted to ensure that there is internal equity in the compensation system. This means that as job rates are set, they are determined on such dimensions as skill, job responsibility, effort, and accountability—not by personal characteristics that may be suspect under employment law.

On the benefits side of the equation, much change has occurred over the past decade. As benefit offerings to employees have become significantly more costly, the benefits administrator (who may also have the title of risk manager) has the responsibility of piecing together a benefits package that meets the needs of the employees, while simultaneously being cost-effective to the organization. As such, much effort is expended searching for lower-cost products, like health insurance, while concurrently maintaining or improving quality. Additionally, various new products are often reviewed, such as flexible benefits programs and utilization reviews, to help in benefit-cost containment.

The benefits administrator also serves as the resource information officer to employees regarding their benefits. Activities such as helping employees prepare for their retirement, looking for various pay-out options, keeping abreast of recent tax law changes, or helping executives with their perquisites, are conducted.[18] This gives this individual a great deal of responsibility, but also high visibility in the organization.

The Employee Relations Department

The final phase in our scheme of HRM operations is the employee relations department. Employee relations (ER) has a number of major accountabilities.

These employees play for their company. By sponsoring teams such as this, the company reinforces the team concept, and indicates its continuing support of employees.

Before we go further, however, we must differentiate between employee relations and labor relations. While the two are structurally similar, labor relations involves dealing with labor unions. As such, because other laws apply, some of the techniques in employee relations may not be applicable. For instance, in a unionized setting, a specific grievance procedure might be detailed in the labor–management contract, and might involve the union, management, and the alleged wronged employee. In a nonunion environment, a similar procedure might exist or the grievance might be handled one-on-one. While these may be subtle differences, the fact remains that labor relations requires a different set of competencies and understanding.

In the nonunion setting, however, we see employee relations specialists performing many tasks. As mentioned earlier, one of their key responsibilities is to ensure that open communications permeates the organization. This is done by fostering an environment where employees talk directly to supervisors and settle any differences that may arise. If needed, employee relations representatives intervene to assist in achieving a fair and equitable solution. ER specialists are also intermediaries in helping employees understand the rules. Their primary goal is to ensure that policies and procedures are enforced properly, and to permit a wronged employee a forum to obtain relief. As part of this role, too, comes the disciplinary process. These representatives are in place to ensure that appropriate disciplinary sanctions are used consistently throughout the organization.

In addition to the communications role, the employee relations department is responsible for additional assignments. Typically in such a department, statistics are collected, tabulated, and written up in the company's affirmative action plan documentation. This material is updated frequently and made available to employees on request. Part of their responsibility is to ensure safe and healthy work sites. This may range from casual work inspections to operating nursing stations and coordinating employee-assistance programs. However involved, the premise is the same—to focus on those aspects that help make an employee committed and loyal to the organization through fair and equitable treatment, and by listening to employees.

Lastly, there is the festive side of employee relations. This department is responsible for company outings, company athletic teams, and recreational and recognition programs. Whatever they do under this domain, the goal remains—having programs that benefit the workers and their families to make them feel part of a community.

Conclusion

Although we have presented four generic areas of HRM, we would be remiss not to recognize the changing nature of HRM in today's organizations. As organizations change structures (to reflect global competition and the like), there has been a movement away from centralization of functional areas toward more self-contained units. In companies where strategic business units, or market-driven units dominate,[19] an HRM professional may be assigned to these units to handle all the HRM operations. In fact, it is estimated that on average one HRM specialist serves the needs of one hundred employees.[20] While a headquarters HRM staff remains to coordinate the activities, the HRM representative is expected to perform all the HR functions. Accordingly, the movement toward generalist positions in HRM appears to be on the rise.

Another trend is also closely aligned with the generalist-versus-specialists discussion. That trend is called **shared services**.[21] In large organizations like AlliedSignal and du Pont, companies that are geographically dispersed are find-

Shared Services Sharing HRM activities among geographically dispersed divisions.

ing it more cost-effective to share their HRM services among the divisions. Under shared services, each location is staffed by a few generalists who handle routine local matters like recruiting, policy implementation, grievances, employee training, and the like. Specialized services, like organization development and compensation and benefits are handled by a staff located at a centralized location. Each location, then, shares these services offered by the centralized unit, and uses only what is necessary for the division. As such, each location gets specialized care on an as-needed basis without the cost of having full-time staff.

HRM in a Small Business

The discussion about the four departments of HRM refers to situations where there are sufficient resources available for functional expertise to exist. However, such is not always the case. Take, for instance, the small business operation. In these organizations, the owner–manager performs these activities. In other situations, small-business human resource departments are staffed with one individual, and possibly a full-time secretary. Accordingly, such individuals are forced, by design, to be HRM generalists.

Irrespective of the unit's size, the same activities are required in small businesses, but on a smaller scale. These small-business HRM managers must be able to properly perform the four functions of HRM and achieve the same goals that a larger department does. The main difference is that they are doing the work themselves without benefit of a specialized staff. There may be a tendency to use outside consultants to assist in HRM activities. For instance, benefit administration may be beyond the capability of the small businessperson. In that case, benefit administration may need to be contracted out. HRM in a small business requires that individuals keep abreast of what is happening in the field. This is especially true of keeping current on legal issues. For example, the Family and Medical Leave Act of 1993 is applicable to those organizations that have fifty or more employees. Accordingly, the small business may be exempt from many laws affecting employment practices. Being aware of this information can save the small business time and money. Before we begin to pity this small business HRM manager, let's look at the benefits from such an arrangement. Often, these individuals feel that they are less constrained in their job. That is, the bureaucratic hierarchy that accompanies larger organizations is often absent in the small business. Furthermore, some small-business HRM managers use this arrangement to their advantage. For instance, in recruiting efforts, a selling point to attract a good applicant might be the aspect of freedom from a rigid structure that the small business opportunity offers. Consequently, the small-business HRM manager may be in an advantageous position.[22] In fact, isn't it ironic that the movement toward self-contained business units having their own human resources generalists closely resembles the small-business setup? Maybe this "back to basics" movement indicates, in part, that HRM in the small-business enterprise may better facilitate HRM goals.

HRM in a Global Marketplace

As a business grows from a regional to a national one, the human resource management function must take on a new and broader perspective. As a national company expands overseas, first with a sales operation, then to production facilities and fully expanded operations or to international joint ventures, the human resources function must adapt to a changing and far more complex environment.

All the basic functions of domestic HRM are more complex when the organization's employees are located around the world, and additional human resource management activities are often necessary that would be considered invasions of employee privacy in domestic operations. This is necessary partially because of the increased vulnerability and risk of terrorism sometimes experienced by American executives abroad.

When a corporation sends its American employees overseas, that corporation takes on responsibilities that add to the basic HRM functions. For example, the staffing, and training and development functions take on greater emphasis. Not only are organizations concerned about selecting the best employee for the job, they must also be aware of the entire family's needs. Why? Many individuals who take international assignments fail because their spouses or family just can't adjust to the new environment. Furthermore, the relocation and orientation process before departure may take months of foreign language training is included (as it should be), and should involve not just the employee, but the employee's entire family. Details such as work visas, travel, and household moving arrangements, and family issues such as the children's schooling, medical care, and housing, all must be provided for.[23] Administrative services for the expatriate employees also must be available once they are placed in their overseas posts. All these additional functions make international human resource management a very costly undertaking.

Study Tools and Applications

Summary

(These summaries relate to the Learning Objectives identified on p. 1.)
After having read this chapter you should know:

1. Management is the process of efficiently achieving the strategic objectives of the organization with and through people. The four main functions of management are planning, organizing, leading, and controlling. Three factors common to the definition of organizations are goals, limited resources, and people.
2. Human resource management is responsible for the people dimension of the organization. It is responsible for getting competent people, training them, getting them to perform at high effort levels, and providing mechanisms to ensure that these employees maintain their productive affiliation with the organization.
3. Human resource management is comprised of the staffing, development, motivation, and maintenance functions. Each of these functions, however, is affected by external influences.
4. Environmental influences are those factors that affect the functions of HRM. They include the dynamic environment of HRM, government legislation, labor unions, and management thought.
5. Management practices affect HRM in a number of ways. As new ideas or practices develop in the field, they typically have HRM implications. Accordingly, once these practices are implemented, they typically require the support from HRM to operate successfully.
6. Labor unions affect HRM practices in a variety of ways. If a union exists, HRM takes on a different focus—one of labor relations as opposed to employee relations.

Additionally, what occurs in the unionized sector frequently affects the activities in organizations where unions are not present.

7. The components of the staffing function include strategic human resource planning, recruiting, and selection. The goal of the staffing function is to locate and secure competent employees. The training and development function includes orientation, employee training, employee development, organization development, and career development. The goal of the development function is to take competent workers, adapt them to the organization, and help them to obtain up-to-date skills, knowledge, and abilities for their job responsibilities.

8. The components of the motivation function include motivation theories, appropriate job design, reward and incentive systems, compensation and benefits. The goal of the motivation function is to take competent, adapted employees, with up-to-date skills, knowledge, and abilities, and provide them with an environment that encourages them to exert high energy levels. The components of the maintenance function include safety and health issues, and employee communications. The goal of the maintenance function is to take competent, adapted employees, with up-to-date skills, knowledge, and abilities, who are exerting high energy levels, to maintain their commitment and loyalty to the organization.

9. The departments of employment, training and development, compensation and benefits, and employee relations support the components of the staffing, training and development, motivation, and maintenance functions respectively.

10. In large HRM operations, individuals perform functions according to their specialization. Such may not be the case with the small business HRM practitioner. Instead, they may be the only individual in the operation, and thus, must operate as an HRM generalist. In an international setting, HRM functions become more complex, and typically require additional activities associated with staffing, and training and development.

Key Terms

communications programs	management thought
controlling	management
employment legislation	organizing
environmental influences	planning
Hawthorne studies	scientific management
leading	shared services

EXPERIENTIAL EXERCISE:

Getting Acquainted

Beginning a new semester is associated with excitement, but also anxiety. New friends can be made, and new frontiers can be crossed. But one of the more basic issues that face us is what is expected in this class. By now, you probably have received a course syllabus that provides some necessary information about how the class will operate. No doubt this information is important to you, and is designed to help you "plan" your semester. But, there is another side to that equation—giving your instructor some indication of what you want/expect from the class. Some information can serve a useful purpose for your instructor.[24] To help collect these data, you'll need to answer some questions. First, take out a piece of paper, place your name at the top, then respond to the following:

1. What do I want from this course (other than a passing grade)?
2. Why is this "want" important to me?
3. How does information covered in this course fit into my career plans?
4. What is my greatest challenge in taking this class?

When you have finished answering the questions, team up with several class members (preferably two or three others who you do not already know) and exchange papers. Get acquainted with one another, using the responses to the four questions above as an ice-breaker. Then, as your professor goes around the room, introduce your team (each member introduces another team member) and share your group's responses to these questions with the class and your instructor.

CASE APPLICATION:
Family-Friendly Benefits Arrive in Corporate America

What do G.T. Water (Plumbing) Products, Fel-Pro, Mattel Toys, Nike, and Procter & Gamble have in common? They each have recently been cited in *Working Mother* magazine as one of the best one hundred companies for women to work for.[25] In what way? Each company provides special benefits to its employees that benefit working moms. For example, G.T. Water offers all twenty-four of its employees time off from work for family matters. Even though a federal law mandates this for many organizations, G. T. Water is exempt because it has fewer than fifty employees. And Fel-Pro, the Skokie, Illinois, gasket-making company, offers its employees $6,500 in tuition assistance for their children.

Companies today are reacting to new demands placed on them by their diversified work force. Whereas three decades ago, when the work force was predominately male and moms stayed home with their 2.5 kids, today's workers are not that homogeneous. Workers are more likely to be female than male. And whether men are willing to admit it or not, most women still have the greater burden and responsibility for child care. But that doesn't have to mean our companies cannot be responsive to the changing work force.

Accompanying today's diversity is the realization that the way we've treated workers with children in the past, and the benefits we offered them, may no longer meet their current needs. Family life is important to our workers, and in many cases will win out in the decision of career versus family. Fortunately, organizational decision makers today are not looking at the situation as a win−lose proposition. Rather, to attract and keep "good talent" requires companies to strongly compete for those skills. One way to successfully compete is to meet the worker's individualized needs. In the 1990s, this might come in the form of time off from work to "bond" with a newly arrived child, or on-site day-care facilities—something that was virtually nonexistent in the 1960s.

Questions:

1. Do companies have the responsibility to provide special benefits for working moms? Explain your rationale.
2. Suppose you have a work force that is evenly divided—50 percent have children and 50 percent do not. Is providing child-care benefits for half of your work force giving those employees something additional that the other half cannot use? What do you think would be the motivational effect on those employees without children?
3. What role do you see Human Resources playing in promoting, and offering these family-friendly benefits? In which function of HRM would you see this activity having the greatest impact? Explain.

Testing Your Understanding

How well did you fulfill the learning objectives?

1. Organizational efficiency is expressed as
   a. planning for long-range goals.
   b. making the best use of scarce resources.
   c. goal attainment.
   d. meeting deadlines.
   e. rewarding and recognizing time-saving activities.

2. When a compensation director reports on successful cost containment with a new health-care package, the primary management function being performed is
   a. planning. b. organizing.
   c. leading. d. controlling.
   e. delegating.

3. All of the following are typical responsibilities for the human resources management professional ex-cept
   a. training employees to function effectively within the organization.
   b. hiring the best qualified candidates.
   c. establishing working conditions that are conducive to retaining the best workers.
   d. providing for continued personal development of employees.
   e. evaluating the performance of managerial employees.

4. Which statement is most likely to be true of Austin Miller, a top-level human resources professional in a large corporation?
   a. She would have worked her way up from a clerical job.
   b. She would have a narrow and well-defined interest.
   c. She would have been vice-president of marketing or finance before getting this assignment.
   d. She would be aware of the strategic importance people have in the attainment of organizational success.
   e. None of the above are true of Austin Miller.

5. A vice-president of human resources of a medium-sized manufacturing firm had to retain a full-time corporate attorney in 1991 after the Americans with Disabilities Act was passed. What external influence most prompted this action?
   a. Government legislation.
   b. Work force diversity
   c. Labor unions.
   d. Management thought.
   e. Restructuring the corporation.

6. What point is made in the external influences section of the text?
   a. Human resources managers need to be aware of their ability to exert influence outside of their organizations on the surrounding community.
   b. Human resources managers need to be aware of

external factors because all human resources management activity undertaken is either directly or indirectly influenced by these factors.
   c. Human resource management goals affect the motivation function, which affects legislation.
   d. Human resource management goals affect the development function, which influences management practices.
   e. Human resource management goals affect the staffing and training and development functions, which influence both management practices and labor unions.

7. Elton Mayo's Hawthorne studies contributed which principles to management practices?
   a. Informal work groups have a significant effect on worker performance.
   b. Wage incentive plans are the most important influence on work group produc-tivity.
   c. Employees who receive training for job skills they already possess are less motivated than other employees.
   d. Union workers are less productive than nonunion workers.
   e. Union workers are more productive than nonunion workers.

8. Which one of the following statements best reflects why labor unions were founded?
   a. To satisfy a social belonging need in workers.
   b. To assist management in hiring and firing workers.
   c. To act on behalf of workers to secure favorable terms and conditions of employment.
   d. To preserve guild ancestries.
   e. To offer an alternative career path for workers.

9. A human resources manager in a medium-sized manufacturing firm sets his pay scale in accordance with local prevailing union rates. Why would he do that if his company is nonunion?
   a. Grievance procedures can occur in any organization.
   b. It is the influence of the spillover effect.
   c. Negotiated agreements are binding by geographical area.
   d. Comparable wages are a good way to get his company in the union.
   e. He balances the high wages with lower benefits.

10. Which one of the following is best descriptive of the selection process?
   a. It assesses probable job success of applicants.
   b. It reaches members of under-represented groups, such as minorities and women.
   c. It builds a large applicant pool.
   d. It provides remedial skill training, when necessary.
   e. It matches goals and objectives to structural changes of the organization.

11. System-wide development functions are part of
    a. employee orientation.
    b. employee training.
    c. organization development.
    d. career development.
    e. employee development.
12. The major objective of the maintenance function is best stated as
    a. retaining productive employees.
    b. reducing grievance procedures and lawsuits.
    c. maintaining recruiting costs.
    d. supporting employee wellness centers.
    e. keeping pay scales in line with geographical peers.
13. What is the difference between employee relations and labor relations?
    a. Labor relations deals with unskilled workers. Employee relations deals with highly-skilled, technical workers.
    b. Labor relations deals with hourly workers. Employee relations deals with salaried workers.
    c. Labor relations deals with manufacturing workers. Employee relations deals with clerical workers.
    d. Labor relations deals with unionized workers. Employee relations deals with nonunion workers.
    e. Labor relations deals with foreign workers. Employee relations deals with U.S. workers.
14. What are the differences between human resources management in a large and a small business?
    a. There is no difference. The activities are the same, just on a grander scale in a lager organization.
    b. Small businesses can afford to hire only specialists.
    c. Small businesses need only employment department activities, and, therefore, hire only recruiters.
    d. Small businesses usually have generalists who perform a variety of HRM tasks.
    e. Small businesses do not need any human resources management professionals.
15. How important is human resources management to an organization?
    a. Human resources management is expendable—the first functional area to be cut in hard times.
    b. Human resources management is important only for social action and public sector organizations.
    c. Human resources management is important only for manufacturing sector organizations.
    d. Human resources management is important for all organizations that want to get and to keep good people.
    e. Human resources management is important only for small companies. Large organizations have professional managers to provide needed support for employees.
16. Mayo's Hawthorne studies contributed which principles to management practices?
    a. Informal work groups have a significant effect on worker performance.
    b. Wage incentive plans are the most important influence on work group produc-tivity.
    c. Employees who receive training for job skills they already possess are less motivated than other employees.
    d. Union workers are less productive than nonunion workers.
    e. Union workers are more productive than nonunion workers.
17. Mary is a human resources consultant hired by a large manufacturing firm to find out why so many new employees were leaving within their first six months of employment. She suggested a formal orientation program. Why?
    a. Mary probably specializes in orientation programs.
    b. Orientation helps new employees adapt to their new surroundings.
    c. Orientation programs provide a "halo effect" for even the worst organization that usually lasts at least six months.
    d. Orientation helps to build the applicant pool.
    e. Training is a necessary first step for all employees.
18. Why is the maintenance function important to an organization?
    a. Commitment from good employees contributes to organizational success.
    b. Most home-based problems an employee faces will not affect job performance.
    c. A safe and healthy work environment maintains OSHA standards.
    d. Organizational loyalty is an old-fashioned idea.
    e. It is not important. Maintenance is the only human resources management function that is optional.

Chapter Two

HUMAN RESOURCES MANAGEMENT IN A DYNAMIC ENVIRONMENT

LEARNING OBJECTIVES

AFTER READING THIS CHAPTER, YOU WILL BE ABLE TO:

1. Describe how globalization affects human resources management practices.
2. Identify the significant changes that have occurred in the composition of the work force.
3. Explain the implications for human resources management of the changing work-force composition.
4. Discuss how changing skill requirements affect human resources management.
5. Describe what is meant by corporate downsizing and identify its effect on human resources management.
6. Explain what is meant by the term *Total Quality Management*, and identify its goals.
7. Discuss the reengineering phenomena of the early 1990s and the role HRM plays in the reengineered organization.
8. Describe the contingent work force and its HRM implications.
9. Explain why work sites may be decentralized and what their implications are for HRM.
10. Define employee involvement and list its critical components.

What would you say about an owner of a small business that had achieved significant growth over the past few years, was making a good profit, gainfully employed thirty-two full-time employees, then decided to completely redo how the company functioned? Crazy? An entrepreneur with a death wish? Neither one! Instead, what this owner is doing typifies a trend that is sweeping businesses today. Today's managers are taking a lot of action that reflects rethinking of how organizations function. They are making radical changes in their practices to achieve results that were "impossible" to even think about years ago. In other words, businesses, both large and small, like Benson Woodworking Company, are making significant changes in their organizations—not just fine tuning what currently exists—to make their companies more quality-oriented.[1] This process in business is known as reengineering.

Tedd Benson, founder and president of Benson Woodworking Company in Alstead, New Hampshire, just felt that things weren't working right. Although the business was profitable, work wasn't fun anymore—for Tedd or his employees. The company had grown over the years, but of late, appeared to consume too much of everyone's time. And as the company grew, it became more structured, with rules, regulations, and strict control mechanisms. Tedd knew that something was drastically needed—an infusion into the organization of the entrepreneurial spirit that once existed. But to do so would change the way that work had been performed over the past decade.

To begin making these radical changes, Benson first began to isolate where the bottlenecks lay. Tedd had to look no further than his own office. As the owner/entrepreneur, Tedd wanted his hand in everything. As a result, things got done more slowly while employees sought Tedd's permission. His desire to control everything was, in effect, stifling productivity throughout the organization. Reengineering for Benson Woodworking, then, meant that the owner had to change his ways of running his company. And Tedd Benson responded! One of the first changes implemented in the organization was employee involvement. Benson Woodworking employees now have a say in how things around them operate. No longer do they have to seek permission for their daily activities. Instead, each employee understands what needs to be done, then has the responsibility, the freedom, and the authority to get the job done.[2] Gone, too, is the organizational structure that constrained productivity. In its place is a leaner organization, one marked by the absence of management levels; replaced by a team effort working toward achieving corporate objectives.

What Benson Woodworking undertook was a rebirth of its operations. Not being satisfied with the status quo—or even attempting to make slight changes—the company has positioned itself for greater efficiency, improved goal attainment, and growth. In fact, by making these changes, Benson expects a 50 percent increase in sales over the next two years. More productivity, higher sales and greater profits—all the results of reengineering in one small timber-frame construction company. Fortunately for Tedd Benson and the employees

Tedd Benson (center) poses for a group picture with some of his employees. After reengineering the company's structure and processes, Benson Woodworking Company has been more profitable. The biggest change for Tedd—letting his employees have the authority to do their work. As a result, his employees are delivering a 50 percent increase in sales. And this is occurring with the same number of employees!

of Benson Woodworking, they didn't rely on the old adage of "If it ain't broke, don't fix it."

Introduction

As we briefly introduced in the last chapter, the world of work is rapidly changing. Even as little as a decade ago, the times were calmer than they are today. But that doesn't mean that ten years ago we didn't experience change. On the contrary, we were then, as we are today, in a state of flux. It's just that today the changes appear to be happening more rapidly.

As part of an organization then, HRM must be prepared to deal with the effects of the changing world of work. For them, this means understanding the implications of globalization, work-force diversity, changing skill requirements, corporate downsizing, total quality management, reengineering, the contingent work force, decentralized work sites, and employee involvement. Let's look at how these changes are affecting HRM goals and practices.

Globalization and Its HRM Implications

Back in 1973, with the first oil embargo, U.S. businesses began to realize the importance that international forces had on profit and loss statements. The world was changing rapidly, with other countries making significant inroads into traditional U.S. markets. Unfortunately, U.S. businesses did not adapt to this changing environment as quickly or adeptly as they should have. The result was that

U.S. businesses lost out in world markets and have had to fight much harder to get in. Only by the late 1980s did U.S. businesses begin to get the message. But when they did, they aggressively began to improve production standards, focusing more on quality (we'll look further at this issue in later in this chapter) and preparing employees for the global village.[3] It is on this latter point that Human Resources will have the biggest effect.

What Is the Global Village?

The **global village** is a term that reflects the state of businesses in our world. The rise of multinational and transnational corporations[4] places new requirements on human resources managers. For instance, human resources must ensure that the appropriate mix of employees in terms of knowledge, skills, and cultural adaptability are available to handle global assignments.

Global Village The production and marketing of goods and services worldwide.

In order for human resources to meet this goal, they must train individuals to meet the challenges of the global village. First of all, there must be means for these workers to gain a working knowledge of the language of the country in which they will work. Understanding the language cannot be overstated. There have been too many examples of embarrassing situations and lost business because executives or lower-level managers were unprepared. Product names or marketing strategies have translated poorly in some foreign countries. It's even happened to the president of the United States! For example, in 1992 in Australia, former President George Bush learned the hard way that what signifies the peace sign in the United States translated into an obscenity for the Australian people. Accordingly, before any organization sends any employee overseas, human resources should ensure that the employee can handle the language.[5]

Language requirements are also going to extend into communication programs for employees. When we go abroad, for instance, searching for people with specific skills, we may be bringing into an organization someone who speaks very little English. Accordingly, we will be required to assist these individuals in learning English as a foreign language—or go even further! That is, while our foreign-born employees may learn English as a second language, it is advantageous for HRM to assure that any communication provided be understood. To achieve that outcome, companies have moved toward multilingual communications. That is, anything transmitted to employees should appear in more than one language to help the message get through. While there are no hard-and-fast rules in sending such messages, it appears safe to say that such a message should be transmitted in the languages that employees speak to assure adequate coverage. If that appears to be a major task, think of Digital Equipment Corporation's process. Currently, their Boston factory employs workers from forty-four countries who speak nineteen different languages. To assure that their messages get across, Digital sends its memos in "English, Chinese, French, Portuguese, Vietnamese, and Haitian Creole."[6]

In addition to the language, human resources must also ensure that workers going overseas understand the host country's culture. All countries have different values, morals, customs, and laws. Accordingly, people going to another country must have exposure to those cultural issues before they can be expected to commence working. It is also equally important for human resource managers to understand how the host society will react to one of these mobile employees. For example, although U.S. laws guard against employers dicriminating against individuals on the basis of such factors as race or religion, similar laws do not exist in all other countries. Consequently, cultural considerations

TABLE 2-1 Countries Sharing Similar Cultural Environments

Latin American	**Central European**
Peru	Switzerland
Mexico	Austria
Argentina	Germany
Colombia	
Chile	**Latin European**
Venezuela	Portugal
	Spain
Anglo-American	Italy
New Zealand	Belgium
South Africa	France
United States	
Australia	**Nordic**
United Kingdom	Norway
Ireland	Finland
Canada	Denmark
	Sweden

Source: Adapted from Simcha Ronen and Allen I. Kranut, "Similarities Among Countries Based on Employee Work Values and Attitudes," *Columbia Journal of World Business* (Summer 1977), p. 94.

are critical to the success of any global business. Although it is not our intent here to provide the scope of cultural issues needed to enable an employee to go to any country, we do want to recognize that some similarities do exist (see Table 2-1). Research findings allow us to group countries according to such cultural variables as status differentiation, societal uncertainty, and assertiveness.[7] These variables indicate a country's means of dealing with its people and how the people see themselves. For example, in an individualistic society, people are primarily concerned with their own family. On the contrary, in a collective society (the opposite of individualistic), people care for all individuals who are part of their group. Thus, a strongly individualistic U.S. manager may not work well if sent to a pacific rim country where collectivism dominates. Accordingly, flexibility and adaptability are key components for managers going abroad. It will be critical, then, for those in human resources to have an understanding "of the working conditions and social systems globally so that they can counsel management on decisions and issues crossing national frontiers."[8]

HRM must also develop mechanisms that will help multicultural individuals work together. As background, language, custom, or age differences become more prevalent, there are indications that employee conflict will increase. HRM must make every effort to acclimate different groups to each other, finding ways to build teams and thus reduce conflict. For instance, at Corning Inc., efforts have been made to assist these issues with respect to African-American and female employees. The purpose of this process is to "identify gender and race issues, find remedial actions, guide program development, and measure results."[9] Such action, however, is not geared to U.S. citizens only;[10] workers from different countries bring with them their own biases toward individuals from other countries, and that also can be problematic. For instance, while initiatives have been underway to bring about peace in the Middle East, the dichotomy between Israel and its surrounding Arab neighbors continues. Accordingly, requiring workers from these two areas to work together could create an uneasiness that must be addressed.

Cultural Environments

Before we leave the issue of globalization, there is one final point to cover. As we have shown, understanding **cultural environments** is critical to the success of an organization's operations, but training employees in these is not the only means of achieving the desired outcomes. Companies like Amadeus Global Travel Distribution, Mars, and Hewlett-Packard are dealing with this issue by hiring nationals in foreign countries in which they operate.[11] What that has meant to these corporations is a ready supply of qualified workers who are well versed in their home country's language and customs. This recruiting has other benefits, too. Because these individuals come from differing backgrounds and are mixed together, there is a spillover training effect: that is, while working closely with one another, individuals informally learn the differences that exist between them and their two cultures. The Mars company, for example, builds on this informal development by providing formalized training that focuses on the "major differences that lead to problems."[12]

HRM also will be required to train management to be more flexible in its practices. Because tomorrow's workers will come in all different colors, nationalities, and so on, managers will be required to change their ways. This will necessitate managers being trained to recognize differences in workers and to appreciate—even celebrate—those differences. The various requirements of workers because of different cultural backgrounds, customs, work schedules, and the like must all be taken into account.[13] In addition, extensive training to recognize these differences and "change the way [managers] think about people different from themselves"[14] has positive outcomes. Companies like Digital, Honeywell, Wang Laboratories, Xerox, and Avon have already begun to formalize this process.[15]

Work-Force Diversity

Forty years ago, human resource management was considerably more simple because our work force was strikingly homogeneous. In the 1950s, for example, the U.S. work force consisted primarily of white males employed in manufacturing, who had wives who stayed at home, tending to the family's two-plus children. Inasmuch as these workers were alike, personnel's job was certainly simpler. Recruiting for these workers was done locally, if in fact, new employees weren't related to a current worker. Because those workers all shared the same interests and needs, personnel's responsibility was to get them in the door, sign them up, tell them about the standardized benefit program, and plan the company's annual Christmas party. Then, when the time came, it was HRM's responsibility to purchase the traditional gold watch, have it engraved, and present it to the employee in a gala event in honor of the employee's retirement. But times have changed. And with these changes have come a new work force, one that by the year 2000 will have fewer than 31 percent white males entering the work force (see Figure 2-1).[16]

The Work Force of Tomorrow

Much of the change that has occurred in the work force is attributed to the passage of federal legislation in the 1960s prohibiting employment discrimination. Based on such laws (we'll look at discrimination legislation in the next chapter), avenues began to open up for minority and female applicants. These

●

Cutural Environments The attitudes and perspectives shared by individuals from specific countries that shape their behavior and how they view the world.

Figure 2-1
Projected entrants to the labor force (1992–2005) (Percent of New Workers From Various Diverse Groups)

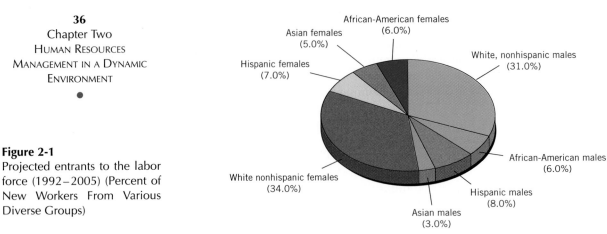

Source: Bureau of Labor Statistics, "Labor Force Entrants, 1992–2005," *BLS Occupational Outlook Quarterly,* (Fall 1993).

two groups have since become the fastest-growing segment in the work force, and accommodating their needs has become a vital responsibility for human resources managers. Furthermore, during this time, birthrates in the United States began to decline. The baby boomer generation had already reached its apex in terms of employment opportunities, which meant that as hiring continued, there were fewer baby boomers left to choose.[17] And as globalization became more pronounced, Hispanic, Asian, and other immigrants came to the United States and sought employment.

Work-Force Diversity The varied personal characteristics that make the work force heterogenous.

Projecting into the future is often an educated guess at best. Trying to predict the exact composition of our **work-force diversity** is no exception, even though we do know it will be made up of "males, females, whites, blacks, Hispanics, Asians, Native Americans, the disabled, homosexuals, straights, and the elderly."[18] Nonetheless, we do have some excellent predictors available to us, the results of which give us a good indication of what is to come. The landmark investigation into work-force composition was conducted by the Hudson Institute and the Department of Labor.[19] Their findings, published in 1987, illuminated the changes we can expect over the next two decades. Although there is some debate over the findings of the Hudson Report and how rapidly the work-force composition change will occur,[20] three groups in particular are projected to supply significant increases of workers to U.S. firms. These are minorities, women, and immigrants (see Figure 2-1).[21]

The Implications for HRM

As women—both natural-born and foreign citizens—become the dominant employee in the work force, HRM will have to change its practices. This means that organizations will need to make concerted efforts to attract and maintain a diversified work force. Like the programs at Xerox, AT&T, Burger King, Seagram, and Levi Strauss, a good diversity program means having customers looking inside the organization and finding people like them (see "Meet Robert Monroe").[22] One means of achieving that goal is through the organizations benefits package. This includes HRM offerings that fall under the heading of the family-friendly organization.[23] A family-friendly organization is one that has flexible work schedules and provides such employee benefits as child care. Even organizations that use part-time and temporary help personnel have found that

Meet

family-friendly benefits are needed by these groups to remain committed to the organization, and productive.[24] We'll look closer at family-friendly organizations in Chapter 14.

In addition to the diversity brought about by gender and nationality, HRM must be aware of the age differences that exist in our work force. Today, there are three distinct groupings.[25] First, there's the **mature workers,** those born prior to 1946. This group of workers—the byproduct of the post–Depression era—are security-oriented and have a committed work ethic. Although mature workers had been viewed as the foundation of the work force, they are regarded by the other generational groups as having obsolete skills and being inflexible in their ways. The **baby boomers,** those born between 1946 and 1964, the largest group in the work force, are regarded as the career climbers—at the right place at the right time. Their career advanced rapidly as organizational growth during their initial years of employment was unsurpassed. Yet, the view of them is that they are unrealistic in their views, and workaholics. Finally,

Mature Workers Those workers born before 1946.

Baby Boomers Those individuals born between 1946 and 1964.

Baby Busters Those individuals born in 1965 and years
after. Often referred to as
"generation Xers."

there's the generation Xers, those born between 1965 and 1975. These twen-
tysomething **baby busters** are bringing a new perspective to the work force—
less commitment, less rule-bound, more into themselves and their own gratifica-
tion,[26] and intolerant of the baby boomers and their attitudes.[27] As a result, they
are viewed as being selfish and not willing to play the "corporate game."
Consequently, blending the three will require much assistance from HRM. That
is, human resource management must train these groups to effectively manage
and to deal with one another, and to respect the diversity of views that each offers.[28] In situations like these, a more participative approach to management
also appears to work better.[29] For example, companies like the Travelers and
the Hartford insurance companies go to great lengths to train their younger
managers how to deal with older employees. Inasmuch as work attitude conflict
is natural, these companies have been successful in keeping problems to a minimum.[30]

Changing Skills Requirements

In any discussion of the changing world of work, the issues of skill requirements
must be addressed. Remember that as recently as the end of the last century the
United States was primarily an agrarian economy. Our great-grandparents
worked the land with sheer brawn, growing food for themselves and those in
the community. As the Industrial Revolution continued to introduce machine
power, assembly lines, and mass production, workers left the farm, moved to
cities, and went to work in factories. For a generation or two, these workers led
the United States in becoming the world's leading industrialized nation, producing quality goods in our smokestack industries. But many of these manufacturing jobs have disappeared—replaced by more efficient machines or sent
overseas to be done by lower-cost labor. Today, the U.S. economy is essentially
driven by service, not manufacturing. Eighty percent of workers are now employed in service. By the year 2000, that number is expected to increase to 88
percent.[31] What does all this imply about our workers?

Segments of our work force are deficient in skills necessary to perform the
jobs required in the twenty-first century. The United States as a whole lags behind Singapore, Denmark, Germany, Japan, and Norway in terms of a skilled
work force.[32] Some new entrants to the work force simply are not adequately
prepared. High-school graduates sometimes lack the necessary reading, writing,
and mathematics skills needed to perform today's high-tech jobs.[33] Others in
the work force are computer illiterate. Just think of what these imply. Imagine
tomorrow's aerospace engineers who cannot read a blueprint or explain how
wing icing affects lift on an airplane. Or tomorrow's traffic engineer who cannot properly adjust the light sequencing at a busy intersection. Just how bad has
it gotten? It is estimated that about 36 percent of all job applicants who were
tested for basic reading and math skills failed to pass the tests.[34] In some cases,
it is even worse. Take, for example, New York Telephone. The initial step in employment requires one to pass a basic skills test. In a recent evaluation, the company reported that more than 57,000 individuals took the exam that emphasizes
reading, math, and reasoning skills. Much to the company's disappointment,
only 2,100 applicants passed the test.[35] That's less than 4 percent!

Skill Deficiencies The lacking
of basic abilities to perform
many of today's jobs.

Skill deficiencies translate into significant losses for the organization in terms
of poor-quality work and lower productivity, increases in employee accidents,
and customer complaints.[36] These losses run into the billions of dollars.[37] This
is a major problem that must be addressed, but it is one that cannot be tackled

by companies alone. To attack and to begin to correct functional illiteracy will require the resources of companies and government agencies.[38] Human resources will become the hub for providing remedial education. For example, in an effort to acquire potentially productive employees, Aetna Life offers a basic course in clerical and mathematical skills to inner-city residents. Such an attempt was made because the company was experiencing a drastic reduction in clerical applications. Since the program's inception, Aetna reports that all individuals who have entered this remedial course have moved on to become productive workers for the company.[39] But such programs do not come cheap. A significant portion of the current $80 billion annually spent on training must be targeted to assisting the functionally illiterate. Ford Motor Company currently spends more than $200 million in remedial education.[40]

Corporate Downsizing

The **downsizing** (sometimes referred to as restructuring, retrenchment, or delayering) of corporate America has swept across the country. American companies have worked to become "lean and mean" organizations.[41] As a result of deregulation in certain industries (like the airlines), foreign competition, mergers, and takeovers, organizations have been forced to trim the fat or the inefficiencies from their ranks. Unfortunately, prior to the changes that occurred during the 1980s, growth patterns typified American industries. Individuals were sometimes hired haphazardly, jobs were frequently ill-defined, and a host of mid-level management positions were created. The cost of such action was often passed on in terms of "invisible" cost increases—cost increases that consumers took for granted. But changing world economies, increases in inflation at home, and reduced profit levels led in part to the changing corporate America that we see today. In fact, by the mid-1990s, almost all Fortune 500 companies were cutting staff and trimming operations. For example, IBM has cut more than 85,000 jobs, Sears has eliminated 50,000 jobs, and Kodak has trimmed more than 12,000 positions from its organization.[42] And to think that downsizing occurs only in the United States would be incorrect. For example, some of Japan's largest organizations, like Matsushita and Toyota, have had to cut jobs and reassign workers to functions in the organizations that are more productive.[43]

Downsizing An activity in an organization aimed at creating greater efficiency by eliminating certain jobs.

The Rationale Behind Downsizing

Whenever an organization attempts to delayer, it is attempting to create greater efficiency.[44] Efficiency, in part, means getting the same output with fewer inputs: That is the foundation of downsizing. Let's look at this issue more closely. The premise of downsizing is, in part, to reduce the number of workers employed by the organization. While individuals actually producing goods and services have not been immune to layoffs, much of the focus of recent downsizing efforts has been on the management ranks. Companies began exploring just what added value they got from management positions and began to consider what would happen if fewer levels of management existed. What is occurring here is a movement toward a greater span of control.

By **span of control,** we mean the number of employees a manager can effectively and efficiently direct. In the most basic assumption, if a manager can direct the activities of more employees, then that manager is more efficient. Figures 2-2 and 2-3 identify two managerial spans of control—one prior to

Span of Control The number of employees a supervisor can effectively and efficiently direct.

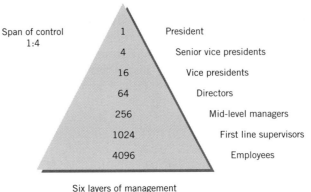

Six layers of management
1365 management personnel

Figure 2-2
SPAN OF CONTROL BEFORE
DOWNSIZING

retrenchment and one post-downsizing. In Figure 2-2, the span of control is four employees. That means that each manager is directly responsible for four individuals. In this simplified case, there are six layers of management totaling 1,365 managers. There are also 4,096 employees—individuals who produce the goods and services. Realizing that the ratio of managers to employees is not very efficient, this company decides to double the span of control to eight. What happens? Figure 2-3 shows the results. After the restructuring, there are now four layers of management, or 585 managers directing the activities of these same 4,096 employees. What are the savings? By increasing the span of control, the company successfully eliminated two layers of management, eliminating 780 positions. Using an average salary of $45,000 per year for all the positions eliminated, this action saved the company more than $35 million in direct pay.[45] For a company that is having financial difficulties, that $35 million provides a significant shot in the arm.

Downsizing raises a number of other issues besides cost savings. First, let's look at the jobs remaining. A job that once required one manager for every four employees has changed overnight. The surviving manager is now doing the work of two or more people.[46] And although our example above focused only on management levels, downsizing in reality is hitting all levels of employees. Accordingly, it is conceivable that a number of today's workers are doing the jobs of three employees, being expected to "produce" what three employees once did. Consequently, restructuring for downsizing's sake without proper job redesign or training of employees may defeat the purpose of the effort or be

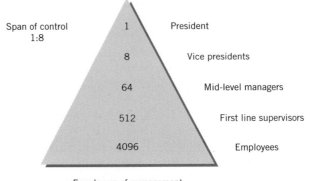

Four layers of management
585 management personnel

Figure 2-3
SPAN OF CONTROL AFTER
DOWNSIZING

counterproductive to the cost savings. Additionally, companies often have downsized without regard to the people dimension of the process. What about the people leaving? What dignity were they afforded in being separated from the company? Were they informed ahead of time, or were they herded into a large auditorium, told their jobs had been eliminated, and escorted out of the building? And what about the surviving employees: How has the company prepared to deal with their anger over friends being dismissed? Their fear that they may be next? Or their job stress from doing the work of several individuals?[47] These effects of corporate restructuring are real issues facing human resource management.

The HRM Implications

So, what should human resource management do to deal with the downsizing of corporate America? In one sense, if they are linked to the strategic direction of the organization, human resources must have input into the downsizing process. HRM must ensure that proper communications occur during this time. They must minimize the negative effects of rumors and ensure that individuals are kept informed with factual data. HRM must also deal with the actual layoff. They must have programs ready to assist the severed workers. For example, employees typically face immediate uncertainties when informed that they're being laid off. Will they receive severance pay? How will health insurance be handled? Will they have any benefits from their retirement plan? These and similar questions should be anticipated, and responses prepared.

The point here is that human resource management cannot be omitted from the downsizing discussion, nor can it ignore or abdicate its responsibilities to its employees. That can be difficult to do when human resource managers are also affected by the retrenchment. They, as with any employee group, are not immune to this corporate action, but they still must maintain their composure in the process.[48]

Finally, although downsizing has been prevalent over the past few years, there's some indication that the significant number of cuts may be declining. In fact, in some organizations, the cuts were so deep that now that economic times have gotten better, they've had to hire some employees back. These new positions are not, however, across the board. Rather, they are in organizations in the service sector, and include professional-level, skilled jobs.[49] That is, where it is prudent to hire full-time staff to assist in achieving organizational goals, and where that hiring does not negatively effect an organization's efficiency, then we can expect some of the "lost" jobs returning. But that is only if they are productive positions leading toward organizational goal attainment. For HRM, then, they must work with top management to show this linkage, and then, attract and retain these people.

Total Quality Management

Total quality management (TQM) is a long-term focus on which an enterprise will operate.[50] It is a continuous improvement process whereby an organization builds a better foundation from which to serve its customers.[51] For TQM, this involves "a company-wide initiative that includes customers and suppliers, supported by top management and implemented in a top-down [manner]."[52] That is, TQM means that a company changes its operations to focus on the customer,

Total Quality Management A continuous process improvement.

These Japanese auto workers continually strive for excellence. Through continuous process improvements, workers at this Nissan Plant continually focus on quality. Why? Not only is it good business, but Nissan quality is one of its competitive advantages. And developing that advantage is a major function of each employee.

Continuous Process Improvement A total quality management concept whereby workers continue toward 100 percent effectiveness on the job.

and to involve workers in matters affecting them.[53] At the heart of the TQM initiative, then, is continuous process improvement.[54]

Continuous process improvement is a process whereby companies make constant efforts to better what they produce. Although perfection is an ultimate goal, reality dictates that we never get there. However, through continuous process improvements, companies strive to improve anything that they do, from hiring quality people, to administrative paper-processing, to meeting customer needs. Therein lies the importance of TQM.

Quality is not a new phenomenon to businesses. In fact, quality concerns date back some fifty years with the pioneering work of W. Edwards Deming. Deming believed that quality could be measured and achieved through a process of statistical controls. These controls were intended to reduce variances in products and achieve a level of uniformity in each one made.[55] That meant, from Deming's perspective, that the 51,084th computer chip produced on an assembly line should have the same quality properties that the first one had. Although Deming's analysis was statistical by nature, he focused on a unique element of quality that was unheard of in those days. His message was that management had more effect on productivity than the actual workers performing their jobs (see Table 2-2). The problems with low productivity, according to Deming, were the fault of management, not the worker.

Deming reinforced this by developing specific requirements for productivity improvements.[56] For reasons unknown, American businesses rebuked Deming's message. Yet, believing in his concept, Deming took his ideas to Japan, a country then rebuilding after World War II. Japanese productivity prior to Deming's arrival was often shoddy; in fact, during the 1950s and 1960s, "Made in Japan" often meant the product was junk. But with Deming's help, many Japanese companies turned themselves around. By applying his principles, these organizations were able to grow to be the industrial giants they are today. And quality is still at the root of their success!

It took much longer for the management of U.S. organizations to recognize the need for quality. Instead of promoting quality, U.S. management promoted short-term profits as opposed to long-term development. They simply removed

1. Plan for the long-term future, not for next month or next year.
2. Never be complacent concerning the quality of your product.
3. Establish statistical control over your production processes and require your suppliers to do so as well.
4. Deal with the fewest number of suppliers—the best ones, of course.
5. Find out whether your problems are confined to particular parts of the production process or stem from the overall process itself.
6. Train workers for the job that you are asking them to perform.
7. Raise the quality of your line supervisors.
8. Drive out fear.
9. Encourage departments to work closely together rather than to concentrate on departmental or divisional distinctions.
10. Do not be sucked into adopting strictly numerical goals, including the widely popular formula of "zero defect."
11. Require your workers to do quality work, not just to be at their stations from 9 to 5.
12. Train your employees to understand statistical methods.
13. Train your employees in new skills as the need arises.
14. Make top managers responsible for implementing these principles.

Source: W. Edwards Deming, "Improvement of Quality and Productivity Through Action by Management," *National Productivity Review* (Winter 1981–82), pp. 12–22. Copyright 1981 by Executive Enterprises Inc., 22 West 21st St., New York, NY 10010–6904. Reprinted by permission of John Wiley & Sons, Inc.

themselves from the reality of impending global competition.[57] In other words, they failed to scan the external environment. Not until American consumers turned their buying power to quality products—products that at times cost even more—did these managers begin to address the problem. To help stave off any further erosion of America's competitive nature, TQM was born.[58] Since that time, TQM has appeared in fashion in almost every organization, private and public—even institutions of higher education.[59]

How successful have these programs been? All indications show progress. For example, at Owens-Corning Fiberglass Corporation's plant in Jackson, Tennessee, the company has salvaged an operation about to go under.[60] Through their TQM efforts, Owens-Corning focused its attention on redefining its goals—both in objectives for the organization and how its work was to be accomplished. The results of this effort led to the production of one quality product, rather than the three that it had in the past. This simplified operation, coupled with the infusion of technology, was able to sustain production at 130 million pounds of fiberglass annually. However, rather than having four layers of management and 540 workers, this same production goal is achieved with one layer of management, and 80 employees. For Owens-Corning, this remake at the Jackson plant has fostered a profitable operation—something that had been missing for seven years.

TQM Today

The focus on continuous process improvements in organizational operations gained momentum in the early 1990s. Unfortunately, TQM is not something that can be easily implemented, nor dictated down through the many levels in an organization. Rather, TQM is likened to an organization-wide development process;[61] that is, the process must be accepted and supported by top management, and driven by collaborative efforts, throughout each segment in the organization.[62]

Every individual must understand what quality means to them on their job and what effort needs to be exerted to achieve the move toward "perfection." These same organizational members must recognize that failing to do so could lead to unsatisfied customers—customers who may take their purchasing power to competitors who do produce quality products and services.[63] And that, too, means knowing just what the customers want. For example, Granite Rock Company is an organization that "produces and sells crushed stone, mixes concrete and asphalt products, and even does some highway paving."[64] There didn't appear to be a serious need for Granite Rock to change its operations. But its management team, headed by Bruce and Steve Woolpert, wouldn't sit still. They knew that they had to continuously get to know their customers, in terms of what quality meant to them, and convey that to their employees. And do you know what they found? By meeting with customers, they determined that each product line had special customers' needs tied to it. For example, in its concrete operations, customers demanded on-time delivery, which meant that Granite Rock had to be prepared to deliver its products whenever the customer wanted. That, they learned, meant an around-the-clock operation.[65] That customer demand was met, affecting such a change even in a union environment, because it could have meant the difference between success or failure of the business. That's what's important: doing what is necessary to keep the company strong and its people employed.

Do unions see the need for this cooperative effort? Early indications are that they do, for they, too, see the need to continuously improve. This has resulted in unions believing that by supporting continuous improvement efforts, the company recognized the importance of its employees.[66] That translates into training, job security, and other rewards. If the organizations don't keep their customers, the employees don't have jobs!

Is there any doubt about why we need to support continuous process improvement? Total perfection may never be achieved, nor may it be economically feasible to do so. For instance, we wouldn't want to spend $500,000 to get perfection if it cost only $2,000 to correct the defects.[67] Or would we? Nonetheless, not attempting to reach that goal may simply be a bad business decision in today's competitive environment.

HRM Support of TQM

Human resource management plays an important role in the implementation of TQM programs. Whenever an organization embarks on any effort like TQM, it is introducing change into the organization. As such, organization development efforts dominate.

Specifically, HRM must prepare individuals for the change. This requires clear and extensive communications of why the change will occur, what is to be expected, and the effects it will have on employees. TQM efforts may result in changes in work patterns, changes in operations, and even changes in reporting relationships. HRM must avail itself to help the affected employees overcome barriers that may result in resistance to the change, That is, the fear dimension that is often associated with change must be overcome.

TQM efforts are also going to result in new ways of doing things. Consequently, HRM must be prepared to train employees in these new processes, and help them to attain new skills levels that may be associated with the "new, improved" operations.[68]

Reengineering Work Processes for Improved Productivity

Although TQM is a positive start in many of our organizations, it focuses on continuous improvement or ongoing incremental change. Such action is intuitively appealing—the constant and permanent search to make things better. Yet, many of our companies function in an environment that is dynamic—facing rapid and constant change. As a result, total quality management techniques may not be in the best interest of the organization.

The problem with continuous process improvements is that it may provide a false sense of security. It may give managers a feeling that they're actively doing something positive. Obviously, this is true. But, ongoing incremental change avoids facing up to the possibility that what the organization may really need is radical or quantum change. Like Tedd Benson and Benson Woodworking, such drastic change results in the reengineering of the organization.

Reengineering occurs when more than 70 percent of the work processes in an organization are evaluated, and altered.[69] It requires organizational members to rethink what work should be done, how it is to be done, and how to best implement these decisions. That is, reengineering in companies like Federal Express, Bell Atlantic, and Vortex Industries, focuses on simplifying the operations and making them more efficient and more customer-focused.[70] As a result, reengineering typically includes three main features: a customer focus, an organizational structure that is production "friendly," and a desire to think about organizational work from scratch. For example, reengineering efforts at Mutual Benefit Life Insurance company focused attention on making its customer insurance applications process more effective. By implementing a new process whereby a case manager has total authority from the time an application is received until the policy is issued, Mutual Benefit has eliminated the work of five separate departments and nineteen different people. Consequently, the application process has decreased from almost one month to as little as four hours.[71] Reengineering efforts, overall, have led to improvements in production quality, speed, innovation, and customer service.[72]

Reengineering Radical, quantum change in an organization.

Although reengineering efforts may prove worthwhile for organizations, some caution is in order. Reengineering is not a one-time process, and as such is not a quick fix. It should also not be a ploy to simply downsize the organization.[73] Instead, it's a continuous review of the organization's structure and its practices—including how managers manage—to increase productivity and meet organizational objectives.[74] And this last point cannot be ignored. Even James Champy and Michael Hammer, the two individuals credited with introducing corporate America to reengineering, have recognized management's role in all of this. In fact, their chief reason cited for why reengineering efforts fails is management itself.[75] That is, reengineering without changing leadership styles, changing the attitude of workers, involving workers in those things that affect them and their jobs, and building work teams, will not bring about the desired results. That's why individuals like Tedd Benson, who recognize their major role in the process, can make the necessary changes that lead to quantum improvements.

Reengineering versus TQM

If you've been reading the last few sections closely, you may be asking yourself: Isn't there a contradiction between TQM and reengineering? On the surface, it may appear so, but consider this. While TQM is necessary for most organizations, it may not always be the right thing to do initially. If what you are producing is outdated, or the like, a new, improved version of the product may not be helpful to the company. Rather, in a number of instances, major change is required. After that has occurred, then continually improving it (TQM) has its rightful place. Let's see how this may be so.[76]

Assume you are the manager responsible for implementing some type of change in your barbeque grill manufacturing process. If you took the continuous improvement approach, your frame of reference would be a kettle drum base made of steel that uses charcoal or propane. Your continuous improvement program may lead you to focus on things like using a different grade of steel for cooking quickness, or adjusting the air flow to make the fire burn more efficiently. Of course your grill might be better than you previously made, but is that enough? Compare your action to that of a competitor who reengineers the process.

To begin, your competitor poses the following question: How does the company design a grill for today's active and environmentally conscious consumer? Starting from scratch, and not being constrained by current manufacturing processes (ala reengineering), the organization completes a redesign with something that looks like a space-age grill—and is electric! That makes this ecologically safe! As a result, this grill is quicker, and doesn't pollute.

In this contrived example, both companies made progress. But which do you believe made the most progress given the dynamic environment they face? It's a moot point, but it clearly reinforces why companies like Union Carbide, GTE, Thermos, or Mutual Benefit Life opted for reengineering as opposed to incremental change.[77] It is imperative in today's business environment for all managers to consider the challenge of reengineering their organizational processes. Why? Because reengineering can lead to "major gains in cost, service, or

Monte Peterson (front), CEO of Thermos, and members of the Lifestyle team proudly display their reengineering barbecue grill. By designing a grill from scratch, this team was able to produce a product that was more ecologically friendly and better met the needs of today's busy customers.

time."[78] And it's these kinds of gains that will take companies well into the twenty-first century.

HRM and Reengineering

If we accept the premise that reengineering will change how we do business, it stands to reason that our employees will be directly affected. As such, generating the gains that reengineering offers will not occur unless we address the people issues.

First of all, reengineering may have left employees, at least the survivors, confused and angry. Although a preferred method of "change" would have been to involve employees throughout the process, we need to recognize that reengineering may have left some of our employees frustrated and unsure of what to expect.[79] Long-time work relationships may have been severed—and stress levels may be magnified. Accordingly, HRM must have mechanisms in place for employees to get appropriate answers and direction of what to expect—as well as assistance in dealing with the conflict that may permeate the organization.

Although the emotional aspect is difficult to resolve, for reengineering to generate its benefits, HRM needs to train its employee population. Whether it's a new process, a technology enhancement, working in teams, having more decision-making authority, or the like, our employees are going to need new skills. Consequently, HRM must be in a position to offer the skills training that is necessary in the "new" organization. Even the best process will fail if employees do not have the requisite skills to perform as the process task dictates.

Furthermore, as many components of the organization have been redefined, so too will be many of the HRM activities that affect employees. For example, if redesigned work practices have resulted in changes on employee compensation packages (e.g., bonus/incentive pay), such changes need to be communicated to employees. Likewise, performance standards and how employees will be evaluated must also be understood.

The Contingent Work Force

Years ago employment patterns in our organizations were relatively predictable. In good times, when work was plentiful, large numbers of employees were hired. Then as the economy went into a recession and fewer goods were being purchased, companies simply laid off their "surplus" employee population.[80] When the economic picture improved, a new cycle started. But downsizing, restructuring, and reengineering have all changed this management practice. Organizations today often do not have the luxury of hiring lots of individuals when times are good and severing them from organizational service when down times occur. Simply the costs of frequently hiring employees, coupled with increases in unemployment insurance rates (based, in part, on how frequently an employer lays off employees) and the costs associated with separating employees (like severance pay) have required employers to rethink their work population.

In a number of organizations, this dynamic situation has led organizations to employ two types of workers. The first group are the core employees. **Core employees** are workers who hold full-time jobs in organizations. These employees usually provide some essential job tasks—like the chief software designer of a high-tech software development company—that require commitment and permanence in the organization. Employees who hold key core positions enjoy the

Core employees An organization's full-time employee population.

Contingent Work Force The part-time, temporary, and contract workers used by organizations to fill peak staffing needs, or perform work unable to be done by core employees.

full slate of employee benefits that typically were provided to full-time employees. Beyond these essential employees are many individuals who "sell" their services to an organization. We collectively call these individuals the **contingent work force.** Contingent workers include individuals who are typically hired for shorter periods of time. They perform specific tasks that often require special job skills, and are employed when an organization is experiencing significant deviations in its work flow. Then, when the special need for them is fulfilled, these workers are let go. But not let go in the traditional layoff sense. Contingent workers have no "full-time" rights in the organization. Consequently, when their project is completed, so, too, may be their affiliation with the organization. Similarly, because of their status, these workers often do not receive any of the employee benefits that are provided to core workers. Upward to 30 percent of the work force in 1995 was comprised of contingent workers,[81] and that number, given the trends in restructuring and reengineering, is expected to climb to almost 50 percent by the turn of the century.[82] So who makes up the contingency pool? Contingent workers are any individuals who work part-time, as temporaries, or as contract workers (see Table 2-3). And they may hold such diverse jobs as secretaries, accountants, nurses, assembly line workers, lawyers, dentists, computer programmers, engineers, marketing representatives, and human resources professionals. Even some senior management positions are filled with contingent workers.[83]

TABLE 2-3   The Contingent Work Force

Part-time Employees:	Part-time employees are those employees who work fewer than forty hours a week. Generally, part-timers are afforded few, if any, employee benefits. Part-time employees are generally a good source of employees for organizations to staff their peak hours. For example, the bank staff that expects its heaviest clientele between 10 A.M. and 2 P.M. may bring in part-time tellers for those four hours. Part-time employees may also be a function of job sharing, where two employees split one full-time job.
Temporary Employees:	Temporary employees, like part-timers are generally employed during peak production periods. Temporary workers also act as fill-ins when some employees are off of work for an extended period of time. For example, a secretarial position may be filled using a "temp" while the secretary is off work during his twelve-week unpaid leave of absence for the birth of his daughter. Temporary workers create a fixed cost to an employer for labor "used" during a specified period.
Contract Workers:	Contract workers, subcontractors, and consultants (may be referred to as freelance individuals) are hired by organizations to work on specific projects. These workers, typically very skilled, perform certain duties for an organization. Often their fee is set in the contract and is paid when the organization receives particular deliverables. Organizations use contract workers because their labor cost is then fixed, and they don't incur any of the costs associated with a full-time employee population. Additionally, some contract arrangements may exist because the contractor can provide virtually the same good or service in a more efficient manner.

Are Contingent Workers Throw-Away Workers?

Undoubtedly, over the past ten to fifteen years, we have witnessed significant changes in how organizations are staffed. As the changing world of work affects our businesses, reality has indicated that today's organizations simply cannot be efficient if they have surplus employees. The strategic nature of both business, and HRM, requires that they both be prepared for "just-in-time" employees. What that means is that organizations must find the proper blend of having a ready supply of skilled workers available when the need arises—not delayed in any manner that might create a serious shortage leading to not meeting the challenge— and not having a surplus pool of workers waiting for something to arise. In order to meet this dual goal, however, organizations must remain flexible in their staffing levels.[84] Contingent workers conveniently fill that void. But at what cost?

Are workers freely becoming contingent workers out of their desire to fulfill personal work, family, lifestyle, or financial needs? Or have individuals been forced into this employment "limbo" as a result to downsizing and the like? The answer to both is unequivocally yes.[85] There are those individuals who prefer the contingent work relationship. This offers workers some of the greatest flexibility in work scheduling—and that's something that workers, especially women, have been requesting from corporate America.[86] With the increasing diversity of the work force, contingent work arrangements permit one to blend family and career goals.[87] Using this logic, contingent positions are, in fact, beneficial to employees.

But we cannot overlook the other side of this issue. Many organizations are using contingent work concepts to save money. Employing contingent workers saves an organization about 40 percent in labor costs, because no benefits are provided. Furthermore, hiring contingent workers protects an organization's

Laura Masurovsky is a contingent worker by choice. As an attorney in a large law firm in Washington, D.C., Laura found she had little time to spend on the things she valued most in her life—her family. As a freelance attorney, Masurovsky can pick and choose her work schedules, thus giving her more time to spend with her family. As a contingent worker, then, Laura now has more autonomy and more flexibility in her daily life as a mother and a career lawyer.

core employees from work fluctuations.[88] For instance, Blue Cross and Blue Shield of Rhode Island was able to trim its work force by more than 40 percent over a five-year period without having to lay off one full-timer. To achieve this, some employees are, in fact, being forced into contingent employee roles. For example, a Bank of America employee with more than fourteen years of experience was given a choice: reduce work time to nineteen hours a week and receive no benefits, or be severed from the bank permanently.[89] This employee, given financial responsibilities, took what was minimally available from the bank and looked elsewhere for another part-time job. Unfortunately, individuals in this situation may work forty hours or more each week, for several organizations, and not have the luxury of the benefits package had those forty hours been spent in one organization. And the Bank of America, like other peer institutions, has repeated this process thousands of times. In fact, entering 1995, this organization employed only 19 percent of its work force on a full-time basis.[90] The rest were contingent workers! Simply, some companies are "dumping" the majority of their full-time work force and replacing it with lower-paid temporaries or contractual workers.[91]

The debate over the use of contingent workers will surely continue. There will always be those who want to be full-time employees, but simply cannot find that opportunity. However, the increasing trend to be lean-and-mean, the increasing competitive nature of business, and the more diverse work force will result in the creation of more temporary jobs (see "HRM in a De-Jobbed Organization"). The IRS is paying close attention this latter activity, though. Failing to withhold payroll taxes or pay social security premiums for temporary workers who are actually working on the company premises for even short durations has led to investigations, and fines and penalties for those companies that have "misclassified" their workers.[92]

HRM Implications of Contingent Workers

When an organization makes its strategic decision to employ a sizable portion of its work force from the contingency ranks, several HRM issues come to the forefront. These include being able to have these "virtual" employees available when needed, providing scheduling options that meet their needs, and making decisions about whether or not benefits will be offered to the contingent work force.[93]

No organization can make the transition to a contingent work force without sufficient planning. As such, when these strategic decisions are being made, HRM must be an active partner in the discussions. After all, it is HRM's responsibility to locate and bring into the organization these temporary workers. Just as employment has played an integral role in recruiting full-time employees, so too, will it play a major part in securing needed just-in-time talent.

As temporary workers are brought in, HRM will also have the responsibility of quickly adapting them to the organization. Although orientation for full-time employees is more detailed, the contingent work force, nonetheless, needs to be made aware of the organization's personality. Along this line, too, is some training may be required. Even a systems analyst brought in to work on a specific computer programming problem will need to be brought up to speed rather quickly on the uniqueness of the organization's system.

HRM will also have to give some thought to how it will effectively attract quality temporaries. As this becomes the status quo in business, there will be significant competition for the "good" talent. Accordingly, HRM will need to reexam-

HRM in a De-Jobbed Organization

If we were able to turn time back almost two hundred years, we would no-tice something strikingly similar to what is happening today. Our ancestors work hard on their jobs, but they did so at home. They were farmers and crafts makers. They produced goods that society needed to survive. Their days were long and hard, they had no set working hours, no supervisors to "tell" them what to do, and they had no job description to rely on for "hints" on what to do at work. As the Industrial Revolution movement brought with it large, centralized work locations, the formalities of work life appeared. But these structured norms are quickly vanishing as workers today handle infor-mation, not physical goods, and the changing environment in which we work demands rapid responses. As a result, we are witnessing the disappear-ance of the job as we know it.

Yesterday's jobs were dominated by the rigidity associated with them. Workers performed the same tasks, day in and day out. Yes, every once in a while those tasks changed, and the job description was rewritten. But once that happened, the routine was reinstated. Today, however, that "luxury" doesn't exist. Tasks change too frequently to be accurately reflected in a job description. As this dynamic situation continues, organizations have to con-tinue to look for new ways of finding the skills necessary to complete the job.

Work, then, will be built around what needs to be done. Individuals will work with other workers for a specified period of time, then move on to an-other project. That project may be in the organization, as well as outside it. Workers will perform their duties as members of project teams, not necessar-ily as representatives of departments within the organization. Workers will be expected to perform whatever tasks the project demands, as opposed to only performing a limited set of jobs that their departmental jobs required. And working with these project teams will be the contingent workers—the part-time, temporary, contract, and consultant individuals.

As a result of these changes, plus the infusion of technology—computers, modems, fax machines, and so on—workers will not have the routine 9-to-5 job. Rather, work hours will be a function of the work to be done. Hours worked may not equate to hours paid. Employees will be paid for project re-sults, at a rate that is consistent to the value the project work added to the organization. Some workers on these project teams, too, may never be seen by their peers. Rather, through the existing technology, some of these work-ers may perform their tasks at locations anywhere in the world, and be linked to the team via telecommuting technology.

Will tomorrow's work be a throwback to yesteryear? If current trends are any indication, there's a strong possibility that this will occur. But the loss of the job as we know it may not be all that bad. Although workers will be los-ing their security and predictability of the traditional jobs, de-jobbed organi-zations may give individuals the opportunity to have the flexible schedules and autonomy that they have been asking for.

Source: Vignette based on William Bridges, "The End of the Job," *Fortune* (September 19, 1994), pp. 62–74. Also see, for example, Peter F. Drucker, "The Age of Social Transformation," *The Atlantic Monthly* (November 1994), pp. 53–80.

ine its compensation philosophy. If temporaries are employed solely as a cost-cutting measure, the pay and benefits offered to contingent workers might be different than those offered to other workers who are used part-time as a result of restructuring and reengineering. HRM, then, will need to begin understanding specifically what these employees want. Is it the flexibility in scheduling, the autonomy these jobs offer, or the control over one's career destiny that such a situation affords individuals that attracts them? Or is it just bad luck, and they are forced into this situation? Understanding the reasons will surely affect the motivation of these workers.[94] For example, Half-Price Books, a Dallas, Texas, book retailer, offers health insurance coverage, retirement, vacation, and sick and holiday pay to its part-time employees. They provide these benefits because they need an ample supply of contingent workers and want to reduce the turnover that often occurs in their industry. By recognizing that many of their workers prefer to work part-time, yet need basic employee benefits, Half-Price Books attracts a higher quality of temporary worker.[95]

Finally, HRM must be prepared to deal with the potential conflict that may arise between core and contingent workers. The core employees may become envious of the higher pay rates and flexibility in scheduling that the contingent workers receive. In the total compensation package, which includes benefits, core employees might earn substantially more money, but these employees may not immediately include the "in-kind" pay (their benefits) in the rate of pay received. For example, paying a training consultant $3,000 for a two-day project management training program might cause some conflict with core HRM trainers. If the consultant offers twenty-five of these two-day programs over the year, earning $75,000 in consulting fees, a $40,000-a-year company trainer might take offense. Consequently, HRM must ensure its communication programs anticipate some of these potential conflicts and address them before they become detrimental to the organization—or worse, provide an incentive for core employees to leave!

Decentralized Work Sites

Perkin-Elmer Company, the Norwalk, Connecticut, manufacturer of scientific and laboratory equipment, recently found itself facing a dilemma.[96] It had closed about thirty-five of its sales offices in the United States and made the decision that several hundred of its sales staff employees would work out of their homes. One employee, Wayne Wolinger, took offense!

It wasn't that Wolinger objected to working out of his home. He clearly saw the benefit of being closer to his customers. What he did challenge, however, was the fact that Perkin-Elmer wouldn't compensate him for the costs he would incur by having his office at home. Although the company was setting up the office—furnishings, supplies, and equipment, Wolinger knew his monthly electric bill, insurance premiums, and the like would increase. Simply put, Wolinger wanted to be reimbursed for added expenses. Furthermore, because the company was saving money on warehousing by requiring employees to have spare parts frequently needed by customers at their homes, Wolinger wanted to be compensated for the "lost" space in his house. But company policy was clear—employees were not going to be paid any additional money for working out of their home. As a result, and an inability to reach a satisfactory compromise, Wayne Wolinger was fired.

What happened to Wayne Wolinger may be an extreme case, but one that will surely come to light as more companies move to having workers do their jobs at home. This **decentralized work site** arrangement has advantages and disadvantages, and will create new issues for HRM.

Work Is Where Your Computer Is

As mentioned in the "HRM in a De-Jobbed Organization" box, if you go back 150 years in U.S. history, it was not uncommon for workers to be performing their "craft" out of their homes. In fact, most workers performed some tasks, produced a finished product, and took it to a market to sell. But the Industrial Revolution changed all that. Large manufacturing companies drew workers away from rural areas and into the cities. Along with this movement came the traditional job—one that required employees to show up at the company's facility and spend their eight-to-twelve-hour work day.

But downsizing and reengineering is changing all of that. Jobs as our parents and grandparents knew them are disappearing. And when you factor technological changes that have occurred in the past decade, even where we do our jobs may change.

Computers, modems, fax machines, and even the telephone are making decentralized work sites attractive. Why? Several reasons have been cited.[97] Telecommuting capabilities that exist today have made it possible for employees to be located anywhere on the globe. With this potential, employers no longer have to consider locating a business near its work force. For example, if Aetna Insurance in Idaho finds that it is having problems attracting qualified local applicants for its claims-processing jobs, and a pool of qualified workers is available in Colorado Springs, Aetna doesn't need to establish a facility in Colorado. Instead, by providing these employees with computer equipment and appropriate ancillaries, the work can be done hundreds of miles away, and then be transmitted to the "home" office.

Telecommuting also offers an opportunity for a business in a high-labor-cost area to have its work done in an area where lower wages prevail. Take the publisher in New York City who finds manuscript editing costs have skyrocketed. By having that work done by a qualified editor in Parkton, West Virginia, the publisher could reduce labor costs. Likewise, not having to provide office space in the city to this editor, given the cost per square foot of real estate in the area, adds to the cost savings.

Decentralized work sites also offer opportunities that may meet the needs of the diversified work force. Those who have family responsibilities, like child care, may prefer to work in their homes, rather than travel to the organization's facility. Telecommuting, then, provides the flexibility in work scheduling that many members of the diversified work force desire. Finally, there's some incentive from government agencies for companies to consider these alternative work arrangements. For example, the federal government, in its effort to address environmental concerns in the United States, may make state highway funds contingent on the state's ability to reduce traffic congestion in heavily populated areas. One means of achieving that goal is for businesses to receive some incentive, like a tax break, for implementing decentralized work sites. In a similar fashion, state departments of labor may also provide an incentive to businesses to relocate their work activities from more affluent communities to economically depressed areas.[98]

This trend is expected to continue. Currently, about 15 percent of the work force works at home, and that number is expected to rise sharply in the future.[99] And these jobs needn't solely exist in processing or sales type jobs. Instead, telecommuting is affording doctors, lawyers, accountants, service workers, and managers the opportunities to conduct their business directly out of their homes.[100] Of course, as this occurs, it is creating some issues that HRM must deal with.

HRM and Decentralized Work Sites

Generally individuals get excited about the opportunities and freedom of working out of their homes. Although there are instances such as those of Wayne Wolinger that must be resolved, many home workers see this work arrangement as a major benefit. For HRM, however, decentralized work sites present a challenge.

Much of that challenge revolves around training managers how to establish appropriate work standards, and ensuring that the work is done on time. Traditional "face-time" is removed in decentralized work sites, and managers' need to "control" the work will have to change. Instead, there will have to be more employee involvement, allowing workers the discretion to make those decisions that affect them. For instance, although a due date is established for the work assigned to employees, managers must recognize that home workers will work at their own pace. That may mean instead of an individual focusing work efforts over an eight-hour period, the individual may work two hours here, three hours at another time, and another three late at night. The emphasis, then, will be on the final product, not the means by which it is accomplished.

Work at home may also require HRM to rethink its compensation policy. Will it pay workers by the hour, on a salary basis, or by the job performed? More than likely, because certain jobs, like claims processing, can be easily quantified and standards set, pay plans will be in the form of pay for actual work done.

Beyond these issues, HRM must also anticipate potential legal problems that may arise from telecommuting.[101] For example, what if the employee works more than forty hours during the work week. Will that employee be entitled to overtime pay? The answer is yes! As such, decentralized work-site activities will have to be monitored by HRM to ensure that employees are not abusing overtime privileges, and that those workers who rightfully should be paid overtime are compensated.

Because employees in decentralized work sites are full-time employees of an organization, as opposed to contingent workers, it will be the organization's responsibility to ensure the health and safety of the decentralized work site. Equipment provided by the company, for example, that leads to an employee injury or illness is the responsibility of the organization. Although HRM cannot constantly monitor workers in their homes, it must ensure that these workers understand the proper techniques for using the equipment. Additionally, if accidents or injuries occur, employees must understand the regulations for reporting them. Generally that means, for instance, reporting them within forty-eight hours, at which time HRM must investigate immediately (see "Ethical Decisions in HRM").

Employee Involvement

Whenever significant changes occur in an organization, subsequent changes in the way work gets done must also occur. With respect to downsizing, many companies today are requiring their employees to do more with less. The sheer magnitude of work alone dictates that it cannot be done without some assistance. Involving employees means different things to different organizations

Ethics Decisions in HRM:

Workers' Compensation and the Home Worker

It is well ingrained into the minds of human resource managers that they are partly responsible for ensuring that the workplace is free from hazards that may cause health-related problems or injuries. Along those lines, too, it is understood that if an employee is injured in the course of performing his or her duties on the job, that employee will be afforded some sort of income continuation—usually through the organization's workers' compensation insurance program. So, for instance, if an employee is required to retrieve supplies from a supply room one flight down, and falls down the steps while attempting to replenish her office supplies, workers' compensation applies. But should that same "courtesy" apply to home workers?

For example, decentralized work sites frequently require employees to store supplies in their house for office use. These supplies, and possibly spare parts, belong to the organization, and were furnished by the organization at no cost to the employee. They are simply being warehoused at the employee's home. Accordingly, if in the course of a day's work, the home worker must go into his or her basement to retrieve supplies, and falls down the basement steps, should the employee be covered by the organization's workers' compensation insurance? What if that same employee decided to take a break from telecommuting, and went into the kitchen for a cup of coffee: If, while on the way there, the employee falls and breaks a leg, should this employee's income be continued under the organization's workers' compensation program?

What responsibility does the organization have for its employees who work at home? Even though a similar situation at the organization's facility might require it to "cover" the employee injury, should the organization be held responsible for worker injuries that occur at home, when the home off-site employee is performing regular duties? What if the employee is injured while using company-furnished equipment for personal business? Should the organization be held responsible? What's your opinion?

and people. But by and large, for today's workers to be successful, there are a number of **employee involvement** concepts that appear to be accepted.[102] These are delegation, participative management, work teams, goal setting, and employer training—the empowering of employees! Let's elaborate on these a bit.

Employee Involvement Affording employees more delegation, participative management, work teams, goal setting, and training.

How Organizations Involve Employees

An employee cannot handle each task of a job and be expected to complete the work of multiple individuals under today's work arrangements. Accordingly, more employees at all levels will need to be required to delegate some of these activities and responsibilities to other organizational members. This means that employees are going to have to be given certain amounts of authority to make

●

Delegation A management activity in which activities are assigned to individuals at lower levels in the organization.

Participative Management A management concept giving employees more control over the day-to-day activities on their job.

Work Teams Formal work groups made up of interdependent individuals who are responsible for attainment of a specific goal.

decisions that directly affect their work. Even though delegation was once perceived as something that managers did with lower levels of management, **delegation** will be required at all levels of the organization.

In addition to being required to take on more responsibilities, employees will be expected to make decisions without the benefit of the "tried and true" decisions of the past. And because all these employees are part of the process today, there is more of a need for them to have a say in the decision-making process. Gone are the days of autocratic management where the strong hand ruled. To facilitate customer demands and fulfill corporate expectations, today's employees need to be more involved. Group decision making enables these employees to have input into the processes, and enables them to have access to needed information, and makes them part of the strategic management process.[103] **Participative management** is also consistent with a work environment that requires increased creativity and innovation.

Another phenomenon of involving employees will be an emphasis on **work teams**.[104] The bureaucratic structure of yesterday—where clear lines of authority existed and the chain of command was paramount—is not appropriate for most of today's companies. Workers from different specializations in an organization are increasingly required to work together to successfully complete complex projects. As such, traditional work areas have given way to more of a team effort, building and capitalizing on the various skills and backgrounds that each member brings to the team. Consider, for example, what kind of group it takes to put together a symphony. One musician could not possibly handle the varied instruments—especially playing them at one time. Accordingly, to blend the music of the orchestra, symphonies have string sections, brass instruments, percussions, and the like. At times, however, a musician may cross over these boundaries, like the trombonist who also plays the piano. The basis of these work teams, then, is driven by the tasks at hand. Involving employees allows them an opportunity to focus on the job goals. By giving them more freedom, employees are in a better position to develop the means to achieve the desired ends.

Implications for HRM

Up until now we have addressed some components of employee involvement. For an organization, however, addressing them is not enough. What is needed is training, and that's where human resources management can make a valuable contribution. Employees expected to delegate, to have decisions participatively handled, to work in teams, or to set goals cannot do so unless they know and understand what it is they are to do. Empowering employees requires extensive training in all aspects of the job. Workers may need to understand how new job design, processes, and the like will affect them. They may need training in interpersonal skills to make participative management and work teams function properly. All in all, we can anticipate much more involvement from HRM in all parts of the organization.

But, make no mistake about it. Employee involvement comes at a price. The question is, then: Is it worth it? From all indications, it appears to be. First of all, better control over one's work activities, coupled with better "tools," has been shown to improve productivity.[105] We are doing more with less, but are doing it smarter and more productively. Additionally, as employees see the commitment the organization and HRM has made to them, there is evidence that commitment and loyalty to an organization will increase.[106]

Study Tools and Applications

Summary

(This summary relates to the Learning Objectives identified on p. 30.)

After having read this chapter, you should know:

1. Globalization is creating a situation where human resources management must begin to search for mobile and skilled employees capable of successfully performing their job duties in a foreign land. This means that these employees must understand the host country's language, culture, and customs.

2. The work force composition has changed considerably over the past thirty years. Once characterized as having a dominant number of white males, the work force composition of the 1990s is comprised of a mixture of women, minorities, immigrants, and white males.

3. The most significant implications for human resources management regarding the changing work force composition are language and skill deficiencies of available workers, changing management practices to accommodate a diverse work group, dealing with conflict among employees, and providing family-friendly benefits.

4. Changing skill requirements necessitate human resource management to provide extensive training. This training can be in the form of remedial help for those who have skill deficiencies, to specialized training dealing with technology changes.

5. Corporate downsizing is a phenomenon that has swept through U.S. corporations in an effort toward making the organizations more efficient. In many cases, this has meant eliminating layers of management by increasing the span of control. In downsizing, HRM acts as the employees' advocate, communicating all necessary information to affected employees.

6. Total quality management (TQM) refers to a process in an organization that promotes continuous improvements. It seeks to build customer satisfaction through these continuous improvements and employee involvement.

7. Reengineering refers to the radical, quantum change that occurs in the organization. HRM is instrumental in reengineering by preparing employees to deal with the change and training them in new techniques.

8. The contingent work force includes those part-time, temporary, consultants, and contract workers who provide services to organizations on an as-needed basis. The HRM implications of a contingent work force include attracting and retaining skilled contingent workers, adjusting to their special needs, and managing any conflict that may arise between core and contingent workers.

9. Organizations use decentralized work sites because telecommuting arrangements enable organizations to find qualified employees without having to relocate business facilities. Decentralized work sites also provide cost savings to the organization, as well as fulfilling some special needs of a diversified work force. For HRM, decentralized work sites will require training for managers on managing and controlling work, and establishing pay systems to reflect this work arrangement. HRM will also have to monitor the hours home workers spend on the job, as well as ensuring the health and safety of workers in the home office.

10. Employee involvement can best be defined as giving each worker more control over his or her job. To do this requires delegation, participative management, work teams, goal setting, and employee training. If handled properly, involving employees should assist in developing more productive employees who are more loyal and committed to the organization.

Key Terms

baby boomers
baby busters
contingent work force
continuous process improvement
core employees
cultural environments
decentralized work sites
delegation
downsizing
employee involvement

global village
mature workers
participative management
reengineering
skill deficiencies
span of control
total quality management (TQM)
work teams
work-force diversity

EXPERIENTIAL EXERCISE:

Generation Similarities and Differences

The diversity that exists in our work force today is exceptionally well documented. Workers come from all walks of life. Yet while these differences can be celebrated, focusing the varied backgrounds toward common organizational goals can be challenging. Something as simple as age difference can reveal this challenge. For example, there are basically three separate generations that co-exist in our work force today—those born before 1946, those born between 1946 and 1964, and those born 1965 or after. In this application, we'll explore some of these differences.

Step 1:   Your professor will divide the class into three groups. Group 1, those born before 1946 (mature workers); Group 2, those born between 1946 and 1964 (the baby boomers); and Group 3, those born 1965 and after (the Generation Xers).

Step 2:   After meeting in your "generational" group, answer the following questions by generating lists to:

a. What do you value in life?

b. What do you want from a "job"?

c. What do you expect from an organization?

d. What are your three most favorite television shows?

e. What are your three most favorite musical groups?

f. What is your ideal vacation?

g. How do you view the other two groups? For instance, if you are a baby boomer, how does your view describe the characteristics of the traditional workers and the generation Xers?

Step 3:   Each group will report to the class its responses to Step 2. This information will be captured by your instructor in some capacity.

Step 4:   As a large group, now that all views have been presented, what similarities are their between the three groups? What differences exist? What challenges do you believe these differences create for organizational members?

CASE APPLICATION:

Nucor Corporation

In the steel business, like the auto industry, you either lead, follow, or get out of the way. Unfortunately, for yesterday's giants, U.S. and Bethlehem Steel, the latter two appear to have occurred. Cheaper-priced foreign steel coming from Japan and Korea, plus labor–management conflicts have all but decimated these prior world leaders. In fact, foreign competition in the steel industry has all but put the United States out of the steel business. Fortunately, though, someone has forgotten to tell Nucor Corporation that a U.S. company cannot effectively compete in this global industry.[107]

Nucor Corporation is a steel-products manufacturer that operates out of sixteen facilities in eight states. Company officials recognized early in its founding that traditional steel manufacturing operations weren't working in today's environment. Rather than build formalized, hierarchial organizational structures, Nucor runs each of these sixteen facilities as separate business units. In all of Nucor Corporation there are only four layers of management—individuals who assist the 6,000-plus nonunion workers in achieving corporate goals. Nucor's management philosophy is quite simple: Involve employees and inspire them to reach great heights.

Both Nucor management and its employees are some of the lowest paid workers in the steel industry. For example, many of the employees are paid a flat rate of $9 an hour—almost 50 percent of what unionized steel workers receive. But that doesn't present a problem for these workers, or create a point of contention between employees and their supervisors. Instead, Nucor employees welcome it, because along with the $9-an-hour pay rate comes an incentive bonus. For example, Nucor's management established a production standard—eight tons of straightened steel an hour. For every ton over eight that is produced, workers receive a bonus. Nucor's employees have responded exceptionally well. They produce somewhere between 35 and 42 tons of steel an hour. That's about four times the industry average of 10 tons. In return, these $9-an-hour employees receive an additional $14—bringing their total wage rate to approximately $23 an hour.

But pay is not the only thing that inspires Nucor workers. They are given the freedom to make meaningful decisions that affect their work lives. Working in teams of up to twenty individuals, Nucor workers establish their work schedules, monitor their own activities and quality of output, evaluate one another, and work diligently to provide a safe work environment. For them, as with Nucor management, as long as they make their "numbers," they're left alone.

Success at Nucor is hard to overlook. Building a company that produces annual sales that exceed $2 billion, and generating a return on investment over 25 percent, is almost an aberration for a U.S. steel company. And it achieved these with its no-frills management and human resources practices. Granted, Nucor practices may not work in every situation—but it's awfully hard to argue with their success!

Questions

1. Nucor Steel focuses its operations solely on production. Its employee involvement practices have all but eliminated the need for traditional HRM functions. Do you believe that such practices could eventually make HRM obsolete in the future? Explain your position.
2. In organizations where employee involvement is advocated, there appears to be an

equivalent incentive system. Do you believe employees value the involvement more, or simply the opportunity to have more control over the amount they earn? Which do you believe is more important to workers? Discuss.

3. In companies like Nucor, where there are fewer layers of management, career opportunities are limited. Employees either don't move up until someone leaves or dies, or they leave the organization themselves. Do you believe that restructuring corporations, such that they are lean and mean, actually works to decrease employee commitment to the organization? Explain.

Testing Your Understanding

How well did you fulfill the learning objectives?

1. Globalization has changed the work of the human resources professional. All of the following statements are globalization issues except
   a. training is often provided through the employing organization.
   b. culture sensitization must be provided, often through the employing organization.
   c. conflict reduction techniques may be needed as workers from different countries are combined into work groups.
   d. management training must include how to deal with workers from many different countries.
   e. in U.S. organizations, HR professionals are responsible for screening future employees to make sure they speak English and share American values.

2. Why has work-force diversity changed the work of the human resources professional?
   a. Most human resources professionals are women, and thus, represent a means of correcting past injustices, like pay differences between men and women.
   b. Workers with different backgrounds, values, and expectations have different needs that must be accommodated with different compensation and benefit packages.
   c. Most human resources departments are now also responsible for on-site day-care centers.
   d. Laws require quotas for the employment of all minority groups.
   e. Work-force diversity is not an issue for the human resources professional.

3. What employee-involvement concepts are accepted in today's organizations?
   a. Delegation is a sign of weakness. Employees need to know that the boss is "in charge" to feel secure.
   b. Participative management gives employees more control over the day-to-day activities of their jobs.
   c. Goals should be set by management and clearly spelled out for each employee.
   d. Don't let employee work teams have responsibility for safety or quality. That action leads to suspicion and mistrust.

   e. Employee involvement can be used to increase productivity, but it stifles creativity, and should never be used in a research and development division.

4. Why are human resources departments assuming responsibilities for language training for employees?
   a. Corporate communications may be sent in multiple languages if no single language or group of languages is shared.
   b. The "wrong" word may cause major ill-will if it is interpreted as an insult.
   c. Hiring people with certain skills may necessitate hiring those who don't speak the host company's language.
   d. Global organizations, by definition, require people of different language backgrounds to work together.
   e. Language training is important for all of these reasons.

5. Why are cultural considerations critical to the success of any global business?
   a. Most people want to work with other cultured people.
   b. Making sure that workers in other countries adhere to American values is an important human resources function.
   c. Managers must be flexible and adaptable to deal with working conditions and social systems throughout the world.
   d. Collective societies stress family values, while individualistic societies stress the work ethic. Therefore, U.S. firms should only do business with organizations in individualistic societies.
   e. It is important to place employees only in positions where they will be most comfortable and familiar.

6. What is the best way to help multicultural individuals work together?
   a. Assign them major projects with other members of their ethnic group.
   b. Pass laws that require them to work together.
   c. Make promotions and raises dependent on working together well.
   d. Engage in cross-cultural team building activities.

Provide training on possible tension-causing areas, and, thus, reduce conflict.

   e. There is no evidence that multicultural work groups have any more conflicts than single-culture work groups.

7. What changes are causing an increased diversity in the U.S. work force?

   a. Most white males are not going to work in the future.

   b. Baby boomers have glutted the labor market. No one else will be able to get jobs for decades.

   c. Increased globalization and changes in employment laws are bringing more women and racial and ethnic minorities into the labor pool.

   d. Work attitudes change as employees get older.

   e. Anti-gay sentiments are decreasing.

8. Luke, vice-president of human resources for a large, multinational firm headquartered in the United States, is planning major staffing requirements. Today, 80 percent of the employees in the organization are white males, under the age of 35. Which statement is probably true, based on the projected labor pool profiles for the next two decades?

   a. Luke will hire more women in the next decade.

   b. The average age of his employees will decrease in the next decade.

   c. Hiring will probably be restricted to U.S. citizens.

   d. New managers will have to be hired from outside the organization, rather than promoted from within.

   e. New managers should be promoted from within.

9. If you were vice-president of a major U.S. corporation and could only do one of the following in the next decade, which action would be most responsive to the work-force diversity issue?

   a. Offer Chinese language classes. Make sure all company communications are in Mandarin and English.

   b. Offer Portuguese language classes. Make sure all company communications are in Portuguese and English.

   c. Offer Russian language classes. Make sure all company communications are in Russian and English.

   d. Offer French language classes. Make sure all company communications are in French and English

   e. Offer Spanish language classes. Make sure all company communications are in Spanish and English.

10. Why should the director of human resources for Ford Motor Company consider hiring grade-school teachers?

   a. Teachers work well with robots on the assembly line.

   b. Teachers work well with the Teamsters on the assembly line.

   c. Teachers who work for the summer go back to their classrooms and make positive comments about the quality of life on the assembly line to grade school students, thus reducing the negative image that union workers have with younger people.

   d. Over $200 million a year is currently spent in remedial education by Ford Motor Company. Employees on the payroll with grade-school teaching credentials would be a good investment.

   e. The mission statement of Ford Motor Company includes a directive to significantly hire from any occupational group that is underemployed.

11. The basis of Deming's pioneering work

   a. was created in Japan.

   b. is about twenty years old.

   c. is that quality can be measured and achieved through a process of statistical controls.

   d. is that workers on the line have more control over the quality of work than the production managers.

   e. all of these.

12. Considering continuous process improvement activities in organizations, should "zero defects" really be a goal?

   a. Yes. Perfection is a reasonable goal.

   b. No. 0.1 percent errors can be corrected much more efficiently than they can be prevented.

   c. Yes. Most industries find this an attainable goal.

   d. No. Current levels of 97 percent accuracy are adequate.

   e. Sometimes. For some mistakes, cost benefits cannot be calculated.

13. What's the difference between reengineering and TQM?

   a. Reengineering involves incremental change focusing on customers while TQM involved radical change in an effort to redesign the organization.

   b. Reengineering involves radical change while TQM involves incremental change.

   c. Reengineering is a function of downsizing and restructuring, while TQM focused on making quantum changes in the organizations' operations.

   d. Reengineering is the application of the tools Deming taught Japanese businesses, while TQM deals with statistical control mechanisms.

   e. There is no difference between reengineering and TQM.

14. Contingent workers offer organizations opportunities to smooth out staffing fluctuations. Which one of the following would not be a reason for an organization to hire contingent workers?

   a. Reducing labor costs

   b. Existing skill deficiencies in the work force

   c. Promoting family-friendly benefits

   d. Replacing core employees who are not productive

   e. Increasing work-force diversity

Chapter Three

EQUAL EMPLOYMENT OPPORTUNITY

LEARNING OBJECTIVES

AFTER READING THIS CHAPTER, YOU WILL BE ABLE TO:

1. Identify those groups afforded protection under the Civil Rights Act of 1964, Title VII.
2. Discuss the importance of the Equal Employment Opportunities Act of 1972.
3. Describe affirmative action plans.
4. Define what is meant by the terms *adverse impact, adverse treatment,* and *protected group members.*
5. Identify the important components of the Vocational Rehabilitation Act of 1974 and the Americans with Disabilities Act of 1990.
6. Explain the coverage of the Pregnancy Discrimination Act of 1978 and the Family and Medical Leave Act of 1993.
7. Discuss how a business can protect itself from discrimination charges.
8. Explain the HRM importance of the *Griggs* v. *Duke Power* case.
9. Define the phenomenon of sexual harassment in today's organizations.
10. Discuss what is meant by the term *glass ceiling.*

What's in a job? For most workers, jobs entail specific work activities that are routinely performed. On occasion, because of the dynamic nature of business today, other duties, many too numerous to name, must also be done. These work activities generally take place in the employers' offices, where many different people come together to achieve certain goals.

Work environments, by nature, differ widely. Just as individuals have personalities, each organization, and each office, has its own culture. Yet, there should be one common element to all work environments. That is, whatever occurs in the office should be related to organizational efforts. Every once in a while, however, this concept evades an employer. When it does, it may be a costly lesson for the organization. Consider the lesson learned at the world's largest law firm, Baker and McKenzie, the San Francisco-based legal giant.[1]

Rena Weeks was hired by the law firm as a secretary. In her duties, she was responsible for a variety of secretarial tasks, including word processing, copying, and answering the phone. What Rena wasn't hired for, however, was to be a playmate for one of the firm's leading trademark attorneys. Yet for twenty-five days, Rena was subjected to some of the most humiliating work behavior any person could imagine. For example, it was alleged that this attorney "grabbed her breast while pouring M&Ms down the front of her shirt pocket, lunged at her in the office with his arms outstretched, and grabbed her hips and pressed himself against her."[2] Needless to say, this created a work environment for Rena in which she could not productively function.

Of course what Rena Weeks experienced was unacceptable work behavior. But when reported by Rena, it apparently fell on deaf ears. In fact, the members of the firm did little to help her. They failed to investigate her allegations and stop this attorney from harassing Rena. As a result, Weeks felt she had no other recourse than to quit her job. Consequently, Rena lost her source of income, and the firm lost a potentially productive employee. But Rena wasn't willing to put this experience behind her—chalking it up to the good old boys and forgetting about her ordeal. Instead, she realized that she was not at fault for these incidents—it was her harasser and her employer who were wrong. And if they just overlooked her complaint, what about others? Hence, she filed suit against the law firm for $600,000 for the emotional trauma she suffered because of the law firm members. After a short trial, a jury agreed with Rena, and awarded her $50,000.

For a large organization like Baker and McKenzie, a $50,000 award may be upsetting, a nuisance, but probably not financially devastating. But this $50,000 award was only half of the picture. In today's legal environment, not only may juries make awards for the damages caused, they may also award the "victim" additional monies in an effort to make a point that tolerating such behavior is unacceptable. And what a point they made to Baker and McKenzie! In addition to the $50,000 for emotional trauma, the jury awarded Rena Weeks an additional

Rena Weeks celebrates with her attorneys after a California jury awarded her $7.1 million for the emotional trauma she suffered as a result of being sexually harassed. The amount of the award has once again sent a clear message to employers that condoning such behaviors will not be tolerated.

$7.1 million ($250,000 to be paid by the harasser).[3] Why? Because it was the jury's belief that the firm "knew of the partner's behavior and condoned it."[4]

What does the Weeks case mean for organizations in the United States today? In essence, sexual harassment is a violation of an employee's civil rights. When it is alleged, the organization had better investigate it, and take appropriate action. Failure to do so could leave the organization legally vulnerable, which may drastically affect the organization's bottom line.

Introduction

What do American Airlines, Texaco, Sears, CBS, and State Farm Insurance have in common? Each has paid out significant amounts of money for practices that allegedly discriminated against minorities or women. In Chapter 1 we introduced the concept of government legislation as it affects employment practices. In this chapter, we will explore this critical influence to provide an understanding of the legislation. Why? Because it is a fact of doing business. Almost every U.S. organization, both public and private, must abide by the guidelines established in the 1964 Civil Rights Act, its subsequent amendment (1972), and other federal laws governing employment practices. Even the United States Congress in early 1995 voted that it, too, would be covered by these same laws! The importance of such legislation cannot be overstated, as these laws permeate all HRM functions in the organization.

Keep in mind that although our discussion will be limited to federal employment legislation, there may also be state or municipal laws that go beyond what the federal government requires. While it is impossible to cover all of these laws, HRM managers must know and understand what additional requirements they face.

Laws Affecting Discriminatory Practices

The beginning of equal employment opportunity is usually attributed to the passage of the 1964 Civil Rights Act. Even though the focus of the activities we will explore in this chapter are rooted in this 1964 act, equal employment's beginning actually goes back more than one hundred years. For instance, Section 1981 of Title 42 of the U.S. Code referred to as the **Civil Rights Act of 1866,** coupled with the Fourteenth Amendment to the Constitution (1868), prohibited discrimination on the basis of race, sex, and national origin. Although these earlier actions have been overshadowed by the 1964 act, they've gained prominence in years past as being the laws that white male workers could use to support claims of reverse discrimination. In such cases, white males used the Civil Rights Act of 1866 and the Fourteenth Amendment to support their argument that minorities were given special treatment in employment decisions that placed the white male at a distinct disadvantage.[5] Under the Civil Rights Act of 1866 employees could sue for racial discrimination.[6] As a result of this act, individuals could also seek punitive and compensatory damages under Section 1981, in addition to the awarding of back pay.[7] However, in 1989, a Supreme Court ruling limited Section 1981 use in discrimination suits in that the law does not cover racial discrimination after a person has been hired.[8] We'll look more at reverse discrimination in our discussion of relevant Supreme Court decisions.

Although earlier attempts were rudimentary in promoting fair employment practices among workers, it was not until the 1960s that earnest emphasis was placed on achieving such a goal. Let's turn our attention, then, to the landmark piece of employment legislation, the Civil Rights Act of 1964.

Civil Rights Act of 1866 Federal law that prohibited discrimination based on race.

The Civil Rights Act of 1964

No single piece of legislation in the 1960s had a greater effect on reducing employment discrimination than the Civil Rights Act of 1964. It was divided into a number of parts, or titles, each dealing with a particular facet of discrimination. For HRM purposes, **Title VII** is especially relevant.

Title VII prohibits discrimination in hiring, compensation, and terms, conditions, or privileges of employment based on race, religion, color, sex, or national origin. Most organizations, both public and private, are bound by the law.[9] However, the law further specifies compliance based on the number of employees in the organization. Essentially, as originally passed, any organization with twenty-five or more (amended to fifteen or more in 1972) employees is covered.[10] This minimum number of employees serves as a means of protecting, or removing from the law, small, family-owned businesses.[11] The organizations initially covered by the EEO regulations, however, found compliance confusing.

Organizations were faced with relatively new requirements, but detailed guidelines for compliance were lacking. Days of purposefully excluding certain individuals from jobs were over, but practices like testing applicants appeared to create the same effect. In an attempt to clarify this procedure, several cases were challenged in the Supreme Court. The outcomes of these cases indicated that any action that had the effect of keeping certain groups of people out of particular jobs was illegal, unless the company could show why a practice was required. The implication of these decisions, for example, was that a company could not hire a maintenance employee using an aptitude test and a high-school diploma requirement unless those criteria could be shown to be directly

Title VII The most prominent piece of legislation regarding HRM, it states that it is illegal to discriminate against individuals based on race, religion, color, sex, or national origin.

•

Griggs* v. *Duke Power Landmark Supreme Court decision stating that tests must fairly measure the knowledge or skills required for a job.

Equal Employment Opportunity Commission The arm of the federal government empowered to handle discrimination in employment cases.

Affirmative Action A practice in organizations that goes beyond discontinuance of discriminatory practices, including actively seeking, hiring, and promoting minority group members and women.

relevant to the job. In one of these cases, ***Griggs* v. *Duke Power Company*** (1971), the company was unable to show job relatedness. Griggs, an applicant for a janitorial job, demonstrated that the power company's tests and degree requirements were unrelated to performance on the job in question. However, that did not mean that specific selection criteria couldn't be used. In the case of *Washington* v. *Davis* (1967),[12] the Supreme Court held that the use of aptitude tests was permissible. In this case, Davis was an applicant for a position as a metropolitan Washington, D.C., police officer. The police force required all applicants to pass a comprehensive aptitude test. The Supreme Court held that the test measured necessary competencies required to be successful as a police officer.

Even though we began to gain a better understanding of what Congress meant in the writing of Title VII, something was clearly lacking—enforcement mechanisms. By 1972, after realizing that the Civil Rights Act was left to interpretation, Congress passed an amendment to the act called the Equal Employment Opportunity Act (EEOA). This act was designed to provide a series of amendments to Title VII. Probably the greatest consequence of the EEOA was the creation of the **Equal Employment Opportunity Commission (EEOC).** The EEOC was granted authority to effectively prohibit all forms of employment discrimination based on race, religion, color, sex, or national origins. The EEOC was given the power to file civil suits (individuals may also file a suit themselves if the EEOC declines to sue) against organizations if it was unable to secure an acceptable resolution of discrimination charges within thirty days. In addition, the EEOA also expanded Title VII coverage to include employees of state and local governments, employees of educational institutions, and employers or labor organizations with fifteen or more employees or members.

Title VII, as it exists today, stipulates that organizations must do more than "just" discontinue discriminatory practices. Enterprises are expected to actively recruit and give preference to minority group members in employment decisions. This action is commonly referred to as **affirmative action.**

Affirmative Action Plans Affirmative action programs were instituted to correct past injustices in our employment processes. Although being critically reviewed and reevaluated by the Clinton Administration and the Republican-controlled Congress, there were four primary reasons for these plans:

1. Affirmative action programs were built on the premise that white males made up the majority of workers in our companies.
2. U.S. companies were still growing and could accommodate more workers.
3. As a matter of public policy and decency, minorities should be hired to correct past prejudice that has kept them out.
4. "Legal and social coercion [were] necessary to bring about the change."[13]

What does that imply about affirmative action programs? What affirmative action means is that an organization must take certain steps to show that it is not discriminating. For example, the organization must conduct an analysis of the demographics of its current work force. Similarly, the organization must analyze the composition of the community from which it recruits. If the work force resembles the community for all jobs classifications, then the organization is demonstrating that its affirmative action program is working. If, however, there are differences, affirmative action also implies that the organization will establish goals and timetables for correcting the imbalance, and have specific plans on how to go about recruiting and retaining protected group members.

In operating an EEO program, a few issues arise. First of all, the company must know what the job requires in terms of skills, knowledge, and abilities (see "HRM in a De-Jobbed Organization"). Candidates are then evaluated on how

HRM in a De-Jobbed Organization

One of the basic premises of human resources management is the requirement that an organization must hire *right*. Right, in these cases, means hiring individuals who possess the necessary skills, knowledge, and abilities in order to successfully perform the essential elements of the job. But if we stop for a moment and think about that practice, we will notice one particular aspect. That is, these skills, knowledge, and abilities are identified through a process of analyzing jobs. That information is then translated into a document that describes the job, and the requisite skills, in detail.

Yet, as we saw in Chapter 2, a fundamental issue of a de-jobbed organization will be the realization that jobs, if they exist, will be ill-defined, if defined at all. Accordingly, it will be difficult to precisely pinpoint what specific skills, knowledge, and abilities will be needed to perform the variety of ever-changing tasks. Consequently, what effect will this have on hiring, and more importantly, equal employment opportunity?

As EEO currently exists, a basic tenant of the laws is the concern that employment practices do not create an adverse impact. HRM practitioners attempt to meet that requirement by selecting the best qualified applicant; the one who best meets the essential requirement of the job. Yet, that may be, at best, a toss of the dice if organizations are unable to describe their jobs. Consequently, what will we be looking at in the next decade as a means of ensuring that discriminatory practices do not exist?

Furthermore, we recognize that in a de-jobbed organization, more and more tasks will be performed by contingent workers—the part-time, or independent contracting worker. Will EEO laws have to be changed to reflect this new cadre of the work force? Or will the laws cease in having the effect that they currently have in guiding HRM activities? On one hand, we can point to the fact that employers will hire smarter, hiring those contingent workers who can successfully perform the tasks. Successful performance, then, will be the key! But how will we know, or track, if certain groups are being adversely affected in the workplace? Will employers have to extend EEO regulations and affirmative action programs to their independent contractors? Will reporting requirements change to reflect this de-jobbed phenomenon? The answer is unknown at this time. However, it would appear reasonable to predict that organizations will have to pay particular attention to this concern. If employment practices revert back to a pre-1964 era where some discriminatory practices were blatant, and organizations fail to "police" themselves, societal pressure to enact some sort of "protective employment" legislation is bound to occur. History has taught us that lesson very well.

Source: The stimulus for this thought-piece comes from William Bridges, "The End of the Job," *Fortune* (September 19, 1994), pp. 62–74.

well they meet these criteria. If candidates meet these criteria, then they are essentially qualified, meaning that they should be successful performers of the job. Nowhere under EEO does the federal government require an organization to hire unqualified workers. They do require organizations to actively search for qualified minorities by recruiting from places like predominantly African-Amer-

Adverse (Disparate) Impact A consequence of an employment practice that results in a greater rejection rate for a minority group than it does for the majority group in the occupation.

ican or women's colleges, but they do not force hiring of these individuals under this process. However, as a result of affirmative action programs, an organization should be able to show significant improvements in hiring and promoting women and minorities, or justify why external factors prohibited them from achieving their affirmative-action goals.

Throughout much of this discussion, we have addressed practices that are designed to assure equal employment opportunity for all individuals. But how do we know if equal employment programs are not operating properly? The answer to that question may lie in the concept of **adverse (disparate) impact.**

Adverse Impact Adverse impact can be described as any employment consequence that results in a greater rejection rate for a minority group than it does for the majority group in the occupation. For example, years ago police departments around the country had height and weight requirements. This height requirement was frequently 5'10" or greater. As such, women who wished to become police officers were unable to. Why? Because the average height of females is shorter than that of males. Accordingly, using this height requirement had the effect of significantly reducing the job opportunities for this group of people. The concept of adverse impact, then, results from a seemingly neutral, even unintentional employment practice consequence.[14]

Adverse (Disparate) Treatment An employment situation where protected group members receive different treatment than other employees in matters like performance evaluations, promotions, etc.

There is another issue that differs from adverse impact, but follows a similar logic. This is called **adverse (disparate) treatment.** Adverse treatment occurs when members of a protected group (those afforded protection under discrimination laws) receive different treatment than other employees.[15] For example, if **protected group members** are evaluated as performing poorly more often, or receive fewer organizational rewards, adverse treatment may have occurred.

Protected Group Member Any individual who is afforded protection under employment discrimination laws.

The Civil Rights Act of 1964 led the way to change how HRM would operate. As the years progressed, other amendments and legislation were passed that extended equal employment opportunity practices to diverse groups. Let's take a look at the most critical of these laws summarized in Table 3-1.

Others Laws Affecting Discrimination Practices

In addition to the Civil Rights Act of 1964, there are a number of other laws and presidential orders that equally affect HRM practices. Specifically, we'll address the Age Discrimination in Employment Act of 1967 (amended in 1978 and 1986), the Vocational Rehabilitation Act of 1973, the Pregnancy Discrimination Act of 1978, the Americans with Disabilities Act of 1990, the Family and Medical Leave Act of 1993, and three Executive Orders—11246, 11375, and 11478.

Age Discrimination in Employment Act of 1967

Age Discrimination in Employment Act Passed in 1967 and amended in 1978 and 1986, this act prohibits arbitrary age discrimination, particularly among those over age 39.

The **Age Discrimination in Employment Act (ADEA) of 1967** prohibited the widespread practice of requiring workers to retire at the age of 65.[16] It gave protected group status to individuals between the ages of 40 and 65. Since 1967, this act has been amended twice—once in 1978, which raised the mandatory retirement age to 70, and again in 1986, where the upper age limit was removed altogether.[17] As a result, anyone over the age of 39 is covered by the ADEA.

Of course, there are exceptions to this law. Employees holding certain types of jobs, such as college professors, just came under full protection as of 1994.[18] Furthermore, other individuals may be forced out of their jobs because of strict

TABLE 3-1   Summary of Discrimination Laws

Civil Rights Act of 1964	Title VII prohibits employment discrimination in hiring, compensation, and terms, conditions, or privileges of employment based on race, religion, color, sex, or national origin.
Executive Order (E.O.) 11246	Prohibits discrimination on the basis of race, religion, color, and national origin, by federal agencies as well as those working under federal contracts.
Executive Order 11375	Added sex-based discrimination to E.O. 11246.
Age Discrimination in Employment Act of 1967	Protects employees 40–65 years of age from discrimination. Later amended to age 70 (1978), then amended (1986) to eliminate the upper age limit altogether.
Executive Order 11478	Amends part of E.O. 11246, states practices in the federal government must be based on merit; also prohibits discrimination based on political affiliation, marital status, or physical handicap.
Equal Employment Opportunity Act of 1972	Established the EEOC.
Vocational Rehabilitation Act of 1973	Prohibits employers who have federal contracts greater than $2,500 from discriminating against individuals with handicaps, racial minorities, and women.
Vietnam Veterans Readjustment Act of 1974	Provided for equal employment opportunities for Vietnam War veterans. Administered and enforced by the Office of Federal Contract Compliance.
Age Discrimination in Employment Act of 1978	Increased mandatory retirement age from 65 to 70. Later amended (1986) to eliminate upper age limit.
Pregnancy Discrimination Act of 1978	Afforded EEO protection to pregnant workers and requires pregnancy to be treated like any other disability.
Americans with Disabilities Act of 1990	Prohibits discrimination against an essentially qualified individual, and requires enterprises to reasonably accommodate individuals.
Civil Rights Act of 1991	Nullified selected Supreme Court decisions. Reinstates burden of proof by employer. Allows for punitive and compensatory damages through jury trials.
Family and Medical Leave Act of 1993	Permits employees in organizations of fifty or more workers to take up to twelve weeks of unpaid leave for family or medical reasons each year.

requirements of the job. For instance, in the airline industry, pilots may not captain a commercial airplane upon reaching the age of 60. Why age 60? That age is a benchmark after which the Federal Aviation Agency believes that medical research can show that the necessary skills to handle an emergency may be lacking, or to significantly decline.[19] Thus, using age 60 as the determining factor, airlines are permitted to remove a pilot at that age for public safety reasons. But that does not mean that they must leave the organization. Should a 60-year-old pilot decide to be a flight engineer, and if an opening exists, the individual may apply for the job. Failure to allow their retiring pilots to do so is in violation of ADEA.[20]

In applying this act to the workplace, a four-pronged test is typically used to determine if age discrimination has occurred. This test involves proving that one is "a member of a protected group, that adverse employment action was taken, the individual was replaced by a [younger] worker, and the individual was qualified for the job."[21] For example, in an organization's attempt to cut salary costs, it lays off senior employees. But instead of leaving the jobs unfilled, the organization hires recent college graduates who are paid significantly less. Should this organization, or any other company be found guilty of age discrimination, punitive damages up to double the amount of the compensatory amount may be awarded by the courts.[22]

Vocational Rehabilitation Act
This act extended to the physically and mentally disabled the same protection afforded racial minorities and women.

The Vocational Rehabilitation Act of 1973 The **Vocational Rehabilitation Act of 1973** requires companies receiving $2,500 or more annually in federal contracts to take action to recruit, employ, and advance all qualified disabled individuals. This includes making reasonable accommodations, removing the barriers an individual faces, and providing a work site that is adaptable to this individual. Much of the protection afforded in this act is now covered under the Americans with Disabilities Act of 1990.

Pregnancy Discrimination Act
Law prohibiting discrimination based on pregnancy.

The Pregnancy Discrimination Act of 1978 The **Pregnancy Discrimination Act of 1978** (and supplemented by various state laws) prohibits discrimination based on pregnancy. Under the law, companies may not terminate a female employee for being pregnant, refuse to make an employment decision based on one's pregnancy, or deny insurance coverage to the individual.[23] The law also requires organizations to offer the employee a reasonable period of time off from work. Although no specific time frames are given, the pregnancy leave is typically six to ten weeks.[24] At the end of this leave, the worker is entitled to return to work. If the exact job they left is unavailable, a similar one must be provided.

It is interesting to note that this law is highly contingent on other benefits the company offers. Should the organization not offer health or disability-related (like sick leave) benefits to its employees, it is exempt from this law. However, any type of health or disability insurance offered, no matter how much or how little, requires compliance. For instance, if a company offers a benefit covering 40 percent of the costs associated with any short-term disability, then it must include pregnancy in that coverage.

Closely aligned with the Pregnancy Discrimination Act is an issue of fetal protection. Fetal protection laws, as the name implies, were passed to protect the unborn child from exposure to toxic chemicals. Many of the Fortune 500 companies, like Exxon, General Motors, and DuPont, had policies restricting female employees, pregnant or not, from holding specific jobs.[25] In doing so, fertile females were restricted from these jobs, causing some to lose out on career opportunities.[26] This led to a charge of discrimination. For example, at Johnson Control Inc., the company would not hire fertile females because of the potential for pregnancy abnormalities due to lead exposure from its battery manufacturing. Accordingly, child-bearing females had two choices: Become sterile, or don't apply.

At issue here was one's right to bear children. Employment at Johnson Control Inc. required one to give up that freedom.[27] Additionally, medical research in fertility matters shed new light on the issue in that males' exposure to toxic chemicals may also result in fetal abnormalities; yet males were not required to be sterilized as a condition of employment. Accordingly, the Supreme Court ruled in 1991 that fetal protection laws violated Title VII on the basis of sex discrimination, and thus must be discontinued.[28]

The Americans with Disabilities Act of 1990 The **Americans with Disabilities Act of 1990 (ADA)** expands the Vocational Rehabilitation Act of 1973.[29] With the passage of the ADA came sweeping changes in terms of discriminatory practices against the disabled, whether the disability is perceived or real.[30] Whereas the Vocational Rehabilitation Act of 1973 granted Civil Rights protection to the physically and mentally disabled, the Americans with Disabilities Act of 1990 extends that protection to most forms of disability status—including those afflicted with AIDS.[31] In addition to the extended coverage, companies are further required to make reasonable accommodations to provide a qualified individual access to the job,[32] as well as eliminating any post–job-offer medical exams. A company may also be required to provide necessary technology to enable an individual to do his or her job. For example, suppose a worker is legally deaf. If special hearing or "reading" equipment is available and could assist this individual in doing the job, then the company must provide it if that accommodation does not present an undue financial hardship.

The ADA extends its coverage to private companies and all public service organizations like "state and local agencies, restaurants, transportation systems, and communication companies."[33] Compliance to ADA was phased in over four years, with full compliance for companies with fifteen or more employees coming on July 26, 1994.[34]

As a final note on this act, it is interesting that contagious diseases, including AIDS, are considered conditions of being disabled. In advancing the decision in the 1987 Supreme Court case of *Arline* v. *Nassau County*,[35] the ADA views contagious diseases as any other medical disability. With respect to AIDS, there are exceptions that can be implemented, but most of these are rare. In restaurants, for example, the individual may simply be assigned other duties, rather than terminated. Under this law, you must treat the AIDS worker in the same way that you would treat a worker suffering from cancer, and all job actions must be based on job requirements.

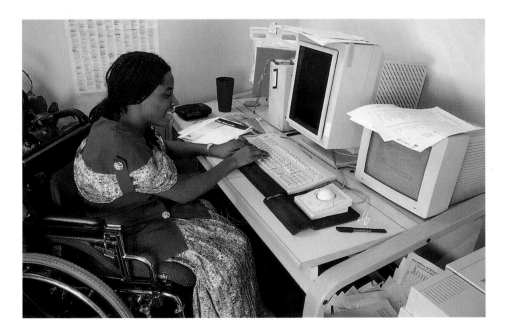

The Americans with Disabilities Act affords EEO protection to all disabled workers and requires the organization to reasonably accomodate them. In this case, that may mean altering work stations and doorways such that this employee's wheelchair can move around freely without barriers.

Family and Medical Leave Act
Federal legislation that provides employees up to
twelve weeks of unpaid
leave each year to care for
family members, or for their
own medical reasons.

The Family and Medical Leave Act of 1993 The **Family and Medical Leave Act
of 1993 (FMLA)** originally was proposed to enhance the Pregnancy Discrimination Act to allow leave for childbirth (as well as adoption) to either parent.
Initially, this bill was vetoed by then-president George Bush in an attempt to let
organizations handle this issue through benefit offerings rather than by a federal mandate. The issue was not dropped, however. There was considerable congressional debate, and twelve states enacted legislation related to family leave.[36]
As a presidential candidate in the 1992 elections, Bill Clinton promised to support the act. In February 1993, less than a month after being inaugurated, President Clinton signed the act into law.

The Family and Medical Leave Act provides employees in organizations employing fifty or more workers the opportunity to take up to twelve weeks of unpaid leave[37] each year for family matters (like childbirth, or adoption, or for
their own illness or to care for a sick family member). These employees are
guaranteed their current job, or one equal to it, upon their return. Furthermore, during this period of unpaid leave, employees retain their employer-of-
fered health insurance coverage (see Figure 3-1). Currently, about 66 percent of
all U.S. workers are covered under FMLA.[38] And it's expected that only about 6
percent of them will opt to take advantage of the law in any given year.[39] This is,
in part, because taking the unpaid leave may create financial hardships for the
individual.

Since being enacted into law, several insights have arisen. Surprisingly, a significant percentage of companies are not complying with the act.[40] In these
companies, either they are not granting the leaves (15 percent), not guaranteeing the job when the employee returns (9 percent), or are not continuing
health benefit coverage during the unpaid leave (10 percent). Some smaller
companies, too, are feeling the effects. Entrepreneurs like Ed Sherman, owner

These Aetna Life and Casualty
workers are but a few of the
500 employees who have
taken a leave of absence from
their jobs since the passage of
the Family and Medical Leave
Act.

Your Rights
Under The
Family and Medical Leave Act of 1993

FMLA requires covered employers to provide up to 12 weeks of unpaid, job-protected leave to "eligible" employees for certain family and medical reasons. Employees are eligible if they have worked for a covered employer for at least one year, and for 1,250 hours over the previous 12 months, and if there are at least 50 employees within 75 miles.

Reasons For Taking Leave:

Unpaid leave must be granted for *any* of the following reasons:

- to care for the employee's child after birth, or placement for adoption or foster care;
- to care for the employee's spouse, son or daughter, or parent, who has a serious health condition; or
- for a serious health condition that makes the employee unable to perform the employee's job.

At the employee's or employer's option, certain kinds of *paid* leave may be substituted for unpaid leave.

Advance Notice and Medical Certification:

The employee may be required to provide advance leave notice and medical certification. Taking of leave may be denied if requirements are not met.

- The employee ordinarily must provide 30 days advance notice when the leave is "foreseeable."
- An employer may require medical certification to support a request for leave because of a serious health condition, and may require second or third opinions (at the employer's expense) and a fitness for duty report to return to work.

Job Benefits and Protection:

- For the duration of FMLA leave, the employer must maintain the employee's health coverage under any "group health plan."

- Upon return from FMLA leave, most employees must be restored to their original or equivalent positions with equivalent pay, benefits, and other employment terms.
- The use of FMLA leave cannot result in the loss of any employment benefit that accrued prior to the start of an employee's leave.

Unlawful Acts By Employers:

FMLA makes it unlawful for any employer to:

- interfere with, restrain, or deny the exercise of any right provided under FMLA:
- discharge or discriminate against any person for opposing any practice made unlawful by FMLA or for involvement in any proceeding under or relating to FMLA.

Enforcement:

- The U.S. Department of Labor is authorized to investigate and resolve complaints of violations.
- An eligible employee may bring a civil action against an employer for violations.

FMLA does not affect any Federal or State law prohibiting discrimination, or supersede any State or local law or collective bargaining agreement which provides greater family or medical leave rights.

For Additional Information:

Contact the nearest office of the Wage and Hour Division, listed in most telephone directories under U.S. Government, Department of Labor.

U.S. Department of Labor
Employment Standards Administration
Wage and Hour Division
Washington, D.C. 20210

WH Publication 1420
June 1993

U S G.P.O.: 353-608

Figure 3-1
Family and Medical Leave Act

of a Hallmark Card shop, feels the law will restrict his growth.[41] Currently employing forty-five individuals, Sherman is exempt from the FMLA. However, adding five more employees mandates his compliance. He's questioning whether growth may be worth the "compliance" costs. On the other hand, Aetna Life and Casualty sees such a law benefiting not only the employee, but the employer. Over the past few years, in providing similar leave benefits to their employees, the company has saved almost $2 million a year by "reducing employee turnover, and hiring and training costs."[42]

Relevant Executive Orders In 1965, President Lyndon Johnson issued Executive Order 11246. This executive order prohibited discrimination on the basis of race, religion, color, or national origin by federal agencies as well as by contractors and subcontractors who worked under federal contracts. This was followed by Executive Order 11375, which added sex-based discrimination to the above criteria. In 1969, President Richard Nixon issued Executive Order 11478 to supersede part of Executive Order 11246. It stated that employment practices in the federal government must be based on merit and must prohibit discrimination based on race, color, religion, sex, national origin, political affiliation, marital status, or physical disability.

These orders cover all organizations that have contracts of $10,000 or more with the federal government. Additionally, those organizations with fifty or more employees and/or $50,000 in federal grants must have an active affirmative action program. The **Office of Federal Contract Compliance Program** administers the order's provisions and provides technical assistance.

Office of Federal Contract Compliance Programs The government office that administers the provisions of Executive Order 11246.

Civil Rights Acts of 1991 Employment discrimination law that nullified selected Supreme Court decisions. Reinstated burden of proof by the employer, and allowed for punitive and compensatory damage through jury trials.

The Civil Rights Act of 1991

The **Civil Rights Act of 1991** was one of the most hotly debated civil rights laws since the 1964 act. The impetus for this legislation stemmed from a number of Supreme Court decisions in the late 1980s that diminished the effect of the *Griggs* decision. Proponents of the 1964 legislation quickly banded together in an attempt to issue new legislation aimed at restoring the provisions lost in these Supreme Court rulings.

The Civil Rights Act of 1991 prohibits discrimination on the basis of race and prohibits racial harassment on the job; returns the burden of proof that discrimination did not occur back to the employer; reinforces the illegality of employers who make hiring, firing, or promoting decisions on the basis of race, ethnicity, sex, or religion; and permits women and religious minorities to seek punitive damages in intentional discriminatory claims.

What impact did this legislation have on employers? The issue dealing with punitive damages may prove to be the most drastic change to have taken place. Since 1964, and particularly in the 1970s, employers significantly changed their HRM practices to come into compliance with the Title VII provision, its amendments, and subsequent legislation. Accordingly, unless these same employers drastically changed their HRM practices after recent Supreme Court rulings, the potential changes brought about by this legislation was minimal.[43] However, for the first time, individuals claiming they have been intentionally discriminated against are able to sue for damages. The amount of these compensatory and punitive charges, however, is prorated based on number of employees in the organization.[44]

Guarding Against Discrimination Practices

Facing a number of laws and regulations, it's critical for HRM to implement practices that are nondiscriminatory. Recall from our earlier discussion that discrimination in employment may stem from a decision that is based on factors other than those relevant to the job. Should that occur frequently, the organization may face charges that it discriminates against some members of a protected group. Determining what constitutes discrimination, however, typically requires more than one individual being adversely affected. To determine if discrimination occurred, one of four tests can be used. These are the 4/5ths rule, restricted policies, geographic comparisons, and the McDonnell-Douglas Test.[45]

Determining Discriminatory Practices

The 4/5ths Rule One of the first measures of determining potentially discriminatory practices is to use a rule of thumb called the 4/5ths rule. Established by the *Uniform Guidelines on Employee Selection Procedures,* this guideline serves as a basis for determining if an adverse impact has occurred. Of course, the 4/5ths rule is not a definition of discrimination. It is, however, a "practical device to keep the attention of the enforcement agencies on serious discrepancies in hiring and promotion rates, or other employment decisions."[46] To see how the 4/5ths rule works, suppose we have two pools of applicants for jobs as sales associates. Our applicants' backgrounds reflect the following—forty members in the majority, and fifteen individuals who comprise the minority population.[47] After we go through a testing process and an interview, the following number of people are hired—twenty-two majority and eight minority members. Is the organization in compliance? Table 3-2 provides the analysis. In this case, we find that the company is in compliance; that is, the ratio of minority to majority members is 80 percent or greater (the 4/5ths rule). Accordingly, even though fewer minority members were hired, no apparent discrimination has occurred. Table 3-2 also shows the analysis of an organization not in compliance.

Remember, whenever the 4/5ths rule is violated, it only indicates that discrimination may have occurred. Should the analysis show that the percentage is less than 80 percent, then more elaborate statistical testing is needed to confirm or reject that there was an adverse impact. That is because too many factors can enter into the picture. For instance, if Company A finds a way to keep most minority group members from applying in the first place, it will only have

4/5ths Rule A rough indicator of discrimination, this rule requires that the number of minority members that a company hires must be at least 80 percent of the majority members in the population hired.

TABLE 3-2 Applying the 4/5ths Rule

In Compliance						
Majority Group (MAJ) = 40 applicants			*Minority Group (MIN) = 15 applicants*			
Item	**Number**	**Percent**	**Item**	**Number**	**Percent**	**%Min/%Maj**
Passed Test	30	75%	Passed Test	11	73%	73%/75% = 97%
Passed Interview	22	73%	Passed Interview	8	72%	72%/73% = 98%
Hired	22	100%	Hired	8	100%	100%/100% = 100%
Analysis	22/40 =	55%	Analysis	8/15 =	53%	
Ratio of Minority/Majority 53%/55% = 96%						

Not in Compliance						
Majority Group (MAJ) = 40 applicants			*Minority Group (MIN) = 15 applicants*			
Item	**Number**	**Percent**	**Item**	**Number**	**Percent**	**%Min/%Maj**
Passed Test	30	75%	Passed Test	11	73%	73%/75% = 97%
Passed Interview	26	86%	Passed Interview	4	36%	36%/86% = 41%
Hired	26	100%	Hired	4	100%	100%/100% = 100%
Analysis	26/40 =	65%	Analysis	4/15 =	26%	
Ratio of Minority/Majority 26%/65% = 40%						

to hire a few of them to meet its 4/5ths rule-of-thumb measure. Conversely, if Company B actively seeks numerous minority group applicants and hires more than Company A, it still may not meet the 4/5ths rule.

Prior to 1984, companies were permitted to use a process commonly referred to as the bottom-line technique. Under this arrangement, as long as the "bottom line" in employment matters indicated that compliance with Title VII was in order (80 percent or greater), then that organization's HRM practices were considered legal. That is, even though a test was discriminatory (failing the 4/5ths rule), as long as other selection criteria corrected this problem, the company was in compliance. However, with the Supreme Court ruling in *Connecticut* v. *Teal,* (1984) the decision stated that all steps in the selection process must conform to the 4/5ths rule.[48]

Restricted Policy An HRM policy that results in the exclusion of a class of individuals.

Restricted Policy A **restricted policy** infraction occurs whenever an enterprise's HRM activities result in the exclusion of a class of individuals. For instance, assume a company is downsizing and laying off primarily individuals who are over age 40. Simultaneously, however, the company is recruiting for selected positions on college campuses only. Because of economic difficulties, this company wants to keep salaries low by hiring people just entering the work force. Those over the age of 40, who were making higher salaries, are not given the opportunity to even apply for these new jobs. By these actions, a restricted policy has occurred: That is, through its hiring practice (intentional or not), a class of individuals (in this case, those protected by age discrimination legislation) has been excluded from consideration.

Geographical Comparisons A third means of supporting discriminatory claims is through the use of a geographic comparison. In this instance, the characteristics of the qualified pool of applicants in an organization's hiring market is compared to the characteristics of its employees. If the organization has a proper mix of individuals at all levels in the organization that reflects its recruiting market, then the company is in compliance. Additionally, that compliance may assist in fostering diversity in the organization. The key factor here is the qualified pool according to varying geographic areas.

McDonnell-Douglas Corp. v. Green Supreme Court case which established a four-pronged test for determining if discrimination exists.

McDonnell-Douglas Test Named for the ***McDonnell-Douglas Corp.* v. *Green*** Supreme Court case,[49] this test provides a means of establishing a solid case.[50] It has four components that must exist. These are:

1. The individual is a member of a protected group.
2. The individual applied for a job for which he or she was qualified.
3. The individual was rejected.
4. The enterprise, after rejecting this applicant, continued to seek other applicants with similar qualifications.[51]

If these four conditions are met, an allegation of discrimination is supported. It is up to the company to refute the evidence by providing a reason for such action. Should that explanation be acceptable to an investigating body, the protected group member must then prove that the reason used by the company is inappropriate.

If any of the above four tests are met, the company might find itself having to defend its practices. In the next section, we'll explain how an enterprise can do that.

Meet

May Snowden
Executive Director—
Diversity, U.S. West Communications

May Snowden is the Executive Director-Diversity at U.S. West Communications. May's responsibilities include Diversity policy, procedure and strategy development, Affirmative Action plans, Consultation services and EEO/AA compliance. From 1991 to 1995 she held the position of Regional Director-Operations, U.S. West Operator and Information Services. Prior to that she was Director of Operations for Information Services.

She has also held positions in Affirmative Action consultation, personnel management and various management assignments in plant and residential services. She established an employee advocacy process while she was in the company's Public Policy organization and she served as a Congressional aide in Washington D.C.

She has a Master's Degree in Public Administration and recently obtained a Master's in Business Administration from the University of Colorado. May has been awarded the Leadership, Commitment and Alignment Chairman's Award, the company's highest leadership honor, and has twice been selected for the company's President's Club. She is in the Leadership America program and is a past participant in Leadership Denver.

For May Snowden, Diversity is a sound, key business strategy that positions the company to meet the growing demands of a diverse customer base and thus provides the company with a strategic advantage. She believes the effort to create a diverse workforce that serves a diverse customer base makes good business sense. May sees a continuation of corporate efforts to recruit and select from a diverse pool of candidates and make available appropriate training, mentoring and developmental opportunities for employees to prepare them to compete for jobs within the corporation.

Providing a Response to an EEO Charge

If an adverse impact results from the HRM practices in an organization, there are a few remedies for the employer dealing with valid allegations. First, the employer should discontinue the practice. Only after careful study should the practice, or a modified version, be reinstated. However, even if enough evidence exists, an employer may choose to defend its practices. Generally, three defenses can be used when confronted with an allegation. The first of these is job relatedness or business necessity; the second is bona fide occupational qualifications; and third is seniority systems.

An organization has the right to operate in a safe and efficient manner, and obtain its goals. These are a business necessity; without it, the survival of the organization could be threatened. A major portion of business necessity involves job relatedness factors, or having the right to expect employees to perform successfully. This means that employees are expected to possess the required skills, knowledge, and abilities needed to perform the essential elements of the job. Job relatedness criteria are substantiated through the validation process. We'll return to this topic in Chapter 6.

The second defense against discriminatory charges is a bona fide occupational qualification (BFOQ). Under Title VII, a BFOQ was permitted where such requirements were "reasonably necessary to meet the normal operation of that business or enterprise." As originally worded, BFOQs could be used only to support sex discrimination. Today, BFOQ coverage is extended to other categories covered. BFOQs cannot, however, be used in cases of race or color.

It is important to note that while BFOQs are "legal" exceptions to Title VII, they are very narrowly defined. Simply using a BFOQ as the response to a charge of discrimination is not enough; it must be directly related to the job. Let's look at some examples.

For years, airlines cited BFOQs as the reason for hiring solely female flight attendants.[52] The airlines' position was that most of their passengers were male and preferred to see stewardesses. The courts, however, did not hold the same view. As a result, it is now common to see both sexes today as flight attendants. Using sex as a criterion for a job is difficult to prove. Even the classic washroom attendant case has seen a change: Many fine restaurants have members of the opposite sex working in washroom facilities. As we mentioned earlier, fetal protection laws as a BFOQ are no longer permissible. However, under certain circumstances sex as a BFOQ has been supported. In a job like modeling, sex can be used as a determining factor.

A religious BFOQ has similar results. An organization can refuse to hire an individual whose religious observances fall on days that the enterprise normally operates. If, in this case, the organization cannot reasonably accommodate these religious observances,[53] then a BFOQ is permissible.[54] To be an ordained minister in a church, religion may be used as a differentiating factor; but a faculty member doesn't have to be Catholic to teach at a Jesuit college. In terms of national origin, BFOQs become rarer. However, if an organization can show that nationality plays a role in a person's being able to perform successfully on the job, then a BFOQ may prevail.

Our last area of BFOQ is age. With subsequent amendments to the Age Discrimination in Employment Act, age BFOQs are very hard to support. As we mentioned in our discussion of age discrimination, there are times when age can be used as a determining factor. However, aside from pilots and a few advertising sales promotions, age as a BFOQ is limited.

Finally, the organization's bona-fide seniority system can serve as a defense against discrimination charges. So long as employment decisions, like layoffs, are the function of a well-established and consistently applied seniority system, decisions that may adversely affect protected group members may be permissible. However, an organization using seniority as a defense must be able to demonstrate the "appropriateness" of its system.

Although three means are available for organizations to defend themselves, the best approach revolves around job-relatedness. BFOQ and seniority defenses are often subject to great scrutiny, and at times, are limited in their use.

Selected Relevant Supreme Court Cases

In addition to the laws affecting discriminatory practices, HRM must be aware of decisions rendered in the Supreme Court. Many of these cases help to further define HRM practices, or indicate activities that are permissible. While it is impossible to discuss every applicable Supreme Court case, we have chosen a few of the more critical ones for what they have meant to the field.

79
Selected Relevant Supreme
Court Cases
•

Cases Concerning Discrimination

Let's return to one of the most important legal rulings affecting selection procedures. In the 1971 *Griggs* v. *Duke Power Company* decision, the U.S. Supreme Court adopted the interpretive guidelines set out under Title VII: that is, tests must fairly measure the knowledge and skills required in a job in order not to discriminate unfairly against minorities. This action, single-handedly, made invalid any employment test or diploma requirement that disqualified African-Americans at a substantially higher rate than whites (even when this was not intended) if this differentiation could not be shown to be job-related. Such action was said to create an adverse (disparate) impact.[55]

The *Griggs* decision had even wider implications. It made illegal most intelligence and conceptual tests used in hiring unless there was direct empirical evidence that the tests employed were valid. This crucial decision placed the burden of proof on the employer. Based on this decision, it was now the responsibility of the employer to provide adequate support that any test used did not discriminate on the basis of non–job-related characteristics. For example, if an employer requires all applicants to take an IQ test, and the results of that test will be used in making the hiring decision, it is the employer's responsibility to prove that individuals with higher scores will outperform on the job those individuals with lower scores. Nothing in the Court's decision, however, precludes the use of testing or measuring procedures. What it did was to place the burden of proof on management to demonstrate, if challenged, that the tests used provided a reasonable measure of job performance.

Although companies began a process of validating these tests, requiring all job applicants to take them raised further questions. In 1975, the Supreme Court decision in the case of *Albemarle Paper Company* v. *Moody* (1975) clarified the methodological requirements for using and validating tests in selection.[56] In the case, four African-American employees challenged their employer's use of tests for selecting candidates from the unskilled labor pool for promotion into skilled jobs. The Court endorsed the EEOC guidelines by noting that Albemarle's selection methodology was defective because:

1. The tests had not been used solely for jobs on which they had previously been validated.
2. The tests were validated for upper-level jobs alone but were also used for entry-level jobs.
3. Subjective supervisory ratings were used for validating the tests, but the ratings had not been done with care.
4. The tests had been validated on a group of job-experienced white workers, whereas the tests were given to young, inexperienced, and often nonwhite candidates.

In addition to these two landmark cases, other Supreme Court rulings have had an effect on HRM practices. We have identified some of the more important ones and their results in Table 3-3. During the late 1980s, however, we began to see a significant change in the Supreme Court's perception of EEO. One of the most notable cases during this period was *Wards Cove Packing Company* v. *Atonio* (1989).[57] Wards Cove operates two primary salmon canneries in Alaska. The issue in this case stemmed from different hiring practices for two types of jobs. Noncannery jobs that were viewed as unskilled positions were filled by predominately nonwhites (Filipinos and native Alaskans). On the other hand, cannery jobs were seen as skilled administrative/engineering positions and were

TABLE 3-3 Summary of Selected Supreme Court Cases Effecting EEO
(1971–1987)

Case	Ruling
Griggs v. *Duke Power* (1971)	Tests must fairly measure the knowledge or skills required for a job; also validity of tests.
Albemarle Paper Company v. *Moody* (1975)	Clarified requirements for using and validating tests in selection.
Washington v. *Davis* (1976)	Job-related tests are permissible for screening applicants.
Connecticut v. *Teal* (1984)	Requires all steps in a selection process to meet the 4/5ths rule.
Firefighters Local 1784 v. *Stotts* (1984)	Layoffs are permitted by seniority despite effects it may have on minority employees.
Wyant v. *Jackson Board of Education* (1986)	Layoffs of white workers to establish racial or ethnic balances are illegal; however, reaffirmed the use of affirmative action plans to correct racial imbalance.
United States v. *Paradise* (1986)	Quotas may be used to correct significant racial discrimination practices.
Sheetmetal Workers Local 24 v. *EEOC* (1987)	Racial preference could be used in layoff decisions only for those who had been subjected to previous race discrimination.
Johnson v. *Santa Clara County Transportation Agency* (1987)	Reaffirmed the use of preferential treatment based on sex to overcome problems in existing affirmative action plans.

held by a predominately white group. Based on the ruling handed down in *Griggs* v. *Duke Power,* an adverse (disparate) impact could be shown by the use of statistics (the 4/5ths rule). However, in the decision, the Court ruled that statistics alone could not support evidence of discrimination. Consequently, the burden of proof shifted from the employer to the individual employee.[58]

The Wards Cove decision had the effect of potentially undermining two decades of gains made in EEO. This case could have struck a significant blow to affirmative action. Inasmuch as the potential was there, businesses appeared to be unwilling to significantly deviate from the affirmative actions plans that had developed over the years. Accordingly, the perception held by many was, "Now that business views affirmative action as a competitive necessity, it (the Supreme Court rulings) just might not matter so much."[59] Of course, it's now a moot point, as the Civil Rights Bill of 1991 nullified many of these Supreme Court rulings.

Cases Concerning Reverse Discrimination

Affirmative action programs are necessary to assure continued employment possibilities for minorities and women. Programs to foster the careers of these two groups have grown immensely. But while this action was needed to correct past abuses, what about the white male?[60] Some white males feel that affirmative action plans work against them. In some situations, this feeling has resulted in less commitment and loyalty to the organization,[61] or to charges of **reverse discrimination.** Although reverse discrimination cases exist, two specific cases of re-

Reverse Discrimination A claim made by white males that minority candidates are given preferential treatment in employment decisions.

verse discrimination have been noteworthy: the Allen Bakke and the Brian Weber cases.

In 1978, the Supreme Court handed down its decision in the case of *Bakke* v. *the Regents of the University of California* at Davis Medical School.[62] Allen Bakke was an applicant to the Davis Medical School for one of the one hundred first-year seats. At that time, U.C. at Davis had a self-imposed quota system to promote its affirmative action plan: That is, of the one hundred first-year seats, sixteen were set aside for minority applicants.

Bakke's charge stemmed from those sixteen reserved seats. His credentials were not as good as those gaining access to the first eighty-four seats, but were better than those minorities targeted for the reserved seats. The issue that finally reached the Supreme Court was, could an institution impose its own quota to correct past imbalances between whites and minorities? The Supreme Court ruled that the school could not set aside those seats, for doing so resulted in "one race being favored over another."[63] Consequently, Bakke was permitted to enter medical school. As a footnote to the case, one often wonders what would have happened if Allen Bakke had waited one more year to apply; a year later, Bakke would have been 40 years old. In an age-protected group, he quite possibly would have been eligible for one of the "reserved" seats.

The Supreme Court's decision in the case of the *United Steelworkers of America* v. *Weber* (1979) appeared to have important implications for organizational training and development practices and for the larger issue of reverse discrimination. In 1974, Kaiser Aluminum and the United Steelworkers Union set up a temporary training program for higher-paying skilled trade jobs, such as electrician and repairer, at a Kaiser plant in Louisiana. Brian Weber, a white employee at the plant who was not selected for the training program, sued on the grounds that he had been illegally discriminated against. He argued that African-Americans with less seniority were selected over him to attend the training due solely to their race. The question facing the Court was: Is it fair to discriminate against whites in order to help African Americans who have been long-time victims of discrimination? The Justices said that Kaiser could choose to give special job preference to African Americans without fear of being harassed by reverse discrimination suits brought by other employees. The ruling was an endorsement of voluntary affirmative action efforts—goals and timetables for bringing an organization's minority and female work force up to the percentages they represent in the available labor pool.

Despite the press coverage that both cases received, as we entered the 1980s many questions remained unanswered. Just how far was a company permitted to go regarding preferential treatment (see "Ethical Decisions in HRM")? In subsequent cases, more information became available. In 1984, the Supreme Court ruled in *Firefighter Local 1784* v. *Stotts*[64] (1984) that when facing a layoff situation, affirmative action may not take precedence over a seniority system: that is, the last in (often minorities) may be the first to go. This decision was further reinforced in *Wyant* v. *Jackson Board of Education*[65] (1986) when the Supreme Court ruled that a collective bargaining agreement giving preferential treatment to preserve minority jobs in the event of a layoff was illegal. And the effects of this case may have been recently felt during the 1993 recession. In a study conducted by both *The Wall Street Journal* and the Government Accounting Office, African Americans and Hispanics were laid off in greater proportions than any other group.[66] On the contrary, in *Johnson* v. *Santa Clara County Transportation,* (1987) the Supreme Court did permit affirmative action goals to correct worker imbalances as long as the rights of nonminorities were protected. This ruling had an effect of potentially reducing reverse discrimination claims.

Ethical Decisions in HRM:

English-Only Rules

Can an organization require its employees to speak English on the job? The answer, for the most part, is yes. At least that is the latest perception, given the Supreme Court's refusal to consider a case involving an employer who has an English-only rule. Accordingly, a Ninth Circuit Court of Appeals decision remains in effect permitting such a policy to exist in organizations located in Alaska, Arizona, California, Hawaii, Idaho, Montana, Nevada, Oregon, and Washington.

At issue here are several items. On the one hand, employers have identified the need to have a common language spoken at the work site. Employers must be able to communicate effectively with all employees, especially when safety or productive efficiency matters are at stake. Of course, if it is a valid requirement of the job, the practice could be permitted. However, at issue in the precedent case in the Ninth Circuit Court was an employer's desire to have one language because "some workers were using bilingual capabilities to harass and insult other workers in a language they could not understand." And with today's ever-increasing concern with protecting employees, especially women, from hostile environments, English-only rules serve as one means of reasonable care.

A counterpoint to this English-only rule firmly rests with the work-force diversity issue. Workers in today's organizations come from all nationalities and speak different languages. It's estimated that in the 1990s, about 32 million workers speak a language other than English. What about their desire to speak their language, to communicate effectively with their peers, and to maintain their cultural heritage? To them, English-only rules are discriminatory in terms of national origin in that they create an adverse impact for non–English-speaking individuals.

Should employers be permitted to require that only English be spoken in the workplace? Even if it's not necessary for successful performance, or doesn't create a safety or health hazard? Should the Supreme Court view this as a discriminatory practice, or render a decision that would create a single, nationwide standard on English-only? What's your opinion?

Source: Commerce Clearing House, Human Resources Management, "English-Only Rules Not Necessarily Invalid, Contrary to EEOC Guidelines," *Ideas and Trends* (July 20, 1994), p. 124.

Enforcing Equal Employment Opportunity

Two U.S. government agencies are primarily responsible for enforcing equal employment opportunity laws. They are the Equal Employment Opportunity Commission (EEOC) and the Office of Federal Contract Compliance Programs (OFCCP).

The Role of the EEOC

Any charge leveled against an enterprise regarding discrimination based on race, color, sex, national origin, age, or wages due to sex falls under the jurisdiction of the EEOC.[67] The EEOC requires that charges be filed within 180 days of an alleged incident,[68] and that these charges be written and sworn under oath. Once the charges have been filed, the EEOC progresses (if necessary) through a four-step process.[69]

1. The EEOC will notify the organization of the charge within ten days of its filing, and then begin to investigate the charge to determine if the complaint is valid. The company may simply settle the case here, and the process stops.
2. The EEOC will notify the organization in writing of its findings within 120 days. If the charge is unfounded, the EEOC's process stops. However, the individual may still file charges against the company in civil court (called a right-to-sue notice). If there is justification to the charge, the EEOC will attempt to correct the problem through informal meetings with the employer. Again, the company, recognizing that discrimination may have occurred, may settle the case at this point.
3. If the informal process is unsuccessful, the EEOC will begin a formal settlement meeting between the individual and the organization (called a conciliation meeting). The emphasis here is to reach a voluntary agreement between the parties.
4. Should Step 3 fail, the EEOC may file charges in court.

The EEOC is staffed by five presidentially appointed commissioners and staff counsels. While acting as the enforcement arm of Title VII, the EEOC has the power to investigate claims, but they do not have the power to force organizations to cooperate. In either the informal meetings or the conciliation meeting, the enterprise participates voluntarily. Only until organizational documents are subpoenaed must the organization cooperate in the process. Even so, it is typically in the best interest of the enterprise to cooperate.[70]

The relief that the EEOC tries to achieve for the individual is regulated by Title VII. Should the charge stand, the EEOC attempts to make the individual whole: That is, under the law, the EEOC attempts to obtain lost wages or back pay, job reinstatement, and other rightfully due employment factors (e.g., seniority or benefits). The individual may also recover attorney fees. However, if the discrimination was intentional, other damages may be awarded. Lastly, under no circumstances may the enterprise retaliate against an individual filing charges. The EEOC monitors that no further adverse action against that individual occurs.

Office of Federal Contract Compliance Program (OFCCP)

In support of Executive Order 11246, the OFCCP enforces the provisions of this order (as amended), as well as Section 503 of the Vocational Rehabilitation Act of 1973 and the Vietnam Veterans Readjustment Act of 1974.[71] Provisions of the OFCCP apply to any organizations, including universities, that have a federal contract or act as a subcontractor on a federal project. The OFCCP operates within the U.S. Department of Labor. Similar to the EEOC, the OFCCP investigates allegations of discriminatory practices and follows a similar process in determining and rectifying wrongful actions. One notable difference is that the OFCCP has the power to cancel an enterprise's contract with the federal government if the organization is not in compliance with EEO laws.

Current Issues in Employment Law

EEO today is addressing the concerns of two important issues: sexual harassment in the workplace and the glass ceiling initiative.

Sexual Harassment

Sexual Harassment Anything of a sexual nature where it results in a condition of employment, an employment consequence, or creates a hostile or offensive environment.

Sexual harassment is a serious issue in our companies. Data indicate that almost all Fortune 500 companies in the United States have had complaints lodged by employees, and about a third of them have been sued.[72] Not only were the settlements in these cases at a substantial cost to the companies in terms of litigation, it is estimated that it costs a "typical Fortune 500 company $6.7 million per year in absenteeism, low productivity, and turnover."[73] That amounts to more than $3 billion annually. And sexual harassment is not just a U.S. phenomenon; it is an issue worldwide.[74] Sexual harassment charges have been filed in such countries as Japan, Australia, Netherlands, Belgium, New Zealand, Sweden, and Ireland.[75] Moreover, sexual harassment creates an unpleasant work environment for people and undermines their ability to perform their job. But just what is sexual harassment?

Sexual harassment can be regarded as any unwanted activity of a sexual nature that affects an individual's employment. Although such an activity was protected under Title VII (sex discrimination), it has not been until recent years that this problem gained recognition. By most accounts, prior to the mid-1980s, this problem was generally viewed as an isolated one, with the individual committing the act being solely responsible (if at all) for his or her actions.[76] Yet, in the 1990s, charges of sexual harassment continue to appear in the headlines on an almost regular basis. Do you remember the fury over the sexual harassment allegations made by Paula Jones against President Bill Clinton?[77] Senator Bob Packwood's staffs' allegations that he sexually harassed them?[78] Sabino Gutierrez's charges against his female supervisor, Maria Martinez, the chief financial officer of California Acrylic Industries?[79] And let us not forget the Clarence Thomas–Anita Hill debate that occurred during a special Senate sub-committee meeting regarding the confirmation of Clarence Thomas as a Supreme Court Justice.

Much of the problem associated with sexual harassment is determining what constitutes this illegal behavior. Sexual harassment can exist under one of three conditions:[80] (1) where such an activity is a condition of employment; (2) where such action has employment consequences (e.g. promotion, dismissal); and (3) where the activity creates a hostile environment. Most would agree that the first two conditions are clear-cut cases of sexual harassment. In fact, these are often referred to as *quid pro quo* sexual harassment cases, or getting something for giving something. Under Title VII, such occurrences were more easily identified and corrected, and management personnel were the only ones who could be involved in *quid pro quo* harassment.[81]

It is the third component that is problematic for organizations. Just what is a hostile environment? Challenging hostile environment situations gained much support from the Supreme Court case of *Meritor Savings Bank* v. *Vinson*.[82] This case stemmed from a situation in which Ms. Vinson initially refused the sexual advances of her boss. However, out of fear of reprisal, she ultimately conceded. But according to court records, it did not stop there. Vinson's boss also "fondled Vinson in front of other employees, followed her into the restroom, and exposed himself to her on various occasions."[83] In addition to supporting hostile environment claims, the Meritor case also identified employer liability: that is, in sexual harassment cases, an organization is held liable for sexual harassment actions by its management team, and, depending on how they treat sexual harassment charges against nonmanagement personnel, may be liable for that, too.[84] This point cannot be taken lightly. An organization's top management can be held liable for the actions of its employees, and even its customers.

Although the *Meritor* case has implications for organizations, how do organizational members determine if something is offensive? For instance, does sexually explicit language in the office create a hostile environment? How about off-color jokes? Pictures of women totally undressed? The answer is: It could! It depends on the people in the organization and the environment in which they work. Take, for example, pin-up photos and calendars. Lois Robinson, a worker at Jacksonville Shipyards, complained to the company that displays of nude and semi-nude women on calendars and posters were offensive. Additionally, because of these photos, she and the other five females out of a work crew of 846 were subjected to abuse. The company, on the other hand, felt that the pictures, while not in the greatest of taste, were not offensive to the average woman. The Supreme Court ruled for Lois Robinson.[85]

What does this tell us? The point here is that we all must be attuned to what makes fellow employees uncomfortable—and if we don't know, then we should ask! Organizational success in the remainder of the 1990s will, in part, reflect how sensitive each employee is toward another in the company. At DuPont, for example, that is exactly what Ed Bardzik is doing with his "A Matter of Respect" program.[86] This program is designed to eliminate sexual harassment through awareness and respect for all individuals. This means understanding one another and, most importantly, respecting others' rights. Similar programs exist at Federal Express, General Mills, and Levi-Strauss.[87]

If sexual harassment carries with it potential costs to the organization, what can a company do to protect itself?[88] Similar to the Rena Weeks case, the courts want to know two things—did the organization know about, or should it have known about, the alleged behavior; and what did management do to stop it? With the number and dollar amounts of the awards against organizations today, there is even a greater need for management to educate all employees on sexual harassment matters and have mechanisms available to monitor employees (see "HRM Skills"). Furthermore, "victims" no longer have to prove that their psychological well-being is seriously affected.[89] That proof was often tied to what was referred to as the "reasonable woman standard," or that the "alleged sexual harassment of a woman be judged on a gender-specific basis."[90] The Supreme Court ruled late 1993 in the case of *Harris* v. *Forklift Systems, Inc.* "that victims do not have to suffer substantial mental distress in order to be awarded big jury awards."[91] That decision has, in essence, made it easier to substantiate hostile environment claims and set in place the "reasonable person" standard. That, in essence, leaves the determination of what behavior may constitute hostile environments up to the reasonable people of the "community of people involved."[92] Unfortunately, the Supreme Court did not clarify how this reasonable person standard is to be applied,[93] nor do all Circuit Courts use it. In those cases, a "reasonable woman" standard is used.

Addressing what is unacceptable behavior at work and then enforcing the policy appears to make better sense than hiring high-priced attorneys and attacking the plaintiffs' sex lives.[94] But this latter tactic is seemingly making its way into the sexual-harassment arena, especially when emotional trauma or psychological well-being issues are raised. How many multi-million dollar awards will it take for all organizations to finally recognize that worker sensitivity and respect

HRM*Skills*

Protecting the Enterprise from Sexual Harassment Charges

1. **Issue a sexual harassment policy describing what constitutes sexual harassment and what is inappropriate behavior.** Just stating that sexual harassment is unacceptable at your organization is not enough. In this policy, specific behaviors that are unacceptable must be identified. The more explicit these unacceptable behaviors, the less chance of misinterpretation later on.

2. **Institute a procedure (or link to an existing one) to investigate sexual harassment charges.** Employees, as well as the courts, need to understand what avenue is available for an employee to levy a complaint. This too, should be clearly stated in the policy and widely disseminated to employees.

3. **Inform all employees of the sexual harassment policy.** Educate these employees (via training) about the policy and how it will be enforced. Don't assume that the policy will convey the information simply because it is a policy. It must be effectively communicated to all employees. Some training may be required to help in this understanding.

4. **Train management personnel how to deal with sexual harassment charges and what responsibility they have to the individual and the organization.** Poor supervisory practices in this area can open the company up to a tremendous liability. Managers must be trained in how to recognize signs of sexual harassment, and where to go to help the "victim." Because of the magnitude of the issue, a manager's performance evaluation should reinforce this "competency."

5. **Investigate all sexual harassment charges immediately.** All means *all*—even those that you suspect are invalid. You must give each charge of sexual harassment your attention, and investigate it by searching for clues, witnesses, as so on. Investigating the charge is also consistent with our societal view of justice.

6. **Take corrective action as necessary.** Discipline those doing the harassing and "make whole" the harassed individual. If you find that the charge can be substantiated, you must take some corrective action, including up to dismissing the individual. If the punishment does not fit the crime, you may be reinforcing or condoning the behavior. The harassed individual should also be given whatever was taken away. For example, if the result of sexual behavior led to an individual's resignation, making whole the person would mean reinstatement, with full back pay and benefits.

7. **Continue to follow up on the matter to ensure that no further harassment occurs, or that retaliation does not occur.** One of the concerns that individuals have in coming forward with sexual harassment charges is that there may be some retaliation against them—especially if the harasser has been disciplined. You must continue to observe what is affecting these individuals—including follow-up conversations with them.

8. **Periodically review turnover situations to determine if a potential problem may be arising.** (This may be EEO audits, exit interviews, and the like.) There may be a wealth of information at your disposal that may indicate a problem. For example, if only females are resigning in a particular department, that may indicate that a serious problem exists. Pay attention to your regular reports and search for trends that may be indicated.

9. **Don't forget to privately recognize individuals who bring these matters forward.** Without their courageous effort, the organization might have been faced with tremendous liability. These individuals took a risk in coming forward. You should show your appreciation for that risk. Besides, if others know that such risk is worth-

while, others may feel more comfortable in coming to you when any type of problem exists.

Sources: Adapted from Anne B. Fisher, "Sexual Harassment: What to Do," *Fortune* (August 23, 1993), pp. 84–88; Clifford M. Koen, Jr., "Sexual Harassment Claims Stem from a Hostile Work Environment," *Personnel Journal* (August 1990), pp. 97–98; Martha E. Eller, "Sexual Harassment: Prevention, Not Protection," *The Cornell H.R.A. Quarterly* (February 1990), p. 87; Maureen P. Woods and Walter J. Flynn, "Heading Off Sexual Harassment," *Personnel* (November 1989), p. 48; and Jacqueline F. Strayer and Sandra E. Rapoport, "Sexual Harassment: Limiting Corporate Liability," *Personnel* (April 1986), pp. 32–33.

toward one another is not only the right thing to do, but a whole lot cheaper? Only time will tell!

The Glass Ceiling Initiative

In years past, many jobs were formally viewed as being male- or female-oriented. For example, librarians, nurses, and elementary schoolteachers were considered typical jobs for women; by contrast, police officers, truck drivers, and top management positions were regarded as the domain of men. Historically, this attitude resulted in the traditional female-oriented jobs being paid significantly less than the male-oriented positions. Thus, differentiation led to concerns over gender-based pay systems, commonly referred to as the **comparable worth** issue.[95] For instance, a nurse may be judged to have a comparable job to that of a police officer. Both must be trained, both are licensed to practice, both work under stressful conditions, and both must exhibit high levels of effort. But they are not typically paid the same; male-dominated jobs have traditionally been paid more than female jobs. Under comparable worth, estimates of the importance of each job are used in determining and equating pay structures. While the 1963 Equal Pay Act requires that workers doing essentially the same work must initially be paid the same wage (later wage differences may exist due to performance, seniority, merit systems, and the like), the act is not directly applicable to comparable worth. Comparable worth proponents want to take the Equal Pay Act one step further. Under such an arrangement, factors present in each job (e.g., skills, responsibilities, working conditions, effort) are evaluated. A pay structure is based solely on the presence of such factors on the job. The result is that dissimilar jobs equivalent in terms of skills, knowledge, and abilities are paid similarly.

Comparable Worth Equal pay for similar jobs, jobs similar in skills, responsibility, working conditions, and effort.

The point of the comparable worth issue revolves around the economic worth of jobs to employers. If jobs are similar, even though they involve different occupations, why shouldn't they be paid the same? The concern here is one of pay disparities: Women still earn less than men. While the disparity is lessening, the fact remains that although significant progress had been made in terms of affirmative action for women, it appears they have reached a plateau in the organization. That is, while laws prohibit organizations from keeping qualified women out of high-paying positions, there appears to be a "glass ceiling" holding them down.

The **glass ceiling** is a term used to reflect why women and minorities aren't more widely represented at the top of today's organizations. The glass ceiling is not, however, synonymous with "classic" discrimination. For example, the Oles Envelope Company, which agreed to pay fifty female employees $220,000 for keeping them in lower-paying jobs, was not necessarily indicative of the glass ceiling issue.[96] Rather, the glass ceiling, according to a Department of Labor

Glass Ceiling The invisible barrier that blocks females and minorities from ascending into upper levels of an organization.

In several organizations like AlliedSignal, Liz Claiborne, General Foods, and Mattel Toys, the glass ceiling has shattered. Women have ascended into senior management positions with significant responsibilities, like that of Jill Barad, CEO of Mattel Toys.

study, is indicative of "subtle attitudes and prejudices that have blocked [these groups] from climbing the corporate ladder."[97] It appears that while significant gains have been made by minorities and women in gaining entry to organizations, fewer than 5 percent of senior management positions are held by women and minorities.[98] Why? Many times these individuals do not have advocates in the organization, lack appropriate networks, or do not have access to executive search firms.[99] To begin to correct this invisible barrier, the OFCCP is working to expand its audit compliance reviews. In these reviews, the auditors will be looking to see if government contractors do indeed have training and development programs operating to provide career growth to the affected groups. Should these be lacking, the OFCCP plans to take legal action to ensure compliance. It did just that when, in its first settlement ever regarding the glass ceiling, the OFCCP got almost $604,000 in back pay and salary increases for fifty-two women workers at a Virginia hospital.[100]

While the OFCCP's initiative to study this phenomenon is promising, the EEOC has not begun a similar investigation. Rather, it will wait to see how the OFCCP's study turns out, and be a little more attuned to possible discrimination cases involving promotions.[101] In the meantime, research into this effort is beginning to identify ways to correct the problem. In one study, it was suggested that an organizational practice such as promoting from within and preparing individuals for top-level positions, may "eventually shatter the glass ceiling."[102] In organizations like Publishers Clearing House, Liz Claiborne, AlliedSignal, Mattel, and General Foods, this practice has worked well.[103] If society puts more pressure on corporations, in terms of boycotting products they sell or not investing in the companies that are inadequately represented by women in upper management, then more cracks in the "glass" are expected.[104]

Study Tools and Applications

Summary

(This summary relates to the Learning Objectives identified on p. 62.)

After reading this chapter, you should know:

1. The Civil Rights Act of 1964, Title VII, gives individuals protection on the basis of race, color, religion, sex, and national origin. In addition to those protected under the 1964 act, amendments to the act, as well as subsequent legislation, give protection to the disabled, veterans, and individuals over age 40. In addition, state laws may supplement this list and include categories like marital status.

2. The Equal Employment Opportunity Act of 1972 is an important amendment to the Civil Rights Act of 1964, as it established the enforcement mechanism to police the provisions of the act. This enforcement arm is the Equal Employment Opportunity Commission.

3. Affirmative action plans are good-faith efforts by organizations to actively recruit and hire protected group members, and to show measurable results. Such plans are voluntary actions by an organization.

4. An adverse impact is any consequence of employment that results in a disparate rate of selection, promotion, or termination of protected group members. Adverse treatment occurs when members of a protected group receive different treatment than other employees. A protected group member is any individual who is afforded protection under discrimination laws.

5. The Vocational Rehabilitation Act of 1973, and the Americans with Disabilities Act of 1990, both provide equal opportunities for the disabled. While the Americans with Disabilities Act is more encompassing, both acts require enterprises to reasonably accommodate these individuals' needs.

6. The Pregnancy Discrimination Act of 1978 affords EEO protection to pregnant workers. If the law is applicable to an organization, it must treat pregnancy as a short-term disability and handle it as it would any other disability. The Family and Medical Leave Act grants up to twelve weeks of unpaid leave for family or medical matters. Fetal protection laws were overturned because they created an adverse impact for women.

7. A business can protect itself from discrimination charges first by having HRM practices that do not adversely affect protected groups, through supported claims of job relatedness, bona fide occupational qualifications, or through a valid seniority system.

8. *Griggs* v. *Duke Power* was one of the most important Supreme Court rulings as it pertains to EEO. Based on this case, items used to screen applicants had to be related to the job. Additionally, post–*Griggs*, the burden was on the employer to prove discrimination did not occur.

9. Sexual harassment is a serious problem existing in today's enterprises. Sexual harassment is defined as any unwelcome sexual advances, requests for sexual favors, or other verbal or physical contact of a sexual nature where the result is a condition of employment, has an employment consequence, or creates a hostile environment.

10. The glass ceiling is an invisible barrier existing in today's organizations that is keeping minorities and women from ascending to higher levels in the workplace.

Key Terms

adverse (disparate) impact	Age Discrimination in Employment Act
adverse (disparate) treatment	Americans with Disabilities Act
affirmative action	Civil Rights Act of 1866

Civil Rights Act of 1991
comparable worth
Equal Employment Opportunity Commission
Family and Medical Leave Act
Firefighter Local 1784 v. *Stotts*
4/5ths rule
glass ceiling
Griggs v. *Duke Power*
McDonnell-Douglas v. *Green*

Office of Federal Contract
    Compliance Programs
Pregnancy Discrimination Act
protected group member
restricted policy
reverse discrimination
sexual harassment
Title VII
Vocational Rehabilitation Act

EXPERIENTIAL EXERCISE:
Know Your Rights

Just as a company should have a policy and educate its work force on sexual harassment issues, so too, should a college. Do you know your college's policy on sexual harassment? Do you know what to do if you are being sexually harassed? If you do, congratulations, your college is getting the information out to you. If you don't know, then you need to find out. For this exercise, contact the office of student affairs (or whatever it is called on your campus) and ask for the college's policy on sexual harassment. You'll probably find that is also in your student handbook. Nevertheless, look at the policy and how it is enforced. Get into groups and discuss the policy and how the college has established a means for one to seek help. Your professor should then lead a discussion on the policy, what constitutes sexual harassment on the campus, and the "complaint procedure" available if one has a problem.

CASE APPLICATION:
The Boundaries of Equal Employment Opportunity

Born and raised in Lebanon, and seeking job opportunities, Ali Boureslan came to the United States, where he became a naturalized citizen in 1977. As a citizen, Ali was granted the same rights as any individual born in the United States. Ali accepted employment with the Arabian American Oil Company (ARAMCO), a U.S. company with significant operations in Saudi Arabia. He later accepted a transfer to Saudi Arabia from the company's Houston location. After some time on the job, Ali was terminated. Ali believes he was fired because of ethnic and racial matters relating to his religious beliefs. According to Ali, he was "harassed by his supervisor (who was not American) because he requested various times off to observe Moslem religious holidays."[105] That is, Ali believed this job action was based on who he was (religious discrimination), not on any ongoing corporate downsizing resulting in the elimination of Boureslan's position, as the company claimed.

   As this case worked its way through the courts, different interpretations became apparent. There appeared to be an indication that Ali's claim was correct—a personnel decision was made using religion as a factor. However, a much bigger question was being raised by the company—the issue of the applicability of U.S. laws to companies when they operate in a foreign country. If Ali Boureslan was terminated from his Houston-based position for religious, ethnic, or racial reasons, it would appear that he had every right to seek justice in the courts. However, the U.S. Supreme Court saw this matter differently. In writing the majority opinion, Justice William Rehnquist stated that equal employment opportunity laws are applicable only within U.S. borders. For Ali Boureslan, being right in the wrong place cost him his job.[106]

Questions:

1. "Equal Employment Opportunity laws should not be limited to only within the borders of the United States. Business today has global implications. Accordingly, a U.S. company should be expected to comply with U.S. EEO laws, no matter on what continents they operate." Do you agree or disagree with the statement? Explain your response.

2. Using the logic of the Boureslan case, wouldn't it appear that a foreign company, say Mitsubishi, could avoid the U.S. EEO laws by being headquartered in another country and abiding solely by their laws with respect to employment matters? Discuss.

3. "In an age of job opportunities abroad, and the diverse work force that may come from any nation on the globe, we have reached a point in time where we need a unifying EEO law that organizations from all 'trading nations' support, implement, and practice—and enforce it by some central legislative body." Build an argument supporting the statement, and one arguing against it.

Testing Your Understanding

How well did you fulfill the learning objectives?

1. Why was the outcome of *Griggs* v. *Duke Power* different from the outcome of *Washington* v. *Davis*?
   a. *Washington* v. *Davis* was heard after *Roe* v. *Wade*. *Griggs* v. *Duke Power* was heard before *Roe* v. *Wade*.
   b. Requirements such as aptitude tests and diplomas were shown to be relevant in one case, but not in the other.
   c. The outcomes were not different. Both men were subsequently hired.
   d. The outcomes were not different. Neither man was subsequently hired.
   e. Police officers are exempt from Title VII. Maintenance workers are not exempt from Title VII.

2. Why was additional discrimination legislation passed in 1972?
   a. Times had changed. New rules were needed.
   b. There was such backlash against the 1964 Civil Rights Act that it was repealed.
   c. The original legislation lacked enforcement mechanisms.
   d. Women were not protected under the original legislation.
   e. Age was not protected under the original legislation.

3. Leisure, Inc. is an Equal Employment Opportunity employer, with an active affirmative action program. What does that mean?
   a. Leisure, Inc. actively pursues female and minority candidates and makes good faith efforts to get them into the applicant pool.
   b. Leisure, Inc. hires only female and minorities during a designated five-year period.
   c. Leisure, Inc. systematically retires and fires more white males than any other group of employees.
   d. Leisure, Inc. hires a larger percentage of minorities and females than white males.
   e. Leisure, Inc. has historically employed large percentages of females and minorities.

4. Which one of the statements is accurate regarding adverse impact?
   a. Adverse impact may result from a seemingly neutral employment practice.
   b. Adverse impact is a deliberate discriminatory practice.
   c. Adverse impact is reverse discrimination against white males.
   d. Adverse impact is a public attitude toward an organization that refuses to hire female and minority job applicants.
   e. Adverse impact is a public attitude toward an organization that refuses to hire white males.

5. A 35-year-old mother of two has been with her firm for fifteen years. She wants to transfer to the computer room of her organization. She is charging adverse impact for which one of the following conditions found in the posted job description for "Computer Room Assistant"?
   a. Must be able to lift fifty pounds.
   b. High-school diploma or GED required.
   c. Prior military experience preferred.
   d. Must be familiar with organizational communications systems and requirements.
   e. Must be able to file and catalog tape and disk resources.

6. What is the difference between *adverse impact* and *adverse treatment*?
   a. There is no difference; the terms are synonymous.
   b. Adverse impact typically refers to organizational hiring practices. Adverse treatment typically refers to organizational promotion and performance evaluation practices.
   c. Adverse impact is physical abuse. Adverse treatment is mental abuse.

d. Adverse impact is emotional and subjective. Adverse treatment is objective and impersonal.

e. Adverse impact is legal. Adverse treatment is illegal.

7. It has just come to your attention that one of your accounting department employees has just tested HIV+. What workplace protection to this employee is provided under the law?

a. Under the 1990 Americans with Disabilities Act, the employee's immediate supervisor and coworkers must be informed within forty-eight hours.

b. Under the 1990 Americans with Disabilities Act, all job actions must be based on job performance requirements.

c. Under the 1990 Americans with Disabilities Act, the employee must be assigned a job with other HIV+ workers within six weeks.

d. Under the 1990 Americans with Disabilities Act, the employee will no longer be allowed to meet with other employees outside of her own area.

e. The 1990 Americans with Disabilities Act does not have provision for people with AIDS.

8. Barbara has worked for a major manufacturing firm for five years and is pregnant with her first child. What benefit provision is she allowed under the 1993 Family and Medical Leave Act?

a. No provision. The law is scheduled to be phased in, starting in 1997.

b. No provision. The law covers only vested employees, those who have been employed seven years.

c. She can take up to twelve weeks of paid leave and resume her old job when she returns.

d. She is entitled to her old job or an equivalent position upon returning to work.

e. She is not entitled to pay during her leave, but she can collect unemployment benefits.

9. Robert is a mortgage loan officer for a large financial institution. He has had a roller-coaster year. He took a six-week leave without pay in May to spend with his newly adopted son. He took a five-week leave without pay in September–October to care for his wife, who had surgery. He is now telling you, the benefits coordinator for his section, that he needs time off (without pay, of course) from Thanksgiving through the first of the year to care for another relative. His father will be out of the hospital around Thanksgiving, but can't be placed in a nursing home until January 1. You need to be sure that he is treated in accordance with the provisions of the 1993 Family and Medical Leave Act. What action will you take?

a. Fire him.

b. Transfer him to a lower paying, less responsible job.

c. Tell him he is entitled to only one additional week this year of unpaid leave, and that other arrangements will have to be worked out with his supervisor and the vice-president of benefits.

d. Grant him the leave. Tell him he is not eligible to apply again for additional unpaid leave for twenty-four months.

e. Grant him the leave.

10. You are accused of discriminatory hiring practices by a Hispanic rights group that says the only minorities your organization hires are African Americans. Which statement is an appropriate application of the 4/5ths rule?

a. In the last year, one hundred African Americans applied for positions, while only ten Hispanics applied.

b. There are no Spanish-speaking neighborhoods in 4/5ths of the geographical locations of the organization.

c. During the interview process, all applicants who were approved by four of the five interviewers were hired.

d. Forty out of eighty white applicants were hired. Two out of three Hispanic applicants were hired.

e. Eighty percent of all applicants were not hired.

11. An allegation of discrimination could best be supported under which one of the following geographical comparisons test?

a. Company position advertisements state that travel is required, approximately ten to twelve days per month.

b. The Leisure, Inc. company has a policy of promoting from within. They only hire inexperienced, newly graduated applicants, mostly from local universities.

c. A large Miami-based financial institution has no Hispanics on the payroll.

d. Jon, an HIV+ postal worker, was passed over for promotion because of his physical condition. He had successfully completed all training requirements and passed the qualifying examination.

e. Company position available announcements are posted in English, Spanish, and French.

Chapter Four

EMPLOYEE RIGHTS AND ETHICAL ISSUES

LEARNING OBJECTIVES

AFTER READING THIS CHAPTER, YOU WILL BE ABLE TO:

1. Describe the intent of the Privacy Act of 1974, and its effect on HRM.
2. Explain the HRM implications of the Drug-Free Workplace Act of 1988, and the Polygraph Protection Act of 1988.
3. Describe the provisions of the Worker Adjustment and Retraining Notification Act of 1988.
4. Discuss the pros and cons of employee drug testing.
5. Describe the use of honesty tests in hiring.
6. Discuss the implications of the employment-at-will doctrine.
7. Identify the four exceptions to the employment-at-will doctrine.
8. Define discipline and the contingency factors that determine the severity of discipline.
9. Describe the general guidelines for administering discipline.
10. Explain how ethical considerations affect Human Resources Management.

Edward Narizzano is a person of honor. He has dedicated his work life in becoming a premier truck mechanic, maximizing his given talents and love for machines. He's also punctual, trustworthy, honest, and law-abiding; an employer's delight. That is, of course, assuming those characteristics are ones valued by the organization. For Narizzano's employer, however, some of them weren't.[1]

Narizzano is an auto and truck mechanic for Beal GMC Truck, Inc., in Bel Air, Maryland. Part of Narizzano's job duties require him to inspect vehicles and issue a certification that the vehicle is safe to be operated on the highways. Over the years, the State of Maryland has enhanced the standards under which vehicles can be licensed in the state. That's because a series of fatal vehicle accidents, especially ones involving large commercial trucks, has revealed the causes of some of these accidents to be related to mechanical failure—vehicle problems, like bald tires or bad brakes. Such problems, when detected, should have prevented the vehicles from being on the road in the first place. Narizzano recognized the importance that his inspections carried—failure to identify potential problems could have a deadly effect. As such, each vehicle Edward inspected was given a "fine-tooth comb" review, and only when he was satisfied that everything was in working order, according to the motor vehicular regulations, would he issue a passing inspection sticker.

But, in June 1993, things didn't turn out as Narizzano expected. On inspecting a 1975 Peterbilt truck, he cited the vehicle for "badly worn brake drums, broken frame cross-members, three badly worn tires, inoperable lights, and brake linings that were chafed and hanging loose." He refused to certify the truck was in safe operating order. But his employer saw things differently. For some reason, the employer wanted this truck to be issued the inspection certificate. In spite of Edward's explanation, the employer wouldn't budge—in fact, his supervisor just kept demanding that the appropriate documentation be issued. Edward refused. And as a result of his ethical decision in steadfastly saying that the truck was not safe for the roads, Edward Narizzano was fired!

Narizzano couldn't believe what was happening to him. He was entrusted with an important job—ensuring that vehicles were safe to be on the highways. Yet, his employer didn't, or wouldn't, understand. If fact, as his attorney stated, "the company forced him to make a choice between keeping his job and obeying the law." But the courts found that Edward Narizzano was terminated illegally, and awarded him $176,000 in back pay and benefits, and punitive damages.

Imagine coming down a steep incline in the mountains and having this truck right behind you. Sure hope the rig's brakes are in working order! That's what most of us would want. But, for Edward Narizanno, his determination to make sure a truck like this, (but with a number of safety violations) would not be on the highways cost him his job. The Courts, however, saw his action as fulfilling the public responsibility his job required.

Introduction

What started out as a routine vehicle inspection turned into a legal battle—a fight for one's job. Shouldn't doing our jobs, and doing them in an appropriate manner be considered? Sure, there's a need for managers to be able to direct the activities of their workers without being questioned, or even second-guessed. But was Edward Narizzano treated fairly? Was his privacy violated? What rights did Narizzano have in the workplace? It is answers to questions such as these that we will address in this chapter.

    Employee rights has become one of the most important issues for human resource management to deal with in the 1990s. Individuals are guaranteed certain rights based on amendments to the U.S. Constitution. For instance, the Fourth Amendment prohibits illegal searches and seizures by the government or its agents. However, this does not mean that those outside the government, like businesses, cannot perform such an activity.[2] This has led to the question: Are employers all-powerful in this arena? The answer is no! In fact, in more and more situations—such as terminating an employee or maintaining health files on employees for insurance purposes—such organizational practices may be more constrained.[3] Consequently, various laws and Supreme Court rulings are establishing guidelines for employers dealing with employee privacy and other matters. Let's now turn to these laws.

Employee Rights A collective term dealing with varied employee protection practices in an organization.

Employment Rights Legislation and their Human Resource Management Implications

Over the past few decades, a number of federal laws have given specific protection to employees. These laws are the Privacy Act of 1974, the Drug-Free Workplace Act of 1988, the Employee Polygraph Protection Act of 1988, and the Worker Adjustment and Retraining Notification Act of 1988.

Privacy Act Requires federal government agencies to make available information in an individual's personnel file.

The Privacy Act of 1974

When an organization begins the hiring process, it establishes a personnel file for that person—a file that is maintained throughout a person's employment. Any pertinent information, like the completed application, letters of recommendation, performance evaluations, or disciplinary warnings, are kept in the file. The contents of these files often were known only to those who had access to the files; often only managers and HRM personnel. The **Privacy Act of 1974** sought to change that imbalance of information. This act, while applicable to only federal government agencies, requires that an employee's personnel file be open for inspection. This means that employees are permitted to review their files periodically to ensure that the information contained within is accurate. The Privacy Act also gives these federal employees the right to review letters of recommendation written on their behalf.

Even though this act applies solely to the federal worker, it provided the impetus for state legislatures to pass similar laws governing employees of state and private-sector enterprises. This legislation is often more comprehensive and includes protection regarding how employers disseminate information on past and current employees.

For human resource management, a key question is: How should employees be given access to their files? Although the information contained within rightfully may be open for inspection, certain restrictions must be addressed. First, any information for which the employee has waived his or her right to review must be kept separate. For instance, job applicants often waive their right to see letters of recommendation written for them. When that happens, human resources is not obligated to make that information available to the employee. Second, an employee can't simply demand to immediately see his or her file; there is typically a twenty-four hour turnaround time. Consequently, organizations frequently establish special review procedures. For example, whether or not the employee can review the file alone or in the presence of an HRM representative is up to each organization. In either case, personnel files generally are not permitted to leave the HRM area. And although an individual may take notes about the file's contents, copying the file often is not permitted.

The increasing use of computers in human resource management has complicated the issue of file reviews. Because much of this information is now stored in computerized employee data systems, access has been further constrained. Yet although computerization of HRM files is a more complicated system, appropriate access to this information should not be any different than when using a paper file; employees still have a right to see the information about them, regardless of where it is kept. Gaining entry into computerized information, however, can be a more time-consuming process. Many times, such access requires certain security clearances to special screens—clearance that is not available to everyone. However, as technology continues to improve, HRM will be better able to implement procedures to give employees access, while simultaneously protecting the integrity of the system.

Fair Credit Reporting Act Requires an employer to notify job candidates of its intent to check into their credit.

Companies are also being held accountable to the **Fair Credit Reporting Act of 1971,** an extension to the Privacy Act. In many organizations, the employment process includes a credit check on the applicant. The purpose of such checks is to obtain information about the individual's "character, general reputation,"[4] and various other personal characteristics. Typically, companies can obtain this information by using two different approaches. The first is through a credit reporting agency, similar to the type that is used when you apply for a loan. In this instance, the employer is required to notify the individual that a credit report is being obtained. However, if an applicant is rejected based on information in the report, the individual must be provided with full details of who conducted the report, and its findings. The second type of credit report is obtained through a third-party investigation. Under this arrangement, not only is one's credit checked, but people known to the applicant are interviewed regarding the applicant's lifestyle, spending habits, and character. For an organization to use this type of approach, the applicant must be informed of the process in writing, and as with the credit report, must be notified of the report's details if the information is used to negatively affect an employment decision. Keep in mind, however, that how the information is used must be job-relevant. If, for example, an organization denies employment to an individual who once filed for bankruptcy and this information has no bearing on the individual's ability to do the job, the organization may be opening itself up to a challenge in the courts.

The Drug-Free Workplace Act of 1988

The **Drug-Free Workplace Act of 1988** was passed to help keep the problem of substance abuse from entering the workplace. Under the act, government agencies, federal contractors, and those receiving federal funds ($25,000 or

Drug-free Workplace Act Requires specific government related groups to ensure that their workplace is drug free.

Organizations like TOYS "Я" US remind all of us, applicants, current employees, and customers, that the store supports a drug-free work environment. Those who are abusing substances will not work for the company!

more) are required to actively pursue a drug-free environment. In addition, the act requires employees of companies regulated by the Department of Transportation (DOT) and the Nuclear Regulatory Commission who hold certain jobs to be subjected to drug tests.[5] For example, long-haul truck drivers, regulated by the DOT, are required to take drug tests.

For all organizations covered under this act, other stipulations are included. For example, the enterprise must establish its drug-free work environment policy and disseminate it to its employees. This policy must spell out what is expected of employees in terms of being substance-free, and detail the penalties regarding infractions of the policy. In addition, the organization must provide substance-abuse awareness programs to its employees.

There's no doubt that this act has created difficulties for organizations. To comply with the act, they must obtain information about their employees. The whole issue of drug testing in today's companies is an explosive one and we'll come back to its applications later in this chapter.

The Polygraph Protection Act of 1988

As a security specialist applicant for the National Security Agency (NSA), you are asked to submit to a polygraph test as a condition of employment. Unsure of what is going to transpire, you agree to be tested. During the examination, you are asked if you have ever snorted cocaine. You respond that you never have, but the polygraph records that you are not telling the truth. Because suspicion of substance use is grounds for disqualification from the job, you are removed from consideration. Can this organization use the polygraph information against you? In the case of a job involving security, it can.

However, the **Polygraph Protection Act of 1988**[6] prohibits employers in the private sector[7] from using polygraph tests (often referred to as lie-detector tests) in employment decisions. Based on the law, companies may no longer use these tests to screen all job applicants.[8] The act was passed because polygraphs were used inappropriately. In general, polygraph tests have been found to have little job-related value, and as such their effectiveness is questionable.[9] However, the Employee Polygraph Protection Act did not eliminate their use in organizations altogether. There are situations where the law permits their use, such as when there has been a theft in the organization, but this process is regulated, too. The polygraph cannot be used as a "witch-hunt." For example, suppose that there has been a theft in the organization. The Employee Polygraph Protection Act prohibits employers from testing all employees in an attempt to determine the guilty party. However, if an investigation into the theft points to a particular employee, then the employer can ask that employee to submit to a polygraph. Even in this case, however, the employee has the right to refuse to take a polygraph test without fear of retaliation from the employer. And in cases where one does submit to the test, the employee must receive, in advance, a list of questions that will be asked. Furthermore, the employee has the right to challenge the results if he or she believes the test was inappropriately administered.[10] Figure 4-1 contains the Department of Labor's Notice of Polygraph Testing explaining employee rights.

Polygraph Protection Act Prohibits the use of lie detectors in screening all job applicants. Often referred to as a "lie-detector" test.

Worker Adjustment and Retraining Notification Act of 1988

In the fall of 1994, General Motors announced its plan to sell its car rental firm, National Car Rental Systems, to Vestar Equity Partners.[11] GM had been looking to divest itself of diversified activities in an effort to reinforce its auto-

---

NOTICE
EMPLOYEE POLYGRAPH PROTECTION ACT

The Employee Polygraph Protection Act prohibits most private employers from using lie detector tests either for pre-employment screening or during the course of employment.

Prohibitions

Employers are generally prohibited from requiring or requesting any employee or job applicant to take a lie detector test, and from discharging, disciplining, or discriminating against an employee or prospective employee for refusing to take a test or for exercising other rights under the act.

Exemptions*

The law does not apply to tests given by the federal government to certain private individuals engaged in national security-related activities.

The act permits *polygraph* (a kind of lie detector) tests to be administered in the private sector, subject to restrictions, to certain prospective employees of security service firms (armored car, alarm, and guard), and of pharmaceutical manufacturers, distributors and dispensers.

The act also permits polygraph testing, subject to restrictions, of certain employees of private firms who are reasonably suspected of involvement in a workplace incident (theft, embezzlement, etc.) that resulted in economic loss to the employer.

Examinee Rights

Where polygraph tests are permitted, they are subject to numerous strict standards concerning the conduct and length of the test. Examinees have a number of specific rights, including the right to a written notice before testing, the right to refuse or discontinue a test, and the right not to have test results disclosed to unauthorized persons.

Enforcement

The Department of Labor may bring court actions to restrain violations and assess civil penalties up to $10,000 against violators. Employees or job applicants may also bring their own court actions.

Additional Information

Additional information may be obtained, and complaints of violations may be filed, at local offices of the Wage and Hour Division, which are listed in the telephone directory under U.S. Government, Department of Labor, Employment Standards Administration.

The Law Requires Employers to Display This Poster Where Employees and Job Applicants Can Readily See It.

*The law does not preempt any provision of any state or local law or any collective bargaining agreement that is more restrictive with respect to lie detector tests.

Source: U.S. Department of Labor, WH Publication 1462 (September 1988), Employment Standards Administration, Wage and Hour Division, Washington, D.C. 20210.

Figure 4-1
Polygraph Protection Notice

motive business. But, had GM been unable to find a buyer, and just decided to close the car rental business, could GM's management have immediately closed the business unit and terminate the 6,400 National employees without prior notification? No![12] Why? Because of the **Worker Adjustment and Retraining Notification (WARN) Act of 1988.**[13] Sometimes called the Plant Closing Bill, this act places specific requirements on employers considering significant changes in staffing levels. Under WARN, an organization employing one hundred or more individuals must notify workers sixty days in advance if it is going to close its facility or lay off fifty or more individuals. Should a company fail to provide this

Worker Adjustment and Retraining Notification Act Federal law requiring employers to give sixty-days' notice of pending plant closing or major layoff.

TABLE 4-1   Summary of Laws Affecting Employee Rights

Law	Effect
Fair Credit Reporting Act	Requires employers to notify individuals that credit information is being gathered and may be used in the employment decision.
Privacy Act	Requires government agencies to make information in their personnel files available to employees.
Drug-Free Workplace Act	Requires government agencies, federal contractors, and those who receive government monies to take steps to ensure that their workplace is drug free.
Employee Polygraph Protection Act	Prohibits the use of lie-detector tests in screening all job applicants. Permits their use under certain circumstances.
Worker Adjustment and Retraining Notification Act	Requires employers with 100 or more employees contemplating closing a facility or laying off 50 or more employees to give 60 days' notice of the pending action.

advance notice, it is subject to a penalty not to exceed "one day's pay and benefits to each employee for each day notice which should have been given."[14]

However, the law does recognize that under certain circumstances, advance notice may be impossible. Assume, for example, a company is having financial difficulties and is seeking to raise money to keep the organization afloat. If these efforts fail and creditors foreclose on the company, no advance notice is required. For example, when Fair Lanes Inc. (of bowling alley fame) was unable to meet its debt obligation, it filed for bankruptcy. Although filing for bankruptcy permitted the bowling alleys to remain open, had they closed immediately,[15] WARN would not have applied.

Plant closings, similar to the employee rights issues raised previously, continue to pose problems for human resource management. What these laws have done is to create specific guidelines for organizations to follow. None preclude the enterprise from doing what is necessary. Rather, the laws exist to ensure that whatever action the organization takes is done in such a way that employee rights are protected. A summary of these laws is presented in Table 4-1.

Current Issues Regarding Employee Rights

Recently, emphasis has been placed on curtailing specific employer practices, as well as addressing what employees may rightfully expect from their organizations. These basic issues are drug testing, honesty tests, employee monitoring, and "right-to-know" information.

Drug Testing

In our earlier discussion of the Drug-Free Workplace Act, we mentioned the legislation applicable to certain organizations. However, because of the severity of substance abuse in our organizations, many organizations not covered by this

1988 act have voluntarily begun a process of **drug testing.** Why? Let's look at some facts. It is estimated that approximately 25 percent of the U.S. work force may be abusing some substance (e.g., drugs or alcohol).[16] Forty percent of all on-the-job injuries and about half of all work-related deaths are attributed to substance abuse.[17] And if that weren't enough, it has been estimated that the United States loses well over $600 billion annually in productivity due to substance abuse.[18]

As a result of the "numbers," many private employers, about 87 percent of major corporations[19] and 80 percent of smaller companies,[20] began to implement programs to curb substance-related problems in their organizations.[21] For instance, Toys R Us and Motorola test all current employees as well as job applicants.[22] In fact, walk into any Toys R Us Store and you'll see prominently displayed at the entrance a sign that says something to the effect that "the employees of this store are drug free. Applicants who cannot pass a drug screening test should not apply." The intent of drug testing is to identify the abusers and either help them to overcome their problem (current employees) or not hire them in the first place (applicants). It is in this arena that many issues arise. For example, what happens if an individual refuses to take the drug test? What happens if the test is positive? Let's look at some possible answers.

A major concern for opponents of drug testing is how the process works and how the information will be used. Drug testing in today's organizations should be conducted to eliminate drugs in the workplace, not to catch those doing drugs.[23] Although many might say that the same outcome is achieved, it's the process, and how employees view the process, that matters. At Motorola, individuals who refuse the drug test are terminated immediately.[24] Although this treatment appears harsh, the ill effect of employing a substance abuser is perceived as too great. But what if that person took the drug test and failed it? Many organizations place these individuals into a rehabilitation program, where they can get help—and the intent here is to help these workers. However, if they don't accept the help, or later fail another test, then they can be terminated.[25]

Applicants, on the other hand, present a different story. If an applicant tests positive for substance abuse, that applicant is generally no longer considered. The company's liability begins and ends there—they are not required to offer those applicants any help. But that needn't imply that applicants can't "straighten" out and try again. For example, the Red Lion Hotels and Inns organization requires all applicants to submit to a drug test. Should they test positive, their application is rejected; however, after a 90-day period, these individuals may reapply, as if nothing occurred previously.[26] It is recommended that employers conduct applicant drug testing only after a conditional job offer is made. That is, the job offer is contingent on the applicant passing a drug test. Why drug test at this stage? To properly administer the test, questions about one's health and medication record need to be addressed. Such questions before a conditional offer is made may be viewed as a violation of the Americans with Disabilities Act.[27]

From all indications, drug testing can work in achieving its goals of lessening the effect of drugs and alcohol on job-related activities like lower productivity, higher absenteeism, and job-related accidents. Nonetheless, until individuals believe that the tests are administered properly and employees' dignity is respected, criticism of drug testing is likely to continue. There have been too many instances where the drug test gave a false reading or the specimen was improperly handled. It is estimated that about 15 percent of all results may be false—that is, attributed to legitimate medication or the food one eats.[28] To

Drug Testing The process of testing applicants/employees to determine if they are using illicit drugs.

Figure 4-2
Alternatives to Body Fluid Testing

Pupillary-Reaction Test
A trained professional can determine if a subject is under the influence of drugs or alcohol by examining the subject's eyes. The pupil will react differently to light (a flashlight is used) if the subject is under the influence of drugs. Follow-up tests by body fluid testings are usually needed.

Positive features: Noninvasive.

Negative features: Must be administered by a trained professional. Some medical conditions may give a false positive result. Follow-up tests are needed.

Hair Analysis
Hair samples are examined using radioimmunoassay, then confirmed by gas chromatography or mass spectrometry. The same techniques are used to test urine samples. Chemicals—drugs, legal or illegal—are left behind in hair follicles and provide a record of past drug use. Type of drug, frequency and duration of use can be determined. Because hair grows about half an inch per month, a relatively small sample can provide a long record of drug use.

Positive features: Accepted by courts in criminal trials. Detailed record of drug use. Cannot be avoided as easily as urinalysis. Less embarrassing than urinalysis.

Negative features: Highly invasive.

Video-based Eye–hand Coordination Test
One company has begun marketing a video-based test of eye–hand coordination. The test takes less than a minute to complete and is self-administered. The test determines only impairment and the employee is actually tested against their own normal performance. Lack of sleep, illness, stress, drugs, or alcohol could cause an employee to fail.

Positive features: Can be used immediately before employee begins work. Noninvasive. Does not make lifestyle judgments. Self-administered. Low cost.

Negative features: So far only implemented at test sites. Follow-up tests necessary.

Source: Reprinted with permission of *HR Magazine,* published by the Society for Human Resource Management, Alexandria, VA: Michael R. Carroll and Christina Heavrin, "Before You Drug Test," *HR Magazine* (June 1990), p. 65.

combat this concern, companies are moving toward more precise tests—ones that do not involve body fluids (see Figure 4-2), and some that involve computers (see also "Meet Harry Letaw, Jr.").

As we move forward in drug-testing methodologies, the process should continue to improve. However, we must not forget the individual's rights. Most employees recognize why companies must drug test, but expect to be treated humanely in the process; they also want safeguards built into the process to challenge false tests. And if there is a problem, they want help, not punishment. For organizations to create this positive atmosphere, several steps must be addressed. This is where human resource management comes into play. HRM must issue its policies on substance abuse and communicate that message to every employee. That policy must state what is prohibited, under what conditions an individual will be tested, the consequences of failing the test, and how the process of testing will be handled.[29]

By making clear what is expected, as well as what the company intends to do, the emotional aspect of this process can be reduced.[30] Where such a policy ex-

Meet

Harry Letaw, Jr.
President, Essex Corporation

Imagine if you could design a computer software program that measured alertness and dexterity. If you could, you'd be able to measure an employee's potential performance level even before he or she gets on the job. Such an invention would surely benefit a lot of companies; especially those that wish to determine if an employee's judgment or abilities are impaired by substances. You would have built a better mousetrap for the 1990s—and that claim today rightfully belongs to Harry Letaw, Jr.

Harry Letaw, Jr., is the president of Essex Corporation, a designer of computer software located in Columbia, Maryland. Harry recognized that testing employees for substance abuse was a growing trend in American businesses. He also realized that the costs of drug testing, coupled with the indignities that may be associated with it, may limit their use. There had to be a way to combine the needs of both employers and employees—a test that met the employers' requirement that workers are drug-free, and one that was "user friendly." The technology that Letaw's firm uses—artificial intelligence and virtual reality systems—led him in the direction of designing a video drug test.

Letaw's video involves some simple mechanics. A blinking blip floats on the computer monitor. The user must keep the blip steady and in the center of the screen by adjusting a control knob. If the employee can achieve those two goals, then their dexterity and reaction time indicates no impairment.

By mid-1994 about a dozen firms had found Harry's "innovation" to be extremely beneficial. For instance, the R. F. White company, a home-heating-oil delivery organization, requires its drivers to take the video test each morning. Those who "pass" the test are then given keys to their tankers and are permitted to make their deliveries. Those who don't are sent home; of course, without pay. For R. F. White, this video test has resulted in fewer accidents and corresponding workers' compensation claims, saving the company more than $30,000 each year in insurance premiums alone. Not a bad return on an investment of $2,500 a year in the leased program.

Although there are skeptics over widespread use of a video game for drug testing, Letaw has high hopes for his product. Not only can impairment be detected, brought about by substance abuse, fatigue, or other factors, but those organizations that require precise eye–hand coordination for successful employee performance have found Essex's product a sound investment.

ists, questions of legality and employee privacy issues are reduced.[31] Additionally, where drug testing is related to preventing accidents and actual job performance, tests have been shown to be more positively viewed.[32]

Honesty Tests

How would you respond to the question: How often do you tell the truth?[33] All the time? Sorry, we can't hire you because everyone has stretched the truth in their lifetime. So you must be lying, and therefore not the honest employee we desire. Most of the time? Sorry again! We can't afford to hire someone who

●

Honesty Tests A specialized paper and pencil test designed to assess one's honesty.

may not have the highest ethical standards. Sound like a Catch-22? Welcome to the world of **honesty tests.** Although polygraph testing has been significantly curtailed in the hiring process, employers have found another mechanism that supposedly provides similar information.[34]

Much of the intent of these tests is to get applicants to provide information about themselves that otherwise would be hard to obtain. These "integrity" tests tend to focus on two particular areas—theft and drug use.[35] But the tests are not simply indicators of what has happened; typically, they assess an applicant's past dishonest behavior and that individual's attitude toward dishonesty.[36] One would anticipate that applicants would try to answer these questions to avoid "being caught," or would even lie; however, research findings suggest otherwise. That is, individuals frequently perceive that "dishonesty is okay as long as you are truthful."[37] As such, applicants discuss questions in such a way that the tests do reveal the information intended. These tests frequently are designed with multiple questions covering similar topic areas, to assess consistency. If consistency in response is lacking, the test may indicate that an individual is being dishonest.[38]

Because of the effectiveness of these tests, coupled with their lower costs versus polygraphs, a number of companies have begun using them in their selection process. In fact, it was estimated that over 5,000 organizations are using some variation of honesty tests to screen applicants, testing some 5 million individuals each year.[39] Surprisingly, however, companies using these tests seldom reveal that they do. The large use of these tests has provoked questions about their validity and their potential for adverse impact. Research to date is promising.[40] Although instances have been recorded that indicate that individuals have been wrongly misclassified as dishonest,[41] other studies have indicated that they do not create an adverse impact against protected group members.[42] Based on the evidence, our conclusion is that these tests may be useful for providing more information about applicants, but should not be used as the sole criterion in the hiring decision.

Whistle-Blowing

Whistle-blowing A situation in which an employee notifies authorities of wrongdoing in an organization.

Over the past few years, more emphasis has been placed on companies being good corporate citizens. Incidents like the Kidder Peabody financial scandal[43] and the breast implant cover-up at Dow Corning have fueled interest in the area. One aspect of being responsible to the community at large is permitting employees to challenge management's practice without fear of retaliation. This challenge is often referred to as **whistle-blowing.**

Whistle-blowing occurs when an employee reports the organization to an outside agency for what the employee believes is an illegal or unethical practice. In the past, these employees were often subjected to severe punishment for doing what they believed was right. For instance, several years ago, an employee in General Electric's nuclear fuel facility operation complained that "radioactive spills in the work setting were not properly cleaned up."[44] As the employee attempted to document her case, she was subjected to personnel actions by the company. The company believed that the employee, instead of leaving the "mess" for all to see, should have cleaned it up. This employee was ultimately terminated,[45] and unfortunately no federal law protected her.

Although federal legislation is lacking (except for a federal law passed during the Bush administration that covers public employees), state laws may be available. However, the extent of these laws, and how much protection they afford, differ greatly.[46] Nonetheless, many firms have voluntarily adopted policies to permit employees to identify problem areas.[47] The thrust of these policies is to

Figure 4-3
Ten Steps to an Effective Whistle-Blowing Policy

1. Develop the policy in written form.

2. Seek input from top management in developing the policy, and obtain their approval for the finished work.

3. Communicate the policy to employees using multiple media. Inclusion in the employee handbook is not sufficient. Active communication efforts such as ethics training, departmental meetings and employee seminars will increase awareness of the policy and highlight the company's commitment to ethical behavior.

4. Provide a reporting procedure for employees that does not require them to go to their supervisor first. Instead, designate a specific office or individual to hear initial employee complaints. Streamline the process and cut the red tape. Make it easy for the employees to use the procedure.

5. Make it possible for employees to report anonymously, at least initially.

6. Guarantee employees who report suspected wrongdoing in good faith that they will be protected from retaliation from any member of the organization. Make this guarantee stick.

7. Develop a formal investigative process and communicate to employees exactly how their reports will be handled. Use this process to investigate all reported wrongdoings.

8. If the investigation reveals that the employee's suspicions are accurate, take prompt action to correct the wrongdoing. Employees will quickly lose confidence in the policy if disclosed wrongdoing is allowed to continue. Whatever the outcome of the investigation, communicate it quickly to the whistle-blowing employee.

9. Provide an appeals process for employees dissatisfied with the outcome of the initial investigation. Provide an advocate (probably from HRM) to assist the employee who wishes to appeal an unfavorable outcome.

10. Finally, a successful whistle-blowing policy requires more than a written procedure. It requires a commitment from the organization, from top management down. This commitment must be to create an ethical work environment.

Source: Timothy R. Barrett and Daniel S. Cochran, "Making Room for the Whistleblower," *HR Magazine* (January 1991), p. 59. Reprinted with permission of *HR Magazine,* published by the Society for Human Resource Management, Alexandria, Virginia.

have an established procedure whereby employees can safely raise these concerns and the company can take correct action. A suggested whistle-blower policy is presented in Figure 4-3.

Employee Monitoring and Workplace Security

Technology, enhanced in part by improvements in computers, has done some wonderful things in our work environment. It has allowed us to be more productive, to work smarter, not harder, and to bring about efficiencies in organizations that were not possible two decades ago. It has also provided us a means of **employee monitoring**—what some would call spying on our employees!

Workplace security has become a critical issue for employees. **Workplace security** can be defined as actions on behalf of an employer to ensure that the employer's interests are protected: That is, workplace security focuses on protecting the employer's property, and its trade business.[48] Without a doubt,

Employee Monitoring An activity whereby the company is able to keep informed of its employees' activities.

Workplace Security A situation in which employers protect their property and trade business.

Ethical Decisions in HRM:

Employee Monitoring

If you worked for Nissan Motors in almost any of their many jobs, and used their e-mail system, how would you feel if your supervisor routinely read your computer messages (especially if in the past you've called your supervisor derogatory terms in e-mail messages to colleagues)? Or how would you feel as a loyal employee of the Boston Sheraton Hotel about you and a friend being secretly videotaped in the men's room at the hotel—even if the videotaping is designed to monitor behavior in hopes of ridding from the premises substance abusers and drug dealers. Technology today makes it possible, even easy, for companies to monitor their employees. And many do so in the hopes that it will help both you and them become more productive and more quality-oriented. The appropriate question for employee rights is, when does such employee snooping become unethical?

Just how pervasive is this practice of monitoring employees? Exact numbers are simply not known, although guestimates in the millions appear reasonable. For example, call most 800-customer-service numbers, like that of Gateway 2000, and you'll likely hear a message that calls are monitored for quality. Or recognize that networked computer stations can be monitored from a central location to assess "real time" productivity. Under such an arrangement, however, employers should issue an "employee monitoring" policy, which details what is monitored, when, and how the information is used. In such instances, employees appear more tolerant of being monitored. Yet, these same employees appear to exhibit more stress-related symptoms than employees who are not monitored.

Are employers overstepping the bounds of decency and respect for employees? Consider that it is almost kids' play to monitor cellular phone conversations or to intercept and copy fax transmissions. Or, take the case of Olivetti, which has employees wearing "smart badges." These identification devices can track the whereabouts of an employee. That can be helpful in having messages transferred to your location, but also means that Olivetti managers may know exactly your every move.

Sure, employee monitoring can help enhance performance and provide valuable feedback to both the employer and the employee. But at what point does the organization's need for that information violate an employee's right to privacy? What's your opinion?

Source: Adapted from Lee Smith, "What the Boss Knows About You," *Fortune* (August 9, 1993), pp. 88–93.

employers must protect themselves. Employee theft, or revealing trade secrets to competition, could be damaging to the company. But how far can this protection extend? Don't we need to consider employees' rights too? Obviously the answer is yes, but how is that balance created?

Consider what happened to Alana Shorts.[49] Arriving at work at Epson America one morning, Alana noticed her boss reading her electronic mail. Although company managers verbally stated that electronic mail messages were private, the company's written policy was different. It was her employer's contention that it owned the system, and accordingly had the right to see what was going on. And they were right! In fact, employers can even film you in the restroom. But whatever employers deem fair game, they should explain for employees in terms of a company policy.[50]

Part of the problem here goes back to the balance of security. Abuses by some employees—for instance, employees using the company's computer system for gambling purposes, to run their own businesses,[51] to waste time playing computer games or to work on personal matters—have resulted in companies implementing a more "policing" role. As employee-monitoring issues become more noticeable, keep a few things in mind. Employers, as long as they have a policy regarding how employees are monitored, will continue to check on employee behavior. Specifically targeted for this monitoring are system computers, electronic mail, and the telephone. In companies like Federal Express, American Airlines, and UPS, employees are continually told that they may be monitored. Undoubtedly, the debate regarding the "ethics" of this action will continue (see "Ethical Decisions in HRM"). Nonetheless, only when employees understand what the company expects and how it will gather its information will their rights be safeguarded.[52]

Other Employee Rights Issues

Although we have addressed a number of employee rights issues, two additional concerns deserve discussion. These are the monitoring of office romances—sometimes called "legislating love"[53] and AIDS testing. We'll leave this section also with a brief discussion of sexual orientation rights.

Legislating Love   **Legislating love** in our companies today is a direct result of the sexual harassment issues facing our organizations. The workplace has long been a place to develop romantic interests; many individuals have met their mates through work or organizational contacts. But what happens when this organizational love reaches another plateau? What if your significant other is now your boss or has moved on to work for a competitor? Many organizations have typically found such situations unacceptable. As a result, they try to keep romantic relationships from developing at the work site, or to control possible conflicts of interest and to maintain secrecy. To do so, they have issued various guidelines on how—if at all—relationships at work may exist. Figure 4-4 lists the policies of several companies.

Some companies, on the other hand, like Mitchell Energy and Development, Interstate Bakeries, and Microsoft, are seeing this dilemma differently.[54] Top management in these organizations views office romance, and possible marriage between their employees, as having a positive effect on employee morale and productivity. For Bill Gates, the CEO of Microsoft, relationships were hard to start and maintain given his eighteen-hour workdays. If a legislating-love policy had existed, it might have prevented Gates from marrying his marketing executive, Melinda French, in January 1994. And for a company like DEC, permitting romantic relationships between employees has helped to foster their "company-centered family."[55]

AIDS Testing   We already know that under the Americans with Disabilities Act, an employer cannot discriminate in employment decisions against anyone who is HIV+ or has AIDS. However, more appropriate for employee rights, does a

Legislating Love Company guidelines on how personal relationships may exist at work.

Figure 4-4
Selected Company Policies on Organizational Romance

AT&T   "Our attitude toward corporate romance is one of benign neglect," says corporate spokesperson Burke Stinson. The company, which is noted for its strong policy on sexual harassment, has never issued formal guidelines against dating, but it discourages direct supervisor–subordinate relationships, and forbids spouses from reporting to each other. "Until the 1980s," says Stinson, "all types of office romance were frowned upon. But the whole environment of corporate America has become a mini-*Love Boat.*" Nationwide, there are an estimated 7,500 married couples at the company.

Prudential   After the Clarence Thomas Supreme Court nomination hearing, the company issued a memo to its employees restating its long-standing policy on sexual harassment and went on to warn that romantic relationships can "influence the quality of decisions and can potentially hurt other people."

"We certainly can't forbid dating," says Don Mann, the company's senior vice president of human resources. "Hundreds of couples met at the company, including the chairman and his wife. The main concern we have is about chain-of-command relationships. A transfer is the typical solution."

DuPont   The company has one of the most extensive sexual-harassment prevention and education programs in the country, including a 24-hour hot line, seminars, and, when necessary, a team of harassment investigators. Dating, however, is allowed, provided that it's not a boss–subordinate relationship. In that case, one person is reassigned.

Source: Ellen Rapp, "Legislating Love," *Working Woman* (February 1992), p. 61.

Years ago, office romances were taboo in organizations. The potential problems that may arise, coupled with the conflict of interest "image" it may project, led many organizations to implement policies prohibiting such actions. Today, however, some organizations are rethinking that policy. Rather than prohibit couples from working together, companies like Parker Hannifin (an auto parts maker) encourage it! Mike and Lois Cawley (pictured) are opening a Parker Hannifin plant in Mexico. Sending one spouse without the other creates more stress on the individual. As such, Parker Hannifin recognizes the benefits of transferring married couples together, which eliminates any marital discord which could eventually hamper productive efforts for the company.

company have a right to know if an employee is HIV positive? The answer is, it depends. If the job requires certain types of contact with other individuals, such as a health-care provider performing invasive surgery, the answer may be yes.[56] In most other cases, it would be difficult to support a reason to know. Although companies have the right to require, and pay for, employees to take a physical exam upon being hired (usually for health-insurance purposes), the more appropriate concern is what happens if the company finds out the employee is infected. Many companies appear to be grappling with this issue, particularly with regard to safeguarding employee confidentiality. IBM and Wells Fargo and Company are two organizations that have taken a leading role in this matter.[57] Both organizations have developed policies regarding how managers are to treat this information, specifically emphasizing the need to protect the privacy of the worker. Irrespective of the number of companies that implement similar policies, one point is clear: failure to protect the individual's privacy may result in a lawsuit.[58]

Sexual Orientation Rights When one considers the laws and court rulings presented in our last chapter, one begins to appreciate what has occurred over the past few decades. Yet although we have made a lot of progress, we clearly have a distance to go. For instance, Cracker Barrel is a retail chain known for its cheese products. If you walk around its stores, you will notice some very fine products. You should also know that no homosexuals work there, at least none who are open about their sexual preference. Discrimination against an individual based on sexual orientation currently does not come under the jurisdiction of Title VII (although some state and local laws do exist). As a result, discriminating in hiring, promoting, and the like on the basis of sexual orientation is legal.[59] Because of the concern about AIDS and the stereotype that it is a homo-

Workers at Lotus Development Corporation work hard at learning to accept one another. Here, straight and gay employees meet to discuss issues that effect their work relationship. Additionally, not only does Lotus not discriminate on the basis of sexual preference, and offers sensitivity training to its employees, the company also provides employee benefits to same-sex partners.

sexual disease, some companies began informally surveying customers about their attitudes toward gay workers. Somewhat begging the question, many customers stated they preferred not to patronize an establishment that hires homosexual workers (how they would know is uncertain). In response to such feedback, these organizations began questioning "suspected" employees about their sexual preference. Some employees had a choice—lie and keep their jobs, turning their backs on their significant others, or tell the truth and be fired. Gay and lesbian groups have targeted companies like Cracker Barrel for boycotts and have held rallies, but federal law has not changed regarding sexual orientation in the workplace. Consequently, as long as it is not in violation of the law, such action by an employer is permitted. However, that may change at some point in the future.

For example, federal legislation that would prohibit employment discrimination because of one's sexual orientation has been introduced before Congress. Called the Employment Non-Discrimination Act (ENDA), the bill "would prohibit sexual orientation discrimination in hiring, firing, promotions, and compensation.[60] The proposed legislation would be similar to the Americans with Disabilities Act (in terms of who is covered), would be enforced by the EEOC, and would permit remedies similar to those of the Civil Rights Act of 1991). But ENDA would not mandate employers to offer employee benefits, like health insurance, to same-sex partners.[61] The liklihood of its passage, however, appears slim in a Republican-controlled congress.

The Role of the Employment-at-Will Doctrine

Background

Employment-at-Will Nineteenth-century common law that permitted employers to discipline or discharge employees at their discretion.

The concept of the **employment-at-will doctrine** is rooted in nineteenth-century common law, which permitted employers to discipline or discharge employees at their discretion. The premise behind this doctrine is to equalize the playing field. If employees can resign at any time they want, why shouldn't an employer have the same right?

Under the employment-at-will doctrine, an employer can dismiss an employee "for good cause, for no cause, or even for a cause morally wrong, without being guilty of a legal wrong."[62] Of course, even then, you can't fire on the basis of race, religion, sex, national origin, age, or disability.[63] Although this doctrine has existed for over one hundred years, the courts, labor unions, and legislation are lessening the use of this doctrine.[64] Jobs are being likened to private property. That is, individuals have a right to these jobs unless the organization has specified otherwise. Employees today are challenging the legality of their discharge more frequently. It is estimated that approximately 2 million workers are discharged each year, with about 10 percent of them being fired for reasons other than just cause.[65] When being fired without cause occurs, individuals like Edward Narizzano (discussed earlier in this chapter), may seek the assistance of the courts to address their wrongful discharge. All fifty states currently permit employees to sue their employers if they believe their termination was unjust.[66] At issue in these suits is that through some action on the part of the employer, exceptions to the employment-at-will doctrine exist.

Exceptions to the Doctrine

While employment-at-will lives today in our organizations, there are four exceptions under which a wrongful discharge suit can be supported. These are through a contractual relationship, public policy violation, implied contracts, and a breach of good faith.[67] Let's take a closer look at these.

Contractual Relationship A contractual relationship exists when employers and employees have a legal agreement regarding how employee issues are handled. Under such contractual arrangements, discharge may only occur if it is based on just cause. Inasmuch as a distinct definition of just cause does not exist, there are guidelines derived from labor arbitration of collective-bargaining relationships (we'll look at discipline in labor–management relationships in Chapter 18) under which just cause can be shown, as follows:

1. Was there adequate warning of consequences of the worker's behavior?
2. Are the rules reasonable and related to safe and efficient operations of the business?
3. Before discipline was rendered, did a fair investigation of the violation occur?
4. Did the investigation yield definite proof of worker activity and wrongdoing?
5. Have similar occurrences, both prior and subsequent to this event, been handled the same and without discrimination?
6. Was the penalty in line with the seriousness of the offense and in reason with the worker's past employment record?[68]

In addition to this contractual relationship, federal legislation may also play a key role. Discrimination laws such as those discussed in Chapter 3 may further constrain an employer's use of at-will terminations. For example, an organization cannot terminate an individual based on his or her age just because such action would save the company some money.

Public Policy Violation Another exception to the employment-at-will doctrine is the **public policy violation.** Under this exception, an employee cannot be terminated for failing to obey an order from an employer that can be construed as an illegal activity. That was the essence of Edward Narizzano's case against Beal GMC Truck. Additionally, should an employee refuse to offer a bribe to a public official to increase the likelihood of the organization obtaining a contract, that employee is protected. Furthermore, employers cannot retaliate against an employee for exercising his or her rights (like serving on a jury). Accordingly, employees cannot be justifiably discharged for exercising their rights in accordance with societal laws and statutes.

Public Policy Violation Prohibiting the termination of an employee for refusing to obey an order the employee considered illegal.

Implied Employment Contract The third exception to the doctrine is the **implied employment contract.** An implied contract is any verbal or written statement made by members of the organization that suggests organizational guarantees or promises about continued employment.[69] These implied contracts, when they exist, typically take place during employment interviews or are included in an employee handbook.

Implied Employment Contract Any organizational guarantee or promises about job security.

One of the earlier cases reaffirming implied contracts was the case of *Toussaint* v. *Blue Cross and Blue Shield of Michigan*.[70] In this case, Toussaint claimed that he was improperly discharged, for unjust causes, by the organization. He asserted that he was told "he'd be with the company until age 65 as long as he did his job."[71] The employee's handbook also clearly reinforced this tenure with statements reflective of discharge for just cause. Even if just cause arose, the discharge could only occur after several disciplinary steps (we'll look at the topic of discipline in the next section) had occurred.[72] In this case, the court determined that the discharge was improper,[73] because permanence of his position was implied by the organization.

Resulting from implied contracts is a change in how human resources management operates. Interviewers are increasingly cautious, avoiding anything that could conjure up a contract. Something as innocent as discussing an annual salary may cause problems, for such a comment implies at least twelve months on the job.[74] Many organizations, because management wants to maintain employment-at-will, have listed disclaimers such as, "This handbook is not a contract of employment," or "Employment in the organization is at the will of the employer," on the covers of their employee handbooks and manuals to reinforce their employment-at-will policy. Yet caution is warranted, as a supervisor's statements may override the printed words.

Breach of Good Faith   The final exception to the employment-at-will doctrine is the breach of good faith. Although this is the most difficult of the exceptions to prove, there are situations where an employer may breach a promise. In one noteworthy case, an individual employed over twenty-five years by the National Cash Register Company (NCR) was terminated shortly after completing a major deal with a customer.[75] The employee claimed that he was fired to eliminate NCR's liability to pay him his sales commission. In the case, the court ruled that this individual acted in good faith in selling the company's product and reasonably expected his commission. Although NCR had an employment-at-will arrangement with its employees, the court held that his dismissal, and their failure to pay commissions, was a breach of good faith.

Breach of good faith, then, can be extended to many activities in which an employer abuses managerial powers, resulting in employees being terminated. Recall from earlier in this chapter the Cracker Barrel terminations of those employees who "confessed" to being homosexual. Although no current federal EEO laws protect sexual preference, these individuals were terminated after an investigation that had little to do with their jobs. These individuals may be able to claim that such action by an employer is in bad faith, but that is for the courts to decide.

Even though the nineteenth-century common law may be used to support a discharge, the courts have been continuously chipping away at its foundation. Some experts estimate that by the year 2000, the employment-at-will doctrine will be eliminated altogether from corporate America.[76] Legislation is also being proposed that would eliminate all terminations for reasons other than just cause.[77] While such legislation appears to be in the distant future, movement today is seen more toward voluntary curtailment. Recall from Chapter 1 that as part of a sound employee relations program, employees should be given a process whereby their complaints can be registered. In companies like Federal Express and IBM, where such programs exist,[78] employees have a disciplinary process that ensures just-cause discharges. In these companies, management has determined that just-cause discharges have a better effect on employee morale and reduce the likelihood of the company having to defend itself against a wrongful discharge suit.

Discipline and Employee Rights

The exceptions to the employment-at-will doctrine mentioned above may be leading you to think that employers cannot terminate employees, or are significantly limited in their action. That's not the point of that discussion. Rather, where exceptions exist, there may be a requirement that such an employment action follow a specific process. That process, and how its works is embedded in the topic we call discipline.

What Is Discipline?

The term **discipline** refers to a condition in the organization where employees conduct themselves in accordance with the organization's rules and standards of acceptable behavior. For the most part, employees discipline themselves. By that we mean that members conform to what is considered proper behavior because they believe it is the right thing to do. Once they are made aware of what is expected of them, and assuming they find these standards or rules to be reasonable, they seek to meet those expectations.

But not all employees will accept the responsibility of self-discipline. There are some employees who do not accept the norms of responsible employee behavior. These employees, then, require some degree of extrinsic disciplinary action, frequently labeled punishment. It is this need to impose extrinsic disciplinary action that we will address in the following sections.

Factors to Consider When Disciplining

Before we review disciplinary guidelines, we should look at the major factors that need to be considered if we are to have fair and equitable disciplinary practices. The following contingency factors can help us analyze a discipline problem:[79]

1. *Seriousness of the Problem.* How severe is the problem? As noted previously, dishonesty is usually considered a more serious infraction than reporting to work twenty minutes late.
2. *Duration of the Problem.* Have there been other discipline problems in the past, and over how long a time span? The violation does not take place in a vacuum. A first occurrence is usually viewed differently than a third or fourth offense.
3. *Frequency and Nature of the Problem.* Is the current problem part of an emerging or continuing pattern of disciplinary infractions? We are concerned with not only the duration but also the pattern of the problem. Continual infractions may require a different type of discipline from that applied to isolated instances of misconduct. They may also point out a situation that demands far more severe discipline in order to prevent a minor problem from becoming a major one.
4. *Extenuating Factors.* Are there extenuating circumstances related to the problem? The student who fails to turn in her term paper by the deadline because of the death of her grandfather is likely to have her violation assessed more leniently than will her peer who missed the deadline because he overslept.
5. *Degree of Socialization.* To what extent has management made an earlier effort to educate the person causing the problem about the existing rules and procedures and the consequences of violations? Discipline severity must reflect the degree of knowledge that the violator holds of the organization's standards of acceptable behavior. In contrast to Point 4, the new employee is less likely to have been socialized to these standards than the twenty-year veteran. Additionally, the organization that has formalized, written rules governing employee conduct is more justified in aggressively enforcing violations of these rules than is the organization whose rules are informal or vague.
6. *History of the Organization's Discipline Practices.* How have similar infractions been dealt with in the past within the department? Within the entire organization? Has there been consistency in the application of discipline procedures? Equitable treatment of employees must take into consideration precedents within the unit where the infraction occurs, as well as previous disciplinary actions taken in other units within the organization. Equity demands consistency against some relevant benchmark.
7. *Management Backing.* If employees decide to take their case to a higher level in man-

Discipline A condition in the organization when employees conduct themselves in accordance with the organization's rules and standards of acceptable behavior.

agement, will you have reasonable evidence to justify your decision? Should the employee challenge your disciplinary action, it is important that you have the data to back up the necessity and equity of the action taken and that you feel confident that your superiors will support your decision. No disciplinary action is likely to carry much weight if violators believe that they can challenge and successfully override their manager's decision.

How can these seven items help? Consider that there are many reasons for why we might discipline an employee. With little difficulty, we could list several dozen or more infractions that management might believe require disciplinary action. For simplicity's sake, we have classified the most frequent violations into four categories: attendance, on-the-job behaviors, dishonesty, and outside activities. We've listed them and potential infractions in Table 4-2. However, these infractions may be minor or serious given the situation, or the industry in which one works. For example, while concealing defective work in a hand-tool assembly line may be viewed as minor, the same action in a pharmaceutical manufacturing plant is more serious. Furthermore, recurrence and severity of the infraction will play a role. For instance, employees who experience their first minor offense might generally expect a minor reprimand. A second offense might result in a more stringent reprimand, and so forth. In contrast, the first occur-

TABLE 4-2 Specific Discipline Problems

Type of Problem	*Infraction*
Attendance	Tardiness
	Unexcused absence
	Leaving without permission
On-the-job Behaviors	Malicious destruction of organizational property
	Gross insubordination
	Carrying a concealed weapon
	Attacking another employee with intent to seriously harm
	Drunk on the job
	Sexually harassing another employee
	Failure to obey safety rules
	Defective work
	Sleeping on the job
	Failure to report accidents
	Loafing
	Gambling on the job
	Fighting
	Horseplay
Dishonesty	Stealing
	Deliberate falsification of employment record
	Clock-punching another's timecard
	Concealing defective work
	Subversive activity
Outside activities	Unauthorized strike activity
	Outside criminal activities
	Wage garnishment
	Working for a competing company

rence of a serious offense might mean not being allowed to return to work, the length dependent on the circumstances surrounding the violation.

Disciplinary Guidelines

All human resource managers should be aware of disciplinary guidelines. In this section, we will briefly describe them.

Make Disciplinary Action Corrective Rather than Punitive. The object of disciplinary action is not to deal out punishment.[80] The objective is to correct an employee's undesirable behavior. While punishment may be a necessary means to that end, one should never lose sight of the eventual objective.

Make Disciplinary Action Progressive. Although the type of disciplinary action that is appropriate may vary depending on the situation, it is generally desirable for discipline to be progressive.[81] Only for the most serious violations will an employee be dismissed after a first offense. Typically, progressive disciplinary action begins with a verbal warning and proceeds through a written warning, suspension, and, only in the most serious cases, dismissal.

Follow the "Hot-stove" Rule. Administering discipline can be viewed as analogous to touching a hot stove (therefore, the **hot-stove rule**).[82] While both are painful to the recipient, the analogy goes further. When you touch a hot stove, you get an immediate response; the burn you receive is instantaneous, leaving no question of cause and effect. You have ample warning; you know what happens if you touch a red-hot stove. Furthermore, the result is consistent: Every time you touch a hot stove, you get the same response—you get burned. Finally, the result is impersonal; regardless of who you are, if you touch a hot stove, you will get burned. The comparison between touching a hot stove and administering discipline should be apparent, but let us briefly expand on each of the four points in the analogy.

Hot-stove Rule Discipline should be immediate, provide ample warning, be consistent, and be impersonal.

The impact of a disciplinary action will be reduced as the time between the infraction and the penalty's implementation lengthens. The more quickly the discipline follows the offense, the more likely it is that the employee will associate the discipline with the offense rather than with the manager imposing the discipline. As a result, it is best that the disciplinary process begin as soon as possible after the violation is noticed. Of course, this desire for immediacy should not result in undue haste. If all the facts are not in, managers may invoke a temporary suspension, pending a final decision in the case. The manager has an obligation to give advance warning prior to initiating formal disciplinary action. This means the employee must be aware of the organization's rules and accept its standards of behavior. Disciplinary action is more likely to be interpreted as fair by employees when there is clear warning that a given violation will lead to discipline and when it is known what that discipline will be.

Fair treatment of employees also demands that disciplinary action be consistent. When rule violations are enforced in an inconsistent manner, the rules lose their impact. Morale will decline and employees will question the competence of management. Productivity will suffer as a result of employee insecurity and anxiety. All employees want to know the limits of permissible behavior, and they look to the actions of their managers for such feedback. If, for example, Bart is reprimanded today for an action that he did last week, for which nothing was said, these limits become blurry. Similarly, if Tanya and Marie are both goofing around at their desks and Tanya is reprimanded while Marie is not, Tanya is likely to question the fairness of the action. The point, then, is that discipline should be consistent. This need not result in treating everyone exactly alike, because that ignores the contingency factors we discussed earlier, but it does put the responsibility on management to clearly justify disciplinary actions that may appear inconsistent to employees.

The last guideline that flows from the hot-stove rule is: Keep the discipline impersonal. Penalties should be connected with a given violation, not with the personality of the violator. That is, discipline should be directed at what employees have done, not the employees themselves. As a manager, you should make it clear that you are avoiding personal judgments about the employee's character. You are penalizing the rule violation, not the individual, and all employees committing the violation can expect to be penalized. Furthermore, once the penalty has been imposed, you as manager must make every effort to forget the incident; you should attempt to treat the employee in the same manner as you did prior to the infraction.

Disciplinary Actions

Discipline generally follows a typical sequence of four steps: written verbal warning, written warning, suspension, and dismissal[83] (see Figure 4-5). Let's briefly review these four steps.

Written Verbal Warning The
first formal step in the disciplinary process.

Written Verbal Warning   The mildest form of discipline is the **written verbal warning.** Yes, the term is correct. A written verbal warning is a temporary record of a reprimand that is then placed in the manager's file on the employee. This written verbal warning should state the purpose, date, and outcome of the interview with the employee. This, in fact, is what differentiates the written verbal warning from the verbal warning. Because of the need to document this step in the process, the verbal warning must be put into writing. The difference, however, is that this warning remains in the hands of the manager; that is, it is not forwarded to HRM for inclusion in the employee's personnel file.

The written verbal reprimand is best achieved if completed in a private and informal environment. The manager should begin by clearly informing the employee of the rule that has been violated and the problem that this infraction has caused. For instance, if the employee has been late several times, the manager would reiterate the organization's rule that employees are to be at their desks by 8 A.M., and then proceed to give specific evidence of how violation of this rule has resulted in an increase in workload for others and has lowered departmental morale. After the problem has been made clear, the manager should then allow the employee to respond. Is she aware of the problem? Are there extenuating circumstances that justify her behavior? What does she plan to do to correct her behavior?

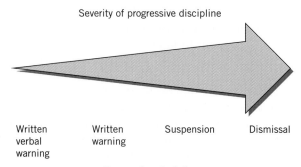

Figure 4-5
The Progressive Discipline
Process

After the employee has been given the opportunity to make her case, the manager must determine if the employee has proposed an adequate solution to the problem. If this has not been done, the manager should direct the discussion toward helping the employee figure out ways to prevent the trouble from recurring. Once a solution has been agreed upon, the manager should ensure that the employee understands what, if any, follow-up action will be taken if the problem recurs.

If the written verbal warning is effective, further disciplinary action can be avoided. If the employee fails to improve, the manager will need to consider more severe action.

Written Warning   The second step in the progressive discipline process is the **written warning.** In effect, it is the first formal stage of the disciplinary procedure. This is because the written warning becomes part of the employee's official personnel file. This is achieved by not only giving the warning to the employee but sending a copy to HRM to be inserted in the employee's permanent record. In all other ways, however, the procedure concerning the writing of the warning is the same as the written verbal warning; that is, the employee is advised in private of the violation, its effects, and potential consequences of future violations. The only difference is that the discussion concludes with the employee being told that a formal written warning will be issued. Then the manager writes up the warning—stating the problem, the rule that has been violated, any acknowledgment by the employee to correct her behavior, and the consequences from a recurrence of the deviant behavior—and sends it to HRM.

Written Warning First formal step of the disciplinary process.

Suspension   A **suspension** or layoff would be the next disciplinary step, usually taken only if the prior steps have been implemented without the desired outcome. Exceptions—where suspension is given without any prior verbal or written warning—occasionally occur if the infraction is of a serious nature.

A suspension may be for one day or several weeks; disciplinary layoffs in excess of a month are rare. Some organizations skip this step completely because it can have negative consequences for both the company and the employee. From the organization's perspective, a suspension means the loss of the employee for the layoff period. If the person has unique skills or is a vital part of a complex process, her loss during the suspension period can severely impact her department or the organization's performance if a suitable replacement cannot be located. From the employee's standpoint, a suspension can result in the employee returning in a more unpleasant and negative frame of mind than before the layoff.

Then why should management consider suspending employees as a disciplinary measure? The answer is that a short layoff, without pay, is potentially a rude awakening to problem employees. It may convince them that management is serious, and shock them into accepting responsibility for following the organization's rules.

Suspension A period of time off from work as a result of a disciplinary process.

Dismissal   Management's ultimate disciplinary punishment is dismissing the problem employee. Dismissal should be used only for the most serious offenses. Yet it may be the only feasible alternative when an employee's behavior is so bad as to seriously interfere with a department or the organization's operation.

A dismissal decision should be given long and hard consideration. For almost all individuals, being fired from a job is an emotional trauma. For employees who have been with the organization for many years and for those over fifty years of age, dismissal can make it difficult to obtain new employment or require the individual to undergo extensive retraining. In addition, management should consider the possibility that a dismissed employee will take legal action to fight the decision. Recent court cases indicate that juries are cautiously building a list of conditions under which employees may not be lawfully discharged.

Positive Discipline: Can It Work?

Although discipline is often regarded as negative—punitive action taken out on someone who has done something wrong—positive discipline attempts to remove the punitive nature from the process. The concept of positive discipline was first reported at Union Carbide Corporation.[84] In its design, positive discipline attempts to integrate the disciplinary process with the performance management system. When problems arise, rather than promptly responding with a written verbal warning (punitive), positive discipline attempts to get the employee back on track by helping to "convince the individual to abide by company performance standards."[85] That is, in using positive discipline, attempts are made to reinforce the good work behaviors of the employee, while simultaneously emphasizing to the employee the problems created by the undesirable performance. The basis of positive discipline is presented in Table 4-3.

Employee Ethics

Ethics Going beyond the law in employment decisions designed to protect employee rights and dignity.

Part of any discussion regarding employee rights should also include a discussion on **ethics.** Employee rights issues often surround very specific behaviors exhibited by those in the company. It is how these behaviors are seen, and their implications, that indicate what individuals will do. For example, if employees

TABLE 4-3   Steps in Positive Discipline

Step 1: An Oral Reminder	Notice here that the word *warning* is removed. The **oral reminder** serves as the initial formal phase of the process to identify to the employee what work problems he or she is having. This reminder is designed to identify what is causing the problem and attempts to correct it before it becomes larger.
Step 2: A Written Reminder	If the oral reminder was unsuccessful, a more formalized version is implemented. This **written reminder** once again reinforces what the problems are and what corrective action is necessary. Furthermore, specific timetables that the employee must accept and abide by, and the consequences for failing to comply, are often included.
Step 3: A Decision-making Leave	Here, employees are given a **decision-making leave**—time off from work, often with pay—to think about what they are doing and whether or not they desire to continue work with the company. This "deciding day" is designed to allow the employee an opportunity to make a choice—correct the behavior, or face separation from the company.

expect personal information to be confidential, but it leaks out, that says something about the organization and its environment.

We can define ethics as those guiding principles that help us decide between what is right and what is wrong. Unfortunately, these guiding principles are not specific rules; rather, they establish acceptable parameters in which we are to operate. During the past decade, these guidelines have come under renewed fire. Major U.S. corporations have been cited as fostering an environment where questionable practices were allowed. Government defense contractors, like General Dynamic, were found to be gouging the government on contracts on which they worked; Wall Street investors and deal-makers came to believe that "greed is good," subtly encouraging unethical behavior and operating questionable schemes. And the list could go on! All managers and employees must consider the ethical dimensions of their decisions, including those in the HRM area.

Ethical Issues in Human Resource Management

When we speak of ethics for HRM practitioners, we are referring to actions that go beyond what is required by the law. As we know, HRM is highly regulated by federal, state, and local laws. But does mere compliance with EEO laws indicate ethical practices? We don't think so. For instance, take the 4/5ths rule. If HRM practices exist such that the exact compliance ratio is reached, then the activities are legal, but the intent is suspect. What we are concerned about is creating an environment where decisions go beyond the law, such that the best interests of our workers are taken into account. Let's look at some ethical issues facing HRM practitioners today.

Ethical Dilemmas in Human Resource Management

We don't profess to have right or wrong answers regarding ethical issues in human resource management. In fact, no one really can state what is right or wrong once you go beyond the laws. However, we can identify a number of instances that raise ethical awareness. How would you react to the following?

Situation 1. Your company has a drug-free policy. For current employees, a drug test is administered only as part of the disciplinary process, and is at the discretion of the immediate supervisor. If performance problems exist and substance abuse is suspected, the supervisor can require the employee to be tested. If the presence of a substance is found, and the test is collaborated with a second sample, the employee is terminated. One of your employees is having performance problems of late, and you've heard rumors that some substance may be involved. This employee, however, has made a great business contact for you and your organization, and you'd really rather not get into this whole issue of drug testing and its implications. You'd rather handle the situation differently to turn this individual's performance around. Is this ethical?

Situation 2. Your company has a poor safety record. Although safety inspectors find no violation, it is clear that you meet only the minimum health and safety requirements. Last year, forty-three injuries were reported, three resulting in fatalities. Even though the company was not liable, should it be doing more?

Situation 3. Your company is in the process of restructuring. You've given your 7,500 employees notice that about 1,500 people will be laid off starting in ninety days. You know precisely which departments and employees will be cut, yet you respond to specific questions about the "who"s with a general statement that you are still in the process of determining where the cuts will be made, and who will be affected. Is this practice ethical?

Situation 4. Your company has had poor relations with the union representing your employees. As you are in the process of negotiating, you notify the union that you desire to have a cap placed on employees' salaries. The union balks at this issue, and claims that if you keep the issue on the table, they will strike. You refuse, they strike, and you immediately hire replacement workers to keep the company operating. Is this ethical behavior?

Situation 5. Your company is comprised of individuals from six different countries who are recruited from your local community. Some of them don't speak English well. Even though supervisors are able to somehow communicate with them, and they get their work done, these same supervisors are upset that these employees converse in their native language at work. Thus, your company is prepared to issue an English-only rule. Is this ethical?

Human resource management faces many dilemmas. Just meeting the law is not enough; until we begin to focus more on our employees' needs and how we affect them, employee problems will continue. Even though you have every right to meet the bare minimum legal requirements, to do so might not be in the best long-term interests of your employees or your organization (see "HRM Skills: Ethics Training").

Ethics Training

1. **Have a policy on ethics.** Such a policy describes what the company perceives as ethical behavior and what it expects employees to do. In doing so, you will clarify what are and what are not permissible practices—its standards of conduct. Without this policy as a guideline, ethics in left to a subjective determination.
2. **Communicate this policy to employees.** Employees must receive and understand the policy. Employees should recognize that this policy is important, and as such should be delivered with the fanfare of a major event.
3. **Train employees to make ethical decisions.** Ethical decision making is never a cut-and-dried process. As such, the training should focus on situations that permit employees to make decisions. Then, these decisions should be analyzed in terms of how ethical they were, or other decisions that may have been more appropriate with company policy. A few training games are on the market that assist in this endeavor.
4. **Reinforce that all decision makers face similar dilemmas.** Decision makers need to know that they are not alone in having to make ethical choices. The organization expects them to make ethical decisions. Accordingly, they need to feel the support of top management, and peers, when unpopular but ethical decisions are made.
5. **Reward ethical decision makers.** Nothing will reinforce the ethics policy more than if decision makers are rewarded for making the "appropriate choice." That situation should be spotlighted in some capacity—especially as a means of reinforcing that there is top management support for such decisions.

Study Tools and Applications

Summary

This summary relates to the Learning Objectives provided on p. 93.

After having read this chapter, you should know:

1. The intent of the Privacy Act of 1974 was to require government agencies to make available to employees information contained in their personnel files. Subsequent state laws have afforded the same ability to nongovernment agencies.

2. The implications of the Drug-Free Act of 1988 were to require government agencies, federal contractors, and those who receive more than $25,000 in government money to take various steps to ensure that their workplace is drug free. Nongovernment agencies with less than $25,000 in government grants are exempt from this law. The Polygraph Protection Act of 1988 prohibits the use of lie-detector tests in screening all job applicants. The act, however, does permit select use of polygraphs under specific circumstances.

3. The Worker Adjustment and Retraining Notification Act of 1988 requires employers with one hundred or more employees contemplating closing a facility or laying off fifty or more workers to provide sixty days' advance notice of the action.

4. Drug testing is a contemporary issue facing many organizations. Because of the problems associated with substance abuse in our society, and our organizations specifically, companies test employees. The costs in terms of lost productivity and the like support such action. On the other hand, however, comes the issue of privacy. Does the company truly have the right to know what employees do on their own time? Additionally, validity of drug tests as well as proper procedures are often cited as reasons for not testing.

5. Honesty testing in hiring has been used to capture the information now unavailable from polygraph in screening applicants. Many companies use these paper-and-pencil tests to obtain information on one's potential to steal from the company, as well as to determine if an employee has stolen before. Validity of honesty tests has some support, and their use as an additional selection device appears reasonable.

6. The employment-at-will doctrine permits employers to fire employees for any reason, justified or not. Although based on nineteenth-century common law, exceptions to employment-at-will have curtailed employers' use of the doctrine.

7. The four exceptions to the employment-at-will doctrine are contractual relationships, public policy violations, implied employment contracts, and a breach of good faith by the employer.

8. Discipline is a condition in the organization when employees conduct themselves in accordance with the organization's rules and standards of acceptable behavior. Whether discipline is imposed and how severe is the action chosen should reflect such contingencies as the seriousness of the problem, duration of the problem, frequency and nature of the problem, the employee's work history, extenuating circumstances, degree of orientation, history of the organization's discipline practices, implications for others employees, and management backing.

9. General guidelines in administering discipline include making disciplinary actions corrective, making disciplinary actions progressive, and following the hot-stove rule — be immediate, provide ample warning, be consistent, and be impersonal.

10. Ethical considerations affect human resource management in a number of ways. To protect employee rights and dignity, ethical consideration means going beyond the law in employment decisions.

Key Terms

discipline

dismissal

drug testing

Drug-Free Workplace Act of 1988

employee rights

employee monitoring

employment-at-will doctrine

ethics

Fair Credit Reporting Act of 1971

hot-stove rule

honesty tests

implied employment contract

legislating love

Polygraph Protection Act of 1988

Privacy Act of 1974

public policy violation

suspension

whistle-blowing

Worker Adjustment and Retraining Notification
    Act of 1988

workplace security

written verbal warning

written warning

EXPERIENTIAL EXERCISE

Drug testing continues to be one of the more intrusive aspects of our hiring process. Many see the need for drug testing, but may object to how it is done. For this exercise, you need to form two groups. One group will develop reasons supporting drug testing of all applicants and all employees; the other will develop reasons against such a process. Once you have generated your facts, the two groups should come together and debate the merits of their case. Each side should prepare a ten-minute, uninterrupted presentation. After both sides have presented, allow ten minutes for each group to respond to questions. After points and counterpoints have been addressed, answer the following questions.

1. What were the main issues raised by both groups?
2. What similarities existed between the two? What differences existed?
3. Based solely on the information presented, which side would you support? Explain.

CASE APPLICATION:

Tina Miller-Silverman and USAir

Today's organizations are recognizing the need to be more flexible in terms of benefit offerings, especially those that support family-related issues. With the work-force diversity that exists, and the realization that about half of the labor force is women, some of these benefits focus on helping mothers manage career and family. In cases where organizations lack this support, it is not highly unusual to find a parents using their vacation leave, or simply calling in sick, to care for a family member. But sometimes an event occurs that becomes difficult to accept. And that's the complaint of Tina Miller-Silverman.[86]

Tina is a flight attendant for USAir. Although Tina is frequently away from home during her flights, she has an excellent support system to help her care for her child. This includes her husband, a regular baby-sitter, and several back-ups. For the most part, caring for her child is no big deal. But one night in the summer of 1994 proved to be the undoing of her system. Tina had called home prior to her last scheduled flight, a shuttle from Boston to New York. During the phone conversation, she learned that her child had become ill. Ordinarily, this would not have been a major ordeal. After all, she would be home shortly after the shuttle landed. But when she arrived in New York at 10 P.M., Tina was notified by a USAir plane scheduler that the plane had to return to Boston immediately, and she would be expected to serve as a member of the flight crew. These changes are not routine, but such unexpected events do occur, and flight attendants are expected to make the trip. But on that night, there was a problem for Tina. Her husband was unavailable to go home immediately, and her baby-sitter had to leave on time. What a frustrating dilemma!

Tina complained to the scheduler, wondering why another flight attendant, who already needed to return from New York to the Boston area, couldn't replace her. After all, this was an unusual situation, and USAir was generally cooperative in giving its employees time off to deal with family matters—especially under sudden circumstances like Tina encountered. She'd fly, but only as a last resort. Ultimately, the Boston-based flight attendant made the trip. But not until Tina Miller-Silverman had been fired for delaying the flight.

Questions

1. Do you believe Tina Miller-Silverman's dismissal is a wrongful discharge? Why or why not?
2. Describe the discipline Tina received in terms of the contingencies that affect the discipline process.
3. Assume the baby-sitter did leave, and Tina complied with the scheduler's request. Would the fact that leaving a child unattended could lead to child abandonment charges brought against Tina and her husband have any effect on supporting a wrongful discharge claim? Discuss.

Testing Your Understanding

How well did you fulfill the learning objectives?

1. Dana is rewriting the section of the policies and procedures manual for her organization regarding employees' access to their employment history files. Which statement is most appropriate?
   a. No employee shall have access to any data in his or her file.
   b. Any employee may have access to any employee file data with supervisor approval.
   c. An employee may have access to his or her file with twenty-four-hour notice to personnel. The file must be reviewed in the human resources area.
   d. Any employee file may be requested by the employee. File contents will be mailed to the employee's official home address.
   e. Any employee may have access to his or her employee file with signatory approval of the immediate supervisor and one additional level of management.

2. The Fair Credit Reporting Act contains which provision?
   a. Job applicants must be informed in writing of third-party credit history investigations.
   b. Job applicants who have filed bankruptcy are guaranteed by a federal agency for seven years.
   c. Job applicants may refuse to submit to a credit check. Organizations must hire them anyway if all other relevant selection criteria are met.
   d. Standards of the act do not apply to female and minority applicants.
   e. Loan payment defaults must be removed from an employee's file in ninety days.

3. You are vice-president of human resources in a federal security agency. Which procedure would be an appropriate pre-employment credit history practice?
   a. Do not tell the applicant of any credit history examinations that you intend to perform.
   b. Do not do any credit history evaluation. No one would apply if they had anything to hide.
   c. Ask the applicant for checking and savings account numbers.
   d. During the screening interview, have applicants sign a statement that informs them they will be subject to a third-party investigation to assess their character and general reputation. Secure names of individuals who may be contacted as personal references.
   e. Ask the candidate to complete a credit history form during the interview. Watch for stress reactions as the individual lists outstanding balances and monthly payment amounts. Ask probing questions if you notice any unusual responses.

4. A vice-president of human resources for a large defense contractor has developed a drug-free workplace compliance policy that defines expected employee behaviors and states penalties for noncompliance. This policy should also include:

a. providing substance-abuse awareness programs for all employees.

b. requiring one hundred hours of community service work for all first time offenders.

c. sponsoring public service announcements on local television or radio stations about substance abuse.

d. working with local school systems to prevent substance abuse in the schools.

e. supplying an article in the company newsletter that identifies offenders.

5. An applicant was given a polygraph test to ascertain general levels of honesty when she applied for a job as a sales associate for a large department store. She "failed" the test and was subsequently removed from the applicant pool. What legal recourse, if any, does the individual have?

a. She can notify the secretary of labor, who will enforce her right to work and require the organization to hire her.

b. She can notify the secretary of labor, who may assess civil penalties up to $10,000 against the employer.

c. She may file criminal action against the human resources professional who administered the test. If guilty, that person could be jailed for five years.

d. The union will issue a walkout if she is employed.

e. None.

6. As a corrections officer applicant, Jim was asked to submit to a routine polygraph test. He was shown the list of questions, and agreed to take the test. When he said, "No," in response to a question about recreational drug usage, the machine indicated a lie. Jim was not hired because suspicion of drug use is grounds for dismissal for corrections officers. What recourse does he have?

a. He can retake the test next month. Law stipulates that he must be given the questions thirty days prior to examination.

b. He should be hired anyway if his drug test was negative.

c. None. Corrections institutions may hire or not hire any job candidate at their discretion.

d. None. The requirement for a security officer is reasonable.

e. If Jim is a minority candidate, he can appeal the decision.

7. An employee has worked for twenty-two years at a twenty-employee branch of a large auto-parts chain. Business has been very bad lately, and there are rumors of consolidation, reorganization, even bankruptcy. What protection does this employee have under the Worker Adjustment and Retraining Notification Act?

a. With over fifteen years' seniority, the employee cannot be laid off with less than six months' notice.

b. No protection. This branch is too small for coverage under WARN.

c. No protection. This industry is not covered by the Plant Closing Bill.

d. The employee will be given sixty days' warning if this location closes.

e. The employee will be given thirty days' warning, but only if the whole organization closes.

8. An accounts payable manager for a 250-employee graphics art manufacturer has been on the job for twenty-seven months. She went to work Monday morning to find the front door locked and a "THIS SPACE FOR LEASE" sign on the front door. She called her office from the local McDonald's and found that the telephone had been disconnected. What protection is given to this accounts payable manager under the Worker Adjustment and Retraining Notification Act?

a. She is entitled to an amount equal to pay and benefits for up to sixty days.

b. No protection. The company was too small for coverage.

c. No protection. This industry was not covered.

d. Her old firm must pay agency fees to have her placed with another organiza-tion.

e. No protection. Managers are not covered by the law.

9. Honesty tests

a. are only legal when they focus on drug use or theft.

b. accept dishonesty as a valid behavior, as long as the respondent is truthful about that behavior.

c. are typically designed to cover similar topic areas with multiple questions to assess consistency.

d. provide information that is easily obtainable by other techniques.

e. are permissible only after a person has been hired.

10. The original premise behind employment-at-will was

a. if employers can fire whenever they want, employees should be able to quit whenever they want.

b. if employers can hire whenever they want, employees should be able to quit whenever they want.

c. if employers can schedule working hours, employees should be able to schedule their own vacations.

d. if employees can quit whenever they want, employers should be able to fire whenever they want.

e. if employees can request vacation leave, employers should be able to schedule working hours.

Chapter Five

STRATEGIC HUMAN RESOURCE PLANNING

LEARNING OBJECTIVES

AFTER READING THIS CHAPTER, YOU WILL BE ABLE TO:

1. Describe the importance of strategic human resource planning.
2. Define the steps involved in the strategic human resource planning process.
3. Explain what Human Resource Management Systems are used for.
4. Define the term *job analysis*.
5. Identify the six general techniques for obtaining job information.
6. Discuss the Department of Labor's Job Analysis and Purdue University's Position Analysis Questionnaire.
7. Explain the difference between job descriptions, job specifications, and job evaluations.
8. Describe the difference between downsizing and rightsizing.
9. List various methods of achieving staff-reduction goals.
10. Explain what is meant by outplacement services.

When you think of General Motors, a number of images may arise. Large, bureaucratic, or automobile manufacturer may be just a few. But, once upon a time, General Motors (GM) depicted everything that was good in the United States. Its management, and leading-edge production processes help the United States become the leader of the industrialized nations. Economically, GM was a winner, employing hundred of thousands of workers and generating sales that, if it had been a country instead of a company, would have placed it in the top ten nations in terms of gross national product. In fact, decades ago, the saying was, what is good for GM is good for the country.

As the years progressed, however, this giant of a company couldn't change quickly enough to compete successfully with the tremendous competition coming from abroad. GM had gotten so large, it appeared at times that it couldn't get out of its own way. Sales were declining rapidly, its product line didn't offer what customers wanted, and GM's management's attempt to hold on to yesterday's practices almost brought this giant down for the final count. How? All told, this once profitable company hit rock bottom in 1991 and 1992, losing $4.5 billion and $23.5 billion, respectively. Something had to be done, and it had to be done now! Chosen to turn around this corporate mammoth was a 33-year company veteran, Jack Smith.[1]

Jack Smith began to quickly assess what was hindering the company. He realized that the organization had gotten away from its mainstay of business—producing quality cars. The large structure that existed in this conglomerate had gotten so big that it failed to adapt to its ever-changing environment. And more importantly, the company lacked a vision. It floundered, in part, because its management didn't know where it wanted to go. To correct these problems, Smith created a direction for the organization. By analyzing the organization's strengths, weaknesses, opportunities, and threats, he was able to focus organizational effort toward a specific purpose. Those things that didn't fit this direction were eliminated. Smith closed plants, sold off subsidiaries that didn't fit the core automotive business, changed various management practices in the company, and cut more than 74,000 jobs. He redesigned work processes, reengineering the work flow such that more productivity was achieved and at a higher quality. Smith had workers trained in new techniques, and sought to generate a production work force of highly skilled technicians. How has Jack Smith fared? In just thirty months on the job, he brought a new life to the ailing company. He's created hope, excitement, and profits. GM reported profits of $2.5 billion in 1993; and is expected to reach profit levels in the $7 billion range by the late 1990s.

Introduction

Jack Smith realized that changes do occur in organizations. But adapting to these changes requires all organizational members to understand where the organization is going and to support what the enterprise is about to do. Individuals like Jack Smith understand that before you can depart on a journey, you have to know your destination. Just think about the last time you took a vacation. For example, if you live in Las Vegas and decide to go to a California beach for spring break, you need to decide specifically what beach—such as Newport or Laguna—you want to go to, and the best route you can take. In an elementary form, this is what planning is all about—knowing where you are going and how you are going to get there. The same holds true for Human Resource Management.

Whenever an organization is in the process of determining its human resource needs, it is engaged in a process we call **strategic human resource planning (SHRP).** SHRP is one of the most important elements in a successful Human Resource Management program,[2] because it is a process by which an organization ensures that it has the right number and kinds of people, at the right place, at the right time, capable of effectively and efficiently completing those tasks that will help the organization achieve its overall objectives. Strategic human resource planning, then, translates the organization's overall plans and objectives into the number and types of workers needed to meet those objectives. Without clear-cut planning, estimation of an organization's human resource needs are reduced to mere guesswork.

Strategic human resource planning cannot exist in isolation. It must be linked to the organization's overall strategy.[3] Twenty years ago, few employees in a typical firm, outside of the firm's top executives, really knew the company's long-range objectives. In fact, it might have been questionable if even top management really knew where the organization was heading. Their strategic efforts were often no more than an educated guess in determining the organization's direction. But things are different today. Aggressive domestic and global competition, for instance, has made strategic planning virtually mandatory. Although it's not our intention to go into every detail of the strategic planning process in this chapter, senior HRM officials need to understand the process because they're playing a more vital role in the strategic process. It is HRM's responsibility to lead the entire management team in "showing the best way to take charge of the new workplace."[4] Let's look at a fundamental strategic planning process in an organization.

Jack Smith, CEO of General Motors has made a significant improvement on GM's bottom line. Prior to his arrival as CEO, the organization posted record losses. Yet, Smith's turnaround efforts in his 30 months at the reigns, have resulted in GM posting over a $2 billion profit in 1993. How did he do this? Through restructuring, reengineering, selling off poorer performing units, and strategic human resource planning.

Strategic Human Resource Planning The process of linking human resource planning efforts to the company's strategic direction.

An Organizational Framework

The strategic planning process in an organization is both long and continuous.[5] At the beginning of the process, the organization's main emphasis is to determine what business it is in. This is commonly referred to as developing the **mission statement.** Without knowing this information, the organization will, at best, flounder. Why is the mission statement important? Take, for instance, a part of Black and Decker's mission statement—to be the premier manufacturer and marketer of tools and electric equipment. What that statement does is clarify for all organizational members what exactly the company is about. Accordingly, the

Mission Statement The reason an organization is in business.

Strategic Goals Organization-wide goals setting direction for the next five to twenty years.

company specifies clearly why it exists and sets the course for company operations: That is, a sound mission statement facilitates the decision-making process. For example, if Black and Decker's managers wanted to sell industrial hand tools, such a decision to enter that market is within the boundaries set by the mission; however, these same managers would know that any effort to expand the company's product lines to include selling washers and dryers would be time ill spent. Yet, that's not to say that mission statements are written in stone; at any time, after careful study and deliberation, they can be changed. For example, the March of Dimes was originally created to facilitate the cure of infantile paralysis (polio). When polio was essentially eradicated in the 1950s, the organization redefined its mission as seeking cures for children's diseases. Nonetheless, the need to specifically define an organization's line of business is critical to its survival.

After reaching agreement on what business the company is in and who its consumers are, senior management then begins to set **strategic goals.**[6] During this phase, these managers define objectives for the company for the next five to twenty years. These objectives are broad statements that establish targets the organization will achieve. For example, Illinois's Continental Banks established broad areas of emphasis. That is, the bank was going to enter three specific banking arenas: corporate and institutional banking, global trading and distribution, and private banking.[7]

After these goals are set, the next step in the strategic planning process begins—the corporate assessment. During this phase, a company begins to analyze its goals, its current strategies, its external environment, its strengths and weaknesses and its opportunities and threats, in terms of whether or not they can be achieved with the current organizational resources. Commonly referred to as a "gap or SWOT (strengths, weaknesses, opportunities, and threats) analysis," the company begins to look at what skills, knowledge, and abilities are available internally, and where shortages in terms of people skills or equipment may exist. For Continental Bank, this meant looking at what people skills were needed in order to be successful in the new markets. Their analysis resulted in their changing the company's recruiting efforts in an attempt to hire people with the specific international marketing skills they wanted.[8] This phase of the strategic planning process cannot be overstated; it serves as the link between the organization's goals and ensuring that the company can meet its objectives—that is, establishes the direction of the company through strategic planning.

The company must determine what jobs need to be done, and how many and what types of workers will be required. In management terminology, we call this *organizing*. Thus, establishing the structure of the organization assists in determining the skills, knowledge, and abilities required of jobholders.

It is only at this point that we begin to look at people to meet these criteria. And that's where Human Resource Management comes in. To determine what skills are needed, HRM conducts a job analysis. Figure 5-1 is a graphic representation of this process. The key message in Figure 5-1 is that all jobs in the organization ultimately must be tied to the company's strategic direction. Recall in Chapter 2 our discussion of effectiveness and efficiency in terms of corporate downsizing. Unless jobs can be linked to the organization's goals and objectives, achieving these goals becomes a moving target. It's no wonder, then, that strategic human resources management has become more critical in organizations. Let's look at how human resource planning operates within the strategic planning process.

Mission	Determining what business the organization will be in
Objectives and goals	Setting goals and objectives
Strategy	Determining how goals and objectives will be attained
Structure	Determining what jobs need to be done and by whom
People	Matching skills, knowledge, and abilities to required jobs

Figure 5-1
The Strategic Direction–
Human Resource Linkage

Linking Organizational Strategy to Human Resource Planning

To ensure that people are available to meet the requirements set during the strategic planning process, human resource managers engage in strategic human resource planning. The purpose of strategic human resource planning is to determine what HRM requirements exist for current and future supplies and demands for workers. For example, if a company has set as one of its goals to double the number of operations over the next five years, such action will require that individuals be available to handle the jobs in the new ventures. After this assessment, strategic human resource planning matches the supplies and demands for labor, supporting the people component.

Assessing Current Human Resources

Assessing current human resources begins by developing a profile of the organization's current employees. This is an internal analysis that includes an inventory of the workers and the skills they currently possess. In an era of complex computer systems, it is not too difficult for most organizations to generate a human resources inventory report. The input to this report would be derived from forms completed by employees and then checked by supervisors. Such reports would include a complete list of all employees by name, education, training, prior employment, current position, performance ratings, salary level, languages spoken, capabilities, and specialized skills.[9]

From a strategic human resource planning viewpoint, this input is valuable in determining what skills are currently available in the organization. They serve as a guide for supporting new organizational pursuits or in altering the organization's strategies. This report also has value in other HRM activities, such as selecting individuals for training and development, promotion, and transfers.

The completed profile of the human resources inventory can provide crucial information for identifying current or future threats to the organization's ability to perform. For example, the organization can use the information from the inventory to identify specific variables that may have a particular relationship to training needs, productivity improvements, and succession planning. A charac-

Human Resource Management System A computerized system that assists in the processing of HRM information.

teristic like technical obsolescence, or workers who are not trained to function with new computer requirements, can, if it begins to permeate the entire organization, adversely affect the organization's performance.

Human Resource Management Systems   To assist in the HR inventory, organizations have implemented a **human resource management system (HRMS).** An HRMS is designed to quickly fulfill the human resource management informational needs of the organization. The HRMS is a database system that keeps important information about employees in a central and accessible location. When such information is required, the data can be retrieved and used to facilitate human resource planning decisions. Its technical potential permits the organization to track most information about employees and jobs, and to retrieve that information when needed. An HRMS may also be used to help track EEO data.[10] Figure 5-2 is a listing of typical information tracked on an HRMS.

HRMSs have grown significantly in popularity in the past decade. This is essentially due to the recognition that management needs timely information on its people and that new technological breakthroughs have cut the cost of these systems.[11] Additionally, HRMS are now more "user-friendly" and provide quick and responsive reports,[12] especially when linked to the organization's management information system.

At a time when quick analysis of an organization's human resources is critical, the HRMS is filling a void in the strategic planning process. With information readily available, companies are in a better position to quickly move forward in achieving their organizational goals.[13] Additionally, the HRMS is useful in other aspects of human resource management, providing data support for compensation and benefits programs, as well as providing a necessary link to corporate payroll.[14]

Replacement Charts HRM organizational charts indicating positions that may become vacant in the near future and the individuals who may fill the vacancy.

Succession Planning An executive inventory report indicating which individuals are ready to move into higher positions in the company.

Replacement Charts   In addition to the computerized HRMS system, some organizations also generate a separate senior management inventory report. This report, called a **replacement chart,** typically covers individuals in middle-to-upper level management positions. In an effort to facilitate **succession planning**— ensuring that another individual is ready to move into a position of higher responsibility—the replacement chart highlights those positions that may become vacant in the near future due to retirements, promotions, transfers, resignations, or death of the incumbent. But not all companies use replacement charts, and this can create confusion, or even worse. For example, when the Coca-Cola Company was trying to pick a successor for current CEO Roberto C. Goizueta,[15] the leading internal candidate, M. Douglas Ivester, wasn't sure if Goizueta was going to step down as planned in the coming months. When Disney sought a replacement for their ill CEO, Michael Eisner,[16] lack of action, in part, resulted in the resignation of the heir apparent.[17] Or when Jim Henson, creator of the Muppets, died suddenly in 1990, no one knew what to do. Would the executive vice-president, David Lazer, ascend to the "throne," or would one of Henson's five children who were involved in the family-owned business succeed their father?[18] In all cases, a replacement chart of internal candidates and timetables would have eliminated much of the confusion.

Against this list of positions is placed the individual manager's skills inventory to determine if there is sufficient managerial talent to cover potential future vacancies. This "readiness" chart then gives management an indication of time frames for succession, as well as helping to spot skill shortages that may exist.

Figure 5-2
Information Categories of Human Resource Management Systems

131
Linking Organizational
Strategy to Human Resource
Planning
●

Group 1 Basic Nonconfidential Information
  Employee name
  Organization name
  Work location
  Work phone number

Group 2 General Nonconfidential Information
  Information in the previous category, plus:
  Social Security number
  Other organization information (code, effective date)
  Position-related information (code, title, effective date)

Group 3 General Information with Salary
  Information in the previous categories, plus:
  Current salary, effective date, amount of last change, type of last change and reason
    for last change)

Group 4 Confidential Information with Salary
  Information in the previous categories, plus:
  Other position information (EEO code, position ranking and FLSA)
  Education data

Group 5 Extended Confidential Information with Salary
  Information in the previous categories, plus:
  Bonus information
  Projected salary increase information
  Performance evaluation information

Source: Joan E. Goodman, "Does Your HRIS Speak English?" *Personnel Journal* (March 1990), p. 81.
Used with permission.

Should skill shortages exist, human resource management can either recruit new employees or intensify employee development efforts (see Chapter 9).

Replacement charts look very similar to organizational charts. With the incumbents listed in their positions, those individuals targeted for replacement are listed beneath with the expected time in which they will be prepared to take on the needed responsibility. We have provided a sample replacement chart in Figure 5-3.

The Demand for Labor

Once an assessment of the organization's current human resources situation has been made and the future direction of the organization has been considered, a projection of future human resource needs can be developed.

It will be necessary to perform a year-by-year analysis for every significant job level and type. In effect, the result is a **human resource inventory** covering specified years into the future. These pro-forma inventories obviously must be comprehensive, and therefore complex. Organizations usually require a heterogeneous mix of people. People are not perfectly substitutable for each other within an organization. For example, a shortage in engineering cannot be offset by transferring employees from the purchasing area where there is an oversupply. If accurate estimates are to be made of future demands in both qualitative and quantitative terms, more information is needed than just to determine that, for example, in sixteen months we will have to hire another 110 people. It

Human Resource Inventory
Describes the skills that are available within the organization.

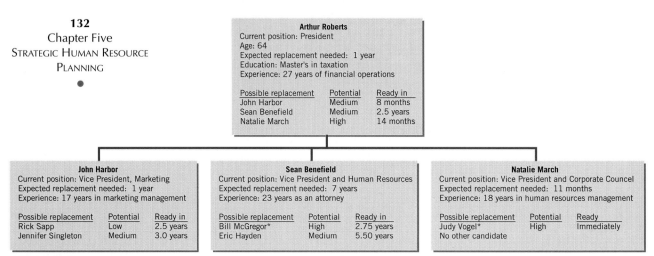

* Denotes minority

Figure 5-3
A sample replacement chart

is necessary to know what types of people, in terms of skills, knowledge, and abilities, are required. Accordingly, our forecasting methods must allow for the recognition of specific job needs as well as the total number of vacancies.

Implementation of Future Supply

Estimating changes in internal supply requires the organization to look at those factors that can either increase or decrease its human resources. As previously noted in the discussion on estimating demand, forecasting of supply must also concern itself with the micro, or unit, level. For example, if one individual in Department X is transferred to a position in Department Y, and an individual in Department Y is transferred to a position in Department X, the net effect on the organization is zero. However, if only one individual is initially involved—say, promoted and sent to another location in the company—it is only through effective strategic human resource planning that a competent replacement will be available to fill the position vacated by the departing employee.

An increase in the supply of any unit's human resources can come from a combination of four sources: new hires, contingent workers, transfers-in, or individuals returning from leaves. The task of predicting these new inputs can range from simple to complex.

New hires and contingent workers are easy to predict, since they are self-initiated. A unit recruits to meet its needs, and hence, at least in the short term, the number and types of new hires or contingent workers that will be added can be determined with high accuracy (see "Meet Suzanne Jones and Bob Freese").

It is more difficult, however, to predict transfers-in to a unit, since they often depend on concurrent action in other units. While the net effect on the total organization by a lateral transfer, demotion, or promotion may be zero, there are clear effects on individual departments and the mix within departments. If, for example, Ms. X is to be promoted from Department A to Department B, the effect on the employees in Department B must be known.

Finally, the net effect on internal supply by people returning from leaves must be considered. Examples of this include absences due to maternity

Meet

Suzanne Jones and Bob Freese

HR Administrator and CEO of Alphatronix

Imagine an organization of about forty people operating in today's environment without the assistance of an HRM professional. Unusual, problematic? Maybe not, especially when the entrepreneurial owner of the company doesn't want to add bureaucracy to the organization. But what if it is revealed that many of your "management" personnel are spending an inordinate amount of time on HR activities? And having forty employees means that the organization is covered under such laws as Equal Employment Opportunity and the Americans with Disabilities Acts. Will these individuals perform the related HRM work in a consistency manner? Are policies enforced uniformly? If not, what liabilities are created for the company? Answers to such questions may be unknown. So what does one do given this scenario? You hire a temporary HR generalist. That's exactly what Bob Freese CEO of Alphatronix, the software developer in Research Triangle Park, North Carolina, did.

Wanting to create an atmosphere where HR activities were functioning properly, and freeing his staff from the day-to-day HRM activities that were consuming much of their time, Freese advertised for a three-day-a-week HR manager. Much to his delight, Freese was overwhelmed with applications. It appeared that there were a number of applicants in the area who wanted to work part-time, but still have the opportunity to keep abreast of the HRM field. In essence, the contingent work force struck HR.

Many of the applicants wanted to spend more time with their children, and were looking for a position that gave them more flexibility. Alphatronix's position provided that opportunity. More importantly, however, hiring a contingent HRM professional did not have to mean getting one who was a novice in the field or lacking good skills. On the contrary, many of the applicants, like his final selection, Suzanne Jones, had many years of HRM experience.

There is obviously a point in time when a company must retain HRM staff on a full-time basis. But for smaller organizations like Alphatronix, a part-time HRM can prove to be beneficial to both parties. Accordingly, the company now has its professional HRM member properly handling the myriad of HR activities required in the company and Suzanne Jones has the opportunity to blend her personal and career goals.

Source: Michael P. Cronin, "The Affordable HR Pro," *Inc.* (October 1994), p. 121.

and other disabilities, international assignments, military service, or sabbatical leaves. Such increases, however, are usually easy to estimate, since they usually last for some fixed duration—twelve weeks, six months, two years, and so forth.

Decreases in the internal supply can come about through retirements, dismissals, transfers-out of the unit, layoffs, voluntary quits, sabbaticals, prolonged illnesses, or deaths. Some of these occurrences are easier to predict than others. The easiest to forecast are retirements, assuming that employees typically retire after a certain length of service, and the fact that most organizations require some advance notice of one's retirement intent. Given a history of the organization, HRM can predict with some accuracy how many retirements will occur over a given time period. Remember, however, that retirement, for the most part, is voluntary. Under the Age Discrimination in Employment Act, an organization cannot force most employees to retire.

At the other extreme, voluntary quits, prolonged illnesses, and deaths are difficult to predict. Deaths of employees are the most difficult to forecast because they are usually unexpected. Although IBM or Chrysler can use probability statistics to estimate the number of deaths that will occur, such techniques are useless for forecasting in small organizations or estimating the exact positions that will be affected in large ones. Voluntary quits can also be predicted by utilizing probabilities when the population size is large. In a company like Dell Computer, managers can estimate the approximate number of voluntary quits during any given year. In a department consisting of two or three workers, however, probability estimation is essentially meaningless. Weak predictive ability in small units is unfortunate, too, because voluntary quits typically have the greatest impact on such units.

In between the extremes, transfers, layoffs, sabbaticals, and dismissals can be forecast within reasonable limits of accuracy. Since all four of these types of action are controllable by management—that is, they are either initiated by management or are within management's veto prerogative—each type can be reasonably predicted. Of the four, transfers out of a unit, such as lateral moves, demotions, or promotions, are the most difficult to predict because they depend on openings in other units. Layoffs are more controllable and forecastable by management, especially in the short run. Sabbaticals, too, are reasonably easy to forecast, since most organizations' sabbatical policies require a reasonable lead time between request and initiation of the leave. For example, at the McDonald's corporation,[19] employees with ten years of continuous service are eligible for an eight-week sabbatical. The sabbatical can be taken during any eight continuous weeks, but with advanced approval of management. This gives the corporation ample time to find a replacement if needed.

Dismissals, based on inadequate job performance, can usually be forecasted in the same method as voluntary quits, using probabilities where large numbers of employees are involved. Additionally, performance evaluation reports are a reliable source for isolating the number of individuals whose employment might have to be terminated at a particular point in time due to unsatisfactory work performance.

Estimated Changes in External Supply

The previous discussion on supply considered internal factors. We will now review those factors outside the organization that influence the supply of available workers. Recent graduates from schools and colleges expand the supply of available human resources. This market is vast and includes everyone from high-school graduates to individuals who have received highly specialized training at the graduate level. Entrants to the work force from sources other than schools include homemakers—both male and female—seeking full-time or part-time work to supplement the family income; individuals returning to work on a full-time basis in the capacity of primary breadwinner; students seeking part-time work; employees returning from military service; job seekers who have been recently laid off; and so on. Migration into a community, increases in the number of unemployed, and employed individuals who are seeking other employment opportunities also represent sources for the organization to consider as potential additions to its labor supply.

It should be noted that consideration of only these supply sources just identified tends to understate the potential labor supply because many people can be retrained through formal or on-the-job training. Therefore, the potential supply can differ from what one might conclude by looking only at the obvious sources of supply. For example, with a small amount of training, a journalist can become qualified to perform the tasks of a book editor; thus, an organization that is having difficulty securing individuals with skills and experience in book editing should consider those candidates who have had recent journalism or similar experience and are interested in being editors. In similar fashion, the potential supply for many other jobs can be expanded.

Demand and Supply

The objective of strategic human resource planning is to bring together the forecasts of future demand for workers and the supply for human resources, both current and future. The result of this effort is to pinpoint shortages both in number and in kind; to highlight areas where overstaffing may exist (now or in the near future); and to keep abreast of the opportunities existing in the labor market to hire good people, either to satisfy current needs or to stockpile for the future.

Attention must be paid to the determination of shortages. Should an organization find that the demand for human resources will be increasing in the future, then it will have to hire additional staff or transfer people within the organization, or both, to balance the numbers, skills, mix, and quality of its human resources. An often-overlooked action, but one that may be necessary because of inadequate availability of human resources, is to change the organization's objectives. Just as inadequate financial resources can restrict the growth and opportunities available to an organization, the unavailability of the right types of people can also act as such a constraint, even leading to changing the organization's objectives.

As organizations like General Motors, IBM, and Union Carbide reorganize and reengineer, another outcome is increasingly likely: the existence of an oversupply. When this happens, human resource management must undertake

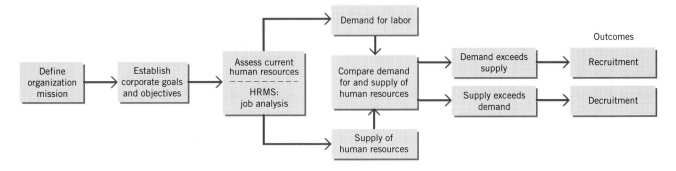

Figure 5-4
The Strategic Human Resource Planning Process

some difficult steps to sever these people from the organization—a process referred to as *decruitment*. We'll return to decruitment under the discussion of corporate downsizing later in the chapter.

Corporate strategic planning and strategic human resource planning are two critically linked processes; one cannot survive without the other. Accordingly, to perform both properly requires a blending of activities. We have portrayed these linkages in Figure 5-4.

Determining Required Skills, Knowledge, and Abilities

Educational Training and Development Systems (ETDS), a corporate training and development firm, has experienced a 20 percent turnover of trainers over the past eighteen months. An analysis of the trainer resignations indicated that the average length of stay has been only six months. Perplexed by this dilemma and the resulting loss to productivity and revenue, senior managers at ETDS insisted on an investigation to find out why such high turnover exists.

The investigation involved contacting most of the individuals who resigned to ask them why they quit. The responses were that what they were *hired* to do and what they were *required* to do were different things. The latter required different skills and aptitudes. Feeling frustrated and bored, and not wanting to jeopardize their career records, they quit. Unfortunately, the company's training costs these past three years had run approximately 300 percent over budget. When one of the senior managers asked what it was about the job that made it so difficult to properly match the job requirements with people skills, no one had an answer. It appeared that no one had conducted job analyses; in other words, no one had taken the time to find out what the jobs were all about.

What Is Job Analysis?

Job Analysis Provides information about jobs currently being done and the knowledge, skills, and abilities that individuals need to perform the jobs adequately.

A **job analysis** is a systematic exploration of the activities within a job. It is a technical procedure used to define the duties, responsibilities, and accountabilities of a job. This analysis "involves the identification and description of what is happening on the job . . . accurately and precisely identifying the required tasks, the knowledge, and the skills necessary for performing them, and the conditions under which they must be performed."[20] Let's explore how this can be achieved (see "HRM Skills: Conducting the Job Analysis").

Job Analysis Methods

The methods that managers can use to determine job elements and the essential knowledge, skills, and abilities for successful performance include the following:

Observation Method A job analysis technique in which data are gathered by watching employees work.

Observation Method. Using the **observation method,** a job analyst watches employees directly or reviews films of workers on the job. Although the observation method provides firsthand information, workers often do not function most efficiently when they are being watched, and thus distortions in the job analysis can occur. This method also requires that the entire range of activities be observable. This is possible with some jobs, but impossible for many—for example, most managerial jobs.

Individual Interview Method Meeting with an employee to determine what his or her job entails.

Individual Interview Method. Using the **individual interview method,** job incumbents are selected and extensively interviewed. The results of these interviews are combined into a single job analysis. This method is effective for assessing what a job entails, but is

HRM *Skills*

Conducting the Job Analysis

1. **Understand the purpose of conducting the job analysis.** Before embarking on a job analysis, one must understand the nature and purpose of conducting the investigation. Recognize that job analyses serve a vital purpose in such HRM activities as recruiting, training, setting performance standards, evaluating performance, and compensation.

2. **Understand the role of the jobs in the organization.** Every job in the organization should have a purpose. Before conducting the job analysis, one must understand the linkage that the job has to the strategic direction of the organization. In essence, one must answer why the job is needed.

3. **Benchmark positions.** In a large organization, it would be impossible to evaluate every job at one time. Accordingly, one should select jobs based on how well they represent other, similar jobs in the organization. This information, then, will be used as a starting point in later analysis of the other positions.

4. **Determine how you want to collect the job analysis information**. Proper planning at this stage permits one to collect the data desired in the most effective and efficient manner. This means developing a "game plan" on how the data are to be obtained. Several methods, or combinations thereof, can be used. Select the ones that best meet your job analyses goals and timetables.

5. **Seek clarification, wherever necessary.** Some of the information collected may not be totally understandable to the job analyst. Accordingly, when this occurs, one must seek clarification from those who possess the critical information. This may include the employee and the supervisor. Failure to understand and comprehend the information will make step 6, writing the job description, more difficult.

6. **Develop the first draft of the job description.** Although there is no specific format that all job descriptions follow, most include certain elements. These include the job title, a summary sentence of the job's main activities, the level of authority and accountability of the position, performance requirements, and working conditions. The last paragraph of the job description typically includes the job specifications, or those personal characteristics the job incumbent should possess to be successful on the job.

7. **Review draft with job supervisor.** Ultimately, the supervisor of the position being analyzed should approve the job description. Review comments from the supervisor can assist in determining a final job description document. When the description is an accurate reflection, the supervisor should sign off, or approve the document.

---

very time-consuming. However, caution is warranted because individuals may inflate the importance or the number of the tasks required for their job.

Group Interview Method. The **group interview method** is similar to the individual interview method except that a number of job incumbents are interviewed simultaneously. Accuracy is increased in assessing jobs, but group dynamics may hinder its effectiveness.

Structured Questionnaire Method. Under the **structured questionnaire method,** workers are sent a specifically designed questionnaire on which they check or rate items they perform on their job from a long list of possible task items. This technique is excellent for gathering information about jobs. However, exceptions to a job may be overlooked, and there is no opportunity to ask follow-up questions or to clarify the information received.

Group Interview Method Meeting with a number of employees to collectively determine what their jobs entail.

Structured Questionaire Method A specifically designed questionaire on which employees rate tasks they perform on their jobs.

Technical Conference Method
A job analysis technique
that involves extensive input
from the employee's supervisor.

Diary Method A job analysis
method requiring job in-
cumbents to record their
daily activities.

**Dictionary of Occupational
Titles** A government publication that lists more than
30,000 jobs.

Technical Conference Method. The **technical conference method** utilizes supervisors with extensive knowledge of the job. Here, specific job characteristics are obtained from the
"experts." Although a good data-gathering method, it often overlooks the incumbent
workers' perceptions about what they do on their job.

Diary Method. The **diary method** requires job incumbents to record their daily activities.
It provides much information, but is seldom applicable to job activities. The diary
method is the most intrusive of the job analysis methods, requiring much work, and
therefore much time, on the part of the incumbent. To capture the entire range of
work activities, this method may have to extend over long periods of time—all adding
to its cost.

These six methods are not meant to be viewed as mutually exclusive; no one
method is universally superior. Even obtaining job information from the incumbents can create a problem, especially if these individuals describe what they
think they should be doing rather than what they actually do. The best results,
then, are usually achieved with some combination of methods—with information provided by individual employees, their immediate supervisors, a professional analyst, or an unobtrusive source such as filmed observations.

Now that we realize that job analysis can be performed in a number of ways,
let us consider other notable job analysis processes: the Department of Labor
Job Analysis Process and the Position Analysis Questionnaire.

The Department of Labor's Job Analysis Process. The Department of Labor's
Job Analysis Process describes what a worker does by having someone observe
and interview the employee. This information is then cataloged into three general functions that exist in all jobs: data, people, and things (see Figure 5-5). An
employment interviewer, for example, might be found to analyze data, speak to
people, and handle things; the job would be coded 2, 6, 7. Figure 5-6 shows the
listing for the employment interviewer's position. This type of coding of key elements has already been done for more than 30,000 job titles listed in the **Dictionary of Occupational Titles,** which is readily available in most libraries. Use of
this publication can significantly reduce the management's burden of gathering

Figure 5-5
Department of Job Analysis Process

Work Functions

Data	*People*	*Things*
0 Synthesizing	0 Mentoring	0 Setting up
1 Coordinating	1 Negotiating	1 Precision working
2 Analyzing	2 Instructing	2 Operating–controlling
3 Compiling	3 Supervision	3 Driving–operating
4 Computing	4 Diverting	4 Manipulating
5 Copying	5 Persuading	5 Tending
6 Comparing	6 Speaking–signaling	6 Feeding–offbearing
	7 Serving	7 Handling
	8 Taking instructions–helping	

Source: U.S. Department of Labor, *Dictionary of Occupational Titles,* 4th ed. revised (Washington,
D.C.: Government Printing Office, 1991), p. xix.

166.267–010   Employment Interviewer
                Alternate title: Placement Interviewer

Interviews job applicants to select persons meeting employer qualifications. Reviews completed application and evaluates applicant's work history, education and training, job skills, salary desired, and physical and personal qualifications. Records additional skills, knowledge, abilities, interests, test results, and other data pertinent to classification, selection, and referral. Searches files of job orders from employers and matches applicant's qualifications with job requirements and employer specifications, utilizing manual search, computer matching services, or employment service facilities. Informs applicant about job duties and responsibilities, pay and benefits, hours and working conditions, company and union policies, promotional opportunities, and other related information. Refers selected applicant to interview with person placing job order according to policy of school, agency, or company. Keeps for future reference records of applicants not immediately selected or hired. May perform reference and background checks. May refer applicants to vocational counseling services. May test or arrange for skills, intelligence, or psychological testing of applicant. May engage in research or follow-up activities to evaluate selection and placement techniques by conferring with management and supervisory personnel. May specialize in interviewing and referring certain types of personnel, such as professional, technical, managerial, clerical, and other types of skilled or unskilled workers. May be known as personnel recruiter and seek out potential applicants and try to interest them in applying for position openings.

Source: U.S. Department of Labor, *Dictionary of Occupational Titles,* 4th ed., revised (Washington, D.C.: Government Printing Office, 1991), p. 99.

information on jobs for its organization. Additionally, the DOL job codes are supplemented with a detailed narrative. So the data on the human resource management job analyst job would also tell us exactly what data are copied, with whom the jobholder speaks, and which things are handled.

The DOL technique allows managers to group jobs into job families that require similar kinds of worker behavior. Candidates for these jobs, therefore, should hold similar worker skills. Obviously this information will benefit managers in identifying the kinds of people that the organization needs.

A variation of the Department of Labor's methodology was developed by a U.S. Employment Service employee, Sidney Fine. Fine developed a process that further described those items listed by the DOL, called the Functional Job Analysis (FJA) (see Figure 5-7). In so doing, the FJA provides a more accurate picture of what the jobholder does.[21]

Position Analysis Questionnaire.   Developed by researchers at Purdue University, the Position Analysis Questionnaire (PAQ) generates job requirement information that is applicable to all types of jobs. In contrast to the DOL approach, the PAQ presents a more quantitative and finely-tuned description of jobs. The PAQ procedure involves "194 elements that are grouped within six major divisions and 28 sections"[22] (see Figure 5-8).

The PAQ allows management to scientifically and quantitatively group interrelated job elements into job dimensions. This, in turn, should allow jobs to be compared with each other. However, research on the usefulness of the PAQ is suspect. For the most part, it appears to be more applicable to lower-level, blue-collar jobs.[23]

Figure 5-7
Fine's Functional Job Analysis (FJA) Scale

Data	*People*	*Things*
1. Comparing	1a. Taking instruction 1b. Serving	1a. Handling 1b. Feeding/off-bearing 1c. Tending
2. Copying	2. Exchanging information	2a. Manipulating 2b. Operating/controlling 2c. Driving/controlling
3a. Computing 3b. Compiling	3a. Coaching 3b. Persuading 3c. Diverting	3a. Precision work 3b. Setting up
4. Analyzing	4a. Consulting 4b. Instructing 4c. Treating	
5a. Innovating 5b. Coordinating	5. Supervising	
6. Synthesizing	6. Negotiating 7. Mentoring	

Source: A.S. Fine, *Functional Job Analysis Scales: A Desk Aid* (Kalamazoo, MI: W.E. Upjohn Institute for Employment Research, 1973). Used with permission.

Other Job Analysis Techniques. In addition to the methodologies just discussed, other job analysis techniques exist. We have summarized them in Table 5-1.

Although a variety of techniques are available, some preparatory work is necessary before implementing any one of them. Job analysis is not difficult per se,

Figure 5-8
Categories and Their Number of Job Elements of the PAQ

Category	*Number of Job Elements*
1. *Information input* Where and how does the worker get the information he or she uses on the job?	35
2. *Mental processes* What reasoning, decision making, planning, etc., are involved in the job?	14
3. *Work output* What physical activities does the worker perform and what tools or devices are used?	49
4. *Relationships with other people* What relationships with other people are required in the job?	36
5. *Job context* In what physical and social contexts is the work performed?	19
6. *Other job characteristics* What special attributes exist on this job (e.g., schedule, responsibilities, pay).	41

Source: Reprinted with permission from the Position Analysis Questionnaire, Copyright 1969, Purdue Research Foundation.

TABLE 5-1 Other Job Analysis Techniques and Their Uses

Device	*Used For*
Management Position Description Questionnaire (MPDQ)	Analyze managerial job activities in terms of responsibilities, restrictions, demands, and activities
Occupational Analysis Inventory (OAI)	Vocational guidance and occupational exploration.
Job Element Inventory (JEI)	An adaptation of the PAQ, but presented at a much lower reading level.
Critical Incident Method	Focuses on behavior that attributes to job success.

Source: Adapted from Wayne Casio, *Applied Psychology in Personnel Management*, 4th ed. (Englewood Cliffs, N.J., Prentice-Hall, 1991), pp. 207, 208, 211. Used with permission.

but detailed. To conduct the job analysis, you should gather as much background information as possible about the job to be analyzed. This information is readily available through old job descriptions and other literature, such as the organization chart. Once you have this information, you need to identify those particular jobs to be reviewed. Remember, all jobs need to be analyzed, but not all at one time. In identifying the job, you also identify those individuals with specific or expert relevant job information. Working with these individuals, you now employ one of the techniques described. Once this has been accomplished, your data-gathering endeavor is over, but you are not finished. You must now analyze the information and produce the end results—the job description and the job specification.

Purpose of Job Analysis

No matter what the method used to gather data, the information gathered and written down from the job analysis process generates three outcomes: job descriptions, job specifications, and job evaluation. It is important to note that these are the tangible products, not the job analysis, which is the conceptual, analytical process or action from which we develop these outcomes. Let's look at them more closely.

Job Descriptions

A **job description** is a written statement of what the jobholder does, how it is done, under what conditions it is done, and why it is done. It should accurately portray job content, environment, and conditions of employment. A common format for a job description includes the job title, the duties to be performed, the distinguishing characteristics of the job, environmental conditions, and the authority and responsibilities of the jobholder. An example of a job description for a faculty member in a school of business and economics is provided in Figure 5-9.

When we discuss employee recruitment, selection, and performance appraisal, we will find that the job description acts as an important resource for:

Job Description A written statement of what the jobholder does, how it is done, and why it is done.

Figure 5-9
Example of a Job Description:

<table>
<tr><td rowspan="2">Job Description</td><td colspan="2">

Faculty Member, School of Business and Economics

Job Title: Faculty Member   **Occupational Code No.** 4554

Reports to: Department Chairperson   **Job No.** 078

Supervises: None   **Date:** 5/14/95

Environmental Conditions: None

Functions: Teach one or more subjects within a prescribed business and economics curriculum.

Duties and Responsibilities:
- Prepare and deliver outside reading assignments.
- Stimulate class discussion.
- Compile, administer, and grade examinations—or assign this work to others.
- Direct research for others working for advanced degree.
- Conduct research in particular field of knowledge and publish findings in professional journals.
- Perform related duties, such as advising students on academic and vocational curricula.
- Serve on faculty committees.
- Provide professional consulting to government and industry.
- Other duties as assigned by department head.

</td></tr>
<tr><td>Job Specifications</td><td>

Job Characteristics: Understanding of instructional methods for traditional and nontraditional students; excellent communication skills; and skilled operation of a personal computer, using word processing, spreadsheet, database management, and statistical packages.

</td></tr>
</table>

Source: Adapted from U.S. Department of Labor, *Dictionary of Occupational Titles,* 4th ed., revised (Washington, D.C.: Government Printing Office, 1991), p. 67.

(1) describing the job (either verbally by recruiters and interviewers or in written advertisements) to potential candidates; (2) guiding newly hired employees in what they are specifically expected to do; and (3) providing a point of comparison in appraising whether the actual activities of a job incumbent align with the stated duties. Furthermore, under the Americans with Disabilities Act, job descriptions have taken on an added emphasis in identifying essential job functions.

Job Specifications

Job Specifications Statements indicating the minimal acceptable qualifications incumbents must possess to successfully perform the essential elements of their jobs.

The **job specification** states the minimum acceptable qualifications that the incumbent must possess to perform the job successfully. Based on the information acquired through job analysis, the job specification identifies the knowledge, skills, education, experience, certification, and abilities needed to do the job effectively. Individuals possessing the personal characteristics identified in the job specification should perform the job more effectively than those lacking these personal characteristics. The job specification, therefore, is an important tool in the selection process, for it keeps the selector's attention on the list of qualifications necessary for an incumbent to perform the job and assists in determining whether candidates are essentially qualified.

Job Evaluations

In addition to providing data for job descriptions and specifications, job analysis is also valuable in providing the information that makes comparison of jobs possible. If an organization is to have an equitable compensation program, jobs that have similar demands in terms of skills, knowledge, and abilities should be placed in common compensation groups. **Job evaluation** contributes toward that end by specifying the relative value of each job in the organization. Job evaluation, therefore, is an important part of compensation administration, as will be discussed in detail in Chapter 13. In the meantime, you should keep in mind that job evaluation is made possible by the data generated from job analysis.

Job Evaluation Specifies the relative value of each job in the organization.

The Pervasiveness of Job Analysis

One of the overriding questions about job analysis is: Are they being conducted properly, if at all? The answer to this question varies, depending on the organization. Generally, most organizations do conduct some type of job analysis. This job analysis extends further, however, than meeting the federal equal employment opportunity requirement. Almost everything that HRM does is directly related to the job analysis process (see Figure 5-10). Recruiting, selection, compensation, and performance-appraising activities are most frequently cited as being directly effected by the job analysis. But there are others. Employee training and career development are assisted by the job analysis process by identifying neccessary skills, knowledge, and abilities. Where deficiencies exist, training and development efforts can be used. Similar effects can also be witnessed in determining safety and health requirements, and labor relations processes, if a union exists. Accordingly, this often lengthy and complex job analysis process cannot be overlooked.

We cannot overemphasize the importance of job analysis, as it permeates most of the organization's activities. If an organization does not do its job analysis well, it probably does not do many of its human resource activities well. If individuals in the organization understand human resource activities, they should understand the fundamental importance of job analysis.

The job analysis, then, is the starting point of sound human resource management. Without knowing what the job entails, the material covered in the fol-

Figure 5-10
The Pervasivenesss of the job analysis

lowing chapters may merely be an effort in futility (see "What If: HRM in a De-Jobbed Organization").

Current Issues in SHRP

Earlier in this chapter, we identified in the strategic planning process a situation in which the supply of workers exceeds demand. When that occurs, organizations must begin a process of decruitment. For the most part, that meant downsizing. Recall from Chapter 2 the necessity for such action. The guiding theme was to make the organization more "lean and mean"; in other words, more efficient. But cutting for efficiency sake may not be appropriate. Rather, companies today are looking at the need to correctly staff the organization with the needed skills, knowledge, and abilities. We call this rightsizing. Let's look at the downsizing/rightsizing issue facing companies.

Downsizing: Past and Present

Over the past few decades, we have witnessed the continued shrinkage of the once-strong smokestack industries—steel, auto, and rubber.[24] Competition in the high-tech industries has also soared during this time, giving rise to massive layoffs at such companies as Apple, DEC, IBM, and Wang. Conglomerates, too, began shedding less-profitable business units, or closing down altogether. And the continual increase in foreign competition creates more problems for U.S. organizations.

Strategic human resource planning tended to ignore issues in managing declining organizations such as those in the industries described above. Going bankrupt (Wang), divesting holdings (GM), or eliminating unprofitable product lines (Chrysler) are activities that are not prevalent in a growing enterprise. These activities have a major impact on the employee population. Human resource planning, as we described earlier, had to change to a more strategic focus.[25] In the latter half of the 1990s, even how we downsize may be changing.

Previously, under downsizing certain topics associated with traditional human resource planning—recruitment and selection—became somewhat irrelevant. It was believed that in order to cut costs and turn around ailing companies, body counts had to be high. So companies embarked on "quick fix" solutions. And these actions were obvious! By 1994, almost every major corporation in the United States had trimmed its work force. AlliedSignal eliminated approximately 5,000 salaried jobs; Goodyear Tire and Rubber, more than 1,100 white-collar jobs; General Motors, almost 75,000 positions; more than 3,000 professional jobs at Ford were lost; Frito-Lay cut 1,800 jobs; and more than 20,000 jobs at IBM were elimanted.[26] It became so commonplace (or we've become so complacent), that today, massive layoffs don't even make front-page news. But there's more to the story.

Cutting employees didn't produce the results that companies were looking for. Operating costs didn't decrease. What it did do, however, was to leave fewer people to do the work that was to be done, and productivity fell. Many companies didn't look at the long-term effects of downsizing.[27] Today, that is changing. In fact, it is estimated that in 1995, two-thirds of companies that laid off employees were also simultaneously hiring. How can that be? Isn't such action contradictory? Is it explainable that American Airlines had cut 5,000 jobs since 1993, while hiring almost 2,500 during the same period?[28] Yes, it's explainable, and its answer lies in strategic human resource planning. That is, companies to-

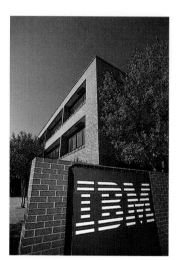

Prior to the 1980s, a company like IBM typically experienced growth. However, less profitable business units, increased foreign competition, and the like forced this organization to restructure its operations. As such, the company downsized in order to cut costs and remain competitive. Unfortunately, this retrenchment effort came at the expense of thousands of jobs!

What If:

HRM in a De-Jobbed Organization

Much of the discussion in this chapter revolves around the importance of having the right people, in the right place, at the right time, in an attempt for the organization to attain its strategic goals and objectives. This meant that the organization had to identify the goals to be met, and put in place a structure that led to goal attainment. A critical component of that structure was the people—those who possessed the necessary skills, knowledge, and abilities (SKAs). Throughout the discussion identifying those SKAs, one element was common. That was the job analysis.

The job analysis, as an activity in HRM is designed to properly assess what skills, knowledge, and abilities are needed for a job incumbent to successfully perform on the job. Furthermore, the results of this analysis permeate almost every activity conducted in HRM. Yet, a basic premise of job analysis is that through a systematic exploration of the jobs and their tasks, we can identify what workers ought to do, and what personal characteristics they must possess. But what if that basic premise is broken?

In a de-jobbed organization, the duties and responsibilities of a job change frequently—at times, almost constantly. As such, it will become almost impossible to accurately evaluate jobs, because a description of what is done now might not apply a short time later. And in situations where employees perform activities according to the "job description," valuable and required critical task activities for a current project may be lost. We've seen some of that already, as many job descriptions include a catch-all phrase at the end like "and other duties as assigned." What if, however, all the work is in fact, "other duties as assigned"? Will this significantly decrease or eliminate the need for the job analysis process? Will HRM activities that revolve around the job description—activities like recruiting, selection, performance appraisals, safety or health, or labor relations—simply become nonexistent? Or will something else replace the job analysis so that some "order" can be restored? In a de-jobbed organization, even that something else may become a moot point.

Source: William Bridges, "The End of the Job," *Fortune* (September 19, 1994), p. 64.

---

day are refocusing their efforts on those things that meet their strategic direction. Organizational activities, and jobs that lead to strategic goal attainment and add value to the corporation are getting the necessary resources. And that includes people. For instance, just ten years ago, AT&T employed fewer than sixty people outside the United States. However, with its strategic direction to go global, the company has increased staffing levels to over 70,000 employees. For American Airlines, of their 5,000 jobs cut, 900 were management personnel. Today, through redirection of work activities, those remaining managers are 26 percent more productive.[29]

Don't let the above paragraph lead you into a false sense of security into be-

•

Rightsizing Linking employee needs to organizational strategy.

lieving that the downsizing trend is over. That's not the point of the discussion. Rather, it indicates that companies are continuously linking their employee needs to the organization's strategy. Those jobs that are not directly linked to strategy are being cut. So instead of downsizing, it's more appropriately called **rightsizing.** That's precisely the point made in Figure 5-4! So what does it mean for employees? Especially those who "survived" these cuts?

What About the Survivors?

There is no doubt that workers' lives have changed.[30] Downsizing efforts, mergers, acquisitions, and the like have thrown employment relationships into a quandary. The job security that employees enjoyed a generation ago is not there. At best, it appears that organizations will have a core group of employees, who will be assisted by a contingent work force. Good work and loyalty to the organization may not be enough. Promotions and career advancement may be significantly limited, if they exist at all. Employees won't have the luxury of knowing precisely what their jobs entail, for they will frequently change—given the direction the company is currently pursuing and the projects it undertakes. And just because employees successfully made it through the merger or the latest cuts, doesn't mean the jobs are forever permanent. Unfortunately, even management may not know when that time is, as the direction of the organization, and the requisite skills, knowledge, and abilities, may go through continuous adaptation. But it must prepare its work force for the inevitable changes that will occur. This means ample training to ensure core employees will be prepared to meet the demands of tomorrow, having flexible management practices, and communicating openly and accurately to the employee population of

How can rightsizing pay off? By having the right mix of skills available, working toward the organization's strategic goals. For example, American Airlines, although cutting some nine hundred management positions in the company, has realigned the remaining managers' work activities and witnessed a 26 percent increase in their productivity.

what is to occur.[31] Even so, as one writer has put it, "The old [game] has changed: Now in good times, companies will fire. In bad times, they'll fire even more."[32] Employees, then, must recognize these facts, and do those things that keep them desirable to employers. This means aspiring to do the work the organization needs, continuously developing and refining skills to do those jobs, and accepting the reality that their tenure with a company may be only as long as the project on which they work.[33]

Methods of Achieving Reduced Staffing Levels

The rightsizing discussion primarily dealt with situations where organizations permanently changed the configuration of its employee staffing levels to meet its strategic focus. Although this has been the dominant activity over the past few years, there are times when reducing staffing levels may require a more temporary nature. This may be due to the seasonal nature of some businesses, or even economic downturns. Under such circumstances, when jobs must be cut and staffing levels temporarily reduced, there are a number of ways to achieve that goal. These include not only the traditional layoffs but also leaves of absence without pay, loaning, work sharing, reduced work hours, early retirement, and attrition.[34] Let's take a closer look at these staff-reducing efforts.

Layoffs Layoffs can take many forms, and can be temporary or permanent. Temporary layoffs usually occur during slack periods when workloads do not warrant such a large work force; as soon as work resumes its normal level, workers are recalled. Although this is a cost-cutting measure, it can result in turning workers into cyclical employees and also increase a company's unemployment insurance premiums.

Proper strategic human resource planning, leveling the work force at the proper staffing level, can help reduce this "yo-yo" effect. For example, by knowing when peak times exist, as well as the valleys, proper staffing can be achieved. However, proper staffing can mean a permanent layoff for other employees—those whose skills, knowledge, and abilities are no longer consistent with the strategic direction of the company.

Leaves of Absence Without Pay One means of cutting labor costs temporarily is to give workers the opportunity to take leaves of absence without pay. This may provide time for an employee who is financially capable to leave the organization to pursue personal interests. These could range from attending college (to increase the employee's marketability and mobility) to engaging in other endeavors, like starting his or her own business. Individuals offered this leave are usually those whose jobs may be eliminated in the future. Thus, this concept serves as a method to help employees prepare for coming changes.

Loaning The loaning of valuable human resources to other organizations is a means of keeping "loaned" employees on the organization's payroll and bringing them back after a crisis has subsided. Usually higher-level managers are loaned for special projects with government or quasi-governmental agencies (e.g., school boards, charitable organizations, or civic associations). The organization pays these "loaned" managers a reduced salary, with the difference usually paid by the agency. While an organization may ultimately lose some of these managers, some who have been loaned do return.

●

Work Sharing A work concept whereby two or more individuals share one full-time job with the remaining time spent on individual pursuits.

Work Sharing Carroll Lindsay is a 48-year-old manager with DataPoint, Inc., a software development firm located in Atlanta, Georgia. Carroll has child-care responsibilities that he shares with his wife, Susan, who also works for DataPoint.[35] Because of their strong convictions to spend more time raising their children, Carroll and Susan share one full-time job. Under their **work-sharing** arrangement, the two split a forty-hour work week, with the remaining time being spent on their individual pursuits. Here two people hold one job, and the cost to the company is no greater than if only one person held the job. In a temporary reduction of staff, this option may keep good employees from leaving the company. They may use the time to do some things they have wanted to do.

The work-sharing technique gained much popularity in the early 1980s. Many Japanese firms, as well as many progressive U.S. companies such as Mony Financial Services, have used this technique to offset some of the problems brought about by economic downturns. The employees' morale flourishes in such cases, as the employees recognize the commitment that management has made to them.[36]

In fact, for the 1990s, the work-sharing concept is getting renewed attention—and not one that focuses solely on cutting employee costs. Faced with a growing diversity in the workplace, and a work force that is about 50 percent female, work-sharing is helping women, like Suzanne Jones, to blend their careers with their personal lives. In offering a variety of work-sharing arrangements, companies like Aetna Life and Casualty, Fel-Pro, Stratco, and Nation's Bank are setting in place what is called the family-friendly organization.[37] A **family-friendly organization** is one in which the organization has policies and practices like flextime, work-sharing, or off-site work that structures the work around employee needs. Although there is some debate over the merits of the family-friendly organization,[38] such work arrangements have generally shown positive results. Because the crux of the family-friendly organization lies in employee

Family-Friendly Benefits Flexible policies and practices that are supportive of caring for one's family.

What is an example of a family-friendly organization? Take a look at Stratco Company, the chemical engineering organization in Leawood, Kansas. In an effort to meet the special needs of its employees, Stratco permits its employees like Debbie (pictured touching baby seat), an accountant, to bring their infants with them to work. Even CEO Diane Graham, has brought each of her three children to work with her for their first six months of life.

benefits, we'll return to this topic in Chapter 14 in our discussion of current issues in benefits administration.

Reduced Work Hours   Reducing staffing levels through **reduced work hours** is based on the concept that there is only so much money an organization is able to spend on its payroll. How it is spent may be up to the workers. For simplicity's sake, let us assume that we have $600,000 a year to spend for labor costs. We originally had twenty workers with annual incomes of $30,000. Now, as the company is experiencing economic hardships, only $480,000 a year is available to pay the workers. With no change in the hours worked, four employees would have to be laid off. To eliminate this dilemma, each worker agrees to work fewer hours and receive less pay, so that the four jobs are saved. In this simplified case, instead of a forty-hour work week, each employee is paid for only thirty-two hours of work. All twenty employees will continue to be employed, but each will earn $6,000 less per year.

> **Reduced   Work   Hours** A staff   reduction   concept where-by employees work fewer than forty hours and are paid accordingly.

While the example is exaggerated, it does reveal an effort on behalf of employees to forgo some of their salaries and benefits in order to keep all workers employed. The rationale is that receiving less is better than receiving nothing at all. However, it takes a strong personal conviction to accept that philosophy unless you are one of the two about to be laid off. For instance, during the early 1990s many state and municipal governments faced severe budget shortages. In some cases, as opposed to laying off a number of workers, these agencies opted for furlough days, or having employees work a number of days without pay. These days without pay added up to the savings that would have been realized if layoffs occurred. The same holds true for a number of other companies with unionized employees, like USAir, which received wage concessions from its pilots in an effort to preserve the financial viability of the company and to save fellow workers' jobs.

Early Retirement   Another staff reduction method is the use of **early retirement.** Many of the industry giants have resorted to using early retirement inducements to reduce the number of workers, especially higher-level management personnel. Regardless of the specifics contained in these offers, the purpose is clear: Buy out some of the highest-paid individuals in the organization and delegate their responsibilities to other employees making less money.

> **Early Retirement** A downsizing effort whereby employees close to retirement are given some incentive to leave the company earlier than expected.

Usually the prime candidate for early retirement is an individual who is two or three years away from retiring. The company may offer this individual a reduced retirement benefit until he or she reaches the agreed retirement age or years of service.

Another option is to buy the years of service remaining until normal retirement, for a sum of money equal to the amount that would have been contributed to the individual's retirement. In either case, the result is the same: a reduction in the cost of paying exorbitant salaries to those individuals. Although this is an effective cost-saving plan, an organization may lose some key executives who decide to bail out.

Attrition   The process of **attrition** occurs when incumbents leave their jobs for any reason (retirement, resignation, transfers, etc.) and those jobs are not filled. Usually accompanying the process of attrition is a hiring freeze. Hiring freezes dictate that no hiring will take place for jobs that are vacated.

> **Attrition** A process whereby the jobs of incumbents who leave for any reason will not be filled.

Attrition and hiring freezes can be implemented organization-wide (used to reduce overall employment numbers) or can be directed toward particular departments or jobs that may no longer be needed. The bottom-line result is that attrition with a hiring freeze is a short-term means of addressing a surplus of employees.

Whenever companies use methods such as those previously described, a philosophical issue arises: Especially in the case of trimming layers of management personnel from the company, what should a company do to help these displaced workers? Does a company have any responsibility, legally or ethically, to these individuals? The answer to such questions lies in the concept of outplacement.

Outplacement Services

Recall that in our discussion in Chapter 1 of the goals of human resource management, we stated the goal of the maintenance function to be such that commitment and loyalty to the organization are maintained. Under growth circumstances, such a goal is possible. However, in downsizing or other staff reduction activities, the emphasis of that goal changes. The company must demonstrate its support for the past commitment and loyalty of the severed employee. **Outplacement** delivers that support. By definition, outplacement is a process of assisting "existing employees" in their search for another job.[39]

This process includes providing career guidance, retraining those employees who can be productively placed elsewhere in the organization, and assisting those who can't with resume writing, interviewing techniques, career and personal counseling, and job-search methods. Companies need to recognize that many of these long-term "loyal" employees have no idea how to go about getting a job outside the company. The crucial period for this employee appears to be the first three to six months,[40] in which a number of key factors come into play. First of all is the psychological aspect of looking for a job. Being unsuccessful for more than six months tends to cause an individual to feel that he or she will never get a job; negative self-image can only hurt in interviewing situations. Second is the money issue: After six months, money—even severance pay—may be running out. And this only adds to the psychological problem. That is why the current aspect of outplacement is so crucial—to help these individuals deal with these tough times. Through proper counseling, networking assistance, and offering space and telephone access, outplacement can help.[41] Outplacement does not come cheap—the costs range into the thousands of dollars per individual—but most employers offering outplacement services indicate that it is money well spent.[42]

Study Tools and Applications

Summary

This summary relates to the Learning Objectives provided on p. 125.

After having read this chapter, you should know:

1. Strategic human resource planning is the process by which an organization ensures that it has the right number and kinds of people capable of effectively and efficiently completing those tasks that are in direct support of the company's mission.

2. The steps in the strategic human resource planning process include mission formulating, establishing corporate goals and objectives, assessing current human resources, estimating the supplies and demand for labor, and matching demand with current supplies of labor. The two outcomes of this process are recruitment and decruitment.

3. A Human Resource Information System is useful for quickly fulfilling human resource management information needs by tracking employee information and having that information readily available when needed.

4. Job analysis is a systematic exploration of the activities surrounding and within a job. It defines the job's duties, responsibilities, and accountabilities.

5. The six general techniques for obtaining job information are observation method, individual interview method, group interview method, structured interview method, technical conference method, and diary method.

6. The Department of Labor's Job Analysis process is a procedure that describes what a worker does in terms of data, people, and things. This coding system allows for jobs to be grouped into job families requiring similar kinds of work. The Position Analysis Questionnaire extends the job analysis process to 194 job elements within six major job divisions.

7. Job descriptions are written statements of what the jobholder does (duties and responsibilities); job specifications identify the personal characteristics required to perform successfully on the job; and job evaluation is the process of using job analysis information in establishing a compensation system.

8. Downsizing refers to the process of restructuring the organization that results in the organization reducing its number of employees. Rightsizing may involve downsizing, but more appropriately focuses on having the right people available to work on activities directly related to the strategic direction of the company.

9. Various methods of achieving staff reductions include layoffs, leave of absences, loaning, work-sharing, reduced work hours, early retirements, and attrition.

10. Outplacement services are programs offered by an employer to assist employees being retrained, or those severed from the organization, in obtaining employment. These services include training, resume writing, interviewing techniques, office and clerical assistance, and career counseling.

Key Terms

attrition
diary method
Dictionary of Occupational Titles
early retirement
family-friendly organization
group interview method
human resource inventory
human resource management system (HRMS)
individual interview method
job analysis

job description
job evaluations
job specifications
layoffs
mission statement
observation method
outplacement
position analysis questionnaire
  (PAQ)
reduced work hours

replacement chart
rightsizing
strategic goals
strategic human resource planning
  (SHRP)

structured questionaire method
succession planning
technical conference method
work-sharing

EXPERIENTIAL EXERCISE:

Downsizing Staff

One of the more difficult tasks any manager faces is deciding whom to lay off. Following is a list of possible candidates. Company records indicate that two full-time positions must be eliminated. Data for your use are provided as follows. All workers function as HRM generalists.

Sara Baker	White female, age 34, seven years with the company in current job. Outstanding performance rating last two years. B.S. in Business Administration. Sara is a single mother, and is currently in week four of her twelve-week leave of absence under the Family and Medical Leave Act. Although her performance has been good the past two years, some decline in performance was noted earlier this year. In fact, a written verbal warning about her performance was given six months ago. Some improvement has been noted; but her performance has not reached its previous level. You believe she is upset because she did not get the promotion to employment manager she applied for six months ago.
Juan Palmiro	Hispanic male, age 39, six months in Human Resource Management, three and one-half years with company. Average performance ratings the last three years. Has an MBA, with a B.S. in Computer Science. Juan is the highest paid HR generalist. He saved the company $200,000 last year through his implementation of an automated benefits communications program. He is about the only one who knows the program and can keep it running.
Tom Kelly	African-American male, age 63, 41 years in Human Resource Management. Started as a clerk and moved up to his current position. Tom has a high-school diploma and has taken some college courses in human resource management. His performance ratings over the past three years were outstanding, average, above average.
Chris Ellerson	White male, age 44. Four years with company, all in human resource management. Chris was a freelance consultant, specializing in career development assessment and training. Chris's excellent consulting work with your organization led to a job offer being made. Chris's performance

the past two years, however, has slipped, going from average to below average. You suspect that he is not happy with the job anymore now that the corporation is putting fewer resources into career development.

Judy Myers — African-American female, age 24. Recent college graduate with a 4.0 average in Industrial Psychology. Just completed her probationary period with the organization. Judy was permanently disabled in an auto accident four years ago, and is about to settle with the insurer of the driver who caused the accident. Rumors cite a settlement in the $4 million range.

Yu Chen — Asian Male, age 27. B.S. in Business Administration, concentrating in Finance. Yu was transferred from accounting and finance to bring into line your benefits costs. To date, he has revamped your benefits program, resulting in a 245 percent decrease in benefits costs for the organization. You accidently saw a copy of the employment section of a regional financial association journal on his desk, lying next to what appeared to be an updated resume.

Based on these five descriptions, decide how you will downsize the unit by the two positions. Then, in your group, reach consensus on how the group would approach the problem. Are there similarities? Differences? On what basis did you make your decision? Could you support it if it were challenged in court? How?

CASE APPLICATION:
Succession Planning at Disney

Anyone growing up in the United States anytime during the past thirty years has seen fads and concepts rise and fall with certainty. The 1960s witnessed the hippie generation, whose long hair and free love eventually gave way to three-piece suits on Wall Street. The 1970s saw the demise of the Beatles; the lime-green leisure suit came and went; disco got hot, but quickly faded away. The 1980s made greed fashionable; ethics and values appeared to go out the window, and some individuals got very rich. The early 1990s witnessed the continual practice of downsizing and restructuring American corporations, three-piece suits were replaced with dress-down Fridays, and jobs as we've come to know them became less and less common.

Throughout these decades, however, one thing remained constant: The Walt Disney Company represented the wholesome and creative talents of the American society. No matter what was happening in society, Disney was fun and imaginative. And although the company had its ailing moments in the early 1980s, its CEO, Michael Eisner, took the organization to new heights. Never before had the company experienced such profits. By the early 1990s, its movies were smashing hits, and Disney's U.S. theme parks even more popular than before. With the exception of some initial difficulties of Euro-Disney, and its battle in the public forum over its proposed new park in Virginia, this company could do no wrong.[43]

Although Eisner is credited with much of Disney's success, he didn't do it alone. He had a team of executives who worked together to bring about this prosperity. Included in this team were the president and chief operating officer, Frank Wells, and Disney's studio chief, Frank Katzenberg. Everything they undertook carried with it the Midas touch. That is, until early 1994.

It all began to unravel in April 1994. Frank Wells, on a well-deserved vacation in Nevada, was killed in a helicopter crash. Then, in July 1994, Michael Eisner underwent emergency cardiac bypass surgery. Questions began to arise about who would be in charge if Eisner couldn't continue because of failing health. Who would succeed him? That proved to be a difficult question for the organization. Wells, the obvious choice, was suddenly gone. Katzenberg, regarded as one of "Hollywood's most talented executives, and Eisner's protégé" wanted the job, and appeared to be the leading candidate. There were also others who were possibilities, but they didn't appear to have the inside track that Wells or Katzenberg had.

Given stockholders' and investors' concerns, Disney had to take some immediate action and name its successor to Eisner. But to the surprise of many, Katzenberg was not named. Eisner, and Disney's board of directors, felt he just wasn't right for the position. Upset about being passed over, Katzenberg resigned. As a result, the team that built a strong Disney the past few years has all but disappeared.

Questions

1. If you were one of Disney's board of directors, what would this case tell you about the importance of succession planning?
2. How could a succession plan, or replacement chart, have helped Disney from losing a talented executive like Katzenberg?

Testing Your Understanding

How well did you fulfill the learning objectives?

1. Diane is vice-president of human resources of a large manufacturing firm. When should she become involved in strategic planning for her organization?
   a. She should do all of it as part of her job.
   b. She should never be involved in it. That function belongs in financial management and marketing.
   c. Her real contribution comes after organizational assessment is completed.
   d. She should be included in mission development.
   e. She should be included in the maintenance phase.
2. Supply and demand forecasts, combined, provide all of the following for human resource managers except
   a. highlighting areas where overstaffing might currently exist.
   b. highlighting areas where overstaffing might exist in the future.
   c. pinpointing anticipated shortages in engineering areas.
   d. pinpointing anticipated budget changes in recruiting and maintenance.

   e. keeping abreast of opportunities to stockpile good people for anticipated needs.
3. The vice-president of human resources in a large manufacturing firm has just received a gap analysis report. It indicated staffing needs over the next five years for one hundred additional shipping clerks, one hundred fewer shop technicians, one hundred additional sales representatives, and one hundred fewer research specialists. What should the vice-president do?
   a. Internal transfers can take care of all these needs.
   b. Corporate outplacement services need to be secured for four hundred employees over the next five years.
   c. Recruiting efforts for research areas need to be increased immediately.
   d. Examine current human resource inventories to determine retirement, internal transfers, and probable dismissals over the next five years.
   e. No additional shipping clerk candidates should be interviewed for five years.
4. Human Resource Management Systems usage has

grown significantly in recent years for all of these reasons except

    a. skill demands have become less complex for most of the work force.

    b. technology costs have come down.

    c. managers are often overwhelmed with information.

    d. systems are more user friendly.

    e. staffing decisions need to be made more quickly.

5. During a job analysis, all of these tasks are performed except

    a. duties and responsibilities of a job are defined.

    b. a description of what happens on a job is provided.

    c. skills and abilities necessary to perform a job are precisely identified.

    d. basic pay ranges for a job are set.

    e. conditions under which a job should be performed are described.

6. Job analysis can be performed in all of these ways except

    a. observing hourly workers.

    b. reviewing exit interviews conducted with departing employees.

    c. studying diaries or daily journals that managers kept over a three-month period.

    d. listening to fifteen assembly line workers in a group discussion.

    e. giving workers checklists to indicate which tasks on the list are performed during job execution.

7. Monique, the director of job analysis, must write job descriptions for two hundred new jobs in a new plant for her large manufacturing firm. The new robotics line will make this location different from the other five sites. Ten new supervisors have been recruited from outside the organization because of their experience with robotics production technology. Ten current supervisors have been sent to robotics production training. In addition, 150 workers have been targeted to work on the line, but none of them has any robotics experience. Which job analysis method should she use?

    a. observation

    b. structured questionnaire

    c. technical conference

    d. diary

    e. gap analysis

8. The Purdue University Position Analysis Questionnaire (PAQ) and the Department of Labor Job Analysis Process (JAP) are accurately compared with which statement?

    a. The PAQ is the same as the JAP.

    b. The PAQ is used to develop the JAP.

    c. The PAQ produces a more quantitative and finely tuned job description than the JAP.

    d. The PAQ works more effectively for white-collar, managerial jobs, while the JAP is more effective for blue-collar, unskilled jobs.

    e. The JAP is used only in the public sector. The PAQ is used only in the private sector.

9. Which statement best compares job specifications and job descriptions?

    a. Job description focuses on qualifications for jobholders. Job specification focuses on what the jobholder does.

    b. Job specification focuses on qualifications for jobholders. Job description focuses on what the jobholder does.

    c. Job specification occurs before job analysis. Job description occurs after job analysis.

    d. Job description is the same as job specification.

    e. Job specification occurs after job analysis. Job description occurs before job analysis.

10. Which statement accurately reflects the current state of job analysis in most organizations today?

    a. Job analysis is not done.

    b. Job analysis is performed by senior human resources professionals.

    c. The primary purpose of job analysis is to assist in the recruiting and selection activities.

    d. Job analysis affects most HRM activities.

    e. Job analysis is developed from the human resource skills inventory.

11. Stan is vice-president of human resources in a medium-sized manufacturing firm. He is being sued under the Americans with Disabilities Act for not hiring Mildred, who is confined to a wheelchair, to work in the plant. Which document will he use in defense?

    a. Job description.   b. Job analysis.

    c. Job evaluation.   d. Job qualification.

    e. Job specification.

12. Jordan is the vice-president of human resources for a large manufacturing organization. His company is in a temporary slump. He has to cut 40 percent of the costs for the current year, but will need all the competent employees he has currently plus 18 percent more at the start of next year when eight major contracts will begin. All of these options should be pursued except

    a. leaves of absence.   b. loans.

    c. layoffs.   d. early retirement.

    e. reduced work hours.

Chapter Six

RECRUITMENT AND THE FOUNDATIONS OF SELECTION

LEARNING OBJECTIVES

AFTER READING THIS CHAPTER, YOU WILL BE ABLE TO:

1. Define what is meant by the term *recruitment*.
2. Identify the dual goals of recruitment.
3. Explain what constrains human resource managers in determining recruiting sources.
4. Describe the principal sources involved in recruiting employees.
5. Discuss the benefits derived from a proper selection process.
6. Identify the primary purpose of selection activities.
7. Describe the selection process.
8. List three types of validity.
9. Explain how validity is determined.
10. Define validity generalization.

Successful strategic human resource planning is designed to identify an organization's human resource needs. Once these needs are known, an organization will want to do something about meeting them. The next step in the staffing function—assuming, of course, that demand for certain skills, knowledge, and abilities is greater than the current supply—is recruitment. This activity makes it possible for a company to acquire the people necessary to ensure the continued operation of the organization. Recruiting is the process of discovering potential candidates for actual or anticipated organizational vacancies. Or, from another perspective, it is a linking activity—bringing together those with jobs to fill and those seeking jobs. Bringing these two together frequently requires creativity and ingenuity. Anyone can place an advertisement in a newspaper and get a response. But will it achieve the kind of response expected? Consider the following position-opening ad that appeared in the summer of 1994 in major news media:[1]

> Help Wanted: CEO for counter-cultural ice-cream empire. Must have social agenda, unfashionable left-of-center politics, and at least one garment tie-dyed before 1970. Unkempt facial hair encouraged. Knowledge of business a plus.

Sound unusual, especially for the number-one job in a large corporation? Well, maybe not, especially if you consider that the company is Ben & Jerry's, the Waterbury, Vermont, ice-cream giant.

Ben & Jerry's has always been known as an organization that bordered on the atypical. For instance, the company's internal slogan, "Are you weird enough?" guides the main corporate policy of "If it isn't fun, why do it!"[2] And to keep this corporate atmosphere from becoming too serious, the founders established the "Joy Gang." Two of the Joy Gang's first accomplishments were to offer in-house professional massages and sponsor a "Barry Manilow Appreciation Day." Three-piece suits, power ties, and wing-tip shoes are dinosaurs in this organization.

With the announced retirement of one of the founders, Ben Cohen, the company needed a new leader. But the founders were not looking for that traditional management leader. Rather, they desired someone who would "fit" the unusual culture of Ben & Jerry's, and would continue its traditions. And what better way to achieve this goal than to make the selection of the CEO a contest. Yes, a "Yo! I'm Your CEO," contest! Rather than resumes, interested applicants are asked to submit an essay stating why they want to run Ben & Jerry's.

Bizarre? Clearly, but hitting its target. Throughout the process, more than 22,000 essays were received. In its own way, Ben & Jerry's had achieved its goal of this recruiting effort, generating a large pool of candidates from which its CEO was selected. And that honor went to Robert Holland, Jr., a former McKensey consultant whose hundred-word essay on "Time, Values, and Ice Cream," advanced him to the forefront of the process.[3]

Goals of Recruiting

For the recruiting process to work effectively, there must be a significant pool of candidates to choose from. And that may not be easy, especially in a tight labor market. For example, CDI, the largest engineering services firm in the United States, was having difficulty filling such jobs as product designer and computer modelers. As an incentive to boost the number of applicants, the company offered a drawing for a multipurpose vehicle, or a Caribbean cruise for two, to those qualified individuals who sent resumes.[4] The first goal of recruiting, then, is to communicate the position in such a way that job seekers respond. Why? The more applications received, the better the recruiter's chances for finding an individual who is best-suited to the job requirements. Simultaneously, however, the recruiter must provide enough information about the job that unqualified applicants can self-select themselves out of job candidacy. For instance, in the Ben & Jerry's advertisement, someone with a conservative political view, with a classical, bureaucratic perspective of management, would not want to apply because that individual wouldn't fit the renowned counter-cultural ways of the company.

Help Wanted! New CEO. Does this look like a typical ad for a CEO of a major corporation? Highly unlikely. But it represents the kind of person Ben & Jerry's is looking for. If this ad appears crazy to you, then maybe you're not the applicant the company is looking to attract.

Why is having potential applicants remove themselves from the applicant pool important to human resource management? Typically, when applications are received, the company acknowledges their receipt. That acknowledgment costs time and money. Then there are the application reviews and a second letter sent, this time rejecting the applications. Again, this incurs some costs. Accordingly, whenever possible, applications from those who are unqualified must be discouraged. A good recruiting program should attract the qualified, and not the unqualified. Meeting this dual objective will minimize the cost of processing unqualified candidates.

Factors that Affect Recruiting Efforts

Although all organizations will, at one time or another, engage in recruiting activities, some do so to a much larger extent than others. Obviously, size is one factor; an organization with 100,000 employees will find itself recruiting continually. So, too, will fast-food firms, smaller-service organizations, as well as firms that pay lower wages. Certain other variables will also influence the extent of recruiting. Employment conditions in the community where the organization is located will influence how much recruiting takes place. The effectiveness of past recruiting efforts will show itself in the organization's historical ability to locate and keep people who perform well. Working conditions and salary and benefit packages offered by the organization will influence turnover and, therefore, the need for future recruiting. Organizations that are not growing, or those that are actually declining, will find little need to recruit. On the other hand, organizations that are growing rapidly, like Microsoft and Rent-A-Center, will find recruitment a major human resource activity.[5]

Recruitment efforts, even in these growing companies, are no easy task. Recall in Chapter 2 the discussion of skill deficiencies. Quality workers are becoming harder to locate. Therefore, HRM will have to develop new strategies to locate and hire those individuals possessing the skills the company needs.[6] United Parcel Service (UPS), for example, found a creative way to locate talented people.[7] Having problems finding workers in its three New Jersey facilities, UPS met with a local public employment agency that offered, among other services, employment counseling. By UPS describing the type of employee it was seeking, this agency sought to match its clients with UPS needs. This cooperation effort resulted in about 1,500 new employees for the company.

Constraints on Recruiting Efforts

While the ideal recruitment effort will bring in a large number of qualified applicants who will take the job if it is offered, the realities cannot be ignored. For example, the pool of qualified applicants may not include the "best" candidates; or the "best" candidate may not want to be employed by the organization. These and other **constraints on recruiting efforts** limit managers' freedom to recruit and select a candidate of their choice. However, we can narrow our focus by suggesting five specific constraints.

Constraints on Recruiting Efforts Factors that can affect maximizing outcomes in recruiting.

Image of the Organization   We noted that the prospective candidate may not be interested in pursuing job opportunities in the particular organization. The *image of the organization,* therefore, should be considered a potential constraint. If that image is perceived to be low, the likelihood of attracting a large number of applicants is reduced.[8] Many college graduates know, for example, that the individuals who occupy the top spots at Disney earn excellent salaries, are given excellent benefits, and are greatly respected in their communities. Among most college graduates, Disney has a positive image. The hope of having a shot at one of its top jobs, being in the spotlight, and having a position of power results in Disney having little trouble in attracting college graduates into entry-level positions. But not all graduates hold a positive image of large organizations. More specifically, their image of some organizations is pessimistic. In a number of communities, local firms have a reputation for being in a declining industry; engaging in practices that result in polluting the environment, poor-quality products, and unsafe working conditions; or being indifferent to employees' needs. Such reputations can and do reduce these organizations' abilities to attract the best personnel available.

Attractiveness of the Job   If the position to be filled is an *unattractive job,* recruiting a large and qualified pool of applicants will be difficult. In recent years, for instance, many employers have been complaining about the difficulty of finding suitably qualified individuals for secretarial positions. Traditionally, these jobs appealed to females. Today, however, women have a wider selection of job opportunities, as well as heightened aspirations—a combination that has resulted in a severe shortage of qualified secretaries. Given the status, pay, and opportunities inherent in most secretarial jobs, many individuals who previously would have sought such positions now consider them unattractive. Any job that is viewed as boring, hazardous, anxiety-creating, low-paying, or lacking in promotion potential seldom will attract a qualified pool of applicants. Even during economic slumps, people have refused to take many of these jobs.[9]

Internal Organizational Policies   Internal organizational policies, such as "promote from within wherever possible," will give priority to individuals inside the organization. Such policies, when followed, will usually ensure that all positions, other than the lowest-level entry positions, will be filled from within the ranks. Although this is promising once one is hired, it may reduce the number of applications.

Government Influence   The government's influence in the recruiting process should not be overlooked. An employer can no longer seek out preferred individuals based on non–job-related factors such as physical appearance, sex, or religious background. An airline wishing to staff all its flight attendant positions with attractive females will find itself breaking the law if comparably qualified male candidates are rejected on the basis of sex. The responsibility, in this case, is on the airline to demonstrate that being female is a bona fide occupational qualification.

Recruiting Costs   The last constraint, but certainly not lowest in priority, is one that centers on recruiting costs. Recruiting efforts by an organization are expensive. Sometimes continuing a search for long periods of time is not possible because of budget restrictions. Accordingly, when an organization considers various recruiting sources, it does so with some sense of effectiveness in mind. That is, recruiting expenditures are made where the best return on the "investment" can be realized. Unfortunately, because of limited resources, these expenditures must be prioritized. Those lower in priority do not get the same resources, and this can ultimately constrain a recruiter's effort to attract the best person for the job.

Recruiting from an International Perspective

When beginning to recruit for overseas positions, the first step, as always, is to define the relevant labor market. For international positions, however, that market is the whole world. As mentioned in Chapter 2, we first must decide if we want to send an American overseas, recruit in the host country where the position is, or ignore nationality and do a global search for the best person available. Thus, our possibilities are to select someone from the United States, the host country, or a third country.

To some extent, this basic decision depends on the type of occupation and its requirements, as well as the stage of national and cultural development of the overseas operations. Although production, office, and clerical occupations are rarely filled beyond a local labor market, executive and sometimes scientific, engineering, or professional managerial candidates may be sought in national or international markets. If the organization is searching for someone with extensive company experience to launch a very technical product in a country where it has never sold before, it will probably want a home-country national. This approach is often used when a new foreign subsidiary is being established and headquarters wants to control all strategic decisions, but technical expertise and experience are needed. It is also appropriate where there is a lack of qualified host-country nationals in the work force.

Host-country national Hiring a citizen from the host-country to perform certain jobs in the global village.

In other situations it might be more advantageous to hire a **host-country national (HCN),** assuming there is a choice. For an uncomplicated consumer product it may be a wise corporate strategic decision to have each foreign subsidiary acquire its own distinct national identity. Clothing has different styles of merchandising and an HCN may have a better feel for the best way to market the sweaters or jeans of an international manufacturer.

Sometimes the choice may not be entirely left to the corporation. In some countries, most African nations for example, local laws control how many expatriates a corporation can send. There may be established ratios, such as twenty host-country nationals must be employed for every American granted working papers. Using HCNs eliminates language problems and avoids problems of expatriate adjustment and the high cost of training and relocating an expatriate with a family. It also minimizes one of the chief reasons international assignments fail—the family's inability to adjust to their new surroundings. Even when premiums are paid to lure the best local applicants away from other companies, the costs of maintaining the employee are significantly lower than with sending an American overseas. In some countries, where there are tense political environments, an HCN is less visible and can somewhat insulate the U.S. corporation from hostilities and possible terrorism.

The third option, recruiting regardless of nationality, develops an international executive cadre with a truly global perspective. On a large scale this type of recruiting may reduce national identification of managers with particular organizational units. For example, automobile manufacturers may develop a Taiwanese parts plant, a Mexican assembly operations, and a U.S. marketing team, creating internal status difficulties through its different treatment of each country's employees.

Recruiting Sources

Recruitment is more likely to achieve its objectives if recruiting sources reflect the type of position to be filled. For example, an ad in the business employment section of *The Wall Street Journal* is more likely to be read by a manager seeking an executive position in the $125,000-to-$175,000-a-year bracket than by an automobile assembly-line worker seeking to find employment. Similarly, an interviewer who is seeking to fill a management training position and visits a two-year vocational school in search of a recent college graduate with undergraduate courses in engineering and a master's degree in business administration is looking for "the right person in the wrong place."

Certain recruiting sources are more effective than others for filling certain types of jobs. As we review each source in the following sections, the strengths

One of the best means of getting the word out to the public that a position is open is to use public newspapers, particularly their employment sections. Doing so, however, can be costly. As such, the ad should be placed in a location where the greatest exposure can be gained.

Internal Search A promotion-
from-within concept.

and weaknesses in attempting to attract lower-level and managerial-level personnel will be emphasized.

The Internal Search

Many large organizations will attempt to develop their own employees for positions beyond the lowest level. These can occur through an **internal search** of current employees, who have either bid for the job, been identified through the organization's human resource management system, or been referred to by a fellow employee. The advantages of such searches—a "promote from within wherever possible" policy—are:

1. It is good public relations.
2. It builds morale.
3. It encourages good individuals who are ambitious.
4. It improves the probability of a good selection, since information on the individual's performance is readily available.
5. It is less costly than going outside to recruit.
6. Those chosen internally already know the organization.
7. When carefully planned, promoting from within can also act as a training device for developing middle- and top-level managers.

There can be distinct disadvantages, however, to using internal sources. It can be dysfunctional to the organization to utilize inferior internal sources only because they are there, when excellent candidates are available on the outside. However, an individual from the outside, in contrast with someone already employed in the organization, may appear more attractive because the recruiter is unaware of the outsider's faults. Internal searches may also generate infighting among the rival candidates for promotion, as well as decreasing morale levels of those not selected.

The organization should avoid excessive inbreeding. Occasionally it may be necessary to bring in some "new blood" to broaden the current ideas, knowledge, and enthusiasm, and to question the "we've-always-done-it-that-way" mentality. As noted in the discussion of human resource inventories in Chapter 5, the organization's HRM files should provide information as to which employees might be considered for positions opening up within the organization. Most organizations can utilize their computer information system to generate an output of those individuals who have the desirable characteristics to potentially fill the vacant position.

In many organizations, it is standard procedure to post any new job openings and to allow any current employee to "bid" for the position. This action, too, receives favorable marks from the EEOC. The posting notification can be communicated on a central "positions open" bulletin board in the plants or offices, in the weekly or monthly organization newsletter, or, in some cases, in a specially prepared posting sheet from human resources outlining those positions currently available. Even if current employees are not interested in the position, they can use these notices to recommend friends or associates for employment within the organization—the employee referral.

Employee Referrals/Recommendations

One of the best sources for individuals who will perform effectively on the job is a recommendation from a current employee. Why? Because employees rarely recommend someone unless he or she believes that the individual can perform adequately. Such a recommendation reflects on the recommender, and when someone's reputation is at stake, we can expect the recommendation to be based on considered judgment. **Employee referrals** also may have acquired more accurate information about their potential jobs. The recommender often gives the applicant more realistic information about the job than could be conveyed through employment agencies or newspaper advertisements. This information reduces unrealistic expectations and increases job survival. As a result of these pre-selection factors, employee referrals tend to be more acceptable applicants, to be more likely to accept an offer if one is made, and, once employed, to have a higher job survival rate. Additionally, employee referrals are an excellent means of locating potential employees in those hard-to-fill positions. For example, because of the difficulty in finding computer programmers, engineers, or nurses with specific skills required by the organization, some organizations have turned to their employees for assistance. In one organization, these specifically identified hard-to-fill positions include a reward if an employee referral candidate is hired. In this case, both the organization and the employee benefit; the employee receives a monetary reward and the organization receives a qualified candidate without the major expense of an extensive recruiting search.

> **Employee Referrals** A recommendation from a current employee regarding a job applicant.

There are, of course, some potentially negative features of employee referral. For one thing, recommenders may confuse friendship with job performance competence. Individuals often like to have their friends join them at their place of employment for social and even economic reasons; for example, they may be able to share rides to and from work. As a result, a current employee may recommend a friend for a position without giving an unbiased consideration to the friend's job-related competence. Employee referrals may also lead to nepotism; that is, hiring individuals who are related to persons already employed by the organization. The hiring of relatives is particularly widespread in family-owned organizations. Although such actions may not necessarily align with the objective of hiring the most-qualified applicant, interest in the organization and loyalty to it may be long-term advantages.

Employee referrals can also lead to an adverse impact. If a predominantly white-male work force recommends other white-male acquaintances for the job and they are subsequently hired, this practice could be keeping minorities out, and the organization could then be in violation of anti-discrimination laws. Employee referrals do, however, appear to have universal application. Lower-level and managerial-level positions can, and often are, filled by the recommendation of a current employee. In higher-level positions, however, it is more likely that the referral will be a professional acquaintance rather than a friend with whom the recommender has close social contact. In jobs where specialized expertise is important, and where employees participate in professional organizations that foster the development of this expertise, it can be expected that current employees will be acquainted with, or know about, individuals they think would make an excellent contribution to the organization.

The External Searches

In addition to looking internally for candidates, it is customary for organizations to open up recruiting efforts to the external community. These efforts include advertisements, employment agencies, school, colleges and universities, professional organizations, and unsolicited applicants.

Advertisements The sign outside the construction location reads: "Now Hiring—Brick Layers." The newspaper advertisement reads:

Advertisement Materials communicating to the general public that a position in a company is open.

Blind-box Ad An advertisement in which there is no identification of the advertising organization.

"Sales Management Trainee. We are looking for someone who wants to assume responsibility and wishes to learn the winter outerwear business. Minimum of two years' sales experience required. College degree or equivalent desired. Salary to $40,000. For appointment, call Ms. Davies at 555-0075."

Most of us have seen both types of advertisements. When an organization wishes to communicate to the public that it has a vacancy, **advertisements** is one of the most popular methods used. However, where the advertisement is placed is often determined by the type of job. Although it is not uncommon to see blue-collar jobs listed on placards outside the plant gates, we would be surprised to find a vice-presidency listed similarly. The higher the position in the organization, the more specialized the skills, or the shorter the supply of that resource in the labor force, the more widely dispersed the advertisement is likely to be. The search for a top executive might include advertisements in a national publication, like *The New York Times,* for example. On the other hand, the advertisement of lower-level jobs is usually confined to the local daily newspaper or regional trade journal.

A number of factors influence the response rate to advertisements. There are three important variables: identification of the organization, labor market conditions, and the degree to which specific requirements are included in the advertisement. Some organizations place what is referred to as a **blind-box ad,** one in which there is no specific identification of the organization. Respondents are asked to reply to a post office box number or to an employment firm that is acting as an agent between the applicant and the organization. Large organizations with a national reputation seldom use blind advertisements to fill lower-level positions; however, when the organization does not wish to publicize the fact that it is seeking to fill an internal position, or when it seeks to recruit for a position where there is a soon-to-be-moved incumbent, a blind-box advertisement may be appropriate. This is especially true when the position that the organization wishes to fill is expected to draw an extraordinary number of applicants. Using the blind ad relieves the organization from having to respond to any individual who applies. Only those individuals the organization wishes to see are notified; the remaining are not, as if the application was never received.

Although blind ads can assist HRM in finding qualified applicants, many individuals are reluctant to answer them. Obviously, there is the fear, usually unjustified, that the advertisement has been placed by the organization in which the individual is currently employed. Also, the organization itself is frequently a key determinant of whether the individual is interested; therefore, potential candidates are often reluctant to reply. Further deterrents are the bad reputation that advertisements have received because of organizations that place ads when no position exists in order to test the supply of workers in the community, to build a backlog of applicants, or to identify those current employees who are interested in finding a new position; or to satisfy affirmative action requirements when the final decision, for the greater part, has already been made.

The job analysis process is the basic source for the information placed in the ad. A decision must be made as to whether the ad will focus on descriptive elements of the job (job description) or on the applicant (job specification). The choice made will often affect the number of replies received. If, for example, you are willing to sift through 1,000 or more responses, you might place a national ad in *The New York Times* or the *Chicago Tribune,* or a regional newspaper's employment section similar to the one in Figure 6-1. However, an advertisement in these papers that looks like Figure 6-2 might attract less than a dozen replies.

The difference between Figures 6-1 and 6-2 is obvious. Figure 6-1 uses more applicant-centered criteria to describe the successful candidate. Most individu-

SALES: CAN YOU LIVE ON $75K–$125K COMMISSION?

THAT MAY LIMIT YOU TO:

- $200K–$300K HOME
- 2 CARS & A BOAT
- A FEW BAHAMAS WEEKENDS
- TIME TO ENJOY IT ALL!

Strangely, it seems few people have the appetite for this type of income. Many have the talent, but neither the courage nor the confidence to pursue it. For the sales-oriented individual who likes to travel, loves weekends, and is truly desirous of high-commission income, call . . .

Source: Anonymous, printed in *The Sunday Sun* (February 23, 1992).

als perceive themselves as having confidence and seeking high "income." More important, how can an employer measure these qualities? The response rate should therefore be high. In contrast, Figure 6-2 describes a job requiring precise abilities and experience. The requirements of at least "seven years of progressive experience in nursing leadership," a master's in Nursing Administration, and a doctorate in a related field are certain to limit the respondent pool.

Employment Agencies   We will describe three forms of employment agencies: public or state agencies, private employment agencies, and management consulting firms. The major difference between these three sources is the type of clientele served.

All states provide a public employment service. The main function of these agencies is closely tied to unemployment benefits, since benefits in some states are given only to individuals who are registered with their state employment agency. Accordingly, most public agencies tend to attract and list individuals

Figure 6-2
Advertisement with a Low Response Rate Likelihood

Vice President, Nursing. Merryvale Medical Center, a 665-bed community teaching medical center located in Cleveland, Ohio, is seeking a top-level, highly creative nursing executive who will be a key member of the leadership team within the Merryvale Health System. The successful candidate will work closely with corporate officers, physicians, and staff in continuing the growth of the Medical Center. The position will be responsible for all aspects of nursing operations, including administration, education, research and practice; will be fiscally accountable for the nursing department; and will be responsible for the delivery of innovative models for interdisciplinary care. This person will possess a progressive vision of professional nursing practice and a proven track record as a leader in the nursing field. A Master's in Nursing Administration, plus the possession of a doctorate (Ph.D., Sc.D., Ed.D.) in a related field; 7–10 years' progressive experience in nursing leadership; and licensure as a registered nurse are required.

Source: Adapted from Christina Murray Younger, Manager, Employment Services, *The Baltimore Sun*, (July 31, 1994).

who are unskilled or have had minimum training. This, of course, does not reflect on the agency's competence, but rather, on the image of public agencies. State agencies are perceived by prospective applicants as having few high-skilled jobs, and employers tend to see such agencies as having few high-skilled applicants. Therefore public agencies tend to attract and place predominantly low-skilled workers. The agencies' image as perceived by both applicants and employers thus tends to result in a self-fulfilling prophecy; that is, few high-skilled individuals place their names with public agencies, and, similarly, few employers seeking individuals with high skills list their vacancies or inquire about applicants at state agencies.

Yet this image may not always be the case. For example, a nationwide computer network at the Employment Security Commission acts as a clearinghouse for professional-level jobs. In this case, a public agency may be a good source for such applicants.

How does a private employment agency, which has to charge for its services, compete with state agencies that give their service away? They must do something different from what the public agencies do, or at least give that impression.[10]

The major difference between public and private employment agencies is their image; that is, private agencies are believed to offer positions and applicants of a higher caliber. Private agencies may also provide a more complete line of services. They may advertise the position, screen applicants against the criteria specified by the employer, and provide a guarantee covering six months or a year as protection to the employer should the applicant not perform satisfactorily. The private employment agency's fee can be totally absorbed by either the employer or the employee, or it can be split. The alternative chosen usually depends on the demand–supply situation in the community involved.

The third agency source consists of the management consulting, executive search, or "headhunter" firms. Agencies of this type are actually specialized private employment agencies. They specialize in middle-level and top-level executive placement,[11] as well as hard-to-fill positions such as computer programmers. In addition to the level at which they recruit, the features that distinguish executive search agencies from most private employment agencies are their fees, their nationwide contacts, and the thoroughness of their investigations. In searching for an individual of vice-president caliber, whose compensation package may be far in excess of $200,000 a year, the potential employer may be willing to pay a very high fee to locate exactly the right individual to fill the vacancy. A fee amounting to 30 percent of the executive's first-year salary is not unusual as a charge for finding and recruiting the individual.[12]

Executive search firms canvass their contacts and do preliminary screening. They seek out highly effective executives who have the skills to do the job, can effectively adjust to the organization, and most important, are willing to consider new challenges and opportunities. Possibly such individuals are frustrated by their inability to move up in their current organization at the pace at which they are capable, or they recently may have been bypassed for a major promotion. The executive search firm can act as a buffer for screening candidates and, at the same time, keep the prospective employer anonymous. In the final stages, senior executives in the prospective firm can move into the negotiations and determine the degree of mutual interest.

Schools, Colleges, and Universities   Educational institutions at all levels offer opportunities for recruiting recent graduates. Most educational institutions operate placement services where prospective employers can review credentials and interview graduates. Whether the educational level required for the job involves a high-school diploma, specific vocational training, or a college background with a bachelor's, master's, or doctoral degree, educational institutions are an excellent source of potential employees for entry-level positions in organizations.[13]

High schools or vocational–technical schools can provide lower-level applicants; business or secretarial schools can provide administrative staff personnel; and two- and four-year colleges and graduate schools can often provide managerial-level personnel. While educational institutions are usually viewed as sources for young, inexperienced entrants to the work force, it is not uncommon to find individuals with considerable work experience using an educational institution's placement service. They may be workers who have recently returned to school to upgrade their skills, or former graduates interested in pursuing other opportunities.

College placements, while a good source of applicants, are costly to the company in terms of the recruiter's expenses in travel, lodging, and the like—that is, unless the school is in the organization's area. An organization must weigh the benefits of this recruiting source with its costs, in many cases over $2,000 per school. This appears to be one of the reasons why, during economic downturns, interviews on campus severely decline.

Professional Organizations Many **professional organizations,** including labor unions, operate placement services for the benefit of their members. The professional organizations include such varied occupations as industrial engineering, psychology, and academics. These organizations publish rosters of job vacancies and distribute these lists to members. It is also common practice to provide placement facilities at regional and national meetings where individuals looking for employment and companies looking for employees can find each other.

Professional organizations, however, can also apply sanctions to control the labor supply in their discipline. For example, although the law stipulates that unions cannot require employers to hire only union members, the mechanisms for ensuring that unions do not break this law are poorly enforced. As a result, it is not unusual for labor unions to control supply through their apprenticeship programs and through their labor agreements with employers. Of course, this tactic is not limited merely to blue-collar trade unions. In those professional organizations where the organization placement service is the focal point for locating prospective employers, and where certain qualifications are necessary to become a member (such as special educational attainment or professional certification or license), the professional organization can significantly influence and control the supply of prospective applicants.

Unsolicited Applicants **Walk-ins,** whether they reach the employer by letter, telephone, or in person, constitute a source of prospective applicants. Although the number of unsolicited applicants depends on economic conditions, the organization's image, and the job seeker's perception of the types of jobs that might be available, this source does provide an excellent supply of stockpiled applicants. Even if there are no particular openings when the applicant contacts the organization, the application can be kept on file for later needs.

Unsolicited applications made by unemployed individuals, however, generally have a short life. Those individuals who have adequate skills and who would be prime candidates for a position in the organization if a position were currently available, usually find employment with some other organization that does have

College Placements An external search process focusing recruiting efforts on a college campus.

Professional Organizations A source of job applicants where placement facilities at regional conferences and national conferences usually occur.

Walk-ins Unsolicited applicants.

an opening. However, in times of economic stagnation, excellent prospects are often unable to locate the type of job they desire and may stay actively looking in the job market for many months.

Applications from individuals who are already employed can be referred to many months later and can provide applicants who (1) are interested in considering other employment opportunities, and (2) regard the organization as a possible employer.

Recruitment Alternatives

Much of the previous discussion on recruiting sources implies that these efforts are designed to bring into the organization full-time, permanent employees. However, economic realities, coupled with management trends such as rightsizing, have resulted in a slightly different focus. Companies today are looking at hiring temporary help (including retirees), leasing employees, and using the services of independent contractors.[14]

Temporary Employees Employees hired for a limited time to perform a specific job.

Temporary Help Services Organizations like the Kelly Temporary Services, Accountemps, and Temp-Force Inc. can be a source of employees when individuals are needed on a temporary basis (see "Ethical Decisions in HRM: Hiring Contingent Workers"). **Temporary employees** are particularly valuable in meeting short-term fluctuations in HRM needs.[15] While traditionally developed in the office administration area, the temporary staffing service has expanded its coverage to include a broad range of skills. It is now possible, for example, to hire temporary nurses, computer programmers, accountants, librarians, and drafters or drafting technicians, as well as temporary secretaries.[16]

In addition to specific temporary help services, another quality source of temporary workers is older workers, those who have already retired or have been displaced by rightsizing in many companies.[17] An aging work force and individuals' desire to retire earlier, has created skill deficiencies in some disciplines. Older workers bring those skills back to the job. In fact, at Monsanto, the company has capitalized on this rich skill base by establishing its own temporary, in-house employment agency, the Retiree Resource Corps (RRC).[18] Then, when there is a need for temporary help somewhere in the organization, the RRC provides the needed talent pool. For Monsanto, such a temporary work force is saving the company almost $2 million a year.

While the reasons many of these older workers wish to continue to work vary,[19] they bring with them several advantages. These include "flexibility in scheduling, low absenteeism, high motivation, and mentoring abilities for younger workers."[20] It was these very attributes that the first ten sales representatives of Everyday Learning Company, the Evanston, Illinois, publishing organization specializing in elementary school math curriculum books, brought to the job.[21] By their fifth year, they had helped the founder, Jo Anne Schiller, build a business that generates more than $2 million annually and has its books in over 2,000 schools.

Employee Leasing Employee leasing is a term used to reflect the hiring of personnel for long periods of time. Whereas temporary employees come into an organization for a specific short-term project, leased employees typically remain with an organization for longer periods of time. Under a leasing arrangement, individuals work for the leasing firm.[22] When an organization has a need for specific employee skills, it contracts with the leasing firm to provide a certain number of trained employees. For example, consider Robert Half Accoun-

Ethical Decisions:

Hiring Contingent Workers

Hiring temporary or contingent workers provides an organization with great flexibility. It enables the organization to deal with peak performance times without having to add permanent staff to its payroll. For many workers, especially older workers and individuals who wish to spend more time on personal matters, like child rearing, this part-time work serves a fundamental need. It permits them to explore those things they prefer to explore, without being hampered by the requirements of a full-time position. But not every contingent worker sees part-time work in the same light. It is suggested that almost several million workers would prefer to work full-time, but can't find anything but part-time employment. As such, the organizational emphasis on a contingent work force is adversely affecting today's workers.

Part-time workers often don't receive the benefits that full-time employees get. They often receive no health insurance benefits, nor enjoy an opportunity to participate in a company-sponsored retirement plan. They have little opportunity, if any, at career advancement, and their tenure with an organization is as long as the project they are working on.

Organizations, however, appear to gain in this scenario. Hiring contingent workers is a cost-effective means of staffing the organization. And, oftentimes, by employing part-time employees, they may be exempt from certain federal EEO regulations. But that may not make it right. Are these organizations exploiting contingent workers? Are they acting responsibly toward a society that keeps them in business? Or are we headed down that proverbial historical path where one day, more federal legislation will be passed to protect the contingent worker? The Clinton administration's desire for 100 percent health coverage of all Americans was brought to the forefront because so many workers, like the contingent work force, did not have health insurance. Are organizations exploiting contingent workers? What do you think?

temps. As a leasing firm, Robert Half has on its staff fully trained accountants ready to meet an organization's accounting needs. If tax season requires additional tax accountants, Robert Half can supply them; the same holds true for other accounting areas. One reason for leasing's popularity is cost.[23] The acquiring organization pays a flat fee for the employees. The company is not responsible for benefits or other costs, like social security payments, it would incur for a full-time employee. This is because leased employees are, in fact, employees of the leased firm. Furthermore, when the project is over, employees are returned to the leasing company, thus eliminating any cost associated with layoffs or discharge.

Leased employees are also well-trained individuals. They are screened by the leasing firm, trained appropriately, and often go to organizations with an unconditional guarantee. Thus, if one of these individuals doesn't work out, the company can get a new employee, or make arrangements to have its fee re-

Independent Contractors Temporary employees offering specialized services to an organization.

turned. There are also benefits from the employee's point of view. Today's workers frequently prefer more flexibility in their lives. Working with a leasing company and being sent out at various times allows these workers to work when they want, for the length of time they desire.

Independent Contractors   Another means of recruiting is the use of **independent contractors.** Often referred to as consultants, independent contractors are taking on new meaning in the 1990s. Companies may hire independent contractors to do very specific work at a location on or off the company's premises. For instance, claims-processing or word-processing activities can easily be done at one's home and forwarded to the employer on a routine basis. With the growing use of personal computers, fax machines, and voice mail, employers can ensure that home work is being done in a timely fashion.

Independent contractor arrangements benefit both the organization and the individual. Because the company does not have to regard this individual as an employee, it saves costs associated with full- or part-time personnel, like social security taxes and workers' compensation premiums. Additionally, such opportunity is also a means of keeping good individuals associated with your company. Suppose an employee wants to work, but also be at home when the kids are home. This cannot be done through typical work arrangements, but allowing the individual to work at home, on his or her time, can generate a win–win solution to the problem.

We have identified a number of sources of potential candidates. If we've achieved our goal and located a number of qualified applicants, it's time to begin to filter through the stack. This filtering process is called selection.

Goals of the Selection Process

A recent HRM graduate went on his first interview.[24] Not knowing what to expect, he prepared as best he could. He was dressed exquisitely in a new navy pinstriped suit and was carrying his new black leather attaché case. As he entered the human resource management office, he encountered two doors. On the first door was, "Human Resource Management Majors." On the second was, "All Other Majors." He entered door 1, which opened up to two more doors. On door 1 was, "3.25 or better GPA"; door 2, "All Other GPAs." Having a 3.68 GPA, he once again entered door 1, and found himself facing yet two more choices. Door 1 stated, "Took Conflict Resolution Techniques Course," and door 2, "Didn't Take Conflict Resolution." Because this course was not required, he went through door 2. Upon opening the door, he found a box with preprinted letters saying, "Your qualifications did not meet the expectations of the job. Thanks for considering our organization. Please exit to the right."

Selection Process The process of selecting the best candidate for the job.

Although fictional, this story illustrates the **selection process.** All selection activities exist for the purpose of making effective selection decisions. Each activity is a step in the process that results in a prediction—managerial decision makers seeking to predict which job applicants will be successful if hired. *Successful,* in this case, means performing well on the criteria the organization uses to evaluate its employees. For a sales position, for example, the criteria should be able to indicate to the assessors which applicants will generate a high volume of sales; for a teaching position, such as a college professor, they should predict which applicants will get high student evaluations or generate many high-quality publications or both.

The Selection Process

Selection activities typically follow a standard pattern, beginning with an initial screening interview and concluding with the final employment decision. The selection process may consist of seven steps: (1) initial screening interview, (2) completing the application form, (3) employment tests, (4) comprehensive interview, (5) background investigation, (6) a medical or physical examination, and (7) the final job offer. Each of these steps represents a decision point requiring some affirmative feedback for the process to continue. Each step in the process seeks to expand the organization's knowledge about the applicant's background, abilities, and motivation, and it increases the information from which decision makers will make their predictions and final choice. However, some steps may be omitted if they do not yield data that will aid in predicting success, or if the cost of the step is not warranted. Applicants should also be advised what specific screening will be done, such as credit checks, reference checking, and drug tests. The flow of these activities is depicted in Figure 6-3. Let us take a closer look at each.

Initial Screening

As a culmination of our recruiting efforts, we should be prepared to initiate a preliminary review of potentially acceptable candidates. This **initial screening** is,

Initial Screening The first step in the selection process whereby inquiries about a job are screened.

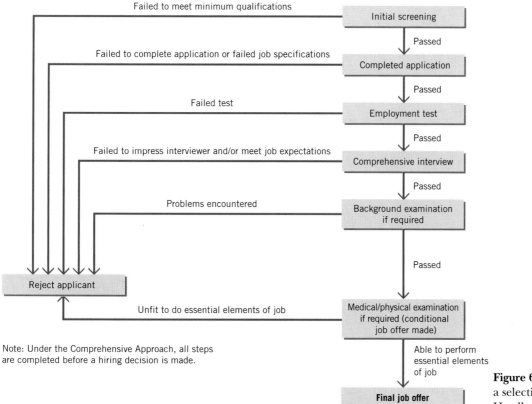

Note: Under the Comprehensive Approach, all steps are completed before a hiring decision is made.

Figure 6-3 Decision points in a selection process: The Hurdle Concept

in effect, a two-step procedure: (1) the screening of inquiries and (2) the provision of screening interviews.

If our recruiting effort has been successful, we will be faced with a number of potential applicants. Based on the job description and job specification, some of these respondents can be eliminated. Factors that might lead to a negative decision at this point include inadequate or inappropriate experience, or inadequate or inappropriate education. The screening interview is also an excellent opportunity for HRM to describe the job in enough detail so the candidates can consider whether they are really serious about applying. Sharing job description information with the individual frequently encourages the unqualified or marginally qualified to voluntarily withdraw from candidacy, with a minimum of cost to the applicant or the organization. Another important point during the initial screening phase is to identify a salary range. Most workers are concerned about their salaries, and while a job opening may sound exciting, a low salary may preclude an organization from obtaining excellent talent. During this phase, if proper HRM activities have been conducted, there should be no need to mask salary data.

Completion of the Application Form

Application Form Company-specific employment forms used to generate specific information the company wants.

Once the initial screening has been completed, applicants are asked to complete the organization's **application form.** The amount of information required may be only the applicant's name, address, and telephone number. Some organizations, on the other hand, may request the completion of a more comprehensive employment profile. In general terms, the application form gives a job-performance-related synopsis of what applicants have been doing during their adult life, their skills, and their accomplishments.

Applications are also useful in that they obtain information the company wants. Additionally, completing the application serves as another hurdle; that is, if the job requires one to follow directions and the individual fails to do so on

Technology is assisting the internal screening process. Here, a recruiter takes some basic information from a potential job applicant and enters it into the computer. Then, the applicant information will be compared to the essential requirements of the job to determine if a match exists. Those that make this "cut" will be moved to the second stage of the selection process, completion of the organization's formal application form.

the application, that is a job-related reason for rejection. Lastly, applications require a signature attesting to the truthfulness of the information given, and to give permission to check references. If at a later point the company finds out the information is false, it can result in the immediate dismissal of the individual.

Employment Tests

Organizations historically relied to a considerable extent on intelligence, aptitude, ability, and interest tests to provide major input to the selection process. Even handwriting analysis (graphology) and honesty tests have been used in the attempt to learn more about the candidate—information that supposedly leads to more effective selection.

In the 1970s and early 1980s, reliance on traditional written tests for selection purposes decreased significantly. This was attributed directly to legal rulings requiring employers to justify as job-related any test that is used.[25] Given the historical difficulty and costs in substantiating this relationship, some organizations merely eliminated employment testing as a selection device.

Since the mid-1980s, however, that trend has reversed. It is estimated that more than 60 percent of all organizations use some type of employment test today.[26] For these organizations, there is recognition that scrapping employment tests was equivalent to "throwing out the baby with the bath water." They have come to recognize that some tests are quite helpful in predicting who will be successful on the job. The key in employment testing, then, is to use a test that accurately predicts job performance. We will discuss the issue of predicting job success later in the chapter.

The Comprehensive Interview

Those applicants who pass the initial screening, application form, and required tests are typically given a **comprehensive interview.** The applicant may be interviewed by HRM interviewers, senior managers within the organization, a potential supervisor, potential colleagues, or some or all of these. In fact, in a company like Disney, applicants are interviewed by some forty people.[27]

The comprehensive interview is designed to probe areas that cannot be addressed easily by the application form or tests, such as assessing one's motivation, ability to work under pressure, and ability to "fit in" with the organization. However, this information must be job-related. The questions asked and the topics covered should reflect the job description and job specification information obtained in the job analysis. We'll take a much more in-depth look at interviews in the next chapter.

Comprehensive Interviews A selection device in which in-depth information about a candidate can be obtained.

Background Investigation

The next step in the process is to undertake a **background investigation** of those applicants who appear to offer potential as employees. This can include contacting former employers to confirm the candidate's work record and to obtain their appraisal of his or her performance, contacting other job-related and personal references, verifying the educational accomplishments shown on the application,[28] verifying an individual's legal status to work in the United States (via the Employment Eligibility Verification, I-9 Form; see Figure 6-4), checking credit references and criminal records; and even using third-party investigators, like Pinkerton Investigation Services, to do the background check.[29]

Background Investigation The process of verifying information job candidates provide.

THE IMMIGRATION REFORM AND CONTROL ACT OF 1986

In an attempt to curtail the hiring of illegal aliens in the United States, Congress passed the Immigration Reform and Control Act. Enforced by the U.S. Immigration and Nationalization Service, all employers are required to verify that the individual about to be hired is a U.S. citizen, has permanent citizen status, or has a valid student visa. The act also prohibits employer discrimination on the basis of national origin (enforced by the Justice Department). All individuals hired are required to complete the accompanying I-9 form.

EMPLOYMENT ELIGIBILITY VERIFICATION (Form I-9)

1 EMPLOYEE INFORMATION AND VERIFICATION: (To be completed and signed by employee.)

Name: (Print or Type) Last	First	Middle	Birth Name
Address: Street Name and Number	City	State	ZIP Code
Date of Birth (Month/Day/Year)		Social Security Number	

I attest, under penalty of perjury, that I am (check a box):

☐ 1. A citizen or national of the United States.
☐ 2. An alien lawfully admitted for permanent residence (Alien Number A _____).
☐ 3. An alien authorized by the Immigration and Naturalization Service to work in the United States (Alien Number A _____ , or Admission Number _____ , expiration of employment authorization, if any _____).

I attest, under penalty of perjury, the documents that I have presented as evidence of identity and employment eligibility are genuine and relate to me. I am aware that federal law provides for imprisonment and/or fine for any false statements or use of false documents in connection with this certificate.

Signature	Date (Month/Day/Year)

PREPARER/TRANSLATOR CERTIFICATION (To be completed if prepared by person other than the employee). I attest, under penalty of perjury, that the above was prepared by me at the request of the named individual and is based on all information of which I have any knowledge.

Signature	Name (Print or Type)		
Address (Street Name and Number)	City	State	Zip Code

2 EMPLOYER REVIEW AND VERIFICATION: (To be completed and signed by employer.)

Instructions:
Examine one document from List A and check the appropriate box, _OR_ examine one document from List B _and_ one from List C and check the appropriate boxes. Provide the _Document Identification Number_ and _Expiration Date_ for the document checked.

List A Documents that Establish Identity and Employment Eligibility	List B Documents that Establish Identity	and	List C Documents that Establish Employment Eligibility
☐ 1. United States Passport ☐ 2. Certificate of United States Citizenship ☐ 3. Certificate of Naturalization ☐ 4. Unexpired foreign passport with attached Employment Authorization ☐ 5. Alien Registration Card with photograph	☐ 1. A State-issued driver's license or a State-issued I.D. card with a photograph, or information, including name, sex, date of birth, height, weight, and color of eyes. (Specify State)_____ ☐ 2. U.S. Military Card ☐ 3. Other (Specify document and issuing authority)		☐ 1. Original Social Security Number Card (other than a card stating it is not valid for employment) ☐ 2. A birth certificate issued by State, county, or municipal authority bearing a seal or other certification ☐ 3. Unexpired INS Employment Authorization Specify form #_____
Document Identification #_____ _Expiration Date (if any)_ _____	_Document Identification_ #_____ _Expiration Date (if any)_ _____		_Document Identification_ #_____ _Expiration Date (if any)_ _____

CERTIFICATION: I attest, under penalty of perjury, that I have examined the documents presented by the above individual, that they appear to be genuine and to relate to the individual named, and that the individual, to the best of my knowledge, is eligible to work in the United States.

Signature	Name (Print or Type)	Title
Employer Name	Address	Date

Form I-9 (05/07/87)
OMB No. 1115-0136

U.S. Department of Justice
Immigration and Naturalization Service

Figure 6-4
Immigration Reform and
Control Act of 1986

Common sense dictates that HRM find out as much as possible about its applicants before the final hiring decision is made. Failure to do so can have a detrimental effect on the organization, both in terms of cost and morale. But getting the needed information may be difficult, especially when there may be a question about invading one's privacy. In the past, many organizational policies stated that any request for information about a past employee be sent to HRM. There, HRM typically only verified employment dates and positions held. Why? Companies wanted to stay away from being sued by a previous employee, and simply verified "the facts." But that has changed.

Based on a concept of "qualified privilege," the courts have ruled that employers must be able to talk to one another about employees. And those discussions are legal and do not invade one's right to privacy so long as the discussion is a legitimate concern for the business. For example, had one McDonald's restaurant learned that one of its applicants had a history of child sexual assault, it might have been able to avert both the sexual assault of a 3-year-old in its restaurant, the embarrassment, and the $210,000 judgment against it.[30]

Physical/Medical Examination

The last step in this process may consist of having the applicant take a **medical/physical examination,** but only after a conditional job offer has been made. Remember, however, that in doing so a company must show that the reasoning behind this requirement is job-related. Physical exams can only be used as a selection device to screen out those individuals who are unable to physically comply with the requirements of a job. For example, firefighters are required to perform a variety of activities that require a certain physical condition. Whether it is climbing a ladder, lugging a four-inch water-filled hose, or carrying an injured victim, these individuals must demonstrate that they are fit for the job.

Aside from its use as a screening tool, there is another purpose for the physical exam: to show that minimum standards of health exist to enroll in company health and life insurance programs. Additionally, a company may use this exam to provide base data in case of an employee's future claim of injury on the job. This occurs, however, after one has been hired. In both cases, the exam is paid for by the employer.

One last event fits appropriately under medical examination: the drug test. As we mentioned in Chapter 4, increasingly more companies require applicants to submit to a drug test. Where in this process that test occurs is somewhat immaterial; the fact remains that failing an employment drug test may result in the rejection of an applicant.

Final Employment Decision

Those individuals who perform successfully in the preceding steps are now considered to be eligible to receive an offer of employment. Who makes that employment offer? The answer is, it depends. For administrative purposes (processing salary forms, maintaining EEO statistics, etc.), the offer typically is made by the human resource management department. But their role should be only administrative. The actual hiring decision should be made by the manager in the department where the vacancy exists. While this might not be the situation in all organizations, the manager of the department should have this authority. First, the applicant will eventually work for this manager and therefore a good "fit" between boss and employee is necessary. Second, if the decision made is not correct, the hiring manager has no one else to blame.

175
The Selection Process
●

Medical/Physical Examination
An examination indicating an applicant is physically fit for essential job performance.

If the organization selection process has been effective in differentiating between those individuals who will make successful employees and those who will not, the selection decision is now in the hands of the applicant. Is there anything management can do at this stage to increase the probability that the individual to whom an offer is made will accept? Assuming that the organization has not lost sight of the process of selection's dual objective—evaluation and a good fit—we can expect that the potential employee has a solid understanding of the job being offered and what it would be like to work for the organization. Yet it might be of interest at this point to review what we know about how people choose a job. This subject—job choice—represents selection from the perspective of the potential employee rather than the organization.

Research indicates that people gravitate toward jobs that are compatible with their personal orientation.[31] Individuals appear to move toward matching their work with their personality. Social individuals lean toward jobs in clinical psychology, foreign service, social work, and the like. Investigative individuals are compatible with jobs in biology, mathematics, and oceanography. Careers in management, law, and public relations appeal to enterprising individuals. This approach to the matching of people and jobs suggests that management can expect a greater proportion of acceptances if it has properly matched the candidate's personality to the job and to the organization, making the good fit.[32]

Not surprisingly, most job choice studies indicate that an individual's perception of the attractiveness of a company is important.[33] People want to work where their expectations are positive and where they believe their goals can be achieved. This, coupled with conclusions from previous research, should encourage management to ensure that those to whom offers are made can see that the job is compatible with their personality and goals.[34]

Before we leave this last step in the selection process—the final employment decision—we should ask, What about those applicants to whom we did not make an offer?[35] We believe that those involved in the selection process should carefully consider how rejected candidates are treated. What is communicated and how it is communicated will have a central bearing on the image that the rejected candidates will have of the organization. And that image may be carried for a lifetime. The young college graduate rejected for a position by a major computer manufacturer may a decade later be the influential decision maker for his or her current employer's computer purchases. The image formed many years earlier may play a key part in the decision. In this same vein, it was said that Richard Nixon never forgave FBI Director J. Edgar Hoover for the Bureau's rejection of Nixon's application following his graduation from law school.

The Comprehensive Approach

We have presented the general selection process as being comprised of multiple hurdles—beginning with a screening interview and culminating with a final selection decision. This discrete selection process is designed so that tripping over any hurdle puts one out of the race. This approach, however, may not be the most effective selection procedure for every job. If, for example, the application form shows that the candidate has only two years of relevant experience, but the job specification requires five, the candidate is rejected without going any further in the process. Yet, in many jobs, negative factors can be counterbalanced by positive factors. Poor performance on a written test, for example, may be offset by several years of relevant job experience. This suggests that sometimes it may be advantageous to do comprehensive rather than discrete selection. In **comprehensive selection,** all applicants are put through every step of the selection process, and the final decision is based on a comprehensive evaluation of the results from all stages.

The comprehensive approach overcomes the major disadvantage of the discrete method (eliminating potentially good employees simply because they receive an acceptable, but low evaluation at one selection step). The comprehensive method is more realistic. It recognizes that most applicants have weaknesses as well as strengths. But it is also more costly, since all applicants must go through all the screening hurdles. Additionally, the method consumes more of management's time and can demoralize many applicants by building up hope. Yet in those instances where many qualities are needed for success in the job, and where finding candidates who are strong on all qualities is unlikely, the comprehensive approach is probably preferable to the typical discrete method.

No matter which approach is used or which steps are involved, one critical aspect must be present: The devices used must measure job-related factors; that is, these devices must be able to indicate how one would perform on the job.

Comprehensive Selection Applying all steps in the selection process before rendering a decision about a job candidate.

Selection from an International Perspective

The selection criteria for international assignments are broader in scope than those for domestic selection. To illustrate the point, in addition to such factors as technical expertise and leadership ability, an international assignment requires greater attention to personality and especially to flexibility in the design. The individual must have an interest in working overseas and a talent for relating well to all kinds of people. The ability to relate to different cultures and environments, a sensitivity to different management styles, and a supportive family are often selection requirements.

Not surprisingly, many corporations consider personal factors of maturity and age, as well as the "family situation factor," far more important in their international assignments than in domestic placements. Although not all **expatriates** are married, many human resource managers believe that marital stability reduces a person's likelihood of returning home early and in many countries enhances the individual's social acceptability.

American women have been successful in the business world and it is unacceptable in our culture to discriminate on the basis of gender in employment, but organizations know that some Middle Eastern countries will not grant working papers to American women executives. On the other hand, in Asia, where common wisdom has held that women executives are less effective, the opposite has proven true! Although few Asian women are at or above middle-management levels, American women are often highly respected because they have risen to be experts in their fields. Thus, past reluctance to assign women to overseas positions where culture rather than law once made them rare is vanishing, and American women in Asia and Latin America are more common. Not only may the candidate's gender be considered, but also the social acceptability of single parents, unmarried partners, and blended families.

In addition, such personal factors as health, background, and education may be considered in international placements. In fact, the ideal candidate for many corporations is an older couple in good health, with no young children at home and a long and stable marital history. These are all factors that would play no role in domestic assignments.

When younger candidates are appropriate, many American corporations seek

Expatriates Individuals who work in a country in which they are not citizens of that country.

foreign students on U.S. university campuses who want to return to their home countries. These students provide a well-educated labor pool with experience in both their home and American cultures.

Key Elements for Successful Predictors

We are concerned with selection activities that can help us predict which applicants will perform satisfactorily on the job. In this section, we want to explore the concepts of reliability, validity, and cut scores. For illustration purposes, we will emphasize these elements as they relate to employment tests, but they are relevant to any selection device.

Reliability

Reliability A selection device's consistency of measurement.

For any predictor to be useful, the scores it generates must possess an acceptable level of **reliability** or consistency of measurement. This means that the applicant's performance on any given selection device should produce consistent scores each time the device is used. For example, if your height were measured every day with a wooden yardstick, you would get highly reliable results, but if you were measured daily by an elastic tape measure, there would probably be considerable disparity between your height measurements from one day to the next. Your height does not change from day to day—the variability is due to the unreliability of the measuring device.

Similarly, if an organization uses tests to provide input to the selection decision, the tests must give consistent results. If the test is reliable, any single individual's scores should remain fairly stable over time, assuming that the characteristic it is measuring is also stable. An individual's intelligence, for example, is generally a stable characteristic, and if we give applicants an IQ test, we should expect that someone who scores 110 in March would score close to 110 if tested again in July. If, in July, the same applicant scored 85, the reliability of the test would be highly questionable. On the other hand, if we were measuring something like an attitude or a mood, we would expect different scores on the measure, because attitudes and moods change.

Validity

Validity The proven relationship of a selection device to some relevant criterion.

High reliability may mean little if the selection device has low **validity**; that is, if the measures obtained are not related to some relevant criterion, such as job performance. For example, just because a test score is consistent is no indication that it is measuring important characteristics related to job behavior. It must also differentiate between satisfactory and unsatisfactory performance on the job. We should be aware of three specific types of validity: content, construct, and criterion-related.

Content Validity The degree to which the content of the test, as a sample, represents all the situations that could have been included (e.g., a typing test for a clerk typist).

Content Validity   **Content validity** is the degree to which the content of the test or questions about job tasks, as a sample, represents the situations on the job. All candidates for that job are given the same test or questions so applicants can be properly compared. A simple example of a content-valid test is a typing test for a word-processing position. Such a test can approximate the work to be done on the job; the applicant can be given a typical sample of typing, and his or her performance can be evaluated based on that sample. Assuming that the tasks on the test, or the questions about tasks, constitute an accurate sample of the tasks on the job (ordinarily a dubious assumption at best), the test is content valid.[36]

Construct Validity   **Construct validity** is the degree to which a test measures a particular trait related to successful performance on the job. These traits are usually abstract in nature, such as the measure of intelligence,[37] and are called constructs. Construct validity is complex and difficult. It takes the effort of a trained industrial psychologist—whom you would typically hire as a consultant should it become necessary—to do this. In fact, it is the most difficult type of validity to prove because you are dealing with constructs, or abstract measures.

Criterion-related Validity   **Criterion-related validity** is the degree to which a particular selection device accurately predicts the level of performance or important elements of work behavior. This validation strategy shows the relationship between some predictor (test score, for example) and a criterion, job performance (e.g., production output or managerial effectiveness). To establish criterion-related validity, either of two approaches can be used: **predictive validity** or **concurrent validity.**

To validate a test predictively, an organization would give the test (with an unknown validity) to all prospective applicants. The test scores would not be used at this time; rather, applicants would be hired as a result of successfully completing the entire selection process. At some prescribed date, usually at least a year after hired, the applicants' job performance would be evaluated by their supervisors. The ratings of the evaluations would then be compared with the initial test scores, which have been stored in a file over the period. At that time, an analysis would be conducted to see if there was any relationship between test scores (the predictors) and performance evaluation (the measure of success on the job, or the criterion). If no clear relationship exists, the test may have to be revised. However, if the organization can statistically show that the employees who scored below some pre-determined score, called a **cut score** (determined in the analysis) were unsuccessful performers, then management could appropriately state that any future applicants scoring below the cut score would be ineligible for employment. What happens to those unsuccessful performers? They are handled like any other employee who has experienced poor evaluations: training, transfer, discipline, or discharge.

The concurrent validity method validates tests using current employees as the subjects. These employees are asked to take a proposed selection test experimentally. Their scores are immediately analyzed, revealing a relationship between their test scores and existing performance appraisal data. Again, if there is a relationship between test scores and performance, then a valid test has been found.

Predictive validity is the preferred choice. Its advantage over concurrent validity is that it is demonstrated by using actual job applicants, whereas concurrent validity focuses on current employees. Both validation strategies are similar, with the exception of the people who are tested and the time that elapses between gathering of predictor and criterion information (see Figure 6-5).

While the costs associated with each method are drastically different, predictive validation strategies should be used if possible. Concurrent validity, although better than no validity at all, leaves many questions to be answered.[38] Its usefulness has been challenged on the premise that current employees know the jobs already and that a learning process takes place. Thus, there may be little similarity between the current employee and the applicant.

Construct Validity The degree to which a particular trait is related to successful performance on the job (e.g., IQ tests).

Criterion-related Validity The degree to which a particular selection device accurately predicts the important elements of work behavior (e.g., the relationship between a test score and job performance).

Predictive Validity Validating tests by using prospective applicants as the study group.

Concurrent Validity Validating tests by using current employees as the study group.

Cut Score A point at which applicants scoring below that point are rejected.

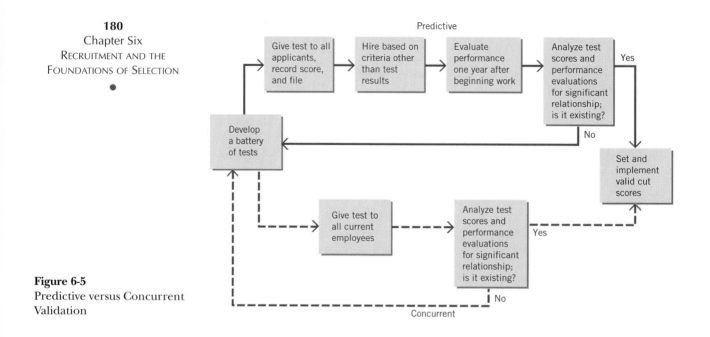

Figure 6-5
Predictive versus Concurrent
Validation

The Validity Analysis

Correlation Coefficients A statistical procedure showing the strength of the relationship between one's test score and job performance.

Correlation coefficients used to demonstrate the statistical relationships existing between an individual's test score and his or her job performance are called validity coefficients. The correlation analysis procedure can result in a coefficient ranging from -1 to $+1$ in magnitude. The closer the validity coefficient is to the extreme $(+1)$, the more accurate the test;[39] that is, the test is a good predictor of job performance. For example, Figure 6-6 contains two diagrams. In each diagram, we are trying to determine if a positive relationship exists between test scores and successful job performance.

In diagram A, there is no relationship. Statistically speaking, the score on the test bears no relationship between test score and performance. In this case, our

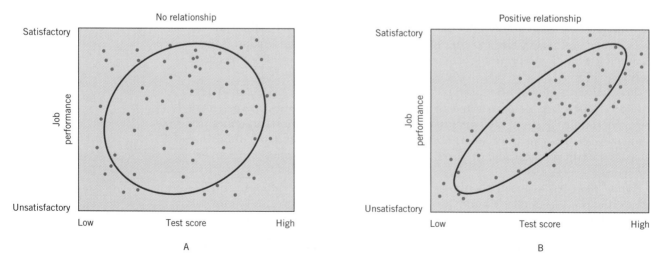

Figure 6-6 Validity Correlation Analysis

test is not valid. It does not help us distinguish between the successful and unsuccessful job performers. Diagram B reveals that there is a positive relationship between test scores and job performance. Those individuals scoring higher on the test have a greater probability of being successful in their jobs than those scoring lower. Based on this relationship, this test appears to be valid. When we have a valid test as determined by our correlation analysis, we are then able to identify the test score that distinguishes between successful and unsuccessful performers (the cut score) (see the experiential exercise).

Cut Scores and Their Impact on Hiring

In this discussion, we have been referring to test scores and their ability to predict successful job performance. By using our statistical analyses, we are able to generate a point at which applicants scoring below that point are rejected. We refer to this as a cut score.[40] However, existing conditions (e.g., availability of applicants) may cause an organization to change the cut score. If cut scores do change, what impact will this have on hiring applicants who will be successful on the job? Let us review again the positive relationship we found in our validity correlation analysis. We have reproduced the main elements in the graph in Figure 6-7.

Let us assume that after our analysis, we determined that our cut score should be 70. At this cut score, we have shown that the majority of the applicants who scored above 70 have a greater probability of being successful performers on the job; the majority scoring below 70, unsuccessful performers. If we change our cut score, however, we alter the number of applicants in these categories. For example, suppose the organization faces a "buyer's market" for

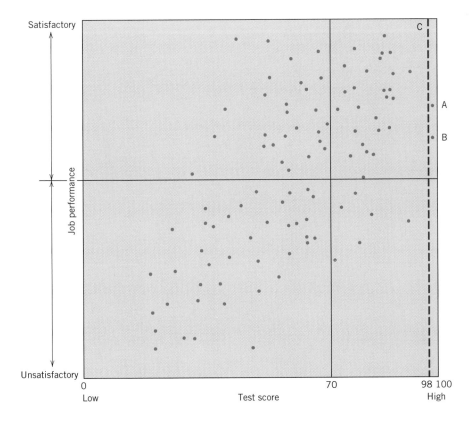

Figure 6-7
Validity Correlation Analysis after Cut Score is Raised

particular positions. Because of the many potential applicants, the organization can afford to be very selective. In a situation such as this, the organization may choose to hire only those applicants who meet the most extreme criteria. To achieve this goal, the organization increases its cut score to 98. By increasing the cut score from 70 to 98, the organization has rejected all but two candidates (areas A and B in Figure 6-7). However, many potentially successful job performers also would be rejected (individuals shown in area C). What has happened here is that the organization has become more selective and has put more faith in the test than is reasonable. If there were one hundred applicants and only two were hired, we could say that the selection ratio (the ratio of number hired to the number of applicants) is 2 percent. A 2 percent selection ratio means that the organization is very particular about who is hired.

Lowering the cut score also has an effect. Using the same diagram, let us lower our cut score to 50 and see what results. We have graphically portrayed this in Figure 6-8. By lowering the cut score from 70 to 50, we have increased our number of eligible hires who have a greater probability of being successful on the job (area D). At the same time, however, we have also made eligible more applicants who could be unsuccessful on the job (area E). Although using a hiring process where we know that more unsuccessful applicants may be hired seems not to make sense, conditions may necessitate the action. Labor market conditions may be such that there is a low supply of potential applicants who possess particular skills. For example, in some cities, finding a good computer modeler may be difficult. Because the supply is low, coupled with many openings, companies may hire individuals on the spot (more commonly referred to as an open-house recruiting effort). In this approach, the organization hires almost all the applicants who appear to have the skills needed (as reflected in a

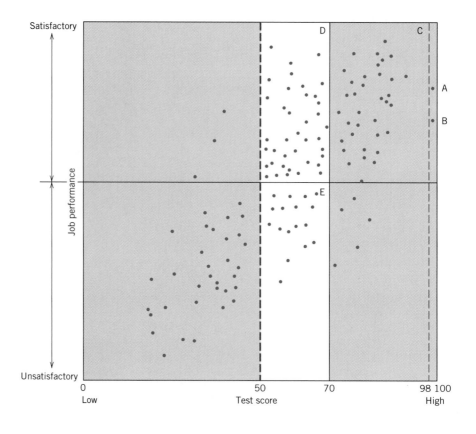

Figure 6-8
Validity Correlation Analysis
after Cut Score is Lowered

score of 50), putting them on the job, and filtering out the unsuccessful employees at a later date. While this may not appear to be effective, the organization is banking on the addition of individuals in area D of Figure 6-8.

Validity Generalization

In the late 1970s, two researchers published a model that was able to support a phenomenon called **validity generalization.**[41] Validity generalization refers to a situation where a test may be valid for screening applicants for a variety of jobs and performance factors across many occupations.[42] For example, the Department of Labor's General Aptitude Test (GATB) was shown to be valid for five hundred jobs studied in terms of the test's ability to predict job performance and training success irrespective of race.[43] What distinguishes validity generalization is its use of a statistical technique called meta-analysis. Through meta-analysis, researchers can determine correlations that may exist among numerous variables, and correct or adjust for any variances that may exist in predictor–criterion relationships.

Validity Generalization Statistically corrected test that is valid across many job categories.

Study Tools and Applications

Summary

This summary relates to the Learning Objectives provided on p. 156.
After having read this chapter, you should know:
1. Recruitment is the discovering of potential applicants for actual or anticipated organizational vacancies.
2. The two goals of recruiting are to generate a large pool of applicants from which to choose while simultaneously providing enough information for individuals to self-select out of the process.
3. Influences that constrain HRM in determining recruiting sources include image of the organization, attractiveness and nature of the job, internal policies, government requirements, and the recruiting budget.
4. The principal sources of recruiting employees include internal search, advertisements, employee referral/recommendations, employment agencies, temporary rental services, schools, colleges, universities, professional organizations, and casual or unsolicited applicants. As we move through the 1990s, employee leasing, temporary employees, and independent contractors are also providing a source of employees.
5. Proper selection can minimize the costs of replacement and training, reduce legal challenges, and result in a more productive work force.
6. The primary purpose of selection activities is to predict which job applicant will be successful if hired. During the selection process, candidates are also informed about the job and organization.
7. The discrete selection process would include the following: initial screening interview, completion of the application form, employment tests, comprehensive interview, background investigation, physical examination, and final employment decision.
8. There are three validation strategies. These are content, construct, and criterion-related validity.

9. Validity is determined either by discovering the extent to which a test represents actual job content, or through statistical analyses that show the test used relates to an important job-related trait, or to performance on the job.

10. Validity generalization refers to a process whereby tests are validated for numerous occupations through the use of meta-analysis.

Key Terms

accept errors	expatriates
advertisements	host-country national (HCN)
application form	independent contractors
background investigation	initial screening
blind-box ad	internal search
comprehensive interview	medical/physical examination
comprehensive selection	predictive validity
concurrent validity	private employment service
conditional job offer	professional organizations
constraints on recruiting efforts	public employment service
construct validity	qualified privilege
content validity	reject errors
correlation coefficients	reliability
criterion-related validity	selection process
cut score	temporary employees
differential validity	validity
employee leasing	validity generalization
employee referrals	walk-ins
executive search	

EXPERIENTIAL EXERCISE

Validating a Test

Determining validity is one of the most critical components in any selection process. To provide you with some idea of how it is done (and to give you an opportunity to apply an HRM Skill), below are presented test scores and performance ratings for forty individuals.[44] Conduct a correlation analysis using the statistical formulas that follow. Determine how strong a relationship exists between test and performance scores, and if a strong relationship exists, calculate the cut score. (Hint: You may wish to review correlation analysis in a statistics textbook. The basis for conducting the analysis is to perform the necessary calculations required in the formula. That is, you'll need to calculate the (ΣX); (ΣY); (ΣXY); $(\Sigma X)^2$; $(\Sigma Y)^2$; (ΣX^2); (ΣY^2); and N, which in this case is 40. From the data below, test scores = the X variables; Performance Scores = the Y variables.)

Applicant Number	Test Scores	Performance Score
1	170	75
2	150	52
3	164	50
4	158	60
5	156	75
6	155	70
7	172	80
8	164	75
9	183	85
10	188	82

11	192	90
12	187	80
13	120	50
14	116	50
15	128	60
16	138	40
17	144	70
18	110	55
19	156	60
20	161	70
21	165	77
22	145	52
23	167	54
24	159	65
25	166	77
26	145	70
27	175	86
28	162	73
29	187	88
30	190	84
31	191	89
32	177	80
33	130	53
34	126	50
35	138	64
36	131	44
37	154	72
38	109	51
39	166	62
40	160	75

The formula for correlation coefficient is:

$$r = \frac{N\Sigma Xy - (\Sigma X)(\Sigma y)}{\sqrt{(N\Sigma X^2 - (\Sigma X)^2)(N\Sigma y^2 - (\Sigma y)^2)}}$$

To determine a cut score, you need to find the slope of the line (b) and the intercept (a).

To find a: To find b:

$$a = \bar{y} - b\bar{x} \qquad b = \frac{N\Sigma Xy - (\Sigma X)(\Sigma y)}{N\Sigma X^2 - (\Sigma X)^2}$$

After finding a and b, calculate the cut score as follows:

$$y = a + bx$$

where $y = 70 =$ satisfactory performance; solve for x, the cut score.

CASE APPLICATION:

Motorola Recruits Internationally

Recruiters often face an unenviable position. They are on the front line trying to locate qualified candidates to fill job openings in the company. In many cases, their success is measured by how well they meet their recruiting goals— or staff the positions that are being recruited for.

In difficult economic times, as we experienced over the past several years, not many jobs were open. In fact, a good number of organizations went the opposite way—eliminating people from the company. In some cases, this elimination hit HRM, especially the recruiters, who were not as readily needed as when an organization gears up for a hiring frenzy. But the past couple of years has witnessed a turnaround. That is, recruiters are more active now, and are attempting to fill very specialized positions that are necessary for the organization to meet its strategic goals. So you'd think recruiters would be having a field day—open positions, and a hungry, plentiful work-force applicant pool. But what if no one is applying? That's exactly what Bill O'Neill must have asked himself.[45]

Working for Motorola as its foreign staff director, Bill was responsible for recruiting highly talented engineers. But to do so, he had to compete directly with Japanese firms for the same quality talent. He advertised extensively, but to no avail. His advertisements simply didn't pay off. No matter what Bill did, it seemed to generate an applicant pool of "second-best" candidates. So Bill O'Neill decided to change the odds to his favor. He began placing company recruiting ads on aluminum cans in an attempt to be different, and make Motorola stand out. And did he score, for shortly after the ads hit the streets, more than 5,000 good applications were received.

Questions:

1. Describe what factors may have been effecting Motorola's efforts to generate a large quality pool of applicants.
2. Why do you think Bill O'Neill's advertisements on aluminum cans generated so many responses when typical newspaper advertisements didn't?
3. What lessons are there in this case that can apply to all recruiters, no matter where they are located or for what type of positions they attempt to fill?

Testing Your Understanding

How well did you fulfill the learning objectives?

1. Recruiting efforts are usually lighter in organizations
   a. that are large, rather than small.
   b. that are growing, rather than declining.
   c. that have poor, rather than good, compensation packages.
   d. that have good, rather than poor, working conditions.
   e. that are service, rather than public, sector.
2. Which of the following indicates effective recruiting efforts for a director of recruiting for a large corporation?
   a. Recruiting costs have increased 8 percent during the last two years.
   b. The applicant pool is increasing in size.
   c. The Director of Recruiting's secretary spends three times as much time acknowledging ad responses from underqualified applicants as she did a year ago.
   d. The director of recruiting's secretary spends less than one-third of the time acknowledging ad responses from underqualified applicants as she did a year ago.
   e. The applicant pool is becoming global.

3. The director of recruiting at a medium-sized East Coast manufacturer, is unable to hire the best people for her company because of a new restriction that no longer pays airfare for college recruiters. Therefore, her staff is limited to going to college job fairs within a 150-mile radius of the company. What one of the following recruiting constraints is most affecting her organization?
   a. Organizational image.
   b. Job unattractiveness.
   c. Internal organizational politics.
   d. Government's influence.
   e. Costs.
4. Bob needs to hire two managers for a Pittsburgh paint manufacturing plant by the end of the year. His organization is under pressure to have females and minorities better represented at top levels of the organization. Currently, all executives are white and male. What recruiting technique should he use?
   a. Employee referrals.
   b. Public employment agencies.
   c. Headhunters.
   d. College placement centers.
   e. Walk-in.

5. A manager of human resources of a small accounting firm needs 2,000 extra person hours of work during the first two weeks of every April for data entry and word processing. What is the manager's best recruiting alternative?
   a. Independent contractors.
   b. Professional organizations.
   c. Employee leasing.
   d. College placement centers.
   e. Temporary help.

6. Which of the following is the most successful selection outcome for the XYZ organization?
   a. Ann was hired by XYZ, but she was unable to perform the job.
   b. Amy was hired by XYZ, but she was bored and left after three weeks.
   c. Andrea was hired by XYZ, and she quit the firm two months later for a better offer.
   d. Angela was not hired by XYZ, but she got an equivalent job with another firm (where she has done very well).
   e. Arnie was not hired by XYZ, and could not get an equivalent job anywhere else in town.

7. A director of recruiting for a large U.S.-based global corporation is looking for a country manager for a newly acquired South American affiliate. Her best choice, to minimize language, culture, and family problems is a
   a. home-country national.
   b. host-country national.
   c. local expatriate.
   d. third-country national.
   e. new foreign subsidiary.

8. Don, director of international staffing for a large U.S.-based manufacturing firm, needs to hire a production manager for an Asian country. He should make all of the following considerations except
   a. an Asian female would not be a likely candidate, being regarded as less effective.
   b. a married employee will be less acceptable than a single one.
   c. health requirements for this assignment are more important than for a domestic assignment.
   d. prior experience in Hong Kong and other Pacific Rim countries would be a plus.
   e. an American female would be highly respected and regarded as an expert in her field.

9. Julie, vice-president of human resources for a large manufacturing firm, is concerned that 40 percent of the clerical workers hired last year lacked basic reading, writing, and filing skills. She thinks these workers should have been eliminated from the applicant pool, as early as the _____ step of the selection process.
   a. application forms
   b. physical examination

c. comprehensive interview
   d. employment tests
   e. background investigation

10. Jan runs an employment agency that provides experienced secretarial help. She gives typing tests to job candidates to make sure they can type as part of the selection process. This test is an example of
   a. content validity.   b. reliability.
   c. construct validity.   d. differential validity.
   e. predictive validity.

11. Ruth runs an employment agency that provides experienced secretarial help. She gives typing tests to applicants during the selection process, but she does not hire based on these scores. She compares these test scores to their performance evaluations six months after employment. What is Ruth doing?
   a. Establishing reliability.
   b. Establishing content validity.
   c. Using cut scores.
   d. Establishing predictive validity.
   e. Decontextualizing construct validity.

12. Mariah is selection manager for a large manufacturing organization. The machinists test has a validity coefficient of .75. Scores typically run evenly from 0 to 100 with 50 as the average. Mariah expects 1,000 employees in this year's applicant pool to fill 75 openings. What cut score is appropriate?
   a. 750.   b. 90.
   c. 100.   d. 50.
   e. She should interview all the applicants.

13. In the recruiting process, positive self-removal happens when
   a. human resources gets out of the hiring loop. Working divisions advertise for and interview their own job candidates.
   b. there is a streamlined human resources office arrangement. Candidates can escort themselves out, thus reducing the need for receptionists and security personnel.
   c. all applicants are encouraged to apply for jobs.
   d. unqualified applicants do not apply for jobs.
   e. women and minority applicants are discouraged and do not apply for jobs.

14. How does the selection process differ when hiring for international versus domestic positions?
   a. There is no difference.
   b. Married employees are preferred for domestic employment. Single employees are preferred for international assignments.
   c. Personality is more important for international assignments. Technical expertise is more important for domestic employment.
   d. Gender discrimination is not allowed in domestic or international situations.
   e. Age discrimination is not allowed in domestic or international situations.

Chapter Seven

SELECTION DEVICES

Which organization would you guess has one of the best selection procedures in corporate America? Southwest Airlines, Toyota Motor Corporation, Wal-Mart? Undoubtedly theirs are good, but the distinction of having the best belongs to Gates Rubber Plant in Siloam Springs, Arkansas.[1]

For several years, Gates Rubber experienced every organization's greatest recruiting nightmare. They simply hired incorrectly. Not having a thorough screening process meant that many of the new hires were, well, as Plant Manager Burt Hoefs explained, incompetent. As a result, the plant suffered. An inordinate number of mistakes were made, which affected the quality of products produced. Workers were being injured too frequently, which left the company short-staffed. Consequently, overtime costs soared in order to meet production schedules. Employee satisfaction was at an all-time low, which led to an increase in work slowdowns and greater turnover of "good" employees. Gates Rubber was in trouble, and it needed to fix its problems. The poison arrow pointed directly to the selection procedures. Hiring new employees required a major overhaul.

To correct the poor hiring decision being made by members of the plant's personnel department, Hoefs and a team of employees redesigned the process. Now, each applicant goes through four stages before they can proudly claim that they've gotten a job at Gates. The first two steps involve personnel. One recruiter interviews a prospective candidate. Then, three days later, a second recruiter conducts a similar interview. The two recruiters then meet to see if their independent evaluations of the candidate agree. Applicants who receive two favorable evaluations go on to stage three.

In this third step, each candidate is interviewed by a panel of three people, one of whom is Hoefs. These individuals focus their interview on an applicant's skills, work attitudes, confidence levels, communication skills, and "fit" into a team environment. If approved by the panel, personnel then conducts an extensive background investigation. Once cleared, the candidate is now ready for stage four.

For many companies, this fourth step may appear peculiar. At this stage, applicants and their guest (spouses or significant others) are invited to attend a two-hour "orientation of the organization" with Hoefs and two Gates employees. During this meeting, applicants are provided with a history of the company, information about the benefits package offered, and explanation of the organization's culture. Sound benign? When you realize that applicants and their guests are being closely watched, this orientation actually serves a vital purpose. For example, Gates requires all employees to work periodic night shifts, and they expect a high level of commitment to the organization from its employees. As applicants and their guests hear of what the plant expects, the panel looks for some response. If there appears to be any conflict between applicant and guest over job expectations, the applicant is not offered the job! Why? As Hoefs ex-

Who holds the distinction of having the best selection process in Corporate America? It's Gates Rubber Plant in Siloam Springs, Arkansas. Their intensive four-stage process has cut turnover, increased quality, and reduced work-related injuries.

plains, this "is designed to bring to light the kinds of problems that usually surface only after someone is hired,"[2] especially problems that begin at home.

Over the past several years, Gates's grueling hiring process has produced significant results. Their turnover rate is down to 8 percent annually; quite an advantage when you consider Gates's biggest competitor in town experiences 100 percent turnover each year. And the problems with quality, injuries, and the like? They've all but disappeared, now that the company is properly matching people to the jobs.

Introduction

As we noted in Chapter 6, the selection process is comprised of a number of steps. Each of these steps provides managers with information that will help them predict whether an applicant will prove to be a successful job performer. One way to conceptualize this is to think of each step as a higher hurdle in a race. The applicant able to clear all the hurdles wins the race—victory being the receipt of a job offer.

The selection steps presented in Chapter 6 attempt to make predictions based on either evaluating the past or sampling the present. The application form, background investigation, and comprehensive interview attempt to find out what the applicant has done in the past and then to project these past experiences and accomplishments into the future. You should be aware that this method of prediction implies certain assumptions concerning the relationship of the past to the future. Specifically, it assumes that a candidate's past behavior can be a guide for predicting future behavior, and that the candidate will remain the same person in the future that he or she was in the past. While these assumptions may be accurate and this approach satisfactory, it appears that devices like job-related tests, where relevant, may also be good predictors because they sample present behavior in order to predict future behavior.

It is logical that selection devices that simulate actual work behavior and are as current as possible should stand the best chance for being good predictors. But is this true in practice? In the following pages, we will review the devices discussed in Chapter 6. Since each of these devices is a potential "tool" in the selector's "tool kit," and using several in combination often is best, we want to look carefully at each in the context of how good a tool it is, and under what conditions it should be used.

The Application Form

The Civil Rights Acts of 1964 and 1991 and subsequent amendments, executive orders, court rulings, and other legislation have made it illegal to discriminate on the basis of sex, race, color, religion, national origin, disability, and age. The only major exceptions to these guidelines involving age, gender, and religion are cases where it can be shown that these criteria are bona fide occupational qualifications (BFOQ).

Many of the items that traditionally appeared on the **application form**—religion, age, marital status, occupation of spouse, number and ages of children, hobbies—may have been interesting to know, but often could not be proved to be job-related. Given this reality, it should not be surprising to find different application forms now (see Figure 7-1). Since the onus is on management to demonstrate that information supplied by applicants is job-related, items that cannot be demonstrated to be job-related should be omitted.

In addition to these changes being made, one important aspect has been added. Note the statement at the bottom of Figure 7-2. Such statements serve a vital purpose, among them giving the employer the right to dismiss an employee for falsifying information. Furthermore, the applicant is giving the company permission to obtain previous work history. Additionally, note how the publisher John Wiley & Sons addresses employment-at-will: "Please note that if you are offered and accept a position with John Wiley & Sons, Inc., your employment is 'at-will' and may be terminated by you or the company at any time with or without cause or prior notice." Of course, an applicant has the right not to sign the application. In that event, however, one's application is removed from consideration.

The fact that application forms have had to be revised should not be interpreted as an indictment of the application form as an effective predictor. Such is not the case; in fact, evidence indicates that hard and relevant biographical data on the application that can be verified—for example, rank in high-school graduating class—may be a more valid measure of potential job performance than many of the intelligence, aptitude, interest, and personality items that traditionally have been used in the selection decision.[3] Additionally, when application form items have been appropriately weighted to reflect job relatedness, we find that the application can successfully predict performance criteria for such diverse groups as salesclerks, engineers, factory workers, district managers, clerical employees, draftspersons, and army officers.[4] A review of studies using biographical data acquired from the application form found a number of items that successfully predicted differences between short-tenure and long-tenure employees.[5] Let's look at how these are used.

The Weighted Application Form

The **weighted application form** appears to offer excellent potential in helping recruiters to differentiate between potentially successful and unsuccessful

Application Form Company-specific employment forms used to generate specific information the company wants.

Weighted Application Form A special type of application form where relevant applicant information is used to determine the likelihood of job success.

Figure 7-1
Pre-Employment Questions and EEO Guidelines

Pre-Employment Questions within Equal Employment Opportunity	Subject	Pre-Employment Questions that may not be within Equal Employment Opportunity Guidelines
Have you ever worked for this company under a different name? Is any additional information relative to name change, use of assumed name, or nickname, necessary to enable a check on your work record? If yes, explain.	Name	Your original name if it has been changed by court order or otherwise. If you have ever worked under another name, state name and dates. Maiden name or Miss, Ms, Mrs.
What is your address? How long have you been a resident of this state or city?	Address	Do you own your own home or rent a house or apartment?
	Race or color	Race, color, ethnic origin, religious affiliation.
	Birthplace	Birthplace of applicant, parents, spouse, or other close relatives.
Will your observed sabbath and religious holidays create a conflict relative to the established work week?	Religion	Your religious denomination, affiliations, or religious holidays observed. An applicant may not be told, "This is a (Catholic, Protestant, or Jewish) organization."
	National origin	Your lineage, ancestry, national origin, descent, parentage, or nationality. Nationality of parents or spouse. What is your native language?
	Sex	Question unlawful unless job related (ex: restroom or locker room attendant)
Marital status information for insurance purposes should only be requested after individual is hired.	Marital status	Are you married? Where does your spouse work? How old are your children? Have you arranged for day care?
Are you over the age of 18? If not, state your age. Can ask for proof after hiring.	Age	How old are you? What is the date of your birth?
Do you have any impairments, physical or mental, which would interfere with your ability to perform the job for which you have applied? If there are any positions for which you should not be considered or job duties you cannot perform, please explain.	Disabilities	Do you have a disability? Have you ever been treated for any of the following diseases? Has any member of your family ever had any of the following diseases? (List questions about emotional maturity and stability.)
May be required after hiring for identification purposes.	Photograph	Attach a photograph to the employment form before hiring. Have pictures taken during interview.

job performers. To create such an instrument, individual form items—such as number of years of schooling, number of months on last job, salary data for all previous jobs, and military experience—are validated against performance and turnover measures and given appropriate weights. Let's assume, for example, that management is interested in developing a weighted applicant form that would predict which applicants for the job of accountant, if hired, would stay with the company. They would select from their files the application forms from each of two groups of previously hired accountants—one, a group that had short tenure with the organization (adjusters who stayed, say, less than one year), and the other, a group with long tenure (say, five years or more). These

EMPLOYMENT APPLICATION

DATE _____

PERSONAL

NAME (Last, First, Middle Initial)	HOME PHONE ( )	BUSINESS PHONE ( )
PRESENT ADDRESS (No., Street, Apt. No.)	(City, State & Zip)	

U.S. CITIZEN? ☐ YES ☐ NO | IF NO, ARE YOU AUTHORIZED TO WORK IN THE U.S.? _____ | VISA STATUS | SOCIAL SECURITY NUMBER

IF YOU ARE UNDER 18, AND WE EMPLOY YOU, CAN YOU FURNISH A WORK PERMIT ? ☐ YES ☐ NO

Have you ever been convicted of or pleaded guilty to commission of a felony in the past 7 years? ☐ YES ☐ NO

If yes, list the court involved unless the record has been sealed. _____

City _____ State _____ Year _____

(Criminal convictions do not automatically disqualify applicants for employment.)

HAVE YOU EVER WORKED FOR OR APPLIED FOR A POSITION WITH JOHN WILEY & SONS, INC? ☐ YES ☐ NO | IF YES, SPECIFY DATES.

ARE ANY RELATIVES OR FRIENDS EMPLOYED BY JOHN WILEY & SONS, INC. ? | IF SO, NAME(s)

HOW WERE YOU REFERRED TO JOHN WILEY & SONS, INC?	POSITION FOR WHICH YOU ARE APPLYING	
		☐ FULL TIME ☐ PART TIME ☐ TEMPORARY
WILL YOU WORK OVERTIME? ☐ YES ☐ NO	MINIMUM SALARY REQUIREMENT	DATE AVAILABLE TO BEGIN WORK

In consideration of John Wiley & Sons, Inc.'s review and evaluation of my application for employment I represent and agree to the following:

• The answers to the questions and information provided by me in this application are true.

• John Wiley & Sons, Inc., may investigate my background, and I authorize all persons and organizations, including schools and law enforcement agencies, to furnish to John Wiley & Sons, Inc., any information concerning me which may be relevant to my employment by John Wiley & Sons, Inc., and release any person or organization furnishing such information from liability for providing same.

• Submission of false information on this application may result in immediate termination of my employment by John Wiley & Sons, Inc., if I am employed by John Wiley & Sons, Inc., or disqualify me from eligibility for employment.

Please note that if you are offered and accept a position with John Wiley & Sons, Inc., your employment is "at-will" and may be terminated by you or the Company at any time with or without cause or prior notice.

SIGNATURE _____ DATE _____

Figure 7-2
Sample Application Form

old application forms would be screened item by item to determine how employees in each group responded. In this way, management would discover items that differentiate the groups. These items would then be weighted relative to how well they differentiate applicants. If, for example, 80 percent of the long-tenure group had a college degree, the possession of a college degree might be given a weight of 4. But if 30 percent of the long-tenure group had prior experience in a Big 6 accounting firm, while 20 percent of the short-tenure did, this item might be given a weight of only 1. Note, of course, that this procedure would have to be done for every job in the organization, and balanced against the factors of those that do not fall into the majority category; that is, while 80 percent of the long-tenure individuals had a college degree, we would need to factor into our weighing scheme those who had a college degree and were successful on the job, but only had short tenure with the company (see "Meet Lisa Staras").

Items that predict long tenure for an accountant might be totally different from items that predict long tenure for an engineer or even an financial analyst. However, with the continued improvement in sophisticated computer software, the task of developing the application for each job may be more manageable.[6]

A Successful Application

The application form, as noted earlier, has had wide success in selection for a number of diverse jobs. For instance, in various positions in the hotel industry, analysis of the application form has been valuable. In one study, it was found

Meet

Lisa Staras
Senior Employment and
Employee Relations Specialist

Lisa Staras is the senior employment and employee relations specialist for John Wiley & Sons, Inc., where she is responsible for sourcing and recruiting high-caliber candidates in a timely, cost-effective, and efficient manner; developing and implementing programs to reduce chronic voluntary and involuntary turnover; counseling employees and managers on performance issues, grievances, and complaints; and promoting diversity through development and implementation of programs designed to attract and retain qualified individuals in protected classes. Prior to working at John Wiley, Lisa was the employment representative for American Express Travel Related Services. She has a bachelor's degree from Rutgers University and a master's degree in Industrial and Labor Relations from Cornell University.

Lisa works with hiring managers at John Wiley to determine the selection criteria necessary to fill an open position—outlining an employee's responsibilities, clarifying expected accomplishments, identifying coworkers, explaining how the job fits the overall department objectives, and identifying the necessary work experience and educational background that a candidate must have. During the interviewing process, Lisa must determine the "can-do," the "will-do," and the "fit" of an applicant. Does the applicant have the necessary capabilities and motivational and behavioral characteristics, as well as the values, style, and personality that will mesh with the company culture and the specific employees in the department?

Lisa believes that making the right match between a candidate and an open position is one of many key factors in a company's success. When a recruitment search is handled thoroughly and methodically, many future problems can be avoided. A "poor hire" can result in a costly, time-consuming problem for an organization that can affect the overall productivity and efficiency of an organization. Lisa also believes in giving candidates a realistic job preview. It is important to convey to an applicant during the interviewing process that the work might be routine or the manager might be very demanding, if that is the case. This enables an applicant to know both the positives and the negatives of a position going into the job.

that seven items on the application were highly predictive of successful performance as measured by job tenure.[7]

Evidence that the application form provides relevant information for predicting job success is well supported across a broad range of jobs. Care must be taken to ensure that application items are validated for each job. Also, since the predictive ability of items may change over time, the items must be continuously reviewed and updated. Finally, management should be aware of the possibility that the application information given is erroneous. A background investigation can verify most of the data.

Employment Tests Any selection examination that is designed to determine if an applicant is qualified for the job.

Employment Tests

In this section, we want to look at **employment tests**—the better-known written tests that attempt to assess intelligence, abilities, and personality traits, as well as

194

the lesser-known performance simulation tests, including work sampling and the tests administered at assessment centers. In addition, we will look at and evaluate the validity of polygraph tests and handwriting analysis as selection devices, and will see how the use of tests may be different in a global environment.

Written Tests

We noted in Chapter 6 that **written tests** historically have served as significant input into the selection decision. And although there was a hiatus after the *Griggs* v. *Duke Power* decision in the mid-1970s, a number of companies recognized that testing served a vital purpose. There has been renewed interest in written tests, since those that have been validated can aid significantly in the acquisition of efficient and effective workers. However, let us remind you that the company has the sole responsibility for demonstrating that tests used for hiring or promotion are related to job performance (see "The Bell Curve Controversy").

There are literally hundreds of tests that can be used by organizations as selection tools.[8] One can use tests that measure intellect, spatial ability, perception skills, mechanical comprehension, motor ability, and personality traits. It is not the purpose of this text to review each of these test categories; that is the province of books on applied industrial psychology.[9]

Written Tests An organizational selection tool designed to indicate whether an applicant will be successful on the job if hired.

Performance Simulation Tests

To avoid criticism and potential liability that may result from the use of psychological, aptitude, and other types of written tests, there has been increasing interest in the use of **performance simulation tests.** The single identifying characteristic of these tests is that they require the applicant to engage in specific behaviors necessary for doing the job successfully. In contrast to the types of tests discussed above, performance simulation tests should more easily meet the requirement of job-relatedness because they are made up of actual job behaviors rather than surrogates.

Performance Simulation Tests Work sampling and assessment centers focusing on actual job activities.

Work Sampling **Work sampling** is an effort to create a miniature replica of a job. Applicants demonstrate that they possess the necessary talents by actually doing the tasks. By carefully devising work samples based on job analysis data, the knowledge, skills, and abilities needed for each job are determined. Then each work sample element is matched with a corresponding job performance element. For example, a work sample for a bank teller at NationsBank involving computation on a calculator would require the applicant to make similar computations. Ever wonder how a check-out clerk at Home Depot is screened for a job to scan the prices of your purchases quickly and accurately? Most go through a similar work-sampling session where supervisors demonstrate how to scan accurately, ensuring that the product did indeed ring up. Then the candidate is given an opportunity to show that he or she can handle the job. Work sampling, then, reflects actual "hands-on" experience.

Work Sampling A selection device requiring the job applicant to actually perform a small segment of the job.

The advantages of work sampling over traditional pencil-and-paper tests are obvious. Because content is essentially identical to job content, work sampling should be a better predictor of short-term performance and should minimize discrimination.[10] Additionally, because of the nature of their content and the methods used to determine content, well-constructed work sample tests should easily meet EEOC content validity requirements.[11] The main disadvantage is the difficulty in developing good work samples for each job. Furthermore, work

The Bell Curve Controversy:

The Case for IQ Tests in Employee Selection

It was undoubtedly the most controversial social-science book published during the first half of the 1990s. *The Bell Curve,* by Richard Herrnstein and Charles Murray, presents evidence that IQ, not education or opportunity, is the key factor determining where a person ends up on the American social scale. Importantly, the evidence they offered to support this point was not the reason for the book's controversy. What stirred up most reviewers, scientists, politicians, and journalists was the authors' claim that economic inequalities between racial groups are related to differences in average IQ levels between different races. But we're only interested in that segment of their work that relates to the issue of IQ and job performance.

Herrnstein and Murray began by making six statements that they categorize as "beyond significant technical dispute":

1. There is such a thing as a general factor of cognitive ability on which human beings differ.
2. All standardized tests of academic aptitude or achievement measure this general factor to some degree, but IQ tests expressly designed for that purpose measure it most accurately.
3. IQ scores closely match whatever it is that people mean when they use the word *intelligent* or *smart* in ordinary language.
4. IQ scores are stable, although not perfectly so, over much of a person's life.
5. Properly administered IQ tests are not demonstrably biased against social, economic, ethnic, or racial groups.
6. A substantial portion of cognitive ability (no less than 40 percent and no more than 80 percent) is inherited through genes.

Using these six points as a foundation, the authors argue forcibly that IQ is a powerful predictor of job performance. Or to use their terms, "a smarter employee is, on average, a more proficient employee."

According to Herrnstein and Murray, all jobs require cognitive ability. This is relatively self-evident in professional occupations such as accountants, engineers, scientists, architects, and physicians. But it's also true for semi-skilled blue-collar jobs and holds, although weakly, even among people in unskilled manual jobs. For instance, they point out that there are better and worse busboys in restaurants. The really good busboy uses his intelligence to solve job-related problems, and the higher his intelligence the more quickly he comes up with solutions and can call on them when appropriate. But as jobs become more complex, IQ becomes more important in determining performance. And this advantage holds over time. Work experience doesn't significantly close the gap. "The cost of hiring less intelligent workers may last as long as they stay on the job."

The authors demonstrate that an IQ score is a better predictor of job performance than any other single criterion—better than a job interview, reference check, or college transcript. They claim that "an employer that is free to pick among applicants can realize large economic gains from hiring those

(continued)

(continued)

with the highest IQs." Current laws in the United States, however, limit the use of intelligence tests as single hiring predictors. Employers must demonstrate that any test they use is job-relevant and the courts have generally been critical of IQ tests on this dimension. Nevertheless, Herrnstein and Murray state that biographical data, reference checks, college transcripts are "valid predictors of job performance in part because they imperfectly reflect something about the applicant's intelligence. Employers who are forbidden to obtain test scores nonetheless strive to obtain the best possible work force, and it happens that the way to get the best possible work force, other things equal, is to hire the smartest people they can find."

Source: Richard J. Herrnstein and Charles Murray, *The Bell Curve: Intelligence and Class Structure in American Life* (New York: The Free Press, 1994).

sampling is not applicable to all levels of the organization. It is often difficult to use for managerial jobs because it is hard to create a work sample test that can address the full range of managerial activities. In the following section, we will look at a type of performance simulation test that is more directly related to mid-level managerial positions.

Assessment Centers A more elaborate set of performance simulation tests, specifically designed to evaluate a candidate's managerial potential, is administered in **assessment centers.** Assessment centers use procedures that incorporate group and individual exercises. Applicants go through a series of these exercises and are appraised by line executives, practicing supervisors, and/or trained psychologists as to how well they perform. As with work sampling, because these exercises are designed to simulate the work that managers actually do, they tend to be accurate predictors of later job performance. In some cases, however, the assessment center also includes traditional personality and aptitude tests.

Assessment Centers A facility where performance simulation tests are administered. These are made up of a series of exercises and are used for selection, development, and performance appraisals.

How are applicants for cashiers at Home Depot screened to determine if they can properly scan customer purchases? They are put through a work sampling test to determine if they can accurately and effectively do the job.

How does an assessment center work? Essentially, the procedure goes something like this:[12]

1. A small group of applicants come to the assessment center.
2. The assessment center has approximately six to eight assessors, some of whom are trained psychologists, while others are managers at least two levels above the individual being assessed, who have been trained as assessors.
3. For about two to four days, the assessees are asked to participate in exercises such as:
   a. Interviews
   b. "In-basket" exercises, where applicants solve day-to-day problems that managers might find in their in-baskets
   c. Case exercises
   d. Leaderless group discussions
   e. Business games
   f. Personality tests
   g. General ability tests
4. Assessors, usually in pairs, observe and record the behavior of applicants in group and individual situational problems. A clinical psychologist summarizes the personality tests.
5. Each assessee is rated on twenty to twenty-five characteristics (such as organization and planning, decision making, creativity, resistance to stress, and oral communication skills).
6. A judgment is made about the assessee's potential for meeting the job requirements.

Assessment centers typically operate as described in Figure 7-3. Evidence supporting the effectiveness of assessment centers is impressive. They have consistently demonstrated results that predict later job performance in professional positions like sales, as well as lower- to mid-level management positions.[13] Even when the costs of conducting assessment center evaluations are taken into account—training of assessors, consultant fees, time away from the job, purchase of tests and exercises, and so on—the payoffs in terms of more effective selection are usually more than justified.[14] For instance, AT&T has assessed thousands of employees in its management development center and has found the center to be very effective in indicating which individuals would be successful on jobs that provide greater responsibility and accountability.[15]

One note of caution has been offered concerning the impressive and consistent results from assessment center selection. It has been proposed that the measures of job performance may be contaminated.[16] Assessment center results may not be valid because they generally use the success measures of promotions and salary increases as determinants of "job performance." Given that promotions and salary increases may not be based solely on performance, assessment evaluators will come up with effective results if they know what factors senior management actually uses to make advancement and salary increment decisions. Accordingly, assessors may not be evaluating true performance, but such nonperformance-related factors as the candidate's social skills, likability, "proper" background, appearance, or attitude. For instance, assessors who correctly realize that upper-level managers like and tend to promote "yes types" and conformists may unintentionally assess candidates for these traits. Whenever assessment center ratings and success measures contain a common component unrelated to job performance, the results will be contaminated and the validity of the procedure questionable.

Other Tests

Two other tests—graphology (handwriting analysis) and polygraph (lie detector) and honesty tests—receive a disproportionate amount of media atten-

Figure 7-3
An Example of an Assessment Agenda

199
Employment Tests
●

Day 1

Orientation Meeting

Management Game: "Conglomerate" Forming different types of conglomerates is the goal, with four-person teams bartering companies to achieve their planned result. Teams set their own acquisition objectives and must plan and organize to meet them.

Background Interview A 90-minute interview conducted by an assessor.

Group Discussion: "Management Problems" Short cases calling for various forms of management judgment are presented to groups of four. In one hour the group, acting as consultants, must resolve the cases and submit its recommendation in writing.

Individual Fact-finding and Decision-making Exercises: "The Research Budget" The participants are told that they have just taken over as division manager. They are given a brief description of an incident in which their predecessor has recently turned down a request for funds to continue a research project. The research director is appealing for a reversal of the decision. The participants are given fifteen minutes to ask questions to dig out the facts in the case. Following this fact-finding period, they must present their decisions orally with supporting reasoning and defend it under challenge.

Day 2

In-basket Exercise: "Section Manager's In-basket" The contents of a section manager's in-basket are simulated. The participants are instructed to go through the contents, solving problems, answering questions, delegating, organizing, scheduling, and planning, just as they might do if they were promoted suddenly to the position. An assessor reviews the contents of the completed in-basket and conducts a one-hour interview with each participant to gain further information.

Assigned Role Leaderless Group Discussion: "Compensation Committee" The Compensation Committee is meeting to allocate $8,000 in discretionary salary increases among six supervisory and managerial employees. Each member of the committee (participant) represents a department of the company and is instructed to "do the best they can" for the employee from their department.

Analysis, Presentation, and Group Discussion: "The Pretzel Factory" This financial analysis problem has the participant role-play a consultant called in to advise Carl Flowers of the C.F Pretzel Company on two problems: what to do about a division of the company that has continually lost money, and whether the corporation should expand. Participants are given data on the company and are asked to recommend appropriate courses of action. They make their recommendation in a seven-minute presentation after which they are formed into a group to come up with a single set of recommendations.

Days 3 and 4

Assessors meet to share their observations on each participant and to arrive at summary evaluations relative to each dimension sought and overall potential.

Source: Reprinted from the *Training and Developmental Journal.* Copyright December 1971, the American Society for Training and Development. Reprinted with permission. All right reserved.

tion. Because of this attention, and the controversy surrounding their validity, we will conclude our discussion of tests with a brief review of these devices, and look at testing issues in a global arena.

Graphology It has been said that an individual's handwriting can suggest the degree of energy, inhibitions, and spontaneity to be found in the writer, disclosing idiosyncrasies and elements of balance and control from which many per-

Graphology Handwriting analysis.

sonality characteristics can be inferred.[17] Although most scientists doubt the validity of handwriting analysis, it is estimated that more than 3,000 U.S. organizations, including Ford, General Electric, and the CIA, consult graphologists to supplement their usual HRM procedures.[18] When used, **graphology** can be considered as an employment test. The argument is made that a large percentage of occupational failures are due to personality defects, not lack of education or ability. Given the inadequacies of many standardized methods for assessing personality characteristics, handwriting analysis, if it really does tell us something about applicants' personality, might have validity, but only if the job analysis had identified these personalities (see Figure 7-4).

In spite of the relatively large number of organizations that admit to using graphology, there is little substantial evidence to support this method as a valid selection device.[19]

Polygraph and Honesty Tests   Recall from Chapter 4 that the use of lie detectors for verifying information on the application form can only be used for specific jobs, such as police officer or federal agents such as those from the National Security Agency, that typically require security clearance. While the polygraph may be a reasonably valid instrument when used by competent examiners, it could be abused in certain situations. Because of this potential for abuse, the Employee Polygraph Protection Act of 1988 (followed by many other state laws) prohibits the use of polygraph testing as a uniform prerequisite of employment. However, a second-generation polygraph technique, honesty tests, is thriving.[20]

As we mentioned in the discussion of employee rights, companies sought to do something to combat the estimated $40 billion lost to employee theft each year.[21] One means of beginning the attack (and without the possible use of polygraph) was the honesty test. Honesty tests are designed to assess an individual's integrity, to predict those who are more likely to steal from an employer[22] or otherwise act in a manner unacceptable to the organization.

Although the questions asked may appear to be relatively innocent, those taking the test do not know how they will be interpreted. For example, the response to "Have you ever cheated on a test in your life?" may not have a correct response on its face value. If you say yes, you admit that you've cheated; a no response might indicate that you are lying. Nonetheless, the question patterns are such that even those who try to "outsmart" the test often fail. These tests often contain questions that repeat themselves in some fashion, and the examiner then looks for consistency in responses.

Since polygraphs are all but unusable for the typical firm, honesty testing has become more widespread. By the early 1990s, it was estimated that nearly 17 percent of all American Management Association affiliated firms used honesty tests.[23] In fact, their use has become so extensive that it has grown into a $50-million-a-year business for these honesty-psychological testing firms.[24]

Although honesty testing is permissible, it is coming under the same attack as

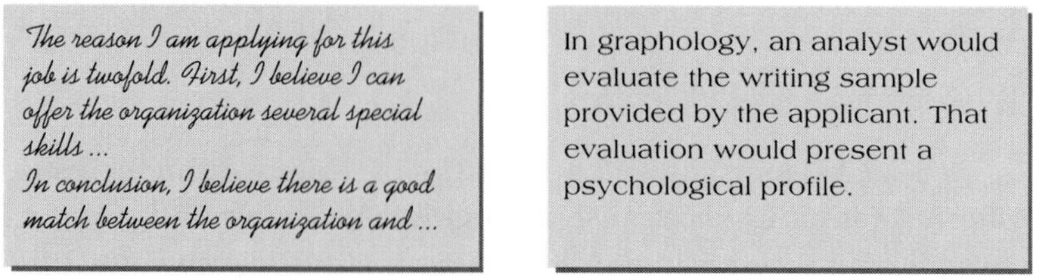

The reason I am applying for this job is twofold. First, I believe I can offer the organization several special skills ...
In conclusion, I believe there is a good match between the organization and ...

In graphology, an analyst would evaluate the writing sample provided by the applicant. That evaluation would present a psychological profile.

Figure 7-4
An Example of Graphology

the polygraph. One of the critical issues for companies using these tests is how job-related they are. If in fact a company cannot demonstrate the job-relatedness of such tests, an adverse impact may occur.[25] Furthermore, companies must also ensure that employee privacy rights are not violated (see Chapter 4).[26]

Testing in a Global Arena Many of the standard selection techniques described in this text are not easily transferable to international situations. Where the decision has been made to recruit and employ host-country nationals, typical American testing will be acceptable in some countries, but not in others. For example, although handwriting or graphology tests are sometimes used in the United States, they are frequently used in France. In Great Britain, most psychological tests like graphology, polygraph, and honesty tests are rarely used in employment. Accordingly, whenever American corporations prepare to do business abroad, their practices must be adapted to the cultures, and regulations, of the country in which they will operate.

Interviews

Whether we're discussing initial screening interviews or comprehensive interviews, a common question arises: Are interviews effective for gathering accurate information from which selection decisions can be made? The **interview** has proven to be an almost universal selection tool—one that can take a number of forms. They can revolve around a one-on-one encounter between the interviewer and the applicant (the traditional interview) or involve several individuals, like stages three and four at Gates Rubber, who interview an applicant at once (the panel interview). Interviews can follow some predetermined pattern wherein both the questions and the expected responses are identified (a **situational interview**[27]). Interviews can also be designed to create a difficult environment in which the applicant is "put to the test" to assess his or her confidence levels. These are oftentimes referred to as the **stress interview** (see "Ethical Decisions in HRM").

Irrespective of how the interview is conducted, it is understood that few people get jobs without one or more interviews. This is extremely interesting, given that the validity of the interview as a selection tool has been the subject of considerable debate. Let's look at the research findings regarding interviews.

Interview A selection method that involves a face-to-face meeting with the candidate.

Situational Interview Structured interview where questions relate directly to actual work activities.

Stress Interview An interview designed to see how the applicants handle themselves under pressure.

The Effectiveness of Interviews

Wouldn't it be nice if all interviews were as clear cut as the following:[28]

After several minutes in an interview, the job applicant interrupted the recruiter and asked what the IBM in the company name stood for.

Another applicant, when asked why he wanted to work for the major regional bank for which he was applying, responded he didn't know because he would really prefer to work for the bank's competitor, which is much closer to his home.

A third applicant, in response to a question why he was applying for a job in a savings and loan, simply stated because the job was available.

Unfortunately for recruiters, situations aren't always this cut and dried. Rather, many other factors enter into the deliberation in determining if a candidate is a "good fit" for the organization.[29] Although interviews are part of every

Ethics Decisions:

The Stress Interview

Your interview day has finally arrived. You are all dressed up to make that lasting, first impression. You finally meet Mr. Henderson, as he shakes your hand and invites you to get comfortable. Your interview has started! This is the moment you've waited for.

The first few moments appear mundane enough. The questions to this point, in fact, seem easy. Your confidence is growing. That little voice in your head keeps telling you that you are doing fine—just keep on going. Suddenly, the questions get tougher. Mr. Henderson leans back, and asks about why you want to leave your current job—the one you've been in for only twenty-four months. As you begin to explain that you wish to leave for personal reasons, he begins to probe more. His smile is gone. His body language is different. All right, you think, be honest. So you tell Mr. Henderson you want to leave because you think your supervisor's incompetent and only got the position because he is related to someone in senior management. This has led to a number of confrontations, and you're tired of dealing with the situation any longer. Mr. Henderson looks at you and replies: "If you ask me, that's a childish reason for wanting to leave. Are you sure you're mature enough and have what it takes to make it in this company?" How dare he talk to you that way! Who does he think he is? So you respond with an angry tone in your voice. And guess what, you've just fallen victim to one of the classic tricks of the interviewing business—the stress interview.

Stress interviews are becoming more commonplace in today's business. Every job produces stress, and at some point in time every worker has a horrendous day. So these types of interviews become predictors of how you may react at work under less than favorable conditions. How so? Interviewers want to observe how you'll react when you are put under pressure. Those who demonstrate the resolve and strength to handle the stress indicate a level of professionalism and confidence. It's those characteristics that are being assessed. Individuals who react to the pressure interview in a more positive manner indicate that they should be more able to handle the day-to-day irritations that exist at work. Those who don't, well . . .

On the other hand, they are staged events. Interviewers deliberately lead applicants into a false sense of security—the comfortable interaction. Then suddenly and drastically, they change. They go on the attack. And it's usually a personal affront that picks on a weakness they've uncovered about the applicant. It's possibly humiliating; at the very least it's demeaning.

So, should stress interviews be used? Should interviewers be permitted to assess professionalism and confidence, and how one reacts to the everyday nuisances of work by putting applicants into a confrontational scenario? Does getting angry in an interview when pressured indicate one's propensity toward violence should things not always go smoothly at work? Should HRM advocate the use of an activity that could possibly get out of control? What's your opinion?

Source: Vignette based on Stephen M. Pollan and Mark Levine, "How to Ace a Tough Interview," *Working Woman* (July 1994), p. 49.

job search process, summaries of research on interviewing have concluded that the reliability and validity of interviews are generally low.[30] Despite its popularity, the interview is expensive, inefficient, and usually not job-related.[31]

More specifically, a review of the research has generated the following conclusions:[32]

1. Prior knowledge about the applicant can bias the interviewer's evaluation.
2. The interviewer often holds a stereotype of what represents a "good" applicant.
3. The interviewer often tends to favor applicants who share his or her own attitudes.
4. The order in which applicants are interviewed often influences evaluations.
5. The order in which information is elicited influences evaluations.
6. Negative information is given unduly high weight.
7. The interviewer may make a decision as to the applicant's suitability in the first few minutes of the interview.
8. The interviewer may forget much of the interview's content within minutes after its conclusion.
9. Structured and well-organized interviews are more reliable.
10. The interview is most valid in determining an applicant's organizational fit, level of motivation, and interpersonal skills.

These conclusions, generated over the past few decades, still hold today. Let's elaborate on a few of them.

When an interviewer has already seen the candidate's resume, application form, possible test scores, or appraisals of other interviewers, bias may be introduced. In such cases, the interviewer no longer relies on the data gained in the interview alone. Based on the data received prior to the interview, an image of the applicant is created. Much of the early part of the interview, then, becomes an exercise wherein the interviewer compares the actual applicant with the image formed earlier.

For example, a classic study of interviewer stereotyping focused on the Cana-

Can this applicant positively influence the interviewer's decision? Impression Management tells us that if he can say or do something that is viewed favorably by the interviewer, then yes, he can influence the decision.

Impression Management Influencing performance evaluations by portraying an image that is desired by the appraiser.

Structured Interviews An interview in which there are fixed questions that are presented to every applicant.

dian Army.[33] In this study, it was concluded that Army interviewers developed a stereotype of what a good job applicant was. But this stereotype was not an individual bias; rather, it was one that was typically shared by all interviewers who had a reasonable amount of experience and who operated in a similar environment. This stereotype changed very little during the interview; in fact, most interviewer decisions changed very little during the interview. Based on this research, which appears to be still valid today, a "good applicant" is probably characterized more by the absence of unfavorable characteristics than by the presence of favorable ones.[34] Thus, negative information in an interview has a greater impact on assessment of evaluations than does positive information.

In addition to interviewer bias is something that is directly related to the applicant's actions. This is referred to as **impression management.** Impression management refers to one's attempt to project an image that will result in receiving a favorable outcome.[35] Thus, if an applicant can say or do something that is viewed favorably by the interviewer, then that person may be viewed more favorably for the position. For example, suppose you find out that the interviewer values workers who can work seven days a week, twelve-plus hours a day, if needed. Understandably, few, if any jobs can sustain this work schedule over a long period of time. But that's the interviewer's view nonetheless. Accordingly, making statements of being a workaholic, which conforms to this interviewer's values, may result in creating a positive impression.

Interviewers have a remarkably short and inaccurate memory. For example, in one study of an interview simulation, a twenty-minute videotape of a selection interview was played for a group of forty managers. Following the playing of the tape, the managers were given a twenty-question test. Although all the questions were straightforward and factual, the average number of wrong answers was ten. The researchers' conclusion? Even in a short interview, the average manager remembers only half of the information.[36] However, taking notes during an interview has been shown to reduce memory loss.[37] Note-taking is also useful—albeit possibly disconcerting for the interviewee—for getting more accurate information and for developing a clearer understanding of the applicant's fit by allowing follow-up questions to be asked. Companies like MPR, a personnel consultant service in Chicago, go even one step further.[38] They tape record each interview. Recruiters at MPR have found that by taping the interview, better, more thorough responses are elicited. Furthermore, taping the interview serves as one means of showing that all candidates were given equal treatment. Of course, a recruiter cannot record the interview without the permission of the applicant.

Evidence lends strong support to the view that **structured interviews** are more reliable and valid than unstructured interviews.[39] When two interviewers are allowed to use their own idiosyncratic pattern for questions and evaluation, they will frequently arrive at two different decisions. This happens, in part, because a different set of questions will elicit different information from the same applicant. Unstructured interviews thus make for very low inter-interviewer reliability.

Another research finding points out that the interview offers the greatest value as a selection device in determining an applicant's organizational fit, level of motivation, and interpersonal skills.[40] This is particularly true of senior management positions. Accordingly, it is not unlikely for candidates for these positions to go through many extensive interviews with executive recruiters, company executives, and even board members before a final decision is made. Similarly, where teams have the responsibility to hire their own members, it is commonplace for each team member to interview the applicant.

One final issue about interviews revolves around when the interviewer actually makes the decision. Early studies, like the Canadian Army example, indicated that interviewers made their choice to hire or not hire a candidate within the first few minutes of the interview. While that belief was widely held, subsequent research does not support these findings.[41] In fact, this research identified that initial impressions may have little effect, unless that is the only information available for an interviewer to use.

So what sense can we make of these issues raised about interviews? And where might interviews be most appropriate? If interviews will continue to have a place in the selection decision, they appear to be more appropriate for the high-turnover jobs, and the less routine ones like middle- and upper-level managerial positions. In jobs where these characteristics are important in determining success, the interview can be a valuable selection input. In nonroutine activities, especially senior managerial positions, failure (as measured by voluntary terminations) is more frequently caused by a poor fit between the individual and the organization than by lack of competence on the part of the individual.[42] Interviewing can be useful, therefore, when it emphasizes the candidate's ability to fit into the organization rather than specific technical skills.

Interviewing: An Interviewer's Perspective

The differences we have described may seem to cast a dark cloud over the interview. But the interview is far from worthless. It can help us to better assess the candidate, as well as be a valuable vehicle for relaying information to prospective employees.

For anyone who interviews prospective job candidates, whether as a recruiter in HRM or in any other capacity, there are several suggestions we can offer for improving the effectiveness of interviews (see "HRM Skills: Interviewing Job Candidates").

Interviewing: A Candidate's Perspective — The Realistic Job Preview

Clara Stevens was a recent graduate of Loyola–Marymount University's MBA program. During the recruiting process with one company, the aspiring marketing manager was guaranteed that she would be closely involved in the company's annual sales meeting—working with several key decision makers in the marketing division. Impressed by the thought of having an active part in the meeting, the job offer seemed very appealing. She accepted the job, and within weeks was actively involved in the sales meetings. She saw to it that coffee was available for both morning and afternoon breaks and made several trips a day to local businesses to pick up audiovisual equipment. This, she was told, was the involvement she had been promised. In frustration, Clara Stevens quit.

The primary purpose of selection devices is to identify individuals who will be effective performers. But it is not in management's best interest to find good prospects, hire them, and then have them leave the organization. Therefore, part of selection should be concerned with reducing voluntary turnover, and its associated costs.[43] One device to achieve that goal is the **realistic job preview (RJP).** What is a realistic job preview? It may include brochures, films, plant tours, work sampling, or merely a short script made up of realistic statements that accurately portray the job. The key element in RJP is that unfavorable as well as favorable information about the job is shared. While the RJP is not nor-

Realistic Job Preview A selection device that allows job candidates to learn negative as well as positive information about the job and organization.

HRM *Skills*

Interviewing Job Candidates

1. **Obtain detailed information about the job for which applicants are being interviewed.** When you are provided with a substantial amount of information about the job, you rely primarily on job-relevant factors in making selection decisions. When such information is unavailable, you may tend to rely more on factors less relevant to the job, allowing bias to enter into the assessment. You should therefore, at a minimum, have a copy of the recent position description as an information source. You are now ready to structure the interview.

2. **Structure the interview so that the interview follows a set procedure.** Reliability is increased when the interview is designed around a constant structure. A fixed set of questions should be presented to every applicant. In the trade-off between structure and consistency versus nonstructure and flexibility, structure and consistency have proved to be of greater value for selection purposes. The structured interview also aids you in comparing all candidates' answers to a like question.

3. **Review the candidate's application form and/or resume.** This step helps you to create a more complete picture of the applicant in terms of what is represented on the resume/application, and what the job requires (from step 1). This will help you to identify specific areas that need to be explored in the interview. For example, areas not clearly defined on the resume but essential for job success become a focal point for interview discussion.

4. **Put the applicant at ease.** Assume the applicant will be nervous. For you to obtain the kind of information you will need, the applicant will have to be put at ease. Introduce yourself, and open with some small talk like the weather, the traffic coming to the interview, etc. But be careful: Don't venture into illegal areas with small talk about the applicant's family. Keep it impersonal!

5. **Ask your questions.** The questions you are asking should be behaviorally based. Such questions are designed to require applicants to provide detailed descriptions of their actual job behaviors. You want to elicit concrete examples of how the applicant demonstrates certain behaviors, the same behaviors that are necessary for successful performance on the job for which the interview is being held. If you are unsatisfied with the applicant's response, probe deeper to seek elaboration. The key here is to let the applicant talk. A big mistake is to do most of the talking yourself. During this part of the interview, take notes. Given the propensity to forget what was actually said during the interview, notes should be taken. This will lead to increased accuracy in evaluation.

6. **Conclude the interview.** Let the applicant know that all of your questioning is finished. Summarize what you have heard from the applicant, and give the applicant an opportunity to correct something that is unclear; or discuss anything that you may have not addressed in the interview. Inform the applicant what will happen next in the process, and when he or she can expect to hear from you.

7. **Complete a post-interview evaluation form**. Along with a structured format should go a standardized evaluation form. You should complete this item-by-item form shortly after the interviewee has departed—while the information and your notes are still fresh in your mind. The information on this evaluation can then be summarized into an overall rating, or impression, for the candidate. This approach increases the likelihood that the same frame of reference is applied to each applicant.

mally treated as a selection device, it does take place during the interview and it has demonstrated effectiveness as a method for increasing job survival among new employees, so we've included it here.

Every applicant acquires during the selection process a set of expectations about the organization and about the specific job the applicant is hoping to be offered. It is not unusual for these expectations to be excessively inflated as a result of receiving almost uniformly positive information about the organization and job during recruitment and selection activities.[44] Evidence suggests, however, that managers may be erring by giving applicants only favorable information. More specifically, research leads us to conclude that applicants who have been given a realistic job preview (as well as a realistic preview of the organization) hold lower and more realistic expectations about the job they will be doing and are better prepared for coping with the job and its frustrating elements. Realistic job previews also appear to work best for those jobs that are more attractive to the individual,[45] resulting in lower turnover rates.[46] Most studies demonstrate that giving candidates a realistic job preview before offering them the job reduces turnover without lowering acceptance rates.[47] Of course, it is not unreasonable to suggest that exposing an applicant to RJP may also result in the hiring of a more committed individual.

Background Investigation

Background investigations are intended to verify that what was stated on the application form is correct and accurate information. And while a chief means of verifying that data comes from reference checks, HRM has witnessed significant changes in this area. For instance, by the late 1980s, organizations began questioning how much information should be given to another employer. These questions arose over the fear of being sued for giving information that had a negative effect on an individual's employment prospects elsewhere. The result is that as employee privacy rights issues began to hit the courts, employers all but abandoned giving references. For instance, consider the following.[48] Larry Buck, an insurance broker with Frank B. Hall and Company, was having trouble getting employment in the field after being fired from Hall. Believing that his previous employer was sabotaging his job-search efforts, Buck hired a private investigator to contact Hall and Company, posing as a prospective employer. What the investigator got was an earful. Buck, it appeared, was referred to as a "Jekyll and Hyde person, a classic sociopath." Those comments by his previous employer cost Frank B. Hall and Company about $2 million in a legal settlement. Why? The Supreme Court held that the comments were malicious and libelous.[49]

Since the late 1980s, however, there has been a changing of the court's opinion toward background investigations and employee privacy issues. This is a result of companies being held liable for the actions of their employees.[50] It is safe to assume that companies today need to expend some effort in investigating an applicant's background. There is documentation that supports the premise that a good predictor of an individual's future behavior is his or her past behavior,[51] as well as data that suggest that one-third of all applicants exaggerate their backgrounds or experiences.[52] Accordingly, companies must assess the liability that potential employees may create, and delve into their backgrounds in as much depth as necessary to limit the risk.[53] For example, local school systems must go to great extremes to assure that potential teachers do not pose a risk to children. Similarly, hospitals need to feel confident that the doctors, nurses, and staff they hire are drug-free. Should an unfortunate event occur, the courts may come down hard on the organization.

In conducting a background investigation, two methods can be used: the internal or the external investigation. In the internal investigation, HRM undertakes the task of questioning former employers, personal references, and possibly credit sources. Although this is a viable option, and one avidly used, unless the investigation process is handled thoroughly, little useful information may be found. On the other hand, the external means involves using a reference-checking firm.[54] Although there is a greater cost associated with this investigation, such firms have a better track record of gathering pertinent information, as well as being better informed on privacy rights issues.[55] However it is done, documentation is the important element.[56] Should an employer be called upon to justify what has or has not been found, supporting documentation is invaluable.

Medical/Physical Examinations

For jobs that require certain physical characteristics, the physical examination has some validity. However, this includes a very small proportion of jobs today. Should a medical clearance be required to indicate that the applicant is physically fit for the essential job elements, a company must be able to show that it is a job-related requirement. Failure to do so may result in the physical examination creating an adverse impact. Also, the company must keep in mind the Americans with Disabilities Act. Thus, even a valid physical examination may only be required after a conditional job offer. Having a physical disability may not be enough to exclude an individual from the job. Companies, as we mentioned in Chapter 3, must make reasonable accommodations for these individuals.

Selection for Self-Managed Teams

Much of the discussion about selection devices throughout the past two chapters has assumed one fact. That is, somewhere in HRM lies the responsibility for the selection process. Today, however, that may not always be the case. Companies like Perdue Farms (the chicken company of Frank Perdue), General Mills, Corning, Toyota, and Federal Express,[57] are more team-oriented, and they empower their employees to take responsibility for the day-to-day functions in their areas. Accordingly, these employees may now work without direct supervision and take on the "management" responsibilities that were once made by their first-line supervisor.[58] One aspect of this change has been a more active role in hiring their coworkers.[59]

Consider a time when you took a course that required a group project. How was your team formed? Did the professor assign you to a group, or were you permitted to form the group yourself? Assuming your professor permitted you to select your own group, what did you look for in a potential group member? Other students who shared your values in getting the work done, on time, and of a high quality? Those who you knew would pull their own weight, and not let one or two in the group do all of the work? Well, that's the same premise behind self-managed work-team selection. In any organization, a critical link to success is how well employees perform their jobs. It is also understood that when those jobs require the interaction of several individuals, or a team, that coming together as a unified unit takes time.[60] The length of that time, however, is a function of how the team views its goals and priorities, and how open and trusting group members are. What better way to begin this team-building than to have the "personalities" involved actually making the hiring decision.

When workers are empowered to hire their coworkers, they bring to the selection process varied experiences and backgrounds. This enables them to "better assess applicants' skills in their field of expertise."[61] They, too, like your class project, want to hire someone they can count on, who will perform his or her duties, and not let the others down. This means that they focus their attention on the job duties required, and those special skills and qualifications needed to be successful. From our previous discussion of validation (Chapter 6), that's precisely the focus of the selection process. In this case, a more objective evaluation may be obtained.

But that's not to say that self-managed work teams are not without problems. If these workers are unfamiliar with proper interviewing techniques, or the legal ramifications of their hiring decisions, they too, could experience many of the difficulties often associated with interviews.

Study Tools and Applications

Summary

This summary relates to the Learning Objectives provided on p. 188.
After reading this chapter, you should know:

1. Selection devices provide managers with information that will help them predict whether an applicant will prove to be a successful job performer.
2. The application form is effective for acquiring hard biographical data—data that can ultimately be verified.
3. Weighted applications are useful in that through statistical techniques, linkage can be determined between certain relevant information and the prediction of job success.
4. Performance simulation tests require the applicant to engage in specific behaviors that have been demonstrated to be job-related. Work sampling and the assessment center, which are performance simulations, receive high marks for their predictive capability.
5. Assessment centers are a type of performance simulation test. They are concluded over a period of a few days with a number of observers studying how the individuals handle or react to various business situations.
6. Graphology is the analysis of handwriting. Its validity is questionable.
7. Interviews consistently achieve low marks for reliability and validity. These, however, are more the result of interviewer problems as opposed to the interview itself. Interviewing validity can be enhanced by using a structured process.
8. Realistic job previews reduce turnover by giving the applicant both favorable and unfavorable information about the job.
9. Background investigations are valuable when they verify hard data from the application; they tend, however, to offer little practical value as a predictive selection device.
10. Medical/physical examinations are valid when certain physical characteristics are required to be able to perform the essential elements of a job effectively. Such examinations are usually given after a conditional job offer is made.

Key Terms

application form

assessment centers

employment tests

graphology

impression management

interview

performance simulation tests

realistic job preview (RJP)

situational interview

stress interview

structured interviews

weighted application form

work sampling

written tests

EXPERIENTIAL EXERCISE:

The Awful Interview[62]

Purpose

1. To practice interviewing skills, especially in dealing with difficult interview questions frequently asked by interviewers.
2. To sharpen your awareness of your strengths and weaknesses in interviewing for a job.

Advanced Preparation

Read the "Introduction" below, and think about some good questions that might be included in the list in Step 1. If you can't think of good, mindboggling questions, ask friends who have some experience in job interviews.

Group Size:	*Trios or quartets.*
Time Required:	*1-1/4 hours (trios), 1-1/2 hours (quartets).*
Special Physical Requirements:	*Trios (or quartets) will need small meeting rooms or an area suitable for holding conversations relatively free of distractions.*

Introduction

Employment interviews are frequently traumatic experiences; interviewers know what they are looking for, and you don't. They are prepared, and you are not. They are relaxed, and you are tense. The cards are all stacked in the interviewer's favor, it seems. Interviewers are also notorious for asking disconcerting questions: "Tell me about your goals in life." "Why do you want to work for International Widgets?" If you answered such questions candidly, but right off the top of your head, you might never get a job. ("My only goal is to get a job so I can begin to find out whether I really like it," or "I want to work for International Widgets because I don't have any other good prospects right now.") If you have been confronted with questions such as these, you will understand why we have titled this exercise, "The Awful Interview." You don't have to let interviewers catch you by surprise. This exercise is based on the assumption that practice can help you prepare for interview situations. We will also assume that honesty really is the best policy. The job-hunter who concentrates on giving a prospective employer the impression that she or he is just the person wanted is employing a defensive strategy. You may become so preoccupied with projecting an "image" that you have little energy left for the real problem of showing the interviewer what careful thought you have given to planning your career.

Procedure

Step 1: 15 minutes

The entire group will develop a list of the ten of the most awful questions one can be asked in a job interview. An "awful" question is one that you would find threatening or difficult to answer honestly in a job interview. When the list is completed, write down the ten. You will need them in the remainder of the exercise. List only questions that have actually been asked in all seriousness in job interviews you or somebody else has experienced. (Note: if you desire a shorter version of this class exercise, have students exchange these lists generated in Step 1, and have another group review them for legalities. Those questions that may raise concern should be identified and discussed with the entire class.)

Step 2: 5 minutes

The group leader will specify whether the total group should break into smaller groups of threes or fours. Choose people with whom you will be comfortable, people who can be most helpful in providing useful feedback on your interviewing style. When the groups are formed, the group leader will tell you where you are to hold your small group meetings.

Step 3: 45 to 60 minutes

Meet with your trio or quartet. Proceed as follows: One member volunteers to answer the first question, another is chosen to ask the question. Choosing a question from the list of the ten most awful, the interrogator asks the interviewee the first question. The interviewee must try to answer the question as truthfully and honestly as he or she can. After the answer, other members of the group provide feedback to the interviewee on how they experienced the answer just given. (Remember the criteria for effective feedback emphasized in the Mill reading.) Upon completion of the feedback, the interviewee becomes the interrogator, chooses a question and a new interviewee, and a new round begins. Continue taking turns until each person has answered at least three questions, or until you are instructed by the group leader to stop.

Step 4: 10 minutes

Take ten minutes and write a brief note to yourself covering the following (this note is for you—nobody else will see it): What questions did I handle well? What were my strengths? What questions did I handle poorly? What questions asked of others would give me problems? What can I do to deal more effectively with the questions that give me problems?

Step 5:

Reconvene with the entire group for discussion of the exercise.

Discussion Questions

1. What did you learn during the exercise about how to answer interviewer's questions more effectively?
2. Do you think employment interviewers obtained valid data in the interview? Why?
3. If you were an interviewer, what kinds of questions would you ask?

CASE APPLICATION:
Applied Computer Technology

Cindy Koehler is a true entrepreneur.[63] She had a vision of building a successful company. She wanted to pursue her individual interests and fulfill a special need she had. So she took some bold steps, accepted the risk, and ventured into business, starting the Fort Collins computer manufacturing company, Applied Computer Technology.

Early in the start-up, Cindy made it a practice to hire family and friends. Her selection criterion? These people wanted to help, and she needed some workers. So on the payroll they went. But before too long, problems erupted. When certain activities were needed, sometimes in a rush, some of her employees couldn't get the work done. It appeared that sometimes they just weren't at work—they left work early, or worse, unilaterally decided to take the day off without any notice. Compounding the problem was the realization that Koehler didn't feel comfortable addressing her displeasure with the employees. After all, these were employees with whom she had a personal relationship. Inasmuch as she didn't want to hurt anyone's feelings, the problems got too far out of hand. They were now threatening her vision of building a successful company. Consequently, Cindy cracked down on her infrequently committed work force. As a result, several friends quit, and the relationship between Cindy and some of her family and friends is, at best, strained.

Although Cindy Koehler has learned a hard lesson, she knows now what went wrong. Simply stated, she mixed work and friendship. Those two often conflict in the selection process.

Questions:

1. In terms of the selection process, diagnose where Cindy Koehler went wrong. What would you recommend she do to correct the problems she experienced?
2. In a small business, it is not uncommon for family and friends to be employees. But no organization can afford to experience what Koehler did over a long period of time. Assuming that family and friends are going to be hired, what would you recommend an entrepreneur do to eliminate a repeat of the Allied Computer Technology hiring fiasco?
3. How could a realistic job preview been used to the benefit of both Cindy and her family and friends? Explain.

How well did you fulfill the learning objectives?

1. A director of selection at a large manufacturing firm is reviewing the selection techniques used by three engineering specialist interviewers. One relies solely on the interview, but does not thoroughly read the application form and never does a background check. A second does not trust the interview outcomes, and conducts extensive background checks on each applicant. A third looks for related work experiences on the application form and asks each applicant to bring a portfolio of current work samples (diagrams, designs, etc.) to the interview. The director concludes
   a. Interviewers one and two are better than interviewer three because they rely on one selection device.
   b. Interviewer three does not assess past or current work-related behaviors.
   c. The three interviewers all perform roughly equivalent processes.
   d. Each interviewee should be seen by all three interviewers to improve the quality of the interview process.
   e. A selection test should be written and added to the devices used.
2. A director of selection for a large manufacturing organization wants to weight application forms for employees in the new robotics plant. That plant, scheduled to open in eighteen months, will utilize new technology that will create substantially different job requirements than any existing organizational jobs. How should the director proceed?
   a. Delay the opening of the plant until a weighted application is developed for current jobs in the robotics plant.
   b. Wait until the plant has been opened a year, then examine the application forms for good and poor workers to identify patterns of differences.
   c. Hire a consultant to conduct the analysis and submit a valid report on the reliability of weighted application forms.
   d. Examine work records from good and poor performers over the last five years. Identify differences in application form items.
   e. A weighted application form is inappropriate for a robotics plant. They work only in the sales and financial areas of a company where hard biographical data are more readily available.
3. College professors interviewing for jobs at a large East Coast university are asked to prepare and deliver a "class" for selected students. Given this information, which one of the following statements is most correct?
   a. This is an example of an in-basket simulation. It is unique to hiring faculty in universities.

b. The class session is a type of work sampling, at least for the teaching part of the job.
   c. The "class" is representative of an assessment center for new faculty to determine the new faculty member's rank.
   d. The "class" is part the interviewing process used to determine attainment of technical degree.
   e. The "class" is an atypical feedback test.
4. As part of the selection process, a day-care center in Boston has each applicant come to work for a day before final hiring decisions are made. Why?
   a. The management has a chance to evaluate the hands-on capabilities of each applicant.
   b. The organization is understaffed. This system provides free help.
   c. Title VII requires this for all child-care providers.
   d. This process takes less time than a real interview.
   e. Workdays have replaced background checking in most child-care organizations.
5. How do employment tests differ from performance simulation tests?
   a. Employment tests are conducted before hiring decisions are made. Performance simulation tests are conducted after hiring decisions are made.
   b. Employment tests are conducted after hiring decisions are made. Performance simulation tests are conducted before hiring decisions are made.
   c. Performance simulation tests are paper-and-pencil exercises. Employment tests are measured by manager observation.
   d. Performance simulation tests have high content validity. Employment tests may also have construct validity.
   e. Employment tests are more expensive than performance simulation tests.
6. What is the difference between work sampling and assessment centers?
   a. Work sampling is another term used to describe the assessment center.
   b. Work sampling is a type of employment test. Assessment centers are a performance evaluation technique.
   c. Work sampling procedures usually have fewer evaluators than assessment centers.
   d. Assessment centers usually take less time to conduct than work sampling procedures.
   e. Assessment centers are usually done for blue-collar work. Work sampling procedures are conducted for managerial job candidates.
7. Jason interviews candidates for technical consultant positions in a large aerospace manufacturing firm. He was trained to do this last year, because of his extensive technical background and job knowledge. At the end of a typical day, he has interviewed eight to ten

people. He asks them all the same questions, in the same order. At 4 P.M. he fills out standard forms for each person, and forwards his recommendations to corporate. He complains that he makes mistakes, and can't really remember facts and details about his candidates while completing the evaluation forms. What should be done to make Jason's interviews more effective?

a. Nothing can be done. Interviews are not effective predictors of successful job performance.
b. Jason should ask a different set of questions with each applicant.
c. Jason should conduct no more than four interviews per day.
d. Jason should learn some memory-enhancing techniques.
e. Jason should take notes.

8. What could have been done differently in the case of Clara Stevens, the Loyola Marymount graduate who quit her job because she had to get coffee and run errands during her first annual sales meeting?

a. The interviewer should have offered Clara coffee during the interview process, to model appropriate behavior.
b. The company should have offered Clara more money to help ease the burden of performing routine tasks.
c. The interviewer should have told Clara that the early part of her assignment would include menial tasks.
d. The interviewer should have been honest with Clara and told her that the firm did not have a job suitable for someone with her credentials.
e. The company should review all of its job descriptions.

9. Realistic job previews are fine, but what do you do when you have a job that no one wants to take? Tom had been interviewing for more than a year for the position of manager in his southeastern furniture manufacturing plant. The hours would be long. The workers were underskilled and unwilling to work. The plant was old, with inefficient and unsafe machinery. Tom spoke frankly to the 1,200 prospective managers he interviewed. No one accepted the job.

a. Tom should consider job redesign or plant relocation. The problem in this case is not with interviewing techniques.
b. Tom should hire a consultant to teach him how to present a realistic job preview in more favorable terms.
c. Tom should keep interviewing. The right person, dedicated and challenge-seeking, will turn up.
d. Tom should raise the salary offer.
e. Tom should let someone else do the interviewing.

10. A vice-president of human resources for a large manufacturing organization wants to start a background investigation process on all new employees in her company who have access to financial information or funding, such as accountants. How should she proceed?

a. Begin a policy of credit checking for new employees.
b. Call former employers of potential employees.
c. Be suspicious of any employee who has held more than two jobs in any five-year period. Hire a professional to follow such an individual for a period of time before hiring.
d. Give candidates polygraph tests.
e. Hire an external investigator for a more thorough job than could be done internally.

11. Don is interviewing Sandy, who is confined to a wheelchair, for a secretarial position in his company. She has passed the usual selection criteria—the employment test, the background check, and all interviews. What should Don do?

a. Have Sandy take a physical examination before hiring her.
b. Recommend that Sandy be hired if she can supply a desk/chair arrangement that would be suitable.
c. Recommend that Sandy be hired.
d. Conduct more interviews with Sandy.
e. Interview employees who would have to work with Sandy.

12. A vice-president of human resources wants to exclude physical examinations from the selection process. In the past year, his firm has been sued four times because of the physical. However, most jobs in the machine shop require moving heavy, sensitive machines. What else can the organization do to protect its equipment investment?

a. Perform a thorough background check.
b. Add weighted items to the application form about health club memberships.
c. Close the production facility.
d. Initiate a work sampling procedure for the jobs in question.
e. Ask applicants about their physical abilities during the intensive interview.

13. Biographical data on job application forms
a. is illegal under civil rights legislation.
b. is often a good predictor of future job success.
c. is seldom a good predictor of future job success.
d. is useful only to identify mental lapses indicated by large time periods between jobs.
e. is standardized across all U.S. organizations.

14. How do organizations use application forms, since civil rights legislation changed the contents?
a. They have no real use. In fact, most companies are eliminating application forms.
b. They are used to avoid adverse impact.
c. Validated information, such as class standing, can be a good predictor of job success.
d. They are used to document ADA compliance.
e. They are used to validate Title VII compliance.

Chapter Eight

EMPLOYEE ORIENTATION

Imagine for a moment you have just been placed into a position where you have the responsibility to assimilate more than 4,000 employees into a newly formed organization. Many of these employees have backgrounds and experiences in a company culture that is significantly different than that of your organization. How will you deal with these employees in helping them adjust to the change they are about to face? Would you plan a gala event, with several hundred colleagues helping you to indoctrinate these employees? Or would you look at the sheer numbers involved and throw your hands up in frustration? When the du Pont and Merck companies joined forces to form the du Pont Merck Pharmaceutical Company, neither of these occurred. Instead, the orientation manager, Sonia Koplowicz, developed the company's *orienteering* program.[1]

Orienteering is designed as a three-staged socialization program. In Phase One, new employees meet with orienteering coaches to discuss the overall goals of their unit. Here employees learn about the company's direction and are introduced to the organization's culture. After a period of one to three months, these new employees are brought back together with their orienteering coaches. Employees have now had several weeks to acclimate themselves into the company, and begin to see how things are going to operate. But Koplowicz recognized more than this summary overview was necessary. Accordingly, in Phase Two, each employee focuses on his or her specific role in making a significant contribution to the organization. That is, each employee learns why his or her job exists, and what role each plays in helping the unit and division in achieving its goals. At the conclusion of this stage, employees return to work with a complete understanding of the linking nature of their jobs performed and company success.

After Phase Two, most employees do have a good perspective of the company. They know what their respective job and departmental goals are. They understand the resources available to them, and the established norms and values. But du Pont Merck wanted more for their employees. They wanted each to understand the bigger picture. And so, Phase Three was developed. During this stage, employees are exposed to the strategic nature of the organization. They review and discuss the company's mission and its long-term goals. By providing employees with a clear picture of what is to come, and the roles they play in achieving that mission, du Pont Merck is able to achieve a greater level of employee commitment to corporate goals. This, as Sonia's plan intended, results in greater productivity.

Programs such as the one at du Pont Merck are designed to help employees fully understand what working in the organization is about. Its intent is to help employees successfully "learn the ropes" on their new jobs. From the company's point of view, knowing the ropes is important. It means that people know and accept behavior that the organization views as desirable. And if you don't think that is important, consider this: It is estimated that the costs of recruiting and selecting for an entry-level position average \$6,000.[2] Furthermore, more than half of all those hired will resign within the first seven months.[3] Consequently, HRM must ensure that the goals of both recruitment and selection are met, and then help these new employees learn what is important in the organization. In this chapter, then, we will show how employees are socialized into their job environments, and the ways that HRM can influence the socialization process.

The Outsider–Insider Passage

When we talk about **socialization,** we are talking about a process of adaptation. In the context of organizations, the term refers to all passages undergone by employees. For instance, when you begin a new job, accept a lateral transfer, or get a promotion, you are required to make adjustments. You must adapt to a new environment—different work activities, a new boss, a different and most likely a diverse group of coworkers, and probably a different set of standards for what constitutes good performance.[4] Although we recognize that this socialization will go on throughout our careers—within an organization as well as between organizations—the most profound adjustment occurs when we make the first move into an organization: the move from being an outsider to being an insider. The following discussion, therefore, is limited to the outsider–insider passage, or what is more appropriately labeled organization-entry socialization.

Socialization A process of adaption that takes place as individuals attempt to learn the values and norms of work roles.

Socialization

Do you remember your first day in college? What feelings did you experience? Anxiety over new expectations? Uncertainty over what was to come? Excitement at being on your own and experiencing new things? Fear based on all those things friends said about how tough college courses were? Stress over what classes to take, and what professors to get? Well, you probably experienced many of these things. And entry into a job is no different. For organizations to assist in the adjustment process, a few matters must be understood. We'll call these the assumptions of employee socialization.[5]

The Assumptions of Employee Socialization

Several assumptions underlie the process of socialization. The first is that socialization strongly influences employee performance and organizational stability. Also, new members suffer from anxiety; socialization does not occur in a vacuum; and the way in which individuals adjust to new situations is remarkably similar. Let's look a little closer at each of these assumptions.

Socialization strongly influences employee performance and organizational stability. Your work performance depends to a considerable degree on knowing what you should or should not do. Understanding the right way to do a job indicates proper socialization. Furthermore, the appraisal of your performance includes how well you fit into the organization. Can you get along with your coworkers? Do you have acceptable work habits? Do you demonstrate the right attitude? These qualities differ among jobs and organizations. For instance, on some jobs you will be evaluated higher if you are aggressive and outwardly indicate that you are ambitious. On another job, or on the same job in another organization, such an approach might be evaluated negatively. As

How does a pharmaceutical company orient new employees? Each is involved in a three-stage process consisting of assimilation into the organization, understanding the corporate culture and strategic direction, and recognizing how his or her job plays an integral role in corporate goal attainment.

Values Basic convictions about what is right or wrong, good or bad, desirable or not.

Norms Tell group members what they ought or ought not do in certain circumstances.

a result, proper socialization becomes a significant factor in influencing both your actual job performance and how it is perceived by others.[6]

Organizational stability is also increased through socialization.[7] When, over many years, jobs are filled and vacated with a minimum of disruption, the organization will be more stable. Its objectives will be more smoothly transferred between generations. Loyalty and commitment to the organization should be easier to maintain because the organization's philosophy and objectives will appear consistent over time. Given that most managers value high employee performance and organizational stability, the proper socialization of employees should be important.

New members suffer from anxiety. The outsider–insider passage is an anxiety-producing situation. Stress is high because the new member feels a lack of identification—if not with the work itself, certainly with a new superior, new coworkers, a new work location, and a new set of rules and regulations. Loneliness and a feeling of isolation are not unusual. This anxiety state has at least two implications. First, new employees need special attention to put them at ease. This usually means providing an adequate amount of information to reduce uncertainty and ambiguity. Second, the existence of tension can be positive in that it often acts to motivate individuals to learn the **values** and **norms** of their newly assumed role as quickly as possible.[8] We can conclude, therefore, that the new member is anxious about the new role but is motivated to learn the ropes and rapidly become an accepted member of the organization.

Socialization does not occur in a vacuum. The learning associated with socialization goes beyond the formal job description and the expectations that may be made by people in human resources or by the new member's manager. Socialization is influenced by subtle and less subtle statements and behaviors offered up by colleagues, management, employees, clients, and other people with whom new members come in contact.

The way in which individuals adjust to new situations is remarkably similar. This holds true even though the content and type of adjustments may vary. For instance, as pointed out previously, anxiety is high at entry and the new member usually wants to reduce that anxiety quickly. The information obtained during the recruitment and selection stages is always incomplete and usually distorted. New employees, therefore, must alter their understanding of their role to fit more complete information they get once they are on the job. The point is that there is no instant adjustment—every new member goes through a settling-in period that tends to follow a relatively standard pattern.

The Socialization Process

Socialization can be conceptualized as a process made up of three stages: prearrival, encounter, and metamorphosis.[9] the first stage encompasses the learning the new employee has gained before joining the organization. In the second stage, the new employee gets an understanding of what the organization is really like, and deals with the realization that the expectations and reality may differ. In the third stage, lasting change occurs. Here, new employees becomes fully trained in their jobs, perform successfully, and "fit" in with the values and norms of coworkers.[10] These three stages ultimately affect new employees' productivity on the job, their commitment to the organization's goals, and their decision to remain with the organization.[11] Figure 8-1 is a graphic representation of the selection process.

The **prearrival stage** explicitly recognizes that each individual arrives with a set of organizational values, attitudes, and expectations. These may cover both the work to be done and the organization. For instance, in many jobs, particularly high-skilled and managerial jobs, new members will have undergone a considerable degree of prior socialization in training and in school.[12] Part of teaching business students is to socialize them to what business is like, what to expect in a business career, and what kind of attitudes that professors believe will lead to successful assimilation in an organization. Prearrival socialization, however, goes beyond the specific job. The selection process is used in most organizations to inform prospective employees about the organization as a whole. In addition, of course, interviews in the selection process also act to ensure the inclusion of the "right type"—determining those who will fit in![13] "Indeed, the ability of individuals to present the appropriate face during the selection process determines their ability to move into the organization in the first place. Thus, success depends on the degree to which aspiring members have correctly anticipated the expectations and desires of those in the organization in charge of selection."[14]

Upon entry into the organization, new members enter the **encounter stage.** Here the individuals confront the possible dichotomy between their expectations—about their jobs, their coworkers, their supervisors, and the organization in general—and reality. If expectations prove to have been more or less accurate, the encounter state merely provides a reaffirmation of the perceptions generated earlier. However, this is often not the case. Where expectations and reality differ, new employees must undergo socialization that will detach them from their previous assumptions and replace these with the organization's pivotal standards.[15] For example, at Micron Technology Inc., of Boise, Idaho, new employees are indoctrinated into the company's use of work teams.[16] Because many new employees were unsure of how to quickly assimilate into work

Prearrival Stage The socialization process stage that recognizes individuals arrive in an organization with a set of organizational values, attitudes, and expectations.

Encounter Stage The socialization stage where individuals confront the possible dichotomy between their organizational expectations and reality.

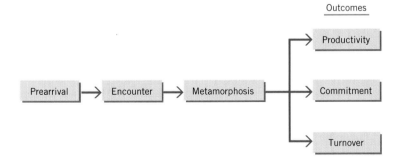

Figure 8-1
A Socialization Model

Metamorphosis Stage The socialization stage whereby the new employee must work out any inconsistencies discovered during the encounter stage.

groups, and what that meant to them as an employee of Micron, the organization created its fifteen-hour "Reaching High Performance" (RHP) program. During this process, employees gain a better understanding of team participation, taking responsibility, employee involvement, and organizational change.

Socialization, however, cannot solve all the expectation differences. At the extreme, some new members may become totally disillusioned with the actualities of their jobs, and resign. It's hoped that proper selection, including the realistic job preview, would significantly reduce this latter occurrence.

Finally, the new member must work out any problems discovered during the encounter stage. This may mean going through changes—hence, we call this the **metamorphosis stage.** But what is a desirable metamorphosis? Metamorphosis is complete—as is the socialization process—when new members have become comfortable with the organization and their work teams. In this situation, they will have internalized the norms of the organization and their coworkers; and they understand and accept these norms.[17] New members will feel accepted by their peers as trusted and valued individuals. They will become confident that they have the competence to complete their jobs successfully. The will have gained an understanding of the organizational system; not only their own tasks but the rules, procedures, and informally accepted practices as well. Finally, they will know how they are going to be evaluated. That is, they've gained an understanding of what criteria will be used to measure and appraise their work. They'll know what is expected of them, and what constitutes a "good" job. Consequently, as Figure 8-1 shows, successful metamorphosis should have a positive effect on new employees' productivity and the employee's commitment to the organization, and should reduce the likelihood that the employee will leave the organization anytime soon.[18]

If HRM recognizes that certain assumptions hold for new employees entering an organization and that new employees typically follow a three-staged socialization process, they can develop a program to begin helping these employees adapt to the company. The onset of that HRM program lies in the orientation process. Let's turn our attention to this aspect of organizational life—socializing our new employees through the new-employee orientation process.

The Purpose of New-Employee Orientation

Orientation Process The process of adapting new employees to the organization.

New-employee **orientation** covers the activities involved in introducing a new employee to the organization and to his or her work unit. It expands on the information received during the recruitment and selection stages, and helps to reduce the initial anxiety we all feel when beginning a new job. For example, an orientation program should familiarize the new member with the organization's objectives, history, philosophy, procedures, and rules; communicate relevant HRM policies such as work hours, pay procedures, overtime requirements, and company benefits; review the specific duties and responsibilities of the new member's job; provide a tour of the organization's physical facilities; and introduce the employee to his or her manager and coworkers. Figure 8-2 illustrates a generic new-employee orientation agenda used in one organization.

Who is responsible for orienting the new employee? This can be done by either the new employee's supervisor, the people in HRM, or some combination thereof. In many medium-sized and most large organizations, HRM takes charge of explaining such matters as overall organizational policies and employee benefits. In other medium-sized and most small firms, new employees will receive their entire orientation from their supervisor. Figure 8-2 demon-

Figure 8-2
A Sample New-Employee Orientation Schedule

NEW EMPLOYEE:	Ryan Bradshaw B.S. in Accounting University of Texas, El Paso, 1996.
JOB TITLE:	Accountant I
DEPARTMENT:	Accounting and Finance
8:00 A.M.	Report to Human Resources Receive orientation package, including brochures describing the organization's history, products, and philosophy.
8:10–8:30	Welcome by company president
8:30–9:00	Ms. Burke, Employment: Review Employment policies and practices.
9:00–10:00	Mr. O'Neal, Training and Development Review Training, Development and Career Development Program offerings.
10:00–10:15	Break
10:15–10:40	Mr. Nash, Compensation Overview and philosophy of company pay practices.
10:40–12:00	Ms. Reed, Benefits Overview and enrollment for eligible benefits.
12:00–12:30	Mr. Harrold, Employee Relations Overview of safety, health, and communications programs.
12:30–1:30	Lunch with Ms. Cosby (new employee's supervisor).
1:30–3:00	Supervisory Orientation Provides a detailed tour of the Accounting Department. Reviews the organization's overall structure, and the organization within the Accounting Department. Discusses daily job routine and department policies and rules. Explains job expectations. Introduces new employee to his coworkers.
3:00–4:00	Tour of physical plant
4:00–5:00	New employee is on his own to familiarize himself with, and set up his office.

strates a situation where the process is shared between the HRM staff and the new member's supervisor.

Of course, the new employee's orientation may not be formal at all. For instance, in many small organizations, orientation may mean the new member reports to her supervisor, who then assigns the new member to another employee who will introduce her to those persons with whom she will be working closely. This may then be followed by a quick tour to show her where the lavatory is, how to make her way to the cafeteria, and how to find the coffee machine. Then the new employee is shown to her desk and left to fend for herself.

Although these programs may function differently, it is our contention that new-employee orientation requires much more. For instance, in today's organizations, it is imperative that new employees understand what the organization is

●

Culture The rules, jargon, customs, and other traditions that clarify acceptable and unacceptable behavior in an organization.

about.[19] More specifically, these individuals need to understand the organization's culture.

Understanding the Organization's Culture

Every organization has its own unique **culture.** This culture includes long-standing, and often unwritten, rules and regulations; a special language that facilitates communication among members; shared standards of relevance as to the critical aspects of the work that is to be done; matter-of-fact prejudices; standards for social etiquette and demeanor; established customs for how members should relate to peers, subordinates, superiors, and outsiders; and other traditions that clarify what is appropriate and "smart" behavior within the organization, and what is not.[20] An employee who has been properly socialized to the organization's culture, then, has learned how things are done, what matters, and which work-related behaviors and perspectives are acceptable and desirable and which ones are not.

To better understand the concept of unique organizational cultures, we should look at the concepts of roles, values, and norms. Every job requires the incumbent to behave in certain specified ways. These behaviors are more or less expected of people who are identified with certain jobs. We call the set of such behaviors **roles.** Your instructor acts a certain way in the classroom, but that is not the way this individual behaves at sporting events. Why? Because your instructor is not "playing teacher" at the game!

Roles Behaviors that job incumbents are expected to display.

Employees do not play out their roles in a vacuum. Their roles are significantly influenced by the values and norms held by members of their work group. Values are basic convictions about what is right or wrong, good or bad, desirable or not. Every individual has a value system, though rarely explicit, that represents a prioritizing or ranking of values in terms of their relative importance. A teacher of business administration courses in a university finds that departmental colleagues often identify with the values of competition, efficiency,

These two employees of the Cadet Uniform company have fully assimilated into the company culture. This socialization process was a function of a three-stage process—the prearrival stage, the encounter stage, and the metamorphosis stage.

free enterprise, and the profit ethic. On the other hand, they tend to place low importance on values like sociability and rewarding employees based on seniority and government intervention. What new organizational members value, then, will significantly influence their behaviors.

The new employee's work group will have its own standards of acceptable behavior. These norms tell members what they ought or ought not do under certain circumstances. They might include not producing too little and thus drawing unnecessary attention to the work unit, defending your coworkers against attacks from management, or avoiding giving any assistance to a competing department.

Note how the concepts of roles, values, and norms interrelate. What a person does on the job depends on the standards that the organization and his or her work group convey as appropriate. Importantly, the parameters of the role—whether one is an accountant, lawyer, teacher, librarian, or salesclerk—change in response to the values and norms in the environment where one performs that role. This explains, for instance, why almost all the employees at Merrill Lynch come to work dressed meticulously in their business attire, while their counterparts at Ben & Jerry's Ice Cream typically wear casual attire.

You may be wondering how these concepts relate to the socialization process. The answer is that individuals, in their work roles, may accept all, some, or none of the organization's standards.[21] Individuals who readily accept all of them may become conformists; their socialization, when complete, can result in the infamous "yes person." At the other extreme is the rebel who rejects all the organization's standards. Such employees are usually quickly labeled as "misfits," since their actions seem to defeat the organization's goals. Rebels rarely last long, being expelled from the organization for their inability to adapt to "the way we do things around here." In between, we get people who accept some standards, but not others. As long as these individuals accept at least the pivotal or key values of the organization, there is no problem if they reject some of the relevant but nonpivotal values. Pivotal values are those deemed essential by the organization; refraining from bad-mouthing the company in public, for example, is often considered a pivotal value. Relevant values, by contrast, are deemed desirable but not absolutely essential for success in the organization. Reading financial periodicals, for example, may be a relevant value for employees at Merrill Lynch, but not for those who work for Ben & Jerry's Ice Cream. People who are able to discriminate between key and relevant standards are often innovative and creative and perform the role of the healthy questioner. They have accepted those standards necessary to maintain membership in the organization. They are comfortable in their jobs and demonstrate commitment to the organization.

Clearly, one objective of the socialization process is to ensure that rebellious types who reject key organizational values are either changed or expelled. But whether management considers most or only some of its standards as truly pivotal depends on management's objectives. If managers want people who are totally loyal to the organization and will fight to maintain its traditions and customs, they will probably utilize different methods of socialization than if they seek highly creative, individualistic employees who accept only the pivotal standards and reject the rest.

Learning the Dos and Don'ts

Regardless of how tolerant management is of individualism, it is realistic to conclude that organizations, particularly large ones, do not enjoy having em-

What effect can an organization's culture have on achieving corporate goals? Plenty! Consider Mary Kay Cosmetics. Corporate culture encourages both the company's 2,200 employees and 375,000 independent beauty consultants by fostering inspiration, excitement, education, and recognition. Sales force members achieving goals receive rewards such as money, diamond jewelry, dream vacations, and the infamous pink Cadillacs, ensuring unparalleled enthusiasm and success.

ployees who continually attack the basic goals of the organization (e.g., the means of attaining business goals, the underlying responsibilities inherent in each person's role, or the organization's basic rules and regulations). But the fact is that new people come into the organization with the potential to bring about change—change that can disturb the organization's "tried and true" ways of doing things.

It may not be management's wish to get every employee to accept all of the organization's standards; to do so could create a conforming and apathetic organizational environment. But the pivotal values must be conveyed and accepted. Without this acceptance, new employees will lack commitment and loyalty to the interests of the organization and will pose a threat to management and experienced members. Furthermore, they will never be accepted as full-fledged members of the organization. Successful socialization will mean having employees who fit in by knowing the dos and don'ts of a "good employee."

A Few Examples

Tenure is a familiar concept to academics. Teachers and professors who are granted tenure, in effect, are given permanent or lifetime employment unless something drastic occurs. While procedures exist for removing tenure, they are time-consuming and difficult for a university to execute. As a result, tenure is a highly-prized possession offering faculty certain rights and allowing for long-term research. To achieve tenure, a prospect must endure the watchful eye of those who are already tenured. This trial period preceding the tenure decision typically lasts five to seven years. Prospects who "measure up" will get tenure. Measuring up means, in actuality, that the individual has been well socialized to the values of the tenured group. Prospects who accept and demonstrate, by their behavior, that they fit in with the tenured members are granted permanent employment. Those who fail may be expelled from the organization. For those who think this practice is an oddity exclusive to educational institutions, consider the process that exists in large accounting and law firms. New employees start out as associates, most with the goal of someday becoming partners in their firms. But partnership (which means owning a piece of the firm and enjoying permanent employment) is withheld for some extended period—usually five to fifteen years—while the associates prove to the current partners that they are worthy. This means that the potential partners must demonstrate through what they say and do that they know the ropes and can be trusted.

The CEO's Role in Orientation

Prior to the mid-1980s, new-employee orientation operated, if at all, without any input from the company's executive management. But that began to change in the 1980s, due in part to consultants and authors such as Tom Peters strongly advocating that senior management "manage by walking around."[22] What Peters and others advocated was that senior managers become highly visible in the organization, meeting and greeting employees, and listening to employee concerns. At the same time, these individuals were given the opportunity to talk about the company—where it is going and how it is going to get there. In management terminology, this was called *visioning*.

As more and more successful companies began to be cited in business literature for their leaders' ability to be involved in the work force, one question arose. If it appeared to work well for existing employees, what would it do for new employees joining the organization? The answer appears to be a lot.[23] Let's look at this more closely.

Earlier we addressed an assumption dealing with one's anxiety. One of the more stressful aspects of starting a new job is the thought of entering the unknown. Although a previous organization may have done something undesirable—like paying considerably lower wages than what the market valued your job—at least you knew what you had. But starting a new job is frightening. Did you do the right thing, make the right choice? Having the CEO present from day one addressing new employees helps to allay some of those fears. The CEO's first responsibility is to welcome new employees aboard and talk to them about what a good job choice they made. In fact, this segment of new-employee orientation can be likened to a cheerleading pep rally. The CEO is in a position to "turn on" these new employees by talking about what it is like to work for the organization. In addition, the CEO is in a position to begin to discuss what really matters in the company—an indoctrination to the organization's culture.[24] For example, at Metropolitan Property and Casualty, new employees are exposed to the company's philosophy and mission from the very beginning.[25] Company managers use the orientation program to begin to instill company values into its new employees. It is also possible at this time to begin to advocate company goals such as "organizational growth" or customer service.[26] For United Hospitals Inc., that is exactly what they've done. In fact, this hospital not only talks about such goals, it also builds techniques like "problem solving" and "conflict resolution" into the orientation program.[27]

When a CEO is present, the company is sending the message that it truly cares for its employees. Employee satisfaction concepts are sometimes thrown around an organization to such an extent that they are nothing more than ruses to pay lip service to the idea. But this senior company official's presence validates that the company really is concerned—the CEO's commitment to making the first day special is evidenced by his or her presence. And even when scheduling conflicts may arise, companies can be prepared: Levi Strauss uses videotaped messages that carry the same message.[28]

As the CEO concludes his or her presentation, a final question-and-answer period can prove worthwhile. During this stage, new employees can get answers from the top about any concerns they may have. Once again the message reinforced is, "Communications are important." Seeing the CEO matches the name to a face and establishes an atmosphere from which to build organizational commitment.

Now that senior management has done its job, it's time for HRM to take over. Let's look at HRM's role in the orientation process.

HRM's Role in Orientation

In our introductory comments we stated that the orientation function can be performed by HRM, line management, or a combination of the two. Inasmuch as Figure 8-2 indicates a preference for a combination strategy, it is our contention that HRM plays a major role in new-employee orientation—the role of *coordination,* which ensures that the appropriate components are in place. In addition, HRM also serves as a participant in the program. Consequently, it is important to recognize what HRM must do. For example, in our discussion of making the job offer (Chapter 6), we emphasized that the offer should come from human resources. This was necessary to coordinate the administrative activities surrounding a new hire. The same holds true for new-employee orientation. Depending on the recruiting that takes place, there should be a systematic schedule of when new employees join a company.

As job offers are made and accepted, HRM should instruct the new employee when to report to work. However, before the employee formally arrives, HRM must be prepared to handle some of the more routine needs of these individuals; for example, new employees typically have a long list of questions about benefits. More proactive organizations like Xerox and AT&T prepare a package for new employees. This package generally focuses on the important decisions that a new employee must make—decisions like the choice of health insurance, institutions for direct deposit of paychecks, and tax withholding information. By providing this information a few weeks before an individual starts work, the HRM unit in these companies gives new hires ample time to make a proper choice—quite possibly, a choice that must be made in conjunction with a working spouse's options. Furthermore, forms often require information that most employees do not readily keep with them; for example, social security numbers of family members and medical histories. Accordingly, having that information before the new-employee orientation session saves time.[29] HRM's second concern revolves around its role as a participant in the process. Most new employees' exposure to the organization thus far has been with HRM, but after the hiring process is over, HRM quickly drops out of the picture unless there is a problem. Therefore, HRM must spend some time in orientation addressing what assistance it can offer to employees in the future. This point cannot be minimized. HRM provides an array of services, like career guidance and training, to other areas of the company. Although these areas generally are unable to go outside the organization for their HRM needs, HR cannot become complacent. They must continue to provide their services to the employees, and departments, of the organization. And one means of affecting this service is to let these new employees know what else HR can do for them.

With these two areas in mind—administrative and educative—let's go through an orientation program that reflects the responsibilities of the four areas of HRM identified in Chapter 1—employment, training and development, compensation and benefits, and employee relations.

Employment's Role

Recall from Chapter 1 that employment is generally regarded as the recruiting arm of HRM. As such, this area has had more contact with applicants and new hires than any other area in HRM. Accordingly, Employment specialists should serve as the coordinating body for the orientation process. These individuals should notify the new employee of the start date and ensure that the pre-employment package has been sent. Questions relating to this package should be addressed initially by Employment representatives, again because of their familiarity with the individual. In addition, because of the relationship that has been built through the selection process, the Employment presenter should serve as host to new-employee orientation, making sure that new employees are greeted as they enter the building, and escorting them to the room where new-employee orientation is taking place. In companies like Apple Computer, much of employee commitment to the organization is often linked to that initial feeling established on the first day on the job.[30]

With the preliminaries taken care of, Employment specialists must then switch hats and become a presenter in the process. During this segment, the Employment representative should provide an overview of its function, describing what it does. Although recruiting is their mainstay operation, new employees may not see the benefit of further dealings with Employment—and for the most part that is true in the immediate future. This is because many organizations have policies that require an individual to be in a current job for a period of time before being permitted to "bid" for another position. During this period, it is true that exposure to the employment aspect will be limited, but beyond that time is a different story.

Accordingly, the employment presenter must address how internal promotions or job transfers work. When these new employees get into that stage of career development, they will be required to follow certain HRM policies. It is important to disseminate these policies when the employee joins the organization, so that the employees can make plans for their future, or know what to expect. For instance, if jobs are posted in a particular way, such as on a bulletin board in the lunchroom, these new employees need to know that. Furthermore, they also need to know if HRM looks at applications from both internal and external sources. So, although current employees may have more advanced knowledge of job openings and more company and job information, they need to know that they must compete for those jobs. There have been instances where current employees wrongly perceived that they would be given preferential treatment for job openings, and did not present themselves in such a way to effectively compete for the job. For instance, Employment specialists are bound to review resumes and applications in search of information indicating that the applicant has the requisite skills to do the job. If current employees do not have an updated resume, or believe that the employment representative will know what skills they possess, they may be making a mistake. Enlightening new employees to this possibility serves an important role.

Employment can also serve as the decruitment branch of HRM. Should downsizing or retrenchment occur, the employment division is generally responsible (in conjunction with other HRM units) for separating the employees from the organization. If policies exist that offer certain rights to employees, these rights should be explained. For example, if layoffs are based solely on seniority and one is targeted for layoff, can the individual bump another employee in another department with less seniority? If so, this should be conveyed. Likewise, if no guarantees are offered, that too has to be communicated.

After employment has been presented, it is time to introduce the presenter of the Training and Development function.

Training and Development's Role

As we will discuss in Chapter 9, many organizations offer a wide range of training programs. Generally speaking, however, training focuses on two elements—job training and personal development. Depending on the structure of the organization, training and development may or may not get involved in the actual job-training process. Should they not be involved, their exposure to new employees will be initially limited. Should they provide job-specific training, then more than likely they will be spending a great deal of time with the new employees over the first few weeks.

For orientation purposes, however, training and development should focus more on the development side of its operation; that is, they should communicate just what development means to employees and what programs and training sessions are available to employees of the organization. During this overview, training and development should highlight its program offerings in which employees may participate shortly, as well as those that are on the long-range horizon. The presenter of training and development should also emphasize its role in the career development process. Services that are available should be mentioned, in addition to how new employees can take advantage of such programs as tuition assistance, computerized career assessments, or any psychological assessments the development specialists are trained to administer.

We should also find training and development personnel spending some time during this presentation discussing corporate culture issues.[31] Generally charged with facilitating the change and maintaining the organization's culture, the training and development presenter should use this opportunity to reinforce what the CEO stated in the opening remarks. Once again, hearing similar messages from different people in new-employee orientation only supports its importance to the organization.

Compensation and Benefits' Role

There is no doubt that new-employee orientation programs help to eliminate many problems for the compensation and benefits area. There are so many forms to be completed when one is hired, having these employees at a convenient location at a specified time facilitates the process. For example, imagine you are the benefits administrator and you need to get new employees enrolled for their health insurance coverage. Suppose that thirty new employees start today, all going to a different location. In order for you to get the forms completed, you must travel to each location, hoping that each employee is available. You spend a minimum of one hour processing the forms with those who are present, and move on. Those who are not available just don't get enrolled. What a nightmare! New-employee orientation eliminates this ordeal. All new employees are brought together for a period of time, wherein the compensation and benefits department has a captive audience. Questions can be answered in a group forum. It is not unusual for this enrollment phase to take up to 50 percent of the time spent in new-employee orientation; that is, if the program spans a four-hour duration, typically two hours are spent completing these forms. What forms may be required? We have listed a number of them in Figure 8-3.

Aside from the form completion phase, other information is necessary for new employees to know. First of all is the question of salary. How are salaries set in the company? During orientation, compensation specialists should discuss how the company establishes its salary grades and ranges—every detail does not need to be explained, but sufficient information should be conveyed so these new employees know their salary offers were based on factual data, not on some whim. Furthermore, compensation must address how performance is evaluated, and how pay increases operate. Are they tied to performance? Are they based on seniority? Just how does the company make its determination? This presenter must be able to address the process in enough detail so that the new employees understand. Included in this discussion should be something that must never be taken for granted—pay dates. Does the company hold back a paycheck? If so, when can these new employees expect to receive their first check? In terms of a realistic job preview, nothing upsets employees more than finding out after they have been hired that they must wait a month for their first pay. Accordingly, this should be conveyed in the hiring process, and elaborated in orientation.

On the benefits side of the function, new employees need to be informed about the benefits they are to receive.[32] Some benefits, like sick and vacation leave, may require employees to be on board for six months before becoming eligible. Employees need to know about this, as well as about observed holidays.

●

Health Insurance Enrollment Form	• may involve multiple forms if an alternative health insurance provider is chosen
Dependent Coverage Forms	• provides health insurance coverage to employee's dependents
Vision and Dental Enrollment Forms	
I-9 Form: Immigration and Naturalization Form	
Direct Deposit Form	• instructs payroll where— i.e., to which financial institution—to deposit your net pay
Credit Union Enrollment Form	
Life Insurance Enrollment Form	
Dependent Life Insurance Form	• extends life-insurance coverage to dependents
Personal History Form	• captures information not permitted to be obtained on application form— (e.g., next of kin, whom to contact in an emergency)
Accidental Death and Dismemberment Enrollment Form	
Retirement Account Enrollment Form	• required when employees may choose how their retirement funds are to be invested

If the company offers personal leave days, how and when they can be used should be addressed. Finally, the retirement issue should be discussed. As we will discuss in Chapter 16, many companies offer a retirement program to which both the employee and the employer contribute. Employees need to know just how much, if any, will be deducted from their pay to contribute toward their pension, and what the company may match.

Employee Relations' Role

As the generalist's function in HRM, employee relations could address many points of interest for new employees. However, a few of these are critical: the company's communications program, its employee assistance program, and its employee recognition programs.

Earlier in this book we stated that the main difference between employee relations (ER) and labor relations lies in the presence of a union. If an organization is concerned with remaining nonunion, then employee relations plays a key role. In that role, communication programs flourish. ER must explain to new employees what the various communication programs are about. For example, the complaint procedure must be carefully reviewed so that employees know what to do if they face a problem in their unit that they cannot get rectified. Remember the discussion of sexual harassment in Chapter 3? One of the necessary components, highlighted in the Rena Weeks case, to protect an organization from being liable for its supervisors' behaviors is an avenue established to raise the sexual harassment concerns. That is exactly what ER must tell new employees—that a process exists, and can be used to their benefit. But not all communication programs are complaint-based. There may be a monthly "town" meeting to discuss the issues or concerns of employees in the organization. New employees should be informed about these meetings, their purposes, and how they can benefit from them.

ER is also frequently responsible for the health and safety of employees. During new-employee orientation, ER should address what the company does to ensure employee welfare, and explain once again what employees should do if they encounter a problem. If that problem is personal, employees may want to use some sort of employee assistance program. For example, a movement spreading rapidly in companies is the creation of the smoke-free office. When companies implement such policies, they should consider the effect it may have on employees. Furthermore, to help foster the smoke-free environment, companies may offer smoking cessation programs to their employees. (We'll take a closer look at employee assistance programs in Chapter 15.) Despite their particular focus, employee assistance programs are designed to help employees with personal problems before they become so large that they affect their work. ER should mention how the program works and how confidentiality is guaranteed.

Finally, employee relations frequently will have various programs recognizing employees for their accomplishments. Whether they are rewards for money-saving suggestions, service awards, or the company-sponsored softball or bowling team, ER should make sure that new employees understand what is available to them. At the end of the four presentations by HRM, the formal orientation program ends. However, that does not mean the process stops. Rather, after the exposure to HRM, the new employees are sent to their respective job areas, where their new managers will continue the orientation process.

Supervisor's Role in Orientation

Just as HRM plays an integral role in orienting new employees, their immediate supervisors also have a responsibility to assist in the adaptation process. When you consider that new employees will be spending almost all their time in their new job location, it's obviously imperative that managers get involved.[33] But what should that involvement be? Typically it involves the initial indoctrination into the unit.

In the initial stage of indoctrination, management must do whatever it can to make the new employee feel welcome. For example, knowing that people are nervous about their new jobs and the people they will work with, the manager can take new employees around and introduce them to their colleagues. This simple gesture goes far in making new employees feel part of the group. There are also other things the manager can do to facilitate this process; for instance, the manager may take the new employee and the other unit employees out for lunch on the first day. In fact, considering that HRM may have the employee for the first half day, meeting the new employee when HRM's program is completed and taking the employee to lunch can once again reinforce the organization's commitment to its people. By including colleagues, the astute manager

These coworkers are helping a new employee to adapt to her new job. Research tells us that this initial informal welcoming session helps increase the likelihood of increasing employee loyalty to the organization, thus reducing the possibility of a quick "turnover."

is laying the groundwork for the new employee's peers to become actively involved in the adaptation process. In fact, studies suggest that new employees not only welcome this **peer orientation,** but often prefer it[34] and rely on it as a source of information.

Lastly, organizations must recognize the importance of these initial few days for employee loyalty. In order to minimize the turnover that accompanies poor socialization processes, organizations must be willing to invest in training managers on just what is required to help new employees adapt. For example, the BOC Distribution Services Limited Company spends considerable time training its managers for such events.[35] This training involves learning how to establish performance standards, how to coach and counsel new employees, and how to be an effective mentor. Even though much of orientation appears to verge on the "touchy-feely" side of HRM, we cannot forget the main reason we hired the new employee—to do a job. Accordingly, managers must be capable of defining job requirements, provide the necessary tools to enable the employee to do the job, and provide ample feedback.

Peer Orientation Coworker assistance in orienting new employees.

Study Tools and Applications

Summary

This summary relates to the Learning Objectives provided on p. 215.
After having read this chapter, you should know:

1. Socialization is a process of adaptation. Organization-entry socialization refers to the adaption that takes place when an individual passes from outside the organization to the role of an inside member.
2. The three stages of employee socialization are the prearrival, the encounter, and the metamorphosis stages.
3. The outsider–insider passage refers to the adaptation to a new work environment resulting in different work activities, a new boss, or a difficult group of coworkers.
4. Orientation is part of socialization and covers the activities involved in introducing a new employee to the organization and to his or her work unit.
5. Organizational socialization attempts to adapt the new employee to the organization's culture by conveying to the employee how things are done and what matters.
6. The critical theme of socializing employees is that new employees accept the organization's pivotal standards.
7. The CEO's role in orientation is to welcome the new employees, reaffirm their choice of joining the company, and discuss the organization's goals and objectives while conveying information about the organization's culture.
8. Each function in HRM has a specific role in orientation. For instance, Employment discusses how the promotion from within process works; Training and Development covers development programs offered; Compensation and Benefits has forms completed and discusses salary and benefit offerings; and Employee Relations discusses the company's health, safety, communications, and complaint procedures.
9. Supervisors serve a role of continuing orientation after HRM's formal program is over. This may include activities like taking the employee to lunch to introducing him or her to colleagues.
10. A sample orientation program involves many parties. Coordinated through HRM, such a program would have a welcome by the senior management member, and presentation by all functions of HRM. Employees' managers would then pick up where HRM leaves off.

Key Terms

culture
encounter stage
metamorphosis stage
norms
organizational stability
orientation

peer orientation
prearrival stage
roles
socialization
values

EXPERIENTIAL EXERCISE
University Orientation

In today's companies, we spend time thinking about planning and implementing orientation programs. Universities, too, have followed suit. In many universities, new students typically are invited to spend a day with university representatives. These representatives go over various aspects of "campus life" that are important to the new student. Among these are campus tours, housing and dining information, major declarations, campus services, and course registration. Inasmuch as this process assists new students to a university, it is often general in nature; specific information for each college or major may be limited.

Therefore, as business students, develop an orientation program to be used in your school. As a group of three to five students, develop an orientation plan that could be given to the dean of the college for immediate implementation. Make sure you address the time frame for the process. Also, decide who should conduct the orientation. Also, consider any modifications to your program to reflect unique needs of women and minority students.

CASE APPLICATION:
Orientation at Marriott Hotels

It should come to no one's surprise that the United States has become a predominantly service economy. In fact, the Bureau of Labor Statistics indicates that almost 80 percent of all employment in the United States is in providing services and that percentage will grow during the next decade. Success in this industry is a function of many factors. Unquestionably, however, is one primary factor—the individuals providing the service. Given this service trend and the importance of people, an appropriate question for service organizations is: What are you doing to attract and keep the best service workers?[36] When the management of Marriott Hotels posed that question to themselves, they responded, "much, much more!"

Marriott Hotels used to hire doormen, bellmen, front desk clerks, and concierges in droves. These front-line people were the first point of contact with customers. As such, you'd expect that the hotel would want to have these people represent the "best" the hotel had to offer. Yet, when these employees were hired, they were often brought together for an hour and told of the benefits they'd receive. After that, they were put to work—often with little idea of what to do, or how Marriott functioned. The results? Customers weren't happy about the service they were getting, and more than 40 percent of the new employees quit within the first three months on the job. That all began to change in the early 1990s, however.

It started when Marriott launched its new employee orientation program. Instead of the one hour, here's-your-benefits speech, new employees go through an intensive ninety-day orientation. It begins with new employees attending an initial eight-hour session. During this session, new employees are overloaded with information about what quality service means. Employees are trained in how to please customers, and what role they play in making the hotel a success. And yes, they still get their benefits information, it just doesn't dominate orientation. And that speech is a bit easier to swallow, especially considering the extravagant lunch that is served as a welcome-aboard gesture.

After the first eight-hour session, employees are not then thrown into their jobs. Rather, they are assigned to a buddy who will continue the orientation with the new employee for the next three months. Employees and their buddies also attend refresher courses, which reinforce the hotel's commitment to both its employees and customers. At the end of the ninety-day orientation, new employees, buddies, and guests are invited to a gala banquet—a reward for "learning the ropes."

How successful has Marriott's orientation program been? If success at the hotels can be measured by customer response times, then they've been highly successful. Prior to its new-employee orientation process, it took an average of fifteen minutes from the time customers stepped onto the curb in front of the hotel until they were in their rooms. Today, that time has been cut to under three minutes!

Questions

1. Describe how Marriott's previous orientation of a one-hour benefit speech adversely affected customer service. How did it affect the hotel's goals and objectives?
2. Identify how Marriott's current employee-orientation program helps new employees through the three-stage socialization process.
3. At two points in time, lunch on the first day and at the conclusion of the ninety-day orientation program, Marriott treats employees to spectacular event. How can such events be related to employees' jobs and customer service?

Testing Your Understanding

How well did you fulfill the learning objectives?

1. Proper socialization is indicated by
   a. cheerfully accepting every assignment you are given.
   b. questioning few assignments you are given.
   c. understanding the right way to do a job.
   d. completing assigned tasks ahead of schedule.
   e. completing assigned tasks error-free.
2. Outsider–insider work passages may be triggered by all of the following changes except
   a. a new boss.
   b. a new occurrence of a disability
   c. new coworkers.
   d. new performance evaluation standards.
   e. new job activities.
3. The metamorphosis stage of socialization is best associated with
   a. permanent change.
   b. reinforcement.
   c. stability and commitment.
   d. none of the above.

4. What is the difference between roles and values?
   a. Values are behaviors that employees display in organizations. Roles are attitudes that employees hold.
   b. Values have no place in organizations. Roles are what is required in organizations.
   c. Roles are expected behaviors. Values are convictions about right and wrong, important and unimportant.
   d. Roles and values are different terms for the same attribute.
   e. Roles determine organization culture. Values are determined by organizational culture.
5. Ray teaches international human resources management at a prestigious eastern business school. He travels every summer to collect data and writes and publishes a short book of comparative human resources practices when he returns. Ray usually wears souvenirs to school through the month of September. For instance, last year he went to Fiji and wore flowered shirts. The year before he went to Argentina and wore gaucho pants. The year before he went to Australia

and wore aboriginal art. The school is known for its conservative, business approach. Suits, ties, and briefcases are the uniform of the day. This year Ray got promoted to full professor and was awarded outstanding scholar status. Which statement is accurate about the organization's culture?

  a. Ray's values are different from most members of the organization.

  b. No norms apply to Ray. Tenured college professors can do whatever they want.

  c. Roles in the business school are different from other parts of the university. Norms cannot be identified in such an institution.

  d. Norms and roles about scholarship are more important in this university than norms and roles about appearance.

  e. Values, roles, and norms in this university are clearly defined and consistent.

6. Military boot camp, the academic tenure system, and becoming a partner in a law firm are all examples of

  a. archaic institutions with rigid cultures that direct most employees' behaviors according to specified rules and regulations.

  b. formal, deliberate processes to teach newcomers the Dos and Don't's of organizational life.

  c. acceptable organizational cultures.

  d. unacceptable organizational cultures.

  e. no such examples were given.

7. The vice-president of human resources wants to include the CEO in the orientation process. What would be the best way to do this?

  a. Have the CEO explain the company benefits packages.

  b. Have the CEO dress up like a clown and sing or do a stunt. That will help employees realize she is just one of the team members.

  c. Have the CEO moderate the film about the first hundred years of company history.

  d. Have the CEO share the vision of the organization, what she hopes to accomplish, and to welcome the new employees to that vision.

  e. Have the CEO go to lunch with each new employee.

8. Some companies send a packet of benefits information to the employee's home a week or so before the new employee starts work. All of these reasons were given for this arrangement except

  a. time is not used during formal orientations to have an employee fill out forms.

  b. decisions about insurance coverage often have to be made in conjunction with coverage already provided by a working spouse.

  c. often, employees change their mind about working for a firm when they see the benefits options in writing. Sending the information home reduces embarrassing scenes in the human resources office.

  d. some of the forms require information that a person would not routinely carry to work.

  e. this process expedites handling routine needs.

9. Managers typically perform all of these functions during the indoctrination process except

  a. taking the new employee to management briefings or helping the new employee to begin networking with other managers.

  b. welcoming the new employee and providing a "welcoming" gift in his or her office.

  c. introducing the new employee to colleagues.

  d. taking the new employee out to lunch.

  e. allowing colleagues to chat informally with the new employee.

10. When a new employee was hired by a large manufacturing organization, his supervisor gave him a few hours to just "get acquainted" with his peers. How was that part of his indoctrination process?

  a. It was not a part of indoctrination.

  b. It gave the boss a chance to observe the new employee in a group setting.

  c. It made the new employee self-reliant and thus, more confident.

  d. It gave the new employee's colleagues a chance to decide whether or not they wanted to work with him.

  e. None of the above.

11. Firms with high organizational stability

  a. are slow to respond to external pressures.

  b. have missions and goals that appear consistent over time.

  c. have higher turnover rates than other firms.

  d. focus on stable production processes.

  e. do not need to spend much time in employee socialization.

12. All of the following are examples of organizational Dos or Don'ts for this human resources class except

  a. Do arrive to class on time.

  b. Don't cut the class more times than the instructor allows.

  c. Don't cheat on exams.

  d. Do turn in papers on time.

  e. Do avoid certain local bars on weekends.

13. Your text describes CEO involvement in orientation programs in all of these ways, except

  a. they welcomed new employees aboard and told them they made a good job choice, like leading a pep rally.

  b. they indoctrinated new employees into the organization's culture by sharing the philosophy and mission of the organization.

  c. they advocated company goals.

  d. they conducted company tours.

  e. they emphasized the importance of communications by having an open question-and-answer period.

Chapter Nine

EMPLOYEE TRAINING AND DEVELOPMENT

LEARNING OBJECTIVES

AFTER READING THIS CHAPTER, YOU WILL BE ABLE TO:

1. Explain why employee training is important.
2. Define training.
3. Discuss the relationship between effective training programs and various learning principles.
4. Describe how training needs evolve.
5. Identify the two types of formal training methods.
6. Define employee development.
7. Explain organizational development and the role of the change agent.
8. Discuss on-the-job and off-the-job employee development techniques.
9. Explain what is meant by the mentoring/coaching process.
10. Identify how employee counseling can be used as a development tool.
11. Describe the methods and criteria involved in evaluating training programs.
12. Explain issues critical to international training and development.

Bill Sanko, CEO of XEL Corporation, the Aurora, Colorado, communications equipment manufacturer, had a dream.[1] He wanted to build a world-class organization, one that produced high-quality products, demonstrated high degrees of workplace efficiency, and performed all this in an enriched team environment. Unfortunately, Bill's dream had one major drawback—his employees. Apparently, the areas from which XEL recruited produced high-school graduates, many of whom lacked sufficient math and English skills. Consequently, organizational activities like team members evaluating one another and statistical process control techniques suffered. Nonetheless, Sanko wasn't about to give up. Rather he sought the help of the local community college and formed a training committee in an effort to develop training programs to correct these deficiencies.

Members of this training committee knew they faced a major challenge. But, they felt that it was not so insurmountable that training couldn't overcome. Yet would typical classroom lectures on the college campus be the answer? That became the critical question. Seeking an answer, the committee learned that employees had special training needs and desires. They also learned that most employees preferred to learn in a specific way—the least desirable of which was to be lectured to. And so, with that information, XEL and the Community College began to develop specifically tailored training programs. Classes consisted of no more than six employees, such that each worker got special attention. Workers got an opportunity to learn at their own pace, trying out what they learned, and discussing problems they still encounter. Today, thirty classes cover a variety of topics, and each of the 230 employees spends more than five hours a month in training.

Companies like XEL, who spend significant money in training, need to address a concern: Are they getting their money's worth? At XEL, after each class, an extensive evaluation is conducted to ensure that what is learned actually transfers to the job. When a problem arises, changes are made. For example, after several statistical process control classes taught by a faculty member at the college, the employees felt that the class was not helping them. Consequently, XEL employees took it upon themselves to develop and implement a new program!

In the four years since the training began at XEL, the company is moving closer to being recognized as a world-class communications equipment producer. In fact, XEL now holds twelve patents in the field; brought about, as Sanko explains, by a better trained work force.

These XEL employees are participating in a training program on statistical process control that they helped develop. Their program, in cooperation with Aurora Community College, limits enrollment to fewer than six participants per program—so that each one gets individual attention.

Introduction

Every organization, like XEL Corporation, needs to have well-trained and experienced people to perform the activities that must be done. As jobs in today's dynamic organizations have become more complex, the importance of employee education has increased. When jobs were simple, easy to learn, and influenced to only a small degree by technological changes, there was little need for employees to upgrade or alter their skills. But that situation rarely exists today. Instead, rapid job changes are occurring, requiring employee skills to be transformed and frequently updated.[2] In organizations, this takes place through what we call employee training.

What Is Employee Training?

Training is a learning experience in that it seeks a relatively permanent change in an individual that will improve the ability to perform on the job. We typically say training can involve the changing of skills, knowledge, attitudes, or behavior.[3] It may mean changing what employees know, how they work, their attitudes toward their work, or their interaction with their coworkers or supervisor.

For our purposes, we will differentiate between **employee training** and **employee development** for one particular reason. Although both are similar in the methods used to affect learning, their time frames differ. Training is more present-day oriented; its focus is on individuals' current jobs, enhancing those specific skills and abilities to immediately perform their jobs.[4] For example, suppose you enter the job market during your senior year of college, pursuing a job as an HRM recruiter. Although you have a Business Administration degree with a concentration in Human Resource Management, when you are hired,

Employee Training Present-oriented training, focusing on individuals' current jobs.

Employee Development Future-oriented training, focusing on the personal growth of the employee.

some training is in order. Specifically, you'll need to learn the company's HRM policies and practices, and other pertinent recruiting practices. This, by definition, is job-specific training, or training that is designed to make you more effective in your current job.

Employee development, on the other hand, generally focuses on future jobs in the organization.[5] As your job and career progress, new skills and abilities will be required. For example, if you become a director of HRM, the skills needed to perform that job are quite different than those required for recruiting candidates. Now you will be required to supervise a number of HRM professionals; requiring a broad-based knowledge of HRM and very specific management competencies like communication skills, evaluating employee performance, and disciplining problem individuals. As you are groomed for positions of greater responsibility, employee development efforts will help prepare you for that day.

Irrespective of whether we are involved in employee training or employee development, the same outcome is required—learning. Learning is critical to making employees more effective and efficient on the job, so let's take a look at what we mean by learning.

Training and Learning

We have previously described training and development as a learning process. Of course, much of an employee's learning about a job takes place outside of specific training activities. This was demonstrated in Chapter 8 on orientation. But if we are to understand what training techniques can do to improve an employee's job performance, we should begin by explaining how people learn.

Theories of Learning

Learning is the process of bringing about relatively permanent change through experience. This can be done through direct experience—by doing, or indirectly, through observation. Regardless of the means by which learning takes place, we cannot measure learning per se; we can only measure the changes in attitudes and behavior that occur as a result of learning. For our discussion, we will emphasize how we learn rather that what we learn.

Two ways have dominated learning research over the years. These are operant conditioning, and social learning theory.

Operant Conditioning A type of conditioning in which behavior leads to a reward or prevents punishment.

Operant Conditioning   **Operant conditioning** views learning as a behavioral change brought about by a function of its consequences. People learn to act in a manner to achieve something they want, or to avoid something they don't want. The tendency for an individual to repeat such behavior, then, is influenced by the reinforcement (or lack thereof) stemming from the consequences of behavior. Reinforcement, therefore, strengthens actions and increase the likelihood that individual will repeat the behaviors.

As originally proposed by B. F. Skinner, operant conditioning (sometimes referred to as behavior modification) focuses on learning from external sources,[6] as opposed to learning that takes place from within. Skinner and his followers have argued that by creating consequences to follow certain behaviors, the frequency of that behavior will be altered. That is, individuals will most likely engage in appropriate behaviors if they are reinforced for doing so. For example, suppose you're unsure about spending the time to answer the "Testing Your

Understanding" questions at the end of each chapter. For the first exam, you do; and you score very highly on the exam. For exam two, however, you didn't have the time, slacked off, and didn't answer them at all. Your second grade was significantly lower. Operant conditioning, then, would indicate that you'll be studying the questions again (the modified behavior), because there was a positive reward (reinforcement) in doing so. This same analogy applies to your work. If by learning, as demonstrated by some proficiency level, you'll be taken off probation, then that reward will foster a learning endeavor.

In operant conditioning, there are four ways in which behavior can be shaped. These are positive reinforcement, negative reinforcement, punishment, and extinction (see "HRM Skills"). **Positive reinforcement** provides a pleasant response to an individual's actions. A raise, promotion, or even praise for a job well done would encourage the behaviors to continue. **Negative reinforcement** involves a reward that is unpleasant. "Writing-up" employees who fight on the job or who take extended lunch breaks would serve as disincentives to not engage in those behaviors. When those behaviors stopped, so too, would the negative reinforcement. **Punishment** penalizes employees for specific undesirable behaviors. Being fired for coming to work under the influence of a substance would be an example of punishment. Finally, if we withhold *any* reinforcement—positive, negative, or punishment—we engage in *extinction*. If your professor never calls on raised hands to ask questions (extinction) sooner or later the hands will no longer go up. Although all four means affect learning, positive appears to have the greatest influence on permanent behavioral change.[7]

Social-Learning Another perspective views learning as a continuous interaction between individuals and their environments. This is called **social-learning theory**.[8] The social-learning theory acknowledges that we can learn by observing what happens to other people, by being told about something, or through direct experience. That is, much of what we learn comes from watching others—family members, teachers, coworkers, the media, and the like. Since much of employee training is observational in nature, this theory appears to have considerable application potential.

Social-learning theory can be viewed as an expansion of behavior modification because it, too, recognizes the importance of consequences on behavior. But social-learning theory also focuses on what individuals observe, and the importance of their perceptions in learning. That is, individuals respond to situations with respect to how they perceive consequences effecting them; not necessarily the consequences themselves. For instance, if you perceive that the "Testing Your Understanding" questions actually will be used by your professor on the exam, then your perception of the consequence not to study them is too negative.

The influence of others and things, which we'll call models, is central to the social-learning viewpoint. Four processes have been found to determine the influence a model will have on an individual:

1. *Attentional Processes* People only learn from models when they recognize and pay attention to their critical features. We tend to be most influenced by models that are attractive, repeatedly available, that we think are important, or that we see as similar to us.
2. *Retention Processes* A model's influence will depend on how well the individual remembers the model's action, even after the model is no longer readily available.
3. *Motor Reproduction Processes* After a person has seen a new behavior by observing the model, the watching must be converted to doing. This process then demonstrates that the individual can perform the modeled activities.

Positive Reinforcement Providing a pleasant response to an individual's actions.

Negative Reinforcement An unpleasant reward.

Punishment Penalizing an employee for undesirable behaviors.

Social Learning Theory Theory of learning that views learning occurring through observation and direct experience.

4. *Reinforcement Processes* Individuals will be motivated to exhibit the modeled behavior if positive incentives or rewards are provided. Behaviors that are reinforced will be given more attention, learned better, and performed more often.

Social-learning theory offers us insights into what a training exercise should include. Specifically, it tells us training should provide a model;[9] grab the trainee's attention; provide motivational properties; help the trainee file away what he or she has learned for later use; and, if the training has taken place off the job, allow the trainee some opportunity to transfer what has been learned to the job (see Table 9-1).

The Learning Curve

Learning begins rapidly, then it plateaus. As such, learning rates can be expressed as a curve that usually begins with a sharp rise, then increases at a decreasing rate until a plateau is reached. Learning is very fast at the beginning, but then plateaus as opportunities for improvement are reduced.

The **learning curve** principle can be illustrated by observing individuals in training to run the mile. At first, their time improves rapidly as they get into

Learning Curve Depicts the rate of learning.

TABLE 9-1   Principles of Learning

Learning Is Enhanced When the Learner Is Motivated.	An individual must want to learn. When that desire exists, the learner will exert a high level of effort. There appears to be valid evidence to support the adage, "You can lead a horse to water, but you can't make him drink."
Learning Requires Feedback.	Feedback, or knowledge of results, is necessary so that learners can correct their mistakes. Feedback is best when it is immediate rather than delayed; the sooner individuals have some knowledge of how well they are performing, the easier it is for them to compare performance to goals and correct their erroneous actions.
Reinforcement Increases the Likelihood that a Learned Behavior Will Be Repeated.	The principle of reinforcement tells us that behaviors that are positively reinforced (rewarded) are encouraged and sustained. When the behavior is punished, it is temporarily suppressed but is unlikely to be extinguished. What is desired is to convey feedback to the learners when they are doing what is right to encourage them to keep doing it.
Practice Increases a Learner's Performance.	When learners actually practice what they have read or seen, they gain confidence and are less likely to make errors or to forget what they have learned.
Learning Begins Rapidly, Then Plateaus.	Learning rates can be expressed as a curve that usually begins with a sharp rise, then increases at a decreasing rate until a plateau is reached. Learning is very fast at the beginning, but then plateaus as opportunities for improvement are reduced.
Learning Must Be Transferable to the Job.	It doesn't make much sense to perfect a skill in the classroom and then find that you can't successfully transfer it to the job. Therefore, training should be designed for transferability.

shape. Then, as their conditioning develops, their improvement plateaus. Obviously, knocking one minute off a ten-minute mile is a lot easier than knocking one minute off a five-minute mile. If you have ever learned to type on a keyboard, you may have had an experience that somewhat follows the pattern shown in Figure 9-1. The specific criterion is words typed per minute, and the time element is in months. Note the shape of the curve in Figure 9-1. During the first three months, the rate of increase is slow as the subject learns the typing technique and becomes familiar with the keyboard. During the next three months, learning accelerates as the subject works on developing speed. After six months, learning slows as progress evolves into refinement of technique.

Training and EEO

Much of our previous discussions of EEO have centered on the selection process. Undoubtedly, it is most prevalent in the hiring process, but its application to training cannot be overlooked. Remember under the definition of adverse impact, we referenced any HRM activity that adversely affects protected group members in hiring, firing, and promoting. So how does fall into the EEO realms? Let's briefly take a look.

Training programs may be required for promotions, job bidding (especially in unionized jobs), or for salary increases. Under any of these scenarios, it is the responsibility of the organization to ensure that training selection criteria are related to the job. Furthermore, equal training must exist for all employees.

Organizations should also pay close attention to training completion rates. If protected group members fail to pass training programs more frequently than the "majority group," this might indicate a disparate impact in the training that is offered. Once again, organizations should monitor these activities, and perform periodic audits to ensure full compliance with EEO regulations.

Determining Training Needs

Now that we have a better understanding of what training is and how individuals learn, we can look at a more fundamental question for organizations. That is, how does an organization assess whether there is a need for training? We propose that management can determine this following a process depicted in Figure 9-2.[10]

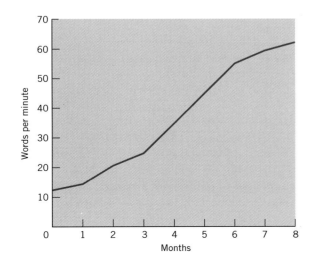

Figure 9-1
Learning Curve on a Computer Keyboard

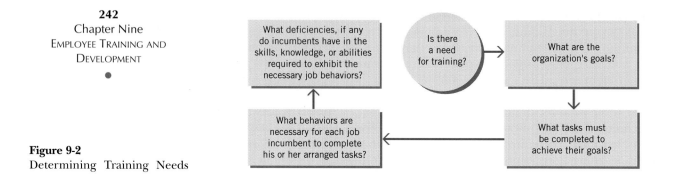

Figure 9-2
Determining Training Needs

Recall from Chapter 5 that these questions demonstrate the close link between strategic human resources planning and the determination of training needs. Based on our determination of the organization's needs, the type of work to be done, and the type of skills necessary to complete this work, our training program should follow naturally. Once we can identify where deficiencies lie, we have a grasp of the extent and nature of our training needs.

What kinds of signals can warn a manager that employee training may be necessary? The more obvious ones relate directly to productivity; that is, inadequate job performance or a drop in productivity. The former is likely to occur in the early months on a new job. When a manager sees evidence of inadequate job performance, assuming the individual is making a satisfactory effort, attention should be given to raising the worker's skill level. When a manager is confronted with a drop in productivity, it may suggest that skills need to be fine-tuned.

In addition to productivity measures, a high reject rate or larger than usual scrappage may indicate a need for employee training. A rise in the number of accidents reported also suggests some type of retraining is necessary. There is also the future element: the changes that are being imposed on the worker as a result of a job redesign or a technological breakthrough. These types of job changes require training that is a preparation for planned change rather than a reaction to immediately unsatisfactory conditions.

If deficiencies in performance are uncovered, it doesn't necessarily follow that the manager should take corrective action. It is important to put training into perspective. It has costs, which are often high, ranging from $350 to $1,400 per employee trained;[11] and training should not be viewed as a panacea. Rather, training should be judged by its contribution to performance, where performance is a function of skills, abilities, motivation, and the opportunity to perform. Managers must compare the value received from the increase in performance that can be attributed to training with the costs incurred in that training.

Once it has been determined that training is necessary, training goals must be established. Management should explicitly state what results are sought for each employee. It is not adequate merely to say the change in employee knowledge, skills, attitudes, or behavior is desirable; we must clarify what is to change, and by how much. These goals should be tangible, verifiable, and measurable. They should be clear to both management and employee. For instance, a firefighter might be expected to jump from a moving fire truck traveling at fifteen miles per hour, successfully hook up a four-inch hose to a hydrant, and turn on the hydrant, all in less than forty seconds. Such explicit goals ensure that both management and the employee know what is expected from the training effort.

Training Methods

The most popular training and development methods used by organizations can be classified as either on-the-job or off-the-job training. In the following pages, we will briefly introduce the better-known techniques of each category.

On-the-Job Training The most widely used training methods take place on the job. The popular use of these methods can be attributed to the simplicity of such methods and the impression that they are less costly to operate. On-the job training places the employees in actual work situations and makes them appear to be immediately productive. It is learning by doing. For jobs that either are difficult to simulate or can be learned quickly by watching and doing, on-the-job training makes sense.

One of the drawbacks of on-the-job training can be low productivity while the employees develop their skills. Another drawback can be the errors made by the trainees while they learn. However, when the damage the trainees can do is minimal, where training facilities and personnel are limited or costly, and where it is desirable for the workers to learn the job under normal working conditions, the benefits of on-the-job training frequently offset the drawbacks. Let's look at two types of on-the-job training; apprenticeship programs and job instruction training (JIT).

People seeking to enter skilled trades—to become, for example, plumbers, or electronic technicians—are often required to undergo **apprenticeship training** before they are elevated to *master* status. Apprenticeship programs put the trainee under the guidance of a master worker. The argument for apprenticeship programs is that the required job knowledge and skills are so complex as to rule out anything less than a period of time where the trainee understudies a skilled master.[12]

During World War II, a systematic approach to on-the-job training was developed to prepare supervisors to train employees. This approach was called **job instruction training (JIT)**. JIT proved highly effective and became extremely popular. JIT consists of four basic steps:

1. preparing the trainees by telling them about the job and overcoming their uncertainties
2. presenting the instruction, giving essential information in a clear manner
3. having the trainees try out the job to demonstrate their understanding
4. placing the workers into the job, on their own, with a designated resource person to call upon should they need assistance[13]

Use of JIT can achieve impressive results.[14] By following these steps, studies indicate that employee turnover can be reduced. Higher levels of employee morale have been witnessed, as well as decreases in employee accidents.[15]

Off-the-Job Training Off-the-job training covers a number of techniques—classroom lectures, films, demonstrations, case studies and other simulation exercises, and programmed instruction. The facilities needed for each of these techniques vary from a small, makeshift classroom to an elaborate development center with large lecture halls, supplemented by small conference rooms with sophisticated instructional technology equipment. We have summarized the majority of these methods in Table 9-2. Because of its growing popularity in today's technology-oriented organizations, however, programmed instruction warrants a closer look.

Apprenticeship A time—typically two to five years—when an individual is considered to be training to learn a skill.

Job Instruction Training A systematic approach to on-the-job training consisting of four basic steps.

TABLE 9-2 Off-the-job Training Methods

Classroom Lectures	Lectures designed to communicate specific interpersonal, technical, or problem-solving skills.
Videos and Films	Using various media productions to demonstrate specialized skills that are not easily presented by other training methods.
Simulation Exercises	Training that occurs by actually performing the work. This may include case analysis, experiential exercises, role playing, or group decision making.
Computer Based Training	Simulating the work environment by programming a computer to imitate some of the realities of the job.
Vestibule Training	Training on actual equipment used on the job, but conducted away from the actual work setting—a simulated work station.
Programmed Instruction	Condensing training materials into highly organized, logical sequences. May include computer tutorials, interactive video disks, or virtual reality simulations.

Programmed Instruction Material is learned in a highly organized, logical sequence, that requires the individual to respond.

Interactive Videos Videos that permit the user to make changes/selections.

Virtual Reality A process whereby the work environment is simulated by sending messages to the brain.

The **programmed instruction** technique can be in the form of programmed tests, manuals, or video displays, while in some organizations teaching machines are utilized. All programmed instruction approaches have a common characteristic: They condense the material to be learned into highly organized, logical sequences that require the trainee to respond. The ideal format provides for nearly instantaneous feedback that informs the trainee if his or her response is correct.

For example, popular today with the purchase of computer software is an accompanying tutorial program. This tutorial walks the user through the software application, giving the individual opportunities to experiment with the program. These tutorials, then, form one basis of programmed instruction.

As technology continues to evolve, we can expect programmed instruction to become more dominant. Two noticeable versions, interactive video disks (IVD) and virtual reality, are gaining momentum in corporate training. **Interactive video disks** (IVDs) (sometimes referred to as multimedia technology), allow users to interact with a personal computer while simultaneously being exposed to video pictures. This "motion picture" enables the trainee to experience the effect of his or her decision in real-time mode.[16] A number of companies, such as Pitney Bowes, Applied Learning, and IBM, have begun using IVDs.[17] In fact, it is estimated that approximately 16 percent of all companies that train use them.[18] In many of these organizations, employees experience greater learning in such areas as mathematics, interpersonal skills, and marketing skills.[19]

Virtual reality is a newer concept in corporate training.[20] Virtual-reality systems simulate actual work activities by sending various messages to the brain. For example, one type of virtual reality requires an individual to place a helmet over his or her head. Inside this helmet are sensors that display both visual and audio simulations of an event. For instance, skiers can be taught to ski through virtual reality. Under the system, an individual standing on dry land can be made to feel like he or she is actually skiing downhill, with the speed, obstacles, and weather being simulated. This sophisticated simulation allows for individuals to interact with their environment as if they were really there. Although such

This virtual reality earthmover simulates the operating of this large piece of equipment. Being used at Caterpillar's plant in Peoria, Illinois, individuals can get "hands-on" experience with the machinery—complete with actual controls and sounds. And yes, the earthmover can even scoop up a load of virtual stones.

systems are promising, their expense at this time precludes their use except for extremely large organizations and very complex jobs.

Employee Development

Employee development, by design, is more future-oriented and more concerned with education than employee training. By education we mean that employee development activities attempt to instill sound reasoning processes—to enhance one's ability to understand and interpret knowledge—rather than imparting a body of facts or teaching a specific set of motor skills. Development, therefore, focuses more on the employee's personal growth.

Successful employees prepared for positions of greater responsibility have analytical, human, conceptual, and specialized skills. They are able to think and understand. Training, per se, cannot overcome an individual's inability to understand cause-and-effect relationships, to synthesize from experience, to visualize relationships, or to think logically. As a result, we suggest that employee development be predominantly an education process rather than a training process.

It is important to consider one critical component of employee development: All employees, at no matter what level, can be developed. Historically, development was reserved for potential management personnel. Although it is critical for individuals to be trained in specific skills related to managing—like planning, organizing, leading, controlling, and decision making—time has taught us that these skills are also needed by nonmanagement personnel. The use of work teams, reductions in supervisory roles, allowing workers to participate in the goals of their jobs, and a greater emphasis on quality and customers, have changed the way developing employees is viewed. Accordingly, organizations now require new employee skills, knowledge, and abilities. Thus, as we go through the next few pages, note that those methods used to develop employees in general are the same as those used to develop managerial personnel.

Employee Development Methods

Some development of an individual's abilities can take place on the job. We will review several methods, three popular on-the-job techniques (job rotation, assistant-to positions, and committee assignments) and three off-the-job methods (lecture courses and seminars, simulation exercises, and outdoor training).

Job Rotation Moving employees horizontally or vertically to expand their skills, knowledge, or abilities.

Job Rotation   **Job rotation** involves moving employees to various positions in the organization in an effort to expand their skills, knowledge, and abilities. Job rotation can be either horizontal or vertical. Vertical rotation is nothing more than promoting a worker into a new position. In this chapter, we will emphasize the horizontal dimension of job rotation, or what may be better understood as a short-term lateral transfer.

Job rotation represents an excellent method for broadening individuals' exposure to company operations and for turning specialists into generalists. In addition to increasing the individual's experience and allowing him or her to absorb new information, it can reduce boredom and stimulate the development of new ideas. It can also provide opportunities for a more comprehensive and reliable evaluation of the employee by his or her supervisors.

Assistant-To Positions   Employees with demonstrated potential are given the opportunity to work under a seasoned and successful manager, often in different areas of the organization. Working as staff assistants or, in some cases, serving on "junior boards," these individual perform many duties under the watchful eye of a supportive coach. In doing so, these employees, get exposure to a wide variety of management activities, and are groomed for assuming the duties of the next higher level.

Committee Assignment   Committee assignments can provide an opportunity for the employee to share in decision making, to learn by watching others, and to investigate specific organizational problems. When committees are of an *ad hoc* or temporary nature, they often take on task-force activities designed to delve into a particular problem, ascertain alternative solutions, and make a recommendation for implementing a solution. These temporary assignments can be both interesting and rewarding to the employee's growth.

Appointment to permanent committees increases the employee's exposure to other members of the organization, broadens his or her understanding, and provides an opportunity to grow and make recommendations under the scrutiny of other committee members. In addition to the on-the-job techniques described above, a number of off-the-job techniques are used, including sensitivity training and transactional analysis. We will briefly discuss three of the more popular ones: lecture courses and seminars, simulations, and outdoor training.

Lecture Courses and Seminars   Traditional forms of instruction revolved around formal lecture courses and seminars. These offered an opportunity for individuals to acquire knowledge and develop their conceptual and analytical abilities. For many organizations, they were offered in-house by the organization itself, through outside vendors, or both.

Today, however, technology is allowing for significant improvements in the training field. A growing trend at companies such as Pacific Bell and British Columbia Telecom[21] is to provide lecture courses and seminars revolving around what we call distance learning.[22] Through the use of digitized computer technology, a facilitator can be in one location giving a lecture, while simultaneously being transmitted over fiber-optic cables, in real time, to several other locations. For example, British Airways uses distance learning to train its employees for supervisory positions.[23] Workers, located in ten different countries, are afforded the opportunity to receive training from five different organizations that otherwise would not be possible without incurring travel costs.[24]

Simulations Simulations were introduced as a training technique. They are probably even more popular for employee development. The more widely used simulation exercises include case studies, decision games, and role plays.

The case-study-analysis approach to employee development was popularized at the Harvard Graduate School of Business. Taken from the actual experiences of organizations, these cases represent attempts to describe, as accurately as possible, real problems that managers have faced. Trainees study the cases to determine problems, analyze causes, develop alternative solutions, select what they believe to be the best solution, and implement it. Case studies can provide stimulating discussions among participants, as well as excellent opportunities for individuals to defend their analytical and judgmental abilities. It appears to be a rather effective method for improving decision-making abilities within the constraints of limited information.

Simulated decision games and role-playing exercises put individuals in the role of acting out managerial problems. Games, which are frequently played on a computer programmed for the particular game, provide opportunities for individuals to make decisions and to consider the implications of a decision on other segments of the organization, with no adverse effect should the decision be a poor one. Role playing allows the participants to act out problems and to deal with real people. Participants are assigned roles and are asked to react to one another as they would have to do in their managerial jobs.

The advantages to simulation exercises are the opportunities to attempt to "create an environment" similar to real situations the managers incur, without

Simulations Any artificial environment that attempts to closely mirror an actual condition.

These individuals may look like they're having a good time, but they are involved in an increasingly popular training trend—outdoor training. The focus of this survival training is to teach them the importance of working together as a team.

Outdoor Training Specialized training that occurs outdoors that focuses on building self-confidence and teamwork.

Mentoring or Coaching Actively guiding another individual.

the high costs involved should the actions prove undesirable. Of course, the disadvantages are the reverse of this: It is difficult to duplicate the pressures and realities of actual decision making on the job, and individuals often act differently in real-life situations than they do in a simulated exercise.

Outdoor Training   A recent trend to employee development has been the use of **outdoor** (sometimes referred to as wilderness or survival) **training.** The primary focus of such training is to teach trainees the importance of working together; gelling as a team.

Outdoor training typically involves some major emotional and physical challenge. This could be white-water rafting, mountain climbing, or surviving a week in the "jungle." The purpose of such training is to see how employees react to the difficulties that nature presents to them. Do they face these dangers alone? Do they "freak"? Or are they controlled, and successful in achieving their goal? The reality that today's business environment does not permit employees to "stand alone" has reinforced working closely with one another, building trusting relationships, and succeeding as a member of a group.[25]

Two Special Cases of Development: Mentoring and Counseling

Two special cases of development continue to gain a great deal of attention. These are the mentoring/coaching process and employee counseling.

Mentoring/Coaching   It has become increasingly clear over the years that employees who aspire to management levels in organizations need the assistance and advocacy of someone higher up in the organization.[26] These career progressions often require having the favor of the dominant "in-group," which sets corporate goals, priorities, and standards.[27]

When a senior employee takes an active role in guiding another individual, we refer to this activity as **mentoring or coaching.** Just as soccer coaches observe, analyze, and attempt to improve the performance of their athletes, "coaches" on the job can do the same. The effective coach, whether on the diamond or in the corporate hierarchy, gives guidance through direction, advice, criticism, and suggestion in an attempt to aid the employee's growth.[28] These individuals offer to assist certain junior employees in terms of providing a support system. This system, in part, is likened to the passing of the proverbial baton—that is, the senior employee shares his or her experiences with the protégé, providing guidance on how to make it in the organization.[29] Accordingly, in organizations such as Motorola, Tenneco, and Prudential,[30] that promote from within, those who aspire to succeed must have the "corporate support system"[31] in their favor. This support system, guided by a mentor, vouches for the candidate, answers for the candidate in the highest circles within the organization, makes appropriate introductions, and advises and guides the candidate on how to effectively move through the system. In one study, this effort generated significant outcomes.[32] For example, these researchers found that where a significant mentoring relationship existed, those protégés had more favorable and frequent promotions, were paid significantly more than those who were not mentored,[33] had a greater level of commitment to the organization, and had greater career success.[34] But there was a caution in this study; that is, those benefits that accrued because of mentoring generally went to white-male employees. Why this outcome? In the past, women and minorities have found it difficult to get a mentor,[35] and therefore their upward mobility was often limited (see "Ethical Decisions in HRM").

Ethical Decisions in HRM:

Special Mentoring Programs for Women and Minorities

We have been witnessing many discussions lately regarding how more women and minorities can break through the glass ceiling. There is no doubt that these groups are underrepresented at the top echelons of organizations. Several reasons have been well documented detailing why this occurred. One of those reasons centers around the issue of mentoring.

Finding, or getting, a mentor to support you is rarely easy. In fact, more often than not, a mentor approaches you to begin the relationship. In the past, many of these individuals happen to be white males; and historically, women and minorities found it difficult to gain the favor of these mentors simply because mentors preferred someone more like them.

With the changing work force composition, employment legislation, and changing societal views of women and minorities in the workplace, mentoring relationships for this group are occurring more frequently. But it is not, as yet, fully ingrained in the minds and hearts of some managers. Consequently, a number of organizations have developed special mentoring programs for women and minorities—formalizing a practice that typically naturally evolved. In some respects, this may be the best way at this time to help further advance these two groups. Leaving it up to nature just doesn't work well. The prevalence of the glass ceiling dilemma attests to that. On the other hand, can a mentoring relationship be forced, and regulated? The crux of these relationships is for an individual to become very close to his or her protégé in an effort to further one's career. Won't forcing these people together—two individuals who have not come together naturally—lead to a constrained relationship? Given the degree of conflict that may arise between the two, it's possible more harm than good for the protégé's career may result.

Should women and minorities be given special treatment in the mentoring relationship by having organizational policies dictating who will mentor and how it will be handled? Should there be special guidelines to ensure that mentoring for women and minorities occurs? And what about the white male? Is he being left out? What do you think?

The technique of senior employees coaching individuals has the advantages that go with learning by doing, particularly the opportunities for high interaction and rapid feedback on performance. Unfortunately, its two strongest disadvantages are: (1) its tendencies to perpetuate the current styles and practices in the organization, and (2) its heavy reliance on the coach's ability to be a good teacher. In the same way that we recognize that all excellent goalies do not make outstanding goalie coaches, we cannot expect all excellent employees to be effective coaches. An individual can become an excellent performer without necessarily possessing the knack of creating a proper learning environment for others to do the same; thus, the effectiveness of this technique relies on the ability of the coach. Coaching of employees can occur at any level and can be most effective when the two individuals do not have any type of reporting relationship.

Recall from Chapter 3 the discussion of the glass ceiling.[36] One of the main reasons for its existence is that women do not have many role models sitting high in the organization who can help them through the system.[37] Although there is no excuse for the continuation of such behavior, there may be some explanation. Mentors sometimes select their protégés on the basis of seeing themselves, in their younger years, in the employee. Since men rarely can identify with younger women, many are unwilling to play the part of their mentor.[38] Of course, as women have battled their way into the inner circle of organizational power, some success is being witnessed.[39]

Additionally, organizations are beginning to explore ways of advocating cross-gender mentoring. This revolves around identifying the problems associated with such an arrangement,[40] deciding how they can be handled effectively, and providing organizational support.[41] Unfortunately, the effects of corporate downsizing in the early 1990s significantly curtailed this effect.[42]

Employee Counseling   In an attempt to assist employees in performing the job they have been assigned, it sometimes may be necessary for the manager to counsel them. In terms of employee counseling, however, a distinction needs to be made. In the discussion above, we've referred to coaching and mentoring techniques as means for helping to develop employees and to assist in their career growth. Although employee counseling is similar in its approach, there is one aspect that differentiates it from coaching. For instance, we typically use employee counseling when a performance problem arises. Thus, the focus of this discussion is more appropriately aligned with the discipline process.

Whenever an employee exhibits work behaviors that are inconsistent with the work environment (i.e., fighting, stealing, unexcused absences, and so forth) or is unable to perform his or her job satisfactorily, a manager must intervene. But before any intervention can begin, it is imperative for the manager to identify the problem. If as managers we realize that the performance problem is ability-related, our emphasis becomes one of facilitating training and development efforts.[43] This type of intervention is then more closely aligned to coaching. However, when the performance problem is desire-related, where the unwillingness is either voluntary or involuntary, employee counseling is the next logical approach.[44]

Employee Counseling A process whereby employees are guided in overcoming performance problems.

Although **employee counseling** processes differ, some fundamental steps should be followed when counseling an employee (see "HRM Skills"). As a prerequisite, a manager must have good listening skills.[45] The purpose of employee counseling is to uncover the reason for the poor performance; a response that must be elicited from the employee. A manager who dominates the meeting by talking may dismiss the benefits of an effective counseling session.

In employee counseling, the manager must attack the inappropriate behavior, not the person. Although they appear difficult to separate, we must deal with only objective performance data. For instance, telling employees they are poor workers is only asking for emotions to run high and confrontation to manifest. Instead, stating that they have been late four times this past month, which has caused a backlog of accounts payables, is better understood and dealt with. In doing so, the manager is dealing with performance-related behaviors. Accordingly, the manager and the employee are in a better position to deal with the problem as adults.

The manager must probe the employee to determine why the performance is not acceptable. It is important to note that the manager is not attempting to be

HRM *Skills*

Counseling Employees

1. **Document all problem performance behaviors.** Document specific job behaviors, like absenteeism, lateness, and poor quality, in terms of dates, times, and what happened. This provides you with objective data.

2. **Deal with the employee objectively, fairly, and equitably.** Treat each employee similarly. That means that one should not be counseled for something that another person did, and nothing was mentioned. Issues discussed should focus on performance behaviors.

3. **Confront job performance issues only.** Your main focus is on those things that affect performance. Even though it may be a personal problem, you should not try to psychoanalyze the individual. Leave that to the trained specialists! You can, however, address how these behaviors are affecting the employee's job performance.

4. **Offer assistance to help the employee.** Just pointing the finger at an employee serves little useful purpose. If the employee could "fix" the problem alone, he or she probably would have. Help might be needed—yours and the organizations. Offer this assistance where possible.

5. **Expect the employee to resist the feedback and become defensive.** It is human nature to dislike constructive, or negative feedback. Expect that the individual will be uncomfortable with the discussion. Make every effort, however, to keep the meeting calm such that the message can get across. Documentation, fairness, focusing on job behaviors, and offering assistance helps to reduce this defensiveness.

6. **Get employee to own up to the problem.** All things said, the problem is not yours, it's the employee's. The employee needs to take responsibility for his or her behavior, and begin to look for ways to correct the problems.

7. **Develop an action plan to correct performance.** Once the employee has taken responsibility for the problem, develop a plan of action designed to correct the problem. Be specific as to what the employee must do (e.g., what is expected and when it is expected); and what resources you are willing to commit to assist.

8. **Identify outcomes for failing to correct problems.** You're there to help, not carry a poor performer forever. You need to inform the employee what the consequences will be if he or she does not follow the action plan.

9. **Monitor and control progress.** Evaluate the progress the employee is making. Provide frequent feedback on what you're observing. Reinforce good efforts.

Source: Adapted from Commerce Clearing House, "The Do's and Don'ts of Confronting a Troubled Employee," *Topical Law Reports* (Chicago: Commerce Clearing House, Inc., October 1990), pp. 4359–60; Gerald D. Cook, "Employee Counseling Session," *Supervision* (August 1989), p. 3; and Andrew E. Schuartz, "Counseling the Marginal Performer," *Management Solutions* (March 1988), p. 30.

---

a psychologist; he or she is only interested in the behaviors that affect performance. If the problem is a personal one, under no circumstances should the manager attempt to "fix" it. Rather, the well-informed manager, when recognizing a personal problem, will refer the employee to an appropriate place in or outside the organization (like the company's employee assistance program).[46] Irrespective of where the problem lies, the manager must get the employee to accept the problem. Until the employee has such an understanding, little hope exists for correcting the problem. When the employee accepts the problem, the manager should work with the employee to find ways to correct the problem. At this point, the manager may offer whatever assistance he or she can. Assistance aside, the employee must understand that it is his or her sole responsibility to make the change; failure to do so will only result in disciplinary procedures.

Organizational Development

Although our discussion so far has been related to the people side of business, it is important to recognize that organizations change from time to time. With the changes experienced with respect to downsizing, rightsizing, total quality management, diversity, and reengineering, it is necessary to move the organization forward through a process we call **organizational development (OD).**

Organizational Development
Process in the organization helping employees adapt to change.

The basis of organizational development is to help people adapt to change. Although there are different perspectives on how that change should occur, one of the best descriptions of the change process was illustrated by Kurt Lewin.[47]

According to Lewin, change occurs over three stages. These include the unfreezing of the status quo, the change to the new state, and refreezing to ensure that the change become permanent. We have graphically portrayed this process in Figure 9-3.

What Lewin identified was the movement in the organization away from the status quo. Portraying the status quo in Figure 9-3 as circles, the change effort helps the organization move in the direction of the squares. Through OD efforts, the intervention can take place, with the change effort supported by continual reinforcement to make it permanent.

OD and Its Methods

Development efforts in human resource management go beyond the individual. There are instances, like changing an organization's culture, where system-wide change and development are required. Organizational development techniques have been created to change the values and attitudes of people and the structure of organizations in order to make them more adaptive.

Included among the more popular OD techniques are three approaches that rely heavily on group interactions, participation, and collaboration. These are survey feedback, team building, and third-party intervention.[48]

Attitude Survey Questionnaires used to elicit responses from employees regarding how they feel about their jobs, work groups, supervisors, and the organization.

Survey Feedback One tool for assessing attitudes held by organizational members, identifying discrepancies among member perceptions, and solving these differences is the **attitude survey.** Organization members may be asked to respond to a set of specific questions or may be interviewed to determine what is-

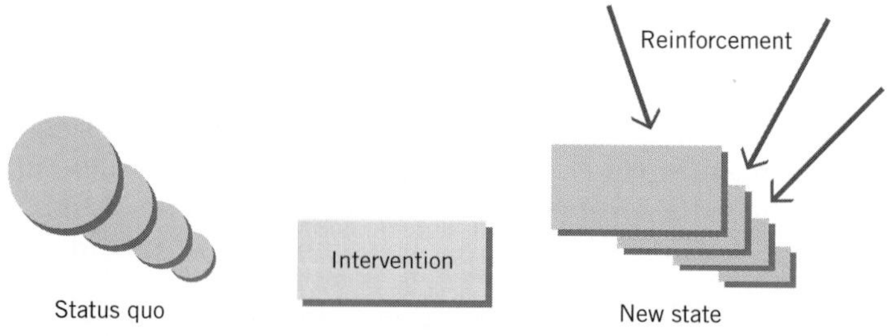

Figure 9-3
Lewin's Change Process

sues are relevant. A questionnaire (see Figure 9-4) typically asks members for their perceptions and attitudes on a broad range of topic, such as decision-making practices; leadership; communication effectiveness; coordination between units; and satisfaction with the organization, job, coworkers, and their immediate supervisor.

The data from this questionnaire are tabulated. These data then become the springboard for identifying problems and clarifying issues that may be creating difficulties for people. Addressing these difficulties hopefully will result in the group agreeing on commitments to various actions that will remedy the problems that have been identified.

Team Building   Organizations are composed of people working together to achieve some common end. Since people are frequently required to work in groups, considerable attention has been focused on OD for team building.

Team building can be applied within groups or at the intergroup level where activities are interdependent. For our discussion, we will emphasize the intragroup level. The activities included in team building typically include goal setting, development of interpersonal relations among team members, role analysis to clarify each member's role and responsibilities, and team process analysis. Of course, team building may emphasize or exclude certain activities depending on the purpose of the development effort and the specific problems with which the team is confronted. Basically, however, team building attempts to use high interaction among group members to increase trust and openness.

Figure 9-4
A Sample Attitude Survey

Rate each of the following statements using the following scale:

    1 = strongly agree
    2 = agree
    3 = undecided
    4 = disagree
    5 = strongly disagree

1. The environment in this organization is conducive to productive work.	5	4	3	2	1
2. Getting ahead in this organization is strictly a function of one's performance.	5	4	3	2	1
3. My salary is fair and competitive.	5	4	3	2	1
4. Employee benefits are appropriate and meet my personal needs.	5	4	3	2	1
5. I have the opportunity to make decisions about my job for those things that affect it.	5	4	3	2	1
6. I have an open and trusting relationship with my boss.	5	4	3	2	1
7. Clear work expectations exist for my job.	5	4	3	2	1
8. My job challenges me to use my skills, knowledge, and abilities.	5	4	3	2	1
9. The organization encourages a team environment.	5	4	3	2	1
10. Managers of this organization have a clear direction for the next ten years.	5	4	3	2	1

Third-party Intervention Third-party intervention seeks to change the attitudes, stereotypes, and perceptions that groups have of each other. For example, in one company, the marketing representatives saw HRM as having a bunch of "smiley-types who sit around and plan company picnics." Such stereotypes have an obvious negative impact on the coordinating efforts between the departments that leads to conflict.

Although there are a number of approaches for third-party intervention, conflict resolution strategies are often dominant.[49] In conflict resolution, the OD practitioner attempts to get both parties to see the similarities and differences existing between them, and focus on how the differences can be overcome. Achieving some movement toward reducing these differences is often gained through consensus building—or finding a solution that is acceptable to both parties.

OD in the Reengineered Organization

Organizational development has taken on a renewed importance today. Brought about by continuous-improvement goals, many organizations have drastically changed the way they do business. For example, companies such as Ryder Trucks, GTE, Motorola, and Union Carbide are making "radical changes in business processes to achieve breakthrough results."[50] Attainment of these goals, however, directly affects the operations, and the people of the organization (see "Meet Peter Senge").

Whenever change occurs, four areas are usually affected: the organization's systems, its technology, its processes, and its people. No matter what the change is, or how minor it may appear, understanding the effect of the change is paramount for it to be supported, and lasting. That is where OD comes in to play.

OD efforts are designed to support the strategic direction of the business. For instance, if work processes change, people will need to learn new production methods, procedures, and maybe skills. OD becomes instrumental in bringing about the change. How so? Whenever change occurs, the effect of that change becomes an organizational culture issue. Accordingly, OD efforts must be expended to ensure that all organizational members support the new culture, and provide whatever assistance is needed to bring the new culture to fruition.

The Role of Change Agents

No matter what role OD takes in an organization, it requires facilitation by an individual well-versed in organization dynamics. In HRM terms, we call this person a **change agent**.[51] Change agents are responsible for fostering the environment in which change can be made, working with the affected employees to help them adapt to the change that is taking place. To achieve this goal, change agents must possess two critical skills—the ability to take risk, and outstanding communication skills.[52] For example, consider Jerry Goldman with the Landover, Maryland-based Hechinger company. As Jerry points out, creativity is essential, but to make that vision a reality requires tenacity, a lot of risk, and being able to deal with people.[53]

Change agents may be either internal employees, often associated with the training and development function of HRM, or external consultants. Successful applications of the change agent role have been witnessed in many organizations, among them W.T. Grant, Sears, Inland Steel, and the New York City Police Department.[54] In all cases, change was brought about through the concerted efforts of one individual who championed the process—the change agent.

Change Agents Individuals responsible for fostering the change effort, and assisting employees in adapting to the changes.

Peter Senge

Champion of the Learning Organization

Imagine you've just entered the grand ballroom of the Loews Anatole in Dallas, and your senses are picking up some strange occurrences. There are several hundred people gathered, milling around with the constant drone of a beating drum in the background. Bird and other animal sounds permeate the air every so often, as your eyes glance at the seaside sunset on the giant projection screen in front of the room. Have you just walked into a religious experience, or a seminar on the latest diet fad? No! You've just been exposed to Peter Senge's Learning Organization Seminar.

Peter Senge is a senior lecturer at MIT, an in-demand consultant, and champion of the learning organization. Based on his research at MIT's Center for Organizational Learning, Senge published a book in 1990 called *The Fifth Discipline*. To Senge and his followers, the book identified a crusade for organizations interested in truly bringing about permanent change—change that will result in the organization radically transforming itself.

Senge describes the learning organization as one that "values, and thinks competitive advantages derive from, continued learning." The learning organization attacks the premise that the status quo is good enough. The learning organization, then, fosters an environment where open, trusting work relationships abound.

To revolutionize today's organizations, Senge identified five prerequisites. These were systems thinking, personal mastery, mental models, shared vision, and team learning. As *Fortune* magazine writer Brian Dumaine summarizes, to fully develop the learning organization, "people should put aside their old ways of doing thinking (mental models), learn to be open with others (personal mastery), understand how their company really works (systems thinking), for a plan everyone can agree on (shared vision), and then work together to achieve that vision (team learning)."

How widespread is the belief in the learning organization as a means of creating an OD metamorphosis? Senge's client list reads like a who's who in corporate America. His ideas and work at Ford, Federal Express, Intel, AT&T, and Motorola have helped these organizations foster a creative and innovative environment that has led each of them to create "excellence" in the organization. For each, that has translated into a bottom line of success.

Source: Brian Dumaine, "Mr. Learning Organization," *Fortune* (October 17, 1994), pp. 147–57.

Evaluating Training and Development Effectiveness

Any training or development effort must be cost-effective. That is, the benefits gained by training must outweigh the costs associated with providing the learning experience. Only by analyzing such programs can effectiveness be determined. In Chapter 7, we discussed the effectiveness of selection devices. We were concerned, for example, with whether employment tests actually differentiated between satisfactory and unsatisfactory job performers. This same concern for effectiveness arises when we discuss training or development activities (referred to collectively as training in this discussion). It is not enough to merely assume that any training an organization offers is effective; we must develop substantive data to determine whether our training effort is achieving its goals—that is, if it is correcting the deficiencies in skills, knowledge, or attitudes that were assessed as needing attention. Note, too, that training and development programs are expensive—estimated to exceed $40 billion annually for American workers.[55] The costs incurred alone justify evaluating the effectiveness.

How Do We Evaluate Training Programs?

It is easy to generate a new training program, but if the training effort is not evaluated, it becomes possible to rationalize any employee-training efforts. It would be nice if all companies could boast returns on investments in training as do Motorola executives, who claim they receive $30 in increased productivity for every dollar spent on training.[56] But such a claim cannot be made without properly evaluating training.

Can we generalize how training programs are typically evaluated? The following is probably generalizable across organizations: Several managers, representatives from HRM, and a group of workers who have recently completed a training program are asked for their opinions. If the comments are generally positive, the program may get a favorable evaluation and the organization will continue it until someone decides, for whatever reason, it should be eliminated or replaced.

The reactions of participants or managers, while easy to acquire, are the least valid; their opinions are heavily influenced by factors that have little to do with the training's effectiveness—things like difficulty, entertainment value, or personality characteristics of the instructor. Therefore let us direct our attention to three approaches, each of which offers more than subjective opinions.

Performance-Based Evaluation Measures

**Post-Training
Performance
Method** Evaluating training
programs based on how
well employees can perform
their jobs after they have received the training.

Post-Training Performance Method The first approach is referred to as the **post-training performance method.** Participants' performance is measured after attending a training program to determine if behavioral changes have been made. For example, assume we provide a week-long seminar for HRM recruiters on structured interviewing techniques. We follow up one month later with each participant to see if, in fact, the techniques addressed in the program were used, and how. If changes did occur, we may attribute them to the training. But caution must be in order, for we cannot emphatically state that the change in behavior was directly related to the training. Other factors, like reading a current HRM journal, may have also influenced the change. Accordingly, the post-training performance method may overstate the benefits of training.

**Pre–post Training Perfor-
mance Method** Evaluating
training programs based on
the difference in perfor-
mance before and after one
receives training.

Pre–Post-Training Performance Method In the **pre–post training performance method,** each participant is evaluated prior to training and rated on actual job performance. After instruction—of which the evaluator has been kept unaware—is completed, the individual is reevaluated. As with the post-training performance method, the increase is assumed to be attributed to the instruction. However, in contrast to post-training performance method, the pre–post-performance method deals directly with job behavior.

Pre–Post-Training Performance with Control Group Method The most sophisticated evaluative approach is the **pre–post-performance with control group method.** Under this evaluation method, two groups are established and evaluated on actual job performance. Members of the control group work on the job but do not undergo instruction. On the other hand, the experimental group is given the instruction. At the conclusion of training, the two groups are reevaluated. If the training is really effective, the experimental group's performance will have improved, and its performance will be substantially better than that of the control group. This approach attempts to correct for factors, other than the instruction program, that influence job performance.

Although a number of methods for evaluating training and development programs may exist, these three appear to be the most widely recognized. Furthermore, the latter two methods are preferred, because they provide a stronger measure of behavioral change directly attributable to the training effort.

Pre–Post-Training Performance with Control Group Evaluating training by comparing pre-and-post-training results with individuals who did not receive the training.

International Training and Development Issues

Important components of international human resource management include both cross-cultural training and a clear understanding of the overseas assignment as part of a manager's development.

Training

Cross-cultural training is necessary for expatriate managers and their families before, during, and after foreign assignments. It is crucial to remember that when the expatriates arrive, they are the foreigners, not the host population. Before the employee and family are relocated to the overseas post, it is necessary to provide much cultural and practical background.[57] Language training is essential for everyone in the family.

Although English is the dominant business language worldwide, relying on English puts the expatriate at a disadvantage. The expatriate will be unable to read trade journals and newspapers, which contain useful business information, and will be reliant on translators, which at best only slow down discussions and at worst "lose things" in the process. Even if an expatriate manager is not fluent, a willingness to try communicating in the local language makes a good impression on the business community—unlike the insistence that all conversation be in English.

Foreign-language proficiency is also vital for family members to establish a social network and accomplish the everyday tasks of maintaining a household. Americans may be able to go to the produce market and point at what they recognize on display, but if the shop has unfamiliar meats or vegetables, it helps to be able to ask what each item is and even better to understand the answers!

But cross-cultural training is much more than just language training. It should provide an appreciation of the new culture including details of its history and folklore, economy, politics (both internal and its relations with the United States), religion, social climate, and business practices. It is easy to recognize that religion is highly important in daily life in the Middle East, but knowledge of the region's history and an understanding of the specific practices and beliefs is important to avoid inadvertently insulting business associates or social contacts.

All this training can be carried out through a variety of techniques. Language skills are often provided through classes and cassette tapes, while cultural train-ing utilizes many different tools. Lectures, reading materials, videotapes, and movies are useful for background information, while cultural sensitivity is more often taught through role playing, simulations, and meetings with former in-ternational assignees,[58] as well as natives of the countries now living in the United States.

While all this training in advance of the overseas relocation is important, cul-tural learning takes place during the assignment as well. One American corpo-ration provides some of the following suggestions for adapting to a foreign envi-ronment: Forget the word *foreign*. Learn how things get done: at work, at home, at schools, at social gatherings. Watch television, even if you don't understand it yet. Read newspapers, as many as possible. Visit parks, museums, and zoos. Make friends with local people and learn from them. Plan vacations and day trips in the new country.[59]

After the overseas assignment has ended and the employee has returned, more training is required for the entire family. All family members must reaccli-mate to life in the United States. The family must face changes in the extended family, friends, and local events that have occurred in their absence. Teenagers find reentry particularly difficult, as they are ignorant of the most recent jargon and the latest trends, but often are more sophisticated and mature than their local friends.

The employee also must adjust to organizational changes, including the in-evitable promotions, transfers, and resignations that have taken place during his or her absence. Returnees are anxious to know where they fit in, or if they have been gone for so long that they no longer are on a career path.

Management Development

In the current global business environment, the overseas assignment should be a vital component in the development of top level executives. However, so

Imagine you've just been as-signed to work in the Middle East, in an organization lo-cated in a country where Farsi is spoken. Your manual (pic-tured) is foreign to you. You can't read it, let alone under-stand what it's saying. As a re-sult, your success on the job might just be significantly di-minished. Language training just might have helped.

far this is truer in Europe and Japan than it is in the United States. Many American managers return with broader experiences than what appears on paper, having been relatively independent of headquarters. Particularly, mid-level managers have experienced greater responsibilities than others at their level, having frequently acquired greater sensitivity and flexibility to alternative ways of doing things. Unfortunately they are often ignored and untapped after their return.

One survey showed that although 70 percent of international assignments were presented as career opportunities, only 30 percent of the sample's respondents were told anything about their career after returning. Only 23 percent reported being promoted upon their return, while 18 percent reported being demoted. Only 54 percent reported there was a specific job waiting for them.[60]

It is vital for the organization to make the overseas assignment part of a career development program. In the absence of such a developmental program, two negative consequences often occur. First, the recently returned manager who is largely ignored or underutilized becomes frustrated and leaves the organization. This is extremely costly, because the investment in developing this individual is lost and the talent the individual has will likely be recruited by a competitor, either at home or overseas.

Second, when overseas returnees are regularly underutilized or leave out of frustration, other potential expatriates become reluctant to accept overseas posts, inhibiting the organization's staffing ability. When the overseas assignment is completed, the organization has four basic options. First, the expatriate may be assigned to a domestic position, beginning the repatriation process. Hopefully, this new assignment will build on some of the newly acquired skills and perspectives. Second, the return may be temporary, with the goal of preparing for another overseas assignment. This might be the case where a manager has successfully opened a new sales territory and is being asked to repeat that success in another region. Third, the expatriate may seek retirement, either in the United States or in the country in which she or he spent the last few years. Finally, employment may be terminated, either because the organization has no suitable openings or because the individual has found opportunities elsewhere.

All of these options involve substantial expenses or a loss in human investment. A well-thought-out and organized program of management development is necessary to make overseas assignments a part of the comprehensive international human resource management program.

Study Tools and Applications

Summary

This summary relates to the Learning Objectives provided on p. 235.
After having read this chapter, you should know:
1. Employee training has become increasingly important as jobs have become more sophisticated and influenced by technological and corporate changes.
2. Training is a learning experience that seeks a relatively permanent change in individuals that will improve their ability to perform on the job.
3. An effective training program should be consistent with the following learning principles: learning is enhanced when the learner is motivated; learning requires feedback; reinforcement increases the likelihood that a learned behavior will be re-

peated; practice increases a learner's performance; learning begins rapidly, then plateaus; and learning must be transferable to the job.

4. An organization's training needs will evolve from seeking answers to these questions: (a) What are the organization's goals? (b) What tasks must be completed to achieve these goals? (c) What behaviors are necessary for each job incumbent to complete his or her assigned tasks? and (d) What deficiencies, if any, do incumbents have in the skills, knowledge, or attitudes required to perform the necessary behaviors?

5. Formal training methods can be classified as on-the-job training, including apprenticeships and job instruction training, and off-the-job training, including seminars, conferences, films, simulation exercises, and programmed instruction.

6. Employee development, in contrast to employee training, is more future-oriented and concerned with education; jobs that require greater skills, knowledge, and abilities.

7. Organization development is the process of affecting change in the organization. This change is facilitated through the efforts of a change agent.

8. On-the-job development techniques include job rotation, assistant-to positions, and committee assignments. Off-the-job development techniques involve lecture courses and seminars, simulation exercises, and outdoor training.

9. Mentoring/coaching is the process whereby senior employees take junior employees under their tutelage and assist them in fostering their career development.

10. Employee counseling is a development effort in that it attempts to have the employee make behavioral changes affecting performance before they reach the extent that discipline becomes required. Employee counseling, then, is a special intermediary step to stave off continued poor performance.

11. Training programs can be evaluated by post-training performance, the pre−post-training performance, or the pre−post-training performance with control group methods. In the evaluation, focus is placed on trainee reaction, what learning took place, and how appropriate the training was to the job.

12. International issues in training and development include cross-cultural training, language training, and economic issues training.

Key Terms

apprenticeship training	negative reinforcement
attitude survey	operant conditioning
change agent	outdoor training
coaching	positive reinforcement
cost−benefit analysis	post-training performance method
employee counseling	pre−post-training performance method
employee development	pre−post-training performance with
employee training	control group method
extinction	programmed instruction
interactive video disks	punishment
job rotation	simulations
job instruction training (JIT)	social-learning theory
learning curve	transactional analysis (TA)
mentors	virtual reality

EXPERIENTIAL EXERCISE:
Evaluating An Orientation Program

In the last chapter, you developed an orientation program for students in the School of Business. Suppose your program was accepted by the dean, and has been running for two semesters. The dean now sends you the following memo:

Dear Students:

   Thank you so much for developing an orientation program for us in the School of Business. I know much work went into the process and your efforts appear to be paying off. Yet, like any other program we offer, I must justify its continuance. Would you design an evaluation system that I can use to show the admistration that we are funding a good program? I look forward to seeing your work.

Based on your orientation program design, put together an evaluation system. How will you evaluate this program? What criteria will you use? How will the evaluation be administered?

CASE APPLICATION:

Hyatt Hotels

Doesn't it make sense that managers who occasionally spend time performing the day-to-day activities that their employees do would have a better appreciation for the problems those employees face? Yes it does, but reality tells us that just a few companies do anything about it. But, that is not the case at Hyatt Hotels.

   Hyatt's president, Darryl Hartley Leonard, recognized the importance of sound corporate training programs. For the corporation to succeed in its highly competitive market, he knows that all employees, from the company president to the hotel cleaning staff, must have a complete understanding of the hotel's daily operation. Consequently, through his actions, Hyatt's "In-Touch Day" program was born.[61]

   The purpose of this training day was to enable management to better understand the day-to-day activities of running the hotel. Not having spent time prior to this program at the grass-roots level, many of these executives were far removed from the problems employees faced in dealing with customers. The object was to bring managers closer through direct experience. For example, one purchasing manager was assigned to spend the day working as a cleaning staff employee at the Hyatt in Chicago. During the course of her day, the purchasing manager encountered a major obstacle—there wasn't enough clean linen to make the beds. What caused this problem? Apparently, corporate managers had not acted on a request to purchase additional linens.

   As fate would have it, this same purchasing manager had been the one delaying the approval of the acquisition of sheets and towels for this hotel. Her action, seemingly innocent at corporate headquarters, meant that she had to strip the beds, launder the sheets and towels, and then return them to the rooms. What a waste of time, and what a learning experience! Darryl Hartley Leonard's In-Touch Day has become a special "treat" for Hyatt employees. By giving corporate executives insight into how their actions affect employees, and ultimately customers, better employee relations and customer service result.

Questions:

1. Using the process of determining training needs described in this chapter, describe how Darryl Hartley Leonard came to the conclusion to develop the "In-Touch" day for Hyatt Hotels.
2. How would you evaluate the training effectiveness of Hyatt's "In-Touch" day? What would you evaluate? Given the information on the program, how effective would you estimate "In-Touch" day to be?

How well did you fulfill the learning objectives?

1. In which of these organizations is employee training least important?
   a. An organization that is switching to a robotics manufacturing facility.
   b. An organization that can easily recruit employees with the skills and experience necessary to perform jobs.
   c. An organization that has been in existence more than a hundred years.
   d. An organization that is developing major new products.
   e. An organization that is entering the global arena for marketing.
2. Dana, with a recent B.S. in Human Resource Management, was hired as a compensation analyst by a major organization. What training is she likely to get before she starts work?
   a. No training. She should be able to function from day one.
   b. Formal training in compensation plans, and alternative financial systems. She could be sent to a local university for some course work.
   c. The company will send her for an MBA before they will let her go to work.
   d. She may need job-specific training, such as a new computer package, or how to interpret internally developed pay graphs and charts.
   e. She should spend several weeks designing her career plans and alternatives for the next ten to fifteen years.
3. Kevin, an eleventh grader who played center field for his high-school baseball team, admired Frank Thomas, the first baseman for the Chicago White Sox. He watched every game Thomas played on television and attended every game the White Sox played in his hometown, Minneapolis. He could mimic, in vivid detail, every part of Thomas's batting stance and swing. Yet, at the end of the season, Kevin still struck out almost every time he was at bat, even though he paid close attention to Thomas and had been nicknamed "the Big Hurt." According to social-learning theory, which statement is correct?
   a. Attentional processes were ineffective.
   b. Retention processes were ineffective.
   c. Motor reproduction processes were ineffective.
   d. Reinforcement processes were ineffective.
   e. Cognitive social processes were ineffective.
4. Chuck, a high-school freshman, played soccer for eight years in grade school. Bored with the sport, he approached the high-school basketball coach and asked for a spot on the team, mentioning his all-star soccer status. The coach had a reputation for letting "stars" skip the tryouts. Why did the coach make him try out anyway, according to social-learning theory?
   a. Socially, the team would not have accepted Chuck without tryouts.
   b. Socially, tryouts are part of the bonding experience.
   c. Chuck needed to learn the right way to have access to desired goals.
   d. The coach questioned the positive transfer potential of soccer to basketball.
   e. The coach held a social desirability bias against soccer.
5. A director of training for a medium-sized computer software manufacturer has just been asked by a systems software development manager, to develop a training program to help fifty programmers "remember" to log off of the system when they have completed online debugging procedures. The system automatically logs off after twenty seconds of keyboard idletime. The training director estimates $10,000 to develop and deliver such a training exercise. The computer time is valued at $.01 for each ten seconds logged on time. He checks around and finds that none of the other five software development managers has a similar log-off problem. What should he do?
   a. Develop the program. The cost of the $10,000 training program is clearly justified by an estimated savings of at least $1 each day.
   b. Develop the program. Training exists to meet the needs of users. Challenging the systems software development manager, or questioning him, would only alienate him.
   c. Do not develop the program. There is no real performance problem identified.
   d. Do not develop the program. The problem is not a training problem.
   e. Develop the program. It could be marketed later to other computer software firms.
6. Jean just qualified for flight school in a military organization. She is learning to fly wearing a helmet that has sensors to project a horizon and the control panel of her plane. She wears a special glove that interfaces with the helmet projection. What kind of training did Jean receive?
   a. Simulation.
   b. Vestibule training.
   c. Virtual reality.
   d. Experiential exercise.
   e. Programmed instruction.
7. The training manager for a small bank that wants to improve the organizational culture for its twenty-three officers. The bank needs to become more open, more

proactive, and more innovative. They are each completing a managerial skills inventory to identify their own (and each other's) perceptions of managerial skill levels in that organization. What OD strategy is the training manager using?

   a. Attitude survey.

   b. Team building.

   c. Transactional analysis.

   d. Third-party intervention.

   e. Employee inventory.

8. Last week, Myra spent the morning watching Myron work. Then, she took Myron to lunch to talk to him about how to improve his job performance. They have been friends for years, and Myra is head teller of the "A" branch and Myron is a teller trainee at the "B" branch of the same bank. What is going on?

   a. Myra and Myron are part of a job rotation program.

   b. Myra is coaching Myron.

   c. Myron is an assistant to Myra.

   d. Myron and Myra are part of a short-term lateral transfer.

   e. None of the above

9. How does mentoring compare to socialization?

   a. Mentoring is done when an employee is being prepared for jobs of greater responsibility. Indoctrination is done when an employee first joins an organization.

   b. Mentoring is done by the supervisor. Indoctrination is conducted by peers.

   c. Mentoring is a required process. Indoctrination is optional.

   d. Mentoring is generally regarded as a negative experience by the employee. Indoctrination is generally regarded as a positive experience by the employee.

   e. Mentoring and indoctrination are the same thing.

10. When is employee counseling an appropriate approach for dealing with performance problems?

   a. When training is too costly.

   b. When the performance problem is ability related.

   c. When the manager cannot identify the problem.

   d. When the performance problem is related to employee willingness to perform the job.

   e. When the performance problem occurs often.

11. Mike, director of training for a large manufacturing organization, has developed a program on sexual harassment in the workplace. All employees are given a questionnaire describing various workplace behaviors and asked to determine whether or not sexual harassment is occurring. They will complete a similar questionnaire at the end of the training program.

What training evaluation method will Mike use with these questionnaires?

   a. Supervisor and incumbent opinion.

   b. Test–retest method.

   c. Pre–post performance method.

   d. Experimental-control group method.

   e. Employee inventory.

12. Don, an MBA from a prestigious school who speaks fluent German, Japanese, and English, was hired by a U.S.-based global organization for international marketing. He was sent to Japan as director of marketing for a year. He returned to the United States for six months and then was sent to Germany for a year as director of marketing. He was expecting a promotion to vice-president of international marketing when he returned to corporate. Instead, he was assigned as West Coast regional manager. Why do you think he received this assignment?

   a. People with prestigious MBAs often have higher opinions of their abilities than do the organizations who employ them.

   b. Don must have made some really big mistakes in his overseas assignments to be demoted like that.

   c. Most foreign assignments result in demotions. The experience is viewed as a vacation and not to be rewarded.

   d. This assignment is not surprising. A recent survey showed that 18 percent of all returning expatriates were demoted upon return.

   e. This assignment only seems like a demotion. The position of regional manager will give him a lot more autonomy than he had as a country-level manager.

13. Training needs may be assessed by answering the questions that are listed here except:

   a. What, historically, has worked well in this organization?

   b. What are the organization's goals?

   c. What behaviors are necessary to complete assigned tasks?

   d. What tasks are needed to achieve the organization's goals?

   e. What skill deficiencies do job incumbents have, related to tasks needed to achieve organizational goals?

14. Why are training programs evaluated in industry?

   a. They cannot be evaluated.

   b. With downsizing, everything in industry is being evaluated.

   c. Evaluation is a necessary component of establishing training effectiveness.

   d. Evaluation is required for Title VII compliance.

   e. Employees have the right to comment on the training they receive.

Chapter Ten

DEVELOPING CAREERS

LEARNING OBJECTIVES

AFTER READING THIS CHAPTER, YOU WILL BE ABLE TO:

1. Describe what is meant by the term *career*.
2. Discuss the focus of careers for both the organization and for individuals.
3. Describe how career development and employee development are different.
4. Explain why career development is valuable to organizations.
5. Identify the five stages involved in a career.
6. List the Holland Vocational Preferences.
7. Describe what is meant by Jungian Personality Typology.
8. Discuss how dual-career couples affect career development.
9. Identify how organizational career development can be made more effective.

What do those born between 1946 and 1964 have going for their careers? A catchy title—baby boomers—and unprecedented growth in corporate America during their career ascent days? An innate ability to organize things? Well, maybe all these things. But baby boomers cannot sit back smugly. There's some new kids on the block, and they're after the boomers' jobs. These are the twenty-somethings, the generation Xers. In spite of the reputation that precedes their generation, they're making some headway on the job scene. For example, consider the story of Robb Gaynor, a 27-year-old manager at Charles Schwab & Company.[1]

Robb Gaynor is quite representative of generation Xers. Believed to be "cynical underachievers, with poor work habits and low ambitions,"[2] Robb fit that role exceptionally well. He attended four colleges, hopping from one to another before he could find himself. For Robb, finding who he was, though, didn't involve college. He dropped out permanently. He jumped from job to job before he finally accepted a position with a Charles Schwab discount brokerage firm in San Francisco. But even on this job, Gaynor didn't conform to the baby boomers' ideal work ethic. In fact, it's believed that Robb leaves his job some afternoons to go to his favorite sunny place to fish. Even his personal affairs appear somewhat messed up to the well-organized boomers. Robb has often missed paying his monthly electric bill, and has been late in his car payments about 25 percent of the time. Sounds like a typical "slacker" from generation X, right? Maybe, but who should care! In spite of Robb's personal demeanor, he's also the "fastest rising star under age 30" at the 6,100-person Charles Schwab organization.

For anyone who does business with Charles Schwab, one thing may be noteworthy—something called Schwablink. It's an electronic trading process that Gaynor developed and manages for the company. And over the past few years, it has helped Schwab add billions of dollars in assets. Just maybe this "misfit," and the thousands like Gaynor, can make a difference in tomorrow's organizations.

Yet, to harness this energy, baby boomers will need to recognize that many of the baby busters' careers will be unorthodox. They will not adhere to the "natural" progression of the past. Instead, generation Xers will stay on a job only for a short period. They'll accept the challenge, work through it, then look for the next exciting thing to do. Come to think of it, isn't that the type of employee a dynamic organization requires to meet future unexpected challenges ahead? Just maybe generation Xers, like Robb Gaynor, have the temperament and the skills, to manage their careers and lead companies well into the next millennium.

●

What Is a Career?

Career development is important to us all. Nevertheless, we know that people sometimes have difficulties achieving their career goals. This reflects the new and unexpected complexities that managers must now confront in their efforts to mobilize and manage their human resources. The historical beliefs that every employee would jump at the chance for a promotion, that competent people will somehow emerge within the organization to fill arising vacancies, and that a valuable employee will always be a valuable employee, are no longer true. Lifestyles are changing; we are becoming increasingly aware of the different needs and aspirations of employees. If managers are to be assured that they will have competent and motivated people to fill the organization's future needs, they should be increasingly concerned with matching the career needs of employees with the requirements of the organization.

Definition

Career The sequence of positions that a person has held over his or her life.

The term **career** has a number of meanings. In popular usage it can mean advancement ("He's moving up in his career"), a profession ("She has chosen a career in medicine"), or stability over time (career military).[3]

For our purposes, we will define career as "the pattern of work-related experiences that span the course of a person's life."[4] Using this definition, it is apparent that we all have or will have careers. The concept is as relevant to transient, unskilled laborers as it is to engineers and physicians. For our purposes, therefore, any work, paid or unpaid, pursued over an extended period of time, can constitute a career. In addition to formal job work, careers can include schoolwork, homemaking, or volunteer work. Furthermore, career success is defined not only objectively in terms of promotion, but also subjectively, in terms of satisfaction.

Individual versus Organizational Perspective

The study of careers takes on a very different orientation, depending on whether it is viewed from the perspective of the organization or of the individual. A key question in career development, then, is, "With whose interests are we concerned?" From an organizational or managerial standpoint, career development involves tracking career paths and developing career ladders. Management seeks information to direct and to monitor the progress of special groups of employees, and to ensure that capable managerial and technical talent will be available to meet the organization's needs. Career development from the organization's perspective is also called organizational career planning.

In contrast, individual career development, or career planning, focuses on assisting individuals to identify their major goals and to determine what they need to do to achieve these goals. Note that in the latter case the focus is entirely on the individual and includes his or her life outside the organization, as well as inside. So while organizational career development looks at individuals filling the needs of the organization, individual career development addresses each individual's personal work career and other lifestyle issues.[5] For instance, an excellent employee, when assisted in better understanding his or her needs and aspirations through interest inventories, life-planning analysis, and counseling, may even decide to leave the organization if it becomes apparent that career aspirations can be best achieved outside the employing organization. Employee ex-

Robb Gaynor may just be the quintessential Generation Xer. He's job hopped, left several colleges, and is often late in paying his bills. But, he's recognized as the fastest rising star at Charles Schwab Brokers. Apparently this technically gifted individual has helped the Schwab organization add billions in assets.

pectations today are different from employee expectations a generation ago. Sex-role stereotypes are crumbling as people are less restricted by gender-specific occupations. Additionally, our lifestyles are more varied, with, for example, more dual-career couples today than ever before. Both of these career approaches (individual and organizational) have value. This chapter blends the interests of both the individual within the organization and the organization itself. However, since the primary focus of human resource management is the interest of careers to the organization, we will emphasize this area.

Career Development versus Employee Development

Given our discussions in Chapter 9 on employee development, you may be wondering what, if any, differences there are between **career development** and employee development. These topics have a common element, but there is one distinct difference—the time frame.

Career Development A process designed to assist workers in managing their careers.

Career development looks at the long-term career effectiveness and success of organizational personnel. By contrast, the kinds of development discussed in Chapter 9 focused on work effectiveness or performance in the immediate or intermediate time frames. These two concepts are closely linked; employee training and development should be compatible with an individual's career development in the organization. But a successful career program, in attempting to match individual abilities and aspirations with the needs of the organization, should develop people for the long-term needs of the organization and address the dynamic changes that will take place over time.

Career Development: Value for the Organization

Assuming that an organization already provides extensive employee development programs, why should it need to consider a career development program as well? A long-term career focus should increase the organization's effectiveness in managing its human resources. More specifically, we can identify several positive results that can accrue from a well-designed career development program.

Ensures Needed Talent Will Be Available   Career development efforts are consistent with, and are a natural extension of, strategic human resource planning. Changing staff requirements over the intermediate and long term should be identified when the company sets long-term goals and objectives. Working with individual employees to help them align their needs and aspirations with those of the organization will increase the probability that the right people will be available to meet the organization's changing staffing requirements.

Improves the Organization's Ability to Attract and Retain High-talent Employees   Outstanding employees will always be scarce, and there is usually considerable competition to secure their services. Such individuals may give preference to employers who demonstrate a concern for their employees' future. If already employed by an organization that offers career advice, these people may exhibit greater loyalty and commitment to their employer. Importantly, career development appears to be a natural response to the rising concern by employees for the quality of work life and personal life planning. As more and more people seek jobs that offer challenge, responsibility, and opportunities for advancement, realistic career planning becomes increasingly necessary. Additionally, social values have changed so that more members of the work force no longer look at their work in isolation. Their work must be compatible with their personal and family interests and commitments. Again, career development should result in a better individual–organization match for employees and thus lead to less turnover.

Ensures that Minorities and Women Get Opportunities for Growth and Development As discussed in previous chapters, equal employment opportunity legislation and affirmative-action programs have demanded that minority groups and women get opportunities for growth and development that will prepare them for greater responsibilities within the organization. The fair employment movement gave impetus to career development programs targeted for these special groups. Recent legislation, such as the Americans with Disabilities Act, offers an even greater organizational career management challenge. Furthermore, courts frequently look at an organization's career development efforts with these groups when ruling on discrimination suits.

Reduces Employee Frustration Although the educational level of the work force has risen, so too, have their occupational aspirations. However, economic stagnation and increased concern by organizations to reduce costs have also reduced opportunities. This has increased frustration in employees who see a significant disparity between their aspirations and actual opportunities. When organizations cut costs by downsizing, career paths, career tracks, and career ladders often collapse.[6] Career counseling can result in more realistic, rather than raised, employee expectations.

Enhances Cultural Diversity Workforce 2000 will provide a more varied combination of race, gender, and values in the organization.[7] Effective organizational career development provides access to all levels of the organization for more varied types of employees. Extended career opportunities make cultural diversity, and the appreciation of it, an organizational reality.

Workers like Eric Woo have found opportunities at AT&T. His move to Hong Kong to sell integrated communications networks is giving Eric the opportunity to maximize his career potential.

Promotes Organizational Goodwill   If employees think their employing organizations are concerned about their long-term well-being, they respond in kind by projecting positive images of the organization into other areas of their lives (e.g., volunteer work in the community). For instance, Joe works for a utility company. He also coaches Little League baseball with other parents. When he expresses his trust of the utility company, because of their expressed career interest, his friends might consider proposed rate hikes in a tolerant light.

Career Development: Value for the Individual

Effective career development is also important for the individual. In fact, it is more important today than ever. Because the definitions of careers and what constitutes success have changed, the value of individual career-development programs has expanded. Career success is no longer measured merely by an employee's income or hierarchical level. Career success now includes using one's full potential, facing expanded challenges, and having greater responsibilities and increased autonomy (see "Meet Michael Giles"). Intrinsic career development, or "psychic income," is desired by contemporary workers who are seeking more than salary and security from their jobs.[8] Contemporary workers seek interesting and meaningful work; such interest and meaning are often derived from a sense of being the architect of one's own career.[9]

Careers are both **external** and **internal**. The external career involves properties or qualities of an occupation or an organization.[10] For example, a career in business might be thought of as a sequence of jobs or positions held during the life of the individual: undergraduate degree in business; store manager for a small retail chain; graduate training in business; management trainee in a large firm; manager; CEO of a small firm; retirement. External careers may also be characterized by such things as career ladders within a particular organization (junior assistant control clerk; assistant control clerk; control clerk; senior control clerk; control supervisor).

The individual career encompasses a variety of individual aspects or themes: accumulation of external symbols of success or advancement (bigger office with each promotion);[11] threshold definition of occupational types (i.e., physicians have careers, dog-catchers have jobs);[12] long-term commitment to a particular occupational field (i.e., career soldier);[13] a series of work-related positions;[14] and, work-related attitudes and behaviors.[15]

With careers being the pattern of work-related experiences that span the course of a person's life, we must understand that both personal relationships and family concerns are also intrinsically valued by employees. Subjective and objective elements, then, are necessary components of a theoretical perspective, which captures the complexity of career.[16] Success can then be defined in external terms. For example, if after five years at the same company you get a promotion, and Dave, a colleague who was hired the same day you were for the same type of job, has not yet been promoted, then you are more successful than Dave. The external definition also states that a certified public accountant is more successful than a dog catcher. However, if you consider the subjective, internal valuation of success, the story may be different. A dog catcher who defines his job as protecting children and others in the community from danger, who goes home proud at night because he has successfully and compassionately captured dogs that day, is successful in his career. Compare that to a CPA who works only to buy a new yacht so she can escape from the drudgery of her day-to-day office life of dealing with clients, accounting forms, and automated systems. Is she more or less successful than the dog catcher?

Michael Giles
Founder, Quick-Wash-Dry Clean USA

What do you do if after spending several years getting your college education, you can't find a job that suits your needs? Although statistics reveal that about 80 percent of all college graduates do find a job within six months after graduation, with three-fourths of these in career starting positions, for some individuals, that's not enough. They want to make their mark on the world, get rich, and simultaneously help enhance the quality of living for all people. For many, such opportunities are limited, especially in the United States. So enterprising individuals, like Michael Giles, find their opportunities by going abroad.

Michael Giles is the kind of person people both wonder about and admire. He was a graduate of the prestigious Columbia Law School and was in high demand when he entered the market. He accepted a position as a marketer for IBM, which paid him an annual salary of $160,000. Working outside of Washington, D.C., Michael appeared to have it all—a challenging and well-paying career, and an endless future for such a bright individual. But Michael wanted more. He wanted the lifestyle great wealth could provide, but he wanted to give something back—especially to the black residents in deplorable living conditions in South Africa. At age 35, he quit his job with

IBM and moved to Soweto, a small South-African township just outside of Johannesburg. Leaving behind the luxury of living in a nice section of the D.C. suburbs, Michael moved into an area where there was no running water or even primitive sewer systems. No doubt many thought he was crazy!

In adversity, however, Michael saw prosperity. He applied for, and received, a $9.3 million loan from the U.S. government's Overseas Private Investment Corporation. With this money, he founded the Quick-Wash-Dry Clean USA Corporation. Today, Michael's firm is completing the building of 108 coin-operated laundromats that will provide laundry services to most of South Africa's black communities. Michael's career dream to give back to the community, while simultaneously making a decent living, appears to be happening. He's making life better for a group of individuals, which fulfills his need to do the right thing! And, his entrepreneurial spirit is being richly rewarded.

Source: Lee Smith, "Landing that First Real Job," *Fortune* (May 16, 1994), p. 94. See also William Echikson, "Young Americans Go Abroad and Strike It Rich," *Fortune* (October 17, 1994), p. 186.

This differentiation of internal from external is important to the manager who wants to motivate employees (see Table 10-1). Different employees may respond to different motivational tools. For instance, Brad is working as your secretary only to earn enough money to purchase a new couch for his living room; as soon as he has the $3,000, he may quit. Diane, your other secretary, joined the company with the expectation that within fifteen years she will have completed her bachelor's degree and be a management trainee. Would they respond equally to the opportunity to be trained in interpersonal skills? Would both of them be as likely to accept (or reject) a transfer to another city? Probably not, because both have different drives. Thus, we can say that internal and

TABLE 10-1 An Integration of Internal and External Event Perspectives and Career Life Stages

Stage	External Event	Internal Event
Exploration	Advice and examples of relatives, teachers, friends, and coaches	Development of self-image of what one "might" be, what sort of work would be fun
	Actual successes and failures in school, sports and hobbies	Self-assessment of own talents and limitations
	Actual choice of educational path—vocational school, college, major, professional school	Development of ambitions, goals, motives, dreams
		Tentative choices and commitments, changes
Establishment	Explicit search for a job	Shock of entering the "real world"
	Acceptance of a job	Insecurity around new tasks of interviewing, applying, being tested, facing being turned down
	Induction and orientation	
	Assignment to further training or first job	Making a "real" choice; to take a job or not; which job; first commitment
	Acquiring visible job and organizational membership trappings (ID card, parking sticker, uniform, organizational manual)	Fear of being tested for the first time under *real* conditions, and found out to be a fraud
	First job assignment, meeting the boss and co-workers	Reality shock—what the work is really like, doing the "dirty work"
	Learning period, indoctrination	Forming a career strategy, how "to make it"—working hard, finding mentors, conforming to an organization, making a contribution
	Period of full performance—"doing the job"	This is "real," what I'm doing matters
		Feeling of success or failure—going uphill, either challenging or exhausting
		Decision to leave organization if things do not look positive
		Feeling of being accepted fully by the organization, "having made it"—satisfaction of seeing "my project"
Mid-Career	Leveling off, transfer, and/or promotion	Period of settling in or new ambitions based on self-assessment
	Entering a period of maximum productivity	More feeling of security, relaxation, but danger of leveling off and stagnation
	Becoming more of a teacher/mentor than a learner	Threat from younger, better trained, more energetic, and ambitious persons—"Am I too old for my job?"
	Explicit signs from boss and co-workers that one's progress has plateaued	Possible thoughts of "new pastures" and new challenges—"What do I really want to do?"
		Working through mid-life crisis toward greater acceptance of oneself and others
		"Is it time to give up on my dreams? Should I settle for what I have?"
Late Career	Job assignments drawing primarily on maturity of judgment	Psychological preparation for retirement
		Deceleration in momentum
	More jobs involving teaching others	Finding new sources of self-improvement off the job, new sources of job satisfaction through teaching others
Decline	Formal preparation for retirement	Learning to accept a reduced role and less responsibility
	Retirement rituals	Learning to live a less structured life
		New accommodations to family and community

Source: Adapted from John Van Maanen and Edgar H. Schein, "Career Development," in *Improving Life at Work,* (ed.) J. Richard Hackman and J. Lloyd Suttle (Santa Monica, CA: Goodyear, 1977), pp. 55–57; and D. Levinson, *The Seasons of a Man's Life.*

external career events may be parallel, but result in different outcomes. We have displayed these events in Table 10-1. They are discussed in the context of career stages, the topic discussed in the next section.

Career Stages

One way to analyze and to discuss careers is to consider them in stages or steps.[17] Progression, from a beginning point through growth and decline phases to a termination point, is a natural occurrence that happens to all employees. Most of us begin to form our careers during our elementary and secondary school years. Our careers begin to wind down as we reach retirement age. We can identify five career stages that are generalizable for most adults, regardless of occupation: **exploration, establishment, mid-career, late career,** and **decline.** These stages are depicted in Figure 10-1.

The age ranges for each stage in Figure 10-1 are general guidelines. For some individuals pursuing certain careers, this model may be too simplistic. The key is, however, to give your primary attention to the stages rather than the age categories. For instance, someone who makes a dramatic change in career to undertake a completely different line of work at age 45 will have many of the same establishment-stage concerns as someone starting at age 25. On the other hand, if the 45-year-old started working at 25, he or she now has twenty years of experience, as well as interests and expectations that differ from those of a peer who is just starting a career at middle age. For example, the 45-year-old college student who begins school once the children are grown has more in common with the 22-year-old sitting next to her than she does with the 45-year-old full professor who is teaching the class. However, for the majority of us, the age generalizations in Figure 10-1 are fairly accurate.

Exploration

Many of the critical choices individuals make about their careers are made prior to entering the work force on a paid basis. What we hear from our relatives, teachers, and friends, what we see on television or on the street corner, and what sports we play, begin to narrow our career choice alternatives and to lead us in certain directions. Certainly, the careers of our parents, their interests, their aspirations for us, and their financial resources will be heavy factors in determining our perception of what careers are available or what schools,

Exploration Phase A career stage that usually ends in one's mid-twenties as one makes the transition from school to work.

Establishment Phase A career stage in which one begins to search for work. It includes getting one's first job.

Mid-career Phase A career stage marked by a continuous improvement in performance, leveling off in performance, or the beginning of deterioration of performance.

Late-career Phase A career stage in which individuals are no longer learning about their jobs, nor is it expected that they should be trying to outdo levels of performance from previous years.

Decline Phase The final stage in one's career, usually marked by retirement.

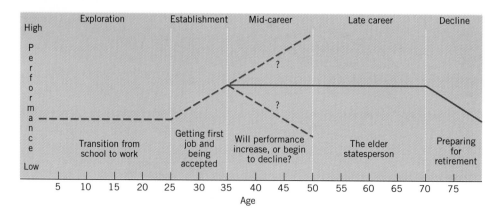

Figure 10-1
Stages in Career Development

colleges, or universities we might consider. Figure 10-2 summarizes information resources.

The exploration period ends for most of us in our mid-twenties as we make the transition from school to work. From an organizational standpoint, this stage has the least relevance, since it occurs prior to employment. It is, of course, not irrelevant. The exploration period is a time when a number of expectations about one's career are developed, many of which are unrealistic. Such expectations may lie dormant for years and then pop up later to frustrate both employee and employer.

Successful career exploration strategies involve trying a lot of potential fields to see what you like or don't like. The college internships and cooperative education programs are excellent exploration tools. You are given the opportunity to see your future coworkers firsthand, and to do, day in and day out, a "real" job. Some successful internships lead to job offers. From a career-stage perspective, an internship that helps you realize that you're bored to death with the work is also a successful one. In the exploration stage we form our attitudes toward work (doing homework, meeting deadlines, taking or avoiding shortcuts, attendance), and our dominant social relationship patterns (easygoing, domineering, indifferent, likable, obnoxious). Therefore, exploration is preparation for work.

Establishment

The establishment period begins with the search for work and includes getting your first job, being accepted by your peers, learning the job, and gaining

Figure 10-2
Information Resources for Career Exploration

Friends and Family:	**People in Industry and Professions:**
Who work in industry or company of interest	Alumni
Who know people in industry or company of interest	Trade associations
Who know people with contacts	Professional societies
	Visiting speakers
Written Sources:	Chamber of Commerce
Career libraries	
Placement offices	**Social, Religious, and Political Organizations:**
Dept. of Labor *Occupational Outlook Handbook*	Kiwanis, etc.
Corporate annual reports	Rotary Club
Investment analyst reports	Church groups
Trade publications and directories	Political parties
Journal articles about companies (e.g., *Forbes*)	**People with Contacts:**
Recruiting brochures	Bankers
Advertisements	Doctors, dentists
Newspaper articles	Lawyers
Industry/company case studies	Insurance agents
	Investment analysts

Source: London and Stumpf, *Managing Careers* (Reading, MA: Addison-Wesley, 1982), p. 51, Table 3.6, Reprinted with permission.

the first tangible evidence of success or failure in the "real world." It begins with uncertainties and anxieties, and is, indeed, dominated by two problems: finding a "niche" and "making your mark."

Finding the right job takes time for many of us. In fact, you may know a 40-year-old who has held a series of seemingly unrelated jobs (for instance, after high school, fast-food worker, three years; clerk in a sporting goods store, three years; construction worker, two years; Army, four years; TV repair, three years; department store clerk, five years; fishing boat operator, now). This person has looked for a niche—or attempted to establish one—for twenty years!

A more typical pattern is to recognize that we may not change as frequently as the individual above. On the other hand, your first "real" job probably won't be with the company from which you retire. Thorough career exploration helps make this part of establishment an easier step.

The second problem of the establishment stage, "making your mark," is characterized by making mistakes, learning from those mistakes, and assuming increased responsibilities. However, individuals in this stage have yet to reach their peak productivity, and rarely are they given work assignments that carry great power or high status. As shown in Figure 10-2, this stage is experienced as "going uphill." The career takes a lot of time and energy. There is often a sense of growth, of expectation, or anticipation, such as a hiker feels when approaching a crest, waiting to see what lies on the other side. And, just as a hiker "takes" a hill when she stands at the crest, the establishment stage has ended when you have "arrived" (made your mark). Technical careers are characterized as having reached *individual contributor* status. You are now responsible for your own mistakes.

Mid-career

Many people do not face their first severe career dilemmas until they reach the mid-career stage.[18] This is a time when individuals may continue their prior improvements in performance, level off, or begin to deteriorate. Therefore, although the challenge of remaining productive at work after you are no longer a "learner" is a major challenge of this career stage, the pattern ceases to be as clear as it was for exploration and establishment. Some employees reach their early goals and go on to even greater heights. For instance, a worker who wants to be the vice-president of HRM by the time she is 35 to 40 years old might want to be CEO by the time she's 55 to 60 if she's achieved the prior goal. Continued growth and high performance are not the only successful outcomes at this stage. Maintenance, or holding onto what you have, is another possible outcome of the mid-career stage. These employees are **plateaued,** not failed. Plateaued mid-career employees can be very productive.[19] They are technically competent and no longer as ambitious as the climbers. They may be satisfied to contribute a sufficient amount of time and energy to the organization to meet production commitments; they also may be easier to manage than someone who wants more. These employees are not deadwood, but good, reliable employees and "solid citizens." An example would be the same HRM vice-president who decides at 40 to not go for the next promotion, but to enjoy life more, pursuing her hobbies, while still performing well on the job.

The third option for mid-career deals with the employee whose performance begins to deteriorate. This stage for this kind of employee is characterized by loss of both interest and productivity at work. Organizations are often limited to shunting such individuals to less conspicuous jobs, reprimanding them, demoting them, or severing them from the organization altogether. The same HRM

Plateauing A condition of stagnating in one's current job.

vice-president could become less productive if, by 42, she realizes that she will never be CEO and tries to "wait it out" for thirteen years until she can take early retirement. Fortunately, some affected individuals can be reenergized by moving them to another position in the organization. This can work to boost their morale and their productivity.[20]

Late Career

For those who continue to grow through the mid-career stage, the late career is usually a pleasant time when one is allowed the luxury to relax a bit and enjoy playing the part of the elder statesperson. It is a time when one can rest on one's laurels and bask in the respect given by younger employees. During the late career, individuals are no longer learning, nor is it expected that they should be trying to outdo their levels of performance from previous years. Their value to the organization lies heavily in their judgment, built up over many years and through varied experiences. They can teach others based on the knowledge they have gained.

For those who have stagnated or deteriorated during the previous stage, on the other hand, the late career brings the reality that they will not have an everlasting impact or change the world as they once thought. Employees who declined in mid-career may fear for their jobs. It is a time when individuals recognize that they have decreased work mobility and may be locked into their current job. One begins to look forward to retirement and the opportunities of doing something different. Mere plateauing is no more negative than it was during mid-career. In fact, it is expected at late career. The marketing vice-president who didn't make it to CEO might begin delegating more to her next in line. The CEO would begin to think seriously about succession planning. Life off the job is likely to carry far greater importance than it did in earlier years, as time and energy, once directed to work, is now redirected to family, friends, and hobbies.

Decline (Late Stage)

The final stage in one's career is difficult for everyone, but, ironically, is probably hardest on those who have had continued successes in the earlier stages. After decades of continued achievements and high levels of performance, the time has come for retirement. These individuals are forced to step out of the limelight and to relinquish a major component of their identity. For those who have seen their performance deteriorate over the years, it may be a pleasant time; the frustrations that have been associated with work are left behind. For the plateaued, it is probably an easy transition to other life activities.

Adjustments, of course, will have to be made regardless of whether one is leaving a sparkling career or a dismal job. The structure and regimentation that work provided will no longer be there. Work responsibilities will be fewer and life will be less structured due to the absence of work. As a result, it is a challenging stage for anyone to confront.

However, as we live longer, healthier lives, coupled with laws removing age-related retirement requirements, 62 or 65 ceases to be a meaningful retirement demand. Some individuals, like former CEO of Kodak, Kay Whitmore, have more personal goals to achieve.[21] Ousted as CEO at age 62, Whitmore moved on to do something he had always wanted—leading the Mormon Mission of Southern England.

Career Choices and Preferences

The best career choice is the choice that offers the best match between what you want and what you need. Good career choice outcomes for any of us should result in a series of positions that give us an opportunity for good performance, make us want to maintain our commitment to the field, and give us high work satisfaction. A good career match, then, is one in which we are able to develop a positive self-concept and to do work that we think is important.[22]

Holland Vocational Preferences

Holland Vocational Preferences An individual occupational personality as it relates to vocational themes.

One of the most widely-used approaches to guide career choices is the **Holland vocational preferences model**.[23] This theory consists of three major components. First, Holland found that people have varying occupational preferences; we do not all like to do the same things. Second, his research demonstrates that if you have a job where you can do what you think is important, you will be a more productive employee. Personality of workers may be matched to typical work environments where that can occur. Third, you will have more in common with people who have similar interest patterns and less in common with those who don't. For instance, assume Brian hates his job; he thinks it is boring to waste his time packing and unpacking trucks on the shipping dock of a manufacturing firm, and would rather be working with people in the recruiting area. Pat, on the other hand, enjoys the routine of her work; she likes the daily rhythm of loading and unloading, and does not want to be troubled by human interaction. Do Pat and Brian get the same satisfaction from their jobs? There's a good chance that they don't. Why? Their interests, expressed as occupational interests, are not compatible.

Even the career pros sometimes have a change of heart. As head of HRM for the plastics molding company, Premix Corporation in North Kingsville, Ohio, Joe Moroski's future looked bright. But after 21 years with the company, Joe quit. To take another job? Who knows? But until Joe decides, he'll be raising Labradors and riding horses on his farm.

Figure 10-3
Holland's General Occupational Themes

Realistic Rugged, robust, practical, prefer to deal with things rather than people, mechanical interests. Best matches with jobs that are Agriculture, Nature, Adventure, Military, Mechanical.

Investigative Scientific, task-oriented, prefer abstract problems, prefer to think through problems rather than to act on them, not highly person-oriented, enjoy ambiguity. Corresponding jobs are Science, Mathematics, Medical Science, Medical Service.

Artistic Enjoy creative self-expression, dislike highly-structured situations, sensitive, emotional, independent, original. Corresponding jobs are Music/Dramatics, Art, Writing.

Social Concerned with the welfare of others, enjoy developing and teaching others, good in group settings, extroverted, cheerful, popular. Corresponding jobs are Teaching, Social Service, Athletics, Domestic Arts, Religious Activities.

Enterprising Good facility with words, prefer selling or leading, energetic, extroverted, adventurous, enjoy persuasion. Corresponding jobs are Public Speaking, Law/Politics, Merchandising, Sales, Business Management.

Conventional Prefer ordered, numerical work, enjoy large organizations, stable, dependable. Corresponding job is Office Practices.

Source: "Adapted from *Making Vocational Choices,* 2nd edition, Psychological Assessment Resources, Inc., Copyright 1973, 1985, 1992. All Rights reserved."

The Holland vocational preferences model identifies six vocational themes (realistic, investigative, artistic, social, enterprising, conventional) presented in Figure 10-3. An individual's occupational personality is expressed as some combination of high and low scores on these six themes. High scores indicate that you enjoy those kinds of activities. Although it is possible to score high or low on all six scales, most people are identified by three dominant scales. The six themes are arranged in the hexagonal structure shown in Figure 10-4. This scale model represents the fact that some of the themes are opposing, while others have mutually reinforcing characteristics.

For instance, Realistic and Social are opposite each other in the diagram. A person with a realistic preference wants to work with things, not people. A person with a social preference wants to work with people, no matter what else they do. Therefore, they have opposing preferences about working alone or with others. Investigative and Enterprising are opposing themes. Can you identify the scale? (Action? Decision making?) Artistic and conventional preferences also oppose each other. Can you identify that dimension also? (Routine? Autonomy?)

An example of mutually reinforcing themes is the Social–Enterprising–Conventional (SEC) vocational preference structure. Sean, for example, likes working with people, being successful, and following ordered rules. That combination is perfect for someone willing to climb the ladder in a large bureaucracy. What about Beth? She is Realistic–Investigative–Artistic, preferring solitary work to large groups, asking questions to answering them, and making her own rules instead of following someone else's. How does Beth fit into a large bureaucracy—as a troublemaker? Where would she fit better? In a research lab! Both the preference of the scientist and the environment of the research lab are characterized by a lack of human interruptions and a concentration on factual material.

The Schein Anchors

Edgar Schein has identified *anchors,* or personal value clusters, that may be satisfied or frustrated by work. When a particular combination of these personal value clusters (technical–functional competence, managerial competence, security–stability, creativity, and autonomy–independence) is held by the worker and characteristically offered by the organization, that person is "anchored" in that job, organization, or industry. Most people have two or three value clusters that are important to them. If an organization satisfies two out of three, that is considered a stable match. For instance, Danny is a new college graduate. He wants to use his human resources degree. His father was laid off when his organization downsized last year, and he never wants to have to deal with that type of uncertainty. Danny's anchors are technical competence and security–stability. His current job choices are marketing on a commission basis for a new credit card company, or college recruiting for an established manufacturing firm. Which job should he take?

Jungian Personality Typology

Carl Jung's theory of psychological types identifies four dimensions of an individual's personality. These personality dimensions can be matched to work environments, much as Holland vocational preferences are used. People with different personality attributes express different job skills, and are compatible with other workers with similar personality structures. The Extraversion–Introversion (EI) dimension measures perception, identifying an individual's orien-

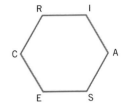

Letters connected by the line indicate reinforcing themes; letters not connected represent opposing themes.

Figure 10-4
Hexagonal Relationships of Holland's Themes

tation toward the inner world of ideas (introversion) or the external world of the environment (extraversion) as a resource and as a source of strength or renewal. The Sensing–Intuitive (SI) dimension indicates reliance on information gathered from either the external world (sensing) or the world of ideas (intuition). The Thinking–Feeling (TF) index indicates a preference to evaluate information using either linear definition and external norms (thinking) or a holistic process and internal values (feeling). The Judging–Perceiving (JP) index identifies an attitude toward the external environment that is either closure-seeking (judging) or information-seeking (perceiving). Each of these preferences tends to produce different and complementary kinds of contributions in work settings. For instance, the EI dimension differentiates the loner from the person who has to be around other people.

Just as we have a **Jungian psychological typology,** so too do jobs. As such, Jung's theory would indicate that we will be better performers if we are appropriately matched. For example, consider the job of a computer programmer. This job requires an individual to work with details, to work autonomously much of the time, and to complete complex programs according to a set schedule. In Jung's terminology, this job would be viewed as having characteristics of introversion, sensing, thinking, judging. Accordingly, to be better matched to the job, Jung would suggest that the employee share the same personality type.

Jungian Personality Typology
Four dimensions of personality matched to work environments.

Making Personal Career Decisions

Considering career stages and individual-job matching issues all at the same time is a larger bite than most of us can chew. Although each of these theoretical perspectives is important, they're influenced and moderated by each other. For the manager who has employees at various life and career stages, with different anchors and preferences, there is no one best answer about how to develop subordinates' careers. Again, career management provides for more satisfied employees.[24] How can the manager provide good career management opportunities for the employees? Several actions may contribute to this process. We offer some suggestions in Table 10-2.

TABLE 10-2   Suggestions for Helping Employees Make Career Decisions

1. **Be aware of an employee's skills and abilities, and preferences.** Understanding who your employees are and what they like is critical to their career success.

2. **Provide opportunities to assess whether employee preferences lie in technical or managerial areas.** Especially during the exploration phase, giving employees an opportunity to work in a number of different type of jobs assists them in determining which they like best, and excel at.

3. **Take into account the life stage of the worker.** A 25-year-old who wants to "climb" in the organization should not be managed the same as a 50-year-old who has plateaued.

4. **Encourage exploration, and opportunity.** Create positive environments employees to explore their career options, and seek change.

5. **Be aware of and honestly present opportunities for growth and advancement within, and external to your organization.** In today's organizations, job growth may be significantly limited. Be open with employees about their potential future with the organization. Be receptive to the realization that job growth for a good employee just might be in another organization.

Contemporary Issues in Career Development

Several current trends are affecting career development for both organizations and individuals. The more popular issues are dual-career couples, downsizing and careers, individual responsibility for career development, and values and career decisions. Let's take a closer look at each of these concerns.

Dual Careers

One of the societal changes that impacts the work force is the increasing incidence of two-career couples. When your grandparents were getting out of school and starting their families, it was expected that Dad would work and Mom would keep house and care for the children. A job change that required moving out of town might be traumatic, but the major issue was usually Dad's work. If Mom worked, it was probably part-time, and merely to supplement Dad's primary income; she could find that kind of job anywhere. Today, almost half the work force is female. Some men do have spouses who are homemakers and do not face dual-career issues in their lives; likewise, some professional women have spouses who are househusbands, also avoiding the pressures and complications of dual careers. When both partners in a household have careers, life may be more complicated. Who takes off a day when a child is ill? Do both partners have the option of considering out-of-town moves to advance their careers? Can employers expect equal commitment from both spouses? Are working women automatically "mommy tracked" (that is, a woman who used to be on a career track with a commitment to an organization, who after leaving the workplace to have one or more children, is assumed to no longer have interest in her career)?

Although each **dual-career couple** is unique, several stress areas have been identified as unique to the relationship of a dual-career couple. Stress may be caused because work roles and family roles may be incompatible. The work role may require a tough, impersonal attitude; the homemaker role is usually one of personal support and encouragement. Stress, then, may be the outcome of too much time pressure for these multiple roles.[25] Competition and jealousy may cloud the relationship of dual-career couples if success is defined in overlapping areas. Juggling career priorities (e.g., who takes the children to the dentist) and adjusting individual career expectations (e.g., "I can't move to Atlanta for my next promotion if my spouse can't find a suitable career spot there") are additional problems. Dual-career couples are at least as happy with their marriages as are traditional families,[26] but they often have developed special coping strategies that are more characteristic of "we" rather than "me" orientations: structural role redefinition, personal role reorientation, and more deliberate time management. Structural role redefinition, the one with the greatest organizational implications, may involve working with management to change their expectations about the job. This includes such activities as developing a flextime schedule and limiting out-of-town travel. Personal role redefinition (i.e., changing your own expectations of involvement) can be seen in the husband who changes diapers or buys groceries, and the woman who hires a housecleaning service. More deliberate time management may mean scheduling a weekend away from the kids rather than counting on spontaneous romantic sparks. These strategies are characterized by active compromise rather than conflict suppression, and by mutual goals rather than expressed self-interest.

Dual-career Couple A situation in which both husband and wife have distinct careers outside the home.

Downsizing and Careers

Some companies and industries go through periodic downsizing. The construction industry, for instance, downsizes after each building season. Park departments hire for the summer, then downsize after the season. But the word downsizing typically conjures the activities that began during the depressed economic times of the early 1990s. Many organizations and industries have experienced the phenomenon, reducing jobs and the number of employees in the organization. Although generally regarded as a negative (society tends to associate growth with health and vitality, while decline suggests decay), downsizing offers unique career opportunities for organizations and employees.[27]

Organizations engage in downsizing activities for various reasons. Reductions in labor costs provide savings. Restructuring an organization, for either business-line viability or unit operations, may result in downsizing. Resource allocation changes, due to internal unit suppliers or managerial layer reductions, may also result in organizational downsizing.[28] Organizational problems that occur after downsizing may also present career management opportunities. Survivors may feel guilty. Workers may have lower confidence in management, lowered motivation to work; they may fear and mistrust other employees and lessen levels of organizational participation and commitment. Higher absenteeism rates, greater incidence of conflict, and scapegoating may also be observed in workers.

Organizations may counter these problems by developing new career paths and ladders. Jobs are redesigned to ensure that work done by laid-off workers is picked up by other workers. Recall in Chapter 2 the discussion of employee involvement. The effect that involving employees has in making work more challenging for employees is applicable to career development. Jobs may be enlarged, as some workers pick up additional skills and responsibilities. Other jobs may be deepened, as a manager picks up details that were handled by subordinates. If career paths are updated to acknowledge these changes, workers are less likely to feel "cut adrift," and morale and commitment may be strengthened. Organizational definitions and clarification, expressed through explicit career pathing, provides stability and a sense of continuity for survivors. Cross-training and job sharing provide opportunities for growth and a sense of security and continuity. Some firms suggest giving raises to survivors to account for their increased workload. Other firms have given pay cuts to survivors, forcing the layoffs of fewer workers, thus reducing the survivors' guilt. Bureaucracies tend to increase rules and regulations to protect remaining territories, further reducing organizational effectiveness and efficiency. Good career paths can reduce some of this maze. When new hires are eventually needed, they often cost more than the displaced workers, and may lack the skills that downsized employees took with them. Also, the downsized organization has sacrificed some sense of security and stability to current and prospective employees.

Individual Responsibility for Careers

Throughout this discussion, we have addressed what the organization can do to assist in career development. Although these actions are necessary for a fully functioning HRM operation, their generalizations across all companies do not exist; that is, we can expect the continued growth of small entrepreneurial firms and the new "contract" that exists between the employee and employer (like temporary help). In both instances, there has been a demise of the commitment to career development that once accompanied employment in large firms. What does that mean for us?

We can no longer expect to have our careers "managed" for us. The responsibility for career development has shifted from the organization to the individual.[29] Although companies such as Intel might forecast where the next demand might be and prepare its workers for the new job requirements, the fact remains: You—the employee—are responsible for your career![30]

Toward More Effective Organizational Career Development

Let's consider the methods or tools that managers can use to better match the career needs of their employees with the requirements of their organization. While these suggestions are not all-encompassing, they are a solid representation of contemporary career development methods.

Challenging Initial Job Assignments

An increasing body of evidence indicates that employees who receive especially challenging job assignments early in their careers do better in later jobs.[31] More specifically, the degree of stimulation and challenge in a person's initial job assignment tends to be significantly related to later career success and retention in the organization.[32] Apparently, initial challenges, particularly if they are successfully met, stimulate a person to perform well in subsequent years.

As we noted in earlier chapters in this book regarding strategic human resources planning, job analysis, recruitment, and selection, there are definite benefits for managers who correctly fill positions with individuals who have the appropriate abilities and interests to satisfy the job's demands. Therefore, managers should be even more concerned with matching new employees to their jobs. Successful placement at this stage can provide significant advantages to both the organization and the individual.

Career Counseling

Although often neglected in the 1980s, career counseling is beginning to return to corporate America, reinstituted in such companies as Schering-Plough and Mellon Bank.[33] As part of employees' performance review, **career counseling** assists employees in setting directions and identifying areas of professional growth. What should take place in this encounter? It has been proposed that the dialogue contain the following four elements:[34]

Career Counseling Assisting employees in setting directions and identifying areas of professional growth.

1. the employee's goals, aspirations, and expectations with regard to his or her own career for the next five years or longer
2. the manager's view of the opportunities available and the degree to which the employee's aspirations are realistic and match up with the opportunities available
3. identification of what the employee would have to do in the way of further self-development to qualify for new opportunities
4. identification of the actual next steps in the form of plans for new development activities or new job assignments that would prepare the employee for further career growth

This career counseling process may not be easy for the manager. If the employee expresses unrealistic aspirations, the manager should be prepared to give a frank appraisal of where or how the individual falls short—an activity that is rarely enjoyable. The resulting dialogue may suggest that the employee needs further assessment and counseling, which should be offered by the orga-

Rachel Vincent just couldn't get her career jump-started in the United States. So rather than complain about how her organization couldn't meet her career expectations, she went international, becoming a public-relations executive in Mexico City.

nization. However, the final outcome should be a mutual understanding between employee and manager about realistic career expectations within the organization. The result, to the organization, will be employees with fewer false hopes and expectations about career opportunities. The key, again, is honesty and the conveyance of realistic data. If we err, it should be on the side of communicating too much information, even if the possibility exists of "turning off" an employee who has his or her unrealistic goals deflated. More employee "turnover, underutilization, and frustrated career development has assuredly resulted from too little realistic information, not too much of it."[35]

Career Development Workshops

Management should consider the value of group workshops to facilitate career development (see "HRM Skills"). By bringing together groups of employees with their managers, problems and misperceptions can be identified and, hopefully, resolved.

Entry workshops are a natural extension of realistic job previews and the orientation and socialization activities discussed earlier in this book. Companies such as Graco and Wendy's also offer psychological assessments to help in this process.[36] In doing so, they provide the opportunity for groups of new employees and their supervisors to share their separate expectations. Discussion can then focus on those areas where mismatches are identified. Where incongruities are significant and not easily resolved, these entry workshops can be extended to work out procedures for reducing the differences by changing the employee's expectations, organizational practices, or both.

Mid-career workshops can be offered to help individuals with similar background and length of tenure in the organization to assess their career development. These workshops frequently include self-diagnostic activities for employees, diagnosis of the organization, and alignment of the separate diagnoses to identify potential mismatches. Where significant differences are found that may

Career Assessment

Individual career development requires people to become knowledgeable of their own needs, values, and personal goals. This can be achieved through a three-step, self-assessment process:

1. **Identify and organize your skills, interests, work-related needs, and values.** The best place to begin is by drawing up a profile of your educational record. List each school attended from high school on. What courses do you remember as liking most and least? In what courses did you score highest and lowest? In what extracurricular activities did you participate? Are there any specific skills that you acquired? Are there other skills in which you have gained proficiency?

   Next, begin to assess your occupational experience. List each job you have held, the organization you worked for, your overall level of satisfaction, what you liked most and least about the job, and why you left. It's important to be honest in covering each of these points.

2. **Convert these inventories into general career fields and specific job goals.** By completing step 1, you should now have some insights into your interests and abilities. What you need to do now is look at how these can be converted into the kind of organizational setting or field of endeavor with which you will be a good match. Then you can become specific and identify distinct job goals.

   What fields are available? In business? In government? In nonprofit organizations? Your answer can be further delineated into areas such as manufacturing, banking, education, social services, or health services. Identifying areas of interest is usually far easier than pinpointing specific occupations. When you are able to identify a limited set of occupations that have interest to you, you can start to align these with your abilities and skills. Will certain jobs require you to move? If so, would this be compatible with your geographic preferences? What type of people will be your coworkers? Do you have the educational requirements necessary for the job? If not, what additional schooling will be needed? Does the job offer the status and earning potential that you aspire to? What is the long-term outlook for jobs in this area? Does the career suffer from cyclical employment? Since no job is without its drawbacks, have you seriously considered all the negative aspects? When you have fully answered questions such as these, you should have a relatively short list of special job goals.

3. **Test these possibilities against the realities of the organization or the job market.** The final step in this self-assessment process is testing your selection against the realities of the marketplace. This can be done by going out and talking with HRM specialists and other knowledgeable people in the fields, organizations, or jobs you desire. These informational interviews should provide reliable feedback as to the accuracy of your self-assessment and the opportunities in the fields and jobs that interest you.

Source: Irving R. Schwartz, "Self-Assessment and Career Planning: Matching Individuals and Organizational Goals," *Personnel* (January-February 1979), p. 48.

create obstacles or frustrations for employees, solutions may take the form of emphasizing the need for individuals to alter their career aspirations, altering the organization's career development practices, or some combination action. Another possible outcome is that the employee will find better career opportunities with another organization.

Finally, the organization may provide late-career workshops. These are particularly useful for employees preparing for retirement, but they can also be used to deal with frustrations over unfulfilled career goals, the responsibilities and role expectations of mentors/coaches, developing new life interests, or coping with young and ambitious coworkers.

Continuing Education and Training

The training and educational development activities presented in Chapter 9 reduce the possibilities that employees will find themselves with obsolete skills. Furthermore, they are consistent with employees taking more responsibility for their development. Additionally, when these development activities are carefully aligned with an individual's aspirations and anticipated future organizational needs, they become an essential element in an employee's career growth.

The education and training in an effective career development program could include on-the-job training; educational or skill courses offered by personnel within the organization; or outside courses provided by colleges, universities, or specialized consultants.

Competency-based training approaches are best for career development.[37] An underlying premise of competency-based training is that a person who already possesses a skill does not need to be taught it.[38] By teaching only skills that are needed, no time is wasted conveying material already mastered. Because employees need to acknowledge their needs for training (work or career management skills), they should be actively involved in the decision-making process of what courses to take and where.

Periodic Job Changes

In addition to encouraging employees to continue their education and training to prevent obsolescence and to stimulate career growth, managers should be aware that periodic job changes within the organization can achieve similar ends.[39] Job changes can take the form of vertical promotions, lateral transfers, job restructuring and sharing, or assignments organized around new tasks, such as being made part of a special committee or temporary task force.

The important element in a job change that offers career development opportunities is the diverse and expanded range of experiences that new job tasks can provide. Varied experiences present to the individual new challenges which, if successfully surmounted, build confidence and provide positive feedback. This process encourages the undertaking of further new challenges and greater responsibilities. Of course, periodic job changes also provide management with more varied information as to the employee's potential to move higher in the organization. When four supervisors rate an employee with high potential for promotion, management can be better assured it is receiving a reliable evaluation than when such appraisal comes from only one supervisor.

Multiple Career Tracks

In some organizations, the only way to get ahead is to be promoted on the managerial track, to move up the management hierarchy. The rewards in this system are for managerial competence. When we examined job-personality fit earlier in this chapter, several other "anchors" and preferences were identified.

Multiple career ladders in an organization recognize these multiple career motivators. Dual-ladder promotion systems may allow good technical contributors to remain in a technical job and to receive the status and financial recognition tendered to those who become managers. For example, IBM promotes managers from project to branch to division to corporate levels of the organization. IBM also promotes systems specialists from analysts to senior analysts to fellows, allowing a good technical expert to remain in a technical job and be "successful." Although dual-career ladders provide good career options for the employee, they frequently necessitate structural change in the organization and modifications of policies and procedures. There are mixed reports of success when dual ladders are put into practice.

Failures appear to be due to one of these reasons: offering technical promotions only when managerial promotion has failed; having unequal compensatory practices; and displaying unequal management support for both ladders.[40] It's tempting to use the alternative ladder as an escape system for the managerial promotion ladder. When a good technician becomes a bad manager and is transferred back to the technical ladder, that action may be perceived by employees as a clear signal that the managerial ladder is preferable, and the technical ladder is devalued. Establishing separate but not equal ladders causes problems in several areas: compensation, evaluation, resource allocations, and responsibility. If the managerial and technical tracks are not compensated in similar fashion, promotion on the technical ladder is quickly regarded as a change in title only, good enough for the plateaued employee, but not for a good performer. Both tracks need to be perceived as supported by senior executives. If X percent of those on the managerial track receive a promotion every year, X percent of employees on the technical track should also be promoted. If the system works only to create a diversion for the managerial stream, that fact will surface in a very few years. If the expectation had been created for equal recognition of technical contribution to the organization, that organization risks substantial loss of technical credibility. Providing dual tracks can reduce the perceived incidence of the plateaued employee by providing lateral growth opportunities in addition to the traditional vertical promotion paths.

Professional Associations

Organizations that employ various groups of professionals can aid career development of those professionals by encouraging involvement in their relevant professional associations. For instance, the Society for Human Resource Management is a professional association for human resource professionals. Chapters in metropolitan areas often meet monthly to network and to sponsor a guest speaker on a current topic. These events help professionals keep abreast of current career demands and expectations. They also provide opportunities for senior staff members to contribute in new ways, and perhaps to meet new people.

Mentor–Protégé Relationships

Mentor–protégé relationships are significant as career development tools.[41] For the protégé, certainly, the relationship has positive career impact, especially for women.[42] For the mentor, the relationship may revitalize the last decade or two of what might have been a stale career. Organizations can encourage these rela-

What If:

HRM in a De-Jobbed Organization

Have you ever pondered the freight-train career ride of the baby-boom generation that occurred from the 1960s through the 1980s? Did you ever wonder what existed that promoted some of these meteoric career heights in such a quick period? Were the baby boomers smarter than the generation Xers; or were they just luckier? A precise answer is difficult to pinpoint, but clearly luck played a major role. How so? Consider that during the 1960s, organizations in the United States experienced unprecedented growth. This meant new markets opened up, bringing along with it many new jobs. Organizations during this period became overly hierarchial, which translated into the creation of managerial positions for almost any task that existed. Undoubtedly, many of the baby boomers were in the right place, at the right time. But don't chalk it up solely to luck. The baby boomers were better educated than the generation preceding them, and they brought an aggressive trait to the work force that was rarely witnessed before. Further-more, accepting most any challenging assignment, being willing to relocate, and having the support of mentors all fostered a career boom. Unfortu-nately, this prosperity didn't last forever. In fact, many of these baby boomers who sky-rocketed to the top in their first ten to fifteen years on the job were the ones hardest hit by the downsizing that began in the late 1980s. For them, and those that follow, fast-tracked career progression may be a thing of the past. Our organizations just cannot afford to promote workers in droves as they once did. And, many of the jobs that served as stepping stones to careers may be lost forever. What, then, can those under 30 do to keep ca-reers alive in today's dynamic organizations? For some, the answer lies in the acronym D.A.T.A.

The *D* stands for *D*esire. Although experience was once perceived as the best preparation for the future, past experience may actually be a hinder-ance. The past may promote a status quo mentality—one that is ill-fitted to a dynamic environment. Instead, workers' desire will be a key factor in career growth. Those individuals who desire to be the best, who continually strive to excel, and who perform under a variety of difficult situations will have an advantage over those who don't possess this trait.

Secondly, workers must have the *A*bility to perform the required work. This means that tomorrow's workers can never sit back on their laurels and bask in their glory. Rather, they must continually upgrade their skills, knowl-edge, and abilities to ensure that they are the best at their jobs. This also means looking closely inside and identifying one's strengths and weaknesses; capitalizing on the strengths, and working to develop the weaknesses.

Tomorrow's employees must also have an appropriate *T*emperament. The security of yesterday's jobs is gone. You are on your own in many circum-stances. And when the job is done, so too, might be your association with the organization. As such, workers must have a disposition that easily adjusts to an ever-changing work situation. Rigidity and the desire for security may be the ultimate killers of one's career.

(continued)

> *(continued)*
>
> Finally, employees must possess a variety of *Assets*. This means that whatever resources the job requires, you must be able to provide. This may be networking contacts, equipment, or even time commitments—all resources that contribute to a successful performer.
>
> Succeeding in tomorrow's organizations needn't be a hopeless cause. We must recognize that career paths of yesterday won't exist. But with proper preparation, and a positive mind-set, the doors to career growth may once again appear. This time, however, it will be solely our responsibility. The organization may be in no position, nor may it desire, to offer this kind of assistance.
>
> *Source:* William Bridges, "The End of the Job," *Fortune* (September 19, 1994), p. 72. See also, Patricia Sellers, "Don't Call Me Slacker!" *Fortune* (December 12, 1994), pp. 181–82.

tionships through networking, through building mentor expectations into managerial job descriptions, and otherwise recognizing and rewarding successful mentoring efforts.[43]

Supportive Environment

An organization that provides a supportive environment for career development is characterized by a concern for employee well-being and a tolerance of the mistakes that can occur during the exploration efforts and growth experiences of those employees. If an employee wants to try the managerial promotion ladder and fails, a mechanism to make a graceful return to a technical track is provided by an organization with a supportive environment. An organization that brands such an employee a failure is not supportive. The existence of career development programs and deliberate career paths, with the expectation that most employees will be long-term employees and that they will grow, is further indication of a supportive environment (see "What If: HRM in a De-Jobbed Organization").

Study Tools and Applications

Summary

This summary relates to the Learning Objectives provided on p. 264.
After having read this chapter you should know:
1. A career is a sequence of positions occupied by a person during a course of a lifetime.
2. Career development from an organizational standpoint involves tracking career paths and developing career ladders. From an individual perspective, career development focuses on assisting individuals in identifying their major career goals and to determine what they need to do to achieve these goals.
3. The main distinction between career development and employee development lies in their time frames. Career development focuses on the long-range career effectiveness and success of organizational personnel. Employee development focuses on more of the immediate and intermediate time frames.

4. Career development is valuable to an organization because it (1) ensures needed talent will be available; (2) improves the organization's ability to attract and retain high talent employees; (3) ensures that minorities and women get opportunities for growth and development; (4) reduces employee frustration; (5) enhances cultural diversity; (6) assists in implementing quality; and (7) promotes organizational goodwill.
5. The five stages in a career consist of exploration, establishment, mid-career, late-career, and decline.
6. The Holland Vocational Preferences are realistic, investigative, artistic, social, enterprising, and conventional.
7. Jungian Personality Typology focuses on four personality dimensions of individuals that can be matched to work environments. These include extraversion–introversion; sensing–intuition; thinking–feeling; and judging–perceiving.
8. Dual-career couples affect career development in that one of the individual's jobs must become priority in terms of advancement and relocation. As such, dual-career couples place added strain on an organization's career development process.
9. Organizational career development can be more effective through (1) challenging initial jobs; (2) career counseling; (3) career development workshops; (4) continuing education and training; (5) periodic job changes; (6) multiple career ladders; (7) professional associations; (8) mentor–protégé relationships; and (9) a supportive environment.

Key Terms

career
career counseling
career development
career stages
decline phase
dual-career couples
establishment phase

exploration phase
Holland vocational preferences model
Jungian personality typology
late career phase
mid-career phase
plateauing

EXPERIENTIAL EXERCISE:
Career Planning

Purpose:

1. To diagnose your occupational strengths and weaknesses.
2. To develop a career plan based on your strengths and weaknesses.
3. To introduce you to commonly used career planning techniques.

Advanced Preparation:

This exercise may require substantial advance preparation. Steps 1 to 5 should be completed before the group meets. Participants may need to read or review one of the exercises or readings discussed in the introduction and body of the exercise. Some participants may need to make trips to the library or arrange discussions with persons in the type of work they are thinking about (see Step 3).

Group Size:

Subgroups of two to six may be used; total group may be of any size.

Time Required:

In-class time depends on size of subgroups; ten minutes per group member plus setup and discussion time (i.e., for subgroups of five, 65 to 85 minutes.)

Special Physical Requirements:

Room or an area large enough to seat small groups comfortably and permit discussions with minimal distraction from others. (Movable chairs will be helpful.) Separate meeting areas for subgroups are desirable, not essential.

Introduction:

Obviously, different occupations and professions require different strengths (skills, abilities, talents, etc.) of the people who are effective in their work. The skills and abilities required for a particular line of work reflect the activities that are involved in the job, which, in turn, are largely dictated by the "raw materials" involved in the work. Broadly speaking, all jobs require dealing with one or more of four types of raw materials: things, data, ideas, and people. These suggest some of the elemental job activities. required for each of these raw materials.

Four Categories of Job Activities

Things	Here are some activities involving **things**: Move, manipulate, machine (saw, drill, finish, etc.), adjust, assemble, design, operate, handle, construct, arrange, inspect, clean, deliver, store, drive, etc.
Data	Here are some job activities involving **data**: Compare, collect, copy, analyze, check, compile, organize, summarize, type, collate, store and retrieve, classify, schedule, observe, diagnose, etc.
People	Here are some job activities involving **people**: Counsel, assist, coach, teach, manage, persuade, interview, consult, advise, criticize, lead, communicate, request, encourage, sell recruit, manage, arbitrate or mediate conflict, negotiate, speak in public, supervise, listen, help others to express themselves.
Ideas	Here are some job activities involving **ideas**: Create, compare, critique, publish, think about, argue, comprehend, decide, plan, interpret, define, establish goals, imagine, invent, synthesize, etc.

Some jobs seem to require the ability to deal with primarily one type of material: bookkeepers work mostly with data, carpenters with things, philosophers with ideas, and sales clerks with people. Most jobs require the ability to deal with at least two types of material. For example, all managers deal with people, but the controller also works with data, the vice-president of engineering is heavily involved with data and things, and the vice-president of marketing with ideas and data.

Individuals vary in their preferences and abilities for dealing with different types of work. As suggested by Jung, these preferences may be fundamental characteristics of personality that differentiate how people collect information (sensing versus intuition) and process information (thinking versus feeling). It seems reasonable to hypothesize that the STs are the individuals primarily oriented toward **things,** since they are drawn to the concrete and impersonal aspects of experience. NTs are clearly those who prefer **ideas** with their "focus on general concepts and issues." NFs value the "personal and social needs of

people," while SFs like detail as it applies to a specific, concrete, immediate situation; that is, **data.**

Effective planning of your career requires that you identify your personal strengths and find a line of work that will let you use those skills that you enjoy exercising the most. Once you have identified a particular vocational area that capitalizes on your strengths, it is also important that you identify any remediable deficiencies or weaknesses that may hinder you from achieving your full potential in your field. You will need to develop specific plans for moving into your chosen line of work (if you are not already in it) and for overcoming your weaknesses.

Step 1:

1. Take four blank sheets of lined, 8-1/2 × 11-inch notebook paper. Put a heading on each sheet, one sheet for each of the four basic areas of:

Things   People

Data   Ideas

2. On the first line of each sheet, write "Satisfying Skills." Beginning with **things,** think of and list all of the things you can do really well with physical materials and objects. Think, in particular, of skills that provide you with a deep sense of satisfaction when you exercise them. When you have listed as many skills and abilities as you can think of for **things,** move on to the sheets labeled **people, data,** and **ideas.** Repeat the process until you feel you have listed all of your really important skills and abilities in each area.

Step 2:

From your lists of "satisfying skills," which are the most important to you? On a fresh sheet of paper, make a list of your **five** most satisfying skills and abilities—those that you enjoy the most (be careful to retain the "things," "people," etc, labels).

Step 3: Do a or b.

a. For people who are not certain about their career interests: What types of careers tend to require the exercise of your most important skills and abilities? Identify as many possibilities as you can before you select the alternative that seems to fit you best. (If you are not sure about some of the possibilities here, there are several ways to get more information. Most colleges and universities have placement and counseling centers that will be glad to discuss your interests with you. If you think certain vocations might be a good fit for you, talk to some people in these jobs—don't be afraid to call someone you don't even know. You might be surprised at how willing most people are to help. If you are really at a loss to think of anything, look up some jobs in the *Occupational Outlook Handbook* or *Dictionary of Occupational Titles* in the nearest library. Once you have identified some likely possibilities, check the card catalog for anything that may be written about these jobs.) As you begin to develop some specific feasible alternatives, pick up any information you can about how people get into this line of work. What are the educational, training, and experience requirements you are going to have to fulfill? Is there a practical way for you to meet these requirements? How? Prepare notes on your findings and conclusions. You will need them in Step 5. You are now ready to establish a tentative career objective. When you have stated your career objective, go on to Step 4.

b. For people who are satisfied with career choices already made: Where do you want to go in your occupation or profession? What does it mean to you to "advance" in your field? Don't restrict yourself to thinking only in terms of traditional measures such as salary and organizational level. For purposes of this activity, define advancement as moving into a new position or redesigning your current job so that it requires you to use even more of your most important and satisfying skills and abilities. Prepare a statement of your career objectives.

Step 4:

Take the original four sheets (Things, Data, People, and Ideas). Turn them over and head up each sheet respectively: weaknesses/deficiencies—things, weaknesses/deficiencies—data; and so on.[44] Respond to the following: Things I do poorly, Things I would like to stop doing, and Things I would like to learn to do well. Which of these deficiencies are most important right now? Which must you do something about first in order to begin moving toward the objective you set for yourself in Step 3? Select and rank order the three most important on the piece of paper where you listed your five most satisfying skills and abilities.

Step 5:

Prepare a brief, written plan showing how you plan to move toward your career objective (from Step 3), and include your plans for dealing with the weaknesses that stand between you and your objective.

Step 6: (Optional)

Share your most important strengths and weaknesses, your statement of your objective, and your plan for achieving your objective with the other(s) in your group. As each person explains his or her inventory and plans, the other members of the group should provide feedback, and offer any suggestions that seem warranted for improving the career plan.

Source: Developed by Donald D. Bowen, in Roy J. Lewicki, Donald D. Bowen, Douglas T. Hall, and Francine S. Hall, *Experiences in Management and Organization Behavior,* 3d ed. (New York: John Wiley, 1988), pp. 261–66. Used with permission.

CASE APPLICATION:

A Demotion of Bay Area

During the winter of 1993, Bill Bateson was described in *Inc.* as "entrepreneur of the year." The article described Bateson as a "winner," destined to one day lead Bay Area Hardware from its regional chain of operations in San Francisco to compete with the Home Depots on a national level.[45]

Bill Bateson was an All-American soccer player at the University of North Carolina in the late 1970s. After graduating with academic honors, and a four-year stay in the Marines, Bill joined his father's hardware business, Bay Area Hardware. He started learning the organization from the ground up, beginning his career as a stock clerk, then cashier, and plumbing supply manager. Concurrently, Bill began studying for an MBA degree at night. In 1989, after obtaining his degree, his father promoted him to vice-president of operations.

But the early 1990s, coupled with the growth potential of the company, made Bay Area a good target for a buyout. In early 1994, Bill's father sold his entire business interest to a management group. One stipulation in the agreement, however, was that Bill Bateson would remain with the company for at least five years.

But, as soon as a new management regime had taken over, sweeping changes were made. Sure, Bill was going to have a job for at least five years with the company, but what he saw was not to his liking. He was immediately demoted to a staff position, one that he had held a number of years ago. No longer was he part of the decision-making process, but rather, a salaried employee who took orders from managers who knew little about the hardware business. Frustrated, Bill made an offer to the CEO—buy out his five-year contract and he would leave immediately. Bill hadn't gotten back to his aisle before the check was written and separation agreements were presented to him.

The demotion and the resignation wasn't the end of Bill's career. Instead, he looked at it as an opportunity to do something he always wanted. He relocated to Nebraska and began working in a company that specializes in hunting gear. His climb to the top may have been stymied, but today, Bill is as happy as he's ever been.

Questions

1. Trace Bill Bateson's career in terms of career stages.
2. How can a demotion, or a change in top management, impede one's career plans? What does this indicate in terms of individual career responsibility? Discuss.

Testing Your Understanding

How well did you fulfill the learning objectives?

1. Joan is a wife and mother. She has raised four children, but feels stifled in that role. She spends most of her time in volunteer activities—save the whales, quilting, great books clubs, church work. What could she change to have a successful career?
   a. Get paid for the work she does.
   b. Stick to only one volunteer activity for a period of more than fifteen years.
   c. Joan does have a successful career.
   d. Joan should have more children.
   e. If Joan felt satisfied as wife, mother, and volunteer worker, her career could be regarded as successful.
2. A vice-president of human resources for a large, high-technology firm fights to attract and retain highly skilled workers. She is hiring a new manager of training and development. She wants a progressive person who is in tune with the needs of the workers and is aware of emerging trends in career management. What comment would be a danger signal on an interview with a prospective candidate?
   a. A major focus of the job is developing career ladders and tracking career paths.
   b. Monitoring the progress of special groups, such as minorities and managers, is an important part of the job.
   c. The needs of dual-career couples should be handled in the same ways as single employees to avoid favoritism.
   d. Lifestyle issues and individual analysis should be part of the career planning services offered to employees.
   e. Employee needs and goals should be assessed. To-

day's worker has different expectations than those of a generation ago.

3. Robin has worked for the same manufacturing firm for twenty years. Last week, after a training session, she decided to quit, return to school, and open a florist shop. What kind of session did Robin attend?
   a. Individual career development.
   b. Organizational career management.
   c. Employee development.
   d. Employee training.
   e. Employee inventory.
4. John, vice-president of human resources, has just cut the career development program from his budget in response to a 35 percent budget cut directive. What is likely to happen?
   a. Good employees will not be affected.
   b. All employee training functions will become more effective and efficient because of this action.
   c. In the short term, employees will work harder.
   d. In the long term, employees will be less committed and satisfied with the organization.
   e. The other training functions can easily replace these programs.
5. A large federal agency conducts career management workshops for its employees. More than 30 percent of workshop attendees leave for employment elsewhere within a year. The program is considered to be a great success in career management because it
   a. keeps those employees out of other training sessions.
   b. increases cultural diversity.
   c. reduces employee frustration.
   d. reduces organizational goodwill.
   e. promotes organizational globalization.

6. Sean is a 27-year-old college senior. He will graduate in the spring with an MBA in Accounting and return to full-time work as a senior accountant for the firm that paid his way through school. Identify Mike's career stage.

   a. Decline.
   b. Maintenance.
   c. Exploration.
   d. Establishment.
   e. Mid-career.

7. Jane is an accounting major and refinishes furniture in her spare time. She is well organized and uses a very impressive time-management calendar. She seems friendly enough, and belongs to several campus groups, but is not an officer in any of them. What is Jane's Holland type?

   a. Realistic-Investigative-Artistic.
   b. Social-Enterprising-Conventional.
   c. Social-Conventional-Realistic.
   d. Investigative-Enterprising-Artistic.
   e. Realistic-Conventional-Artistic.

8. Gloria works for a large bank as a teller manager. She likes the steady hours, the predictable schedule, the pleasant coworkers, the good working relationships with her subordinates, and the status of the bank. What Schein anchors are important to Gloria?

   a. Security, managerial competence.
   b. Security, creativity.
   c. Technical competence, security.
   d. Creativity, autonomy, technical competence.
   e. Creativity, autonomy, security.

9. Based on a comparison of Holland's vocational preferences and the Jungian typology, which statement is accurate?

   a. A realistic person is likely to be intuitive.
   b. A social person is likely to be an extrovert.
   c. An investigative person is likely to be thinking.
   d. An artistic person is likely to be judging.
   e. An enterprising person is likely to be an introvert.

10. Jo is an Extrovert-Sensing-Thinking-Judging Jungian type. What job would be best for her?

    a. A shoe clerk. She could meet lots of people, measure feet, sell the shoes, and move on to the next customer.
    b. A waitress. She could meet lots of people, anticipate their dining needs, make sure everyone in the dining party was happy, and look forward to repeat business.
    c. A rocket scientist. She could work in her lab, away from people, and make whatever experiments she wanted, whenever she wanted.
    d. A veterinarian. She could work with animals, not people, extend the limits of physical diagnosis in her treatments, and move on to the next dog.
    e. A grade-school teacher. She could work with children, help them be creative, help socialize them, and know that, for years to come, she influenced their lives.

11. Sid and Nancy, a dual-career couple, work in a large East Coast metropolitan area. Nancy works for a bank. Sid works for a tool and die manufacturer. Nancy is involved in an individual career assessment activity at her bank. In which of these exercises will the dual-career couple pressure appear?

    a. Jungian typology.
    b. Schein's anchors.
    c. Holland vocational preference profiles.
    d. Role-play exercise about real-life priorities.
    e. Employee inventory.

12. Matt quit school when he was 16 to work full-time at the local fast-food emporium to pay for his car and his video games. Now, at 36, he wants to try something else. What should Matt do?

    a. Finish high school.
    b. Get into the management training program at the fast-food emporium.
    c. Spend some time sorting and identifying his skills, interests, needs, and values.
    d. Just say, "No."
    e. Check the want ads and interview for other jobs.

13. Individual career management is different today than it was a generation ago for all of these reasons except

    a. sex-role stereotypes are crumbling.
    b. employee expectations are different.
    c. the impact of other life roles and responsibilities on work life has been recognized.
    d. choices are more important. There is little opportunity today to change a career, once it has been launched.
    e. lifestyles are more varied.

14. Which statement best reflects the relationship between career development and employee development?

    a. Employee development should replace organizational career management programs.
    b. The goals of employee development should be compatible with the goals of career development.
    c. The goals of employee development should be considered independently of career development.
    d. The relationship is an adversarial one.
    e. Employee development should be done before individual career development and after organizational career development.

Chapter Eleven

MOTIVATION AND JOB DESIGN

LEARNING OBJECTIVES

AFTER READING THIS CHAPTER, YOU WILL BE ABLE TO:

1. Define motivation.
2. Identify the three critical components of motivation in an organizational setting.
3. Discuss the process of motivation.
4. Describe how unsatisfied needs create tension.
5. Explain the difference between functional and dysfunctional tension.
6. Discuss the effort–performance relationship, the performance–organizational goal relationship, and the organizational goal–individual goal relationships.
7. Identify the five core characteristics of the job characteristics model.
8. Describe the motivational effects of job enrichment and work-at-home.
9. List several suggestions that can be used to motivate employees.
10. Describe how you might motivate low-tech and high-tech employees.

Imagine the surprise of Bill Mork when he found out the employee suggestion program he had recently implemented at Modern of Marshfield, a furniture manufacturer in Marshfield, Wisconsin, had failed miserably.[1] This program was supposed to be the textbook copy of success stories at a number of companies. Mork had attended a seminar on improving organizational quality and had visited Milliken & Company, a recipient of a prestigious U.S. award for outstanding quality. Given what he had heard and seen, and witnessing how successful it had been at Milliken, Mork began the process of implementing a similar program at Modern.

The process at Modern was simple. Each month, a group of managers would evaluate all the suggestions made by employees during the previous month. The author of the best suggestion would be given special parking privileges for the month, and would be recognized at a short ceremony in front of all of his or her coworkers. Surprisingly, very few, if any, suggestions appeared with any kind of frequency. Why this was happening was unclear to Mork. But one day he thought he found the answer. An individual being recognized for his suggestion asked that the ceremony not take place. Since being cited for his efforts, the employee had been teased and called a brown-noser by his peers for participating in the suggestion program. Mork had the startling revelation that his suggestion program was working just the opposite from what was intended. It was not motivational and promoting productivity; it had become something to avoid at all costs. But, Bill Mork was not about to admit defeat. He knew such programs had merit. He just had to figure out what his employees really needed. So he backtracked and sought employee input into the process.

As a result of his investigation, the employee suggestion program at Modern was significantly changed, Now, every suggestion submitted is eligible for up to 10 percent of the cost savings it generates. And there can be several winners at the same time! A portion of the cost savings the company receives is also set aside to honor all employees who have made suggestions during the previous year and to cover monthly drawings for such "rewards" as televisions. Furthermore, managers no longer decide the winners. An employee committee has been empowered for this determination.

Since the restart of Modern's employee suggestion program, its 100 employees have made more than 1,200 suggestions. These suggestions helped the company save more than $50,000 and doubled its sales from $4 million to nearly $8 million in 1993. Workers with cost-savings suggestions shared in more than $10,000 in rewards. Now, as Mork states, "people have a different attitude when they see someone getting a check. Instead of a brown-noser, the winners become someone who can buy the next round."[2]

Introduction

In any organization, success is contingent on how well its employees perform. Up to this point in HRM, we have focused our attention toward productive employees through the use of job analysis, proper recruitment and selection techniques, and adaptation and training of employees. Although these activities are critical, we cannot assume that they will give us our desired result—highly energized employees. We can hire individuals with extraordinary competencies, adapt them to the organization, and further develop their abilities, but this will not assure satisfactory **performance.** We know that an individual's performance is a function of their ability to do the job, and their willingness to do it. Recruitment, selection, and training typically focus only on the ability side; thus, a major missing ingredient is one's willingness. Motivation, then, becomes a process of activating this potential in all our employees. For example, even the most mundane topics in a college course can be made exciting by a professor who knows how to "excite" his or her students. By doing those things necessary to keep students involved and their interest piqued, the professor is activating the learning "energies" of these individuals.

In whatever forum—a university, a company, or a one-on-one relationship—the issue at hand is finding ways to motivate people. Let's take a closer look at motivation and how it manifests itself in our organizations.

Characteristics of Motivation

The Motivation Process

Motivation can be defined in terms of some outward behavior. People who are motivated exert a greater effort to perform some task than those who are not motivated. However, saying such is only relative and tells us little. Rather, a more descriptive definition of motivation would be the willingness to do something, where this something is conditioned by its ability to satisfy some need for the individual.[3] For instance, consider the amount of effort (willingness) you put into a class you take on a pass/fail basis. Human nature tells us that you exert only enough effort to meet the minimum requirements necessary to pass. That effort is typically less than if you attempted to get an A in the class. So, an individual's level of effort should be considerably higher when the need is to "earn an A," in contrast to merely passing.

Although in a generic sense this definition is correct, it needs to be modified for organizational reasons; that is, the effort put forth by employees can be misguided. Therefore, it must be focused toward some **organizational goal.** We often assume that this factor is implied, but it is our contention that it is too important to be left to an assumption. For example, if your goal is to pass the HRM class you are currently enrolled in, you don't put your energies into studying for a chemistry test to prepare for your HRM mid-term examination. Thus, the focus on goals becomes crucial in channeling the effort in the right areas.

There is another reason why this definition needs to be modified. That reason lies in satisfying both organizational and individual needs. As employers, we must ensure that employee needs are met, but in doing so, we must have something tangible on which to base our reward. That something is productive work—effort that assists the organization in meeting its goals and objectives. Consequently, employee motivation can be defined as an individual's willing-

Bill Mork was willing to make an effort to find a way to recognize and motivate his employees. Unfortunately, his initial program met with much resistance. However, altering the program in such a way that it better met employee needs led to the desired result—organizational goal attainment and an increase in employee satisfaction.

Performance Effective and efficient work, which also considers personnel data such as measures of accidents, turnover, absence, and tardiness.

Motivation The willingness to do something, conditioned by the action's ability to satisfy some need.

Organizational Goals Meeting company objectives.

ness to exert effort to achieve the organization's goals, conditioned by this effort's ability to satisfy individual needs. Inherent in this definition, then, are three components: effort, organizational goals, and individual needs. We have portrayed these three components graphically in Figure 11-1. Although we have a general understanding of effort and organizational goals, let's focus for a moment on **individual needs.**

An individual need, in our terminology, means some internal state that makes certain outcomes appear attractive. Regarding Figure 11-1, note that although individual needs can be satisfied without the achievement of organizational goals (by, for example, winning a $5 million lottery), our purpose here is to focus only on those needs satisfied through work effort in an organization. Needs, and how they relate to our behavior, are depicted in Figure 11-2.

Our process of motivation begins with an unsatisfied need. Unsatisfied needs are anything that we desire, of which we are deprived. For instance, what if you would just love to purchase a new car? The fact that you don't have one creates an unsatisfied need. Until you do get the automobile, you are deprived of its pleasure.

Whenever we are in a state of **deprivation,** having unsatisfied needs, this results in tension. Tension, as we've come to know it, has a negative connotation. But some tension is absolutely necessary. Rather than group all forms of tension into one term, let's recognize both the positive and negative forms—functional and dysfunctional tension. For motivation to occur, we must have **functional tension.** This "hype" is what gives us the energy to perform. Think about what athletes do before a sporting event: They get themselves "pumped up," which is functional tension. As a result of this tension, individuals are able to perform at peak levels. We'll come back to dysfunctional tension shortly.

Given that individuals are experiencing some unsatisfied needs and have the desire to change that, the functional tension they have will cause them to exhibit a particular behavior—in our model, called **effort.** Effort is the outward action of individuals that focuses on a particular goal. These actions are performed so that the required goals can be achieved.

If our efforts are successful in achieving our goal, then we expect our needs to be satisfied. Satisfied needs then reduce or eliminate the deprivation we initially experienced. If we worked hard and saved for that car, when we finally make our purchase, we have satisfied that need. Furthermore, when this need is satisfied, our tension is reduced for that particular need, resulting in a temporary calming effect until the next need (like purchasing a house) becomes unsatisfied.

Therefore, we can say that motivated employees are in a state of tension. To relieve this tension, they engage in organizational activities. The greater the tension, the greater the drive to bring about relief. Accordingly, when we see people working hard at some activity, we can conclude that they are driven by a desire to achieve some goal that they perceive as having value to them. The problem, however, is that this is a fragile process, one that requires the blending of many "pieces of the puzzle." If any of these linkages are missing, the willingness to exert energy will decrease.

Individual Needs A basic want or desire.

Deprivation A state of having an unfulfilled need.

Functional Tension Positive tension that creates the energy for an individual to act.

Effort Outward action of individuals directed toward some goal.

Process Flow

Figure 11-1
Components of Motivation

Figure 11-2
The Process of Motivation

Barriers to the Process

Because we are dealing with people—individuals who view things in their own idiosyncratic way—a number of barriers may exist to prevent motivation. These barriers can lie either in the individual or in the organization. Despite the actual reasons for reduced motivation, we can identify some common problems. Let's look again at our diagram of the process of motivation (Figure 11-2).

Dysfunctional Tension Tension that leads to negative stress.

Apathy Significant dysfunction tension resulting in no effort being made.

Problems begin to become apparent in the tension phase. During this activity, two major obstacles can exist: **dysfunctional tension** and **apathy.** As we mentioned, some tension is crucial to effort. But when that tension becomes dysfunctional, we witness a change in individuals. For instance, suppose that initially an individual was putting forth the effort, but didn't satisfy his or her need. Maybe a second attempt was made, with the same result. At some point, the tension takes a turn for the worse—creating stress and leading to dysfunctional tension. For example, suppose we have two employees working in an admissions office at a local community college. Yearly performance evaluations conducted on employees result in a pay raise. In this college, three evaluation outcomes are possible—outstanding, satisfactory, and needs improvement. The pay increases for each are 6 percent, 3 percent, and 0 percent, respectively. Furthermore, assume the college has a means of quantifying this evaluation based on student applications processed, and their quality. To be rated "outstanding," one needs a quantitative score of 114 percent with less than a 1 percent error rate; for "satisfactory," 78 percent with less than a 5 percent error rate; and "needs improvement" is anything under 78 percent or an error rate above 5 percent. During the first evaluation, employee A has a score of 109.6 percent with no recorded errors; employee B, 86 percent with a 4 percent error rate. What pay raise do both get? Three percent! For employee A, this is disturbing; a 6 percent pay raise is what she wants (unsatisfied need). So for period two, she tries even harder to get to 114 percent. Employee B, on the other hand, is satisfied with the 3 percent raise. At the end of period two, the evaluations indicate: employee A, 111.1 percent, no errors; employee B, 78.9 percent, 3 percent errors. Their pay raises? Three percent. By now, employee A is frustrated. She has done all she can to satisfy her needs, but apparently she is unable to do so. So how does dysfunctional tension come into play? This employee knows that she can get an 80 percent rating by working hard until Wednesday afternoon. So she slows down, thus losing her drive. In the end, she gives the company what she believes is fair—effort consistent with a 3 percent pay raise!

Apathy also can play a role in this process. By *apathy* we mean a condition of little or no drive, or just not caring. Although people often encounter problems in an organization—such as being disciplined—when a manager's actions result in "making" someone apathetic, the manager has broken the employee's spirit. Sadly, there is little that can be done to correct this problem. For instance, consider when a new manager took over a Bay Area hardware chain in

San Francisco, bringing in an all new management team, current management employees were displaced.[4] Although they were productive, this new manager saw them as a remnant of the old regime. As such, many were either let go or demoted to lesser positions in the hardware store. When they are cast aside, these employees' dignity is stripped away, and it may only be a short period of time before they all leave. But before they do, there is little doubt as to how much productivity the organization will get from them. Because of this manager, their effort toward goal achievement is nil.

For motivation to exist, then, it is imperative that certain conditions exist. For HRM, these parameters are the effort–performance relationship; the performance–organizational goal relationship; and the organizational goal–individual goal relationship.[5] However, before we get into these relationships, a few words are in order about our view of motivation. Whenever discussions of motivation occur, there is a tendency to spend considerable time discussing the likes of Abraham Maslow,[6] Douglas McGregor,[7] Frederick Herzberg,[8] David McClelland,[9] J. Stacey Adams,[10] and Victor Vroom.[11] Since you have undoubtedly reviewed these theorists' contributions in earlier courses, we assume you're already familiar with their theories. Nonetheless, we've summarized them briefly in Table 11-1.

A Model of Motivation

The motivation process is complex. Because individuals, and organizations for that matter, are multifaceted, there must exist an appropriate blend of factors

TABLE 11-1   Recap of Classic Motivational Theories

Theory	*Individual*	*Summary*
Hierarchy of Needs	Abraham Maslow	Five needs rank in an hierarchical order from lowest to highest: physiological, safety, belonging, esteem, and self-actualization. An individual moves up the hierarchy and, when a need is substantially realized, moves up to the next need.
Theory X–Theory Y	Douglas McGregor	Proposes two alternative sets of assumptions that managers hold about human beings: motivations—one, basically negative, labeled Theory X; and the other, basically positive, labeled Theory Y. McGregor argues that Theory Y assumptions are more valid than Theory X and that employee motivation would be maximized by giving workers greater job involvement and autonomy.
Motivation–Hygiene	Frederick Herzberg	Argues that intrinsic job factors motivate, whereas extrinsic factors only placate employees.
Achievement, Affiliation, and Power Motives	David McClelland	Proposes that there are three major needs in workplace situations: achievement, affiliation, and power. A high need to achieve has been positively related to higher work performance when jobs provide responsibility, feedback, and moderate challenge.
Equity Theory	J. Stacey Adams	An individual compares his or her input/outcome ratio to relevant others. If there is a perceived inequity, the individual will augment his or her behavior, or choose another comparison referent.
Expectancy Theory	Victor Vroom	Proposes that motivation is a function of valence (value) of the effort–performance and the performance–reward relationships.

that promote needs satisfaction. Furthermore, the factors that must exist may also change frequently—what one has as an unfulfilled need today may not be important tomorrow. Research has shown us that people do change over time; that at various stages in their careers, certain goals are more important than others. For example, consider just two possible "outcomes"—a three-day weekend for the summer months, or a $4,000 annual bonus. That is what Tina Irwin of Friendship Cards[12] posed to her employees. Tina believed that all her employees would value a $4,000 bonus; most of them were under 30 years of age, and she thought that an infusion of that kind of money—almost 10 percent of their salary—would be welcomed. But Tina was mistaken: When she asked her employees what they valued more, the majority asked for the three-day weekend.

Although another group of employees might have responded differently, there's an important message here: That is, to be sure that specific needs are satisfied, you might have to ask employees what those needs are.[13] Even the best motivational device is useless if it misses its intended target. For that direct hit to occur, HRM must ensure that all the potential traps that can sap an individual's motivation are removed. To begin, HRM must ensure that employees clearly see a strong relationship between effort and performance.[14]

The Effort–Performance Relationship

Whenever we hire an employee, there is an implied understanding that we have hired the individual who best fits the job requirements. Accordingly, one of the initial components of the **effort–performance relationship** focuses on one's ability to exert the appropriate effort. We said earlier that effort is an inward reaction that is witnessed as outward behavior. But what should that effort be? For motivation to occur, we must be able to specify what effort is needed. For HRM, this means that jobs must be analyzed properly (and updated frequently) to ensure that the job is defined in terms of the tasks, duties, and responsibilities (Chapter 5). Furthermore, HRM must identify what the job incumbent must possess to be successful. Once these two concepts are in place, HRM must ensure that it has selected the appropriate person for the job (Chapters 6 and 7), adapted them to the organization (Chapter 8), and trained them in doing the job the company way (Chapter 9). In fact, the effort component is indeed the first two legs of our HRM model—staffing, and training and development. By defining the job properly and selecting the appropriate person, we have those competent, adapted individuals with up-to-date skills, knowledge, and abilities. For job performance purposes, staffing and training and development functions serve to address the "ability" component.

In addition to ability, effort also implies job design. Although we'll look at job design in greater detail later in this chapter, here we want to make sure the organization facilitates productive performance. In doing so, a company must assure that employees have the best equipment available to do the job. Even the best ability on a paper-oriented spreadsheet may not provide the same productivity and quality that a computerized version and laser printer would. Consequently, for effort to be exerted, the right tools must be present.

In addition to their existence, the necessary resources must also be readily available. Consider an individual who must spend a considerable part of each day using specific tools. If the tools are located a distance from the job sight, this individual will be less productive than if the tools were readily accessible. Dave Miller, of Lemco Miller Custom Machine Parts, found that just correcting this tool location problem increased worker productivity by almost 20 percent.[15]

Effort–performance Relationship The likelihood that putting forth the effort will lead to successful performance on the job.

Inasmuch as ability and job design are critical to effort, so, too, is the performance dimension. All the effort in the world will be lost if it is not directed toward some end. For HRM, that end is performance. Hence, an individual will make the effort as long as there is a good likelihood that he or she will be a successful performer. But what is successful performance? At this stage of the motivation model, performance must be defined. Managers must be trained in establishing work standards and communicating these expectations to their employees. These same managers must be able to coach their employees and assist them in achieving their performance levels. And for managers to be proficient at this, they must be trained by HRM staff in performance-appraisal processes. Only by showing employees that their effort is required for specified performance, and that if such effort exists they will be successful on the job, will the effort–performance linkage be completed. When that milestone has been achieved, it's time to tie this performance to organizational goals.

The Individual Performance–Organizational Goal Relationship

Whenever employees perform their duties, their effort should be guided toward some end.[16] As we discussed in Chapter 5, that end is meeting organizational goals. If we have determined the strategic nature of our jobs and linked them accordingly to company objectives, then we can best facilitate their attainment by promoting the appropriate performance. Just as we modified the definition of motivation to include organizational goals, so, too, do we need to reveal to employees this critical linkage.

The **individual performance–organizational goal relationship** is designed to provide something of value to the organization. Just as individuals have unsatisfied needs that cause them to behave in a certain manner, so, too, do organizations. But the organization's unsatisfied needs (unfulfilled goals) cannot be satisfied without the effort of its people. If employees' performance is not adequate to meet company objectives, the company will be less able to "reward" its people.

For example, consider Lincoln Electric Company. Known for decades as an organization with some of the highest paid blue-collar workers in the world, Lincoln Electric's methodology is one in which employees share in company profits. Each year, management and employees determine what goals are to be met. If those goals are achieved, then employees receive a specified amount. Additionally, if the goals are surpassed, as they have been for years, then the employees receive a bonus. How much will they receive? That amount is directly related to the level of worker performance. Accordingly, through a profit-sharing process, the more the employee performance exceeds organizational goals, the greater their share of the profits. In fact, in situations like this, a performance–organizational goal relationship creates a win–win situation for all involved. Even so, caution is in order. Such a linkage does not occur automatically. Rather, it is a function of many parts of the organization, like an extensive performance-appraisal system—being led in part by HRM.

For the performance–organizational goal relationship to function effectively, the organization must set a clear direction. That is, the organization must set its plans for given time periods and communicate those plans downward in the organization, and employees must have control over the performance measures. At each successive level, then, the plans take on more detail, such that at employee levels, each individual knows why his or her job exists and what role it plays in achieving the organization's objectives. At these levels, then, jobs must be clearly focused. Just as in our first relationship, effort–performance, employ-

Individual Performance–Organizational Goal Relationship The likelihood that successful performance on the job will lead to the attainment of organizational goals.

•

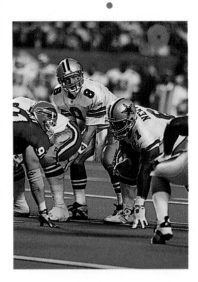

For the performance–organizational goal relationship to function effectively, a clear directive must be set. For Troy Aikman of the Dallas Cowboys, the ultimate goal is to reach the Super Bowl. Once this goal is explicitly defined, Troy and his teammembers must then understand what is expected of them to reach this goal.

Organizational Goal–Individual Goal Relationship The expectation that achieving organizational goals will lead to the attainment of individual goals.

ees must know what is expected of them. Furthermore, they must know what goal performance is, and how it will be determined.

In most of our organizations, the linkage to successful performance is measured through some performance evaluation instrument. But too often, what we measure, or how we go about the process, may be inappropriate. For example, consider a college professor. Assuming the university has set its objectives, we recognize that one measurement of these objectives is how much students learned. In one simple way, we might assess this information through student evaluations. Are these evaluations an accurate reflection of the performance–organizational goal relationship?

The answer is: it depends. Obviously, student reaction is one piece of information. As we mentioned in Chapter 9 on evaluation training effectiveness, participants' reactions are important. Yet they are not the only thing. What about student testing and other assignments the faculty members evaluate? Aren't they better predictors of what was learned? If learning is the outcome, measured by a quantifiable student evaluation score, can we be certain that a high score is a valid prediction of high learning? Or that a low score indicates the opposite? Suppose one faculty member is viewed as being easy—a high grader, who entertains the class with a variety of stories. If this individual is rated high, was the university's goal met? Quite possibly, no. Conversely, another professor who is rigid in grading, not overly charismatic in the classroom, and demands quite a bit of work from students may be rated lower, but has helped students learn more.

Whatever the case may be, HRM must ensure that performance evaluations operate properly. Doing so requires significant time and effort by both HRM and the managers who evaluate employees. Because of the intricacies involved, we'll reserve further comments on performance evaluation until the next chapter.

If all is going as planned, we are getting into a better position to motivate our employees. We have defined our jobs, linked them to the strategic nature of the business, communicated to the employees what they must do to be successful, and then measured that effort properly. It is now time to complete the cycle. We have shown employees what they can do for the company; it is now time to show what the organization will do for them (see "Meet Don Miller"). This part is called the **organizational goal–individual goal relationship**.

The Organizational Goal–Individual Goal Relationship

Mediatech, a midwestern videocassette duplicating company, recognized that something was needed to help its employees feel better about work.[17] Like Modern of Marshfield, Mediatech's management apparently noticed that employees tended to be less productive on Friday afternoons—if, in fact, they were on the job at all. To turn around this situation, the company's management decided to institute a lottery. Each week, the company placed $250 into a lottery drawing, which would be held at the close of business on selected Fridays. Employee pay stubs would then be placed into a drum, with the winner receiving the cash award. The only stipulation was that you had to be present to win. Mediatech's game has resulted in better morale, greater productivity, and much better attendance on Fridays.

The point of the Mediatech example is not the lottery drawing; rather, it is that doing something differently excites employees and reinforces attendance. In the past, however, companies generally did not look for unique and creative ways to "turn on" employees; rather, managers became complacent about what

Meet

Don Miller
CEO, Roppe Corporation

Finding appropriate techniques to motivate employees is often likened to building a better mousetrap. Well, maybe the cat is out of the bag for Don Miller, CEO of the Fostoria, Ohio-based Roppe Corporation, producers of such rubber products as baseboards, stair treads, and floor tiles.

In the early 1990s, Miller noticed that his company was not producing at capacity. Instead, his employees were only reaching approximately 75 percent of production standard, and when they hit that mark, they just stopped working. In fact, at times, they couldn't continue, for mysteriously, the machines suddenly broke down.

Unhappy about the turn of events, Miller sought a workable solution. To confront the workers and become more stringent in his dealing with them, however, was not the answer he felt would work. Rather, he proposed the following to them. He would develop a new production standard, one that was 10 percent greater than originally set. When employee productivity reached this new standard, each employee would receive a 10 percent increase in their hourly pay. And, although the new standard would be set according to what time estimates showed could be achieved in an eight-hour work period, employees could go home whenever they were finished—still receiving the 10 percent pay increase. However, Mr. Miller stipulated one thing: that higher production would not mean sacrificing quality.

Almost overnight, Miller noticed significant changes. Employee productivity rose dramatically. For instance, the old standard for rubber baseboards was 26,000 feet per day, per line. In the past, workers stopped after producing just over 21,000 feet. Under Miller's new plan, the goal was increased to 29,000 feet per day, per line and workers produced every foot of it—about a 35 percent increase over what was being produced the week before! Even more surprising, they often did it in less than seven hours of work—then they were free to leave for the day.

By eliminating a "clock-punching" environment, and giving workers more freedom to act responsibly on their jobs, the Roppe Corporation has been maintaining its 35 percent increase in productivity. And it only increased company costs by the 10 percent raise in hourly pay. Needless to say, both organizational goals and individual goals are being met under Miller's plan.

Source: Michael P. Cronin, "No More Clock Watchers, *Inc.* (February 1994), p. 83.

---

people really wanted out of their jobs. For years, companies held that rewarding employees meant giving pay raises, some recognition here and there, and providing for an occasional guest motivational speaker.[18] Unfortunately, while their efforts were commendable, what they were trying to achieve actually backfired. If each of us has specific unsatisfied needs that cause us to behave in a particular manner, how can we be expected to meet all those different needs with one reward system? We can't, generally. Rather, we must tailor our rewards to meet those individual needs, if for no other reason than that such a diverse work force exists, one that indicates various needs must be met. That is the thrust of this last linkage. The organization requires specific activities to be met to accomplish its goals; why should employees be any different? Hence, if we truly want to enhance motivation, we must make sure individual goals are met.

How can this be done? Through careful assessment of employee needs and a reward system that reflects individual preferences. If you were to poll every member of your class, you might find that each has a different reason for being there. Some attend because they want to learn more about the subject; some go because it is required, or they fear that missing classes will result in poorer test scores and a lower grade. Some may even be there out of habit—they go to class because that's what they think they're supposed to do. (This latter group often believes that learning will occur "just by showing up"!) Whatever the reason, each student has a compelling drive that brings him or her to class. Therefore, to satisfy each class member, the instructor must address these diverse needs. But professors will not know what these needs are unless they ask. Ever wonder why some classes start by asking you for your expectations of the course? The instructor is gathering information on your specific needs so that throughout the semester, they can be met. In cases where a student's expectations go outside the intended class syllabus, the instructor knows that additional materials or reading lists may be needed to fulfill that student's expectations. Unfortunately, businesses have not entirely gotten to this point. There are cases at companies, like TRW and Primerica, where individual rewards are tailored to meet specific individual needs. In such companies, this is done through a process called *flexible compensation*. Let's look at how this works.

In organizations, there is a tendency to provide uniform benefits. Everyone, for instance, may get medical coverage and reimbursement for night courses taken at the local college. But flexible compensation programs allow people to choose the mix that best fits their needs. Suppose, for example, an individual values more time off from work rather than a bonus or other benefits. Where this freedom to choose does exist, individual choices can be handled. In such companies, employees are presented with a pool of money that reflects increases due to achieving organizational goals through successful performance. Each employee is also presented with a menu of what options are available for the next year and how much each will cost. Employees can choose the benefits they want until they've spent their budgeted amount. Someone wanting more health or life insurance coverage might choose that over more pension contribution, more time off, or extended day care—the employer can purchase those things that are best-suited to his or her individual needs.

Flexible compensation, then, gives choices and allows employees to tailor benefits to their unique needs. Although flexible compensation systems are expensive to implement and administer, where they exist the benefits have outweighed the costs.[19] We'll revisit this topic in Chapter 14.

In addition to formulating compensation programs, companies also need to review how their reward and recognition programs operate. For example, suppose the Taco Bell food chain puts the "associate of the month's" name on a sign beside the counter. Not everyone places a high value on recognition. Doing something that employees see as low in value does not create the desired effect on motivation we want. That's precisely the lesson Bill Mork learned from his employees at Modern. Consequently, we may want to recognize superior performance by giving employees a choice and letting them select the reward they most value. For example, maybe an employee would like $100 in cash, or tickets for two to the local symphony. Maybe an employee would like dinner for herself and her spouse, or a night at a downtown luxury hotel. Or maybe an employee wants to pick out something from a catalog that he has wanted for a long time. Our point is that the same amount of money spent on a plaque might be better spent letting employees select their rewards.

HRM, then, must ensure that processes are in place that result in employees getting something they want. Yet above all, these rewards must be perceived as being directly attributable to their performance. Only by creating and supporting the performance–reward link will both the employee be motivated and rewarded and the organization be more productive and moving toward meeting its goals.

Putting the Pieces Together

The model we have presented has a number of implications. For one, it shows the need for sound inception and development efforts on the part of HRM. It also reveals that **pay-for-performance** can be beneficial to both employee and company. Until we begin to reinforce that productivity and show that only productivity matters, we will continue to get things other than the productivity that we reward.

Yet there is another point of the model that is interesting: The motivation process can be adapted to reflect corporate values of what is important for both the organization and the employee. We have portrayed this adaptation in Figure 11-3.

Pay-for-performance Rewarding employees based on their performance.

Implications of the Model for Motivating Employees

Organizations today are recognizing the importance of having a highly energized work force. To bring this about, they're using more self-managed work teams, allowing for more worker participation, and empowering their employees. But it is still a long way from being ingrained into the everyday life of most companies.

For example, it has been suggested that managers, for whatever reasons, are not providing accurate feedback to individuals about their performance. Managers find that identifying group-task goals and linking them to task responsibilities of individual members is a time-consuming operation. Mutual goal setting (the sharing of the goal-setting task with the employee) is avoided by some managers because they believe this is an infringement of management prerogatives. In some cases, task goals are identified, performance is evaluated, and the results are conveyed to the employee; yet the employee remains unsure of management's view of his or her accomplishments in terms of preestablished goals. In summary, it appears that many managers fail to recognize the importance of establishing goals and performance feedback as would be suggested by the model.

Furthermore, the model suggests that managers should ensure that high productivity and good work performance lead to the achievement of personal goals. Again, a review of actual organizational practices reveals many exceptions. Unfortunately, organizations too often fail to allocate rewards in such a way as to optimize motivation. While individual performances tend to be widely divergent—that is, a few outstanding, a few very poor, and the majority surrounding the average—rewards tend to be allocated more uniformly. The result is the over-rewarding of incompetence and the under-rewarding of superior

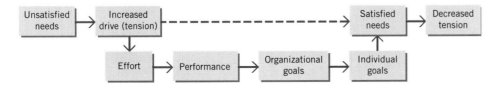

Figure 11-3
Motivation Process for a Work Environment

performance. Employees perceive that hard work does not necessarily pay off; they place a low probability on its leading to organizational rewards, and eventually the attainment of personal goals. As such, they do just enough to get by (see Figure 11-4).[20]

Internal politics is also a vital determinant of who and what will be rewarded. For example, group acceptance may be a personal goal, and high productivity may hinder rather than support achievement of this goal—that is, if the work team one has joined works at a slower pace, leaves exactly at the end of their shift, and takes their breaks precisely on schedule (irrespective of the work that may need to get done at that moment), one must exhibit those same work behaviors to become "part of the gang." Although, at times, these are the realities of work behavior, our motivational theories tend to overemphasize the decision-making, goal-oriented rationality of human beings. For example, when unemployment is high, there may be a tendency for work groups to work at a pace that helps keep their jobs.

While the above discussion presents a rather pessimistic view, we offer some suggestions to help motivate employees, summarized in Table 11-2. These suggestions focus on getting tomorrow's managers to understand their employees as individuals, rather than trying to judge them based on their own value system. Again, with a diverse work group, it is unlikely that a manager's employees will share all of his or her values.

TABLE 11-2 Suggestions for Motivating Employees

1. **Address individual differences.** Recognize that employees are not homogeneous. Rather, each individual possesses a unique set of needs. Accordingly, to effectively motivate any individual, you must understand what those needs are that make them provide the effort.

2. **Properly place employees.** Employees should be properly matched to the job. The best intention will do little for productive behavior if the employee lacks the ability to get the job done. Proper recruiting and selection techniques should assist in creating this match.

3. **Set achievable goals.** Employees often work best when challenging, but achievable goals are mutually set. These hard and specific goals provide the direction employees may need. Continuous feedback on how well employees are performing helps to reinforce their effort.

4. **Individualize rewards.** Realizing that employees have different needs should indicate that rewards, too, may need to be different. What works for one individual may not "motivate" another. As such, one should use their understanding of employee differences and tailor rewards to meet these various needs.

5. **Reward performance.** Rewarding individuals for anything other than performance only reinforces that performance may not matter most. Each reward (individual rewards) must be shown to be the result of achieving organizational goals.

6. **Use an equitable system.** The rewards individuals receive should be viewed as comparable to the effort they have expended. Although perceptions may vary in what is equitable, effort must be made to ensure the reward system used is fair, consistent, and objective.

7. **Don't forget money.** It's easy to get caught up in identifying needs, tailoring rewards, and the like. But don't forget the primary reason most individuals work—money. While it cannot be the sole motivator, failure to use money as a motivator will significantly decrease employee productivity.

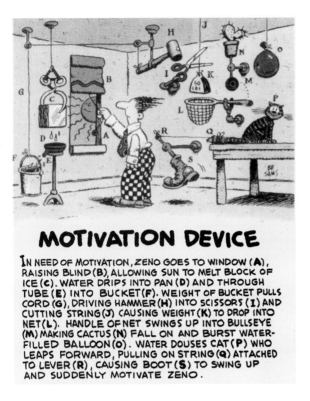

Figure 11-4
A Motivation Device

Job Designs to Increase Motivation

The Job Characteristics Model

If the type of work a person does is important, can we identify those specific job characteristics that affect productivity, motivation, and satisfaction? A model has been developed by J. Richard Hackman and Greg R. Oldham that identifies five such job factors and their interrelationship. It is called the **job characteristics model.**[21] The research with this model indicates that it can be a useful guide in redesigning the jobs of individuals.[22]

The model specifies five core characteristics or dimensions:

1. Skill variety—the degree to which a job requires a variety of different activities so one can use a number of different skills and talents.
2. Task identity—the degree to which the job requires completion of a whole and identifiable piece of work.
3. Task significance—the degree to which the job has a substantial impact on the lives or work of other people.
4. Autonomy—the degree to which the job provides substantial freedom, independence, and discretion to the individual in scheduling the work and in determining the procedures to be used in carrying it out.
5. Feedback—the degree to which carrying out the work activities required by the job results in the individual obtaining direct and clear information about the effectiveness of his or her performance.

Figure 11-5 presents the model. Notice how the first three dimensions—skill variety, task identity, and task significance—combine to create meaningful work; that is, if these three characteristics exist in a job, we can predict that the incumbents will view their job as being important, valuable, and worthwhile.

Job Characteristics Model A framework for analyzing and designing jobs. JCM identifies five primary job characteristics and their interrelationship.

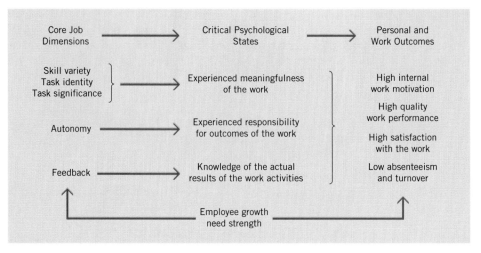

Figure 11-5
The Job Characteristics Model
of Work Motivation

Notice, too, that jobs that possess autonomy give the job incumbents a feeling of personal responsibility for the results; and that if a job provides feedback, the employees will know how effectively they are performing. From a motivational standpoint, the model says that internal rewards are obtained by individuals when they learn (knowledge of results) that they personally (experienced responsibility) have performed well on a task that they care about (experienced meaningfulness).[23] The more that these three conditions are present, the greater will be the employees' motivation, performance, and satisfaction and the lower will be their absenteeism and likelihood of turnover. As the model shows, the links between the job dimensions and the outcomes are moderated, or adjusted for, by the strength of the individual's growth need; that is, the employee's desire for self-esteem and self-actualization.[24]

This means that individuals with a high growth need are more likely than their low-growth-need counterparts to experience the critical psychological states when their jobs are enriched, and to respond more positively to the psychological states when they are present.

An example of how this model works can be seen at Chaparral Steel, the Midlothian, Texas, steel producer.[25] The industry has had severe problems in the past few decades, but Chaparral Steel has become one of the world's lowest-cost producers. To achieve that distinction, the company, headed by CEO Gordon Forward, began to change the jobs of the employees. Employees were trained to do a variety of jobs that increased task variety, task identity, and task significance. In fact, employees were given the opportunities to redesign production-process machinery to make life easier for them, and to cut costs for the organization. Furthermore, employees are given a lot of freedom to complete their jobs (autonomy), and are recognized by management for a job well done (feedback).

Motivating Potential Score A predictive index suggesting the motivation potential of a job.

The core job dimensions can be analyzed and combined into a single index called the **motivating potential score** (MPS) as shown in Figure 11-6. Jobs that are high on motivating potential—as derived by answers to specific questions

Figure 11-6
Computing the Motivating
Potential Score

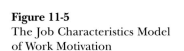

$$\text{Motivating potential score} = \frac{\text{Skill variety} + \text{Task identity} + \text{Task significance}}{3} \times \text{Autonomy} \times \text{Job feedback}$$

for each dimension—must be high on at least one of the three factors that lead to experiencing meaningfulness, and they must be high on both autonomy and feedback. If jobs score high on motivating potential, the model predicts that motivation, performance, and satisfaction will be positively affected, while the likelihood of absence and turnover is lessened.

Research findings on the job characteristics model have been generally supportive.[26] These studies have shown:

1. People who work on jobs with high-core job dimensions are more motivated, satisfied, and productive than those who do not.
2. People with strong growth needs respond more positively to jobs that are high in motivating potential than do those with weak growth dimensions.
3. Job dimensions operate through the psychological states in influencing personal and work outcome variables, rather than influencing them directly.[27]

These findings support a position that the structure of work is an important influence on an employee's motivation level. Certainly the decision about how a job is to be structured reflects other considerations (such as technology, the environment, plant and equipment, and skill levels) besides its motivational potential. But the design of a job and the way work is scheduled are variables that (1) management can readily influence, and (2) affect an employee's motivation.

Job Enrichment

The most popularly advocated structural technique for increasing an employee's motivational potential is **job enrichment.** To enrich a job, management allows the worker to assume some of the tasks executed by his or her supervisor. Enrichment requires that workers do increased planning and controlling of their work, usually with less supervision and more self-evaluation. From the standpoint of increasing the internal motivation from doing a job, it has been proposed that job enrichment offers great potential.[28] However, job enrichment is successful only when it increases responsibility, increases the employee's freedom and independence, organizes tasks so as to allow individuals to do a complete activity, and provides feedback to allow individuals to correct their own performance.[29] These aspects are precisely what the job characteristics model advocates. In addition, we can say that these factors lead, in part, to a better quality of work life (QWL). Furthermore, job enrichment efforts will only be successful if the individuals in the enriched jobs find that their needs are met by the "enrichment." If these individuals did not want increased responsibility, for example, then increasing responsibility will not have the desired effect. Successful job enrichment, then, is contingent on worker input.

A successful job enrichment program should ideally increase employee satisfaction and commitment. But since organizations do not exist to create employee satisfaction as an end, there must also be direct benefits to the organization. There is evidence that job enrichment, and QWL programs, produce lower absenteeism, reduce turnover costs,[30] and increase employee commitment,[31] but on the critical issue of productivity, the evidence is inconclusive, or poorly measured. In some situations, job enrichment has increased productivity; in others, productivity has been decreased. However, when it decreases, there does appear to be a consistently conscientious use of resources and a higher quality of product or service. In other words, in terms of efficiency, for the same input a higher quality of output is obtained; so fewer repairs could increase productivity if the measure included the number of repairs.

Job Enrichment The process of expanding the depth of the job by allowing employees to do more planning and controlling of their work.

Job Rotation

In Chapter 9 we identified job rotation as an on-the-job employee development technique. Job rotation also offers a potential for dealing with the problem of general worker dissatisfaction caused by over-structuring or career plateauing.[32] It allows employees to diversify their activities and offset the occurrence of boredom.

Horizontal job transfers can break up the monotony inherent in almost any job after the employee's skills have been refined and the newness has worn off. In some cases, this may be after only a few weeks, while in other cases it may be years.

Opportunities for diversity, to learn new skills, change supervisors, relocate, or make new job acquaintances can deter or slow the onset of boredom from jobs that have become habitual. Job rotation, therefore, can renew enthusiasm for learning and can motivate workers to better performance.[33]

Work at Home

Technology today is providing an unusual opportunity for employees of the 1990s. With the advent of home computers, fax machines, modems, and networked communication lines, certain types of jobs can be completed in the comfort of one's own home. As we mentioned in Chapter 2, many in the work force—especially women—find that work at home affords them the opportunity to combine both their careers and family responsibility. Furthermore, permitting work to be done at a worker's home also gives the organization an opportunity to save money. By having decentralized work sites and supported through telecommunication technology (see Chapter 2), organizations are able to reduce the work space they must either purchase or lease, thus cutting some overhead costs.

Most of the findings about working at home appear promising. Although home-work requires different management techniques—like planning and controlling the productive work flow—the flexibility such a practice offers clearly has a positive motivational effect on employees.[34]

Flexible Hours

Flextime A scheduling system in which employees are required to work a number of hours per week but are free, within limits, to vary the hours of work.

Another approach toward increasing workers' freedom and their motivation is **flextime.** Flextime is a system whereby employees contract to work a specific number of hours a week but are free to vary the hours of work within certain limits. Each day consists of a common core, usually six hours, with a flexibility band surrounding the core. For example, the core may be 10 A.M. to 4 P.M., with the office actually opening at 7:30 A.M. and closing at 6 P.M. All employees are required to be at their jobs during the common core period, but they are allowed to use their other two hours before and/or after the core time. Some flextime programs allow extra hours to be accumulated and turned into a free day off each month.

Under flextime, employees assume responsibility for completing a specific job, and that increases their feeling of self-worth. It is consistent with the view that people are paid for producing work, not for being at their job stations for a set period of hours; hence, its motivational aspects.

Flex time has been implemented in a number of organizations, such as American Express, IBM, Levi Strauss, and PepsiCo.[35] In the United States, it is estimated that such scheduling exists in almost 40 percent of all companies.[36] And for many of these organizations, there has been some good news. Flextime appears to contribute to decreased tardiness, reduced absenteeism, less job fatigue, increased organizational loyalty, and improved recruitment. In fact, when you recall the discussion of the composition of our work force, a more positive light is shed on flexible arrangements—for example, flextime enables dual-career couples a better opportunity to balance work and family responsibilities.[37] And with more and more single parents coming into the work force, flexible work arrangements can only better serve both the employer and employee.[38]

Although the benefits of flexible scheduling appear plentiful, there is still one major drawback. It produces problems for managers in directing employees outside core time periods, or may cause difficulty in evaluating the performance of an employee who may not be seen eight hours a day.[39] But inherent in that statement is part of the problem. Rather than evaluating employees on how much they've been seen—often called "face-time" in organizations—managers should concern themselves with "results and productivity."[40] As we described in our motivation model, that should be the only thing that matters. Thus, if a scheduling arrangement permits better performance, there is no logical reason for not implementing one.

Unique Motivation Challenges for HRM

Recall from Chapter 2 the discussion of the changing work force. Inherent in that discussion is the possibility that we are witnessing a bimodal work force—those individuals who work in the low-tech jobs of our society, and those who hold the more prestigious, high-tech positions. Let's explore some of the issues facing managers both in meeting the needs of these two groups, as well as in getting the diversified work force to exert high-effort levels.

Low-Tech Employees

Consider you are the first-line supervisor at the local McDonald's. Working in your restaurant are nineteen employees who are aged 16 to 18, three who are over 70, and one disabled employee. You know the nineteen teen-agers are full-time students and most will leave within the next year. In fact, your turnover averages 50 percent a year. You pay $4.75 to $5.35 per hour, depending on the shifts employees work and whether they are responsible for opening or closing for the day. How do you motivate these employees? Too often, you consider yourself fortunate if they just show up. When they do, you want them to work, not spend time talking to their visiting friends. And you certainly don't want them giving food away. You could give them a pay raise to increase motivation levels, but would it do much good? Any significant increase will add to your costs, raise your prices, and likely cut customer demand.

Low-paying jobs with limited advancement opportunities, such as those in fast-food restaurants, create challenges for employers. Sadly, there doesn't appear to be a readily available solution. A lot of the linkage may not apply. These workers may not have "career" needs; in fact, they may just want to earn a few dollars so they can enjoy their leisure time, pay for automobile insurance, or purchase clothing. Still, the McDonald's of this world must go on, and they need energized people. So what can managers do? Let's look at three possibilities: respect, nonfinancial rewards, and autonomy.[41]

One of the first concerns in motivating these workers is to assess how you feel about them. If your attitude is that these are low-level employees lucky to work for you, you may be sending the wrong message. If your employees are made to feel inferior, they won't respond to what is needed to work effectively. Thus, common sense dictates that respect is required here. We all have a need to be respected for what we do; we want to be treated with kindness, even if we aren't the superstar employee. Giving these employees the respect and dignity they deserve can change their perception of you and the job. A little caring, kindness, and concern can go a long way to get these individuals to perform more productively for the company.

Furthermore, employees are capable of knowing that employers cannot continue to raise salaries. But just because money isn't available doesn't mean that you can overlook them. Rather, you need to look at a variety of nonfinancial rewards. This may be something as simple as a pat on the back, a smile, or more responsibility on the job. Letting them know you trust them and are willing to help them learn can create a positive work environment for them. You may also search for some appropriate award like permitting your "crew member of the month" to have a friend over for a meal on the premises, and extend the employee's dinner break for the special occasion.

Finally comes the issue of autonomy. Low-paying jobs are not necessarily correlated to activities that must be closely monitored. If you know the employees are well trained, giving them the responsibility to complete the tasks without a "watchful" eye allows them the opportunity to take responsibility. By giving them the freedom to make limited choices, you are sending a message that they are important to your operation.

On a final note, let's not forget about fun.[42] A little enjoyment in the office can go far to create a positive atmosphere. The old saying, "All work and no play makes Johnny a dull boy," may have special meaning in our workplaces. When people laugh, they are happy. If we allow happiness to become contagious, people will feel better about their jobs, their bosses, and hopefully themselves.

High-Tech Employees

You would intuitively think that employees who are higher paid create fewer motivational problems for organizations. Their motivation, by and large, would seemingly be more intrinsic, and garnered from the job itself. But organizations today cannot leave it up to individuals to seek their own satisfaction. Instead, they must put into place a variety of mechanisms to retain this "worker elite."

Many of the issues discussed in Chapter 2 with respect to employee involvement have been recognized as helping to create an environment that is conducive for motivating high-tech employees.[43] These include delegation, participative management, job enrichment, challenging work, and recognition.

Hi-tech employees bring with them a set of skills that are generally in high demand in the marketplace. As such, they are generally highly marketable, and will move to another organization that best meets their needs. Delegation gives these individuals the opportunity to make decisions about the various work elements of their job. Coupled with participative management, these employees are able to control their day-to-day activities. High-tech employees also need to be given the opportunity to continuously grow and excel. Job enrichment provides for them the means for undertaking a variety of tasks, thus eliminating boredom. Challenging work permits them to stretch in their abilities, thus ac-

Motivating high-tech employees requires special attention. Beth Malloy, a lab technician at Genetech in San Francisco, analyzes rare proteins found in human blood. Traditional motivational techniques may not motivate people like Beth. For her, and her high-tech peers, exerting high effort levels is a function of delegating, participating management, job enrichment, challenging work, and recognition.

centuating organizational and personal goals. But it is the last component that may be the greatest motivation—recognition.[44] Because these workers are generally adequately paid, money does not become a dominant issue. Rather, their thirst for success dominates! And they need to know that others appreciate, and recognize, the efforts that they make.

The Diversified Work Force

As we begin to experience the influx of different groups of people into our work-force composition, it will become increasingly more critical to recognize individual differences and individual needs—and to individualize rewards. We know from experience that American managers have not done this well when there was a relatively homogeneous group. Now that there is increasing diversity, reasons have never been better to recognize differences and act on them.

For example, we know that different cultures place value on widely different things. In Japan, for example, leisure time is not highly prized, although it is in the United States. Similarly, the Japanese place much higher importance on respect and conforming to group norms than Americans. Employees with young children frequently place a higher value on day care and flexible work hours than other employees. This suggests that hours worked, scheduling, recognition, group membership, day care, and similar variables should be considered when trying to optimize the motivation of a diversified work force.

Study Tools and Applications

Summary

This summary relates to the Learning Objectives provided on p. 294.
After having read this chapter you should know:

1. Motivation is the willingness to make every effort to achieve organizational goals conditioned by this effort's ability to satisfy individual needs.
2. The three major components for motivation in an organization setting are effort, organizational goals, and individual needs.
3. The process of motivation begins with an unsatisfied need that creates an increase in tension. This tension causes one to behave in a manner (effort) such that the needs can be satisfied, and tension ultimately reduced.
4. An unsatisfied need is a state of deprivation. Because these needs are something you desire, they cause tension.
5. Tension can be viewed in two forms—functional and dysfunctional. Functional tension is positive and causes an individual to act toward goal attainment. Dysfunctional tension is negative and may lead to problems in performance or attitudes.
6. The effort–performance relationship focuses on the energy exerted by employees and its outcome in terms of performance. The premise of this relationship is that if appropriate effort is exerted, an employee will give a successful performance.
7. The performance–organizational goal relationship focuses on the work achieved and how well it relates to organizational objectives. The premise of this relationship is that if successful performance levels are achieved, then the organization will be meeting its stated goals.
8. The organizational goal–individual goal relationship focuses on the reward for the employees as it relates to organizational goals. The premise of this relationship is that if organizational goals are met, employees are to be rewarded for their performance. Their rewards will be such that they satisfy individual needs.
9. The job characteristics model consists of skill variety, task identity, task significance, autonomy, and feedback.
10. Job enrichment refers to a situation where workers assume increased responsibility for planning and self-evaluation of their work. This provides an opportunity to fulfill intrinsic and autonomous needs. Working at home enables employees to meet organizational job requirements while simultaneously fulfilling personal needs. Work at home provides the diverse work force with opportunities to combine both work and family.
11. A number of suggestions can be made regarding how to motivate employees. Among them are: addressing individual differences, properly placing employees, setting achievable goals, individualizing rewards, and rewarding performance.
12. Although no one means of motivating low-tech employees is universally accepted, some action can be taken. In addition to addressing individual differences, properly placing employees, setting achievable goals, individualizing rewards and rewarding performance, these individuals can be given more responsibility. Furthermore, a kind, caring, concerned manager can help to create an environment whereby the workers are willing to exert higher energy levels. Hi-tech employees, on the other hand, appear to respond to delegating, participative management, job enrichment, challenging work, and recognition.

314

Key Terms

apathy
autonomy
deprivation
dysfunctional tension
effort
effort–performance relationship
feedback
flextime
functional tension
individual needs

individual performance–organizational goal relationship
job enrichment
motivating potential score
motivation
organizational goal–individual goal relationship
organizational goals
pay-for-performance
performance
skill variety
task identity
task significance

EXPERIENTIAL EXERCISE

I:AM Assessment

Motivation processes are based, in part, on needs satisfaction. Although we all have changing needs, there are often certain needs that remain dominant for us over a period of time. This assessment is designed to identify those needs. Follow the instructions for the assessment and then answer the following questions:

1. Do these needs seem accurate to you? How do you know?
2. How do these needs affect you (a) in the classroom, and (b) on a job?
3. What does this assessment tell you about what it may take to motivate you?

Instrument: I:AM

I:AM is a simple questionnaire for examining one's own motivations and interests. It should be used before getting into any detailed discussion of motivational theories, to avoid self-consciousness on the part of individuals. The result can be used as part of an overview presentation on theories of motivation.

Interpretation

The four need scores correspond to the four "higher order" categories of needs (or motives) identified by Abraham Maslow. The "lowest level" need category, physiological needs (food, shelter, water, etc.) is not included, since most of those who will read this and use this instrument have little personal concern for these needs. One must remember, however, that most of the world's people are most concerned with this need category.

CASE APPLICATION:

Motivation Explains Behavior

Jerald Greenberg, a faculty member at Ohio State University, has found that when employees face turbulent times and their managers pay little attention to their needs, employees tend to get even.[45] Greenberg studied three plants of a large manufacturing organization. He recognized that this organization was dealing with many of the difficulties facing American companies—lower productivity and increased competition. In addition, this organization had implemented a pay cut to attempt to keep the organization afloat. Greenberg wanted to know how all this was affecting employee morale. How did the employees react? Surprisingly worse than anticipated!

One of the basic tenets of motivation is that individuals need to feel as if they are getting something from the organization, like pay or benefits, that is consistent with their level of effort, education, experience, and anything else they bring to the job. This something provided, then, must equate to the amount of work each performs. For example, if employees feel the organization is not paying them a "fair wage," these employees are more likely to make certain adjust-

---

TABLE 11-3 I:AM Instrument

I:AM An Inventory for Assessing One's Primary Interests

Instructions: Place a check mark in the blank under the response that best describes your own feelings about the statement. There are no "right" or "wrong" answers; the purpose of this questionnaire is simply to organize your own thoughts about your personal preferences.

	Strongly Agree	Agree	Neither Agree nor Disagree	Disagree	Strongly Disagree
1. My friends mean more to me than almost anything else.	——	——	——	——	——
2. I don't believe in "blowing my own horn" just to be heard.	——	——	——	——	——
3. Searching for and finding what makes me feel happy is the most important thing in life.	——	——	——	——	——
4. I prefer to be by myself a lot of the time.	——	——	——	——	——
5. A secure job and a good salary are "number one" for me.	——	——	——	——	——
6. Chasing dreams is a waste of one's time and energy.	——	——	——	——	——
7. I get furious when someone else tries to take credit for what I know I did.	——	——	——	——	——
8. I really don't worry about a particular job or what I get for doing it, as long as it's fair.	——	——	——	——	——

Scoring Form

Item	SA	A	?	D	SD		Score	Need Scale
5	5	4	3	2	1	+ =	☐	Safety/security
8	1	2	3	4	5			
1	5	4	3	2	1	+ =	☐	Belongingness/social
4	1	2	3	4	5			
2	1	2	3	4	5	+ =	☐	Self-esteem
7	5	4	3	2	1			
3	5	4	3	2	1	+ =	☐	Self-actualization
6	1	2	3	4	5			

Scores range from 2 to 10 on each of the four need scales.

Source: Marshall Sashkin and William C. Morris, *Experiencing Management* (Reading, MA: Addison-Wesley Publishing Co., 1987), p. 110. Used with permission.

ments in their work habits. They might work slower, reduce quality, or even resign. Accordingly, any personnel action by the organization will ultimately result in employees comparing what the company has done to them to the amount of effort they give the employer.

Employees in the three plants Greenberg studied, once told of the pending pay cuts, decided to change their behavior to compensate for less income. How was this done? By stealing! In two of the plants, employee theft skyrocketed. These employees stole an amount from the company that they considered was approximately equivalent to the amount of their pay cut. Not necessarily what the firm had in mind when it implemented pay cuts!

Questions

1. Discuss this case in terms of the behavioral process, and equity theory. Was the behavior of these employees rational? Explain your response.
2. What suggestions would you make to an organization that faced difficult times and had to cut employee costs by implementing drastic HRM practices? How would these suggestions affect employee motivation? Discuss.

Testing Your Understanding

How well did you fulfill the learning objectives?

1. Employee performance is a function of the employee's ability to do a job and
   a. the employee's willingness to do the job.
   b. the manager's ability to monitor performance.
   c. effective communication throughout the organization.
   d. the employee's salary.
   e. the organization's culture, plus a good work environment.
2. A vice-president of human resources for a large manufacturing firm conducted an employee survey to improve employee benefits and working conditions. The survey showed 97 percent of employees wanted a 30-hour (or less) work week. Why didn't the vice-president recommend that change to the benefits manager, according to organizational motivation theory?
   a. The vice-president's ability to exert effort was ineffective.
   b. Organizational goals were not defined.
   c. Employees' individual needs changed.
   d. Employees' individual needs would not be satisfied.
   e. Organizational goals would not be met.
3. Why are beer commercials set in the desert, according to motivation theory?
   a. The contrast makes beer look drinkable.
   b. An individual's sense of deprivation is heightened by the parched surroundings.
   c. It's easier to attain a calm state in the desert.
   d. Dysfunctional tension is reduced when distractions are removed.
   e. Most human drives are intensified by heat.

4. How can a teacher produce dysfunctional tension in a straight-A student?
   a. Give boring lectures.
   b. Give difficult tests.
   c. Grade term papers on a curve.
   d. Require oral presentations as part of the class.
   e. Assign grades in a random manner, ranging from A to C, for all written work.
5. Roberta, Ernie's secretary, likes her job and her boss, but she types 40 words per minute and has a 5 percent error rate. Standard performance in the company is 80 words per minute and a 3 percent error rate. Should Ernie send Roberta to secretarial school, according to motivation theory?
   a. No. It would embarrass Roberta.
   b. Yes. It would strengthen the effort–performance link.
   c. No. It would weaken the effort–performance link.
   d. Yes. It would strengthen the performance–organization relationship.
   e. No. It would weaken the performance–organization relationship.
6. If the goal of an undergraduate business school program is to produce qualified graduates who obtain suitable entry-level positions upon graduation, which question best measures the performance–organizational goal linkage?
   a. How many articles do the faculty publish each year, compared to faculty at other similar institutions?
   b. How high are the GPAs of graduates, compared to non-business majors in the university?
   c. What percentage of the graduates get jobs they

want, compared to graduates from other programs during the same year?

d. What positions do graduates hold in organizations seven years after graduation, compared to other graduates from the same year?

e. What percentage of graduates go on for MBA degrees within ten years, compared to graduates of other undergraduate business programs?

7. A vice-president of human resources for a large service organization has instituted a program that allows employees to choose up to $1,500 worth of goods or services from a range of annual options, such as more time off, a cash bonus, tuition reimbursement, or new office furniture. What is the vice-president doing?

a. Instituting a flexible compensation program to satisfy individual needs.

b. Saving the company money during a downsizing cycle.

c. Simplifying the accounting mechanisms for the entire human resources function.

d. Reducing the number of complaints from workers about their immediate supervisors.

e. Changing the organization to comply with Title VII stipulations.

8. Jobs that score high on the core dimensions are associated with all of these work outcomes in employees with high growth needs except

a. high work satisfaction.

b. experienced responsibility for outcomes.

c. high quality work performance.

d. high internal work motivation.

e. lower absenteeism.

9. Job enrichment is successful when all of the following are present except

a. responsibility is increased for the employee.

b. pay-for-performance is increased.

c. the employee's freedom and independence is increased.

d. tasks are reorganized so that an individual performs a complete activity.

e. feedback is provided so that the employee may correct his or her own performance.

10. Don pays minimum wage to the thirty workers who help him run the local food bank. How can he motivate them?

a. Make sure he tells them they are appreciated.

b. Make work fun.

c. Let them have as much autonomy as possible.

d. Involve them in day-to-day decisions about the work to be done.

e. All of these.

11. Motivation is all of the following except

a. the process of activating a willingness to work in employees.

b. evident in "energized" students, who want to learn.

c. found in workers who are involved and interested in their work.

d. a necessary component of good job performance.

e. usually measured during the recruitment and selection process.

12. What is the difference between functional tension and dysfunctional tension?

a. There is no difference.

b. Functional tension leads to action that will attain the desired organizational goal. Dysfunctional tension leads to action that thwarts the desired organizational goal.

c. Functional tension leads to action. Dysfunctional tension leads to inaction.

d. Functional tension satisfies needs. Dysfunctional tension does not satisfy needs.

e. Functional tension is more intense than dysfunctional tension.

13. Managers can do all of the following to strengthen the effort–performance link for their employees except

a. coach employees.

b. assist employees in achieving their performance levels.

c. give raises.

d. establish work standards.

e. communicate performance expectations to employees.

14. Marty won a $10 million lottery Saturday. Why, according to motivation theory, did he quit his job on Monday?

a. Marty's ability to exert effort had changed.

b. Organizational goals changed.

c. Marty's individual needs changed.

d. Marty's individual interests changed.

e. Organizational needs were realigned.

15. In the motivation theory presented, how is tension created?

a. Pressure is exerted from outside sources.

b. An individual becomes aware of an unsatisfied need.

c. Pleasure is anticipated.

d. Force for action is triggered.

e. Needs are balanced with equity.

Chapter Twelve

EVALUATING EMPLOYEE PERFORMANCE

LEARNING OBJECTIVES

AFTER READING THIS CHAPTER, YOU WILL BE ABLE TO:

1. Describe the link between performance management systems and motivation.
2. Identify the three purposes of performance management systems and who is served by them.
3. Explain the six steps in the appraisal process.
4. Discuss what is meant by absolute standards in performance management systems.
5. Describe what is meant by relative standards in performance management systems.
6. Discuss how MBO can be used as an appraisal method.
7. Explain why performance appraisals might be distorted.
8. Identify ways to make performance management systems more effective.
9. Describe what is meant by the term 360-degree appraisal.
10. Discuss how performance appraisals may differ in foreign countries.

Every year, most employees experience an evaluation of their past performance. This may take the form of a five-minute, informal discussion between employees and their supervisors, or a more elaborate, several-week process involving many specific steps. Irrespective of their formality, however, employees generally see these evaluations as having some direct effect on their work lives. They may result in increased pay, a promotion, or assistance in personal development areas for which the employee needs some training. As a result, any evaluation of employees's work can create an emotionally charged event. Consider what happened at Bates Mechanical Services, the Orlando, Florida, surveying company.[1]

The policy at Bates is that each employee is evaluated on the anniversary of their date of hire. Based on the evaluation, the supervisor makes recommendations for an increase in the employee's hourly rate of pay. Joe Barranger, the supervisor, has asked Adam Welsh to come to his office at 11 A.M. today. Although Adam is somewhat certain that it is time for his performance evaluation, he is not totally sure. Nonetheless, he leaves his surveying crew around 10:15, and heads for the office. As he arrives, he notices Joe in his office working on a standardized form used for evaluation. Adam sits quietly until Joe has finished. With the final touches complete, Joe begins his meeting. Let's eavesdrop on that conversation.

JOE: Adam, glad you were able to make it here today. As you know, this is the anniversary of your hire date, and I am required to fill out an evaluation on you. Sorry I didn't have it done before you got here, it's been just one of those mornings. Well, let me see . . .

ADAM: Joe, I've been through this five times before, so just give it to me. What's my raise? I'd really like to get back to my work crew. We're trying to finish up on that Henderson job—the builders want to start the excavation early next week.

JOE: Adam, there's more than just the pay increase. I want to talk about your performance. I believe, overall, you've done some good work, but you have some problem areas, too.

ADAM: What do you mean problem areas? I've done my job better than most on my work crew. In fact, you've been using me to train our new surveyors.

JOE: Well Adam, that's your opinion. Yes, you're helping to train new surveyors, but I have had some complaints from them over the past few months. I think that needs to be addressed.

ADAM: So get to the bottom line, Joe. What's my raise? Let's stop the charade.

JOE: Okay, Adam, I am recommending a 50 cents an hour raise. I'd like for you to look over this evaluation, and sign it.

ADAM: Just give me a pen, let me sign the paper, and I'll get out of here.

Effective performance evaluation? Absolutely not! But maybe not unlike the many that are performed each day. What's missing is that neither Joe nor Adam really understand what the appraisal process is about. That's too bad, because in order to compete effectively and meet employee and organizational goals, either within the United States or abroad, companies need to assess how well employees are performing!

Introduction

Because performance evaluations aren't the simple process they once were, it is now more critical to perform them while simultaneously focusing on key activities of the job. For example, what should Adam have been evaluated on? His ability to perform surveying tasks in a timely and accurate manner? How well he interacts with customers and builders who depend on his work? How about how well he serves as a mentor to new employees? Such questions cannot be overlooked. And that's exactly how senior management at Ameritech Corporation viewed a similar situation.[2]

To answer what employees did, management established a task force to identify the key performance measures of a specific job. During the course of one review, a task force developed eight specific measurable skills, in this case for a position of secretary in the company. These skills were business awareness, communication skills, decision making, flexibility, adaptability, initiative, interpersonal skills, and organizational skills[3]—all requisites for success on the job. Taking information from a job analysis, the task force then developed the standards from which performance would be measured.

If we want to know how well our employees are doing, we've got to measure their performance—not necessarily an easy task. Many factors go into the performance evaluation process, such as why do we do them, who should benefit from the evaluation, what type of evaluation should be used, and what problems might we encounter. This chapter seeks answers to these and several other important factors in the **performance-appraisal process.** By developing a valid performance management system, we can maximize the relationship in our motivational model that focuses on the effort–performance linkage. Let's review that linkage for a moment.

The Linkage to Motivation

As we discovered in the last chapter, just because employees have the ability to do the job does not ensure that they will perform satisfactorily. Another critical dimension is their willingness to exert high energy levels—their motivation. Theoretically, as managers we should be interested in ends, not means; that is, getting the job done![4] As one football coach remarked in appraising his ungraceful but effective field goal kicker: "It ain't pictures, it's numbers." Similarly, managers should be concerned with quality results.[5] It's performance that counts! It may be difficult for some managers to accept, but they should not be appraising employees on how they look, but rather on whether they can score. We propose, therefore, that organizations exist to "score," rather than to provide an environment for individuals to "look like players." Just like the football coach, managers must be concerned with evaluating their personnel on "numbers" and not on "pictures."

Performance is a vital component of the motivation model.[6] Specifically, we must be concerned with the link between effort and performance, and between performance and rewards (see Figure 12-1). Employees have to know what is expected of them, and they need to know how their performance will be measured. Furthermore, employees must feel confident that if they exert an effort within their capabilities, it will result in a better performance as defined by the criteria by which they are being measured. Finally, they must feel confident that if they perform as they are being asked, they will achieve the rewards they

Performance appraisals are designed to provide feedback on an employee's past performance, to assist in the development of future plans, and to provide supportive documentation for personnel decisions. Unfortunately, when we are judging people during the process, emotions can run high. Unless managers are trained in the proper techniques of performance evaluation, scenes like the one at Bates Mechanical Services can occur.

Performance-Appraisal Process A formal process in an organization whereby each employee is evaluated to determine how he or she is performing.

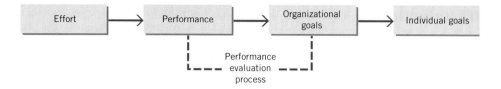

Figure 12-1
Performance Appraisals and the Motivation Process

value.[7] Do people see effort leading to performance, and performance to the rewards that they value?

In summary, performance appraisals and their outcomes play a vital part in the model of motivation. If the objectives that individual employees are seeking are unclear, if the criteria for measuring that objective attainment are vague, and if employees lack confidence that their efforts will lead to a satisfactory appraisal of their performance or feel that there will be an unsatisfactory payoff by the organization when their performance objectives are achieved, we can expect individuals to work considerably below their potential. If we have done our job to acquire capable people and develop their basic abilities to do the job, we must also make sure that they know what behaviors are required of them; understand how they are going to be appraised; and believe that the appraisal will be conducted in a fair and equitable manner, and that they can expect their performance to be recognized by proper rewards.[8]

Performance Management Systems

The Purposes

Two decades ago performance evaluations were designed primarily to tell employees how they had done over a period of time, and to let them know what pay raise they would be getting. Although this may have served its purpose then, today there are other reasons for performance appraisals. Specifically, performance evaluations should also address development and documentation concerns.[9]

Performance appraisals must convey to employees how well they have performed on mutually set goals and measures. As our motivation model suggested, without proper two-way feedback about one's effort and its effect on performance, we run the risk of decreasing an employee's "drive." However, equally as important to feedback is the issue of development.[10] By development, we are referring to those areas in which an employee has a deficiency or weakness, or an area that simply could be better if some effort was expended to enhance performance. For example, suppose a college professor demonstrates extensive knowledge in his or her field and conveys this knowledge to students in an adequate way. Although this individual's performance may be regarded as good, his or her peers may indicate that some improvement could be made. In this case, then, development may include exposure to different methods of teaching, such as bringing into the classroom more experiential exercises, computer applications, case analyses, or the like.[11]

Documentation Used as a record of the performance appraisal process outcomes.

Finally comes the issue of **documentation.** A performance evaluation system would be remiss if it did not concern itself with the legal aspects of employee performance. Recall in Chapter 3 the discussion about EEO and the need for job-related measures. Those job-related measures must be performance-supported when an HRM decision affects current employees. For instance, suppose a manager has decided to terminate an employee. Although the manager cites performance matters as the reason for the discharge, a review of recent performance appraisals of this employee indicates that performance was evaluated as satisfactory. Accordingly, unless this employee's performance significantly decreased (and assuming that proper methods to correct the performance deficiency were performed), personnel records do not support the manager's decision. In fact, in our discussion of sexual harassment in Chapter 3, we addressed the need for employees to keep copies of past performance appraisals. If retaliation (like termination) for refusing a manager's advances occurs, existing documentation can show that the personnel action was inappropriate, for it was not consistent with past performance.

Because documentation issues are prevalent in today's organizations, effort must be made to ensure that the evaluation system used supports the legal needs of the organization. However, even though the performance appraisal process is geared to serve the organization, we should also recognize two other important players in the process: employees and their appraisers. Through timely and accurate feedback and development we can better serve employees' needs. In doing so, we may also be in a better position to show the effort–performance linkage (see "HRM Skills").

Next, we should keep in mind the needs of the appraiser. If feedback, development, and documentation are to function effectively, appraisers must have a performance system that is appropriate for their needs—a system that facilitates giving feedback and development information to their employees, and one that allows for employee input. For example, if appraisers are required to evaluate their employees using inappropriate performance measures, or answer questions about employees that have little bearing on the job, then the system may not provide the same benefits as one where such negatives are removed. To create the performance management system we desire, we must recognize the difficulties that may exist and look for ways to either overcome them or deal with them more effectively. Let's turn to these difficulties.

Difficulties in Performance Management Systems

When you consider that three constituencies coexist in this process—employees, appraisers, and organizations—coordinating the needs of each may cause problems. By focusing on the difficulties, we can begin to address them in such a way that we can reduce their overall impact on the process. In terms of difficulties, two categories can be addressed—the focus on the individual, and the focus on the process.

Focus on the Individual Do you remember the last time you received a graded test from a professor and felt that something was marked incorrect that wasn't wrong, or that your answer was too harshly penalized? How did you feel about that? Did you accept the score and leave it at that, or did you question the instructor? Whenever performance evaluations are administered (and tests are one form of performance evaluations), we run into the issue of having people seeing "eye-to-eye" on the evaluation. Appraising individuals is probably one of the more difficult aspects of a manager's job. Why? Because emotions are involved, and sometimes managers just don't like to do appraisals.[12] We all think we are performing in an outstanding fashion, but that just may very well be our perception. And although our work is good, and a boss recognizes it, it may not be seen as outstanding. Accordingly, in evaluating performance, emotions may arise. And if these emotions are not dealt with properly (we'll look at ways to enhance performance evaluations later in this chapter), they can lead to greater

HRM*Skills*

Conducting the Performance Appraisal

1. **Prepare for, and schedule, the appraisal in advance.** Before meeting with employees, some preliminary activities should be performed. You should at a minimum review employee job descriptions, period goals that may have been set, and performance data on employees you may have. Furthermore, you should schedule the appraisal well in advance to give employees the opportunity to prepare their data, too, for the meeting.

2. **Create a supportive environment to put employees at ease.** Performance appraisals conjure up several emotions. As such, every effort should be made to make employees comfortable during the meeting, such that they are receptive to constructive feedback.

3. **Describe the purpose of the appraisal to employees.** Make sure employees know precisely what the appraisal is to be used for. Will it have implications for pay increases, or other personnel decisions? If so, make sure employees understand exactly how the appraisal process works, and its consequences.

4. **Involve the employee in the appraisal discussion, including a self-evaluation.** Performance appraisals should not be a one-way communication event. Although as supervisor, you may believe that you have to talk more in the meeting, that needn't be the case. Instead, employees should have ample opportunity to discuss their performance, raise questions about the facts you raise, and add their own data/perceptions about their work. One means of ensuring that two-way communications occurs is to have employees conduct a self-evaluation. You should actively listen to their assessment. This involvement helps to create an environment of participation.

5. **Focus discussion on work behaviors, not on the employees.** One means of creating emotional difficulties is to attack the employee. As such, you should keep your discussion on the behaviors you've observed.

6. **Support your evaluation with specific examples.** Specific performance behaviors help to clarify to employees the issues you raise. Rather than saying something wasn't good (subjective evaluation) you should be as specific as possible in your explanations.

7. **Give both positive and negative feedback.** Performance appraisals needn't be all negative. Although there is a perception that this process focuses on the negative, it should also be used to compliment and recognize good work. Positive, as well as negative, feedback helps employees to gain a better understanding of their performance.

8. **Ensure employees understand what was discussed in the appraisal.** At the end of the appraisal, especially where some improvement is warranted, you should ask employees to summarize what had been discussed in the meeting. This will help you to ensure that you have gotten your information through to employees.

9. **Generate a development plan.** Most of the performance appraisal revolves around feedback and documentation. But, another component is needed. Where development efforts are encouraged, a plan should be developed to describe what is to be done, by when, and what you, the supervisor, will commit to aid in the improvement/enhancement effort.

conflict. In fact, consider the aforementioned test example, assuming you confronted the professor. Depending on the encounter, especially if it is an aggressive one, both of you may have become defensive. And because of the conflict, nothing but ill feelings arose. For appraisers, the same thing applies. You both differ on the performance outcomes.[13]

When that occurs, it may lead to a situation in which emotions overcome both parties. This is no the way for evaluations to be handled. Accordingly, our first concern in the process is to remove the emotion difficulty from the process. When emotions do not run high in these meetings, employee satisfaction of the process increases,[14] and additionally, this satisfaction carries over into future job activities, where both the employee and supervisor have opportunities to have ongoing feedback in an effort to fulfill job expectations.[15] For Joe and Adam at Bates Mechanical Services, this latter function did not occur.

Focus on the Process Wherever performance evaluations are conducted, there is a rigid structure that must be followed. This structure exists to facilitate the documentation process that often allows for a quantifiable evaluation. Additionally, policies often exist that dictate performance outcomes. For example, if a company ties performance evaluations to pay increases, consider the following potential difficulty. Sometime in the spring of the year, managers develop budgets for their units—budgets that are dictated and approved by upper management. Now in this budget for next fiscal year, each manager's salary budget increases by 4 percent. As we enter the new fiscal year, we evaluate our employees. One in particular has done an outstanding job, and is awarded a 6 percent raise. What does this do to our budget? To average 4 percent, some employees will get less than the 4 percent salary increase. Consequently, company policies and procedures may present barriers to a properly functioning appraisal process.

Furthermore, to get these numbers to balance means that rather than accentuating the positive work behaviors of some employees, an appraiser focuses on the negative.[16] This can lead to a tendency to search for problems, which can ultimately lead to an emotional encounter. We may also find from the appraiser's perspective some uncertainty about how and what to measure, or how to deal with the employee in the evaluation process.[17] Frequently, appraisers are poorly trained in how to evaluate an employee's performance. Because of this lack of training, appraisers may make errors in their judgment, or permit biases to enter into the process. We'll talk more about these problems later.

Because difficulties may arise, we should begin to develop our performance appraisal process so that we can achieve maximum benefit from it. This maximum benefit can be translated into employee satisfaction with the process. Such satisfaction is achieved by creating an understanding of the evaluation criteria used, permitting employee participation in the process, and allowing for development needs to be addressed.[18] To begin doing so requires us to initially understand the appraisal process.

Performance Appraisals and EEO

Performance evaluations are an integral part of most organizations. Properly developed and implemented, the performance-appraisal process can help an organization achieve its goals by developing productive employees. Although there are many types of performance evaluation systems, each with its own ad-

Ethical Decisions in HRM:

The Inaccurate Performance Appraisal

Most individuals recognize the importance of effective performance management systems in an organization. Not only are they necessary for providing feedback to employees and for identifying personal development plans, they serve a vital legal purpose. Furthermore, organizations that fail to accurately manage employee performance often find themselves facing difficult times in meeting their organizational goals.

Most individuals would also agree that performance appraisals must meet Equal Employment Opportunity requirements. That is, they must be administered in such a way that they result in a fair and equitable treatment for the diversity that exists in the workplace. Undeniably, this is an absolute necessity. But what about those gray areas—instances where an evaluation meets legal requirements, but verges on a questionable practice. For example, what if a manager deliberately evaluates a favored employee higher than one he likes less, even though the latter is a better promotional candidate? Likewise, what if the supervisor avoids identifying areas for employee development for individuals, knowing that the likelihood of career advancement for these employees is stalemated without the better skills?

Supporters of properly functioning performance appraisals point to two vital criteria that managers must bring to the process—sincerity and honesty. Yet, there are no legislative regulations, like EEO laws, that enforce such ethical standards. Thus, they may be, and frequently are, missing from the evaluation process.

Can an organization have an effective performance-appraisal process without sincerity and honesty dominating the system? Can organizations develop an evaluation process that is ethical? Should we expect companies to spend training dollars to achieve this goal? What do you think?

Source: Larry L. Axline, "Ethical Considerations of Performance Appraisals," *Management Review* (March 1994), p. 62.

vantages and disadvantages, we must be aware of the legal implications that arise.

EEO laws require organizations to have HRM practices that are bias-free. For HRM, this means that performance evaluations must be objective and job-related. That is, they must be reliable and valid! Furthermore, under the Americans with Disabilities Act, performance appraisals must also be able to measure "reasonable" performance success. To assist in these matters, two factors arise: (1) The performance appraisal must be conducted according to some established intervals; and (2) appraisers must be trained in the process.[19] The reasons for this become crystal-clear when you consider that any employee action, like a promotion or termination, must be based on valid data—data prescribed from the performance evaluation document[20] (see "Ethical Decisions in HRM"). This objective data often support the "legitimacy" of employee actions.[21]

The Appraisal Process

The appraisal process (see Figure 12-2) begins with the establishment of performance standards in accordance with the organization's strategic goals. These should have evolved out of the company's strategic direction—and, more specifically, the job analysis and the job description discussed in Chapter 5. These performance standards should also be clear and objective enough to be understood and measured. Too often, these standards are articulated in ambiguous phrases that tell us little, such as "a full day's work" or "a good job." What is a "full day's work," or a "good job"? The expectations a manager has in terms of work performance by her employees must be clear enough in her mind so that she will be able to, at some later date, communicate these expectations to her employees, mutually agree to specific job performance measures, and appraise their performance against these established standards.

Once performance standards are established, it is necessary to communicate these expectations; it should not be part of the employees' job to guess what is expected of them. Too many jobs have vague performance standards, and the problem is compounded when these standards are set in isolation and do not involve the employee. It is important to note that communication is a two-way street: Mere transference of information from the manager to the employee regarding expectations is not communication! The third step in the appraisal process is the measurement of performance. To determine what actual performance is, it is necessary to acquire information about it. We should be concerned with how we measure and what we measure.

Four common sources of information are frequently used by managers regarding how to measure actual performance: personal observation, statistical reports, oral reports, and written reports. Each has its strengths and weaknesses; however, a combination of them increases both the number of input sources and the probability of receiving reliable information. What we measure is probably more critical to the evaluation process than how we measure, since the selection of the wrong criteria can result in serious, dysfunctional consequences. And what we measure determines, to a great extent, what people in the organization will attempt to excel at. The criteria we measure must represent performance as it was mutually set in the first two steps of the appraisal process.

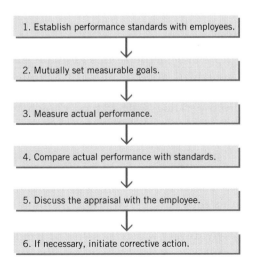

1. Establish performance standards with employees.

2. Mutually set measurable goals.

3. Measure actual performance.

4. Compare actual performance with standards.

5. Discuss the appraisal with the employee.

6. If necessary, initiate corrective action.

Figure 12-2
An Appraisal Process

The fourth step in the appraisal process is the comparison of actual performance with standards. The point of this step is to note deviations between standard performance and actual performance so that we can proceed to the fifth step in the process—the discussion of the appraisal with the employee. As we mentioned earlier, one of the most challenging tasks facing managers is to present an accurate appraisal to the employee. Appraising performance may touch on one of the most emotionally charged activities—the assessment of another individual's contribution and ability. The impression that employees receive about their assessment has a strong impact on their self-esteem and, very importantly, on their subsequent performance. Of course, conveying good news is considerably less difficult for both the manager and the employee than conveying the bad news that performance has been below expectations. In this context, the discussion of the appraisal can have negative as well as positive motivational consequences.

The final step in the appraisal is the initiation of corrective action where necessary. Corrective action can be of two types: One is immediate and deals predominantly with symptoms, and the other is basic and delves into causes. Immediate corrective action is often described as "putting out fires," whereas basic corrective action gets to the source of deviation and seeks to adjust the difference permanently. Immediate action corrects something right now and gets things back on track. Basic corrective action asks how and why performance deviated. In some instances, managers may rationalize that they do not have the time to take basic corrective action and therefore must be content to "perpetually put out fires." Good managers recognize that taking a little time to analyze the problem today may save more time tomorrow when the problem may get bigger.

Appraisal Methods

The previous section described the appraisal process in general terms. In this section, we will look at specific ways in which management can actually establish performance standards and devise instruments that can be used to measure and appraise an employee's performance. Three different approaches exist for doing appraisals: Employees can be appraised against (1) absolute standards, (2) relative standards, or (3) objectives. No one approach is always best; each has its strengths and weaknesses.

Absolute Standards

Absolute Standards Measuring an employee's performance against some established standards.

Our first group of appraisal methods uses **absolute standards.** This means that subjects are not compared with any other person. Included in this group are the following methods: the essay appraisal, the critical incident appraisal, the checklist, the adjective rating scale, forced choice, and behaviorally anchored rating scales.

Essay Appraisal A performance appraisal method whereby an appraiser writes a narrative about the employee.

The Essay Appraisal   Probably the simplest method of appraisal is to have the appraiser write a narrative describing an employee's strengths, weaknesses, past performance, potential, and suggestions for improvement. The strength of the **essay appraisal** lies in its simplicity. It requires no complex forms or extensive training to complete, but its weaknesses are many. Because the essays are unstructured, they are likely to vary widely in terms of length and content. This makes it difficult to compare individuals across the organization. And, of course, some raters are better writers than others. So a "good" or "bad" evaluation may be determined as much by the rater's writing skill as by the employee's actual level of performance. However, the essay appraisal can provide considerable information, much of which can be easily fed back and assimilated by the employee. But this method provides only qualitative data, and HRM decisions improve when useful quantitative data, which can be compared and ranked more objectively, are generated. However, the essay appraisal is a good start and is beneficial if used in conjunction with other appraisal methods.

The Critical Incident Appraisal   **Critical incident appraisal** focuses the rater's attention on those critical or key behaviors that make the difference between doing a job effectively and doing it ineffectively. The appraiser writes down anecdotes describing what the employee did that was especially effective or ineffective. For example, the college dean might write the following critical incident about one of her instructors: "Outlined the day's lecture on the chalkboard at the beginning of class." Note that with this approach to appraisal, specific behaviors are cited, not vaguely defined personality traits. A behavior-based appraisal such as this should be more valid than trait-based appraisals because it is clearly more job-related. It is one thing to say that an employee is "aggressive," "imaginative," or "relaxed," but that does not tell us anything about how well the job is being done. Critical incidents, with their focus on behaviors, judge performance rather than personalities.

Critical Incident Appraisal A performance appraisal method that focuses on the key behaviors that make the difference between doing a job effectively or ineffectively.

The strength of the critical incident method is that it looks at behaviors. Additionally, a list of critical incidents on a given employee provides a rich set of examples from which employees can be shown which of their behaviors are desirable and which ones call for improvement. Its drawbacks are basically that: (1) Appraisers are required to regularly write these incidents down, and doing this on a daily or weekly basis for all subordinates is time-consuming and burdensome for managers; and (2) critical incidents suffer from the same comparison problem found in essays—mainly, they do not lend themselves to quantification. Therefore the comparison and ranking of subordinates is difficult.

The Checklist Appraisal   In the **checklist appraisal,** the evaluator uses a list of behavioral descriptions and checks off those behaviors that apply to the employee. As Figure 12-3 illustrates, the evaluator merely goes down the list and checks off "yes" or "no" to each question.

Checklist Appraisal A performance appraisal type in which a rater checks off those attributes of an employee that apply.

Once the checklist is complete, it is usually evaluated by the HRM staff, not the manager doing the checklist. Therefore the rater does not actually evaluate

Figure 12-3
Sample Checklist Items for Appraising Customer Service Representative

	Yes	No
1. Are supervisor's orders usually followed?	_____	_____
2. Does the individual approach customers promptly?	_____	_____
3. Does the individual suggest additional merchandise to customers?	_____	_____
4. Does the individual keep busy when not servicing a customer?	_____	_____
5. Does the individual lose his or her temper in public?	_____	_____
6. Does the individual volunteer to help other employees?	_____	_____

the employee's performance; he or she merely records it. An analyst in HRM then scores the checklist, often weighing the factors in relationship to their importance. The final evaluation can then be returned to the rating manager for discussion with the subordinate, or someone from HRM can provide the feedback to the employee.

The checklist reduces some bias, since the rater and the scorer are different, but the rater usually can pick up the positive and negative implications in each item so bias can still be introduced. From a cost standpoint, this appraisal method may be inefficient if there are a number of job categories, because a checklist of items must be prepared for each category.

The Adjective Rating Scale Appraisal One of the oldest and most popular methods of appraisal is the **adjective rating scale.**[22] An example of some rating scale items is shown in Figure 12-4. Rating scales can be used to assess factors such as quantity and quality of work, job knowledge, cooperation, loyalty, dependability, attendance, honesty, integrity, attitudes, and initiative. However, this method is most valid when abstract traits like loyalty or integrity are avoided, unless they can be defined in more specific behavioral terms.[23] The assessor goes down the list of factors and notes the point along the scale or continuum that best describes the employee. There are typically five to ten points on the continuum. In the design of the graphic scale, the challenge is to ensure that both the factors evaluated and the scale points are clearly understood and are unambiguous to the rater. Should ambiguity occur, bias is introduced.

Why are rating scales popular? Although they do not provide the depth of information that essays or critical incidents do,[24] they are less time-consuming to develop and administer, they provide a quantitative analysis and comparison,

Adjective Rating Scales A performance appraisal method that lists a number of traits and a range of performance for each.

Figure 12-4
Sample of Adjective Rating Scale Items and Format

Performance Factor	Performance Rating				
Quality of work is the accuracy, skill, and completeness of work.	☐ Consistently unsatisfactory	☐ Occasionally unsatisfactory	☐ Consistently satisfactory	☐ Sometimes superior	☐ Consistently superior
Quantity of work is the volume of work done in a normal workday.	☐ Consistently unsatisfactory	☐ Occasionally unsatisfactory	☐ Consistently satisfactory	☐ Sometimes superior	☐ Consistently superior
Job knowledge is information pertinent to the job that an individual should have for satisfactory job performance.	☐ Poorly informed about work duties	☐ Occasionally unsatisfactory	☐ Can answer most questions about the job	☐ Understands all phases of the job	☐ Has complete mastery of all phases of the job
Dependability is following directions and company policies without supervision.	☐ Requires constant supervision	☐ Requires occasional follow-up	☐ Usually can be counted on	☐ Requires very little supervision	☐ Requires absolute minimum of supervision

and, in contrast to the checklist, there is more generalization of items so that comparability with other individuals in diverse job categories is possible.[25]

The Forced-Choice Appraisal When you were in elementary or secondary school, did you ever complete one of those tests that presumably gives you insights into what kind of career you should pursue? (Questions might be, for example, "Would you rather go to a football game with a group of friends or stay home and read a nonfiction book in your room?") If so, then you are familiar with the forced-choice format. The **forced-choice appraisal** is a special type of checklist, but the rater must choose between two or more statements, all of which may be favorable or unfavorable. The appraiser's job is to identify which statement is most (or in some cases least) descriptive of the individual being evaluated. For instance, students evaluating their college instructor might have to choose between: "(a) is patient with slow learners; (b) lectures with confidence; (c) keeps interest and attention of class; or (d) acquaints classes in advance with objectives for each class." All the preceding statements are favorable, but on another checklist, the choices could all be unfavorable. As with the checklist method, to reduce bias, the right answers are not known to the rater; someone in HRM scores the answers based on the key. This key should be validated so management is in a position to say that individuals with higher scores are better-performing employees.

The major advantage of the forced-choice method is that, because the appraiser does not know the "right" answers, it reduces bias and distortion.[26] For example, the appraiser may like a certain employee and intentionally want to give her a favorable evaluation, but this becomes difficult if one is not sure which response is most preferred. On the negative side, appraisers tend to dislike this method; many dislike being forced to make distinctions between similar-sounding statements. Raters also may become frustrated with a system in which they do not know what represents a "good" or "bad" answer; hence they may try to second-guess the scoring key in order to get the formal appraisal to align with their intuitive appraisal.

The Behaviorally Anchored Rating Scales An approach that has received considerable attention by academics in past years involves **behaviorally anchored rating scales (BARS)**. These scales combine major elements from the critical incident and graphic rating scale approaches. The appraiser rates the employees based on items along a continuum, but the points are examples of actual behavior on the given job rather than general descriptions or traits. The enthusiasm surrounding BARS grew from the belief that the use of specific behaviors, derived for each job, should produce relatively error-free and reliable ratings. Although this promise has not been fulfilled,[27] it has been argued that this may be due partly to departures from careful methodology in the development of the specific scales themselves rather than to inadequacies in the concept;[28] they also may be just too time-consuming.

Behaviorally anchored rating scales specify definite, observable, and measurable job behavior. Examples of job-related behavior and performance dimensions are generated by asking participants to give specific illustrations of effective and ineffective behavior regarding each performance dimension; these behavioral examples are then translated into appropriate performance dimensions. Those that are sorted into the dimension for which they were generated are retained. The final group of behavior incidents are then numerically scaled to a level of performance that each is perceived to represent. The incidents that are retranslated and have high rater agreement on performance effectiveness

Forced-choice Appraisal A type of performance appraisal method in which the rater must choose between two specific statements about an employee's work behavior.

Behaviorally Anchored Rating Scales (BARS) A performance appraisal technique that generates critical incidents and develops behavioral dimensions of performance. The evaluator appraises behaviors rather than traits.

are retained for use as anchors on the performance dimension. The results of these processes are behavioral descriptions, such as *anticipates, plans, executes, solves immediate problems, carries out orders,* and *handles emergency situations.* Figure 12-5 is an example of a BARS for an employee relations specialist's scale.

The research on BARS indicates that while it is far from perfect, it does tend to reduce rating errors. Possibly its major advantage stems from the dimensions generated, rather than from any particular superiority of behavior over trait anchors.[29] The process of developing the behavioral scales is valuable in and of itself for clarifying to both the employee and the rater which behaviors connote good performance and which bad. Unfortunately, it, too, suffers from the dis-

Figure 12-5
Sample BARS for an Employee Relations Specialist

Performance dimension scale development under BARS for the dimension "Ability to Absorb and Interpret Policies for an Employee Relations Specialist."

This employee relations specialist

	9 Could be expected to serve as an information source concerning new and changed policies for others in the organization
Could be expected to be aware quickly of program changes and explain these to employees	8
	7 Could be expected to reconcile conflicting policies and procedures correctly to meet HRM goals
Could be expected to recognize the need for additional information to gain a better understanding of policy changes	6
	5 Could be expected to complete various HRM forms correctly after receiving instruction on them
Could be expected to require some help and practice in mastering new policies and procedures	4
	3 Could be expected to know that there is always a problem, but go down many blind alleys before realizing they are wrong
Could be expected to incorrectly interpret guidelines, creating problems for line managers	2
	1 Could be expected to be unable to learn new procedures even after repeated explanations

Source: "Reprinted from *Business Horizons* (August 1976), Copyright 1976 by the Foundation for the School of Business at Indiana University. Used with permission."

tortions inherent in most rating methods.[30] These distortions will be discussed later in this chapter.

Relative Standards

In the second general category of appraisal methods, individuals are compared against other individuals. These methods are **relative standards** rather than absolute measuring devices. The most popular of the relative methods are group order ranking, individual ranking, and paired comparison.

Group Order Ranking **Group order ranking** requires the evaluator to place employees into a particular classification, such as "top one-fifth" or "second one-fifth." This method is often used in recommending students to graduate schools. Evaluators are asked to rank the student in the top 5 percent, the next 5 percent, the next 15 percent, and so forth. But when used by managers to appraise subordinates, managers deal with all their subordinates. So if a rater has twenty subordinates, only four can be in the top fifth; and, of course, four also must be relegated to the bottom fifth.

> **Group Order Ranking** A relative standard of performance characterized as placing employees into a particular classification, such as the "top one-fifth."

The advantage to this group ordering is that it prevents raters from inflating their evaluations so everyone looks good or from homogenizing the evaluations so everyone is rated near the average—outcomes that are not unusual with the graphic rating scale. The predominant disadvantages surface when the number of employees being compared is small. At the extreme, if the evaluator is looking at only four employees, it is quite possible that all may be excellent, yet the evaluator may be forced to rank them into top quarter, second quarter, third quarter, and low quarter! Theoretically, as the sample size increases, the validity of relative scores as an accurate measure increases; but occasionally the technique is implemented with a small group, utilizing assumptions that apply to large groups.

Another disadvantage, which plagues all relative measures, is the "zero-sum game" consideration. This means that any change must add up to zero. For example, if there are twelve employees in a department performing at different levels of effectiveness, by definition, three are in the top quarter, three are in the second quarter, and so forth. The sixth-best employee, for instance, would be in the second quartile. Ironically, if two of the workers in the third or fourth quartiles leave the department and are not replaced, then our sixth-best employee now falls into the third quarter. Because comparisons are relative, an employee who is mediocre may score high only because he or she is the "best of the worst"; in contrast, an excellent performer who is matched against "stiff" competition may be evaluated poorly, when in absolute terms his or her performance is outstanding.

Individual Ranking The **individual ranking** method requires the evaluator merely to list the employees in order from highest to lowest, and only one can be "best." If the evaluator is required to appraise thirty individuals, this method assumes that the difference between the first and second employee is the same as that between the twenty-first and the twenty-second. Even though some of these employees may be closely grouped, this method allows for no ties. In terms of advantages and disadvantages, the individual ranking method carries the same pluses and minuses as group order ranking.

> **Individual Ranking** Ranking employees' performance from highest to lowest.

> **Paired Comparison** Ranking individuals' performance by counting the number of times any one individual is the preferred member when compared with all other employees.

Paired Comparison The **paired comparison** method is calculated by taking the total of $[n(n-1)]/2$ comparisons. A score is obtained for each employee by simply counting the number of pairs in which the individual is the preferred member. It ranks each individual in relationship to all others on a one-on-one basis. If ten people are being evaluated, the first person is compared, one by one, with each of the other nine, and the number of times this person is preferred in any of the nine pairs is tabulated. Each of the remaining nine persons, in turn, is compared in the same way, and a ranking is formed by the greatest number of preferred "victories." This method ensures that each employee is compared against every other, but the method can become unwieldy when large numbers of employees are being compared.

Objectives

The third approach to appraisal makes use of objectives. Employees are evaluated by how well they accomplish a specific set of objectives that have been determined to be critical in the successful completion of their job. This approach is frequently referred to as **management by objectives (MBO).**[31] Management by objectives is a process that converts organizational objectives into individual objectives. It consists of four steps: goal setting, action planning, self-control, and periodic reviews.

In goal setting, the organization's overall objectives are used as guidelines from which departmental and individual objectives are set. At the individual level, the manager and subordinate jointly identify those goals that are critical to fulfill the requirements of the job as determined by job analysis. These goals are agreed upon and then become the standards by which the employee's results will be evaluated.

In action planning, the means are determined for achieving the ends established in goal setting; that is, realistic plans are developed to attain the objectives. This step includes identifying the activities necessary to accomplish the objective, establishing the critical relationships between these activities, estimating the time requirements for each activity, and determining the resources required to complete each activity.

Self-control refers to the systematic monitoring and measuring of performance—ideally, by having the individual review his or her own performance. Inherent in allowing individuals to control their own performance is a positive image of human nature. The MBO philosophy is built on the assumption that individuals can be responsible, can exercise self-direction, and do not require external controls and threats of punishment to motivate them to work toward their objectives. This, from a motivational point of view, would be representative of Douglas McGregor's Theory Y.

Finally, with periodic progress reviews, corrective action is initiated when behavior deviates from the standards established in the goal-setting phase. Again, consistent with the MBO philosophy, these manager–subordinate reviews are conducted in a constructive rather than punitive manner. Reviews are not meant to degrade the individual but to aid in future performance. These reviews should take place at least two or three times a year. What will these objectives look like? It is important that they be tangible, verifiable, and measurable. This means that, wherever possible, we should avoid qualitative objectives and substitute quantifiable statements. For example, a quantitative objective might be "to cut, each day, 3,500 yards of cable to standard five-foot lengths, with a maximum scrap of 50 yards," or "to prepare, process, and transfer to the treasurer's office, all accounts payable vouchers within three working days from the receipt of the invoice."

MBO's advantages lie in its results-oriented emphasis. It assists the planning

Management by Objectives (MBO) A performance appraisal method that includes mutual objective setting and evaluation based on the attainment of the specific objectives.

and control functions and provides motivation, as well as being an approach to performance appraisal, because employees know exactly what is expected of them and how they will be evaluated, and that their evaluation will be based on their success in achieving their objectives. Additionally, employees should have a greater commitment to objectives they have participated in developing than to those unilaterally set by their boss.

The major disadvantage of MBO is that it is unlikely to be effective in an environment where management has little trust in its employees; that is, where management makes decisions autocratically and relies heavily on external controls. The amount of time needed to implement and maintain an MBO process may also cause problems. Many activities must occur to set it up, such as meetings between managers and subordinates to set and monitor objectives; these meetings take an inordinate amount of the manager's time. Additionally, it may be difficult to measure whether the MBO activities are being carried out properly. The difficulty involved in properly appraising the managers' efforts and performance as they carry out their MBO activities may cause it to fail.

Factors that Can Distort Appraisals

The performance appraisal process and techniques that we have suggested present an objective system in which the evaluator is free from personal biases, prejudices, and idiosyncrasies. This is defended on the basis that objectivity minimizes the potential capricious and dysfunctional behavior of the evaluator, which may be detrimental to the achievement of the organizational goals. Thus, our goal should be to utilize direct performance criteria where possible.

It would be naive to assume, however, that all practicing managers impartially interpret and standardize the criteria upon which their subordinates will be appraised. This is particularly true of those jobs that are not easily programmable and for which developing hard performance standards is most difficult if not impossible. These would include, but are certainly not limited to, such jobs as researcher, teacher, engineer, and consultant. In the place of such standards, we can expect managers to utilize nonperformance or subjective criteria against which to evaluate individuals.

A completely error-free performance appraisal is only an ideal we can aim for,[32] with all actual appraisals falling short of this ideal. However, we can isolate a number of factors that significantly impede objective evaluation.[33] In this section, we will briefly review the more significant of these factors.

Leniency Error

Every evaluator has his or her own value system that acts as a standard against which appraisals are made. Relative to the true or actual performance an individual exhibits, some evaluators mark high and others low. The former is referred to as positive **leniency error,** and the latter as negative leniency error. When evaluators are positively lenient in their appraisal, an individual's performance becomes overstated; that is, rated higher than it actually should. Similarly, a negative leniency error understates performance, giving the individual a lower appraisal.

If all individuals in an organization were appraised by the same person, there would be no problem. Although there would be an error factor, it would be applied equally to everyone. The difficulty arises when we have different raters with different leniency errors making judgments. For example, assume a situa-

Leniency Error A means by which performance appraisal can be distorted by evaluating employees against one's own value system.

tion where both Jones and Smith are performing the same job for a different supervisor, with absolutely identical job performance. If Jones's supervisor tends to err toward positive leniency while Smith's supervisor errs toward negative leniency, we might be confronted with two dramatically different evaluations.

Halo Error

Halo Error The tendency to let our assessment of an individual on one trait influence our evaluation of that person on other specific traits.

The **halo error** or effect is a "tendency to rate high or low on all factors due to the impression of a high or low rating on some specific factor."[34] For example, if an employee tends to be conscientious and dependable, we might become biased toward that individual to the extent that we will rate him or her positively on many desirable attributes.

People who design teaching appraisal forms for college students to fill out in evaluating the effectiveness of their instructor each semester must confront the halo effect. Students tend to rate a faculty member as outstanding on all criteria when they are particularly appreciative of a few things he or she does in the classroom. Similarly, a few bad habits—like showing up late for lectures, being slow in returning papers, or assigning an extremely demanding reading requirement—might result in students evaluating the instructor as "lousy" across the board. One method frequently used to deal with the halo error is "reverse wording" the evaluation questions so that a favorable answer for, say, question 17 might be 5 on a scale of 1 through 5, while a favorable answer for question number 18 might be 1 on a scale of 1 through 5. Structuring the questions in this manner seeks to reduce the halo error by requiring the evaluator to consider each question independently. Another method, which can be used where there is more than one person to be evaluated, is to have the evaluator appraise all ratees on each dimension before going on to the next dimension.

Similarity Error

Similarity Error Evaluating employees based on the way an evaluator perceives himself or herself.

When evaluators rate other people in the same way that the evaluators perceive themselves, they are making a **similarity error.** Based on the perception that evaluators have of themselves, they project those perceptions onto others. For example, the evaluator who perceives himself or herself as aggressive may evaluate others by looking for aggressiveness. Those who demonstrate this characteristic tend to benefit, while others are penalized.

Low Appraiser Motivation

What are the consequences of the appraisal? If the evaluator knows that a poor appraisal could significantly hurt the employee's future—particularly opportunities for promotion or a salary increase—the evaluator may be reluctant to give a realistic appraisal. There is evidence that it is more difficult to obtain accurate appraisals when important rewards depend on the results.[35]

Central Tendency

Central Tendency The tendency of a rater to give average ratings.

It is possible that regardless of who the appraiser evaluates and what traits are used, the pattern of evaluation remains the same. It is also possible that the evaluator's ability to appraise objectively and accurately has been impeded by a failure to use the extremes of the scale; that is, **central tendency.** Central tendency is "the reluctance to make extreme ratings (in either direction); the inability to distinguish between and among ratees; a form of range restriction."[36] Raters who are prone to the central tendency error are those who continually rate all employees as average. For example, if a manager rates all subordinates as 3, on a scale of 1 to 5, then no differentiation among the subordinates exists. Failure to rate subordinates as 5, for those who deserve that rating, and as 1, if the case warrants it, will only create problems, especially if this information is used for pay increases.

Inflationary Pressures

A middle manager in a large South Carolinian company could not understand why he had been passed over for promotion. He had seen his file and knew that his average rating by his supervisor was 86. Given his knowledge that the appraisal system defined "outstanding performance" at 90 or above, "good" as 80 or above, "average" as 70 or above, and "inadequate performance" as anything below 70, he was at a loss to understand why he had not been promoted, with his near-outstanding performance appraisal. The manager's confusion was somewhat resolved when he found out that the "average" rating of middle managers in his organization was 92. This example addresses a major potential problem in appraisals—inflationary pressures. This, in effect, is a specific case of low differentiation within the upper range of the rating choices.

Inflationary pressures have always existed but appear to have increased as a problem over the past three decades. As "equality" values have grown in importance in our society, as well as fear of retribution from disgruntled employees who fail to achieve excellent appraisals, there has been a tendency for evaluation to be less rigorous and negative repercussions from the evaluation reduced by generally inflating or upgrading appraisals.

Inappropriate Substitutes for Performance

It is the unusual job where the definition of performance is absolutely clear and direct measures are available for appraising the incumbent. In many jobs it is difficult to get consensus on what is "a good job," and it is even more difficult to get agreement on what criteria will determine performance. For a salesperson the criteria is affected by factors such as economic conditions and actions of competitors—factors outside the salesperson's control. As a result, the appraisal is frequently made by using substitutes for performance; criteria that, it is believed, closely approximate performance and act in its place. Many of these substitutes are well chosen and give a good approximation of actual performance. However, the substitutes chosen are not always appropriate. It is not unusual, for example, to find organizations using criteria such as effort, enthusiasm, neatness, positive attitudes, conscientiousness, promptness, and congeniality as substitutes for performance. In some jobs, one or more of these criteria are part of performance. Obviously, enthusiasm does enhance the effectiveness of a teacher: You are more likely to listen to and be motivated by a teacher who is enthusiastic than by one who is not; and increased attentiveness and motivation typically lead to increased learning. But enthusiasm may in no way be relevant to effective performance for many accountants, watch repairers, or copy editors. So what may be an appropriate substitute for performance in one job may be totally inappropriate in another.

Attribution Theory A theory of performance evaluation based on the perception of who is in control of an employee's performance.

Attribution Theory

There is a theory in management literature called **attribution theory.** According to this theory, employee evaluations are directly affected by "managers' perceptions of who is believed to be in control of the employee's performance—the employer or the manager."[37] Attribution theory attempts to differentiate between those things that the employee controls (internal) versus those that the employee cannot control (external). For example, if an employee fails to complete a project that he has had six months to complete, a manager may view this negatively if he or she believes that the employee did not manage either the project or his time well (internal control). Conversely, if the project is delayed because top management requested that something else be given a higher priority, a manager may see the incomplete project in more positive terms (external control).

One research study found support for two key generalizations regarding attribution:[38]

1. When managers attribute an employee's poor performance to internal control, the judgment is harsher than when the same poor performance is attributed to external factors.
2. When an employee is performing satisfactorily, managers will evaluate the employee favorably if the performance is attributed to the employee's own efforts than if the performance is attributed to outside forces.

Impression Management Influencing performance evaluations by portraying an image that is desired by the appraiser.

While attribution theory is interesting and sheds new light on rater effects on performance evaluations, much more study of the topic is needed. Yet it does provide much insight on why unbiased performance evaluations are important. An extension of attribution theory relates to what is called **impression management.** Impression management takes into account how the employee influences the relationship with his or her supervisor. In one study, impression management was viewed as having an effect on performance ratings. In such a case, when the employee "positively impressed his or her supervisor," the outcome was seen as a higher performance rating.[39]

Creating More Effective Performance Management Systems

The fact that managers frequently encounter problems with performance appraisals should not lead us to throw up our hands and give up on the concept. There are things that can be done to make performance appraisals more effective. In this section, we offer some suggestions that can be considered individually or in combination.

Behavior-based Measures

As we have pointed out, the evidence favors behavior-based measures over those developed around traits. Many traits often considered to be related to good performance may, in fact, have little or no performance relationship. Traits like loyalty, initiative, courage, reliability, and self-expression are intuitively appealing as desirable characteristics in employees. But the relevant question is: Are individuals who are evaluated as high on those traits higher performers than those who rate low? We cannot answer this question. We know that there are employees who rate high on these characteristics and are poor performers. We can find others who are excellent performers but do not score well on traits such as these. Our conclusion is that traits like loyalty and initiative may be prized by managers, but there is no evidence to support that certain traits will be adequate synonyms for performance in a large cross-section of jobs.

A second weakness in traits is the judgment itself. What is "loyalty"? When is an employee "reliable"? What you consider "loyalty," I may not. So traits suffer from weak inter-rater agreement. Behavior-derived measures can deal with both of these objections. Because they deal with specific examples of performance—both good and bad—we avoid the problem of using inappropriate substitutes. Additionally, because we are evaluating specific behaviors, we increase the likelihood that two or more evaluators will see the same thing. You might consider a given employee as "friendly" while I rate her "standoffish." But when asked to rate her in terms of specific behaviors, we might both agree that in terms of specific behaviors, she "frequently says `good morning' to customers," "rarely gives advice or assistance to coworkers," and "almost always avoids idle chatter with coworkers."

Combine Absolute and Relative Standards

A major drawback to individual or absolute standards is that they tend to be biased by positive leniency; that is, evaluators lean toward packing their subjects into the high part of the rankings. On the other hand, relative standards suffer when there is little actual variability among the subjects. The obvious solution is to consider using appraisal methods that combine both absolute and relative standards. For example, you might want to use the graphic rating scale and the individual ranking method. This dual method of appraisal, incidentally, has been instituted at some universities to deal with the problem of grade inflation. Students get an absolute grade—A, B, C, D, or F—and next to it is a relative mark showing how this student ranked in the class. A prospective employer or graduate school admissions committee can look at two students who each got a B in their cost accounting course and draw considerably different conclusions about each when, next to one grade it says "ranked 4th out of 26," while the other says "ranked 17th out of 30." Obviously, the latter instructor gave a lot more high grades!

Ongoing Feedback

A few years back, a nationwide motel chain advertised, "The best surprise is no surprise." This phrase clearly applies to performance appraisals. Employees like to know how they are doing. The "annual review," where the manager shares the employees' evaluations with them, can become a problem. In some cases, it is a problem merely because managers put off such reviews. This is particularly likely if the appraisal is negative. But the annual review is additionally troublesome if the manager "saves up" performance-related information and unloads it during the appraisal review. This creates an extremely trying experience for both the evaluator and employee. In such instances it is not surprising that the manager may attempt to avoid confronting uncomfortable issues that, even if confronted, may only be denied or rationalized by the employee.[40]

The solution lies in having the manager share with the employee both expectations and disappointments on a day-to-day basis. By providing the employee with frequent opportunities to discuss performance before any reward or punishment consequences occur, there will be no surprises at the time of the annual formal review. In fact, where ongoing feedback has been provided, the formal sitting-down step should not be particularly traumatic for either party. Additionally, in an MBO system that actually works, ongoing feedback is the critical element.

Multiple Raters

As the number of raters increases, the probability of attaining more accurate information increases.[41] If rater error tends to follow a normal curve, an increase in the number of raters will tend to find the majority congregating about the middle. If a person has had ten supervisors, nine of whom rated him or her excellent and one poor, then we must investigate what went into that one. Maybe this rater was the one who identified an area of weakness where training is needed, or an area to be avoided in future job assignments. Therefore, by moving employees about within the organization to gain a number of evaluations, we increase the probability of achieving more valid and reliable evaluations (see "What If: HRM in a De-Jobbed Organization").[42]

Peer Evaluations Have you ever wondered why a professor asks you to evaluate the contributions of each other's work when a group assignment is used in a classroom? The reasoning behind this is that the professor cannot tell what every member did on the project, but only what the overall product quality was. And at times, that may not be fair, especially if a member or two in the group left most of the work up to the remaining group members.

Similarly, managers find it difficult to evaluate their employees' performance because they are not working with them every day. Unfortunately, unless they have this information, they may not be making an accurate assessment. And if their goal of the performance evaluation is to identify deficient areas and provide constructive feedback to their employees, they have been providing a disservice to these workers by not having all the information. Yet how do they get this information? One of the better means is through **peer evaluations.** Peer evaluations are conducted by employees' coworkers, people explicitly familiar with the behaviors involved in jobs mainly because they too are doing the same thing.[43] For example, at Digital Equipment Corporation, all team members evaluate one another.[44] This is done because coworkers are the ones most aware of each others' day-to-day work behavior and should be given the opportunity to provide the management with some feedback.[45]

The main advantage to peer evaluation is that (1) there is a tendency for coworkers to offer more constructive insight to each other so that, as a unit, each will improve; and (2) their recommendations tend to be more specific regarding job behaviors. Unless specificity exists, constructive measures are hard to gain.[46] But caution is in order because these systems, if not handled properly, could lead to increases in halo effects and leniency errors,[47] and fear among employees.[48] Thus, along with training our managers to appraise employee performance, so too must we train peers to evaluate one another.

A slight deviation from peer assessments is a process called the **upward appraisal,** or the reverse review.[49] Used in such companies as Pratt and Whitney and AT&T, upward appraisals permits employees to offer frank and constructive feedback to their managers on such areas as leadership and communication skills.[50]

Peer Evaluations A performance evaluation situation in which coworkers provide input into the employee's performance.

Upward Appraisals An employee appraisal process whereby employees evaluate their supervisors.

What If:

HRM in a De-Jobbed Organization

The foundation of the performance appraisal process is the concept that performance standards are clearly identified. This fundamental fact implies that for workers to perform effectively, they must know and understand what is expected of them. This thesis, however, applies only where clear job descriptions exist, and where variations to the job are minimal. In other words, conventional performance appraisals were designed to fit the needs of the traditional organization. But what happens to these when the organization is de-jobbed? Let's look at some possibilities.

First, setting goals between a supervisor and an employee may be a thing of the past. Tomorrow's worker's are likely to go from project to project, with the demands and requirements of this work rapidly changing. No formalized performance appraisal system will be able to capture the intricacies of the jobs being done. Second, employees, either part of the core group, or the contingent work force, will have several bosses, not just one individual who directs the work. Just who will have the responsibility for the performance appraisal? It is more likely to be the team members themselves—setting their own goals and evaluating each other's performance. One can even speculate that this will take the format of an on-going informal process, rather than some formal "ritual" held every twelve months or so.

The traditional outcomes of performance evaluations are likely to change also. Because many of tomorrow's workers will not be permanent employees of the organization, the "rewards" component of performance's linkage to motivation may be nonexistent in terms of how we currently view rewards. Instead, how individuals work on a project and how they performed their duties as a team player, will probably give rise to continued use of their services; or at the least, serve as a reference for other organizations.

All in all, while we surmise a drastic change in the performance appraisal process, it should not be interpreted that organizations will become less concerned with evaluating employee performance. On the contrary, individual performance will matter most. And employee performance information is likely to be collected from a number of sources—from anyone who's familiar with the employee's work. As such, it's just the formalized measurement systems existing today that will rarely apply in the de-jobbed organization.

Source: William Bridges, "The End of the Job," *Fortune* (September 19, 1994), p. 64.

360-Degree Appraisals An appraisal device that seeks performance feedback from such sources as oneself, bosses, peers, team members, customers, suppliers, and the like is gaining in popularity.[51] It's called the **360-degree appraisal.**[52] It's being used in such companies as DuPont, General Electric, Motorola, Procter & Gamble, and UPS.[53] In today's dynamic organizations, traditional performance evaluations systems are archaic. Delayering has resulting in supervisors

360-Degree Appraisal Performance appraisal process in which supervisors, peers, employees, customers, and the like evaluate the individual.

having greater work responsibility and more employees reporting directly to them. Accordingly, in some instances, it is almost impossible for supervisors to have extensive job knowledge of each of their employees. Furthermore, the growth of project teams and employee involvement in today's companies places the responsibility of evaluation where people are better able to make an accurate assessment.

The 360-degree feedback process also has some positive benefits for development concerns (see "Meet Joe Malik"). Many managers simply do not know how their employees truly view them, and the work they have done. For example, Jerry Wallace, GM's Saturn plant's head of personnel viewed himself being up-to-date on all the latest management techniques.[54] While Jerry viewed himself open to change and flexible to new ideas, feedback from his employees indicated that Jerry was a "control" freak. After some soul-searching, plus an assessment from an external leadership group, Jerry realized his employees were right. He finally understood why nobody wanted to be on a team with him, and why he had to do everything himself.[55] In this case, the 360-degree feedback instrument eliminated a strong barrier to Jerry's career progression.

While 360-degree feedback is a relatively recent phenomenon, early research studies are reporting positive results where such a system operates. These stem from more accurate feedback, empowering employees, the reduction of subjective factors in the evaluation process, to the development of a leadership competitive advantage in an organization.[56]

Selective Rating

It has been suggested that appraisers should only rate in those areas in which they have significant job knowledge. If raters make evaluations on only those dimensions for which they are in a good position to rate, we can increase the inter-rater agreement and make the evaluation a more valid process. This approach also recognizes that different organizational levels often have different orientations toward ratees and observe them in different settings. In general, therefore, we recommend that, in terms of organizational level, appraisers should be as close as possible to the individual being evaluated. Conversely, the more levels separating the evaluator and evaluatee, the less opportunity the evaluator has to observe the individual's behavior and, not surprisingly, the greater the possibility for inaccuracies.

The specific application of these concepts results in having immediate supervisors or coworkers as the major input into the appraisal and having them evaluate those factors that they are best qualified to judge. For example, it has been suggested that when professors are evaluating secretaries within a university, they use such criteria as judgment, technical competence, and conscientiousness; whereas peers (other secretaries) use such criteria as job knowledge, organization, cooperation with coworkers, and responsibility.[57] Such an approach appears both logical and more reliable, since people are appraising only those dimensions of which they are in a good position to make judgments.

In addition to taking into account where the rater is in the organization or what he or she is allowed to evaluate, selective rating should also consider the characteristics of the rater. If appraisers differ in traits, and if certain of these traits are correlated with accurate appraisals while others are correlated with inaccurate appraisals, then it seems logical to attempt to identify effective raters. Those identified as especially effective could be given sole responsibility for doing appraisals, or greater weight could be given to their observations.

Joe Malik
Engineering Manager, AT&T

Joe Malik is the manager of a team of engineers at AT&T in New Jersey. Joe is an individual who prides himself on recognizing his strengths and weaknesses. He makes every attempt to capitalize on those strengths, and works fervently on developing efforts to overcome the weaknesses. His biggest problem, he thought, was his temper. In the past, Joe just blew his stack—and it was no surprise to anyone when Joe flew off the handle at work. He understood that this interfered with his work and with relationships he had on the job. Understandably, Joe has been working very hard to overcome this problem. No 360-degree appraisal was needed to confirm that this was a problem.

Although an active believer in getting and receiving feedback, Joe was startled to learn that his employees viewed him as having a bigger problem. A function of his temperament, Joe thought? No, his employees thought Joe had no vision for where the group was heading!

Team members reported to Joe that whenever any of them asked about the future plans for their work group, Joe would just "scrunch up in his chair." Everyone perceived this as Joe's way of evading the question—a tough one at that. Moreover, his body language indicated to these employees that he may know some unsettling news, and just didn't want to share it. Fear became rampant! Sadly, though, their perceptions were the furthest from the truth. Interestingly enough, Joe prided himself as being a visionary.

How else could he manage a group of professions developing prototypes for the phone systems networking system? Unfortunately, Joe kept his visions to himself. Through AT&T's 360-degree evaluation process, Joe was able to appreciate and understand the results of his behavior. Joe now knows that his employees have a strong desire to understand where they are going, and what his future plans for the unit are. He now communicates such information to team members regularly. As a result, team members are less frustrated, and Joe has overcome one of his shortcomings.

By providing this constructive feedback through the 360-degree appraisal, team members' needs are being better met. As for Joe, he still scrunches up in his chair, but not because he doesn't know the answer to employee questions. That's just Joe, and it doesn't bother his employees any longer!

Source: Brian O'Reilly, "360-Feedback Can Change Your Life," *Fortune* (October 17, 1994), p. 64–65.

Trained Appraisers

If you cannot find good raters, the alternative is to make good raters. Evidence indicates that the training of appraisers can make them more accurate raters.[58] Common errors such as halo and leniency can be minimized or eliminated in workshops where managers can practice observing and rating behaviors. Why should we bother to train these individuals? Because a poor appraisal is worse than no appraisal at all.[59] These negative effects can manifest themselves as demoralizing employees, decreasing productivity, and making the company "liable for wrongful termination damages."[60]

Rewards for Accurate Appraisers

Our final suggestion is obvious, but is frequently overlooked when organizations establish a performance appraisal system. The managers doing the evaluation must perceive that it is in their personal and career interest to conduct accurate appraisals. We noted earlier in the chapter that in most organizations the consequences for the appraiser of assigning accurate performance ratings to poor performers are negative. This must be overcome by encouraging and rewarding accurate appraisers.

International Performance Appraisal

In evaluating employee performance in international environments, other factors come into play. For instance, the cultural differences between the parent country and the host country must be considered. The cultural differences between the United States and England are not as great as those between the United States and China, for example. Thus, hostility or friendliness of the cultural environment in which one manages should be considered when appraising employee performance.

Should a Chinese manager of this McDonald's be required to use the corporate evaluation developed and used extensively in the U.S.? If so, will it need to be translated into Chinese? Questions such as these need responses when evaluating employees in the international arena.

Who Performs the Evaluation?

There are also issues to consider regarding who will be responsible for the evaluations: the host-country management or the parent-country management? Although local management would generally be considered a more accurate gauge, it typically evaluates expatriates from its own cultural perspectives and expectations, which may not reflect those of the parent country. For example, in the United States a participatory style of management is quite acceptable, while in some Asian countries, hierarchical values make it a disgrace to ask subordinates for ideas. This could vastly alter a manager's performance appraisal.[61]

Confusion may arise from the use of parent-country evaluation forms if they are misunderstood, either because the form has been improperly translated or not translated at all, or because the evaluator is uncertain what a particular question means. The home-office management, on the other hand, is often so remote that it may not be fully informed on what is going on in an overseas office. Because they lack access and because one organization may have numerous foreign operations to evaluate, home-office managements often measure performance by quantitative indices, such as profits, market shares, or gross sales.[62] However, "simple" numbers are often quite complex in their calculations and data are not always comparable. For example, if a company has many operations in South America, it must be aware of the accounting practices in each country. Peru, for instance, counts sales on consignment as firm sales, while Brazil does not. Local import tariffs can also distort pricing schedules, which alter gross sales figures, another often-compared statistic. Even when the measurements are comparable, the comparison country will have an effect. For instance, factory productivity levels in Mexico are well below those of similar plants in the United States, but American-owned plant productivity in Mexico is far above that of similar Mexican-owned plants. Depending on where the manager's results are compared, different results may occur. Accordingly, such issues complicate parent-country management performance evaluations by numerical criteria, or indices.

Which Evaluation Format Will Be Used?

Other issues surround the question of selecting the best format to use in performance appraisals. If we have an overseas operation that includes both parent-country nationals (PCNs) and host-country nationals (HCNs), we must determine if we will use the same forms for all employees. While most Western countries accept the concept of performance evaluation, some cultures interpret it as a sign of distrust or even an insult to an employee. This complicates a decision to use one instrument like a graphic rating scale for all employees. On the other hand, using different formats for PCNs and HCNs may create a dual track in the subsidiary, in turn creating other problems.

The evaluation form presents other problems. If there is a universal form for the entire corporation, an organization must determine how it will be translated accurately into the native language of each country. English forms may not be readily understood by local supervisors. For example, clerical and office jobs do not always have identical requirements in all cultures. As a result, some U.S. multinationals may be hesitant about evaluating HCNs and TCNs (third-country nationals). In some countries, notably the formerly Communist countries, individual performance was not assessed. Under Communist ideology, all workers were rewarded only when the group performed—with punishment or discipline being highly limited. Without the ability to reward good individual performance or to punish poor performance, there was little motivation to have any evaluation at all.[63] This is expected to change with the conversion of the former USSR and Soviet-bloc nations to capitalism, but the new format has yet to unfold. However, the system still exists in the People's Republic of China, where the United States is involved in numerous joint ventures, particularly in the hotel industry.

Although the subject of international performance appraisal continues to receive research attention, two general recommendations have been suggested as follows.

1. Modify the normal performance criteria of the evaluation sheet for a particular position to fit the overseas position and site characteristics. Expatriates who have returned from a particular site or the same country can provide useful input into revising criteria to reflect the possibilities and constraints of a given location.[64]
2. Include a current expatriate's insights as part of the evaluation. This means that nonstandardized criteria, which are difficult to measure, will be included, perhaps on a different basis for each country. This creates some administrative difficulties at headquarters, but in the long run will be a more equitable system.[65]

Study Tools and Applications

Summary

This summary relates to the Learning Objectives provided on p. 319.
After having read this chapter, you should know:
1. Performance management systems serve in the process of linking effort and performance. Only through effective means of making this linkage apparent can an organization develop its rewards based on performance.
2. The three purposes of performance management systems are feedback, development, and documentation. They are designed to support the employees, the appraisers, and the organization.

3. The six-step appraisal process is to: (1) establish performance standards with employees; (2) manager and employee set measurable goals; (3) measure actual performance; (4) compare actual performance with standards; (5) discuss the appraisal with the employee; and (6) if necessary, initiate corrective action.

4. Absolute standards refer to a method in performance management systems whereby employees are measured against company set performance requirements. Absolute standard evaluation methods involve the essay appraisal, the critical incident approach, the checklist rating, the adjective rating scale, the forced-choice inventory, and the behaviorally anchored rating scale (BARS).

5. Relative standards refer to a method in performance management systems whereby employees' performance is compared to other employees. Relative standard evaluation methods include group order ranking, individual ranking, and paired comparisons.

6. MBO is used as an appraisal method by establishing a specific set of objectives for an employee to achieve and reviewing performance based on how well those objectives have been met.

7. Performance appraisal might be distorted for a number of reasons, including: leniency error, halo error, similarity error, central tendency, low appraiser motivation, inflationary pressures, and inappropriate substitutes for performance.

8. More effective appraisals can be achieved with behavior-based measures, combined absolute and relative ratings, ongoing feedback, multiple raters, selective rating, trained appraisers, peer assessment, and rewards to accurate appraisers.

9. In 360-degree performance appraisals evaluations are made by oneself, supervisors, employees, team members, customers, suppliers, and the like. In doing so, a complete picture of one's performance can be assessed.

10. Performance management systems may differ in the international spectrum in terms of who performs the evaluation, and the format used. Cultural differences may dictate that changes in the U.S. performance management system are needed.

Key Terms

absolute standards	halo error
adjective rating scale	impression management
attribution theory	individual ranking
behaviorally anchored rating scale (BARS)	leniency error
central tendency	management by objectives (MBO)
checklist appraisal	paired comparison
critical incident appraisal	peer evaluations upward appraisals
documentation	performance-appraisal process
essay appraisal	relative standards
forced-choice appraisal	similarity error
group order ranking	360-degree appraisal

EXPERIENTIAL EXERCISE:

The Performance Appraisal

Purpose

1. To practice skills in performance appraisal and supervising employees.
2. To develop skills in communications and problem-solving in the performance appraisal process.

Introduction

Any kind of system, whether it be a person, organization, or a spacecraft, needs feedback from its environment to tell how close it is to being on target in achieving its objectives. One of the most important and useful sources of feedback to an employee is his supervisor. However, in the day-to-day course of our work experiences, we usually obtain little direct feedback on our performance from our supervisors, and we give an equal amount to our own employees.

One of the most common mechanisms for feedback between employees and employers is the performance appraisal process. In many organizations, this is a formal process in which the supervisor fills out a standard form describing the employee's work, they discuss it, and the employee signs it. Then it is sent to higher-level managers, and is finally placed in the employee's personnel file.

Senior managers in most organizations will describe their performance appraisal system in detail, stressing the requirements, such as the employee's signature, that ensure the appraisal will, in fact, be conducted. However, when employees are asked about their performance appraisals, the response is often a blank stare. Many employees do not even know what a performance appraisal is. Others report that it is conducted in a cursory manner; many seem to be conducted in brief encounters in the hallway or by the coffeepot. Thus, there is a mysterious process whereby the performance appraisal is there when one talks to senior managers, but gone when one talks to employees. One reason for this is that supervisors feel uncomfortable giving feedback in a one-to-one encounter. This occurs, in part, because they have rarely been trained to do so.

Procedure

1. Working in groups of three, one member will play the role of J.J. Stein, and another, the role of T.T. Burns. (Your instructor will provide you with the roles.) The third member (and others, if necessary) will act as observer. Guidelines for observer's role will also be given to you.
2. The supervisor conducts the appraisal interview with the employee (20 minutes). The observer is silent and takes notes on the process of the interviewer, using the "general instructions" as a guide. At the conclusion of the evaluation meeting, the observer gives feedback to the two participants.
3. After all groups have completed their appraisals, the large group will discuss the following: Supervisors—what evaluation method did you use? How effective was it? Employee—how did you react to the appraisal method? What did you like? Dislike? Observers—What strengths did you witness in the evaluation? The weaknesses?

Source: Roy J. Lewicki, Donald D. Bowen, Douglas T. Hall, and Francine S. Hall, *Experiences in Management and Organizational Behavior,* 3d ed. (New York: John Wiley, 1988), pp. 41–43. Used with permission.

CASE APPLICATION:

Jeannie Rice of Vanderbilt University

How open will an individual be to receiving feedback from anyone who has contact with the employee? That depends on many factors. Is the organization supportive of a multifaceted feedback process? Has the organization adopted the 360-degree appraisal into its value system? Do employees feel comfortable saying what they really think? For Jeannie Rice, the picture is a bit clearer.[66]

Jeannie Rice is the manager of buildings and property information at Vanderbilt University. Not unlike any individual in her position, Jeannie felt she was doing her job to the best of her abilities. She was successful! She set department goals that supported the mission of the university and, with the help of her staff, achieved them. There didn't appear to be anything unusual operating here, nor any underlying dissension among her staff. Oh sure, there were trying times for Jeannie, but there are for any manager, right? But her staff saw things differently. Most viewed Jeannie as being too demanding. She was creating a stressful work environment that was not only affecting Jeannie, herself, but many of those who had daily dealings with her.

As part of Jeannie's personal development plan, she was sent to the Center for Creative Leadership, where she was provided with numerous assessments and feedback instruments from her colleagues and employees. As a result of this feedback, a program was established for Jeannie to correct her behavior. One aspect was to return to her job and meet individually with the staff. There she shared the comments that were provided to her, and sought some clarification and elaboration. In many cases, however, staff members began with statements such as "I didn't say that about you," or "You used to be that way." Fortunately, however, Jeannie was able to overcome this initial barrier, and delve deeper into the issues. As a result, Jeannie has changed the way she does business, and has created a more positive work climate for her staff. And Jeannie, too, is now a bit more relaxed.

Questions

1. Describe how a 360-degree appraisal aids in developing an evaluation process that effectively supports the employee and the organization.
2. What role do organizational values play in having an effective 360-degree appraisal? Describe some problems that may arise if these values are not present.
3. Could a 360-degree appraisal work in a college classroom? Explain your position.

Testing Your Understanding

How well did you fulfill the learning objectives?

1. Performance management systems lead to employee motivation in all of these ways except
   a. work objectives are clarified.
   b. criteria for measuring work objectives are specified.
   c. employees have confidence that their efforts will lead to satisfactory job performance.
   d. employees have confidence that satisfactory job performance will lead to an acceptable reward.
   e. individual value systems are identified.
2. A director of computing services always has trouble with his people after performance appraisals. They quit, call in sick for a week, or sabotage operations. During a conversation with Terry, the vice-president of human resources, about the performance evaluation process, the director complained,"I have a bunch of babies working for me. They all expect me to tell them what good performance is. Part of their job is figuring out what they are supposed to do." What would be the best response from Terry?
   a. Commiserate. Agree that the director's employees are babies.
   b. Help the director develop corrective action steps for his employees.
   c. Tell the director that performance standards should be set with employees, and objectives should be clearly agreed to.

d. Tell the director to set clear performance expectations for his employees. It is his job, not theirs.
e. Show the director the performance objectives Terry uses for her employees. Suggest that the director use those objectives.

3. Marie is a marketing analyst. Her boss periodically observes her work on specific parts of her job (client calls, conducting meetings, attending seminars, etc.) and writes down, using specific behavioral descriptions, what he sees her doing. What appraisal technique is he using?
   a. graphic rating scale
   b. critical incident
   c. BARS
   d. checklist appraisal
   e. forced-choice comparison
4. Compare the group order ranking and the individual ranking techniques for performance evaluation.
   a. The techniques are the same.
   b. Individual ranking is disadvantaged because you may be forced to identify the "best of the best" in one set of employees and the "best of the worst" in another set. Group order ranking does not have this problem.
   c. Group order ranking is disadvantaged because you may be forced to identify the "best of the best" in one set of employees and the "best of the worst" in another set. Individual ranking does not have this problem.

d. Individual ranking forces the evaluator to compare all employees to each other. Group order ranking does not.

e. Individual ranking allows no ties. Group order ranking allows ties.

5. If you had an MBO agreement with your professor about what to do to get an A in this class, which would be the best (in terms of MBO standards) objective?

a. Get an A for doing the best you can.

b. Get an A for excellent work on tests, quizzes, and projects.

c. Get an A for a score of 96 or better on this test.

d. Get an A for interesting contributions to class.

e. Get an A if you are in the better part of the class.

6. Tony rates Al, an average worker, "excellent" on all of his performance evaluations. The rest of the staff suspect that Al gets high ratings because he graduated from the same prestigious university and was a member of the same fraternity as Tony. What rating error has the staff identified?

a. similarity error

b. halo error

c. leniency error

d. central tendency

e. inflationary pressures

7. According to attribution theory, if in a manager's judgment an employee's poor performance is attributable to external factors,

a. the employee will be more harshly rated.

b. the employee will be favorably rated.

c. the manager's perception will be jaded by impression management influence.

d. there exists an internal focus of control.

e. the poor performance will be viewed in more positive terms.

8. Which of the following is an example of an upward appraisal?

a. A manager refers to earlier performance appraisals of subordinates before evaluating them.

b. Peer evaluation is employed.

c. Several managers form teams to evaluate all their employees collectively.

d. Subordinates evaluate their managers.

e. Managers evaluate employees' traits, rather than their behaviors.

9. The 360-degree appraisal process

a. provides feedback from a variety of individuals who have knowledge of an employee's performance.

b. works best in large organizations.

c. aids in developing competitive intelligence about competing organizations.

d. diminishes the effect of development in the performance appraisal process.

e. all the above

10. Sarah, vice-president of a large transnational firm, explains that because of cultural and language differences between the parent and most subsidiary countries, her organization has chosen to evaluate performance only "by the numbers." Gross sales figures and factory productivity levels are used. What is wrong with this approach?

a. Nothing. Most firms are using this technique for international performance evaluation.

b. Each country's accounting practices must be considered when recording sales. (For example, some countries record consignments as sales.)

c. Language differences affect factory productivity levels.

d. Sales figures cannot be easily converted to a common currency designation.

e. The effort is redundant. Either gross sales or factory productivity levels should be sufficient.

11. Good performance management systems are designed to provide

a. performance information and salary updates.

b. disciplinary action and salary updates.

c. feedback, development, and documentation.

d. training, documentation, and salary updates.

e. communication and documentation.

12. Performance management systems must satisfy the needs of

a. employees, appraisers, organizations.

b. employees, customers, supervisors.

c. customers, managers, human resources professionals.

d. employees, organizations, customers.

e. human resources professionals, supervisors, managers.

13. The three approaches for performance appraisal are

a. absolute standards, tangential standards, nominal standards.

b. absolute standards, relative standards, objectives.

c. absolute standards, objectionable standards, peer review.

d. absolute standards, relative standards, peer review.

e. relative standards, peer review, objectives.

14. MBOs are likely to be ineffective in

a. global organizations.

b. hierarchical organizations that are implementing TQM.

c. service-sector organizations.

d. manufacturing plants with more than three production facilities.

e. hierarchical organizations where managers traditionally do not trust subordinates and do not delegate.

15. Advantages of MBO include all of the following except

a. employees have greater commitment to objectives they set.

b. employees know what is expected of them.

c. MBO provides a basis for performance evaluation.

d. MBO is a time-saving way to set goals.

e. employees know that performance is defined in terms of successfully meeting stated objectives.

Chapter Thirteen

REWARDS AND COMPENSATION

LEARNING OBJECTIVES

AFTER READING THIS CHAPTER, YOU WILL BE ABLE TO:

1. Describe the link between rewards and motivation.
2. Explain the various classifications of rewards.
3. Discuss why some rewards are membership-based.
4. Define the goal of compensation administration.
5. Discuss job evaluation and its four basic approaches.
6. Explain the evolution of the final wage structure.
7. Describe competency-based compensation programs.
8. Discuss why executives are paid significantly higher salaries than other employees in an organization.
9. Identify what is meant by the balance sheet approach to international compensation.

It's quickly approaching the end of the fiscal year for the organization, and a number of employees are getting excited. Year-end means only one thing—closing out the books and determining bonuses! But a closer look reveals something startling—those anxious for the bonus share one thing in common. They are the company's management team; the individuals generally higher paid to begin with. How did this select group earn their bonuses? On the efforts and sweat of their employees. What a motivator for workers—produce so well that your bosses get handsomely rewarded! Well, that may exist in a number of companies, but it doesn't at Remediation Technologies (RETEC). Company president, Robert Dunlap, knows who the real heroes are, his employees; and he makes sure the employees get their fair share first—even before any management person is rewarded![1]

Each year, RETEC, the Concord, Massachusetts environmental engineering firm, places 20 percent of pre-tax profits into a profit-sharing pool. The first dispersement of this money is to match contributions, up to 6 percent, of the money employees have set aside for their retirement. Monies that remain are then divided up as follows. Employees are recommended for a bonus based on their performance. Those who performed the best get a bigger piece of the pie than those who were just "satisfactory." The average, however, is approximately 3 percent of salary. Then, and only then, if monies still remain, are management personnel given cash bonuses. But don't think Dunlap's system penalizes management personnel. Some years, they do get a cash bonus. Some years they don't. But irrespective of the monies set aside for bonuses, these managers, as well as 20 percent of the employees, are given company stock and stock options.

Although Dunlap admits that his plan will never please everyone, he wants all to understand that it is the employee population that drives the company. Without their efforts, there'd be little need to concern themselves with dividing up pre-tax profits—they wouldn't exist. That organization culture, coupled with open communications about the company financial picture, has resulted in some of the most satisfied workers in the area.

Robert Dunlap knows how to keep his employees motivated. He rewards them well. In fact, in his company, Remediation Technologies, employees get their rewards before management personnel get theirs. This way, employees are certain to be rewarded for their efforts.

Intrinsic Rewards Rewards one receives from the job itself, such as pride in one's work, a feeling of accomplishment, or being part of a team.

Extrinsic Rewards Rewards one gets from the employer, usually money, a promotion, or benefits.

Introduction

"What's in it for me?" That is a question every person consciously or unconsciously asks before engaging in any form of behavior. Our knowledge of motivation tells us that people do what they do to satisfy some need. Before they do anything, therefore, they look for a payoff or reward.

The most obvious reward employees get from work is pay, and we will spend the major part of this chapter addressing pay as a reward as well as how compensation programs are established. However, rewards also include promotions, desirable work assignments, and a host of other less obvious payoffs—a smile, peer acceptance, a kind word of recognition, or even a professional massage![2]

The Linkage to Motivation

The place of rewards in our motivation model was made clear in Chapter 11. Since people behave in ways that they believe are in their best interests, they constantly look for payoffs for their efforts. They expect good job performance to lead to organizational goal attainment, which in turn leads to satisfying their individual goals or needs (see Figure 13-1).

Organizations, then, use rewards to motivate people. They rely on rewards to motivate job candidates to join the organization. They certainly rely on rewards to get employees to come to work and perform effectively once they are hired.[3]

In the following section, we will review the various types of rewards over which managers have discretion, and look at the properties of effective rewards, with particular emphasis on using rewards in ways that are consistent with the motivation model.

Types of Organizational Incentives

There are a number of ways to classify rewards. We have selected three of the most typical dichotomies: intrinsic versus extrinsic rewards, financial versus nonfinancial rewards, and performance-based versus membership-based rewards. As you will see, these categories are far from being mutually exclusive, yet all share one common thread—they assist in maintaining employee commitment.[4]

Intrinsic versus Extrinsic Rewards

Intrinsic rewards are the satisfactions one gets from the job itself. These satisfactions are self-initiated rewards, such as having pride in one's work, having a feeling of accomplishment, or being part of a team. Job enrichment, for instance, discussed in Chapter 11, can offer intrinsic rewards to employees by making work seem more meaningful.[5] **Extrinsic rewards,** on the other hand, include money, promotions, and benefits. Their common thread is that they are

Figure 13-1
Rewards and the Link to Motivation

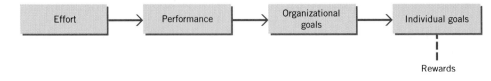

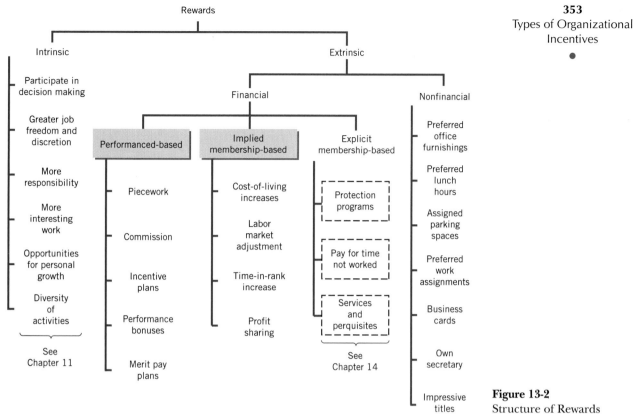

Figure 13-2
Structure of Rewards

external to the job and come from an outside source, mainly, management. For example, Apple Computer gives a PC to each of its employees. After one year on the job, the PC becomes the employee's personal property.[6] Thus, if an employee experiences feeling of achievement or personal growth from a job, we would label such rewards as intrinsic. If the employee receives a salary increase or a write-up in the company magazine, we would label these rewards as extrinsic. The general structure of rewards has been summarized in Figure 13-2.

Financial versus Nonfinancial Rewards

Rewards may or may not enhance the employee's financial well-being. If they do, they can do this directly—through wages, bonuses, profit sharing, and the like—or indirectly—through supportive benefits such as pension plans, paid vacations, paid sick leaves, and purchase discounts.

Nonfinancial rewards cover a smorgasbord of desirable "extras" that are potentially at the disposal of the organization. Their common link is that they do not increase the employee's financial position. Instead of making the employee's life better off the job, nonfinancial rewards emphasize making life on the job more attractive. The nonfinancial rewards that we will identify represent a few of the more obvious; however, the creation of these rewards is limited only by managers' ingenuity and ability to assess "payoffs" within their jurisdiction that individuals within the organization find desirable.

The old saying, "One man's food is another man's poison," applies to the entire subject of rewards, but specifically to the area of nonfinancial rewards. What one employee views as "something I've always wanted," another might find useless. Therefore, care must be taken in providing the "right" nonfinancial reward for each person. Yet where selection has been done properly, the benefits by way of increased performance to the organization should be significant.

Some workers are very status-conscious. A paneled office, a carpeted floor, a large walnut desk, or a private bathroom may be just the office furnishing that stimulates an employee toward top performance. Similarly, status-oriented employees may value an impressive job title, their own business cards, their own administrative assistant, or a well-located parking space with their name clearly painted underneath the "Reserved" sign. Similarly, if lunch is normally from noon to 1 P.M., the benefit of being able to take lunch at another, more preferred, time can be viewed as a reward. Having a chance to work with congenial colleagues, and achieving a desired work assignment or an assignment where the worker can operate without close supervision, are all nonfinancial rewards within management's discretion and, when carefully used, can provide stimulus for improved performance.

Performance-based versus Membership-based Rewards

The rewards that the organization allocates can be said to be based on either performance criteria or membership criteria. While managers in most organizations will vigorously argue that their reward system pays off for performance, you should recognize that this isn't always the case. Few organizations actually reward employees based on performance—a point we will discuss later in this chapter. Without question, the dominant basis for reward allocations in organizations is membership.

Performance-based Rewards
Rewards exemplified by the use of commissions, piecework pay plans, incentive systems, group bonuses, or other forms of merit pay.

Membership-based Rewards
Rewards that go to all employees regardless of performance.

Performance-based rewards are exemplified by the use of commissions, piecework pay plans, incentive systems, group bonuses, merit pay, or other forms of pay-for-performance plans. On the other hand, **membership-based rewards** include cost-of-living increases, benefits, and salary increases attributable to labor-market conditions, seniority or time in rank, credentials (such as a college degree or a graduate diploma), or future potential (e.g., the recent MBA out of a prestigious university). The key point here is that membership-based rewards are generally extended irrespective of an individual's, group's, or organization's performance. The difference between the two is not always obvious. In practice, performance may be only a minor determinant of rewards, despite academic theories holding that high motivation depends on performance-based rewards.

What Is Compensation Administration?

Why do aerospace engineers at AlliedSignal Technical Engineering Services in Houston, Texas, earn more than security guards? Intuitively, you would say that the engineers are more skilled, so they should earn more. But how about satellite technicians at AlliedSignal who keep satellites in space and capture the data that are being returned to the ground station? Should they make more or less than the aerospace engineers who design new satellites? The answer to questions such as these lies in job evaluation.

Job Evaluation Specifies the relative value of each job in the organization.

Job evaluation is the process whereby an organization systematically establishes its compensation program. In this process, jobs are compared in order to arrive at each job's appropriate worth. In this section we will discuss the broader topic of compensation, narrow our discussion to job evaluation methods, and conclude with a review of an increasingly controversial topic—executive compensation.

Employees exchange work for rewards. Probably the most important reward, and certainly the most obvious, is money. But employees don't earn the same amount of money. Why? The search for this answer moves us directly into the topic of compensation administration.

The goals of **compensation administration** are to design a cost-effective pay structure that will attract, motivate, and retain competent employees, and that also will be perceived as fair by these employees. *Fairness* is a term that frequently arises in the administration of an organization's compensation program. Organizations generally seek to pay the least that they have to in order to minimize costs, so fairness means a wage or salary that is adequate for the demands and requirements of the job. Of course, fairness is a two-way street: Employees also want fair compensation. As we pointed out in our earlier discussion of motivation, if employees perceive an imbalance in the relation of their efforts–rewards ratio to some comparative standard, they will act to correct the inequity. So the search for fairness is pursued by both employers and employees.

Compensation Administration
The process of managing a company's compensation program.

Government Influence on Compensation

In Chapter 3, we described how government policies shape and influence HRM. This influence, however, is not equally felt in all areas. For example, collective bargaining and the employee selection process are heavily constrained by government rules and regulations. In contrast, this influence is low in the areas of strategic human resource planning and orientation. Compensation administration falls into the former category. Government policies set minimum wages and benefits that employers must meet, and these policies provide protection for certain groups (see Figure 13-3). The laws and regulations we will discuss are not meant to comprehensively cover government's influence on compensation administration. Rather, they are presented as highlights. The point of these highlights should be to make you aware that government constraints reduce management's discretion on compensation decisions. An abundance of laws and regulations define the general parameters within which managers decide what is fair compensation. Let's look at some of these.

The **Fair Labor Standards Act** stipulates that nonexempt employees must be paid time-and-one-half for overtime work beyond forty hours a week. This act, when coupled with protective state laws, also establishes that organizations must pay at least the minimum wage. For instance, in 1995, all organizations except for the smallest businesses and a few exempt classes had to pay their employees at least $4.25 an hour. And the Clinton administration in 1995 proposed legislation to increase the hourly rate. Both federal and state governments have enacted laws requiring employees who contract with the government to pay prevailing rates. In the federal sector, the secretary of labor is required to review industry rates in the specific locality to set a prevailing rate which becomes the minimum under the contract prescribed under the Walsh–Healy Act. Under this act government contractors must pay also time-and-a-half for all work in excess of eight hours a day or forty hours a week.

The Civil Rights Act and the Equal Pay Act, among other laws, protect employees from discrimination. Just as it is illegal to discriminate in hiring, organi-

Fair Labor Standards Act
Passed in 1938, this act established laws outlining minimum wage, overtime pay, and maximum hour requirements for most U.S. workers.

YOUR RIGHTS

UNDER THE FAIR LABOR STANDARDS ACT

Federal Minimum Wage

$4.25

Minimum Wage of at least $4.25 per hour beginning April 1, 1991.

Certain full-time students, student learners, apprentices, and workers with disabilities may be paid less than the minimum wage under special certificates issued by the Department of Labor.

Tip credit — The tip credit which an employer may claim with respect to "Tipped Employees" is 50 percent of the applicable minimum wage.

Overtime Pay

At least 1½ times your regular rate of pay for all hours worked over 40 in a workweek.

Child Labor

An employee must be at least **16** years old to work in most non-farm jobs and at least **18** to work in non-farm jobs declared hazardous by the Secretary of Labor. Youths **14** and **15** years old may work outside school hours in various non-manufacturing, non-mining, non-hazardous jobs under the following conditions:

No more than —
- **3** hours on a school day or **18** hours in a school week;
- **8** hours on a non-school day or **40** hours in a non-school week.

Also, work may not begin before 7 a.m. or end after 7 p.m., except from June 1 through Labor Day, when evening hours are extended to 9 p.m. Different rules apply in agricultural employment.

Training Wage

A training wage of at least 85 percent of the applicable minimum wage, or $3.35 per hour, whichever is greater, may be paid to most employees under 20 years of age for up to 90 days under certain conditions. Individuals may be employed at a training wage for a second 90-day period by a different employer if certain additional requirements are met. No individual may be employed at a training wage, in any number of jobs, for more than a total of 180 days. Employers may not displace regular employees in order to hire those eligible for a training wage. **The training wage provisions expire March 31, 1993.** Note to Employers: The requirements for use of a training wage are very specific. If you need assistance, you should contact the nearest Wage and Hour office.

ENFORCEMENT

The Department of Labor may recover back wages either administratively or through court action, for the employees that have been underpaid in violation of the law. Violations may result in civil or criminal action.

Fines of up to $10,000 per minor may be assessed against employers who violate the child labor provisions of the law and up to $1,000 per violation against employers who willfully or repeatedly violate the minimum wage or overtime pay provisions. This law prohibits discriminating against or discharging workers who file a complaint or participate in any proceedings under the Act.

Note: ■ Certain occupations and establishments are exempt from the minimum wage and/or overtime pay provisions.
- Special provisions apply to workers in Puerto Rico and American Samoa.
- Where state law requires a higher minimum wage, the higher standard applies.

FOR ADDITIONAL INFORMATION, CONTACT the Wage and Hour Division office nearest you — listed in your telephone directory under United States Government, Labor Department.

The law requires employers to display this poster where employees can readily see it.

U.S. Department of Labor
Employment Standards Administration
Wage and Hour Division
Washington, D.C. 20210

WH Publication 1088
Revised April 1991

*U.S. Government Printing Office: 1991 — 300-812

Figure 13-3
Federal Minimum Wage

zations cannot discriminate in pay on the basis of race, color, creed, age, or sex. Interestingly, if you recall our discussion of EEO protection for same-sex partners in Chapter 4, you'll remember that sexual orientation is not a protected category. Early research indicates that sexual orientation is adversely affecting one's pay levels. For example, a study out of the University of Maryland, published in the *Industrial and Labor Relations Review,* indicates that homosexual males earn between 11 and 27 percent less than heterosexual men.[7]

The **Equal Pay Act** of 1963 mandates that organizations compensate men and women doing the same job in the organization the same rate pay. The Equal Pay Act was designed to lessen the pay gap between male and female pay rates. Although progress is being made, women in general still earn roughly 76 percent of what their male counterparts earn.[8] Some of this difference is attributable to perceived male- versus female-dominated occupations, but the Equal Pay Act requires employers to eliminate pay differences for the same job. That is, all salaries must be established on the basis of skill, responsibility, effort, and working conditions.[9] For example, if an organization is hiring computer programmers, new employees, irrespective of their sex, must be paid the same initial salary because the attributes for the job are the same. However, it is important to note that the Equal Pay Act typically affects only initial job salaries. If two workers, one male and one female, perform at different levels during the course of the year, it is conceivable that if performance is rewarded, in the next period their pay may be different. This is permitted under the act.

Equal Pay Act Passed in 1963, this act requires equal pay for equal work.

Recall also from Chapter 3 our discussion on comparable worth. Although job evaluation techniques, described later, can reduce this concern, comparable worth is not an Equal Pay Act concern. Rather it is a societal issue designed to further reduce the male–female pay disparity. Yet it is interesting to note that while comparable worth continues to be debated, especially in this era of workforce diversity, other countries have moved forward to correct the situation. For instance, in Canada, the 1988 Ontario Pay Equity Act went into effect.[10] Under this law, Canadian employers must equate salaries in the female-dominated jobs in their organizations with those in the male-dominated ones. For example, in reviewing this law, Canadian lawmakers found that the skills, knowledge, and abilities of nursing assistants in hospitals were comparable to plumbers working in the same location. Accordingly, under the law, these nursing assistants were given a 17 percent pay increase.[11]

Job Evaluation and the Pay Structure

The essence of compensation administration is job evaluation and the establishment of a pay structure. Let us turn now to a definition of job evaluation and a discussion of how it is done.

What Is Job Evaluation?

In Chapter 5, we introduced job analysis as the process of describing the duties of a job, authority relationships, skills required, conditions of work, and additional relevant information. We stated that the data generated from job analysis could be used to develop job descriptions and specifications, as well as to do job evaluations (see "HRM in a De-Jobbed Organization"). By job evaluation, we mean using the information in job analysis to systematically determine the value of each job in relation to all jobs within the organization. In short, job

What If:

HRM in a De-Jobbed Organization

Job evaluation, the systematic examination of jobs in organizations, is designed to specify the relative value of each job to the organization. Similar to the discussion of job analysis, the process of job evaluation is contingent on having accurate and complete job descriptions. Without these prerequisites, however, job evaluation becomes a process of subjectively determining how much to pay any position. The question becomes, without the job analysis serving as the foundation of the job-evaluation process, has this salary-determining event been rendered obsolete? In its current form, more likely, yes.

However, job evaluation will unlikely disappear altogether. Rather than being based on the job-analysis process and job descriptions, job evaluation is likely to change its focus. That is, rather than focus on the jobs themselves, the process may focus on individual workers. How so? Consider the following. There is a movement today to rethink how employees are paid. Rather than focusing on the value of the job to the company, this new process looks at what value the individual adds to the organization. For example, under this new job-evaluation method, employees will be paid according to the degree of skill, knowledge, and specific behaviors they bring to the job. Those who possess these "competencies" in greater detail will be paid a higher wage rate. Consequently, pay systems will move away from the traditional approach of paying the job to one in which the individual worker becomes the primary focus.

When you consider such a system, paying employees according to what they add to the organization is consistent with most aspects of HRM we've discussed. The specific competencies required of employees should be detailed in the strategic human resource planning process. In this manner, organizations are paying specifically for those "things" that will help them achieve their goals. Likewise, knowing that the organization rewards competencies, rather than other factors, helps individuals to better manage their career growth. Those who wish to be paid higher salaries know unquestionably what is required for the next "step." Furthermore, such a process is critically linked to the motivation process, in that performance dictates the rewards one receives.

Traditional job-evaluation techniques, then, may not be losing ground in today's organizations. Rather, they may be appropriately changing to reflect the new work force we employ. When you consider the contingent work force that exists, and the number of consultants employed for projects, paying people for their value added makes more sense. For example, have you ever wondered why some consultants can command $250 per hour, while others may struggle to get $25? The answer lies in the skills, knowledge, and behaviors that each brings to the client organization. Those who possess special competencies are "worth" more to an organization, and as such are paid accordingly. Wouldn't you prefer to be compensated based on what value you bring to the organization? In many respects, that is precisely what employees have been wanting for years—fair and equitable payment for the services they render.

evaluation seeks to rank all the jobs in the organization and place them in a hierarchy that will reflect the relative worth of each. Importantly, this is a ranking of jobs, not people. Job evaluation assumes normal performance of the job by a typical worker. So, in effect, the process ignores individual abilities or the performance of the jobholder.

The ranking that results from job evaluation is the means to an end, not an end in itself. It should be used to determine the organization's pay structure. Note that we say should; in practice, we will find that this is not always the case. External labor market conditions, collective bargaining, and individual differences may require a compromise between the job evaluation ranking and the actual pay structure. Yet even when such compromises are necessary, job evaluation can provide an objective standard from which modifications can be made.

Isolating Job Evaluation Criteria

The heart of job evaluation is the determination of what criteria will be used to arrive at the ranking. It is easy to say that jobs are valued and ranked by their relative job worth, but there is far more ambiguity when we attempt to state what it is that makes one job higher than another in the job structure hierarchy. Most job-evaluation plans use responsibility, skill, effort, and working conditions as major criteria,[12] but each of these, in turn, can be broken down into more specific terms. Skill, for example, is often measured "through the intelligence or mental requirements of the job, the knowledge required, motor or manual skills needed, and the learning that occurs."[13] But other criteria can and have been used: supervisory controls, complexity, personal contacts, and the physical demands needed.[14]

You should not expect the criteria to be constant across jobs. Since jobs differ, it is traditional to separate jobs into common groups. This usually means that, for example, production, clerical, sales, professional, and managerial jobs are evaluated separately. Treating like groups similarly allows for more valid rankings within categories, but still leaves unsettled the importance of criteria between categories. Separation by groups may permit us to say the position of die-design engineer in the production group requires more mental effort than that of a production supervisor, and hence gets a higher ranking; but it does not readily resolve whether greater mental effort is necessary for die-design engineers than for office managers.

Methods of Job Evaluation

There are four basic methods of job evaluation currently in use: ranking, classification, factor comparison, and point method.[15]

Ranking Method The **ranking method** requires a committee, typically composed of both management and employee representatives, to arrange jobs in a simple rank order, from highest to lowest. No attempt is made to break down the jobs by specific weighted criteria. The committee members merely compare two jobs and judge which one is more important or difficult. Then they compare another job with the first two, and so on until all the jobs have been evaluated and ranked.

Ranking Method Rating employees from highest to lowest.

The most obvious limitation to the ranking method is its sheer unmanageability when there are a large number of jobs; imagine the difficulty of trying to rank hundreds or thousands of jobs in the organization! Other drawbacks to be

Classification Method Method of job evaluation that focuses on creating common job grades based on skills, knowledge, and abilities.

considered are the subjectivity of the method—there are no definite or consistent standards by which to justify the rankings—and because jobs are only ranked in terms of order, we have no knowledge of the distance between the ranks.

Classification Method   The **classification method** was made popular by the U.S. Civil Service Commission, now the Office of Personnel Management (OPM). The OPM requires that classification grades be established. These classifications are created by identifying some common denominator—skills, knowledge, responsibilities—with the desired goal being the creation of a number of distinct classes or grades of jobs. Examples might include shop jobs, clerical jobs, sales jobs, and so on, depending, of course, on the type of jobs the organization requires.

Once the classifications are established, they are ranked in an overall order of importance according to the criteria chosen, and each job is placed in its appropriate classification. This latter action is generally done by comparing each position's job description against the classification description. At the OPM, for example, evaluators have classified both Budget and Finance Clerk I and Typist III positions as GS-5 grades, while Contracts and Procurement officers, and IRS Audit Supervisory jobs have both been graded as GS-13.

The classification method shares most of the disadvantages of the ranking approach, plus the difficulty of writing classification descriptions, judging which jobs go where, and dealing with jobs that appear to fall into more than one classification. On the plus side, the classification method has proven itself successful and viable in classifying millions of kinds and levels of jobs in the civil service.

Factor Comparison Method A method of job analysis in which job factors are compared to determine the worth of the job.

Factor Comparison Method   **Factor comparison method** is a sophisticated and quantitative ranking method. The evaluators select key jobs in the organization as standards. Those jobs chosen should be well known, with established pay rates in the community, and they should consist of a representative cross-section of all jobs that are being evaluated. Typically, fifteen to fifty key jobs are selected by the committee.[16]

What factors in the key jobs will the other jobs be compared against? These criteria are usually mental requirements, skill requirements, physical requirements, responsibility, and working conditions. Once the key jobs are identified and the criteria chosen, committee members rank the key jobs on the criteria. The next step is the most interesting dimension in the factor comparison method. The committee agrees on the base rate (usually expressed on an hourly basis) for each of the key jobs and then allocates this base rate among the five criteria (see Table 13-1). For example, in one organization the job of maintenance electrician was chosen as a key job with an hourly rate of $17.40. The committee allocated $4.25 to mental effort, $5.15 for skill, $2.50 for physical effort, $3.50 to responsibility, and $2.00 for working conditions. These amounts then became standards by which other jobs in the organization could be evaluated.

The final step in factor comparison requires the committee to compare its overall judgments and resolve any discrepancies. The system is in place when the allocations to the key jobs are clear and understood, and high agreement has been achieved in committee members' judgments about how much of each criteria every job has.

Drawbacks to factor comparison include its complexity; its use of the same five criteria to assess all jobs, when, in fact, jobs differ across and within organi-

TABLE 13-1   Factor Comparison Method (Selected Positions)

Jobs	Hourly Pay	Mental Requirements	Skill Requirements	Physical Requirements	Responsibility	Working Conditions
Maintenance Electrician	$17.40	$4.25	$5.15	$2.50	$3.50	$2.00
Inventory Control Specialists	14.95	4.05	4.65	2.00	3.25	1.00
Warehouse Stocker	12.60	2.75	3.50	1.80	2.30	2.25
Administrative Assistant	11.15	3.25	3.00	1.00	2.65	1.25
Maintenance Electrician Helper	10.45	2.65	2.00	2.20	1.60	2.00

zations; and its dependence on key jobs as anchor points. "To the extent that one or more key jobs change over time either without detection or without correction of the scale, users of the job comparison scale are basing decisions on what might be described figuratively as a badly warped ruler."[17] On the positive side, factor comparison requires a unique set of standard jobs for each organization, so it is a tailor-made approach. As such, it is automatically designed to meet the specific needs of each organization. Another advantage is that jobs are compared with other jobs to determine a relative value, and since relative job values are what job evaluation seeks, the method is logical.

Point Method   The last method we will present breaks down jobs based on various identifiable criteria (such as skill, effort, and responsibility) and then allocates points to each of these criteria. Depending on the importance of each criterion to performing the job, appropriate weights are given, points are summed, and jobs with similar point totals are placed in similar pay grades.

An excerpt from a **point method** chart for clerical positions is shown in Figure 13-4. Each clerical job would be evaluated by deciding, for example, the degree of education required to perform the job satisfactorily. The first degree might require the equivalent of skill competencies associated with ten years of elementary and secondary education; the second degree might require competencies associated with four years of high school; and so forth.

The point method offers the greatest stability of the four approaches we have presented. Jobs may change over time, but the rating scales established under the point method stay intact. Additionally, the methodology underlying the approach contributes to a minimum of rating error. On the other hand, the point method is complex, making it costly and time-consuming to develop. The key criteria must be carefully and clearly identified, degrees of factors have to be agreed upon in terms that mean the same to all raters, the weight of each criterion has to be established, and point values must be assigned to degrees. While it is expensive and time-consuming to both implement and maintain, the point method appears to be the most widely-used method. Furthermore, this method can be effective for addressing the comparable worth issue.[18]

Point Method Breaking down jobs based on identifiable criteria and the degree to which these criteria exist on the job.

Establishing the Pay Structure

Once the job evaluation is complete, its data become the nucleus for the development of the organization's pay structure.[19] This means pay rates or ranges will be established that are compatible with the ranks, classifications, or points arrived at through job evaluation.

Figure 13-4

Excerpts from a Point Method

Job Class: Clerk

Factor	1st Degree	2nd Degree	3rd Degree	4th Degree	5th Degree
Skill					
1. Education	22	44	66	88	110
2. Problem solving	14	28	42	56	70
Responsibility					
1. Safety of others	5	10	15	20	25
2. Work of others	7	14	21	28	35

2. Problem solving:

This factor examines the types of problems dealt with in your job. Indicate the one level that is most representative of the majority of your job responsibilities.

Degree 1: Actions are performed in a set order per written or verbal instruction. Problems are referred to supervisor.

Degree 2: Solves routine problems and makes various choices regarding the order in which the work is performed within standard practices. May obtain information from varied sources.

Degree 3: Solves varied problems that require general knowledge of company policies and procedures applicable within area of responsibility. Decisions made based on a choice from established alternatives. Expected to act within standards and established procedures.

Degree 4: Requires analytical judgment, initiative, or innovation in dealing with complex problems or situations. Evaluation not easy because there is little precedent or information may be incomplete.

Degree 5: Plans, delegates, coordinates, and/or implements complex tasks involving new or constantly changing problems or situations. Involves the origination of new technologies or policies for programs or projects. Actions limited only by company policies and budgets.

Source: Material reprinted with permission of The Dartnell Corporation, Chicago, IL 60640.

Any of the four job evaluation methods can provide the necessary input for developing the organization's overall pay structure. Each has its strengths and weaknesses, but because of its wide use, we will use the point method to show how point totals are combined with wage survey data to form wage curves.

Wage Surveys   Many organizations use surveys to gather factual information on pay practices within specific communities and among firms in their industry.[20] This information is used for comparison purposes. It can tell management if the organization's wages are in line with those of other employers and, in cases where there is a short supply of individuals to fill certain positions, may be used to actually set wage levels.[21] Where does an organization get wage salary data? The U.S. Department of Labor, through its Bureau of Labor Statistics, regularly publishes a vast amount of wage data broken down by geographic area, industry, and occupation. Many industry and employee associations also conduct surveys and make their results available. But organizations can conduct their own surveys, and many large ones do.

It would not be unusual, for instance, for the HRM director at Rockwell International in Texas to regularly share wage data on key positions. Jobs such as maintenance engineer, electrical engineer, computer programmer, or administrative assistant would be identified, and comprehensive descriptions of these jobs would be given to firms in the community like TRW, Litton, Hewlett-Packard, NCR, Control Data, and Motorola. This is most often done by way of a mailed questionnaire, but personal interviews and telephone interviews also can be used.[22] When organizations do their own **wage surveys,** they are not limited in what they can ask. In addition to the average wage level for a specific job, other information frequently requested includes entry-level and maximum wage rates, shift differentials, overtime pay practices, vacation and holiday allowances, the number of pay periods, and the length of the normal workday and workweek.

Wage Curves When management arrives at point totals from job evaluation and obtains survey data on what comparable organizations are paying for similar jobs, then a wage curve can be fitted to the data. An example of a **wage curve** is shown in Figure 13-5. This example assumes use of the point method and plots point totals and wage data. A separate wage curve can be constructed based on survey data and compared for discrepancies.

A completed wage curve tells management the average relationship between points of established pay grades and wage base rates. Importantly, it can identify jobs whose pay is out of the trend line. When a job's pay rate is too high, it should be identified as a "red circle" rate. This means that pay is frozen or below-average increases are granted until the structure is adjusted upward to put the circled rate within the normal range. Of course, there will be times when a wage rate is out of line but not red circled. The need to attract or keep individuals with specific skills may require a wage rate outside the normal range. To continue attracting these individuals, however, may ultimately upset the internal consistencies supposedly inherent in the wage structure. It also should be pointed out that a wage rate may be too low. Such undervalued jobs carry a

Wage Surveys Used to gather factual data on pay practices among firms and companies within specific communities.

Wage Curve The result of the plotting of points of established pay grades against wage base rates to identify the general pattern of wages and find individuals whose wages are out of line.

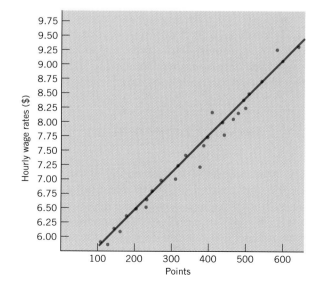

Figure 13-5
A Wage Curve

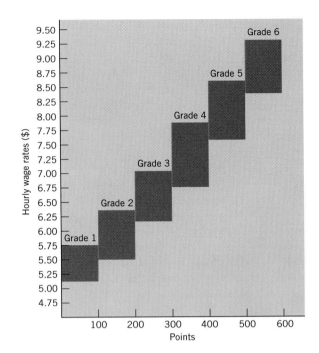

Figure 13-6
A Wage Structure

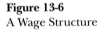

Wage Structure A pay scale showing ranges of pay within each grade.

"green circle" rate, and attempts should be made to grant these jobs above-average pay increases.

The Wage Structure   It is only a short step from plotting a wage curve to developing the organization's **wage structure.** Jobs that are similar—in terms of classes, grades, or points—are grouped together. For instance, pay grade 1 may cover the range from 0 to 150 points, pay grade 2 from 151 to 300 points, and so on. As shown in Figure 13-6, the result is a logical hierarchy of wages.[23] The more important jobs are paid more; and as individuals assume jobs of greater importance, they rise within the wage hierarchy. Jobs may also be paid in accordance to what is commonly referred to as knowledge-based pay.[24]

Irrespective of the determinants, notice that each pay grade has a range and that the ranges overlap. Typically, organizations design their wage structures with ranges in each grade to reflect different tenure in positions, as well as levels of performance. Additionally, while most organizations create a degree of overlap between grades, employees who reach the top of their grade can only increase their pay by moving to a higher grade.

Some Special Cases of Compensation

As traditional organizations are rapidly changing in the dynamic world in which we live, so, too, are compensation programs. Most notably, organizations can no longer continue to increase wage rates by a certain percentage each year (a cost-of-living raise), without some comparable increase in performance. Accordingly, more organizations are moving to varied themes of the pay-for-performance systems. These may include incentive compensation plans, and competency and team-based compensation.

Incentive Compensation Plans

In addition to the basic wage structure, organizations that are sincerely committed to developing a compensation system that is designed around performance will want to consider the use of incentive pay. Typically given in addition to—rather than in place of—the basic wage, incentive plans should be viewed as an additional dimension to the wage structure we have described. Incentives can be paid based on individual, group, or organization-wide performance—a pay-for-performance concept.

Individual Incentives   Individual incentive plans pay off for individual performances.[25] For the 1990s, these plans have been the biggest trend in compensation administration in the United States.[26] Popular approaches include merit pay, piecework plans, time-savings bonuses, and commissions.

One popular and almost universally used incentive system is **merit pay.**[27] Under a merit pay plan, employees who show merit have a sum of money added to their base salary. Somewhat likened to a cost-of-living raise, merit pay should differ in that the percentage of increase to the base wage rate is attributable solely to performance. Those who perform better should receive more merit pay. Often, though, this is not the case, and merit pay is just a substitute for cost-of-living raises.[28] And similar to the cost-of-living raise, merit monies accrue permanently to the base salary, and become the new base from which future percentage increases are calculated. The problem with merit pay, or a cost-of-living system, is that pay increases are always expected. But what if the company has a bad year, or employees don't produce what is expected of them? Under these traditional systems, wage increases still are expected.

Organizations today are refuting that logic. AlliedSignal, for example, will give employees a 3 percent raise only if they increase productivity by 6 percent. A 6 percent raise requires a 9 percent productivity gain. But, although a pay-for-performance incentive exists, the company will raise pay by 2 percent even if all goals are missed.[29] Why? Even today, not giving a pay increase, no matter how nominal, can lead to decreased morale, and further productivity problems.

Merit Pay An increase in one's pay, usually given on an annual basis.

How can this employee get a bigger pay raise next year? At AlliedSignal's Fostoria, Ohio, spark-plug plant, by increasing productivity 9 percent in the coming year, she can double her pay increase to 6 percent. The incentive, then, is to help the organization achieve its goals, while simultaneously, getting something in return for the effort.

●

Piecework Plans A compensation plan whereby employees are typically paid for the number of units they actually produce.

While the merit pay plan is the most widely used, the best-known incentive is undoubtedly piecework. Under a straight **piecework plan,** the employee is typically guaranteed a minimal hourly rate for meeting some preestablished standard output. For output over this standard, the employee earns so much for each piece produced. Differential piece-rate plans establish two rates—one up to standard, and another when the employee exceeds the standard. The latter rate, of course, is higher to encourage the employee to beat the standard.

Individual incentives can be based on time saved as well as output generated. At Jacobs Engineering Group in Pasadena, California, engineers are not given annual pay raises. Rather, based on their performance, these individuals are given an incentive bonus. For the past few years, this bonus has averaged more than 5 percent of their annual salary—greater than the cost-of-living adjustments if tied to inflation.[30] As with piecework, the employee can expect a minimal guaranteed hourly rate, but in this case, the bonus is achieved for doing a standard hour's work in less than sixty minutes. Employees who can do an hour's work in fifty minutes obtain a bonus that is some percentage (say 50 percent) of the labor saved.

Sales personnel frequently work on a commission basis. Added to a lower base wage, they get an amount that represents a percentage of the sales price. On encyclopedias, it may be a hefty 25 or 30 percent. On sales of multimillion-dollar aircraft or city sewer systems, commissions are frequently 1 percent or less.

Individual incentives work best where clear performance objectives can be set and where tasks are independent.[31] If these conditions are not met, individual incentives can create dysfunctional competition or encourage workers to "cut corners." Coworkers can become the enemy, individuals can create inflated perceptions of their own work while deflating the work of others, and the work environment may become characterized by reduced interaction and communications between employees. And if corners are cut, quality and safety may also be compromised. For example, when Monsanto tied workers' bonuses to plant safety, covering up accidents was encouraged.[32]

A potentially negative effect with incentive for performance is that you may "get what you pay for." Since the incentives are tied to specific goals (which are only part of the total outcomes expected from a job), people may not perform the not measured, and thus not rewarded, activities in favor of the measured, rewarded ones. For example, if your school held a colloquium and brought in a guest speaker, and your instructor decided to take your class, would you go? Your response might be contingent on whether the colloquium was a requirement, the content of which could be included on an exam, and where attendance was taken. But if it was just for your information, attending might not be as high a priority. Despite the potential negative repercussions that individual incentives can cause in inappropriate situations, they are undoubtedly widespread in practice.

Group Incentives   Each of the individual incentives we described also can be used on a group basis; that is, two or more employees can be paid for their combined performance. When are group incentives desirable? They make the most sense where employees' tasks are interdependent and thus require cooperation.[33]

Plant-wide Incentives An incentive system that rewards all members of the plant based on how well the entire group performed.

Plant-wide Incentives   The goal of **plant-wide incentives** is to direct the efforts of all employees toward achieving overall organizational effectiveness. This type of incentive, like that of E.I. DuPont de Nemours Company, produces rewards for all employees based on organization-wide cost reduction or profit sharing.[34]

Kaiser Steel, for example, developed in one of its plants a cost-reduction plan that provides monthly bonuses to employees.[35] The amount of the bonus was determined by computing one-third of all increases in productivity attributable to cost savings as a result of technological change or increased effort. Additionally, Lincoln Electric has had a year-end bonus system for decades, which in some years has provided an annual bonus "ranging from a low of 55 percent to a high of 115 percent of annual earnings."[36] The Lincoln Electric plan pays off handsomely when employees beat previous years' performance standards. Since this bonus is added to the employee's salary, it has made the Lincoln Electric workers the highest-paid electrical workers in the United States.[37]

One of the best-known organization-wide incentive systems is the **Scanlon Plan.**[38] It seeks to bring about cooperation between management and employees through the sharing of problems, goals, and ideas. (It is interesting to note that many of the quality circle programs instituted in the 1980s were a direct outgrowth of the Scanlon Plan.[39]) Under Scanlon, each department in the organization has a committee composed of supervisor and employee representatives. Suggestions for labor-saving improvements are funneled to the committee and, if accepted, cost savings and productivity gains are shared by all emploees, not just the individual who made the suggestion. Typically, about 80 percent of the suggestions prove practical and are adopted.

Another incentive plan that gained momentum in the early 1990s is called IMPROSHARE.[40] **IMPROSHARE,** which is an acronym for Improving Productivity through Sharing, uses a mathematical formula for determining employees' bonuses.[41] For example, if workers can save labor costs in producing a product, a predetermined portion of the labor savings will go to the employee. Where IMPROSHARE exists, productivity gains up to 18 percent have been identified, with most of the gains coming from reduced defects and less production downtime.[42]

Profit-sharing plans, or gainsharing plans, are also plant-wide incentives. They allow employees to share in the success of a firm by distributing part of the company's profits back to the workers. In essence, employees become owners of the company. The logic behind profit-sharing plans is that they increase commitment and loyalty to the organization. For instance, at Science Applications International Corporation, a high-tech research and engineering company in San Diego,[43] workers own almost half of the business. Each employee is entitled to a number of shares of company stock based on how profitable the company is over the year. As such, when employees encounter problems with customers, or the work process, it is in their best interest to take corrective action; you are more likely to be cost-conscious if you share in the benefits. On the negative side, employees often find it difficult to relate their efforts to the profit-sharing bonus. Their individual impact on the organization's profitability may be minuscule. Additionally, factors such as economic conditions and actions of competitors—which are outside the control of the employees—may have a far greater impact on the company's profitability than any actions of the employees themselves.[44]

All the plant-wide incentives suffer from a dilution effect. It is hard for employees to see how their efforts result in the organization's overall perfomance. These plans also tend to distribute their payoffs at wide intervals; a bonus paid in March 1997 for your efforts in 1996 loses a lot of its reinforcement capabilities. Finally, we should not overlook what happens when organization-wide incentives become both large and recurrent. When this happens, it is not unusual

How has American Express provided an incentive to its employees? Based on how well workers fulfill customer satisfaction, employee productivity, and stockholder wealth creation goals, employees are eligible for a bonus up to 4 percent of their base salary. And in 1993, 98 percent of these employees at the Phoenix operations center received a bonus.

Scanlon Plan An organization-wide incentive program focusing on cooperation between management and employees through sharing problems, goals, and ideas.

IMPROSHARE A special type of incentive plan using a specific mathematical formula for determining employee bonuses.

for the employee to begin to anticipate and expect the bonus. Employees may adjust their spending patterns as if the bonus were a certainty. The bonus loses some of its motivating properties then, because it comes to be perceived as a membership-based reward.[45]

Competency-based Compensation

So far in our discussion of establishing pay plans, we've implied one specific aspect of the process. That is, we pay jobs. People who hold those jobs just happen to get the salary assigned to that position. That assumption, however, may be changing. Organizations like Towers Perrin are advocating something radically different.[46] Rather than thinking of the job as the most critical aspect to the organization, such organizations view the people as an organization's competitive advantage. When that conviction dominates, compensation programs become one of rewarding competencies, or the "skills, knowledge, and behaviors"[47] employees possess (see "Meet Marc E. Lattoni"). Let's look at how this system works.

Competency-based Compensation Programs Organizational pay system that rewards skills, knowledge, and behaviors.

The premise behind **competency-based compensation programs** is that individuals progress through a four-staged model of development—apprentice, doer, mentor, and strategic leader—sometimes referred to as job families.[48] During the first stage, *apprentice,* workers are dependent on the assistance of others. They perform their work under direct supervision, and can be considered a new learner to the job. Salaries in this stage are the lowest. At the *doer* stage, employees begin to learn the job for which they were hired. They contribute significantly to achieving unit goals, and have assumed some sense of independence and autonomy in performing their work. In other words, at the doer stage, we have an empowered employee. Hence, Stage II employees have greater competencies, and thus are compensated at a greater rate than apprentices. At Stage III, the *mentor* stage, the employee now accepts greater responsibility for achieving unit goals. This may include developing others, setting unit goals, and having the responsibility and being held accountable for the unit's performance. In other words, the mentor becomes the facilitator and leader of the unit. Because of these added responsibilities, mentors are paid a higher salary than doers. The final stage is the *strategic leader.* Whereas the mentor has unit responsibilities, the strategic leader has organizational responsibilities. This means establishing the organization's direction, as well as having responsibility for achieving those goals. The highest rate of pay, therefore, goes to individuals possessing strategic leader competencies.

What in essence has occurred is a pay scheme based on the specific competencies an employee possesses. These may include knowledge of the business and its core competencies, skills to fulfill these core requirements, and demonstrated employee behaviors such as leadership, problem solving, decision making, and planning.[49] Based on the degree to which these competencies exist, pay levels are established. For example, all individuals who are evaluated at the apprentice stage would be paid according to some pre-set level. In competency-based pay plans, these pre-set levels are called **broad-banding** (see Figure 13-7). That is, those who possess a level of competencies within a certain range will be grouped together in a pay category. Pay increases then, are awarded for growth in personal competencies, as well as the contribution one makes to the organization. Accordingly, career and pay advancement will not be tied to a promotion, per se, but rather to how much more one is capable of contributing to the organization's goals and objectives.

Broad-banding Paying employees at preset levels based on the level of competencies they possess.

If you are making the connection to a few pages ago when we discussed the

Marc E. Latoni

Practice Manager for
Employee Pay
Towers Perrin, Canada

Mark Latoni is a member of the Calgary Human Resources consulting team and is Practice Manager for Employee Pay consulting for Towers Perrin in Canada. Prior to joining Towers Perrin, Marc was a senior consultant and manager for a major actuarial and consulting firm in their Montreal, Toronto, and Calgary offices. Prior to that he was a partner in a wellknown Canadian firm of human resources consultants. Marc holds a Bachelor of Commerce degree in Management from Loyola College and a masters in Business Administration from Concordia University in Montreal. He has authored several articles on compensation and competency development, and is a frequent speaker on compensation issues.

Marc consults to a wide variety of clients in the areas of total compensation design, compensation strategy development, competency based rewards, and salary management. He has worked with a diverse cross section of organizations, large and small, in the private, para-public and public sectors, assisting them to develop and implement cost-effective compensation strategies that reflect and reinforce organization values. In what ways?

Marc has been spending much of his time helping organizations to understand competency-based pay systems. The Towers Perrin approach views competency pay systems on a three-phased approach. Phase one involves strategy clarification and capabilities assessment. It's during this phase that the organization defines its business goals and identifies its capabilities. In phase two, these business goals are translated into the individual skills, experiences, and behaviors required by employees to maintain organizational capabilities and reach corporate goals. Once this framework has been established, phase three focuses on implementation. During this phase, cultural change in the organization will take place—most notably, involving employees in most aspects of the organization that affect them. From employee communications to new ways of dealing with performance and pay issues, substantial HRM activities will occur to support and foster the competency-based compensation approach.

Competency-based pay systems aren't a company decision to be taken lightly. Instead, they represent a change from the status quo to a system where employees are viewed as adding economic value to the organization. In organizations that have found value in this approach, better financial results have occurred. Involving employees creates an environment where both the organization and its members can succeed.

point method of job evaluation, you are reading attentively. However, the point method looked specifically at the job, and its worth to the company. Competency-based pay plans assesses these "points" based on the value added by the employee in assisting the organization in achieving its goals.

As more organizations move toward competency-based pay plans, HRM will play a critical role. Just as we discussed on Chapter 5 on SHRP, once the direction of the organization is established, attracting, developing, motivating, and retaining competent individuals becomes essential. This will continue to have implications for recruiting, training and development, career development, performance appraisals, as well as pay and reward systems.[50] Not only will HRM ensure that it has the right people at the right place, but it will have assembled a competent team of employees who add significant value to the organization.

●

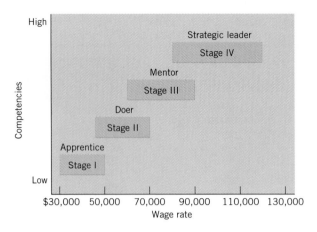

Figure 13-7
Competency-based

Team-based Rewards Rewards
based on how well the team
performed.

Team-based Compensation

You've just been handed a copy of the course syllabus for the business policy course you're taking this semester, and quickly your eyes glance at how the final grade will be calculated: two tests—a midterm and a final—and a class project. Intrigued, you read further about the class project. You and four other classmates will be responsible for thoroughly analyzing a failing company. You are to make recommendations about the company's financial picture, human resources, product lines, competitive advantage, and strategic direction. The group is to turn in a case paper of no less than fifty pages, double-spaced, and make a thirty-minute presentation to the class about your suggested turnaround. The case paper and presentation accounts for 50 percent of the course grade, and each member will receive the grade given by the instructor for the project. Not fair? Too much riding on the efforts of others? Welcome to the world of **team-based rewards.**

In today's changing organizations, much more emphasis has been placed on involving employees in most aspects of the job that affect them. When organizations group employees into teams and empower them to meet their goals, teams reap the benefits of their productive effort. That is, team-based rewards are tied to team-based performance. And that translates directly into their compensation. For example, at MacAllister Machinery, distributors of Caterpillar tractors in Indianapolis, bonus goals were established for its managers. If goals were achieved, they all shared in the "glory." If any of the managers failed, the entire team would not receive a dime of bonus money. How did the managers react? They pulled together and helped one another, resulting in sales increasing almost 25 percent and profits rising nearly 30 percent. Consequently, each manager received a bonus amounting to 50 percent of his or her salary.[51] The concept is now being driven down to the employee population! Similar programs also exist at DuPont, Monsanto, American Express,[52] DEC, and General Motors.[53]

Under a team-based compensation plan, team members who have worked on achieving, and in many cases, exceeding established goals, often share equally in the rewards (although, in the truest sense, teams allocate their own rewards). By providing for fair treatment of each team member, group cohesiveness is encouraged.[54] Yet, this does not occur overnight. Rather, it is a function of several key components being in place.[55] For instance, for teams to be effective, they must have a clear purpose and goals. They must understand what is expected of them, and that their effort is worthwhile. Teams must also be provided the necessary resources to complete their tasks. Because their livelihood may rest on accomplishing their goals, a lack of requisite resources may doom a team effort before it begins. And finally, there must be mutual trust among the team members. They must respect one another, effectively communicate with one another, and treat each member fairly and equitably. Without these, serious obstacles to teams may exist, which might defeat the purpose that group cohesiveness can foster.

Executive Compensation Programs

Executive pay is merely a special case within the topic of compensation, but it does have several twists that deserve attention. First, the base salaries of executives are higher than those of low-level managers or operative personnel, and we want to explain why this is so. Second, executives frequently operate under bonus and stock option plans that can dramatically increase their total compensation. A senior executive at Disney, Hewlett-Packard, or General Mills can, in a good year, earn $5 million, $10 million, or more on top of the base salary.[56] We want to briefly look at how such compensations come about and why. Finally, executives receive perquisites or special benefits that others do not. What are these, and how do they impact on executive motivation? These are the topics in this section on compensation.

Salaries of Top Managers

Michael Eisner, chairman of the Walt Disney Company, was recently awarded a salary that made people stop to check if the numbers were correct. In 1993, Eisner collected $203,010,590 in salary, bonuses, and stock-based incentives.[57] Disney's success under Eisner can't be overlooked. During his tenure with the creative entertainment company, Disney has grown significantly. And along with this growth came increases in company profits and stock prices. But 1993 and 1994 were unusual years for the organization. EuroDisney was an initial fiasco. It just didn't have the same success that Disneyland and Disney World had in the United States. In fact, it led to a significant drain on the organization's finances, and resulted in a 40 percent decrease in company profits. And Disney's effort to build a theme park in Virginia was met by strong public opposition. Yet despite this poor showing, and profit losses, Eisner was awarded a salary in the $200-million-plus range! But don't look at this solely as a big business phenomenon. Ely R. Callaway, president of Callaway Golf, the producer of oversized golf clubs, earned more than $21 million in 1993.[58] Ten other small-company CEOs, likewise, earned in excess of $2 million![59]

It is well-known that executives in the private sector receive considerably higher compensation than their counterparts in the public sector. Middle-level executives regularly earn base salaries of $100,000 to $180,000; the CEO of a billion-dollar corporation can expect a minimum total compensation package in excess of $2 million, while base salaries of $1 million or more are not unusual among senior management of Fortune 100 firms. In fact, 502 of the top two executives in the nation's largest 361 companies had salaries exceeding $1 million.[60]

How do organizations justify such extraordinary salaries for their executives (see "Ethical Decisions in HRM")? The answer is quite simple: economics and motivation.[61] In economic terms, we know that top managers are expected to demonstrate good decision-making abilities. This attribute may not be widely held by all workers. As a result, the supply of qualified senior executives is scarce, and organizations have bid up the price for this talent. They must keep

Who's one of the highest paid women executives in the United States? It's Sherry Lansing, Chair of Paramount Pictures Motion Picture Group. Sherry's 1994 salary was in the $3 million range, placing her in the top five of women executive salaries.

Ethical Decisions in HRM:

Are Executives Overpaid?

Are U.S. executives overpaid? Is an average salary in excess of $3 million justifiable? In any debate, there are two sides to the issue. In support of this salary is the fact that these individuals have tremendous responsibilities, not only to manage the organization today, but to keep it moving into the future. Their jobs are not 9-to-5 jobs, but rather six to seven days a week, often ten to fourteen hours a day. If jobs are evaluated on the basis of skills, knowledge, abilities, and responsibilities, executives surely should be highly paid. Furthermore, there is the issue of motivation and retention. If you want these individuals to succeed and stay with the company, you must provide a compensation package that motivates them to stay. Incentives based on various measures also provide the impetus for them to excel.

On the other hand, most of the research done on executive salaries questions the linkage to performance. Even in down years, executives are paid handsomely. In fact, American company executives are regarded as some of the highest paid people in the world. It is estimated that these individuals make nearly 150 times the salary that their employees do; average CEOs make almost $1,500 an hour, whereas the average worker makes just over $10 an hour. The difference of almost 150 times the average worker salary reinforces the attitude that employees of the organization are second-rate. Furthermore, U.S. executives make three to six times the salaries of their foreign counterparts. That's an interesting comparison, especially when you consider that some executives in Japan perform better.

Are our executives overpaid? What's your opinion?

Source: Ford S. Worthy, "Still Making Out on Wall Street," *Fortune* (April 6, 1992), p. 71. See also Judith H. Dobrzynski, "CEO Pay: Something Should Be Done—But Not by Congress," *Business Week* (February 3, 1992), p. 29; and Michael A. Verespej, "Pay-for-Skills, Its Time Has Come," *Industry Week* (June 15, 1992), p. 29.

their salaries in line with the competition or potentially lose an executive to another organization. High salaries also act to attract both top executives and lower-level managers. For instance, when Susan Angelo, vice-president of Brunswick Savings Bank, wanted to attract excellent executive candidates, she put together a unique compensation package.[62] Under her program, executives are able to go beyond salary deferrals to include deferring their bonuses also. What this has achieved is a flexible compensation system that can be tailored to each executive's needs. High pay not only encourages top-level managers to perform well in order to keep their jobs, but also acts to stimulate lower-level managers to work hard so that they can someday move up the ladder to "the big money."

Supplemental Financial Compensation

In 1993, the average compensation for executives in the Fortune 500 companies in the United States was $1.7 million.[63] This figure includes their total compensation—base salary plus bonuses and stock options. Bonuses and stock options dramatically increase the total compensation that executives received. Much of this additional compensation is obtained through a deferred bonus—that is, the executive's bonus is computed on the basis of some formula, usually taking into account increases in sales and profits. This bonus, although earned in the current period, is distributed over several future periods. Therefore, it is not unusual for an executive to earn a $1 million bonus but have it paid out at $50,000 a year for twenty years. The major purpose of such deferred compensation is to increase the cost to the executive of leaving the organization. In almost all cases, executives who voluntarily terminate their employment must forfeit their deferred bonuses. One of the main reasons why there are so few voluntary resignations among the ranks of senior management at General Motors is that these executives would lose hundreds of thousands of dollars in deferred income.

Interestingly, another form of bonus, the "hiring bonus," has arisen in the last decade, purposely designed to help senior executives defray the loss of deferred income. It is now becoming increasingly popular to pay senior executives a hiring bonus to sweeten the incentive for them to leave their current employer and forfeit their deferred bonuses and pension rights. These bonuses often do provide deferred income to compensate for loss of pension rights. For example, Kodak paid George Fisher a $5 million signing bonus and IBM paid Louis Gerstner $4.9 million to join the company to compensate them for giving up deferred compensation and pension and retirement rights.[64]

Stock options also have been a common incentive offered to executives. They generally allow executives to purchase, at some time in the future, a specific amount of the company's stock at a fixed price. Under the assumption that good management will increase the company's profitability and, therefore, the price of the stock, stock options are viewed as performance-based incentives. It should be pointed out, however, that the use of stock options is heavily influenced by the current status of the tax laws. In recent years, tax-reform legislation has taken away some of the tax benefits that could accrue through the issuance of stock options.[65] The success, however, of these IRS changes to curb CEO compensation is limited at best. Deferred pay[66] and supplemental retirement plans appear to be vehicles that skirt around the legalities of tax regulations.

Supplemental Nonfinancial Compensation: Perquisites

Executives are frequently offered a smorgasbord of **perquisites** not offered to other employees. The logic of offering these *perks,* from the organization's perspective, is to attract and keep good managers and to motivate them to work hard in the organization's interest. In addition to the standard benefits offered to all employees (see Chapter 14), some benefits are reserved for privileged executives. They range from an annual physical examination (worth several hundred dollars) to interest-free loans of millions of dollars, which can be worth $100,000 a year or more. Popular perks include the payment of life insurance premiums,[67] club memberships, company automobiles, liberal expense accounts, supplemental disability insurance, supplemental retirement accounts, post-retirement consulting contracts, and personal financial, tax, and legal counseling.[68] Some also may be given mortgage assistance;[69] for example, in organizations like Kaiser Permanente, mortgage loans up to $380,000 are given. At Church and Dwight of Piscataway, New Jersey, not only are individuals able to get up to 15 percent of their mortgage from the employer, if they remain on the

Perquisites Attractive benefits, over and above a regular salary, granted to executives ("perks").

Golden Parachute A protection plan for executives in the event that they are severed from the organization.

job for five years, and are active in the community as a volunteer, their debt is considered paid in full.[70]

A popular benefit for top executives that came about in the 1980s and continues today is the **golden parachute.** The golden parachute was designed by top executives as a means of protecting themselves if a merger or hostile takeover occurred. These "parachutes" provide either a severance salary to the departing executive or a guaranteed position in the newly created (merged) operation.

International Compensation

Probably the most complex function of international human resource management is the design and implementation of an equitable compensation program.[71] The first step in designing an international compensation package is to determine if there will be one policy applying to all employees or whether parent-country nationals (PCNs), host-country nationals (HCNs), and third-country nationals (TCNs) will be treated differently. Currently American PCNs and HCNs are commonly treated separately, often also differentiating among types of expatriate assignments (temporary or permanent transfer) or employee status (executive, professional, or technical). It is also necessary to thoroughly understand the statutory requirements of each country to ensure compliance with local laws.[72] International compensation packages in the United States generally utilize the "balance-sheet approach," which considers four factors: base pay, differentials, incentives, and assistance programs.[73]

Base Pay

Ideally this is equal to the pay of employees in comparable jobs at home, but the range of pay scales in most countries is far narrower than in the United States. Thus, where a middle manager in a U.S. factory might earn $60,000 a year, the same manager in Germany might earn $90,000. However, the U.S. higher-level executive might earn $500,000 and her counterpart in Germany only $150,000. How can human resource managers satisfy the middle manager who earns a third less than the counterpart where he works, while also satisfying the German executive who earns less than her U.S. counterpart?

In addition to considerations of fairness among overseas employees, foreign currencies and laws must be considered. Should expatriates be paid in U.S. dollars, or the local currency—or a combination of the two? How will the organization deal with changes in currency values? Are there restrictions on either bringing in or taking out dollars or the local currency? If so, how will savings be handled? Should salary increases be made according to the same standards as for domestic employees or according to local standards? Will the expatriate pay U.S. or foreign income taxes?

Taxation is a major factor in calculating equitable base pay rates. If there are substantial differences in tax rates, as for instance in Sweden, where income taxes are about 50 percent, will the base pay be adjusted for the actual loss of net income? While the U.S. Department of State has negotiated agreements with every country to determine where income will be taxed, the protection of income from a tax rate other than the domestic one creates new administrative requirements for the organization. Almost all multinational corporations have some tax protection plan so that the expatriate doesn't pay more in taxes than if she were in her home country.

Differentials

The cost of living is not the same around the world, although the value of the dollar to foreign currencies will affect price; a six-pack of Coca-Cola may cost $2.65 in New York, $3.75 in Paris, and $5.81 in Tokyo, and a gallon of premium gasoline $1.56 in New York, $3.89 in Paris, and $4.49 in Tokyo.[74] Differentials are intended to offset the higher costs of overseas goods, services, and housing. The Department of State, which has employees in almost every country in the world, publishes a regularly updated comparison of global costs of living that is used by most multinational corporations for providing differentials to maintain the standards of living the expatriate would enjoy as if at home.[75]

Incentives

Not all employees are willing to be separated for long periods of time from family, friends, and the comfort of home support systems. Thus, mobility inducements to go on foreign assignments are regularly offered. These may include monetary payments or services, such as housing, car, chauffeur, and other incentives. But how should a hardship premium be paid? As a percent of salary? In a lump sum payment? In the home or the foreign currency? If foreign housing is provided, what happens to the vacant home back in the States or to the family housing situation when they eventually return? Incentives require careful planning before, during, and after the overseas assignment.

Assistance Programs

As with any relocation, the overseas transfer requires a lot of expenditures for the employee's family. Some of the assistance programs commonly offered by multinational corporations include: household good shipping and storage; major appliances; legal clearance for pets and their shipment; home sale/rental protection; automobile protection; temporary living expenses; travel, including pre-relocation visits and annual home leaves; special/emergency return leaves; education allowances for children; club memberships (for corporate entertaining); and security (including electronic systems and bodyguards).

Clearly the design of a compensation system for employees serving overseas is complex and requires enormous administrative expertise, particularly when an organization has expatriates posted in forty or fifty different countries.

Study Tools and Applications

Summary

This summary relates to the Learning Objectives provided on p. 350.

After having read this chapter, you should know:

1. Rewards are the final link in the motivation model. After the effort has been expended, successful performance happens, organizational goals achieved, individuals are now ready to have their individual goals met. These goals, or rewards, can come in a variety of types.

2. Rewards can be classified as (1) intrinsic or extrinsic, (2) financial or nonfinancial, or (3) performance-based or membership-based.

3. Some rewards are membership-based because one receives them for simply belonging to the organization. Employee benefits are an example of membership-based rewards, in that every employee gets them irrespective of performance levels.

4. Compensation administration seeks to design a cost-effective pay structure that will not only attract, motivate, and retain competent employees, but also be perceived as fair by these employees.

5. Job evaluation systematically determines the value of each job in relation to all jobs within the organization. The four basic approaches to job evaluation are: (1) the ranking method, (2) the classification method, (3) the factor comparison method, and (4) the point method.

6. The final wage structure evolves from job evaluation input, wage survey data, and the creation of wage grades.

7. Competency-based compensation views employees as a competitive advantage in the organization. Compensation systems are established in terms of the knowledge and skills employees possess, and the behaviors that they demonstrate. Possession of these three factors is evaluated and compensated according to a broad-banded salary range established by the organization.

8. Executive compensation is higher than that of rank-and-file personnel and also includes other financial and nonfinancial benefits not otherwise available to operative employees. This is done to attract, retain, and motivate executives to higher performance levels.

9. The balance sheet approach to international compensation takes into account base pay, differentials, incentives, and assistance programs.

Key Terms

broad-banding	merit pay
classification method	performance-based rewards
compensation administration	perquisites
competency-based compensation programs	piecework plans
Equal Pay Act	plant-wide incentives
extrinsic rewards	point method
factor comparison method	ranking method
Fair Labor Standards Act	Scanlon Plan
golden parachute	team-based rewards
IMPROSHARE	wage curves
intrinsic rewards	wage structure
job evaluation	wage surveys
membership-based rewards	

EXPERIENTIAL EXERCISE:
Determining Pay Increases

For most people, their annual pay raise may be the most concrete information they have on how the organization evaluates their performance. Therefore, whether you as a manager intend it or not, the pay raise will be seen by the employee as either a reward or a punishment for last year's work performance. In behavioral terms, with the pay raise, you either positively or negatively reinforce last year's performance. Therefore, the pay raise can either be motivating or demotivating, depending on how the employee views the connection between good performance and financial issues. Issues of fairness, equity, and the motivation process are thus involved in people's reaction to pay decisions.

Purpose

1. Provide practice in making salary decisions.
2. Evaluate and weigh different sources of information about employee performance.
3. Develop skills in applying motivation theory to compensation decisions.

Step 1

Read the instructions on the "Employee Profile Sheet" (provided by your instructor), and then individually decide on a percentage pay increase for each of the eight employees.

Step 2

Form teams of three to five members. Each team member should report his or her pay increase, and the team should reach consensus on a pay increase for the eight employees. Your team should also justify these raises, explaining the criteria for these choices.

Step 3

Each team will turn in to the instructor their percentage increase, and the new salary for each of the eight employees. Your instructor will record and post them. Each group will then briefly explain its criteria for their decisions. Specifically, (1) What factors affected your pay raise decisions? (2) What are the reasons for basing pay raises on each of these factors? (3) What do you believe the behavioral effects will be for basing pay increases on these factors?

Step 4

The entire class will briefly discuss the differences between the sets of pay raises, and the factors that went into these decisions. Particular attention should be directed for employees for whom there was a wide variation among the various teams.

Source: Based on "Motivation Through Compensation," in Roy J. Lewicki, Donald D. Bowen, Douglas T. Hall, and Francine S. Hall, *Experiences in Management and Organizational Behavior* (New York: John Wiley, 1988), pp. 49–51. Used with permission.

CASE APPLICATION:
Advanced Network Design

Dave Wiegard believes he's found a better mousetrap. As president of the La Mirada, California-based telecommunications company, Advanced Network Design, Inc. (AND), Dave knew there had to be a better way to get his employees to be more productive.[76] Earlier, AND had what many considered a good incentive program. Dave Wiegard ensured that those employees who produced well in accordance with established company goals would receive awards at weekly, monthly, and quarterly intervals. Something, however, was not working right. It appeared to Dave that after an award was given, productivity would slack off until the next major award was nearing. Furthermore, if any reward program was discontinued, the "incentive" to excel followed suit.

To end this roller-coaster phenomenon, Dave implemented his new system—one in which no systematic process was in place to provide rewards. Rather, Dave now takes it upon himself to administer the rewards as he sees fit. This means that AND employees don't know when they may be rewarded, but understand that any reward given is attributed solely to company profitability.

Since its beginning, this unusual incentive plan has resulted in significant changes in the company. Productivity has shot up, while simultaneously AND's work force has shrunk; company sales records are being broken each year; and employees are receiving more rewards than ever before. One difference, however, is that these rewards are tailored to the unique needs of each employee; that is, rather than a rigid incentive plan whereby employees receive a similar reward, AND employees are now afforded the opportunity to receive what they want. And what are some of these tailored rewards? One employee got a five-day, all-expenses-paid trip to Disney World for the entire family; another got an expensive suit and a set of pearls for his wife; yet another got an expensive clock radio.

Questions

1. Why do you believe the initial incentive plan at Advanced Network Design failed to generate continuous productivity growth, as opposed to spurts close to the time incentives were to be given? What might that indicate about the incentive plan that was operating?
2. Describe how Dave Wiegard has linked his self-determined reward system to the motivation process.
3. Would you consider AND's new incentive plan to be fair, when one employee can get a trip to Disney World for the entire family, while another got an expensive clock radio? Explain your position.

Testing Your Understanding

How well did you fulfill the learning objectives?

1. Employees respond to organizational rewards for all of these reasons except
   a. people behave in ways that they believe are in their best interests.
   b. people constantly look for payoffs for their efforts.
   c. people expect that good job performance will lead to organizational goal attainment that will lead to satisfying individual needs or goals.
   d. organizations use rewards to motivate employees.
   e. employees often respond to peer pressure.
2. What is the difference between financial and nonfinancial rewards?
   a. financial rewards (such as salary) are taxable. Nonfinancial rewards (such as day-care spending accounts) provide tax shelters.
   b. financial rewards are a matter of public record. Nonfinancial rewards are not a matter of public record.
   c. financial rewards make life better off the job. Nonfinancial rewards make life better on the job.
   d. financial rewards are fixed according to a compensation schedule. Nonfinancial rewards are variable in nature.
   e. financial rewards provide the same motivation levels for all employees. Nonfinancial rewards provide differing levels of motivation.
3. Good organizational reward systems have all of the following qualities except
   a. they are individualized to reflected differences in what employees consider important to them.
   b. they are perceived as equitable.
   c. they are visible and flexible.
   d. they are based on seniority.
   e. they are allocated at a relatively low cost.

4. Fairness, in the context of a compensation system, means all of the following except
   a. a wage adequate for the demands of the job, from the organization's perspective.
   b. employees' perception of an appropriate balance in terms of their efforts–rewards ratio compared to a relevant standard.
   c. employees' perception that they are treated better than similar workers in competing organizations.
   d. pay rates are established according to a job's comparative worth.
   e. reasonable cost-minimization by organizations.
5. A compensation analyst for a large firm is completing a job evaluation for her organization. Identifiable criteria for jobs (skill, effort, responsibility) were determined and points were assigned, based on weighting factors. Several degrees of competency were identified for each of the job criteria. All jobs were then categorized according to these rating scales. What job evaluation method was used?
   a. ranking
   b. classification
   c. factor comparison
   d. point method
   e. core specification
6. Rachel works for a textile manufacturer as a seamstress. She is paid $.05 for each sleeve she sews an hour, up to 100 sleeves. She is paid $.09 for each sleeve she produces over the first 100. What kind of compensation system is used?
   a. piecework
   b. time-saving bonus
   c. commission
   d. Scanlon Plan
   e. IMPROSHARE
7. Last year, an aerospace engineer made $110,000. His annual base pay was $100,000. The remainder was calculated based on his ability to work faster than the

standard hour's work. What kind of compensation system was used?

   a. piecework   b. time-saving bonus

   c. commission   d. Scanlon Plan

   d. IMPROSHARE

8. Competency-based compensation systems can best be described as

   a. paying employees according to their knowledge, skills, and demonstrated behaviors.

   b. paying employees according to how educated and the number of advanced degrees they possess.

   c. pay systems that promote team-based incentives.

   d. incentive systems whereby strategic goals of the organization are replaced by the value-added nature of employee skills.

   e. paying employees according to a piecework system whereby a sophisticated formula is used to determine the dollar value of the employee's bonus.

9. Team-based compensation programs reward employees for achieving unit and organizational goals. Under which situation would a team-based compensation most likely function well?

   a. a situation where a team of workers perform mutually exclusive, independent tasks

   b. a situation where a team of workers have mutual distrust for one another

   c. a situation where work tasks are woven together such that the work of any one individual is difficult to assess

   d. a situation where competition among employees is encouraged and fostered

   e. a situation where group values conform to limiting production

10. U.S. organizations justify high salaries for their executives in all of these ways except

   a. good decision-making ability is not widely represented in the work force.

   b. global competition requires that the United States match the salaries given to executives in other countries.

   c. organizations must pay high prices for scarce executives.

   d. high salaries are necessary to keep executives from going over to the competition.

   e. high executive salaries attract good workers throughout managerial levels of an organization.

11. Bill, a U.S. computer programmer, reluctantly moved his family to Saudi Arabia for a three-year assignment with his firm. A hardship premium, equal to his annual U.S. salary, was deposited in a U.S. account for each six months of his assignment. What kind of pay factor was used?

   a. base pay   b differentials

   c. bonuses   d incentives

   e. assistance programs

12. All of the following questions should be addressed when considering base pay for expatriates except:

   a. Is the cost of living the same in the host country as in the United States?

   b. Will the expatriate pay U.S. or foreign income tax?

   c. Should expatriates be paid in U.S. dollars or local currency?

   d. Are there restrictions on taking money into or out of the host country?

   e. Should salary increases be made according to local standards or U.S. standards?

13. Membership-based rewards include all of the following except

   a. cost-of-living allowances.

   b. benefit provisions.

   c. pay increases for seniority.

   d. pay increases for completion of a college degree.

   e. commissions.

14. Compensation administration is

   a. more heavily influenced by government policies than is strategic human resource planning.

   b. less influenced by government policies than is strategic human resource planning.

   c. less influenced by government policies than is orientation.

   d. influenced at the state, but not the national, level.

   e. influenced at the national, but not the state, level.

15. Specific provisions of the Fair Labor Standards Act include all of the following except

   a. child labor laws for workers aged 14 through 17.

   b. overtime pay of at least 1 1/2 times regular pay for all hours worked over forty per week.

   c. some categories of workers, such as apprentices or full-time students, may be paid less than the minimum wage under special certificates issued by the Department of Labor.

   d. where federal law differs from state law, federal law prevails.

   e. minimum wage and other relevant information must be posted publicly where employees can readily see it.

16. Pay adjustments designed to maintain the standard of living for an expatriate that she would enjoy at home are called

   a. base pay.   b differentials.

   c. bonuses.   d. incentives.

   e. assistance programs.

Chapter Fourteen

EMPLOYEE BENEFITS

Just how important are employee benefits to workers in a community? If employee benefits can make the difference between joining one company over another, can employee benefits help generate support for a community to "woo" an organization considering relocating to an area? Even if the benefits offered by the organization are counter-cultural to the area? Residents of Williamson County, Texas, clearly voiced their opinion in the matter.[1]

In late 1993, Apple Computer approached elected officials of Williamson County about the prospects of building an $80 million complex in Round Rock, Texas. Apple's projects were that such an operation would yield 1,400 new jobs to the community of 140,000 people. Likewise, the company and its employees would generate an estimated $300 million in annual tax revenues for Williamson County. Initially, county commissioners viewed Apple's proposal as a genuine windfall for the area. Competition for key businesses to relocate into an area is keen, and having a partnership with Apple would clearly serve Williamson County, and the surrounding area well. The decision appeared to be a "no-brainer." Move forward with blazing speed!

As the process was underway, some startling information was learned about Apple. That is, Apple Computer is one of about fifty companies in the United States that offer a special benefit to its employees. That benefit is health-care coverage for an employee's unmarried live-in partner. Furthermore, Apple doesn't differentiate between heterosexual or homosexual relationships. Domestic partners are covered, period! Apple recognized how such a benefit could attract and retain skilled professionals.

Unfortunately, the community of Williamson County viewed the benefit differently. They did not want to have people in their community that such a benefit might draw. After emotionally long and arduous public debates, county commissioners voted not to approve a tax break for Apple to build in Round Rock—one incentive for Apple to come to the area. Consequently, Apple threatened to take its business elsewhere. But the community debate did not subside. Here was an organization that could add million of dollars into an area that was being stymied by the community's prejudice over an employee benefit. In the end, the dollar prevailed; one commissioner changed his vote, giving Apple the tax break, and opening the doors for Apple to move into the community—domestic benefits and all!

Employee benefits are supposed to provide something of value to employees. In attempting to meet this goal, sometimes companies find themselves in a quandry. At Apple, the company offers domestic partner benefits to its employees, in part, because that is something they understood their employees wanted. However, public sentiment in Williamson County, Texas, about the benefit, almost killed the deal that was to bring more than 1400 jobs to the area.

Employee Benefits Membership-based, nonfinancial rewards offered to attract and keep employees.

Introduction

When an organization is designing its overall compensation program, one of the critical areas of concern is what benefits should be provided. Today's workers expect more than just an hourly wage or a salary from their employer; they want additional considerations that will enrich their lives. These considerations in an employment setting are called **employee benefits.**[2]

Employee benefits have grown in importance and variety over the past several decades. Once perceived as an added feature for an organization to provide its employees, employee benefit administration has transformed itself into a well-thought-out, well-organized package. Employers realize that the benefits provided to employees have an impact on whether applicants accept their employment offers or, once employed, whether workers will continue to stay with the organization. Benefits, therefore, are necessary components of an effectively functioning compensation program.

The irony, however, is that while benefits must be offered to attract and retain good workers, benefits as a whole do not directly affect a worker's performance. Benefits are generally membership-based, offered to employees regardless of their performance levels. While this does not appear to be a logical business practice, there is evidence that the absence of adequate benefits and services for employees contributes to employee dissatisfaction and increased absenteeism and turnover.[3] Accordingly, because the negative impact of failing to provide adequate benefits is so great, organizations spend tens of billions of dollars annually to ensure that valuable benefits are available for each worker.

Over the decades, the nature of benefits has changed drastically. The benefits offered in the early 1900s clearly were different from those offered today. In the early 1900s, much emphasis was placed on time off from work. As the first personnel departments arrived on the scene, their main emphasis was to ensure that workers were "happy and healthy." This meant that their responsibility was to administer such benefits as scheduled vacations, company picnics, and other social activities for workers. Later, around the late 1930s, the practice of having employees complete a sign-up card for some type of health insurance came about. Those days of simplicity for the organization, unfortunately, are long gone. Federal legislation, labor unions, and the changing work force have all led to growth in benefit offerings. Today's organizational benefits are more widespread, more creative, and clearly more abundant. As indicated in Table 14-1, the benefits offered in the 1990s clearly are designed to ensure something of value for each worker.

The High Costs of Benefits

Most of us are aware of inflation and the impact it has had on the wages and salaries of virtually every job in the United States. It seems incredible that only sixty years ago, a worker earning $100 a week was ranked among the top 10 percent of wage earners in the United States. Although we are aware that hourly wages and monthly salaries have increased in recent years, we often overlook the more rapid growth in benefits offered to employees. Since the cost of employing workers includes both direct compensation and the corresponding benefits and services, the growth in both benefits and services has resulted in dramatic increases in labor costs to organizations. What do these dramatic cost increases mean for employers? In the 1980s the cost of employee benefits was just over 9 percent of corporate revenues generated.[4] In fact, from 1979 to

TABLE 14-1 Major Employee Benefits Offered (Percent of Employers Participating)

HEALTH INSURANCE:		OTHER BENEFITS:	
Medical Care (noncontributory)	83	Employee Parking	88
Extended Care Facility	66	Educational Assistance	72
Dental	60	Employee Assistance Programs	56
Vision	23	Travel Insurance	42
Substance Abuse Treatment	81	Severance Pay	41
		Flexible Spending Accounts	36
RETIREMENT PLANS:		Wellness Programs	35
Defined Benefit	59	Relocation Allowance	31
Defined Contribution	41	Elder Care	9
401(k)s	29	Child Care	8
Deferred Profit Sharing	16		
Employee Stock Plans	3		

Source: U.S. Bureau of the Census, *Statistical Abstracts of the United States: 1994* (Washington, D.C.: Government Printing Office, 1994), p. 434.

LIFE/DISABILITY:	
Life	94
Accident	45
Long-term Disability	40

PAID TIME OFF:	
Vacations	96
Holidays	92
Jury Duty Leave	86
Funeral Leave	80
Sick Leave	67
Military Leave	54
Personal Leave	21

1992, the cost of providing something of value to each employee increased from $5,560 per year to $13,631 per year,[5] with the greatest cost being incurred in retiree benefits.[6] That's more than a doubling of costs in thirteen years.

Employers have also found that benefits present attractive areas of negotiation when large wage and salary increases are not feasible. For example, if employees were to purchase life insurance on their own, they would have to pay for it with net dollars; that is, with what they have left after paying taxes. If the organization pays for it, the benefit is nontaxable (the premiums paid on insurance up to $50,000) for each employee.[7]

Benefits for the Year 2000

There has been a dramatic increase in the number and types of benefits offered and an equally sensational increase in their costs. What has triggered the sweeping changes in benefits offerings that will carry us into the next millennium? The answer to that question lies, in part, in the demographic composition of the work force.

Benefits offered to employees reflect many of the trends existing in our labor force. As the decades have witnessed drastic changes in educational levels, family status, and employee expectations, benefits have had to be adjusted to meet the needs of the workers.[8] What specifically have we seen over the past few decades with respect to demographic changes? Let's explore a few factors to show why the benefits offered today are different than those of thirty years ago.

Recall from Chapter 2 our discussion of the changing work force. Let's look at this issue with an eye on benefits. As recently as the early 1960s, the work force was comprised of a relatively homogeneous group—predominately males. This typical male had a wife who stayed home and cared for their children, thus necessitating a relatively standard benefit need. That is, most of these workers required a retirement plan, sick leave, vacation time, and health insurance. Providing these to workers was customary, and for the most part, uncomplicated. However, the typical worker of the early 1960s is rare in today's work force. Dual-career couples, singles, singles with children, and individuals caring for their parents (elder care) are now widely prevalent in the work force. And, while not as widespread, equally important is the issue of benefit coverage for a worker's significant other. As a result of such events, organizations must be able to satisfy diverse benefit needs. Consequently, organizational benefit programs are being forced to take on different focuses. This is required in order to achieve the goal of "something of value" for each worker (see "What If: HRM in a De-Jobbed Organization").

The Linkage to Motivation

Wait a minute! The linkage to motivation? In the last chapter, and even a few paragraphs ago, we stated that benefits are membership-based, and are provided to employees regardless of performance. How, then, can they be linked to the motivation process? If you're seeing this potential contradiction, you're paying close attention.

Let's review the motivation process we laid out several chapters ago (see Figure 14-1). Benefits may become a critical link to this process if organizations tai-

What If:

HRM in a De-Jobbed Organization

Benefits in a de-jobbed organization. Even the sound of that is something of an anomaly. Unquestionably, there are those in the contingent work force who would argue that working part-time, or even on a temporary basis, better serves their personal needs. That is really not the point. The issue is what major changes those who are thrust into this de-jobbed arena will expect. For several areas of HRM, we have been laying out the what-ifs, but none will hit home more than the area of benefits.

Our work force is comprised of several generations of workers, many of whom enjoyed the richness that benefits administration had to offer. We felt comfortable that our health insurance would cover us in the event of a catastrophic illness. We knew that some retirement would be ours, so long as we put in the many years of hard work. We also planned our vacations to coincide with our children being out of school—heading to family gatherings, resorts, the beaches, and the like to bask in friendship, stress-free environments, and the warm sun. But these benefits, and many others that we have grown accustomed to, simply may be a thing of the past.

For one thing, we will be working when the organization needs us. Our income will be determined largely by the actual work we perform. We will not have the luxury of having sick leave, for if we are not available to work on our projects for organizations, we won't get paid. Like the consultant who gets paid based on the number of hours actually worked, if you can't work today, you simply don't get your fees. Vacations, too, will become yesterday's dream. A vacation will likely be hard to plan, because vacation will occur when you are between jobs. One project finishes up on Friday, and the next doesn't begin until Monday, two weeks hence. Well, then, there's your vacation.

Similar analogies can be drawn to such benefits as leaves of absences, long-term disability, and other paid time off from work. They simply won't exist in their current form—that is, employer offered. Rather, we as independent contractors will be expected to provide our own coverages through our own insurance plans. And don't forget about retirement. Over the past decade we've been hearing we need to save more for our own retirement—to augment Social Security and the retirement we may get from a company. That advice becomes even more prominent tomorrow, where we, the individual, have full responsibility for funding our retirement income, especially if financial problems continue to plague Social Security.

The days of having something added to make organizational life sweeter may be ending. As employees, we've always wanted benefits that best fit our needs. Benefits in the de-jobbed organization will permit just that. How so? Simply, we will personally buy only what we want. Clearly not the vision flexible-benefit advocates have had in mind, but organizational life, like life itself, continues to evolve.

Source: Based on William Bridges, "The End of the Job," *Fortune* (September 19, 1994), p. 72–73.

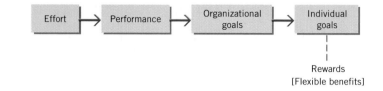

Figure 14-1
Benefits and the Link to Motivation

lor them to meet the specific needs of employees. For instance, if each employee is given the same benefits package, regardless of their situation or needs (the traditional approach), then, yes, benefits may have little effect on one's motivation. But, if employees have the opportunity to pick and choose the benefits most useful to them, then behavior can be influenced. Let's explain this using a classroom analogy.

Your professor has laid out a syllabus that attempts to meet your specific needs. In the syllabus, the instructor informs students that his policy is to permit each student to drop one test score—their lowest grade of the four exams scheduled in the course. While that consideration (benefit) may be available to everyone, it may not be appealing enough. After all, you still have to take all four exams, and generally, you have done well in classes like this. Getting four "A's" on an exam, and getting to drop one for final grade determination, may not meet your individual goal. Hence, its effect on your performance may be minimal. However, this professor is well known and respected in the surrounding business community. You know that a letter of recommendation from him to specific company representatives could provide you that edge you need to land that "great" job you want after graduation. But, he doesn't write letters of recommendation freely. Instead, you notice on his syllabus that he will only write letters for students who achieve a class standing in the top 5 percent. You value this benefit, so you have to perform so as to be one of the "chosen," and fulfill your individual goal.

So while it's generally true that organizations may not get the most out of their benefits packages, there are avenues available that can change that outcome. Before we discuss some of those mechanisms, however, it's important to frame what we mean by the term *benefit administration*.

In putting together a benefits package, two issues must be considered: (1) what benefits *must* be offered by law, and (2) what benefits *should* be offered to make the organization attractive to applicants and current workers (see "Ethical Decisions in HRM"). First we'll explore the **legally required benefits.**

Legally Required Benefits
Employee benefits that are required by law.

Legally Required Benefits

The organization must provide certain benefits to its employees regardless of whether it wants to or not, and they must be provided in a nondiscriminatory manner. With a few exceptions, the hiring of any employee requires the organization to pay Social Security premiums,[9] unemployment compensation, and workers' compensation. The payment of these premiums is either shared with employees (as in the case of Social Security), or borne solely by the organization, in an effort to provide each employee with some basic level of financial protection at retirement, termination, or as a result of injury. These benefits also provide a death benefit for dependents in case of a worker's death. Finally, employers must permit employees to take time off from work for certain personal reasons. Let's take a closer look at these legally required benefits.

Ethical Decisions in HRM:

Benefits and the Contingent Work Force

Hiring contingent workers can be a blessing for organizations. Contingent workers provide employees with a rich set of diverse skills on an as-needed, cost-effective basis. Likewise, workers who desire to work less than full time are also given the opportunity to keep their skills sharp, while at the same time, balancing their commitment to personal matters and career.

Unfortunately, many contingent work force members are not there by choice. Jobs have disappeared all too frequently, and the trend is growing. In fact, by the beginning of 1994, about 30 percent of the work force was made up of contingent workers, including part-time employees, people who contract directly with companies for specific projects, and temporary workers. Furthermore, many of these workers receive a lower rate of pay and accompanying benefits than those given to full-time, core employees.

So, is the movement toward contingent workers a management windfall, one that exploits workers? Should organizations be required to provide full benefits to its contingent work force? Is legislation necessary to mandate this coverage? Or, do we simply argue that no change is necessary because many contingent workers choose their employment status, thereby reaping other benefits from blending personal and career factors? What's your opinion?

Source: J. Fierman, "The Contingent Work Force, *Fortune* (January 24, 1994), pp. 30–36.

Social Security

A source of income for American retirees, disabled workers, and for surviving dependents of workers who have died, has been the benefits provided by **Social Security** insurance. Social Security also provides some health insurance coverage through the federal-government-sponsored Medicare program. In 1988, Social Security benefits exceeded $136 billion a year,[10] covering about 155 million workers in the United States.[11]

Social Security insurance is financed by contributions made by the employee and matched by the employer, computed as a percentage of the employee's earnings. In 1995, for instance, the rate was 7.65 percent (levied on both the employee and the employer) of the worker's earnings up to $61,200, or a maximum levy of $4,681.80 (see Figure 14-2).[12] Of this tax, 6.2 percent is allocated to the retirement portion of Social Security; 1.45 percent for medicare. Those earning more than $61,200 continue to pay the medicare portion, and that amount, too, is matched by the employer.[13]

To be eligible for Social Security, employees must be employed for a minimum of forty quarters, or ten years of work. During this work period, employees must have also earned a minimum of $630 per quarter. Prior to 1983, employees became eligible for full benefits at age 65. With revisions to Social Security

Social Security Retirement, disability, and survivor benefits, paid by the government to aged, former members of the labor force, the disabled, or their survivors.

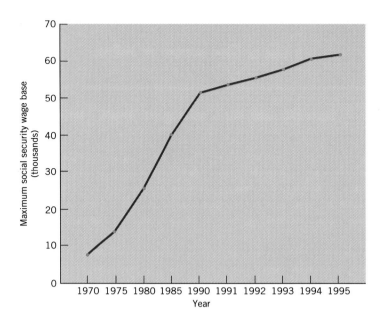

Figure 14-2
Escalating Costs of Employee
Benefits

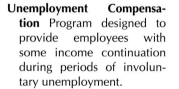

Unemployment Compensation Program designed to provide employees with some income continuation during periods of involuntary unemployment.

laws, those born after 1938 will have to wait an additional two years before receiving full retirement benefits.

Keep in mind, however, that Social Security is not intended to be employees' sole source of retirement income. Social Security benefits vary, based on the previous year's inflation, one's additional earnings, and the age of the recipient.[14] For 1995, the maximum Social Security retirement check is $1,199. Consequently, workers are expected to supplement this income with their own retirement plans (we'll look at these shortly).

Unemployment Compensation

Unemployment compensation laws provide benefits to employees who meet the following conditions: are without a job, have worked a minimum number of weeks, submit an application for unemployment compensation to their State Employment Agency, register for available work, and are willing and able to accept any suitable employment offered them through their State Unemployment Compensation Commission. The premise behind unemployment compensation is to provide an income to individuals who have lost a job through no fault of their own (e.g., layoffs, plant closing).

The funds for paying unemployment compensation are derived from a combined federal and state tax imposed on the taxable wage base of the employer. At the federal level, the unemployment tax is 6.2 percent on the first $7,000 of earnings of employees.[15] States that meet federal guidelines are given a 5.4 percent credit, thus reducing the federal unemployment tax to .08 percent, or $56 per employee.[16]

State unemployment compensation tax is often a function of a company's unemployment experience; that is, the more an organization lays off employees, the higher its rate. Rates for employers range from 0.0 to 3.0 percent of state-established wage bases.[17] Eligible unemployed workers receive an amount that varies from state to state but is determined by the worker's previous wage rate and the length of previous employment. Compensation is provided for only a limited period—typically, the base is twenty-six weeks[18] but may be extended by the state another twenty-six weeks during times when unemployment runs excessively high.

Unemployment compensation and parallel programs for railroad, federal government, and military employees cover more than 75 percent of all members in the work force. Major groups that are excluded include self-employed workers, employees who work for organizations employing fewer than four individuals, household domestics, farm employees, and state and local government employees. As recent recessions have demonstrated, unemployment compensation provides stable spending power throughout the nation. In contrast to the early 1930s, when millions of workers lost their jobs and had no compensatory income, unemployment compensation provides a floor that allows individuals to continue looking for work while receiving assistance through the transitory period from one job to the next.[19]

Workers' Compensation

Every state currently has some type of **workers' compensation** to compensate employees or their families for death or permanent or total disability resulting from job-related endeavors, irrespective of fault for the accident. Federal employees and others working outside the U.S. border are covered by separate legislation. The rationale for workers' compensation is to protect employees' salaries and to attribute the cost for occupational accidents and rehabilitation to the employing organization. This accountability factor considers workers' compensation costs as part of the labor expenses incurred in meeting the organization's objectives.

Workers' compensation benefits are based on fixed schedules of minimum and maximum payments. For example, the loss of an index finger may be calculated at $500, or the loss of an entire foot at $5,000. When comprehensive disability payments are required, the amount of compensation is computed by considering the employee's current earnings, future earnings, and financial responsibilities.

The entire cost of workers' compensation is borne by the organization. Its rates are set based on the likelihood of an accident, the actual history of company accidents, the type of industry and business operation, and the likelihood of accidents occurring. The organization, then, protects itself by covering its risks through insurance. Some states provide an insurance system, voluntary or required, for the handling of workers' compensation. Some organizations cover their workers' compensation risks by purchasing insurance from private insurance companies. Finally, some states allow employers to be self-insurers. Self-insuring, while usually limited to large organizations, requires the employer to maintain a fund from which benefits can be paid.

Most workers' compensation laws stipulate that the injured employee will be compensated by either a monetary allocation or the payment of medical expenses, or a combination of both. Almost all workers' compensation insurance programs, whether publicly or privately controlled, provide incentives for employers to maintain good safety records. Insurance rates are computed based on the organization's accident experience, hence employers are motivated to keep accident rates low.[20]

Workers' Compensation Payment to workers or their heirs for death or permanent or total disability that resulted from job-related activities.

Family and Medical Leave Act

The last legally required benefit facing organizations is the Family and Medical Leave Act of 1993. Recall from our discussion in Chapter 3, the FMLA was passed to provide employees the opportunity to take up to twelve weeks of unpaid leave each year for family or medical reasons.

Voluntary Benefits

The voluntary benefits offered by an organization are limited only by management's creativity and budget. As Table 14-1 revealed, many different benefits are offered—almost all of which carry significant costs to the employer. Some of the most common and critical ones are health insurance, retirement plans, time off from work, and disability and life insurance benefits. We will delay the discussion of benefits that deals with health issues, like employee assistance programs, until the next chapter.

Health Insurance

Health Insurance An employee benefit designed to provide coverage in the event of an injury or illness.

All individuals have health-care needs that must be met, and most organizations today offer some type of **health insurance** coverage to their employees. This coverage has become one of the most important benefits for employees because of the tremendous increases in the cost of health care.[21] In fact, health care costs U.S. businesses more than $174 billion annually.[22] Estimates also indicate that costs may continue to increase throughout 1990s,[23] with some claiming that employee layoffs and major corporate restructuring will be the only ways to deal with the cost increases. Without health insurance, almost any family's finances could be depleted at any time if they had to pay for a major illness—that's why the Clinton administration worked so fervently for health-care reform.[24] The purpose of health insurance is to protect the employee and his or her immediate family from the catastrophes of a major illness, and to minimize their out-of-pocket expenses for medical care.

Any type of health insurance offered to employees generally contains provisions for coverage that can be extended beyond the employee. An employee, an employee and spouse, an employee with child, or the family can be covered. Coverage generally focuses on hospital and physician care, and also major medical expenses. The specific types of coverage offered to employees will vary based on the organization's health-care policy. Generally, three types appear more frequently than others: traditional health-care coverage, Health Maintenance Organizations (HMOs), and Preferred Provider Organizations (PPOs) (sometimes referred to as point-of-service (POS) or network plans).[25] All three are designed to provide protection for employees, but each does so in a different way. There is also increasing interest in employer-operated options such as self-funded insurance. Let's look at each of these various types.

Traditional Health Insurance   When health insurance benefits began decades ago, generally one type of health insurance was offered: the traditional membership program. The cost of this insurance to the employee, if any, was minimal. This traditional insurance generally was provided (and is to some extent today) through a Blue Cross and Blue Shield Organization.[26]

Since its inception in 1929, Blue Cross and Blue Shield (BC/BS) insurance has served as the dominant health-care insurer in the United States. Blue Cross and Blue Shield plans offer special arrangements to their members in return for a guarantee that medical services will be provided. Blue Cross organizations are concerned with the hospital end of the business. These hospitals contract with **Blue Cross** to provide hospital services to members, and agree to receive reimbursement from the health insurer for their fees incurred. The reimburse-

Blue Cross A health insurer concerned with the hospital side of health insurance.

ment is often paid on a per diem basis for days stayed in the hospital or by paying a percentage of the total bill.[27]

The other component of the health insurer is the **Blue Shield** organization. Whereas Blue Cross has special arrangements with the hospitals, Blue Shield tries to achieve the same by signing up doctors to participate in Blue Shield coverage. This participation feature means that a doctor is willing to accept the payment from Blue Shield as payment in full for services rendered. These payments are generally based on what are called "Usual, Customary, and Reasonable" (UCR) fees. The UCR fees are reflective of physician fees charged in an area.[28]

For many organizations, the costs associated with the "cadillac" of the health insurance plan are too prohibited. As such, traditional health-care coverage is rapidly being replaced by the other two plan types. Traditional insurers like Blue Cross and Blue Shield, too, have begun to offer other types of health insurance coverage options to employers in order to help contain rising health-care benefit costs.

Health Maintenance Organizations Health Maintenance Organizations **(HMOs)** are designed to provide quality health care at a fixed expense for its members. People's needs have changed, and with these changing needs comes the expectation that they can obtain good health care at a reasonable cost. Under traditional coverage, preventive care is not covered, and the costs of such are borne by the employee. For instance, visiting a physician for routine baby immunizations or gynecological exams would not be paid for under the terms of traditional health insurance coverage. To meet this need and provide the desired services to employees, HMOs were created. This creation stemmed from the passage of the **Health Maintenance Act of 1973,** which required employers who extended traditional health insurance to their employees to also offer alternative health-care coverage options. HMOs seek efficiencies by keeping health-care costs down; one means of achieving that goal is by providing preventive care.

Blue Shield A health insurer concerned with the provider side of health insurance.

Health Maintenance Organization Provide comprehensive health services for a flat fee.

Health Maintenance Act Established the requirement that companies offering traditional health insurance to its employees must also offer alternative health-care options.

How can a company help to control its runaway health care costs? For ones like Deere and Company, that may mean starting its own health maintenance organization. Originally designed for Deere employees, the HMO now provides medical services to employees of 300 other companies. Not only has Deere helped control its health care expenditures, it has opened up a new line of business for the Moline, Illinois, agricultural-equipment manufacturer.

An HMO like Kaiser Permanente is "an organization that generally delivers broad, comprehensive health care to a specific, voluntary enrolled population . . . on a fixed, periodic payment basis."[29] Since their inception, they have grown rapidly in the United States. It is estimated that there are more than 300 HMOs operating in the United States, providing services to more than 24 million members, and growing "at a 25 percent annual pace."[30] Table 14-2 is a sample of HMO coverage. The major disadvantage, however, it that under an HMO, to get "full" coverage, one must receive services from the service center location that is selected. Furthermore, to be seen outside of the HMO, or for other services, individuals must either receive permission from their HMO physician or incur a greater out-of-pocket expense. Accordingly, under an HMO arrangement, freedom of health-care choice is significantly limited.

Preferred Provider Organization Organization that requires using specific physicians and health-care facilities to contain the rising costs of health care.

Preferred Provider Organizations   Preferred Provider Organizations (PPOs) are health-care arrangements where an employer or insurance company has agreements with doctors, hospitals, and other related medical service facilities to provide services for a fixed fee. In return for accepting this fixed fee, the employer or the insurer promises to encourage employees to use their services. The encouragement often results in additional services being covered. PPOs offer lower premiums to the employer in return for a greater quantity of services provided. Table 14-3 is a sample of PPO coverage.

TABLE 14-2   Sample Health Maintenance Organization Coverage (Selected Items)

Coverage Conditions	*Coverage (HMO Facility Only)**
Physician	
Primary Care	$5 Co-pay
Specialists	$10 Co-pay
In-patient care	100% (If Approved by HMO physician)
Out-patient care	100% (If Approved by HMO physician)
Hospital	100% for 365 days (If approved by HMO physician)
Surgery	100% (If approved by HMO physician)
Maternity Benefits	100% (If approved by HMO physician)
Well-baby Care	$5 Co-pay
Immunizations	100% (If approved by HMO physician)
Dental Coverage	
Diagnostic	100%
Preventive	100%
Deductibles	
Individual	None
Family	None
Out-of-Pocket Maximums	
Individual	None
Family	None

* All medical services must be provided through the HMO participating providers and facilities, and must be authorized by the HMO.

Source: State of Maryland, *Benefit Comparisons and Costs, Calendar Year 1995* (November 1994), pp. 43–44.

TABLE 14-3 Sample Preferred Provider Organization (Point-of-Service Network) Coverage (Selected Items)

Coverage Conditions	Coverage in Network	Coverage Out of Network
Physician		
Primary Care	$15 Co-pay	80% after deductible
Specialists	$20 Co-pay	80% after deductible
In-patient care	100%	80% after deductible
Out-patient care	100%	80% after deductible
Hospital	100% for 365 days	80% after deductible
Surgery	100%	80% after deductible
Maternity Benefits	100%	80% after deductible
Well-baby Care	$15 Co-pay	80% after deductible
Immunizations	100%	80% after deductible
Deductibles		
Individual	None	$250
Family	None	$500
Out-of-Pocket Maximums		
Individual	None	$3,000
Family	None	$6,000

Source: State of Maryland, *Benefit Comparisons and Costs, Calendar Year 1995* (November 1994), pp. 32–35.

PPOs also provide valuable information to employers. Through utilization review procedures, the PPO can provide data to help the employer determine unnecessary plan use. These "quality" checks can act as "gatekeepers" to ensure that health-care costs are contained. How can a PPO benefit the employee? Through the agreement reached, a PPO can provide much the same service that an HMO provides; the difference is that an individual is not required to use a specific facility, like a hospital. In those cases, the PPO takes the form of traditional health insurance. If an employee decides to go elsewhere for services, then the service fee is reimbursed according to specific guidelines. For example, at AT&T, those employees who use the services of a physician associated with the PPO network are reimbursed for 100 percent of medical expenses incurred after a $150 annual individual deduction. For those going outside the PPO, the reimbursement is 85 percent, after a $200 deductible has been met.[31]

PPOs are trying to combine the best of both worlds—the HMO and traditional insurance. They may well be the fastest growing form of health plan in the 1990s, which suggests that by the end of this decade HMOs and PPOs will be providing the dominant health-care coverage in the United States.[32] PPOs alone are "expected to increase from 1 percent to an estimated 8 percent of the U.S. population by 1990, and to 20–25 percent by [the late 1990s], surpassing the growth of HMOs."[33]

Employer Operated Coverage Although the types of insurance programs mentioned above are the most popular means of health insurance today, many companies are looking for other options that will assist them in containing the rising health-care costs they incur. To this end, some companies have begun reviewing the concept of being self-insured, and in many of these instances, using the assistance of a third-party administrator. A movement in health-insurance coverage in the 1980s was the formation of self-funded programs. Some organizations, such as the State of Maryland and General Binding Corporation, have ventured into the insurance business to reduce health insurance costs. Under a self-funding arrangement, an "employer provides a formal plan to employees under which the employer directly pays and is liable for some or all of the benefits promised under the plan."[34] This insurance plan is customarily established and operated under an arrangement called a voluntary employees beneficiary association (VEBA). In this case, the employer typically establishes a trust fund to pay for the health benefits used.[35] For the most part, this employer trust fund has received favorable treatment from the IRS.

Health Insurance Continuation   What happens to an employee's health insurance coverage if that employees leaves the organization, or maybe is laid off? The answer to that question lies in the **Consolidated Omnibus Budget Reconciliation Act (COBRA).** One of the main features established by the CO-BRA was the continuation of employee benefits for a period up to three years after the employee leaves the company.[36] Because of high unemployment rates in the early 1980s, supplemented by the downsizing of corporate America, large numbers of individuals were out of work, and more importantly, no longer had medical insurance. To combat this problem, COBRA was enacted in 1985. When employees resign or are laid off through no fault of their own—like the expansive downsizing that occurred in the early 1990s—they are eligible for a continuation of their health insurance benefits. The cost of this coverage is paid by the employee, but COBRA requires employers to offer this benefit through the company's current group health insurance plan.

Retirement Programs

Retiring from work today does not guarantee a continuation of one's standard of living. Social Security cannot sustain the lifestyle most of us grow accustom to in our working years. Accordingly, we cannot rely on the government as the sole source of our retirement income. Instead, Social Security payments must be just one component of a properly designed retirement system.[37] The other components are retirement we receive from our organization, and savings we have amassed over the years. Irrespective of the retirement vehicles used, it is important to recognize that retirement plans are highly regulated by the Employee Retirement Income Security Act.

The **Employee Retirement Income Security Act (ERISA)** of 1974 was passed to deal with the largest problems imposed by private pension plans—that people were not getting their benefits. That was due chiefly to the design of these pension plans, which almost always required a minimum tenure with the organization before the individual had a guaranteed right to pension benefits, regardless of whether or not they remained with the company. These permanent benefits—or the guarantee to a pension when one retires or leaves the organization—are called **vesting rights,** and were typically withheld until employees served ten to fifteen years with the company. In some cases, no vesting privileges were identified. This meant, for instance, that a 60-year-old employee with twenty-three years of service who left the company—for whatever reason—would have no right to a pension benefit. ERISA was enacted to prevent such abuses.

ERISA requires employers who decide to provide a pension plan to design a retirement program under specific rules. Typically, each plan must convey to employees "new eligibility requirements for coverage, breaks in service, restoration of service following a break, plan payment methods, and new vesting re-

Consolidated Omnibus Budget Reconciliation Act Provides for the continuation of employee benefits for a period up to three years after an employee leaves a job.

Employee Retirement Income Security Act Law passed in 1974 designed to protect employee retirement benefits.

Vesting Rights The permanent right to pension benefits.

quirements."[38] Currently, vesting rights in organizations comes after five years of service, and pension programs must be available to all employees over age 21.[39] This shorter vesting period is crucial for employees, especially when one considers that the length of service in companies today is shorter. With this shorter vesting period, employees who leave companies after five years generally can carry their retirement rights with them; that is, ERISA enables pension rights to be portable.[40]

ERISA also created guidelines for the termination of a pension program. Should an employer voluntarily terminate a pension program, like the LTV Corporation did in 1986,[41] the **Pension Benefit Guaranty Corporation (PBGC)** must be notified. Similarly, the act permits the PBGC, under certain conditions (such as inadequate pension funding), to lay claim on corporate assets—up to 30 percent of net worth to pay benefits that had been promised to employees. Furthermore, when a retirement plan is terminated, the PBGC requires the employer to identify to workers and retirees any financial institution that will be handling future retirement programs for the organization.[42]

Another key aspect of ERISA is its requirement for a company to include what is commonly called a **Summary Plan Description (SPD).** Summary Plan Descriptions are designed to serve as a vehicle to inform employees about the benefits offered in the company in terms the "average" employee can understand.[43] This means that employers are required to inform employees on the details of their pension plans, including such items as "the retirement plan requirements (including eligibility, forfeiture, complaint procedures); their rights under ERISA; information on how the plan is funded; and their accumulated benefits."[44]

Defined Benefit Plans In years past, the most popular pension was a **defined benefit plan.** This plan specifies the dollar benefit workers will receive at retirement. The amount typically revolves around some fixed monthly income for life; or a variation of a lump sum cash distribution. The amount and type of the benefit is set, and the company contributes the set amount each year into a trust fund. The amount contributed each year is figured on an actuarial basis; that is, by considering variables such as how long plan participants are expected to live, their lifetime earnings, and how much return the trust portfolio will receive (e.g., 5 percent or 10 percent annually) contributions are made. The pension payout formulas used to determine retirement benefits vary widely.

Over the past decade, defined benefit plans have received some criticism. Employees have identified a need to receive more retirement benefits, and to be permitted to make contributions to their retirement plans. At the New York Mercantile Exchange, for example, employees requested that management consider making changes to the retirement plan in effect. Recognizing that another retirement vehicle met employees needs better, the company discontinued its defined benefit plan and implemented a money purchase plan and 401(k) combination.[45]

Defined Contribution Plans **Defined contribution plans** are different from defined benefit plans in at least one very important area—no specific dollar benefits are fixed. That is, under a defined contribution plan, each employee has an individual account, to which both the employee or the employer may make contributions.[46] The plan establishes rules for contributions. For example, the Humana, Inc. defined contribution pension plan allows employees to select both a money purchase plan (described next) and a defined contribution with the company matching up to 6 percent of salary. In a defined contribution plan, the money is invested and projections are offered as to probable retirement in-

Pension Benefit Guaranty Corporation The organization that lays claim to corporate assets to pay or fund inadequate pension programs.

Summary Plan Description An ERISA requirement of explaining to employees their pension program and rights.

Defined Benefit A type of retirement program whereby a retiring employee receives a fixed amount of retirement income based on some average earnings over a period of time.

Defined Contribution Plans A retirement plan whereby an employer only agrees to contribute to employees' retirement funds. The amount contributed is not fixed.

come levels. However, the company is not bound by these projections, and accordingly, unfunded pension liability problems do not occur. For this reason, defined contribution plans have become a popular trend in new qualified pension plans. Additionally, variations in plan administration frequently allow the employee some selection in the investment choices; that is, one may select bonds for security, common stocks for appreciation and an inflation hedge, or some type of money market fund.

Money Purchase Pension Plan   Money purchase pension plans are variants of defined contribution pension plans. The difference between the two justify its being listed separately. Under this arrangement, the organization commits to deposit into the fund annually, a fixed amount of money or a percentage of the employee's pay.[47] Under IRS regulations, however, the maximum permitted is 25 percent of worker pay. Under money purchase plans no specific retirement dollar benefits are fixed as they are under a defined benefit plan. However, companies do make projections of probable retirement income based on various interest rates, but the company is not bound to the projection.

Profit-Sharing Plans   Profit-sharing pension plans are yet another variation of defined contribution plans. Under these plans, companies, like Fisher-Price, contribute to a trust fund account an optional percentage of each worker's pay (maximum allowed by law is 15 percent). This, of course, is guided by the profit level in the organization. The operative word in profit-sharing plans here is "optional." The company is not bound by law to make contributions every year. It should be noted, however, that although employers are not bound by law, the majority of employers feel a moral obligation to make a contribution. Often they will keep to a schedule, even in times when profits are slim or nonexistent.[48]

Individual Retirement Accounts   From 1982 to 1986, the Individual Retirement Account (IRA) was the darling of retirement planning. The law permitted each worker to defer paying taxes on up to $2,000 of earned income per year ($2,225 for employee and spouse where spouse did not work) with interest on these accounts also accumulating on a tax-deferred basis. This was a tax shelter for the average person, a good way to build a nest egg. Anyone who had earned income could invest in an IRA. The purpose of an IRA was to make the individual partly responsible for his or her retirement income.

IRAs were very popular for the few years they received favorable tax status; however, with the Tax Reform of 1986, IRAs became significantly limited for many workers. To be eligible for deferring income to an IRA, workers now must meet specific conditions, such as not participating in a recognized pension program at work and falling under limits on the adjusted annual income. For instance, a single individual making $35,000 a year ($50,000 for married taxpayers) with a company-paid pension would no longer qualify for a tax deduction from their IRA contribution. The purpose of the tax reform was to focus IRAs on lower income workers who might not have a pension program at their place of work, or for those who deserve to augment the one they have. The future of IRAs appears to be a matter of debate. Both the Democrats and the Clinton administration, as well as the Republican Congress, have made proposals to reinstate IRAs, making them more available to a broader group of workers. To date, the issue has not been settled.

401(k)s   Under the Tax Equity and Fiscal Responsible Act (TEFRA), capital accumulation programs, more commonly known as **401(k)s** or thrift-savings plans,

401(k)s Tax code section that permits employees to set aside a part of their salary for retirement on a pretax basis.

were established. A 401(k) program is named after the IRS tax code section that created its existence. These programs permit workers to set aside a certain amount of their income on a tax-deferred basis. In many cases, what differentiated the 401(k) from an IRA was the amount permitted to be set aside, and the realization that many companies contributed an amount to the 401(k) on the employee's behalf.[49] Because of this matching feature, many companies call their 401(k) a matching-contribution plan, meaning that both the employer and the employee are working jointly to create a retirement program. For instance, at Critical Care America, for every dollar of gross income employees defer to the plan, the company makes a matching contribution of 25 cents, up to a maximum match of 6 percent of salary.

The 401(k) programs have been popular with employees since their inception. Both employers and employees have found that there are advantages to offering capital accumulation plans. The cost of providing these plans is low for the employer, and employees can supplement their retirement program and dabble in investments. Most companies have offered their employees the ease of contributing to their 401(k) through payroll deductions. Additionally, in some instances, the matching-contribution program may be offered to supplement the employer's noncontributory (defined benefit) retirement plan.

Other Retirement Vehicles   While we've described the major retirement plans, we would be remiss not to mention the following that are appropriate retirement vehicles for selected groups of workers. These are 403(b)s, Simplified Employee Pension Plans (SEPs), Keogh Plans, and Stock Option Plans (ESOPS— Employee Stock Ownership Plans), PAYSOPS (Payroll-Based Stock Ownership Plans), and TRASOPS (Tax-Benefit Based Stock Ownership Plans). Table 14-4 provides a summary of these retirement alternatives for special groups of workers.

Time Off with Pay

There are a number of benefits that provide pay for time off from work. The most popular of these are vacation and holiday leave and disability insurance, which includes sick leave and short- and long-term disability programs.

TABLE 14-4   Other Retirement Plan Options

Plan	About the Plan
403(B)	Designed to be the 401(k) counterpart for educational and non-profit organizations.
Simplified Employee Retirement Plans	Designed for an employer or the self-employed individual. Permits contributions up to 15 percent of net profit, or $30,000 (whichever is less).
Keogh Plans	Available to the self-employed, permits contributions of 15 percent of net profit, or $30,000 (whichever is less). The main distinction between a Keogh and an SEP lies in the annual report filing requirement of the IRS.
Stock Option Plans	Under these plans, an individual can purchase company stock through payroll deductions. The stock is generally sold at a discount to the employee, or at straight market value without the use of, or commissions for, a broker.

Vacation and Holiday Leave   After employees have been with an organization for a specified period of time, they usually become eligible for a paid vacation. Common practice is to relate the length of vacation to the length of tenure and job classification in the organization. For example, after six months' service with an organization, an employee may be eligible for one week's vacation; after a year, two weeks; after five years, three weeks; and after ten or more years, four weeks. It is interesting to note that U.S. workers have one of the shortest vacation periods of many industrialized nations. For example, while U.S. workers enjoy fifteen to twenty days off each year, on average, employees in France, England, Germany, and Hong Kong are offered up to thirty days a year.[50]

The rationale behind the paid vacation is to provide a break in which employees can refresh themselves. This rationale is important, but is sometimes overlooked. For example, in a situation where employees accrue a certain amount of vacation time and can sell back to the company any unused vacation days, the regenerative "battery charging" intent is lost. While the cost may be the same to the employer (depending on how long vacation time can be accrued), employees who do not take a break ultimately may be adversely affecting themselves.

Holiday pay is paid time off while observing some special event—federally mandated holidays (like New Year's Day, President's Day, Martin Luther King's Birthday, Memorial Day, Labor Day, Thanksgiving, and Christmas), company-provided holidays (like Christmas Eve and New Year's Eve), or personal days (days employees can take off for any reason). In the United States, employees average ten paid holidays per year.[51] Most other countries are similar, with averages of nine paid holidays in the United Kingdom, eleven in Brazil, seventeen in Japan, and a maximum of nineteen in Mexico.[52]

Disability Insurance Programs   Employees today recognize that salary continuation for injuries and major illnesses is almost more important than life insurance. For most employees, there is a greater probability that they will have a disabling injury requiring an extended absence from work of more than ninety days than that they will die before their retirement.[53] Programs to address this area of need can be broken down into two broad categories—short-term disability and long-term disability programs.

Almost all employers offer some type of short-term disability plan (STD). Categories under this heading include the company sick-leave policy, short-term disability programs,[54] state disability laws, and workers' compensation. The focus of each is to provide replacement income in the event of an injury or a short-term illness.[55] For many, this short-term period is defined as being six months or less in duration.

One of the most popular types of short-term disability programs is a company's sick-leave plan. Most organizations, such as Chrysler and Black & Decker, provide their employees with pay for days not worked because of illness. Sick leave is allocated on the basis of a specific number of days a year,[56] accrued on a cumulative basis, or expanded relative to years of service with the organization. In the first case, an individual may take off up to a specific maximum number of days due to illness, while receiving full pay. In the latter case, some organizations expand their sick leave with tenure. Each year of employment may entitle the worker to two additional days' sick leave. Regardless of whether sick leave is used, it would continue to accumulate (usually up to some maximum number of days); those individuals who have been with the company the longest would have accumulated the most sick-leave credit.

Sick-leave abuse has often been a problem for organizations. The belief that one should amass sick leave for use later in life is quickly diminishing. That belief may have been popular when a person joined an organization early in life and retired from that company, but with today's mobility, long-term focus has little meaning, especially when we consider that sick days are not usually transferable to another organization. Thus, the "use them or lose them" concept may only hinder productivity. Attempts have been made recently to combat this potential for sick-leave abuse. This has come in the form of financial incentives to individuals who do not fully use their sick leave for the year. In a number of union settings, for example, in an effort to reward attendance, companies have what is called "well pay"—that is, there is some monetary inducement for workers not to use all of their sick leave. This inducement can be in the form of buying back the unused sick leave, or in other cases, lumping sick-leave days into the years of service in calculating retirement benefits. These incentives intend to serve as a bonus and encourage judicious use of sick time.[57]

If health insurance coverage was unable to prevent a major illness from occurring, and an extended period of time off work did not provide for ample recuperation, then employees may need the benefits provided under a long-term disability program. Similar to their short-term disability counterparts, long-term disability programs (LTDs) are designed to provide replacement income for an employee who is no longer able to return to work and where short-term coverage has expired. The period of time before long-term disability becomes effective is usually six months. Some type of long-term disability coverage is in effect in almost 99 percent of all companies and is provided on a temporary or permanent basis.[58] By definition, a temporary disability is one in which an individual cannot perform his or her job duties for the first twenty-four months after injury or illness. Permanent, long-term disability is when an individual is unable to perform in any occupation.[59]

The benefits paid to employees is customarily set between 50 and 67 percent, with 60 percent salary replacement the most common (see "HRM Skills"). In most plans, there is a maximum monthly payment of replacement income that lies between 70 and 80 percent of gross pay.[60] This may be as little as $2,000, or greater than $10,000.[61] In most cases, long-term disability payments continue until the individual reaches age 65.[62]

Survivor Benefits

To provide protection to the families of employees, many companies offer life insurance as a benefit. Life insurance programs offered to employees typically come in two varieties—noncontributory and contributory policies. Our major focus in this context is on the noncontributory variety, for that is the one generally completely employer funded.

Group Term Life Insurance   When a company offers group term life insurance to its employees,[63] the standard policy provides for a death benefit of one to five times their annual rate of pay, with most including a double indemnity provision—that is, should an employee's death result from an accident, the benefit is twice the policy value. Almost 74 percent of all companies provide this coverage.[64]

Death benefits offered are generally linked to one's position in the organization. Generally speaking, the more "valuable" an employee is defined in terms of his or her level in the organization, the greater the death benefit offered. Those at lower levels of the organization typically receive one and one-half their annual wage as a benefit, whereas top-level employees may receive as much as three times their salary.[65]

HRM*Skills*

Calculating Long-Term Disability Payments

Determining long-term disability payments can be easily formulated with the appropriate background information. To demonstrate this process, let's present the necessary data, and show the calculations.

Suppose an employee makes $36,000 per year, or $3,000 per month. The organization offers its employees a long-term disability (LTD) insurance at 65 percent of earnings, with a monthly cap at $4,000. The company's LTD is also integrated with Social Security disability payments (SSDI) such that no more than 70 percent of salary is covered. The employee has a verifiable illness, is unable to work in any occupation, and has been covered under the company's short-term disability plan for the past six months (the required time before long-term disability starts). To determine what the payment made to this employee would be, we need to determine the amount of the SSDI monthly payment. For example's sake, let us assume that this employee is entitled to $8,400 in SSDI benefits a year, or $700 per month. We now have enough data to calculate the employee's LTD payment. After the calculations have been completed, we see that this employee, given his specific set of circumstances, is eligible for a payment of $500 from SSDI, and $900 from the LTD policy. Even though the LTD limit of 65 percent of the employee's salary would be $1,300, when integrated with SSDI, the employee may not receive more than $1,400 (70 percent of monthly salary). The following reflects the LTD calculations.

65% of annual earnings/month = LTD coverage	=	$1,950 ($3,000 × 65%)
70% of monthly income for integration with Social Security	=	$2,100 ($3,000 × 70%)
SSDI benefit $8,400/12 = $700	=	$ 700 (Given)
Proposed total monthly payment without Social Security integration	=	$2,650 ($1,950 + $700)
Proposed total monthly payment with Social Security integration	=	$2,100 (Maximum)
Overage	=	$ 550 ($2,650 − $2,100)
Actual LTD payment	=	$1,400 ($1,950 − $550) (LTD − overage)

Source: This example was directly influenced by a similar example given in Jerry S. Rosenbloom and G. Victor Hallman, *Employee Benefits Planning*, 3d ed. (Englewood Cliffs, N.J.: Prentice-Hall, 1991), p. 225. Actual benefits received under SSDI vary according to family status, average annual income, and the consumer price index. Therefore, only an estimate is given.

Travel Insurance   Another insurance plan offered to many employees is travel insurance. Under this policy, employees' lives are covered in the event of death while traveling on company time. This insurance typically provides a lump sum payment, from $50,000 to $1 million. Depending on any unique provisions of a policy, as long as an employee is conducting business-related activities when the death occurs, the insurance will be paid. For example, if a salesperson's day typically begins by traveling to a client's place of business from his or her residence, coverage begins as soon as this person gets into the car. If he or she is killed going to that location, then this insurance is activated. The key element is when death occurred. An employee who normally commutes to work would not be covered if an accident happened on the way.

An Integrative Perspective on Employee Benefits

When an employer considers offering benefits to employees, one of the main considerations is to keep costs down. Traditionally employers attempted to do this by providing a list of benefits to their employees—whether employees wanted or needed any particular benefit, or used it at all. Rising costs, and a desire to let employees choose what they want, led employers to search for alternative measures of benefits administration. The leading alternative to address this concern was the implementation of **flexible benefits.**[66] Although flexible benefits offer greater choice to employees (and may have a "motivational" effect), we must understand that they are provided mainly to contain benefit costs.[67] The term *flexible benefits* refers to a system whereby employees are presented with a menu of benefits and asked to select, within monetary limits imposed, the employee benefits they desire. Today, more than 25 percent of all major corporations in the United States, like PepsiCo, AT&T, and Xerox, offer flexible benefits.[68] A number of types of flexible benefits exist. Specifically, three plans are popular: flexible spending accounts, modular plans, and core-plus options.[69]

Flexible Benefits A benefits program in which employees are permitted to pick benefits that most meet their needs.

Flexible Spending Accounts

Flexible spending accounts, approved and operated under Section 125 of the Internal Revenue Code, are special types of flexible benefits that permit employees to set aside up to $5,000 annually to pay for particular services. For example, Abbott Laboratories has a flexible spending account that enables employees to pay for such items as health-care premiums, certain medical expenses (like dental), dependent child-care premiums, and specific group legal services with pre-tax dollars.[70] By placing a specified amount into a spending account, the employee is permitted to pay for these services with monies not included in W-2 income. This can result in a lower tax rate for an employee, and can increase the amount of take-home pay.

While tax benefits exist for employees, workers must understand that flexible spending accounts are heavily regulated. Each account established must operate independently. For instance, money set aside for dependent care expenses can be used only for that purpose. One cannot decide later to seek reimbursement from one account to pay for services where no account was established, or to pay for services from another account because all monies in the designated account have been withdrawn. Additionally, money that is deposited into these accounts must be spent during the period, or forfeited. Unused monies do not revert back to the employee in terms of a cash outlay; forfeited monies typically revert back to the company. This point must be clearly communicated to employees to avoid misconception of the plan requirements.

Modular Plans

The **modular plan** of flexible benefits is a system whereby employees choose a pre-designed package of benefits. As opposed to selecting "cafeteria style," modular plans contain "a fixed combination of benefit plans put together to meet

Modular Plans A flexible benefit system whereby employees choose a pre-designed package of benefits.

the needs of a particular segment of the employee population."[71] For example, suppose a company offers its employees two separate modules. Module 1 benefits consist of no dental or vision coverage, a life insurance policy at two times annual earnings, and HMO health-care insurance; this policy is provided to all employees at no cost to them. Module 2 benefits consist of dental and vision coverage, a life insurance policy of two times annual earnings, and traditional health insurance. This plan, however, requires a biweekly payroll deduction of $57. While a choice does exist, it is limited to selecting either of the packages in its entirety.

Core-plus Options Plans

A **core-plus** options flexible benefits plan exhibits more of a menu selection than the two programs just mentioned. Under this arrangement, employees typically are provided with coverage of core areas—typically medical coverage, life insurance at one time annual earnings, minimal disability insurance, a pension program, and standard time off from work with pay.[72] With these minimum benefits in place, not only are employees provided basic coverage from which they can build more extensive packages, but the core-plus option helps to eliminate **adverse selection.**[73] Under this type of plan, employees are given the opportunity to select other benefits. These additional benefits may range from more extensive coverage of the core plan, to other benefits like spending accounts. Employees are generally given credits to purchase their additional benefits. These credits are often calculated according to an employee's tenure in the company, salary, and position held. As a rule of thumb, in first-time installations, the credits given to an employee equal the amount needed to purchase the identical plan in force before flexible benefits arrived; that is, no employee should be worse off. If the employee decides to select exactly what was previously offered, the employee would be able to purchase such benefits with no added out-of-pocket expenses (co-payments) other than what he or she had previously paid.

The Service Side of Benefits

In addition to the benefits described above, organizations offer a wealth of services employees may find desirable. These services can be provided to the employee at no cost, or at a significant reduction from what might have been paid without the organization's support.

Services provided to employees may be such benefits as sponsored social and recreational events, employee assistance programs, credit unions, housing, tuition reimbursement, jury duty, uniforms, military pay, company-paid transportation and parking, free coffee, baby-sitting services or referrals, and the like. Companies can be as creative as they like in putting together their benefits program. The crucial point is to provide a package containing those benefits in which employees have expressed some interest and perceive some value in its offering.

Current Issues in Benefit Administration

Over the past few decades, as we have described, there have been considerable changes in the composition of employee benefits offered to workers. Although many of these changes have brought a new philosophy, and a new administration of employee benefits, all indications point to a continual expansion and re-

Core-plus Plans A flexible benefits program whereby employees are provided core benefit coverage, and then are permitted to buy additional benefits from a menu.

Adverse Selection A situation in flexible benefits administration where those in greatest need of a particular benefit choose that benefit more often than the average employee.

definition of employee benefits packages. What benefit predictions can we make as we move closer to the year 2000? Even though predictions are just an educated guess, based on what we have been seeing, a sound forecast can be made. Specifically, we can expect more activities surrounding domestic partner benefits, reduction of retiree benefits and family-friendly benefits.

Domestic Partner Benefits

Traditionally, health insurance benefits have been offered to employees, and their immediate family. However, this construct of what family life is about has been changing in the American society. Living arrangements, either heterosexual or homosexual, are different today than they were three decades ago, resulting in "demands" from employees to have the same opportunity as their married counterparts to medical coverage for their significant others. Although in the past only a few companies had offered such a benefit to employees, that trend appears to be reversing, and may even become law.[74] Organizations like Apple Computer, Lotus Development, Ben & Jerry's, Levi Strauss, and the City of San Diego, offer full domestic partner benefits, regardless of the sex of the significant other.[75] Not surprisingly, though, there are still some concerns for companies. Two key issues facing domestic-partner benefits are homosexual partners and abuse of the system—like signing up anybody close to you so that person can have health insurance.

Like the attitude Apple faced in Williamson County, many associate this benefit as supporting a homosexual lifestyle. In many people's minds, this may result in the organization incurring more medical insurance premium expenses. Ironically, this fear of higher costs doesn't appear to be well founded.[76] For instance, Lotus Development Company in Cambridge, Massachusetts, has implemented a policy that offers "domestic partners of homosexual employees" the same benefits it offers to spouses of married employees.[77] Lotus requires these employees to sign affidavits attesting that they have a marriage-like relationship with another individual. And for those individuals who want to turn the discussion to such illnesses like AIDS, Lotus has determined the cost of a heart attack or can-

Employees of Lotus Development are provided with a unique benefit among corporate America. It's called the domestic partner's benefit. This benefit provides health insurance coverage to one's significant other, irrespective of the sex of the partner.

cer closely approximates the medical costs of AIDS.[78] Therefore, from their perspective, the cost issue, coupled with the relatively small employee population eligible for the coverage, made the decision easy. By doing so, Lotus and companies that offer similar coverage have a policy that "represents an issue of fairness and equality."[79]

A similar response can be made about potential abuse in the system. Just claiming that one has a domestic partner may not be enough. Rather, employees must be able to show that they are in a relationship that resembles a "marriage." That may mean substantiating that this relationship has existed for some time, and that assets of both individuals are used to share household costs. Understandably, no organization would be willing to provide health benefit coverage to an employee's significant other, if that "other" changes several times a year. Certain safeguards can protect from that occurring.

Reduction of Retiree Health Benefits

Initially, companies had hoped that Medicare programs administered by the federal government would lessen the costs of covering retiree health care once the retiree was age 65 or older. This was to be achieved through coordination with the Medicare program. Unfortunately, this cost reduction never fully materialized. Today, health benefits for retirees is a complex and convolute process. Factors affecting this benefit have "legal, accounting, and financial constraints, as well as HRM concerns."[80] For example, a relatively new Financial Accounting Standards Board rule requires companies to decrease company earnings by a proportion of their retirement obligations.[81] For companies like Chrysler, this ruling meant a $4 to $6 billion write-off in 1992;[82] now Chrysler will offer full health benefits only to its retirees who meet 30-years-of-service and 60-years-of-age criteria. For other companies, such as Ralston Purina and Boise Cascade, this ruling meant the elimination of retiree health benefits altogether.[83]

Cutting retiree health benefits is a strategic move to cut costs, but what is it doing to the motivation of current employees? The answer, although common sense may dictate the worst, is unknown at this time.[84] Some companies, like DuPont, are not willing to take that chance. Rather, they treat all employees, active or retired, the same (see "Meet Robert McNutt").[85]

Family-Friendly Benefits

Family-Friendly Benefits Flexible benefits that are supportive of caring for one's family.

Another major trend affecting corporations today is the push for benefits that fall under the category called **family-friendly benefits.** Family-friendly benefits are so named because they represent flexible benefits that are supportive of caring for one's family. These would include such benefits as flextime, child care, dependent-care flexible spending account, part-time employment, relocation programs, summer day camp, adoption benefits,[86] and parental leave.[87] Some of the more notable companies that offer such benefits are AT&T, Hewlett-Packard, the Prudential Insurance Company,[88] and IBM.[89] At the heart of such programs, however, is a means for increasing child- and elder-care benefits.[90] While flexible spending accounts mentioned earlier have assisted in "affording" this care, more employees are seeking ways of having quality child care and elder care in close proximity to them; this is especially true of organizations that operate staggered shifts or around the clock.

A number of societal issues are at stake here. Dual-career couples with children and/or elderly live-in parents need to have some assurance that child- or elder-care programs are available to them without major disruptions to their lives. No longer is it acceptable to assume that other family members or friends

Meet

Robert McNutt
Manager, Compensation and Benefits, DuPont & Company

Robert P. McNutt is currently the manager of Compensation and Benefits at the E. I. DuPont de Nemours & Company. He has also written about compensation and benefit changes and has addressed the Conference Board, the American Management Association (AMA), and the American Compensation Association (ACA) on the compensation and benefits issues.

McNutt was selected to join the teaching faculty of ACA in 1990. He joined DuPont in 1966 and has held a variety of marketing, manufacturing, product, and business management assignments in the Textile, Carpet, and Industrial market segments of the Fibers Department. For more than ten years, McNutt has been adjunct professor of business administration in the College of Business and Economics at the University of Delaware. He received an MBA from the University of Delaware in 1969.

Lately, one of McNutt's major concerns has been the rapidly rising costs associated with employee benefits. For example, at DuPont, health-care benefits had been rising so dramatically that by 1993, the company was paying about $6,000 per employee per year. That amounted to almost $1.5 million a day—for just health insurance. Needless to say, it was time to act, and act quickly, but properly. To deal with the escalating costs, McNutt's group implemented a four-pronged approach to health-insurance cost-cutting.

First, DuPont became active in the national debate on health care. The company believes that there should be managed health-care competition, and that all employees should receive some type of health-care insurance. Internally, McNutt advocated prevention and wellness in the organization. One means of cutting costs is to prevent the major illness that may arise. DuPont also came to the realization that employees had to share in their health-care costs. Although this had existed for about a decade, the company's failure to index health-care costs to inflation led to DuPont paying more than 90 percent of the share. And finally, the organization implemented managed care—cost-effective, preferred provider arrangements.

Has the change worked? Overall, McNutt thinks that the change has been successful. Employees appear to be getting used to the new changes (with the assistance of an extensive communications program). They see the benefit of this action for the strategic competitiveness of DuPont, and the company is beginning to regain control of their health-care costs.

Source: Based on the Robert McNutt interview appearing in Commerce Clearing House, "DuPont Revamps Its Health Plan to Rein in Costs," *Human Resources Management: Ideas and Trends* (January 5, 1994), pp. 1–2.

Bright Horizons Children's Center provides child-care services to employees of such companies as New York Hospital, Mattel Toys, du Pont, and Duke Power. It's eighty service locations, like this one pictured in Cambridge, Massachusetts, not only provide a location for children to be safely cared for, but also focus on a curriculum that is designed to help these children develop themselves.

will provide this care—although in many cases that is what occurs. Nonetheless, companies are beginning to recognize that when its employees are faced with a choice between their jobs and their families, the vast majority of employees clearly place their job second. For example, although sick leave is supposed to be used for the employee's illness only, when a child of that employee is sick and no child care is available, it is likely the employee will call in sick in order to care for their dependent. One company, Nyloncraft, Inc., recognized that it was experiencing tremendous turnover because of child-care conflicts; accordingly, it instituted what is now regarded as the nation's first employer-owned child-care facility.[91] The purpose was to promote increased productivity, improve attendance, lessen turnover, and the like.[92] While there are legal and insurance ramifications to be addressed, in locations where these programs operate, employee morale has increased. In addition, companies have also developed cooperative efforts to address this issue; for example, American Express, IBM, Work Family Directions, and Allstate Insurance have joined forces to offer quality child care at a facility that is in close proximity to all of their employees.[93]

Similar to the need for child care is the need for elder care. Elder care refers to a situation in which children become more responsible for the care of an aged parent. The same issues regarding facilities, quality providers, and so forth, arise. Although child care has been given more attention, elder care is a matter that will need further investigation as we move closer to the year 2000.

Organizations have come a long way during the past decade in their concern for family-oriented benefits. But don't think that these benefits exist in every organization. Rather, today's business climate, and the need for greater productivity, have made some companies less friendly.[94] Downsizing, selling off diversfied divisions, cutting salaries or reducing pay increases, hiring contingent workers, and the like indicate that the once-paternalistic companies may have become relics of the past. Maybe the de-jobbing of America will ultimately curtail this family-friendly benefit trend!

Study Tools and Applications

Summary

This summary relates to the Learning Objectives provided on p. 380.

After having read this chapter, you should know:

1. The linkage of benefits to motivation may not exist unless the benefits offered are tailored to the specific needs of the workers (their rewards). Traditional benefit administration, treating benefits as membership-based rewards, may not generate the increased productivity like that of flexible-benefit options.

2. Employers offer benefits to employees to attract and retain them. Benefits are expected by today's workers, and as such, must be offered in such a way that they provide meaning and value to the employees.

3. Social Security is an insurance program funded by current employees to provide (1) a minimum level of retirement income, (2) disability income, and (3) survivor benefits. Unemployment compensation provides income continuation to employees who lose a job through no fault of their own. Unemployment compensation typically lasts for twenty-six weeks. Workers' compensation provides income continuation for employees who are hurt or disabled on the job. Workers' compensation also provides compensation for work-related deaths or permanent disabilities. All three are legally required benefits.

4. The three major types of health insurance benefits offered to employees are traditional, health maintenance organizations, and preferred provider organizations. The latter two are designed to provide a fixed out-of-pocket alternative to health-care coverage.

5. The most popular types of retirement benefits offered today are defined benefit plans, defined contribution plans, money purchase pension plans, profit-sharing plans, Social Security, individual retirement accounts, and 401(k)s. For special groups, however, 403(b)s, stock option programs, simplified employee pension plans, and Keough plans may be used.

6. The Employment Retirement Income Security Act (ERISA) has had a significant effect on retirement programs. Its primary emphasis is to ensure that employees have a vested right to their retirement monies, to ensure that appropriate guidelines are followed in the event of a retirement plan termination, and to ensure that employees understand their benefits through the Summary Plan Description.

7. The primary reason for a company to provide a vacation benefit is to allow employees a break from work in which they can refresh/reenergize themselves.

8. Disability benefit programs are designed to ensure income replacement for employees in the event of a temporary or permanent disability arising from an injury or extended illness (typically originating off the job).

9. Flexible benefits programs come in a variety of packages. The most popular versions existing today are flexible spending accounts, modular plans, add-on plans, and core-plus options.

10. Family-friendly benefits refers to a variety of benefits that are supportive of blending family and career. This may include on-site child care, flexible work schedules, dependent spending accounts, and part-time employment.

Key Terms

adverse selection
Blue Cross
Blue Shield
Consolidated Omnibus Budget
    Reconciliation Act (COBRA)
core-plus plans
defined benefit plan
defined contribution plans
employee benefits
family-friendly benefits
flexible benefits
flexible spending accounts
401(k)s
health insurance

Health Maintenance Act
health maintenance organization (HMO)
legally required benefits
modular plans
Pension Benefit Guarantee Corporation (PBGC)
preferred provider organization (PPO)
Social Security
summary plan description (SPD)
unemployment compensation
vesting rights
Voluntary Employees Beneficiary Association (VEBA)
workers' compensation

EXPERIENTIAL EXERCISE:

Flexible Benefits Choices

Form into groups of three to five members. Using Table 14-5, determine the mix of benefits that would best fit your needs. After doing so, answer the following questions in your group.

1. Explain the reasons for the choices you made. What compelled you to make those specific choices?

2. Compare what you have chosen with the members of your group. Are there similarities? In which benefit coverage? Are there differences? In which benefit coverage?

3. How can you best explain the reasons for the differences—that is, what factors from question 1 affected the differences in benefits selection?

4. Do you think your benefits selection choices will be the same five years from now? Ten years? Explain.

TABLE 14-5   Sample Flexible Benefit Selection Sheet

NAME: MANNY CHOICES[1]			YEARS OF SERVICE:	4
ANNUAL EARNINGS:	$35,000		CREDITS TO SPEND:	2565[2]

Health Care			Vacation[6]		
HMO	Core[3]		1 week	Core	
PPO	840		2 weeks	673	
Traditional	1680		3 weeks	1346	
			4 weeks	2019	

Life Insurance
- $1 \times AE$ Core[4]
- $2 \times AE$ 252
- $3 \times AE$ 504
- $4 \times AE$ 756

Paid Holidays
- 7 days   Core

Personal Days
- 1 day   Core
- 2 days   134
- 3 days   268

Disability Insurance
- 50% AE   Core
- 55% AE   138
- 60% AE   276
- 65% AE   414

Vision Coverage
- HMO   Core
- PPO   194

Dental Coverage
- No coverage   Core
- PPO   210

Retirement[5]
- Non-Contributory Core
- 401(k) with 1% match   350
-              with 2% match   700
-              with 3% match   1050
-              with 4% match   1400

[1] All cost figures represent single employee coverage only, where applicable. For additional family coverages for health insurance, see footnote 3.

[2] All flexible credits are based on 37 percent of salary (AE). Flexible spending credits are those credits available to you to spend on benefits. Credits available for spending are the difference between total flexible credits and those costs associated with core coverage. Any amount over the credits will be deducted evenly over your twenty-six biweekly pays.

[3] Health-care core coverage is based on $190 per month for employee-only coverage. Add $70 for employee plus one; and $140 for employee plus two or more. Add $35 and $56 for PPO, and $190 and $281 for traditional respectively, depending on family status. (No increase for dental or vision based on family status.)

[4] Life insurance rate is calculated at 7.20 cents per $1,000 of life insurance.

[5] Retirement costs are calculated at 16 percent of total earnings; 401(k) reflects a maximum 4 percent contribution.

[6] Vacation costs are determined at 1/52nd of annual earnings. Paid holidays and personal days are based on a 2,080 work-hour year and a cost per hour rate.

CASE APPLICATION:
Sick-Child Care at Scitor

Imagine your dilemma. You're scheduled to attend a major project-launch meeting late this morning—a meeting that has been set for several weeks now. As you pull the covers off your child, however, your stomach sinks. The kid feels hot. The thermometer confirms it—the temperature is 102.3! What do you do? Call in sick yourself, and miss the meeting? After all, it's your meeting and you're expected to be there. Or do you leave the child home "for just a couple of hours"? Not a good idea—child endangerment! And you know that your regular baby-sitter will be of little help, because you cannot bring a child to day care who has anything other than a common cold. No problem, you work for Scitor, the Sunnyvale, California, systems engineering and program management company.[97]

Back in 1990, Scitor offered its employees a unique benefit. If they had a child who was ill, too ill for regular day care, then that child would be cared for by an independent day-care center called Feeling Better—child-care professionals in the area specializing in the caring of sick children. And Scitor would pay 100 percent of the costs. During its first full year as a benefit, Feeling Better services were used more than twenty-one times, at a cost to the company of nearly $2,500.

In deciding to offer this benefit to its employees, the company viewed it as a classic benefit/cost analysis. Under a typical situation, parents would generally miss work, either taking a personal day, or in other cases, just calling in sick themselves. Company records indicate that each day an engineer is working, he or she bills clients an average of $817. In contrast, Feeling Better's services are about $115 a child per day. Accordingly, offering this benefit netted the company more than $700.

Scitor continues to look for ways to help its employees deal with this issue. Although using Feeling Better has been successful overall, some parents are still apprehensive about leaving their ill child in a strange place. Consequently, Scitor is now exploring other options, including having care-givers come to the employee's home for the day.

Questions:

1. Describe Scitor's sick-child-care benefit in terms of the motivation process. Explain how you envision its effect on employee productivity.
2. Do you believe any benefit offered to employees should be scrutinized in terms of its benefits to the organization? What if the costs are greater than the benefit? Should the program not become part of the employee benefit package? Explain.

Testing Your Understanding

How well did you fulfill the learning objectives?

1. Employee benefits are important in today's organizations for all of these reasons except
   a. employees expect more than monetary rewards from their jobs.
   b. benefits packages are instrumental in recruiting the best workers for an organization.
   c. benefits packages increase employee productivity.
   d. benefits packages help to retain good workers in an organization.
   e. benefits packages are designed to meet the needs of a wide variety of workers.
2. Mavis worked for a manufacturing organization for sixteen years. She quit her job when she moved out of state to marry. Which of the following would provide the most information about her company pension retirement benefits?

a. Social Security Administration Review
b. COBRA
c. Summary Plan description
d. Section 89 reports
e. Pension Benefit Guaranty Corporation publications

3. Social Security, workers' compensation, and unemployment compensation are accurately compared by all of these statements except
   a. all programs are legally required.
   b. Social Security and workers' compensation are funded by employees and employers. Unemployment compensation is funded by employees and state government.
   c. Social Security and unemployment compensation provide monetary allocations to recipients. Workers' compensation may provide monetary allocation or payment for services.

d. Social Security is administered by the federal government. Workers' compensation and unemployment compensation are administered at the state level.

e. All three programs are designed to provide income protection or continuation.

4. Which statement best compares traditional health insurance, HMOs, and PPOs?

a. PPOs try to combine the best features of the traditional and the HMO coverages.

b. Most U.S. workers have PPO coverage. Fewest U.S. workers have traditional coverage.

c. Traditional health insurance provides access to a qualified physician. HMOs and PPOs are usually staffed by physicians' assistants.

d. Traditional coverage has no limit, or cap, on services provided. Both HMOs and PPOs have maximum benefit amounts.

e. Traditional coverage usually has an annual deductible amount. HMOs and PPOs usually do not have a deductible.

5. Michael, a 55-year-old engineer, works for a large manufacturing organization. Each year he contributes 10 percent of his earnings to an individual account and the company contributes an additional 6 percent. Michael has the option to choose whether the funds will be invested in stocks or bonds, and can change his choice every quarter. Projections are made as to probable retirement benefit levels from this account. What kind of retirement program does Michael have?

a. defined benefit plan

b. defined contribution plan

c. money purchase pension plan

d. capital accumulation program

e. Individual Retirement Account

6. Mason, a plant manager, has worked for an automotive parts manufacturer for twenty years. Usually he takes his four weeks of vacation to go fishing in the North Woods. This year, with three children in college, he wants to "sell" three weeks back to the company for additional income and take one week in September to help all the children move into their school dorms. Why would his human resources department advise against such action?

a. There is no time to go through his files if he is not out of the office.

b. Such a practice is against the law.

c. Mason might suffer "burnout" without the rejuvenating effects of his vacation.

d. It is too costly to allow people to have the additional salary.

e. Such action would lower morale in the plant and damage future recruiting efforts.

7. Dana, director of employee benefits, wants to change the company's liberal sick leave policy. Currently, employees are entitled to four hours of paid sick leave for each month of service with the company. When employees leave or retire, unused sick leave is forfeited. Dana noticed that many employees are "sick" just before major holiday periods, such as Christmas or Independence Day, leaving critical areas of the company understaffed. Also, many employees are "sick" for a day or two after their annual vacations, creating scheduling problems for other employees who are then asked to rework their own vacation plans. Which of the following would be the best change for Dana's sick leave policy?

a. Require employees to produce a physician's excuse for all sick leave taken.

b. Designate time periods of before and after major holidays and before and after annual leave ineligible for sick leave. Any time off taken during those periods must be without pay and unexcused.

c. Have someone on the human resources staff telephone to make sure employees are home, sick, when they say they are.

d. Allow unused sick leave to accumulate. Fold it into retirement benefits to be credited and compensated as length of service.

e. Cease to offer paid sick leave as a benefit.

8. Jeri, who earned $100,000 as a year vice-president of marketing for a manufacturing firm, died in a plane crash on the way to an industry convention in Chicago. She had group term life insurance of four times her annual salary with a double indemnity provision, a $500,000 travel insurance policy, a $250,000 maximum short-term disability insurance plan, an additional purchased group life insurance plan of two times her annual salary (without double indemnity), and a $1,000,000 AD&D policy. How much money did Jeri's widower receive?

a. $400,000   b. $1,100,000

c. $2,100,000   d. $1,350,000

e. $2,500,000

9. Denise works for a company that provides HMO medical insurance, short-term disability, two-times life insurance, one week paid vacation, and a basic pension plan to all employees. Denise also has the option of purchasing $4,000 (amount calculated from 1 percent of salary × years of service) worth of additional benefits from such areas as additional life or health insurance coverages, more pension, child-care or elder-care accounts, tuition reimbursement, and more vacation. What kind of flexible spending plan is Denise's company using?

a. flexitime   b. flexible spending accounts

c. modular   d. core-plus options

e. none of the above

10. Which one of the following is a not a family-friendly benefit?

a. employee assistance programs

b. dependent spending accounts

c. part-time employment

d. summer camp

e. relocation programs

Chapter Fifteen

SAFETY AND HEALTH

LEARNING OBJECTIVES

AFTER READING THIS CHAPTER, YOU WILL BE ABLE TO:

1. Describe the organizational effect of the Occupational Safety and Health Act.
2. List the Occupational Safety and Health Administration's (OSHA) enforcement priorities.
3. Identify what punitive actions OSHA can impose on an organization.
4. Explain what companies must do to comply with OSHA record-keeping requirements.
5. Discuss three contemporary areas for which OSHA is setting standards.
6. Describe the leading causes of safety and health accidents.
7. Explain what companies can do to prevent workplace violence.
8. Define stress and the causes of burnout.
9. Discuss what is meant by creating a healthy work site.

Traveling by air in the United States has often been regarded as one of the safest means of transportation available. Although throughout the years an occasional incident would occur, most travelers tend to believe that flying is safe. But in 1994, people have begun questioning that claim. Two plane crashes in North Carolina that year claimed dozens of lives. A seemingly easy, last leg of a several-city stopover was met by ill-fate, as the Pittsburgh-bound plane unexpectedly rolled over, went into an uncontrollable nose dive, and plunged headfirst into the surrounding wooded terrain. The plane disintegrated, as did the 100-plus passengers on board. Several weeks later, a similar event occurred, when a commuter plane in the Midwest iced-up, leaving the aircraft unable to fly.

Pilots and their crews are trained extensively to deal with potential emergencies. Air-traffic controllers, advanced monitoring devices, warning signals, ground crews, pilots, and others combine to ensure we can safely get to our destinations. Undoubtedly, the captains of these planes face hazardous elements each day in flight—some brought on by nature, like wind shear, and others due to mechanical failures. What pilots, and everyone else associated with the airline industry, don't expect is for their safety to be endangered by those on the plane. For Federal Express pilot David Sanders and his flight crew, the unbelievable occurred.[1]

Sanders was flying a DC-10, cruising at an altitude of 27,000 feet. The flight appeared normal enough. The cargo plane was fully loaded, and would be landing in a few hours to ensure the packages would reach their destination overnight. The only noticeable deviation from the norm was a pilot colleague who had "caught" a ride. Pilots and crew who are needed in other locations often ride along on another crew's flight. So even having a passenger onboard was not highly unusual. The passenger, however, wasn't being sent to handle a flight in another location. Instead, he was returning to headquarters for a disciplinary hearing, where he was to answer questions about lying on his resume.

Suddenly, this individual attacked the flight crew with a hammer and a spear he had brought on the plane. At the altitude the plane was flying, no one needed great distractions, let alone trying to defend oneself from a "madman" violently swinging a hammer and attempting to spear human flesh. The melee must have appeared to last for hours to the crew! But Captain Sanders didn't lose his cool. Rather, he placed the plane into a violent roll, and then a nose dive, to disorient the attacker enough so that he could be subdued, and ultimately arrested.

Fortunately, no lives were lost! But, it just reinforces that no one is totally safe from violence at work—even when the workplace is several miles up in the sky!

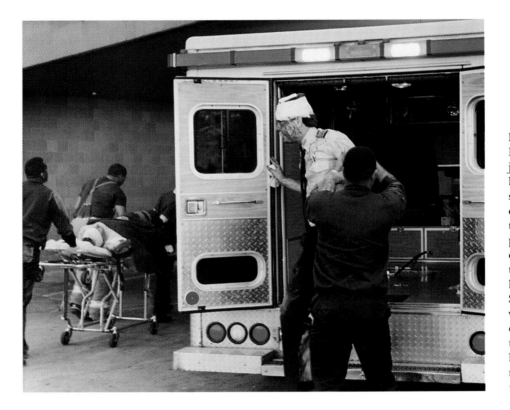

Federal Express Cargo Pilot David Sanders recognizes his job is hazardous. The unknown elements a pilot faces several miles up in the sky are enough to keep anyone on their toes—awaiting the unexpected. What Sanders didn't expect, however, was to be attacked with a hammer by a fellow pilot. Yet, quick action by Sanders and his crew prevented a major disaster from occurring. Injured, but alive, this Federal Express crew knows first-hand just what is meant by the term *work place violence.*

Introduction

Management has a legal responsibility, if not a moral one, to ensure that the workplace is free from unnecessary hazards and that conditions surrounding the workplace are not hazardous to employees' physical or mental health. Of course, accidents can and do occur, and the severity of these may astound you. There are approximately 10,000 reported work-related deaths and 2 million injuries each year in the United States, resulting in over 90 million days lost of productive time.[2] Heartless as it sounds, employers must be concerned about employees' health and safety if for no other reason than that accidents cost money.

From the turn of the century through the late 1960s, remarkable progress was made in reducing the rate and severity of job-related accidents and diseases. Yet the most significant piece of legislation in the area of employee health and safety was not enacted until 1970. This law is called the Occupational Safety and Health Act (OSHA). Let's take a closer look.

The Occupational Safety and Health Act

Any discussion of employee safety and health is different from what it would have been three decades ago. The passage of the **Occupational Safety and Health Act** dramatically changed the role that management must play in ensuring that the physical working conditions meet adequate standards. What the Civil Rights Act did to alter the organization's commitment to affirmative action, OSHA has done to alter the organization's health and safety programs.

Occupational Safety and Health Act Set standards to ensure safe and healthful working conditions and provide stiff penalties for violators.

OSHA legislation established comprehensive and specific health standards, authorized inspections to ensure the standards are met, empowered the Occupational Safety and Health Administration to police organizations' compliance, and required employers to keep records of illness and injuries and to calculate accident ratios. The act applies to almost every U.S. business engaged in interstate commerce, which means that 5 million workplaces employing approximately 64 million workers are covered. Those organizations not meeting the interstate commerce criteria are generally covered by state occupational safety and health laws.

The safety and health standards OSHA established are quite complex. Standards exist for such diverse conditions as noise levels, air impurities, physical protection equipment, the height of toilet partitions, and the correct size of ladders. And OSHA has recently moved into researching repetitive motion disorders, problems associated with the eye strain that accompanies video display terminal use, and developing training and education programs for businesses.

The initial standards took up 350 pages in the Federal Register, and some of the annual revisions and interpretations are equally extensive. Nevertheless, employers are responsible for knowing these standards and ensuring that those that do apply to them are followed (see Figure 15-1).

Its Enforcement Priorities

Enforcement procedures of OSHA standards vary depending on the nature of the event and the organization. Typically, OSHA enforces the standards based on a five-item priority listing. These are, in descending priority: imminent danger; serious accidents that have occurred within the past forty-eight hours; a current employee complaint; inspections of target industries with a high injury ratio; and random inspections.

Imminent danger refers to a condition where an accident is about to occur. Although this is given top priority and acts as a preventive measure, imminent danger situations are hard to define. In fact, in some cases, the definition of imminent danger appears to be an accident in progress, and interpretation leaves much to the imagination. For example, suppose you were leaving school and driving home on a dangerous mountain road. As your car begins to pick up too much speed, you notice that your brakes don't work! Are you in imminent danger? No, according to one interpretation of imminent danger, not until the car has gone off the roadside, and over an embankment. By that time it is too late.

This has given rise to priority-two accidents—those that have led to *serious injuries* or death. Under the law, an organization must report these serious accidents to the Occupational Safety and Health Administration field office within forty-eight hours of occurrence. This permits the investigators to review the scene and try to determine the cause of the accident.

Priority three, *employee complaints,* is a major concern for any manager. If an employee sees a violation of the OSHA standards, that employee has the right to call OSHA for investigation. The worker may refuse to work on the item in question until OSHA has investigated the complaint; this is especially true when there is a union. In some union contracts, workers may legally refuse to work if they believe they are in significant danger; they may stay off the job with pay until OSHA arrives and either finds the complaint invalid or cites the company and mandates compliance.[3]

Next in the priority of enforcement is the *inspection of targeted industries.* Earlier we stated that more than 5 million workplaces are covered under OSHA. To

Imminent Danger A condition where an accident is about to occur.

JOB SAFETY & HEALTH PROTECTION

The Occupational Safety and Health Act of 1970 provides job safety and health protection for workers by promoting safe and healthful working conditions throughout the Nation. Provisions of the Act include the following:

Employers

All employers must furnish to employees employment and a place of employment free from recognized hazards that are causing or are likely to cause death or serious harm to employees. Employers must comply with occupational safety and health standards issued under the Act.

Employees

Employees must comply with all occupational safety and health standards, rules, regulations and orders issued under the Act that apply to their own actions and conduct on the job.

The Occupational Safety and Health Administration (OSHA) of the U.S. Department of Labor has the primary responsibility for administering the Act. OSHA issues occupational safety and health standards, and its Compliance Safety and Health Officers conduct jobsite inspections to help ensure compliance with the Act.

Inspection

The Act requires that a representative of the employer and a representative authorized by the employees be given an opportunity to accompany the OSHA inspector for the purpose of aiding the inspection.

Where there is no authorized employee representative, the OSHA Compliance Officer must consult with a reasonable number of employees concerning safety and health conditions in the workplace.

Complaint

Employees or their representatives have the right to file a complaint with the nearest OSHA office requesting an inspection if they believe unsafe or unhealthful conditions exist in their workplace. OSHA with withhold, on request, names of employees complaining.

The Act provides that employees may not be discharged or discriminated against in any way for filing safety and health complaints or for otherwise exercising their rights under the Act.

Employees who believe they have been discriminated against may file a complaint with their nearest OSHA office within 30 days of the alleged discriminatory action.

Citation

If upon inspection OSHA believes an employer has violated the Act, a citation alleging such violations will be issued to the employer. Each citation will specify a time period within which the alleged violation must be corrected.

The OSHA citation must be prominently displayed at or near the place of alleged violation for three days, or until it is corrected, whichever is later, to warn employees of dangers that may exist there.

Proposed Penalty

The Act provides for mandatory civil penalties against employers of up to $7,000 for each serious violation and for optional penalties of up to $7,000 for each nonserious violation. Penalties of up to $7,000 per day may be proposed for failure to correct violations within the proposed time period and for each day the violation continues beyond the prescribed abatement date. Also, any employer who willfully or repeatedly violates the Act may be assessed penalties of up to $70,000 for each such violation. A minimum penalty of $5,000 may be imposed for each willful violation. A violation of posting requirements can bring a penalty of up to $7,000.

There are also provisions for criminal penalties. Any willful violation resulting in the death of any employee, upon convic-

Continued

Figure 15-1
Job Safety and Health Protection *(Continued)*

tion, is punishable by a fine of up to $250,000 (or $500,000 if the employer is a corporation), or by imprisonment for up to six months, or both. A second conviction of an employer doubles the possible term of imprisonment. Falsifying records, reports, or applications is punishable by a fine of $10,000 or up to six months in jail or both.

Voluntary Activity
While providing penalties for violations, the Act also encourages efforts by labor and management, before an OSHA inspection, to reduce workplace hazards voluntarily and to develop and improve safety and health programs in all workplaces and industries. OSHA's Voluntary Protection Programs recognize outstanding efforts of this nature.

OSHA has published Safety and Health Program Management Guidelines to assist employers in establishing or perfecting programs to prevent or control employee exposure to workplace hazards. There are many public and private organizations that can provide information and assistance in

this effort, if requested. Also your local OSHA office can provide considerable help and advice on solving safety and health problems or can refer you to other sources for help such as training.

Consultation
Free assistance in identifying and correcting hazards and in improving safety and health management is available to employers, without citation or penalty, through OSHA-supported programs in each State. These programs are usually administered by the State Labor or Health department or a State university.

Posting Instructions
Employers in States operating OSHA approved State Plans should obtain and post the State's equivalent poster.

Under provisions of Title 29, Code of Federal Regulations, Part 1903.2(a)(1) employers must post this notice (or facsimile) in a conspicuous place where notices to employees are customarily posted.

More Information

Additional information and copies of the Act, specific OSHA safety and health standards, and other applicable regulations may be obtained from your employer or from the nearest OSHA Regional Office in the following locations:

Atlanta, GA   (404) 347-3573
Boston, MA   (617) 565-7164
Chicago, IL   (312) 353-2220
Dallas, TX   (214) 767-4731
Denver, CO   (303) 844-3061
Kansas City, MO   (816) 426-5861
New York, NY   (212) 337-2378
Philadelphia, PA   (215) 596-1201
San Francisco, CA   (415) 744-6670
Seattle, WA   (206) 442-5930

To report suspected fire hazards, imminent danger safety and health hazards in the workplace, or other job safety and health emergencies, such as toxic waste in the workplace, call OSHA's 24-hour hotline: 1-800- 321-OSHA.

This information will be made available to sensory impaired individuals upon request. Voice phone: (202) 523-8615; TDD message referral phone: 1-800-326-2577

Lynn Martin, Secretary of Labor, U.S. Department of Labor, Occupational Safety and Health Administration, Washington, D.C., 1992 (Reprinted) OSHA 2203 U.S. GOVERNMENT PRINTING OFFICE:1992 0-320-762 QL 3

investigate each would require several hundred thousand full-time inspectors; however, OSHA only employs about 1,200 inspectors who conduct about 70,000 inspections a year.[4] So, in order to have the largest impact, OSHA began to direct its attention to those industries with the highest injury rates: chemical processing, roofing and sheeting metal, meat processing, lumber and wood products, mobile homes and campers, and stevedoring. In addition, a new rule established in 1990 requires employers who handle hazardous waste (i.e., chemicals, medical waste) to follow strict operating procedures;[5] any employer who handles hazardous waste is required to monitor employee exposure, develop and communicate safety plans, and provide necessary protective equipment.[6]

The final OSHA priority is the *random inspection.* Originally, OSHA inspectors were authorized to enter any work area premise, without notice, to ensure that the workplace was in compliance. In 1978, however, the Supreme Court ruled in **Marshall** v. **Barlow's Inc.**[7] that employers are not required to let OSHA inspectors enter the premises unless the inspectors have search warrants. This decision, while not destroying OSHA's ability to conduct inspections, forces inspectors to justify their choice of inspection sites more rigorously. That is, rather than trying to oversee health and safety standards in all of their jurisdictions, OSHA inspectors find it easier to justify their actions and obtain search warrants if they appear to be pursuing specific problem areas.

But don't let the warrant requirement mislead you into a false sense of security. If needed, an OSHA inspector will obtain the necessary legal document. Attorneys who deal with OSHA suggest that companies cooperate rather than viewing this event as confrontational.[8] This cooperation focuses on permitting the inspection, but only after "agreeing to the exact facility and entity to be inspected as well as the scope of the inspection."[9] That's not to say that you can keep inspectors from finding violations, however. Consider what happened at the electronics and refrigeration facility of Ford Motor Company.[10] On a routine inspection of the facility, in an area the company knew would be seen, an OSHA inspector witnessed unsafe equipment being used. Because the inspector determined that its use was condoned by management at the plant, the company was fined and paid $1.2 million for past violations. Finally, it is recommended that any information regarding the company's safety program be discussed with the OSHA inspector, emphasizing how the program is communicated to employees, and how it is enforced.[11]

Should an employer feel that the fine levied is unjust, or too harsh, the law permits the employer to file an appeal. This appeal is reviewed by the Occupational Safety and Health Review Commission, an independently operating safety and health board. Although this commission's decisions are generally final, employers may still appeal commission decisions through the federal courts.[12]

OSHA's Record-Keeping Requirements

To fulfill part of the requirements established under the Occupational Safety and Health Act, employers in industries listed in Table 15-1 who have eleven or more employees must maintain safety and health records.[13] Organizations not listed in Table 15-1, such as universities, still must comply with the law itself; their only exception is the reduction of time spent on maintaining safety records. The basis of record-keeping for OSHA is the completion of OSHA Form 200 (see Figure 15-2). On this form, employees must identify "when the occupational injury or illness occurred, to whom, the regular job of the injured or ill person at the time of injury or illness exposure, the department in which

Marshall v. **Barlow, Inc.** Supreme Court case that stated an employer could refuse an OSHA inspection unless OSHA had a search warrant to enter the premises.

Bureau of Labor Statistics
Log and Summary of Occupational
Injuries and Illnesses

NOTE:	This form is required by Public Law 91-596 and must be kept in the establishment for *5 years*. Failure to maintain and post can result in the issuance of citations and assessment of penalties. *(See posting requirements on the other side of form.)*	RECORDABLE CASES: You are required to record information about every occupational death; every nonfatal occupational illness; and those nonfatal occupational injuries which involve one or more of the following: loss of consciousness, restriction of work or motion, transfer to another job, or medical treatment (other than first aid) *(See definitions on the other side of form.)*

Case or File Number	Date of Injury or Onset of Illness	Employee's Name	Occupation	Department	Description of Injury or Illness
Enter a nonduplicating number which will facilitate comparisons with supplementary records.	Enter Mo./day.	Enter first name or initial, middle initial, last name.	Enter regular job title, not activity employee was performing when injured or at onset of illness. In the absence of a formal title, enter a brief description of the employee's duties.	Enter department in which the employee is regularly employed or a description of normal workplace to which employee is assigned, even though temporarily working in another department at the time of injury or illness.	Enter a brief description of the injury or illness and indicate the part or parts of body affected.

Typical entries for this column might be: Amputation of 1st joint right forefinger; Strain of lower back; Contact dermatitis on both hands; Electrocution--body. |
(A)	(B)	(C)	(D)	(E)	(F)
					PREVIOUS PAGE TOTALS ⟶
					TOTALS (Instructions on other side of form.) ⟶

OSHA No. 200   ★U.S.GPO:1990-262-256/15419

Figure 15-2
OSHA Form 200

418

U.S. Department of Labor

For Calendar Year 19 _____   Page ____ of ____

Form Approved
O.M.B. No. 1220-0029
See OMB Disclosure Statement on reverse.

Company Name _____

Establishment Name _____

Establishment Address _____

Extent of and Outcome of INJURY						Type, Extent of, and Outcome of ILLNESS											
Fatalities	Nonfatal Injuries					Type of Illness							Fatalities	Nonfatal Illnesses			
Injury Related	Injuries With Lost Workdays				Injuries Without Lost Workdays	CHECK Only One Column for Each Illness *(See other side of form for terminations or permanent transfers.)*							Illness Related	Illnesses With Lost Workdays				Illnesses Without Lost Workdays
Enter DATE of death. Mo./day/yr.	Enter a CHECK if injury involves days away from work, or days of restricted work activity, or both.	Enter a CHECK if injury involves days away from work.	Enter number of DAYS away from work.	Enter number of DAYS of restricted work activity.	Enter a CHECK if no entry was made in columns 1 or 2 but the injury is recordable as defined above.	Occupational skin diseases or disorders	Dust diseases of the lungs	Respiratory conditions due to toxic agents	Poisoning (systemic effects of toxic materials)	Disorders due to physical agents	Disorders associated with repeated trauma	All other occupational illnesses	Enter DATE of death. Mo./day/yr.	Enter a CHECK if illness involves days away from work, or days of restricted work activity, or both.	Enter a CHECK if illness involves days away from work.	Enter number of DAYS away from work.	Enter number of DAYS of restricted work activity.	Enter a CHECK if no entry was made in columns 8 or 9.
(1)	(2)	(3)	(4)	(5)	(6)	(a)	(b)	(c)	(d)	(e)	(f)	(g)	(8)	(9)	(10)	(11)	(12)	(13)
									(7)									

Certification of Annual Summary Totals By _____ Title _____ Date _____

OSHA No. 200   **POST ONLY THIS PORTION OF THE LAST PAGE NO LATER THAN FEBRUARY 1.**

Figure 15-2 (*continued*)
OSHA Form 200

TABLE 15-1 Industries Required to Keep OSHA Records

Agriculture, Forestry, and Fishing

Oil and Gas Extraction

Construction

Manufacturing

Transportation and Public Utilities

Wholesale Trade

Building Materials and Garden Supplies

General Merchandise and Food Stores

Hotels and Other Lodging Places

Repair Services

Amusement and Recreational Services

Health Services

Source: U.S. Department of Labor, Bureau of Labor Statistics, *A Brief Guide to Recordkeeping, Requirements for Occupational Injuries and Illness* (Washington, D.C.: Government Printing Office, June 1986), p. 1.

the person was employed, the kind of injury or illness, how much time was lost, and whether the case resulted in a fatality."[14] Employers are required to keep these safety records for five years.

In complying with OSHA record-keeping requirements, one issue arises for employers—that is, just what is a reportable accident or an illness? According to the act, OSHA distinguishes between the two in the following ways: Any work-related illness (no matter how insignificant it may appear) must be reported on Form 200. Injuries, on the other hand, are reported only when they require medical treatment (besides first aid), involve loss of consciousness, restriction of work or motion, or transfer to another job.[15]

To help employers decide whether an incident should be recorded, OSHA offers a schematic diagram for them to follow (see Figure 15-3). By using this "decision tree," companies can decide if, in fact, an event should be recorded. Should that occur, the organization is responsible for recording it under one of three areas: fatality, lost workday cases, or neither fatality nor lost workdays.[16] Part of this information is then used to determine a company's **incident rate.** An organization's incident rate reflects the "number of injuries, illnesses, or (lost) workdays related to a common exposure base rate of 100 full-time workers."[17] This rate is then used by OSHA for determining industries and organizations that are more susceptible to injury. To calculate the incident rate, the formula $(N/EH) \times 200,000$ is used,[18] where:

Incident Rate Number of injuries, illnesses, or lost workdays as it relates to a common base of 100 full-time employees.

N is the number of injuries and/or illnesses or lost workdays;
EH is the total hours worked by all employees during the year; and,
200,000 is the base hour rate equivalent (100 workers $\times$ 40 hours per week $\times$ 50 weeks per year).

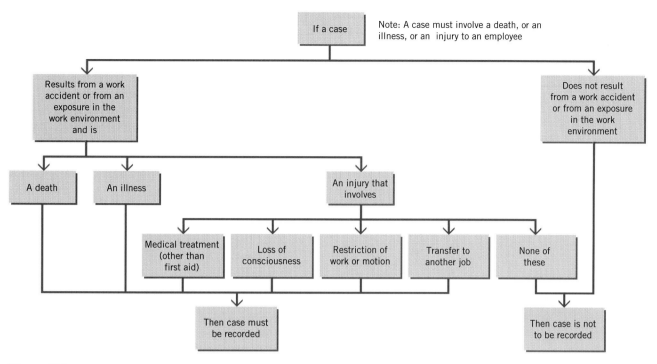

Figure 15-3
Determining Recordability of Cases Under OSHA

In using the formula and calculating an organization's accident rate, assume we have an organization with 1,800 employees that experienced 195 reported accidents over the past year. We would calculate the incident rate as follows: $(195/3,600,000) \times 200,000$.[19] The incident rate, then, is 10.8. What does that 10.8 represent? That depends on a number of factors. If the organization is in the meat-packing industry where the industry average incident rate is 44.4,[20] then they are doing well. If, however, they are in the insurance industry, where the industry incident rate is 2.4,[21] then a 10.8 indicates a major concern.

Its Punitive Action

An OSHA inspector has the right to levy a fine against an organization for noncompliance. While levying the fine is more complicated than described here, if an organization does not bring a "red-flagged" item into compliance, it can be assessed a severe penalty. As originally passed in 1970, the maximum penalty was $10,000; however, with the **Omnibus Budget Reconciliation Act of 1990,** that $10,000 penalty can increase to $70,000 if the violation is severe, willful, and repetitive.[22] Although in its first twenty years questions arose regarding the value of OSHA to workers' health and safety,[23] such questions appear to be abating. Great inroads have been made by the director of OSHA in redirecting OSHA's efforts. The agency has increased inspections and has been viewed as taking a tougher stance on workplace health and safety issues—and a number of companies have seen what that focus can mean. For example, the Budd Company was fined and paid $1.5 million for "843 willful violations."[24] But fines are not for safety violations alone: If a company fails to keep its OSHA records properly, it, too, can be subjected to stiff penalties. For instance, the USX Corporation faced more than $7.3 million in fines, and Union Carbide more than

Omnibus Budget Reconciliation Act of 1990 Law that increased OSHA penalties from $10,000 to $70,000 for a severe, willful, and repetitive OSHA violation.

$1.3 million, for failing to have adequate record-keeping procedures for the company's safety and health matters.[25] And if fines are not enough, OSHA has had court backing to impose criminal charges against the management of a company that willfully violates health and safety laws.

Much of this legal support is the result of a case involving the Chicago Magnet Wire Company. An employee in the company died after prolonged exposure to and inhalation of cyanide fumes. During the course of its investigation, OSHA determined that the company was aware of the dangers employees faced, but did little to take corrective action. Consequently, the company's top three managers were charged with criminal negligence in the employee's death.[26] Although the case was ultimately appealed to the Supreme Court on the grounds that such charges were impermissible based on OSHA regulations, the Supreme Court refused to hear the case. This action paved the way for states to bring criminal actions against such employers.[27]

OSHA: A Critique

Has OSHA worked? The answer is a qualified yes. In fact, OSHA has had a direct and significant impact on almost every business organization in the United States. In some of the largest organizations, an additional administrator has been created who is solely responsible for safety. The impact of OSHA standards has made organizations more aware of health and safety. The standards may have been initially extreme in their specificity, and their red tape a nuisance, but that has been changing. Recent standard modifications have made them more realistic. Also, one result of the Republican party's victory in the 1994 elections could be a decrease in some of the reporting requirements, in line with the theme of their "Contract With America" to cut government regulation.[28]

What can we expect from OSHA over the next decade? Although its efforts will continue to concentrate on safety and health violations in organizations, OSHA is addressing problems associated with contemporary organizations, concentrating its efforts through the **National Institute for Occupational Safety and Health (NIOSH)** for researching, and in setting standards in such areas as blood-borne pathogens, and chemical process safety. Similarly, OSHA continues to explore motor vehicle safety.[29]

Setting standards for blood-borne pathogens is designed to protect individuals, like medical personnel, from becoming infected with such diseases as AIDS[30] and hepatitis. In doing so, OSHA has established guidelines regarding protective equipment (like latex gloves, eye shields), and in cases where a vaccine is available, ensures that exposed workers have access to it.[31]

Chemical processing standards reflect specific guidelines that must be adhered to when employees work with chemicals or other hazardous toxic substances. This requires companies to "perform hazardous analyses" and take any corrective action required.[32]

These concerns over chemical hazards developed in a roundabout way; in the early 1980s, a number of states passed what were commonly called Right-to-Know Laws, which helped begin the process of identifying hazardous chemicals in the workplace, and required employers to inform employees of the chemicals they might be exposed to, the health risk associated with that exposure, and other policies guiding their use.[33] Although these state laws made progress in providing information regarding workplace toxins, there were enough variations in each state (and some states didn't have the law) to warrant protection from the federal level. Recognizing that need, OSHA developed the **Hazard**

National Institute for Occupational Safety and Health (NIOSH) The government agency that researches and sets OSHA standards.

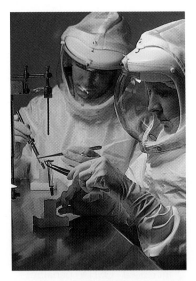

OSHA's new direction is focusing on protecting workers like this lab technician from exposure to harmful elements. Through their research, recommendations have been made to provide protective gear for anyone who comes in contact with such elements as chemicals, or human fluids.

Figure 15-4
Material Safety Data Sheet Checklist

Each MSDS must contain:

_____ 1. Identity used on the label.
_____ 2. Chemical and common names of each hazardous ingredient (except as provided in 29 CFR 1910.1200(i)).
_____ 3. Physical and chemical characteristics of the hazardous chemical (such as vapor pressure or flashpoint).
_____ 4. The physical hazards of the hazardous chemical including the potential for fire, explosion and reactivity.
_____ 5. Health hazards of potential health risks, including signs and symptoms of exposure, and medical conditions aggravated by exposure.
_____ 6. Primary routes of entry.
_____ 7. OSHA, PEL, ACGIH TLV or other exposure limits.
_____ 8. Whether any ingredient is listed as a carcinogen by OSHA, NTP, or IARC.
_____ 9. Hygienic practices.
_____ 10. Procedures and precautions for safe handling.
_____ 11. Protective measures for repair and maintenance of contaminated equipment.
_____ 12. Spill and clean-up procedures.
_____ 13. Control measures such as engineering controls, work practices or personal protective equipment required such as gloves or goggles.
_____ 14. Emergency and first-aid procedures.
_____ 15. Date of MSDS preparation or revision.
_____ 16. Name, address and telephone number of responsible party, who can provide additional information on emergency procedures.

Source: State of Maryland, Department of Licensing and Regulation
Division of Labor and Industry.

Communication Standard in 1983.[34] This policy "requires employers to communicate chemical hazards to their employees by labeling containers, and by distributing data information (called Material Safety Data Sheets [see Figure 15-4]) provided by the manufacturer"[35] to the employees. In addition, employees exposed to various hazardous chemicals must be trained in their safe handling.[36] As enacted in 1983, this standard applied only to manufacturing industries; by mid-1989, however, meeting the requirements of the Hazard Communication Standard became the responsibility of all industries.[37]

The third area, motor vehicle safety, reflects OSHA's interest in addressing the problems associated with workers who drive substantially as part of their job duties. This interest is due, in part, because approximately 36 percent of all worker deaths in any given year are attributed to motor vehicle accidents.[38] Although specific safety standards are currently unavailable at this time, we can expect for them to place emphasis on substance-abuse testing of drivers, safety equipment, and driver's education.

Hazard Communication Standard Requires organizations to communicate to its employees hazardous chemicals they may encounter on the job, and how to deal with them safely.

Job Safety Programs

If businesses are concerned with efficiency and profits, you may ask, why would they spend money to create conditions that exceed those required by law? The answer is the profit motive itself. The cost of accidents can be, and for many organizations is, a substantial additional cost of doing business. The direct cost of an accident to an employer shows itself in the organization's worker's compensation premium. This cost, as noted in the last chapter, is largely determined by the insured's accident history. Indirect costs, which generally far exceed direct costs, also must be borne by the employer. These include wages paid for time lost due to injury, damage to equipment and materials, personnel to investigate and report on accidents, and lost production due to work stoppages and personnel changeover. The impact of these indirect costs can be seen in statistics that describe the costs of accidents for American industry as a whole.[39]

In the early 1990s, workers' compensation premiums were costing U.S. employers almost $100 billion a year, an increase of almost 300 percent in a little under a decade.[40] Accidents cost employers additional billions of dollars in wages and lost production. The significance of this latter figure is emphasized when we note that this cost is approximately ten times greater than losses caused by strikes, an issue that historically has received much more attention. It's also interesting to note that on average, Japanese organizations have up to seven times fewer accidents in the workplace.[41] For Japanese firms, this has positively affected productivity.

Causes of Accidents

The cause of an accident can be generally classified as either human or environmental.[42] Human causes are directly attributable to human error brought about by carelessness, intoxication, daydreaming, inability to do the job, or other human deficiency. Environmental causes, in contrast, are attributable to the workplace and include the tools, equipment, physical plant, and general work environment. Both of these sources are important, but in terms of numbers, the human factor is responsible for the vast majority of accidents. No matter how much effort is made to create a work environment that is accident-free, a low accident rate record can only be achieved by concentrating on the human element.

One of the main objectives of safety engineers is to scrutinize the work environment to locate sources of potential accidents. In addition to looking for such obvious factors as loose steps, oil on the walkway, or a sharp protrusion on a piece of equipment at eye level, safety engineers will seek those that are less obvious. Standards established by OSHA provide an excellent reference to guide the search for potential hazards.

Preventative Measures

What traditional measures can we look to for preventing accidents? The answer lies in education, skill training, engineering, protection devices, and regulation enforcement. We have summarized these in Table 15-2.

Ensuring Job Safety

One way management can be assured that rules and regulations are being enforced is to develop some type of feedback system. This can be provided by inspection of the work surroundings. Management can rely on oral or written reports for information on enforcement. Another approach is to get firsthand information by periodically walking through the work areas to make observations. Ideally, managers will rely on reports from supervisors on the floor and employees in the work areas, and support these by their own personal observations.

TABLE 15-2   Accident Prevention Means

425
Job Safety Programs
●

Education	Create safety awareness by posting highly visible signs that proclaim safety slogans, placing articles on accident prevention in organization newsletters, or exhibiting a sign proclaiming the number of days the plant has operated without a lost-day accident.
Skills Training	Incorporate accident prevention measures into the learning process.
Engineering	Prevent accidents through both the design of the equipment and the design of the jobs themselves. This may also include eliminating those factors that promote operator fatigue, boredom, and daydreaming.
Protection	Provide protective equipment where necessary. This may include safety shoes, gloves, hard hats, safety glasses, and noise mufflers. Protection also includes performing preventative maintenance on machinery.
Regulation Enforcement	The best safety rules and regulations will be ineffective in reducing accidents if they are not enforced. Additionally, if such rules are not enforced, the employer may be liable for any injuries that occur.

Although safety is everyone's responsibility, it should be part of the organization's culture (see "HRM Skills").[43] Top management must show its commitment to safety by providing resources to purchase safety devices and maintaining equipment. Furthermore, safety should become part of every employee's performance appraisal. As we mentioned in Chapter 12 on performance evaluations, if something isn't included, there's a tendency to diminish its importance. Holding employees accountable for evaluating their performance sends the message that the company is serious about safety.

Another means of promoting safety is to empower the action. In organizations like General Electric, such employee groups are called safety committees.[44] Although chiefly prevalent in unionized settings, these committees serve a vital role in helping the company and its employees implement and maintain a good safety program.

A Safety Issue: Workplace Violence

Inasmuch as there is growing concern for the job safety for our workers, a much greater emphasis today is being placed on the increasing violence that has erupted on the job. No organization is immune from such happenstance, and the problem appears to be getting worse. Shootings at a local post office by a recently disciplined employee, an upset purchasing manager who stabs his boss because they disagreed over how some paperwork was to be completed, or another employee who disliked working for women and goes on a shooting rampage[45]—incidents like these have become all too prevalent. Consider the following statistics: Homicide has become the number-three cause of work-related death for men in the United States, just behind automobile accidents and machinery mishaps.[46] For women, it's the number-one cause of work-related death![47] In the United States, almost 1,100 employees were murdered on the job in 1993, with more than 2 million physically attacked, and more than 6 million threatened with bodily harm.[48]

HRM*Skills*

Developing a Safety and Health Program

1. **Involve management and employees in the development of a safety and health plan.** If neither group can see the usefulness, and the benefit of such a plan, even the best plan will fail.
2. **Hold someone accountable for implementing the plan.** Plans do not work by themselves. They need someone to champion the cause. This person must be given the resources to put the plan in place, but also must be held accountable for what it's intended to accomplish.
3. **Determine the Safety and Health Requirements for Your Work Site.** Just as each individual is different, so, too, is each workplace. Understanding the specific needs of the facility will aid in determining what safety and health requirement will be necessary.
4. **Assess what workplace hazards exist in the facility.** Identify the potential health and safety problems that may exist on the job. By understanding what exists, preventive measures can be determined.
5. **Correct hazards that exist.** If certain hazards were identified in the investigation in Step 4, fix or eliminate them. This may mean decreasing the effect of the hazard, or controlling it through other means (e.g., protective clothing).
6. **Train employees in safety and health techniques.** Make safety and health training mandatory for all employees. Employees should be instructed how to do their jobs in the safest manner, and understand that any protective equipment provided must be used.
7. **Develop the mind-set in employees that the organization is to be kept hazard-free.** Often employees are the first to witness problems. Establish means for them to report their findings, including having emergency procedures in place, if necessary. Ensuring that preventive maintenance of equipment follows a recommended schedule can also prevent their breakdowns from becoming a hazard.
8. **Continuously update and refine the safety and health program.** Once the program has been implemented, it must continuously be evaluated, and necessary changes must be made. Documenting the progress of the program is necessary for use in this analysis.

Source: Adapted from Maryland Occupational Safety and Health, *Developing a Workplace Safety and Health Program* (Baltimore; Maryland Occupational Safety and Health Agency, 1993), pp. 5–16.

Many individuals note that in U.S. cities, drug abuse is spilling over into the workplace, as are other behaviors that lead to violence. Clear examples are cab drivers or convenience store clerks who are killed during robberies.[49] Although these are terrible events, our discussion centers more on workplace violence as a function of two factors—domestic violence and disgruntled employees.[50] The issue for companies, then, is how to prevent the violence from occurring on the job.

Because the circumstances of each incident are different, a specific plan of action for companies to follow is difficult to detail. However, several suggestions can be made.[51] First, the organization must develop a plan to deal with the issue. This may mean reviewing all corporate policies to ensure that they are not adversely affecting employees. In fact, in many of the cases where the violent individuals caused mayhem in an office setting, and didn't commit suicide, one common factor arose. That is, these employees were not treated with respect or dignity. They were laid off without any warning, or treated too harshly, in their mind, in the discipline process. Sound HRM practices can help to ensure that respect and dignity exist for employees, even in the most difficult of issues like terminations.

Organizations must also train their management personnel to identify troubled employees before the problem results in violence.[52] Employee assistance programs (EAPs) can be designed specifically to help these individuals. As we'll see shortly in our discussion of EAPs, rarely does an individual go from being happy, to shooting coworkers overnight! Furthermore, if supervisors are better able to spot the types of demonstrated behaviors that may lead to violence, then those who cannot be helped through the EAP can be removed from the organization before others are harmed. Organizations should also implement stronger security mechanisms. For example, many women who are killed at work, following a domestic dispute, die at the hands of someone who didn't belong on company premises. These individuals, as well as violence paraphernalia—guns, knives, and the like— must be kept from entering the facilities altogether.

Sadly, no matter how careful the organization is, and how much it attempts to prevent workplace violence, some will occur. In those cases, the organization must be prepared to deal with the situation.[53] As one researcher has stated, we need to "teach employees what to do when someone goes berserk,"[54] and we need to be prepared to offer whatever assistance we can to deal with the aftermath.

Maintaining a Healthy Work Environment

Unhealthy work environments are a concern to us all. If workers cannot function properly at their jobs because of constant headaches, watering eyes, breathing difficulties, or fear of exposure to materials that may cause long-term health problems, productivity will decrease. Consequently, creating a healthy work en-

Just how healthy is this office building? For it to get the "seal of approval" as a healthy work site, it must be free from harmful airborne chemicals, asbestos, germs, fungi, and indoor pollution.

●

Sick Building An unhealthy work environment.

vironment not only is the proper thing to do, it also benefits the employer. Often referred to as **sick buildings,** office environments that contain harmful airborne chemicals, asbestos, or indoor pollution (often caused by smoking) have forced employers to take drastic steps. For many, it has meant the removal of asbestos from their buildings. Because extended exposure to asbestos has been linked to lung cancer, companies are required by various federal agencies like the EPA to remove it altogether, or at least seal it so that it cannot escape into the air.

But asbestos is not the only culprit! Germs, fungi, and a variety of synthetic pollutants cause problems, too. For example, in the mid-1980s, employees at Eastman Kodak were experiencing symptoms of lung inflammation.[55] It took many months and several million dollars to locate the cause, and "cure" it. Kodak had to replace the entire germ-infested ventilation system.[56]

Although specific problems and their elimination go beyond the scope of this text, there are some suggestions for keeping the workplace healthy, which are listed in Table 15-3. One in particular, however, is noteworthy for us to explore: the smoke-free environment. Let's turn our attention to this growing phenomenon.

The Smoke-Free Environment

Should smoking be prohibited in a public place of business? Even, say, in a bar, where forbidding smoking could put the establishment out of business?[57] The dangers and health problems associated with smoking have been well communicated—and this is translating into increased health insurance costs. For example, studies have shown that the premiums paid for insuring an employee who smokes cost up to $5,000 more than one who doesn't.[58] Furthermore, smokers were found to be absent more than nonsmokers, lose productivity due to smoke breaks, damage property with cigarette burns, require more routine maintenance (ash/butt cleanup),[59] and create problems for other employees through secondhand smoke disorders. Recognized as a means to control these maladies associated with smoking, in conjunction with society's renewed em-

---

TABLE 15-3   Suggestions for Keeping the Workplace Healthy

---

1. **Make sure workers get enough fresh air.** The cost of providing it is peanuts compared with the expense of cleaning up a problem. One simple tactic: unsealing vents closed in overzealous efforts to conserve energy.

2. **Avoid suspect building materials and furnishings.** A general rule is that if it stinks, it's going to emit an odor. Substitute tacks for smelly carpet glue, natural wood for chemically treated plywood.

3. **Test new buildings for toxins before occupancy.** Failure to do so may lead to potential health problems. Most consultants say that letting a new building sit temporarily vacant allows the worst fumes to dissipate.

4. **Provide a smoke-free environment.** If you don't want to ban smoking entirely, then establish an area for smokers that has its own ventilation system.

5. **Keep air ducts clean and dry.** Water in air ducts is a fertile breeding ground for fungi.

6. **Pay attention to workers' complaints.** Dates and particulars should be recorded by a designated employee.

Source: Faye Rice, "Do You Work in a Sick Building?" *Fortune* (July 2, 1990), p. 88.

Phil Thompson, President of Industrial Supply company in Salt Lake City, Utah, implemented a strict ban on smoking on company premises several years ago. As a result of creating this smoke-free environment, Industrial Supply has witnessed a 30 percent increase in productivity, while simultaneously controlling runaway health insurance premium hikes.

phasis on wellness, **smoke-free policies** have appeared. In fact, about 250 U.S. companies have banned smoking altogether, while another 31 percent have smoking restricted to designated areas.[60]

Although many nonsmokers would agree that a total ban on smoking in the workplace is the most desirable, it may not be the most practical. For those employees who smoke, quitting immediately may be impossible. The nicotine addiction prohibits this "cold-turkey" approach for the most ardent smoker. Accordingly, a total ban on smoking must be viewed as a phased-in approach.[61] For example, this gradual process should begin with the involvement of representative employees to determine what the organization's smoke-free goals should be. This means deciding if the organization will ban smoking altogether over a period of time; or if special areas will be designated as smoking rooms. If the latter is chosen, then these rooms must be properly ventilated to keep the smoke fumes from permeating other parts of the facility. For many companies, this option is quite expensive; Texas Instruments found the cost for constructing these rooms averages $70,000 each.[62]

Consequently, the organization needs to look at incentives for getting people not to smoke. As mentioned earlier, health-care premiums for smokers are significantly higher than for nonsmokers. Employers may decide to pay only the nonsmoking premium, and pass the additional premium costs on to the smokers. Companies also need to have in place various options for individuals to seek help. Through various assistance programs, smoking cessation sessions, and the like, the organization can show that it is making a deliberate commitment to eliminate the problems associated with smoking in the workplace (see "Ethical Decisions in HRM").

Smoke-Free Policies Organization policies that reduce or prohibit smoking on company premises.

Repetitive Motion Disorders

Whenever workers are subjected to a continuous motion like typing, without proper work station design (seat and keyboard height adjustments), they run

●

Ethical Decisions in HRM:

Rights for the Smoker

It has become well-documented that smoking can create health problems. Accordingly, health insurance premiums, as well as other premiums like life insurance, are significantly higher to those who "light-up." And in most cases, employers have passed these increased premium costs on to the worker. Companies have become more stringent in developing policies on smoking, and many have banned smoking on company premises altogether. Clearly, the smoker today is disadvantaged, but how far can that go?

Can an organization refuse to hire someone simply because they smoke? Depending on the organization, the requirement of the job, and the state in which one lives, they might! Even so, employers may take this one step further. Companies may, in fact, be able to terminate an individual for smoking off the job—on an employee's own time. Do you believe companies have the right to dictate what you do outside of work? If an organization can take such action against employees for smoking, and justify it on the grounds that it creates a health problem, what about other things we do? Eating too much fatty food can create a health problem, so should we be susceptible to discipline for being caught eating a Big Mac? Some members of the medical community cite how one or two alcoholic drinks a day may in fact be therapeutic and prevent the onset of certain diseases. Yet, alcohol can be damaging to humans. Accordingly, should we be fired for having a glass of wine with dinner, or drinking a beer at a sporting event?

What do you think? How far should we permit regulating "wellness" in our organizations?

Repetitive Motion Disorder Injuries sustained by continuous and repetitive movements, usually of the hand.

Cumulative Trauma Disorder An occupational injury that occurs from repetitively performing similar physical movements.

Ergonomics The process of matching the work environment to the individual.

the risk of developing **repetitive motion disorders,** referred to as **cumulative trauma disorders.** These disorders, costing U.S. companies several billion dollars annually, arise out of headaches, dizziness, and nerve damage. The most frequent of this disorder is in the wrist and is called carpal tunnel syndrome.[63] Carpal tunnel has been found to be directly linked to office designs and the way that work is performed.[64]

One chief means of reducing the potential effects of cumulative trauma disorders for an organization is through the use of **ergonomics.**[65] Ergonomics involves fitting the work environment to the individual. Reality tells us that every employee is different—different shape, size, height, and so on. Expecting each worker to adjust to "standard" office furnishings is just not practical. Instead, recognizing and acting on these differences, ergonomics looks at customizing the work environment such that it is not only conducive to productive work, but keeps the employee healthy. For example, to reduce the likelihood of cumulative trauma disorders, Chevron purchased and installed ergonomically designed work stations.[66] Not only has the organization begun to lessen the chances for this disorder, but they have also found that employees have become more productive. As one of Chevron's legal support service members stated, "It costs us about $1,000 per employee [for ergonomically designed adjustable desk add-ons] . . . but our employees are more productive because they don't have backaches, headaches, and don't complain as much."[67]

When we speak of ergonomics, we are primarily addressing two main areas: the "office environment and office furniture."[68] Organizations are reviewing their office settings, their work environment, and their space utilization in an effort to provide more productive atmospheres. This means that new furniture is being purchased—furniture that is designed to reduce back strain and fatigue. Properly designed and fitted office equipment, like Chevron's adjustable desk add-on for a keyboard stand, can also help reduce repetitive motion disorders. Furthermore, they are using colors, like the mauves and grays, that are more pleasing to the eye, and experimenting with lighting brightness as a means of lessening employee exposure to harmful eyestrain associated with today's video display terminals.

Stress

Stress is a dynamic condition in which an individual is confronted with an opportunity, constraint, or demand related to what he or she desires, and for which the outcome is perceived to be both uncertain and important.[69] This definition is complicated, so let us look at it more closely. Stress can manifest itself in both a positive and a negative way. Stress is said to be positive when the situation offers an opportunity for one to gain something; for example, the "psyching-up" that an athlete goes through can be stressful, but this can lead to maximum performance. It is when constraints or demands are placed on us that stress can become negative. Let us explore these two features—constraints and demands.

Constraints are barriers that keep us from doing what we desire. Purchasing a condominium may be your desire, but if you cannot afford the $145,000 price, you are constrained from purchasing it. Accordingly, constraints inhibit us in ways that take control of a situation out of our hands. If you cannot afford the condominium, you cannot get it. Demands, on the other hand, may cause us to give up something we desire. If you wish to attend a concert on campus Thursday night but have a major examination Friday morning, the examination may take precedence. Thus, demands preoccupy our time and force us to shift priorities.

Constraints and demands can lead to potential stress. When they are coupled with uncertainty about the outcome and importance of the outcome, potential stress becomes actual stress.[70] Regardless of the situation, if you remove the uncertainty or the importance, you remove stress. For instance, you may have been constrained from purchasing the car because of your budget, but if you know you will get one for graduating from college, the uncertainty element is significantly reduced. Accordingly, if you are auditing a class for no grade, the importance of the major examination is also reduced. However, when constraints or demands have an impact on an important event and the outcome is unknown, pressure is added—pressure resulting in stress.

Causes of Stress

Stress can be caused by a number of factors called **stressors.** These factors that create stressors can be grouped into two major categories—personal factors and organizational factors. Both of these categories directly affect the person, and ultimately, the job. For the moment, we will postpone our discussion of

Stress A dynamic condition in which an individual is confronted with an opportunity, constraint, or demand related to what he or she desires and for which the outcome is perceived to be both uncertain and important.

Stressors Something that causes stress in an individual.

Controlling stress for a better quality of life is a necessity for all individuals. For executives like Karen Horn, CEO of Bank One in Cleveland, failure to control it can lead to failure on the job. Horn relaxes by getting out into the country and riding horses. As a dressage rider, she reduces her stress by taking these beautiful animals through ballet-precision paces. Such "motionless" effort provides her a sense of tranquility.

organizational factors and cover them in the "burnout" section of this chapter. However, because personal factors affect and are affected by organizational factors, we will address them now.

Almost anything can cause stress for an individual. We all have our levels of resistance, but once the stressors become too great, we exhibit some different behavior. The main fact to remember about stress from personal factors is that the good can cause as much stress as the bad. Certainly we all know that the death of a family member, a divorce, or being fired from work can cause major stress, but so can getting married, the birth of a child, or landing that new job. For example, remember the time you finally got that date with the person of your dreams? Was it a happy time? Yes. But what did you go through to get ready for it? You debated over what clothes to wear, where to go, whether you looked good, and so on. You were nervous when you finally arrived (or your date arrived). All in all, you had a good time on the date, but this good time caused you a lot of stress. While we are not attempting to minimize stress in people's lives, it is important to recognize that both good and bad personal factors may cause stress. Of course, when you consider the changes, like downsizing, that are occurring in U.S. companies, it is little wonder that stress is so rampant in today's companies. Just how rampant? A recent Northwestern National Life Insurance study cited that more than 60 percent of the workers surveyed experienced significant job stress.[71] And stress on the job knows no boundaries. In Japan, worker stress has been identified in 70 percent of the workers by a Fukoku Life Insurance Company study.[72] In fact, in Japan there is a concept called **karoshi,** which means death from overworking. Many Japanese employees literally work themselves to death.

Karoshi A Japanese term meaning death from overworking.

Symptoms of Stress

Although death is seldom the outcome of job stress, there are a number of symptoms that manifest themselves. What are these symptoms of job stress? If we are under stress, we can exhibit one or more of three types of symptoms: physiological, psychological, or behavioral.[73]

Physiological symptoms of stress are the most difficult to detect with the naked eye. They relate to the medical changes that can occur internally in the individual. Such changes as increased heart and breathing rates, higher blood pressure, headaches, and heart attacks can be brought on by stress, but are not easy to spot early. Accordingly, they become less important for us with respect to helping individuals change their actions.

Psychological symptoms of stress manifest themselves as tension, anxiety, irritability, boredom, and procrastination. These, individually, or in combinations, can cause harm in an organization because they lead to significant dissatisfaction with the job.

But it's the third group, the **behavioral symptoms,** that have the greatest effect on the organization. These are observable in terms of decreased productivity, increased absenteeism and turnover, and increased smoking and alcohol consumption.

Where one or more of these symptoms exists for a prolonged time, even greater problems may arise—for both the individual and the company. This extended stress symptom is commonly referred to as **burnout.**

Chronic Stress: Burnout

Worker burnout is costing U.S. industry billions of dollars. One estimate revealed that almost $90 billion is lost each year due to burnout and its related implications.[74] Burnout is a multifaceted phenomenon, the byproduct of both personal variables and organization variables. It can be defined as a function of three concerns: "chronic emotional stress with (a) emotional and/or physical exhaustion, (b) lowered job productivity, and (c) dehumanizing of jobs."[75] Note that none of the three concerns includes long-term boredom. While boredom is often referred to as burnout, it is not!

Causes and Symptoms of Burnout   The factors contributing to burnout can be identified as follows: organization characteristics, perceptions of organization, perceptions of role, individual characteristics, and outcomes.[76] Table 15-4 sum-

Physiological Symptoms Characteristics of stress that manifest themselves as increased heart and breathing rates, higher blood pressure, and headaches.

Psychological Symptoms Characteristics of stress that manifest themselves as tension, anxiety, irritability, boredom, and procrastination.

Behavioral Symptoms Symptoms of stress characterized by decreased productivity, increased absenteeism and turnover, and increased smoking and alcohol/substance consumption.

Burnout Chronic and long-term stress.

TABLE 15-4   Variables Found to Be Significantly Related to Burnout

Organization Characteristics	Perceptions of Organization	Perceptions of Role	Individual Characteristics	Outcomes
Caseload	Leadership	Autonomy	Family/friends support	Satisfaction
Formalization	Communication	Job involvement	Sex	Turnover
Turnover rate	Staff support	Being supervised	Age	
Staff size	Peers	Work pressure	Tenure	
	Clarity	Feedback	Ego level	
	Rules and procedures	Accomplishment		
	Innovation	Meaningfulness		
	Administrative support			

Source: Baron Perlman and E. Alan Hartman, "Burnout: Summary and Future Research," *Human Relations*, Vol. 25, No. 4 (1982), p. 294.

marizes these variables. While these variables can lead to burnout, their presence does not guarantee that burnout will occur. Much of that outcome is contingent on the individual's capability to work under and handle stress. Because of this contingency, stressful conditions result in a two-phased outcome—the first level being the stress itself, and the second level being the problems that arise from the manifestation of this stress.[77]

Reducing Burnout   Recognizing that stress is a fact of life and must be channeled properly, organizations must establish procedures for reducing these stress levels before workers burn out. Although no clear-cut remedies are available, four techniques have been proposed:

1. Identification. This is the analysis of the incidence, prevalence, and characteristics of burnout in individuals, work groups, subunits, or organizations.
2. Prevention. Attempts should be made to prevent the burnout process before it begins.
3. Mediation. This involves procedures for slowing, halting, or reversing the burnout process.
4. Remediation. Techniques are needed for individuals who are already burned out or are rapidly approaching the end stages of this process.[78]

The key point here is that accurate identification is made and then, and only then, is a program tailored to meet that need. Because of the costs associated with burnout, many companies are implementing a full array of programs to help alleviate the problem. Many of these programs are designed to do two things: increase productivity and make the job more pleasant for the worker.

The Employee Assistance Program

No matter what kind of organization or industry one works in, one thing is certain: At times, employees will have personal problems. Whether that problem is job stress, legal, marital, financial, or health-related,[79] one commonality exists: If an employee experiences a personal problem, sooner or later it will manifest itself at the workplace in terms of lowered productivity, increased absenteeism, or turnover (behavioral symptoms of stress).[80] To help employees deal with these personal problems, more and more companies are implementing **employee assistance programs (EAPs).**[81]

Employee Assistance Programs (EAPs) Specific programs designed to help employees with personal problems.

A Brief History

EAPs as they exist today are extensions of programs that had their birth in U.S. companies in the 1940s. Companies like DuPont, Standard Oil, and Kodak recognized that a number of their employees were experiencing problems with alcohol.[82] To help these employees, formalized programs were implemented on the company's site to educate these workers on the dangers of alcohol and to help them overcome their "addiction."[83] The premise behind these programs, which still holds today, is getting a productive employee back on the job as swiftly as possible. Let's examine this for a moment.

Throughout this text thus far, we have discussed the various aspects of HRM designed to create an environment where an employee can be productive. Emphasis is placed on finding the right employee to "fit" the job, training them to do the job, then giving them a variety of opportunities to excel. All of this takes considerable time and money. Think back to the learning curve discussed in Chapter 9. We know it takes considerable time for employees to become fully productive—a process that requires the company to make an investment in its people. As with any investment, the company expects an adequate return. Now, how does this relate to EAPs?

Suppose you have a worker, Beverly, who has been with you for a number of years. Beverly has been a solid performer throughout her tenure, but lately something has happened. You notice Beverly's performance declining: The quality of her work is diminishing, she has been late three times the past five weeks, and rumor has it that Beverly is having marital problems. You could, and would, have every right to discipline Beverly according to the company's discipline process. But it is doubtful discipline alone would help; consequently, you may end up firing Beverly. You've now lost a once good performer, and must fill her position with another—a process that may take eighteen months to finally achieve the productivity level Beverly had. However, instead of firing Beverly you decide to refer her to the company's EAP. This confidential program[84] works with Beverly to determine the cause(s) of her problems, and seeks to help her overcome them. Although Beverly meets more frequently at first with the EAP counselor, you notice that after a short period of time, she is back on the job, improving her performance. And after four months, she is performing at the level she once did. In this scenario, you now have your fully-productive employee back in four months, as opposed to possibly eighteen months had you fired and replaced Beverly. As for the return on investment, it is estimated that U.S. companies spend almost $1 billion each year on EAP programs.[85] For most, studies suggest that these companies save up to $5 for every EAP dollar spent.[86] That, for most of us, is a significant return on investment!

EAPs Today

Since their early focus on alcoholic employees, EAPs have ventured into new areas. One of the most notable areas is the use of EAPs to help control rising health insurance premiums, especially in the areas of "mental health and substance abuse services."[87] For example, at the Campbell's Soup Company, the company's EAP program is the first stop for individuals seeking psychiatric or substance-abuse help. By doing this, Campbell's was able to trim insurance claims by 28 percent.[88] These cost savings accrue from such measures as managing "inpatient length of stays, outpatient treatment days, disability days, and stress-related claims."[89]

No matter how beneficial EAPs may be to an organization, one aspect cannot be taken for granted: employee participation. EAPs must be perceived as being worthwhile to the employee. They must see the EAP as an operation that is designed to help them deal with such problems as "alcohol and chemical dependency, emotional problems, stress, pre-retirement planning, marital problems, careers, finances, legal matters, or termination."[90] In addition, EAPs are becoming more involved in helping employees who have AIDS, as well as counseling employees on cultural diversity issues.[91] For employees to accept EAPs, a few criteria must exist: These are "familiarity with the program, and the perception of the trustworthiness and opportunity for personal attention."[92] Accordingly, there must be extensive information given to employees regarding how the EAP works, how employees can use its services, and how confidentiality is guaranteed.[93] Furthermore, supervisors must be properly trained to recognize changes in employee behaviors and to refer them to the EAP in a confidential manner. And with the AIDS issue, confidentiality has become of even greater importance.

Although EAPs can help employees when problems arise, companies have given much support to finding ways to eliminate some factors that may lead to personal problems. In doing so, some organizations such as the Adolph Coors Company, have promoted wellness programs.[94]

Wellness Programs

Wellness Programs Organizational programs designed to keep employees healthy.

When we mention **wellness programs** in any organization, we are talking about any type of program that is designed to keep employees healthy. These programs are varied, and may focus on such things as smoking cessation, weight control, stress management,[95] physical fitness, nutrition education, high blood-pressure control,[96] and so forth. Wellness programs are designed to help cut employer health costs,[97] and to lower absenteeism and turnover by preventing health-related problems.[98] For instance, it is estimated that over a ten-year period, the Adolph Coors Company saved almost $2 million in decreased medical premium payments, reduced sick leave, and increased productivity.[99] For Coors, that represents a more than $6 return for every $1 spent on wellness.[100] Although savings like those achieved at Coors are not often calculated, there is evidence that the effects on health-care premiums and productivity are positive.[101] However, such results may not occur in all wellness programs.[102]

It is interesting to note that, as with EAPs, wellness programs don't work unless employees view them as worthwhile. Unfortunately for wellness, the numbers across the United States are not as promising. It is estimated that only about 20 percent of employees who have access to these programs actually use them.[103] To help combat this low turnout, a number of key criteria must exist.[104] First of all, there must be top management support—without their support in terms of resources, and in personally using the programs, the wrong message may be sent to employees. Second, there appears to be a need to have the programs serve the family as well as the employees themselves. This not only provides an atmosphere where families can "get healthy together," it also reduces possible medical costs for the dependents. And finally comes the issue of employee input: If programs are designed without considering employees' needs, even the best ones will fail. Companies need to invite participation by asking employees what they'd use if available. Although many companies know that exercise is beneficial, few initially addressed how to get employees involved. But after finding out that employees would like such things as on-site exercise facilities, aerobics, and the like, organizations were able to begin appropriate program development.[105] For example, at AT&T in Kansas City and New Jersey, an on-site fitness facility is made available to all employees.[106] In addition to the regular exercise equipment and aerobics, AT&T also offers T'ai-chi, the Chinese meditative art that exercises all muscle groups.[107]

As wellness programs continue to expand in corporate America, the question regarding top management support is still crucial, but questions about that support being present are lessening. Why? Because in finding out how to get senior executives involved, it was discovered that they, too, wanted a place to go for exercise. Many of these executives, as one of their perks, are provided with a membership in a health club; executives at such companies as Merrill Lynch, Revlon, and Tenneco enjoy such memberships as a means of maintaining their physical fitness.[108] Whether it is executives or support staff participation, wellness or EAPs, U.S. organizations appear to be continuing their efforts to support a healthy work environment. The companies reap a good return on their investments; programs such as EAP and wellness have proven to be win–win opportunities for all involved.

International Safety and Health

It is important to know the safety and health environments of each country in which an organization operates. Generally, corporations in western Europe, Canada, Japan, and the United States put great emphasis on the health and welfare of their employees. However, most businesses in less-developed countries have limited resources and thus cannot establish awareness or protection programs.

Most countries have laws and regulatory agencies that protect workers from hazardous work environments. It is important for American firms to learn the often complex regulations that exist, as well as the cultural expectations of the local labor force. Manufacturers, in particular, where there are a myriad of potentially hazardous situations, must design and establish facilities that meet the expectations of the local employees—not necessarily those of Americans.

The Union Carbide pesticide plant in Bhopal, India, provides a dramatic example of the impact of local cultural attitudes toward health and safety. Union Carbide built its plant with all the safety devices that would be available in a comparable plant in the United States, as well as with the expectation that managers and employees who worked there would react to an emergency like American workers. A great deal of money was invested in worker training regarding safety procedures. However, after the disaster that took thousands of lives, it was reported that an on-duty supervisor was informed of the lethal chemical leak during his tea break. He reportedly said he would follow it up after he finished his break—a perfectly reasonable expectation in India, where a very high value is placed on human relations and much less on machinery. By the time his tea break was over, the situation was already beyond control.

International Health Issues

For corporations preparing to send executives on overseas assignments, a few basic health-related items appear on every checklist.

1. An Up-to-date Health Certificate. Often called a "shot book," this is the individual's record of vaccinations against infectious diseases such as cholera, typhoid, and smallpox. Each country has its own vaccination requirements for entry inside its borders, but in addition, the U.S. Department of State Traveler Advisories "hotline" provides alerts to specific problems with diseases or regions within a country. For example, in 1991, cholera was a serious health concern in Peru and certain parts of other South American countries.

2. A General First Aid Kit. This should include all over-the-counter medications such as aspirin, cold and cough remedies, and so on, the employee or family members would usually take at home, but that might not be available at the overseas drugstore. In addition, any prescription drugs should be packed in twice the quantity expected to be used. In case of an accidental dunking, overheating, or other problem, it is wise to pack the two supplies of drugs separately. It also is advisable to know the generic name—not the U.S. trade name—of any prescription drug. Finally, include special items such as disinfectant solutions to treat fresh fruit or vegetables, and water purifying tablets, as the sanitation system of the host country warrants.

3. Emergency Plans. Upon your arrival at the foreign destination, check out the local medical and dental facilities and plan on what care can be expected in the host country or where the closest appropriate medical care is. This might include evacuation of a sick or injured employee or family member to another city or even another country. For example, expatriates in China often prefer to go to Hong Kong even for regular medical checkups. It is always wise to take along copies of all family members' medical and dental records.

International Safety Issues

Safety for the expatriate executive has become increasingly an issue of security, both while traveling and after arrival. Again, the U.S. Department of State provides travel alerts and cautions on its "hotline." These can be general or very specific. In early 1990, the China alert included: "Be cautious about bringing in documents, letters, etc., that might be regarded as objectionable." At the same time, the message for Sudan was: "High potential for terrorist acts exists in Khartoum. Curfew rules are strictly enforced."[109]

But safety precautions begin before the overseas journey. While it may be a matter of status and comfort to fly first class, experience with skyjacks has shown that it is safer to fly economy class. The goal is to blend into the crowd as much as possible, even if the corporation is willing to pay for greater luxury. Many corporations offer some of the following advice for traveling executives: Blending in includes wearing low-key, appropriate clothing, not carrying obviously expensive luggage, avoiding luggage tags with titles like "vice-president," and, if possible, traveling in small groups. Upon arrival at the airport, it is advisable to check in at the airline's ticket counter immediately and go through security checkpoints to wait in the less public gate area. The wisdom of this advice was confirmed in Rome, Athens, and other airport bombings.

Once the expatriate family has landed, the goal remains to blend in. These individuals must acquire some local "savvy" as quickly as possible; in addition to learning the language, they also must adapt to the local customs and try to dress in the same style as the local people.

Foremost on many individuals' minds when they go abroad is security. Many corporations now provide electronic safety systems, floodlights, and the like for home and office, as well as bodyguards or armed chauffeurs—but individual alertness is the key factor. It is suggested that kidnappers select their potential targets by seeking someone who is valuable to either a government or corporation, with lots of family money or a wealthy sponsor, and where there is opportunity to plan and execute the kidnapping. This last criterion means it is important to avoid set routines for local travel and other behaviors. The employee should take different routes between home and office, and the children should vary their paths to school. The family food shopping should be done at varying times each day, or in different markets, if possible. These and other precautions, as well as a constant awareness of one's surroundings, are important for every member of the family.

Study Tools and Applications

Summary

This summary relates to the Learning Objectives provided on p. 411.
After having read this chapter, you should know:
1. The Occupational Safety and Health Act (OSHA) outlines comprehensive and specific safety and health standards.
2. OSHA has an established five-step priority enforcement process consisting of imminent danger, serious accidents, employee complaints, inspection of targeted industries, and random inspections.
3. OSHA can fine an organization up to a maximum penalty of $70,000 if the violation is severe, willful, and repetitive. For violations not meeting those criteria, the maxi-

mum fine is $7,000. OSHA may, at its discretion, seek criminal or civil charges against an organization's management if they willfully violate health and safety regulations.

4. Companies in selected industries must complete OSHA Form 200 to record accidents, injuries, and illnesses that are job-related. This information is then used to calculate the organization's incident rate.
5. OSHA is setting standards to protect workers exposed to blood-borne pathogens, chemicals and other work-related toxins; and is setting standards for motor vehicle safety.
6. The leading causes of accidents are human or environmental factors.
7. A company can help prevent workplace violence by ensuring that its policies are not adversely affecting employees, by developing a plan to deal with the issue, and to train its managers in identifying troubled employees.
8. Stress is a dynamic condition in which an individual is confronted with an opportunity, constraint, or demand for which the outcome is perceived as important and uncertain. Burnout is caused by a combination of emotional and/or physical exhaustion, lower job productivity, or dehumanizing jobs.
9. Creating a healthy work site involves removing any harmful substance, like asbestos, germs, fungi, cigarette smoke, and so forth, thus limiting employee exposure.
10. Employee assistance and wellness programs are designed to offer employees a variety of services that will help them to become mentally and physically healthy, which in turn helps to contain the organization's health-care costs.

Key Terms

behavioral symptoms
burnout
cumulative trauma disorder
employee assistance programs (EAPs)
ergonomics
hazard communication standard
imminent danger
incident rate
karoshi
Marshall v. *Barlow, Inc.*
National Institute for Occupational

Safety and Health (NIOSH)
Occupational Safety and Health Act
Omnibus Budget Reconciliation Act of 1990
physiological symptoms
psychological symptoms
repetitive motion disorder
sick building
smoke-free policies
stress
stressors

EXPERIENTIAL EXERCISE

Stress and Life Events

The list of life events provided in Table 15-5 (p. 440) is designed to provide you some indication of the level of stress in your life. Look at each item, noting those that apply to you. When you have finished, determine your sum total of points. After its completion, answer the following questions:

1. What does this assessment tell you about the level of stress in your life? Do you feel you are managing your stress well? Explain.
2. What are the main factors that contribute to your stress?
3. What would you suggest you do to lessen this effect of stress?
4. If many of your stressors were job-related, would you consider giving up your job, and possibly changing your lifestyle to a more calm state? Explain why or why not.

CASE APPLICATION:

Imperial Food Products

Most employees, regardless of their position in the organization, status, or motivation level, share one common requirement: They expect to work in an envi-

TABLE 15-5   Life-Event Stress Sheet

Life Events	Mean Value	Life Events	Mean Value
1. Death of spouse	100	24. In-law troubles	29
2. Divorce	73	25. Outstanding personal achievement	28
3. Marital separation from spouse	65	26. Spouse beginning or ceasing work outside of home	26
4. Detention in jail or other institution	63	27. Beginning or ceasing formal schooling	26
5. Death of a close family member	63	28. Major change in living conditions (e.g., building a new home, remodeling, deterioration of home or neighborhood)	25
6. Major personal injury or illness	53		
7. Marriage	50	29. Revision of personal habits (dress, manners, associations, etc.)	24
8. Being fired at work	47	30. Troubles with the boss	23
9. Marital reconciliation with spouse	45	31. Major changes in working hours or conditions	20
10. Retirement from work	45	32. Change in residence	20
11. Major change in the health or behavior of a family member	44	33. Changing to a new school	20
12. Pregnancy	40	34. Major change in usual type and/or amount of recreation	19
13. Sexual difficulties	39	35. Major change in church activities (e.g., a lot more or a lot less than usual)	19
14. Gaining a new family member (e.g., through birth, adoption, parent moving in, etc.)	39	36. Major changes in social activities (e.g., clubs, dancing, movies, visiting, etc.)	18
15. Major bankruptcy readjustment (e.g., merger, reorganization, bankruptcy, etc.)	39	37. Taking on a loan (e.g., purchasing a car, TV, freezer, etc.)	17
16. Major change in financial state (e.g., a lot worse off or a lot better off than usual)	38	38. Major changes in sleeping habits (a lot more or a lot less sleep, or change in part of day when asleep)	16
17. Death of a close friend	37	39. Major change in the number of family get-togethers (e.g., a lot more or a lot less than usual)	15
18. Changing to a different line of work	36		
19. Major changes in the number of arguments with spouse (e.g., either a lot more or a lot less than usual regarding child rearing, personal habits, etc.)	35	40. Major changes in eating habits (a lot more or a lot less food intake, or very different meal hours or surroundings)	15
20. Taking on a significant mortgage (e.g., purchasing a home, business, etc.)	31	41. Vacation	13
21. Foreclosure on a mortgage or loan	30	42. Christmas	12
22. Major change in responsibilities at work (e.g., promotion, demotion, lateral transfer)	29	43. Minor violations of the law (e.g., traffic tickets, jaywalking, disturbing the peace, etc.)	11
23. Son or daughter leaving home (e.g., marriage, attending college, etc.)	29		

Source: Adapted from T.H. Holmes and R.H. Rahe, "The Social Readjustment Rating Scale, *Journal of Psychosomatic Research* (Pergamon Press, Ltd., 1967), pp. 217–18. Used with permission. All rights reserved.

ronment that is free from unnecessary hazards that can cause injury, illness, or even death. We are rightly angered when employees are injured or die because of management negligence or lack of safety concerns. Anger is exactly the emotion felt by residents of Hamlet, North Carolina.

Hamlet is the home of a chicken-processing plant for Imperial Food Products. This plant was the scene of one of the most horrifying episodes in the annals of U.S. corporate safety and health. Early in the morning of September 3, 1991, workers were made aware that a fire had broken out in the plant when a hydraulic line on the conveyor belt burst and erupted in flames. The blaze quickly spread out of control, fueled by the grease from the processing operations. Normal exits became inaccessible. The operation lacked fire alarms, and didn't have in place adequate sprinkler systems in the event something like this occurred. Fleeing for their lives, employees frantically raced to the exits. Unfortunately, many of these exits were locked, leading to the deaths of twenty-five Imperial Food employees.[110]

By December 1991, the North Carolina State Safety and Health Agency had completed its investigation, and fined the company more than $800,000 for its violations. Furthermore, its owner, Emmett Roe, and two other management personnel were indicted in March 1992 on charges of involuntary manslaughter. In September, Roe plead guilty to twenty-five of the counts, and received a jail sentence of about twenty years. Charges against other management personnel were dropped as part of Roe's plea. Finally, by November 1992, a settlement had been reached in the lawsuits filed in the case. Claimants were awarded a total of $16 million.[111]

What happened at Imperial Food was a disaster. The sad fact is that if those doors hadn't been locked, if fire prevention measures existed, or if the State Health and Safety Office had conducted a recent inspection of the plant and cited Imperial for these violations, those lives undoubtedly would have been saved.[112]

Questions

1. Given that there existed several safety violations at the Hamlet plant, describe how you believe such violations could have escaped detection for so long.
2. "Emmett Roe's conviction of twenty-five counts of voluntary manslaughter is justified given the facts of this case." Build an argument to support this statement. Develop a counterargument.
3. What responsibility or liability do you believe the State's Safety and Health Office had in this case? Explain.

Testing Your Understanding

How well did you fulfill the learning objectives?

1. OSHA legislation did all of the following except
   a. established comprehensive and specific health standards.
   b. authorized inspections to ensure the standards are met.
   c. required employers to keep records of illnesses and injuries.
   d. required employers to calculate hospitalization and medical treatment costs for job-related injury and illness.
   e. required employers to calculate accident ratios.
2. If OSHA wants to inspect your facility, you should do all of the following except
   a. discuss the company's safety program with the OSHA inspector.
   b. agree with OSHA, before the inspection, on the exact facility and entity to be inspected.
   c. insist on seeing the search warrant.
   d. tell the OSHA representative how safety programs are communicated to employees.
   e. explain to the OSHA representative how safety programs are enforced.

3. An OSHA safety inspector is scheduled to inspect a meat-processing plant the day after tomorrow. All of the following could preempt that inspection except
   a. A complaint from an automotive distributor.
   b. A complaint from a sawmill.
   c. A serious accident at a chemical plant.
   d. A serious accident at a shipyard.
   e. A refusal to allow entry without a search warrant by an electronics firm.
4. Last month, the OSHA inspector in a chicken-processing plant "red-flagged" a production area for an old and faulty water boiler. Yesterday, the boiler exploded, injuring thirty-one workers. There were no fatalities, and all but two of the twenty-seven workers who were sent to the hospital were treated and released the same day. The two hospitalized employees are expected to return to work within sixty days. What OSHA penalty can this firm expect?
   a. No penalty. A report would not be filed without a fatality.
   b. The firm will be fined at least $70,000 for failing to fix the boiler.
   c. The shift supervisor will be imprisoned for the to-

tal amount of time the injured workers are hospitalized.

   d. No penalty. This minor incident would result in only a report being filed.

   e. The plant would be closed.

5. All of the following are accurate statements about the current status and impact of OSHA except

   a. OSHA has refocused its energy from enforcing the intent of the law to stipulating the law.

   b. many unions argue that OSHA enforcement efforts have not been extensive enough.

   c. in some large organizations, an additional administrative position has been created with a sole responsibility of safety.

   d. OSHA standards have become more realistic in recent years.

   e. in the last few years, OSHA standards have focused more on health than on safety.

6. A chemical engineer for a pharmaceutical plant was blinded when a pipe he was adjusting cracked and spewed hot vapor into his face. He wasn't wearing safety glasses or a hard hat, although both were specified for the job he was doing. John's report indicated that he knew about the safety equipment, but that for the last five years, had gotten along quite well without the cumbersome gear. What means of preventing accidents was not being used effectively in this situation?

   a. Education.

   b. Skills training.

   c. Engineering.

   d. Protection.

   e. Regulation enforcement.

7. In academic life, the year that tenure is decided for a professor is usually a very stressful one. The tenure decision means that a professor can either stay at that university until retirement or must leave that university within a year to find employment elsewhere. Bob, an untenured assistant professor, cut a "deal" with the provost and the dean, two key decision makers in his tenure process, well in advance of the decision. Bob was not stressed during his tenure decision year due to the lack of which stress contributor?

   a. Constraints.

   b. Demands.

   c. Outcome importance.

   d. Outcome uncertainty.

   e. Burnout.

8. Why do companies use EAPs?

   a. Two years of treatment usually returns up to 80 percent of employees to the workforce. Costs of hiring and training new employees amount to over four years' salary.

   b. Studies suggest that $5 is saved for each EAP dollar spent.

   c. EAPs are more popular with employees than traditional health insurance coverage.

   d. Title VII compliance requires either EAP or wellness programs. EAPs are cheaper.

   e. EAPs are required in most health insurance packages.

9. Which one of the following is not a recommended measure for preventing workplace violence?

   a. have police agencies from the local area frequently visit the office facility

   b. train supervisors to identify troubled employees and refer them for help

   c. install security measures such as guards and electronic detection equipment

   d. establish an employee assistance program

   e. instruct employees on what to do if someone becomes violent

10. Which statement applies to OSHA's "random inspection" level of enforcement?

   a. OSHA may inspect any facility, at any time, without warning.

   b. Employers are not required to admit OSHA inspectors without a search warrant.

   c. OSHA is so understaffed that they never conduct "random inspections."

   d. Employers in noncritical industries are notified at the start of each month if they are to be potentially investigated by OSHA during that month.

   e. Any organization that has had a legitimate OSHA complaint filed against it is subject to "random inspections" of the facility at any time during the next five years.

11. Which of the following statements best describes OSHA's enforcement mechanisms?

   a. Fines can be levied for noncompliance, up to $70,000 per violation, if the violation is severe, willful, and repetitive.

   b. Top company officials have been convicted of manslaughter.

   c. Government contracts have been canceled with noncompliant firms.

   d. Firms with repeated violations are required to keep, at their own expense, an OSHA inspector on site at all times.

   e. Fines up to $100,000 per violation can be levied against firms that do not comply with record-keeping requirements.

12. Indirect costs of accidents that must be borne by the employer include all of the following except

   a. wages paid for time lost due to injury.

   b. damage to equipment and material.

   c. the workers' compensation premium.

   d. personnel to investigate and report accidents.

   e. lost production due to stoppages and changeovers.

Chapter Sixteen

COMMUNICATIONS PROGRAMS

LEARNING OBJECTIVES

AFTER READING THIS CHAPTER, YOU WILL BE ABLE TO:

1. Discuss how communication serves as the foundation for HRM activities.
2. Explain the legally required communications with respect to benefit administration and safety and health.
3. Describe the purpose of HRM communications programs.
4. Discuss how corporate culture is affected by effective communication.
5. Explain the role of the chief executive officer promoting communications programs.
6. List information employees should receive under an effective communications program.
7. Describe the purpose of the employee handbook.
8. Explain what information should be included in an employee handbook.
9. List four popular communication methods used in organizations.
10. Discuss the critical components of an effective suggestion program.

Almost every successful organization has a rich history associated with it. Thriving companies usually got started through the entrepreneurial spirit of a well-focused risk taker. And although such organizations as IBM, Ford, and Microsoft can be traced to their inspirational founders, it's hard to fathom that these giants were once run out of someone's basement. For instance, unless you've read a profile of Bill Gates, you probably don't recognize that this software genius started his company in his home. Accordingly, today's employees are often out of luck in appreciating what went into growing their business. Lou Bucelli, president of CME Conference Video, however, just won't let the beginnings be forgotten.[1]

CME Conference Video, the medical video production company in Mount Laurel, New Jersey, was founded in 1989. From a company that once occupied only 800 square feet of "office space" and generated sales of about $75,000, Bucelli has nurtured the business dramatically. In 1994, CME's sales surpassed the $9 million mark. Lou and his twenty employees are now housed in a 16,000-square-foot facility that is "state of the art." But growth in sales, employees, and space is not the point here. Rather, Bucelli wants his employees to appreciate how far the company has come. He regularly ropes off some 800 square feet in the facility and requires his employees to join him in the office of the past. He wants the employees to feel the cramped nature of the early company. Even some of his early employees are asked to tell "war-stories" from those first few years—like how they used to take up to two months to produce a video that today can be done in under ten days.

Why the emphasis on communicating the past? That's simple to Bucelli. He feels reminiscing about the past not only gives employees a better appreciation of where the company has been, but also helps them to envision the future. By seeing how the company has transformed itself over the past five years, Bucelli is confident that his employees will use that mental process to see the future of the business.

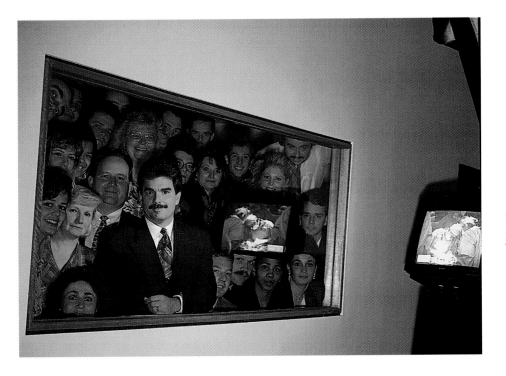

Lou Bucelli, Founder and president of CME Conference Video in Mount Laurel, NJ, requires all his employees to experience first-handedly the company's history. By going back to days of old, Bucelli has strong beliefs that it helps his employees to shape the future.

Introduction

For fifteen chapters, we have been discussing a variety of HRM activities. Inherent in all of these activities is one common thread—effective **communication.** Although we may not have elaborated specifically on how HRM involves itself in the communication process, we have addressed its needs on several occasions. For example, in Chapter 2 the discussion of worker diversity identified the need for better communications with employees, especially those who do not speak the native language. Communications in work-force diversity also means letting these individuals know that they are welcome in the corporation and that the company will make every attempt to provide them equal opportunity in the organization.[2]

We also addressed the need to communicate with respect to the recruiting and selection process (in terms of understanding what the job entails, and realistic job previews), in orientation (acclimating employees to HRM activities and policies), and training (understanding how to do the job). Yet probably the most critical HRM activities emphasizing communications came in the discussion of motivation, performance evaluations, benefits, and safety and health. In motivation, we discussed the need to be able to communicate the relationship that exists between one's efforts and individual goal attainment. In that discussion we highlighted the need for performance goals to be communicated—goals that will, when met, facilitate achieving organization-wide objectives. Specificity for doing so was discussed in performance evaluations, and how the interaction between an employee and manager can affect performance outcomes. When these outcomes are positive, individuals should be rewarded; when they are not positive, effort must be expended to correct the problem. For that, we introduced employee counseling, which relies heavily on effective communications.

Communication The transference of meaning and understanding.

For benefits and safety and health, we discussed not only the importance of informing employees of the benefits offered them, and availability of EAP and wellness programs, but the legal issues of providing certain information. That is, with respect to benefits, HRM is responsible for providing each employee with a Summary Plan Description, which describes in understandable terms employee rights under ERISA, their pension plan requirements, and updated benefits accumulations.[3] Likewise, OSHA, under its Hazard Communication Standard, requires employers to notify employees of potential dangers and protective measures when exposed to workplace hazardous chemicals or toxins.

As we move into the twenty-first century, we recognize that our companies will be different. Factors like global competition and computerization are making our companies rethink how they are organized. We've witnessed extensive delayering, mergers, and acquisitions in the late 1980s through the mid 1990s. When such occurrences are frequent, employee stress levels increase. One way of allaying such stress is to reduce the uncertainty that surrounds the situation—in our terms, effective communications.[4]

We know the years ahead will continue to witness change in our companies.[5] Our movement toward leaner structures, continuous improvement, employee involvement, and work teams will work best if effective communication exists.[6] And where good communications programs are operating, benefits accrue to the company. For instance, one study credits communications with "better work relations; greater trust between employees and managers; greater employee satisfaction, and leading to lower turnover rates."[7] And with our diverse work force, this means communicating in different languages to ensure that the message is understood by all employees.

Achieving these goals is not easy. Effective communication does not just happen; rather, it evolves after careful thought, implementation, and evaluation. For much of that, we rely on HRM. Although we've highlighted many of these items throughout the text, there are still a few that warrant exposure. Specifically, in this chapter we want to focus on HRM's role in the communications process, look at the purpose of employee handbooks and newsletters, and close with a discussion of suggestion systems/complaint procedures that exist in companies. Let's now turn our attention to HRM communications programs.

HRM Communications Programs

The Purpose

Human resource management communications programs are designed to keep employees abreast of what is happening in the organization, and knowledgeable of the policies and procedures affecting them.[8] Whereas public relations departments are created to keep the public informed of what an organization does, HRM communications focus on the internal constituents—the employees.[9] As we mentioned in Chapter 1 regarding the role of the employee relations department in the maintenance function, communication programs serve as a basis for increasing employee loyalty and commitment.[10] How? By building into the corporate culture a systematic means through which information is free-flowing, timely, and accurate, employees are better able to perceive that the organization values them.[11] Such a system builds trust and openness among organizational members, even assisting the sharing of "bad news."[12]

For example, at Georgia Power Company, company executives were able to use communications effectively to stave off any further deterioration of the company's operations.[13] Georgia Power had been experiencing several crises during the latter part of the 1980s. Failure to act on these problems, like profitability and customer service, may have led to significant changes in the organization and the employees' lives. Instead, Georgia Power's top management decided to take the issue to the people. By empowering its nine-person communications department to get employees motivated to achieve the company's objectives, several programs were implemented. One program involved calling employees at home to determine if they knew corporate goals; those who did were monetarily rewarded. Various other communications programs were also instituted, again to reinforce what the company was about. As a result of these efforts, by the early 1990s, Georgia Power's employees had helped turn the company around, while simultaneously indicating that employee morale was at its highest level in years.[14]

HRM communications has the ability to bring about many positive changes in an organization. This process, by whatever means it exists, should stay focused on keeping employees informed, thereby setting the stage for enhancing employee satisfaction. For employees at Hewlett-Packard, that is what has been happening. Because of the efforts of its managers to enhance communications with employees, Hewlett-Packard has witnessed more employee job satisfaction and a higher quality of work life for its organization members.[15] And at Challenger Electrical Equipment Corporation in Allentown, Pennsylvania, it took a union organizing campaign before company managers realized that employees were dissatisfied with the information they had (or hadn't) been getting.[16] With these in mind, let's look at some fundamental requirements for an effective HRM communications program.

Guidelines for Supporting Communications Programs

Building effective HRM communications programs involves a few fundamental elements. These include top management commitment, effective upward communication, determining what is to be communicated, allowing for feedback, and information sources. Let's look at each of these.

Top Management Commitment Before any organization can develop and implement an internal organizational communications program it must have the backing, support, and "blessing" of the CEO.[17] Any activity designed to facilitate work environments must be seen by employees as being endorsed by the company's top management. In doing so, these programs are given priority and are viewed as significant components of the corporate culture.[18] Just as it is critical for employees to see top management supporting communications, so, too, is it for them to see communications effectively operating at all levels—that is, effective communications does not just imply that top management sends information down throughout the company. It also implies that information flows upward as well, and laterally to other areas in the organization.

Effective Upward Communication The upward flow of communication is particularly noteworthy because it is often the employees, the ones closest to the work, who may have vital information that top management should know. For instance, let's take a situation that occurs in HRM.[19] We've witnessed this changing field and recognize its ever-changing nature. Legislation at any level—federal, state, or local—may add new HRM requirements for the organization. Unless top management is made aware of the implications of these requirements—like knowing how to ensure that sexual harassment charges are thoroughly investigated—severe repercussions could occur. Thus, that information must filter up in the company.

A similar point could easily be made for any part of an organization. And in keeping with the spirit of employee empowerment, as employees are more involved in making decisions that affect them, that information must be communicated "up the line." Furthermore, it's important for top management to monitor the pulse of the organization regarding how employees view working for the company. Whether that information is obtained from walking around the premises, through formal employee suggestions, or through employee satisfaction/morale surveys, such information is crucial. In fact, on the latter point, with the advent of technology, some of the employee satisfaction measures can be captured in almost "real time." At IBM, such surveys are "on-line," making it easier for the employee to use, more expedient in its analysis, and more timely for company use.[20]

Determining What to Communicate   At the extreme, if every piece of information that exists in our organizations were communicated, no work would ever get done; people would be spending their entire days on information overload. Employees, while wanting to be informed, are not concerned with every piece of information, like who just retired, was promoted, or what community group was given a donation yesterday.[21] Rather, employees need pertinent information—addressing those things employees should know to do their jobs. This typically includes where the business is going (strategic goals),[22] current sales/service/production outcomes, new product or service lines, and human resource policy changes.[23]

One means we advocate is a "what-if, so-what" test. When deciding the priority of the information to be shared, managers should ask themselves *what if* this information is not shared: Will my employees be able to do their jobs as well as if it were shared? Will they be disadvantaged in some way by not knowing? If the answers are no, then that may not be a priority item. And then, the *so-what* test: Will employees care about the information? Will they see it as an overload of meaningless information? If they may, then that, too, is not priority information. That's not to say this information may never be exchanged; it only means that it's not important for employees to get the information immediately.

For example, let's assume we have two pieces of information to share. One item is that the company's health insurance plan is changing from traditional coverage to a preferred provider organization. Would this meet our what-if, so-what test? What if we didn't communicate this in a timely fashion? Would the employees be affected? When you are talking about their welfare, you bet they would. And as we discussed in terms of individual goals being met for motivation purposes, such a change matters, thus passing the so-what test. But contrast a benefit change with information regarding the information systems department installing a Novell computer network. Will employees be adversely affected if the information is delayed a day or a week? Probably not! But this delaying of information must be considered on an individual basis—that is, while many employees may not need the immediate information on the network, certain areas of the company, like purchasing and systems maintenance, would find it a necessity.

Allow for Feedback   We cannot assume that our communication efforts are achieving their goals. Consequently, we must develop into the system a means of assessing the flow of information, and for fostering employee feedback. How that information is generated may differ from organization to organization. For

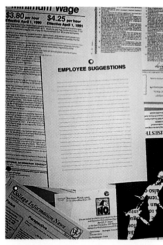

What is one means of getting feedback from employees? The company suggestion program. Through such a device, employees can tell management what they think, and have management take some action on these suggestions.

TABLE 16-1 Employee Preferences for Information Sources

1. Immediate supervisor

2. Company bulletin board

3. Company newsletter

4. Letter sent directly to employee's home

5. Company magazine

6. Coworkers (grapevine)

7. Union steward (if union is present)

Source: Adapted from David N. Bateman, "Communications," in *Human Resources Management: Ideas and Trends* (Chicago: Commerce Clearing House, Inc., July 26, 1988), p. 28.

some, it may be a casual word-of-mouth assessment. Others may use employee surveys to capture the data, or provide a suggestion box where comments can be given. For others, there is a formalized and systematic communications audit program.[24]

Irrespective of how that information is gathered, employees must be involved. Otherwise, not only will measurement of the effectiveness of the communications program be difficult,[25] but you may also lose its benefits from its appearing to be less of a commitment to employees.

Information Sources   HRM communications should serve as a conduit in promoting effective communications throughout the organization. Although HRM plays an important role in bringing this to fruition, they are not the only, or the main, source of information. For that, we have to turn to one's immediate supervisor.[26] If successful programs can be linked to the immediate supervisor, then HRM must ensure that these individuals are trained in how to communicate properly. Even our benefit change, cited a few paragraphs ago, if implemented would likely result in a number of questions for one's supervisor. Thus, HRM must make every effort to empower these supervisors with accurate data to deal with the "frontline" questions. From an HRM point of view, where is information best conveyed? Table 16-1 lists the top seven sources where employees prefer to go to satisfy their information needs. Note that these items are areas that HRM can directly influence by either providing the training, publishing periodicals, or through word-of-mouth dissemination of factual data.

Although these sources are varied and serve vital purposes, there is one medium that is central to providing information to employees: the employee handbook.

A Guide for Employees: The Employee Handbook

During the orientation of new employees, we inform them of a number of important facts regarding employment in the organization. But we must recognize that stating this information once will not be enough. There's often too much for the employee to absorb, especially during the excitement of the first day on the job, so a permanent reference guide is needed. This reference guide for employees is called the employee handbook.

Employee Handbook A booklet describing the important aspects of employment an employee needs to know.

The Purpose of an Employee Handbook

An **employee handbook** is a tool that, when developed properly, serves both employee and employer. For the employee, a well-designed handbook provides a central information source that conveys such useful information as "what the company is about, its history, and employee benefits."[27] The handbook, then, gives employees an opportunity to learn about the company, and what the company provides for them, in a way that permits each employee an opportunity to understand the information at his or her own pace.[28] By having this resource available, questions that may arise over such benefits as vacation accrual, matching contributions, vesting, and so forth, can be more easily answered. Serving as an easy reference guide, the employee handbook can be used by employees whenever it is warranted.[29] Table 16-2 lists the purposes of an employee handbook. Beyond just being a source of information, employee handbooks also generate some other benefits. Where they exist, it has been found that they assist in creating an atmosphere in which employees become more productive members of the organization, and increase their commitment and loyalty to the organization.[30] Furthermore, a good handbook also helps create a sense of security for employees.[31] By being thorough in its coverage, an employee handbook will address various HRM policies and work rules, which set the parameters within which employees are expected to perform.[32] For example, the handbook may express information on discipline and discharge procedures and a means of redressing disciplinary action should the employee feel that it was administered unfairly. The handbook, then, serves to ensure that any HRM policy will be fair, equitable, and consistently applied.[33]

Employers, too, can benefit from using an employee handbook. In addition to any benefits accrued from having a more committed and loyal work force, handbooks can also be used in the recruiting effort.[34] Remember, we advocated the use of realistic job previews for helping to "sell" recruits on the organization; a well-written employee handbook, shown to an applicant, can be useful in providing some of the necessary information an applicant may be seeking. Although employee handbooks are designed to "educate, inform, and guide" em-

TABLE 16-2 The Dos of an Employee Handbook

A well-designed, well-written employee handbook should convey such information as:

1. **What the organization expects from its employees.** Employees need to be informed of company policies. This includes such items as work hours, employee conduct, performance evaluations, disciplinary process, moonlighting, vacations, holiday, and sick and personal leave usage.

2. **What the employee can expect from the organization.** What benefits does the employee receive? These should be detailed enough such that the employee fully understands the "fringes" of the job. The company's HRM policies regarding salary increases, promotions, and so on, also need to be conveyed.

3. **The history of the organization.** The history section provides an opportunity to help employees understand where the organization has been, and where it is heading. This section also includes the philosophy/culture of the organization.

4. **A glossary section.** Words have different meanings to different people, and may differ depending on the context used. To eliminate confusion, the terms used in the handbook should be defined.

Source: Adapted from "The (Handbook) Handbook: A Guide to Writing the Perfect Manual for Employees You Care About," *Inc.* (November 1993), pp. 60–61.

This handbook is not a contract, expressed or implied, guaranteeing employment for any specific duration. Although [the company] hopes that your employment relationship with us will be long-term, either you or the company may terminate this relationship at any time, for any reason, with or without cause of notice.

Figure 16-1
Sample Employee Handbook
Disclaimer

ployees in the organization,[35] a word of caution is in order. In Chapter 4, in our discussion of employee rights and employment-at-will, we addressed the issue of implied contracts. Recall that an implied contract is anything expressed, verbally or in writing, that may be perceived by the individual to mean that she or he can't be terminated. For example, telling an employee that as long as her performance is satisfactory, she will have a job until retirement, could be construed as an implied contract. Over the years, the courts have viewed that various statements made in employee handbooks may be binding on the company.[36] To prevent this from occurring, many legal advocates and HRM researchers recommend a careful choice of words in the handbook, and a disclaimer.[37] We have reproduced a disclaimer from one business in Figure 16-1.

Before we move into the specific components of a handbook, there is one other important aspect for management to consider; that is, an employee handbook is of little use if employees don't read it. To facilitate that goal, we recommend that, first of all, the handbook should be pertinent to employees' needs.[38] Providing information that is viewed as unnecessary, or having a handbook that contains unclear wording or excessive verbiage,[39] may diminish meeting this goal. Consequently, employers should, through feedback mechanisms, assess how employees perceive the usefulness of employee handbook information, gather their input, and make modifications where necessary.[40] HRM should not assume that once developed and disseminated to employees, the employee handbook is final; rather, it should be viewed as something to be updated and refined on a continuous basis. Employers often find that using some sort of loose-leaf binder system more readily allows for corrections/updates/ additions.[41]

As a second requirement, it is recommended that the handbook be well organized to make it easy to find the needed information.[42] Just as this book has a table of contents and an index to help you find specific information more quickly, so too should the employee handbook. HRM must remember that the handbook will be helpful to employees, and it must do whatever possible to make it easy to use. To assist in achieving this goal, we have summarized some "Dos" for employee handbooks in Table 16-3.

Employee Handbook Contents

Although there are no right or wrong ways of putting together the contents of an employee handbook, there is a recommended format.[43] As a means of facilitating this discussion, we will present an outline from an actual employee handbook (see Table 16-4). Let's elaborate on these components.

Introductory Comments   In this section, the company conveys various introductory information to the employees. Carroll Tree Service begins by having its top management send a letter of greetings to the employees, welcoming them into the organization. The purpose of this letter is to describe to employees

TABLE 16-3   Suggestions for Making Employee Handbooks More Employee Friendly

Use simple language that can be understood by all employees.

Keep sentences short—20 words or less.

Keep discussion of each item to less than one page.

Use graphics wherever possible.

Use wide margins (top, bottom, and sides).

Keep the handbook under 35 pages.

Source: Adapted from James W. Wimberly, Jr., "How to Prepare and Write Your Employee Handbook," in Commerce Clearing House, *Topical Law Reports* "Handbook: The Format—How You Want It to Look" (Chicago: Commerce Clearing House, Inc., October 1990), p. 5410.

TABLE 16-4   Sample Employee Handbook Table of Contents

(Effective February 1995—Carroll Tree Service)

what the company is about, its mission and goals. Furthermore, the company conveys to its employees the corporate value of customer satisfaction, and how by achieving that goal the firm can provide those things that employees may desire (e.g., job security, pay increases, better benefits).

These introductory remarks also tell new employees that they are valuable assets to the organization. By making employees feel important, and letting them know the roles they play and what the company will do to help them grow as employees, the organization fosters an environment where effective worker performance and loyalty and commitment can be realized (see "Meet Carol Ruprecht").

There is often a final component to this introductory section; that is, a brief history of the organization. Although not all employees will value this information, it does provide them with a better understanding of how the company progressed to its current state. That's exactly what CME Conference video is attempting to achieve. This is another means of expressing the company philosophy the organization wishes its employees to share.

What You Should Know   This section is designed to inform all employees of the rules and policies regarding employment in the company. Those items of importance to employees, such as attendance, work hours, and so forth, are presented so that there is no misunderstanding by employees. For example, in this company, specific information regarding the length of one's lunch period, paydays, work hours, and how employees will be evaluated is laid out in such clear terms that confusion is avoided.

In Chapter 12 on performance appraisals we discussed the need for managers to explicitly state what is required of employees. If, for example, you expect employees on the job by 8 A.M., tell them so, and hold employees accountable for being on time. The handbook, then, reinforces those work behaviors a company expects of its employees.

Your Benefits   No matter how much value we place on the introductory remarks of any employee handbook, the section on employee benefits is probably the most widely read and most important to employees. This section should thoroughly explain the benefits employees receive, when they are eligible (if not immediately upon employment), and what, if any, costs the employee might incur. As we explained in Chapter 14 on employee benefits, although these benefits are membership-based, they are important to keep employee morale high. Hence, we must make every effort to convey the full slate of benefits to employees in such a manner that they know what they have, and how they can use them.

Your Responsibility and Safety Procedures   Just as employers are responsible for creating a safe and healthy workplace, workers must also do their part. Accordingly, this section provides information regarding company policies on reporting accidents, alcohol and substance abuse, and personal conduct, among others, explained in such terms that employees know what compliance requires. Furthermore, failure to comply with these policies and subsequent outcomes is thoroughly explained.

Other Vehicles for Employee Communications

In the spirit of finding various vehicles to ensure that communication takes place, there are a number of other means available besides the employee hand-

Meet

Carol Ruprecht

Employee handbooks have the potential to provide a wealth of information to employees—information that is important to them, and is critical to their employment. Simultaneously, however, the handbook can also provide specific information that "protects" the organization from claims being made against it at a later date. This documentation, then, almost creates the necessity that handbooks be thorough, detailed, and "legally cleared." For Carol Ruprecht, International Sales Manager of the Fountain Valley, California, Kingston Technologies, nothing could be closer from the truth.

Several years ago Kingston's management recognized the need to have in place an accurate and technically correct employee handbook. To achieve that goal, they hired a consultant to develop the manual and submit it to the company in camera-ready format for duplication and binding. Several weeks later, the company got just what it wanted. The handbook was done—another project completed. Or so the company thought!

Ruprecht later recognized that the finished product was poor. In fact, she "never expected anybody would be offended by it. But it contained all this legal butt-covering language—which made it seem as if the company didn't trust [employees]." Employees hated the manual, which got the attention of the founders of the organization. Kingston Technologies operated as a wholesome company. Its president's philosophy is to build trust and loyalty with every member of the company. The president wanted to make that statement on the first day of hiring, yet the thing new employees left with that first day, the handbook, created just the opposite view. Consequently, the handbook had to be redone; not by outsiders, but by an individual in the organization, like Carol, who understood the philosophical underpinnings of Kingston.

Kingston's new employee handbook has been a big success. Ruprecht has met her goal of providing the information that employees need, but this time in a simple and straightforward manner. Each of the twenty pages of the handbook addresses important questions employees may have, and embellishes on the company's philosophies—courtesy, compassion, modesty, and honesty.

Source: "The (Handbook) Handbook: A Guide to Writing the Perfect Manual for Employees You Care About," *Inc.* (November 1993), pp. 63–64.

---

book. The following sections discuss the four most popular means: bulletin boards, company newsletters, company-wide meetings, and electronic media.

Bulletin Board

Bulletin Board A means a company uses to post information of interest to its employees.

A **bulletin board** in any organization serves several purposes in communicating with employees. Bulletin boards are generally centrally located in the organization where a majority of employees will have exposure to it. For many, these bulletin boards are found near company cafeterias (if they exist), or by the main office.

The information posted on a bulletin board will vary among organizations. Job postings, upcoming company-sponsored events, new HRM policies, and the like may be posted in this highly visible location to help "get the information out." Furthermore, if employees know that important information is placed on these boards, they will be more inclined to peruse them periodically. Bulletin boards also can be used for activities other than employer-related business; that is, employees can post information for other employees to see. For example, companies may permit employees to advertise personal belongings for sale, or promote a charitable event an employee is associated with. Although the information employees place on the bulletin board is given great latitude, most organizations require such information to have HRM approval before it is posted. By following this procedure, inappropriate or offensive information can be eliminated before any problems arise.

Company Newsletter

The **company newsletter** or newspaper is designed to provide sound internal communication to employees regarding important information they need to know, activities happening in the organization, and anything else of interest.[44] Just as a town's daily newspaper discusses current events, sports, and human-interest stories, so too should the company newsletter. Company newsletters provide employees with a permanent record they can keep and refer to at some future time. Furthermore, some information, like technical and detailed information, may be better communicated in this written format.

While there is no definitive design for company newsletters, they should focus attention on activities of concern to employees of the company, problems the company may be experiencing, successes the company has enjoyed, updates on newsworthy company items (such as company-sponsored sporting events and United Way campaigns), and stories about employees (those receiving awards, recognition, retiring, and so forth) (see "Ethical Decisions in HRM"). Company newsletters also can be enhanced with sections devoted to questions raised by employees and answered by someone in management; and by having employees writing articles.[45]

Company Newsletter A means of providing information for employees in a specific recurring periodical.

Company-wide Meetings

Every so often, there is a need to inform all employees at once in a face-to-face encounter. Should an organization be facing a merger, going into a new product line, or changing its culture, to name a few, it may be useful for the CEO to address all employees en masse. In doing so, the CEO can add emphasis to this new direction, while simultaneously answering questions and addressing concerns.

One of the most notable uses of this "town meeting" was the company-wide session held by former GM Chairman Robert Stemple. Faced with pending layoffs and possible restructuring, Stemple, through electronic hook-ups, was able to send his message to all GM employees at once, wherever the plant was located. This process was repeated when plant closings were announced in 1992.

In addition to opening up the channels of communications for employees, **company-wide meetings** permit all employees to have the same information at once. This, for many operations, reduces the grapevine rumors that may occur, especially when the company is facing difficult times.[46]

Company-wide Meetings Frequently held meetings used to inform employees of various company issues.

The Electronic Media

Technology has served organizational communications well. Whether it be an interactive video sent to employees or having access to on-line information, technology is enhancing the effectiveness of communications.[47] And this technology is no more noteworthy than in HRM.

Whenever a company wishes to provide employees with up-to-date, even real-time information regarding their pay and benefits, nothing serves that purpose

Ethical Decisions in HRM:

The Whole Story

Effective communications in organizations is built on the premise that appropriate and accurate information must be conveyed. Organization members should be afforded the respect and dignity that factual information can deliver. But at what point is it best to withhold information from employees?

We've addressed a so-what test—if it really matters to individuals, the information should be conveyed. But reality tells us that even factual information can, at times, be difficult to deliver, and may best be withheld for a number of reasons. For example, confidentiality is a must in matters that affect employees personally. Assume, then, that you have just been informed by one of your employees that he has Hodgkin's lymphoma, a treatable form of lymph-node cancer. Consequently, he may be absent frequently at times, especially during his chemotherapy treatments. Yet, he doesn't anticipate his attendance to be a problem, nor will it directly affect his work. After all, some of his duties involve direct computer work, so he can work at home and forward the data electronically to the appropriate people.

On several occasions, the employee has either called in sick or has had to leave early because he felt ill. Your employees are beginning to suspect something is wrong, and have come to you to find out what is wrong. There are even rumors going around that the employee might be HIV-positive, and that is causing quite a stir. You simply, and politely, decline to discuss the issue about an employee with other individuals. However, a number of your employees think that you are giving this employee preferential treatment. You know if they only knew what was going on they'd understand, but you can't disclose the nature of the illness. On the other hand, continued "favoritism" will surely be a disruptive force in your department. You are stumped. What do you do? Should employees be given the whole story? What's your opinion?

Electronic Media Any technological device that enhances communications.

better than the **electronic media.** For AT&T and IBM, this has meant developing an in-house television station.[48] Through their television stations, these companies are able to send information faster and with less chance of distraction. At Levi Strauss, the company has greatly expanded the use of personal computers to assist employees in getting up-to-date information on their compensation packages.[49] Through the system called Oliver, employees can access their records to gain information on such topics as "compensation, disability insurance, health care, pension employee investment plans, and survivor benefits."[50] Workers also can use this system to "obtain financial projections regarding future income and retirement benefits, as well as getting information on upcoming training and development workshops."[51] Through computers, flexible benefits programs can also be better implemented, giving employees opportunities to examine what is offered to find what will best serve them.[52] Such computerized systems can be used to provide employees with personalized benefits statements.[53] Not only do these statements provide employees information on their selections, they also reinforce the "hidden pay" they are receiving.[54]

Communications and the Off-Site Employee

Communications in many of today's organization no longer follow the traditional downward or upward flows so typical of hierarchial organizations. Instead, as our work changes, as well as our work force, communication mechanisms, too, must adapt. As we described in Chapter 2, the trend today is the movement to the off-site worker. Worker needs, coupled with technology advancements, have enabled some workers to work at home. How, then, can effective communications be fostered with off-site employees? The answer typically lies in the technology that has become routine today—electronic (e-) mail, facsimile (fax) machines, and the computer modem.

With the use of home computer systems, employees can remain in close contact with their employers, even though they are miles away. For instance, modems can be used to receive and transmit data to main-frame computers at a company location. Data downloaded to an employee can be properly manipulated, and sent back to the organization in its final form. Where electronic wires won't do, fax machines can send documents in hard copy formats almost instantaneously to anywhere in the world. Finally, **e-mail** allows written messages to be sent between parties that have computers that are linked together with an appropriate software. They are fast, cheap, and permit the reader to retrieve the message at his or her convenience.

E-mail An electronic device that allows for messages to be left for another party.

We know that communication to our employees is important, in whatever form, but there still remains one final aspect to be addressed: Is there a mechanism in the organization that allows employees to raise their concerns? In the next section, we'll briefly look at employee complaint and suggestion systems.

Mechanisms for Effective Upward Communications

Any communications system operating in an organization will only be effective if it permits information to flow upward. For HRM, enabling this process revolves around two central themes—complaint procedures and a suggestion system.[55]

The Complaint Procedure

An organization's **complaint procedure** is designed to permit employees to question actions that have occurred in the company, and to seek the company's assistance in correcting the problem. For example, if the employee feels her boss has inappropriately evaluated her performance, or believes the behavior of the boss to be counterproductive, a complaint process allows for that information to be heard. Typically under the direction of employee-relations specialists, complaints are investigated and decisions made regarding the validity of the alleged wrongdoings are made.

Complaint Procedure A formalized procedure in an organization through which an employee seeks resolution of a work problem.

Complaint procedures implemented in nonunionized organizations are called by a variety of titles. Irrespective of their names, most follow a set pattern; that is, given the structure of HRM laid out in Chapter 1, a nonunionized complaint procedure may consist of the following:

Step 1: Employee–Manager   This is generally regarded as the initial step to resolve an employee problem. Here, the employee tries to address the issue with her manager, seeking some resolution. If the issue is resolved here, nothing further need be done. Accordingly, this is considered an informal step in the process. Furthermore, depending on the problem, this step may be skipped altogether, should the employee fear retaliation from the manager.

Step 2: Employee–Employer Relations   Not getting the satisfaction desired in Step 1, the employee then proceeds to file the complaint with the employee-relations representative. As part of his or her job, the ER representative investigates the matter, including gathering information from both parties, and renders a decision. Although this is the first formal step, the employee may continue upward, should the recommended solution be unsatisfactory.

Step 3: Employee–Department Division Head   If employee relations fails to correct the problem, or if the employee wishes to further exercise her rights, the next step in the complaint procedure is to meet with the senior manager of the area (e.g., vice-president). Once again, an investigation will take place and a decision rendered. It is important to note, however, that if employee relations found no validity in the individual's charge, they are not responsible for providing continued assistance to the employee.

Step 4: Employee–President   The final step in the process involves taking the issue to the president. Generally, although employee rights may be protected under various state laws, the president's decision is final.

Inasmuch as this is a generic portrayal of a complaint process, it is important to recognize that this serves as the foundation of an internal complaint procedure. We have graphically portrayed these steps in Figure 16-2. Keep in mind that in actuality, more levels of management could be included in the picture. In either case, however, employees must be notified that this is how the company will resolve employee complaints. And this communication should occur initially during orientation, appear in employee handbooks, and be posted throughout the company.

Finally, we mentioned that this process is generally useful in nonunionized settings. Why not in a unionized company? The answer to that question lies in

Figure 16-2
A Sample Complaint Procedure in a Nonunionized Work Environment

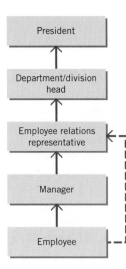

Note: This is a sample process; in some states where unfair dismissal laws exist, the flow may not be valid.

the various labor laws that are unique to labor–management relationships. Although there is a complaint procedure, called a grievance procedure, its uniqueness requires us to discuss it as part of the "Collective Bargaining Process" (Chapter 17).

The Suggestion Program

Similar to the complaint procedure, a **suggestion program** is designed to allow employees opportunities to tell management what it is doing inefficiently, and what the company should do from an employee's point of view. That is, suggestion programs give employees the chance to tell management "what they are doing right; and what they are doing wrong."[56] In many companies, in conjunction with TQM processes and employee involvement, management welcomes such suggestions.[57] In fact, as we discussed in Chapter 13, companies such as Lincoln Electric, and those that use plans such as Scanlon or IMPROSHARE, actually monetarily reward individuals for their suggestions that are implemented. But although employees value the "reward," the most important aspect of a suggestion program is for individuals to witness management action.[58] That is, whether the suggestion is useful or not, employers must recognize employees submitting suggestions and inform them of their outcome. Even if the idea wasn't appropriate for the company, employees still should be told what management's decision was. Failure to do so will more than likely decrease employees' willingness to make suggestions. And if the suggestion is good, in the spirit of employee communication, not only reward them, but recognize their input in the company's next newsletter!

Suggestion Program A process whereby employees have the opportunity to tell management how they perceive the organization is doing.

Study Tools and Applications

Summary

This summary relates to the Learning Objectives provided on p. 443.
After reading this chapter, you should know:

1. Effective communication surrounds the effective operations in HRM activities in that it enables understanding to occur between the organization and its employees, assists in recruiting and selection, and specifies what activities must be performed to successfully perform one's job. Effective communication also implies keeping employees informed of happenings in the organization.
2. Communications in benefits administration and health and safety is mandated by law. In benefits administration, employers must provide employees with a summary plan description. In health and safety, employees must be given information concerning exposure to hazardous and toxic materials.
3. Human resources management communication programs are designed to keep current employees abreast of events occurring in the organization, including the various policies and procedures that affect them.
4. Effective communications can affect corporate culture in that open, frank discussions indicate a culture where employees are valued.
5. The CEO of an organization is the one individual responsible for setting the foundation from which the culture is built. If this individual promotes and practices open communications, then that activity will filter down through the company.
6. A communication program should, at the minimum, inform employees what is ex-

pected of them, what they can expect from the company, and what the various personnel policies are.

7. The employee handbook is a tool that provides one central source of organizational information for employees regarding the company and its HRM policies.

8. Although employee handbooks differ, most include introductory comments about the organization, information about what employees need to know about the workplace, their benefits, and employee responsibility.

9. Four popular means of communication program vehicles include bulletin boards, company newsletters, company-wide meetings, and electronic media.

10. A critical component of an organizational suggestion program is the recognition that employees' suggestions will be heard. Failure to pay attention to employees' suggestions may decrease the value of the program to them.

Key Terms

bulletin board	electronic media
communication	e-mail
company newsletter	employee handbook
company-wide meetings	suggestion program
complaint procedure	

EXPERIENTIAL EXERCISE:

The Student Handbook

In any communication program, there is a need to ensure that the information conveyed is appropriate and necessary. For this exercise, you will need to obtain a copy of your school's student handbook. In your group, go through this publication and analyze what information it is giving you. You might consider using the information in this text regarding what is contained in employee handbooks to assist your analysis.

After analyzing the material, identify those things your group feels are good points of information for students to know. Explain why your group feels the way it does. Also, identify areas that you feel may be missing, or areas that need to be expanded. How would you suggest that be done?

CASE APPLICATION:

Communications at General Motors

General Motors had been long regarded as the classical bureaucratic organization. For years, the company existed with many layers of management, with power and information being carefully controlled by the top echelons of the corporation. In recent years, however, this giant organization has come to recognize that employees at all levels of the company need to know what is going on. In other words, employees need communication.

To bring this feat to fruition, Ron Actis, director of Communications and Public Affairs for General Motors, set out to implement a sound employee communications program.[59] Starting with the company's Saginaw Division, Actis believed that such a program could be beneficial for both employees and the company. Employees not only would gain valuable information that would help them do their jobs better, but also have a better understanding of what the company was doing for them. GM, on the other hand, would benefit from employees' understanding of corporate goals, thus leading to better performance effectiveness.

To bring about this dual success, Actis relied on a number of communications programs, including employee newsletters, a video magazine, and routine meetings between top management and employees. Furthermore, Actis wanted managers to deal more with employees on a one-on-one basis. Prior to this time, the primary one-on-one meetings occurred either during performance evaluations or while administering discipline. As such, to break the tradition that one-on-one meetings were often confrontational in nature, Actis wanted both the employees and managers to see face-to-face meetings as a natural part of the work environment. For the Saginaw Division, Ron Actis's communication program was a success. In studies conducted before and after its implementation, this division posted "better budget performance, sales per employee, profits, and return on investments"[60] attributable directly to enhanced organizational communications.

Questions

1. Describe how communications programs such as the one implemented by Ron Actis have helped to shape corporate culture in GM.
2. How does effective communications influence worker performance and productivity?
3. Do you believe that one-on-one meeting between supervisors and employees in union settings is an attempt by an organization to eliminate, or significantly reduce, the union's power? Explain your position.

Testing Your Understanding

How well did you fulfill the learning objectives?

1. Effective communication is an important contributor to successful work-force diversity because
   a. it lets minority workers know that the company will make every attempt to provide them equal opportunity in the organization.
   b. it ensures realistic job previews.
   c. it helps employees understand how to do their jobs.
   d. it helps employees understand the relationship between their efforts and individual goal attainment.
   e. it helps to increase positive outcomes for interactions between managers and their employees.

2. Human resource management communications programs are designed to
   a. keep employees knowledgeable about policies and procedures affecting customers.
   b. keep customers informed about policies and programs designed to increase service.
   c. keep employees knowledgeable about policies and programs affecting them.
   d. keep customers informed about policies and programs affecting employees.
   e. improve interactions between employees and their managers.

3. How does HRM communication affect corporate culture?
   a. HRM communications do not affect corporate culture.

   b. HRM communications can be used to state corporate culture effectively.
   c. HRM communications often replace corporate culture in large, hierarchical organizations.
   d. A free-flowing, timely, and accurate HRM communications system can help to build trust.
   e. A free-flowing, timely, and accurate HRM communications system can help to improve productivity.

4. A CEO of a 300-employee electronics manufacturer had just been convinced by her vice-president of human resources that an "open door" management policy would help to improve worker morale. Agreeing to the idea, how can she best show support for this program?
   a. Support can be shown by "opening" her own door to employees.
   b. Support can be shown by making a video to endorse the program to be shown to all employees.
   c. Support can be shown by announcing the program herself, over the company address system.
   d. Support can be shown by writing a column endorsing the new system for the next issue of the company newsletter.
   e. Support can be shown by feigning ignorance of the new program.

5. Why is upward communication important in empowered organizations?
   a. Upward communication is the definition of an empowered work force.

b. Empowered employees make more decisions about how to do their work. These decisions need to be communicated to top management.

c. Workers feel empowered when they can communicate with top management.

d. There is no upward communication in empowered organizations. Top management has been removed, and most decisions are made by individuals closest to the problem.

e. Customer information and satisfaction are top priorities in an empowered organization.

6. A well-written employee handbook will provide all of these benefits to the organization except
   a. create an atmosphere in which employees become more productive.
   b. create an atmosphere in which employee commitment is increased.
   c. create a sense of security for employees.
   d. provide an implied employment contract.
   e. provide a source of information for many employee work-related questions.

7. A small, family-run electronics firm has just been acquired by an aggressive transnational organization. What is the best way to inform employees?
   a. employee handbook   b. bulletin board
   c. company-wide meeting   d. company newsletter
   e. electronic media

8. If you have a complaint about the grade you receive in this course, who should you go to first?
   a. the professor
   b. the department chairperson who is the "boss" of the professor
   c. the dean of the school in which the professor teaches
   d. your academic advisor
   e. another professor

9. Compare suggestion programs and complaint processes.
   a. Suggestion programs are found only in union shops. Complaint processes are found only in nonunion shops.
   b. Both suggestion programs and complaint processes allow the upward flow of information in an organization.
   c. Suggestion programs allow employees to tell management what it is doing right. Complaint processes allow employees to tell management what it is doing wrong.
   d. Suggestion programs target individual performance. Complaint processes target group performance.
   e. Suggestion program events are initiated by managers. Complaint process events are initiated by employees.

10. Effective communication is an important contributor to the recruiting and selection process because
    a. it lets minority workers know that the company will make every attempt to provide them equal opportunity in the organization.
    b. it helps to increase positive outcomes for interactions between managers and their employees.
    c. it helps employees understand how to do their jobs.
    d. it helps employees understand the relationship between their efforts and individual goal attainment.
    e. it ensures realistic job previews.

11. The Summary Plan Description is all of the following except
    a. a presentation of ERISA rights.
    b. a presentation of OSHA requirements.
    c. information about pensions.
    d. a statement of updated benefits accumulations.
    e. required by law.

12. Diane has just been promoted to director of HRM communications. She is writing a mission statement for her department. What item should be included?
    a. departmental reason for its existence and what services it will provide to the organization.
    b. organizational policies and programs for retirement options and financial planning.
    c. organizational efforts to assist in improving interactions between employees and their managers.
    d. departmental issues regarding benefits and services provided to employees.
    e. organizational policies and programs regarding achieving excellence in customer services.

13. If new HRM communications programs are endorsed by top management,
    a. they are bound to fail.
    b. they are viewed as significant components of corporate culture.
    c. they are more slowly accepted by the rest of the organization.
    d. they are viewed with suspicion by the rest of the organization.
    e. they replace the authority of the top management.

14. All of the following questions are appropriate for managers to use in determining how to filter information to their employees except
    a. Will my employees be able to do their jobs as well if this information is not shared?
    b. Will my employees be disadvantaged in some way by not knowing this information?
    c. Will employees care about the information?
    d. Will my employees think badly of me for telling them?
    e. Will my employees view this information as information overload?

Chapter Seventeen

INTRODUCTION TO LABOR RELATIONS

LEARNING OBJECTIVES

AFTER READING THIS CHAPTER, YOU WILL BE ABLE TO:

1. Define what is meant by the term unions.
2. Identify the main thrust of the Clayton Act against union activity.
3. Explain the key elements of the Norris–LaGuardia Act.
4. Discuss what effect the Wagner Act, the Taft–Hartley Act, and the Landrum–Griffin Act had on labor–management relations.
5. Identify the significance of Executive Orders 10988 and 11491, and the Civil Service Reform Act of 1978.
6. Explain the structure of the AFL–CIO.
7. Discuss why a union would affiliate with the AFL–CIO.
8. Describe the union organizing process.
9. Explain what is meant by the terms *union avoidance* and *union busting*.
10. Discuss how sunshine laws affect public sector collective bargaining.

The history of the labor movement in the United States is rich in character. Decade after decade, whenever workers tried to unite and defend themselves against various management practices, management, usually with the backing of the courts, was able to successfully squelch any employee efforts. And although laws were finally passed in the 1930 and 1940s that legitimized unions' right to exist, the relationship between labor and management was strained—often exhibiting open hostilities and serious confrontations.

Yet, as the 1970s dawned, management began to recognize that unions might not be the "enemy." Rather, global competition, technological changes, and the like, made both sides recognize that they needed to be more cooperative. Fighting each other served no useful purpose—and more importantly, threatened the survival of both. Something was drastically needed—new ideas on how to increase production, quality improvements, more open discussion giving employees a say in what affects their jobs, and more joint problem solving to establish, implement, and achieve common goals. As a result, the late 1970s witnessed the birth of joint labor committees—committees comprised of both union members and management personnel whose charge was to identify problem areas in the organization and jointly determine and implement a solution. Finally, maybe the confrontational days of yesteryear could be put to rest. Sadly, that never materialized in all cases.

There are a number of reasons why this cooperative relationship was never accepted by all labor and management groups. Some reflected the changing world of work, and the dynamic environment in which it operates. Others, the personality of the key players involved. But just about no one expected this to be the result of the law. After all, most labor legislation attempts to balance the power between unions and organizations. Inasmuch as that is true, in 1992, the labor board that oversees labor and management activities ruled that these joint labor committees were illegal![1] Why? Simply stated, some of the discussion that occurs in these committees touches on such issues as wages, benefits, or working conditions. Those, according to the law, may only be discussed in actual contract negotiations. Joint labor–management committees that delve into these areas may result, then, in them becoming "company dominated labor organizations.[2]

It is interesting to note that court rulings and decisions about labor–management relationships are subject to change or reinterpretation.[3] In fact, as a result of the 1994 elections in which the Republican party gained control of both the House of Representatives and the Senate, labor law reform is expected. The Republican party is more favorably inclined to set as one of its priorities making these joint labor–management committees legal. However, even then, the committees will have to refrain from any discussions that approach issues, like wages, that are rightfully left to the collective bargaining process.

Introduction

A **union** is an organization of workers, acting collectively, seeking to promote and protect its mutual interests through collective bargaining. However, before we can examine the activities surrounding the collective bargaining process, it is important to have an understanding of what unions are and how they have developed over the years, and identify laws that govern this process. As we progress, one major aspect should be noted: As we demonstrate the pursuit of union goals, realize that these pursuits may impose constraints on HRM practices.

While it is true that only about 11 percent of the private sector work force is unionized,[4] the successes and failures of this body's activities affect all segments of the work force in two important ways. First, since major industries in the United States—such as automobile, steel, and electrical manufacturers, as well as all branches of transportation—are unionized, unions have a major effect on some of the important sectors of the economy (see Figure 17-1). Second, any gains made by unions typically spill over into other nonunionized sectors of the economy. So, the wages, hours, and working conditions of nonunion employees at a Baltimore lumber yard may be affected by collective bargaining between the United Auto Workers and General Motors at the latter's Baltimore Minivan facility.

For many managers, HRM practices in a unionized organization consist mainly of following procedures and policies laid out in the labor contract. This labor contract was agreed to by both management and the labor union, stipulating, among other things, the wage rate, the hours of work, and the terms and conditions of employment for those covered by the negotiated agreement. Decisions about how to compensate employees, employee benefits offered, procedures for overtime, and the like, are no longer unilateral prerogatives of management for jobs within the unions' province. Such decisions may be made at the time the labor contract is negotiated.

The concept of labor relations may mean different things to different individuals depending on their experience, background, etc. One means of providing some focus in this arena is to have an understanding of the laws that serve as the foundation of labor–management relationships.

Union Organization of workers, acting collectively, seeking to protect and promote their mutual interests through collective bargaining.

This group represents workers from both labor and management. Although their discussions focus on a variety of issues concerning the workplace of these employees, such groups may be illegal. That is, if discussions approach topics like wages and benefits, then this group is concentrating on something that rightfully belongs in contract negotiations.

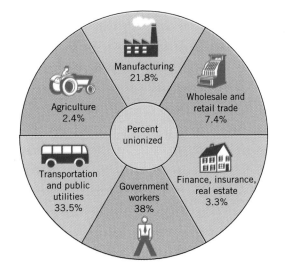

Figure 17-1
Union Membership by Industry Concentration

Labor Legislation

The legal framework for labor–management relationships has played a crucial role in its development. In this section, therefore, major developments in labor law will be discussed. An exhaustive analysis of these laws and their legal and practical repercussions is not possible within the scope of this book;[5] in our discussion, however, key labor legislation will be presented chronologically to enhance appreciation of the evolution of labor law in the United States. We have also provided a quick reference guide to these laws in Table 17-1.

The Sherman Antitrust Act of 1890   The purpose of the Sherman Antitrust Act was to "protect trade and commerce against unlawful restraints and monopolies, for every contract, combination in the form or otherwise, or conspiracy, in restraint of trade or commerce . . . is declared to be illegal."[6]

It should be noted that the word "union" is not mentioned anywhere in this act. Yet, under this act, organized labor was considered to be a trust. It was believed that unions had the same anticompetitive effects as organizations like Standard Oil—thus, the justification for the use of injunctions. Interpretation and application of this act caused many hardships for emerging unions. When unions tried to organize workers, employers enlisted the courts to hold unions in restraint of trade, significantly hindering union organization and growth.

Clayton Act Labor legislation that attempted to limit the use of injunctions against union activities.

The Clayton Act of 1914   The main thrust of the **Clayton Act** was to limit the use of injunctions against union activity, especially strikes in support of recognition for representational and collective bargaining purposes. Although the act was an attempt to exclude the impact of the Sherman Antitrust Act in labor disputes;[7] it did not achieve this objective; not only did the courts continue to invoke the Sherman Antitrust Act against unions, the Clayton Act also made it easier for management to obtain injunctions on their own. Consequently, in-

TABLE 17-1   Summary of Major Labor Legislation

Sherman Antitrust Act (1890)	As applied to unions, allowed the use of court-imposed injunctions to prevent union activities.
Clayton Act (1914)	Tried to limit the use of injunctions in labor disputes; but resulted in them being more easily obtained by companies.
Railway Labor Act (1926)	Permitted transportation workers to join unions and have their representatives bargain with management.
Norris–LaGuardia Act (1932)	Limited the use of injunctions in labor disputes. Made yellow-dog contracts unenforceable.
National Industrial Recovery Act (1933)	Permitted employees to choose their representatives. Later declared unconstitutional.
Wagner Act (1935)	Legitimized union activities, giving them the right to exist. Cited unfair employer practices and created the NLRB.
Taft–Hartley Act (1947)	Identified union unfair labor practices. Declared the closed shop illegal. Set means for employees to vote unions out. Enabled states to enact right-to-work legislation.
Landrum–Griffin Act (1959)	Held unions accountable for their funds. Curtailed some types of union boycotts and picketing activities. Established voting procedures for union elections.

junctions continued to be issued against unions. The Clayton Act did, however, indicate that attitudes were beginning to change where unions were concerned.

The Railway Labor Act of 1926

The **Railway Labor Act** provided the initial impetus for widespread collective bargaining in the United States.[8] Although the act covers only the transportation industry, it was important because workers in these industries were guaranteed the right to organize, bargain collectively with employers, and establish dispute settlement procedures in the event that an agreement was not reached at the bargaining table. This dispute settlement procedure allows congressional and presidential intercession in the event of an impasse. For example, in June 1992, when the Machinists Union and CSX railroad reached an impasse in their negotiations, President George Bush signed a bill requiring the three-day impasse to end.[9] Although such intervention is permissible when an impasse has the potential to create an economic crisis, some lawmakers and union supporters are questioning its use in modern labor–management relations;[10] many believe it distracts from the intent of having two parties reach a mutually acceptable contract.

Railway Labor Act Provided the initial impetus to widespread collective bargaining.

The Norris–LaGuardia Act of 1932

The **Norris–LaGuardia Act** of 1932 was one of the most progressive pieces of federal labor legislation of the early 1900s. This act is best known for making yet another attempt to limit the use of injunctions in labor matters unless there was evidence of violence or irreparable harm. This opened the door for legalizing picketing and other union tactics against the employer. Norris–LaGuardia made **yellow-dog contracts** unenforceable, but did not prevent their use. Unfortunately, there was no enforcement arm for this act, so it was often difficult to match the intent of the legislation with labor relations practices. Nevertheless, this act provided insight into changing public opinion about unions and was a harbinger of impending developments in U.S. labor legislation.

Norris–LaGuardia Act Labor law act that set the stage for permitting individuals full freedom to designate a representative of their choosing to negotiate terms and conditions of employment.

Yellow-Dog Contract An agreement whereby employees state that they are not now, nor will they be in the future, union members.

Labor relations in the transportation industry fall under the jurisdiction of the Railway Act. This piece of federal legislation first gave transportation workers the right to join unions and to bargain with management over such issues as wages, benefits, and working conditions.

The National Industrial Recovery Act of 1933

The National Industrial Recovery Act (NIRA) was the first piece of legislation that enabled workers to form unions and select a representative of their own choosing. This representative was empowered to deal directly with employers on matters concerning wages, hours, and working conditions. Like the Norris–LaGuardia Act, this act also lacked an enforcement mechanism, and the result was that it was ignored by both courts and employers. Ultimately, the Supreme Court declared the act unconstitutional.[11]

The National Labor Relations Act of 1935

Wagner Act Also known as the National Labor Relations Act of 1935, this act gave employees the legitimate right to form and join unions and to engage in collective bargaining.

The National Labor Relations Act, commonly referred to as the **Wagner Act,** is the basic "bill of rights" for unions, guaranteeing workers the right to organize and join unions, bargain collectively, and act in concert to pursue their objectives. In terms of labor relations, the Wagner Act specifically requires employers to bargain in good faith over mandatory bargaining issues—wages, hours, and terms and conditions of employment.

This act shifted the pendulum of power to favor unions, for the first time in U.S. labor history. Most of the provisions of the Wagner Act addressed specific activities employers must avoid or face an unfair labor practice charge. Specifically, it is unfair labor practice for an employer to:

> Interfere with, restrain, or coerce employees in the exercise of the rights to join unions and to bargain collectively; dominate or interfere with the formation or administration of any labor organization; discriminate against anyone because of union activity; discharge or otherwise discriminate against any employee because he or she filed or gave testimony under the Act; and refuse to bargain collectively with the representatives chosen by the employees.[12]

National Labor Relations Board Established to administer and interpret the Wagner Act, the NLRB has primary responsibility for conducting union representation elections.

Another noteworthy change from past legislation was the emphasis on enforcement. This was achieved through establishment of the **National Labor Relations Board (NLRB).** This administrative body, consisting of five members appointed by the president,[13] was given the responsibility for determining appropriate bargaining units, conducting elections to determine union representation, and interpreting and applying the law with respect to unfair labor practice charges. The NLRB, however, has only remedial and no punitive powers.

The Wagner Act provided the legal recognition of unions as legitimate interest groups in American society. However, many employers opposed its purposes and failed to live up to the requirements of its provisions. The Wagner Act also provided no protection for management from unfair union labor practices. Thus, the belief that the balance of power had swung too far to labor's side, and the public outcry stemming from post–World War II strikes, led to the passage of the Labor–Management Relations (Taft–Hartley) Act in 1947.

The Labor–Management Relations Act of 1947

Taft–Hartley Act Legislation that attempted to balance the power between unions and management.

The major purpose of the Labor–Management Relations Act, also known as the **Taft–Hartley Act,** was to specify unfair union labor practices. Under Section 8(b), Taft–Hartley states that it is an unfair labor practice for unions to:

> restrain or coerce employees in joining the union, or coerces the employer in selecting his bargaining or grievance representatives; discriminate against an employee to whom union membership has been denied, or to cause an employer to discriminate

against an employee; refuse to bargain collectively; engage in strikes and boycotts for purposes deemed illegal by the Act; charge excessive or discriminatory fees or dues under union-shop contracts; and obtain compensation for services not performed or not to be performed.[14]

In addition, Taft–Hartley declared illegal one type of union security arrangement: the closed shop. Until Taft–Hartley's passage, the closed shop was dominant in labor contracts. By declaring it illegal, Taft–Hartley began to shift the pendulum of power away from unions. Furthermore, in doing so, the act enabled states to enact laws that would further reduce compulsory union membership. Taft–Hartley also prohibited yellow-dog contracts, included provisions that forbade secondary boycotts,[15] and gave the president of the United States the power to issue an eighty-day cooling-off period when labor–management disputes affect national security. The act also set forth procedures for workers to decertify, or vote out, their union representatives.

Whereas the Wagner Act required only employers to bargain in good faith, Taft–Hartley imposed the same obligation on unions. Although the negotition process is described in Chapter 18, it is important to understand what is meant by the term "bargaining in good faith." This does not mean that the parties must reach agreement, but rather that they must come to the bargaining table ready, willing, and able to meet and deal, open to proposals made by the other party, and with the intent to reach a mutually acceptable agreement.

Realizing that unions and employers might not reach agreement and that work stoppages might occur, Taft–Hartley also created the **Federal Mediation and Conciliation Service (FMCS)** as an independent agency separate from the Department of Labor. The FMCS's mission is to send a trained representative to negotiations to "prevent or minimize interruptions of commerce . . . and to help the parties to settle their dispute through conciliation and mediation."[16] Both employer and union have the responsibility to notify the FMCS when

Federal Mediation and Conciliation Service A government agency that assists labor and management in settling their disputes.

When contract negotiations reach a stalemate, a neutral and objective third-party individual may intervene. When that happens, the individual usually comes from the Federal Mediation and Conciliation Service (FMCS). The mediator's job is to help both parties to uncover where the problems lie and get both back to the negotiating table. Pictured here is Mediator W. J. Usery (right) with Major League Baseball owners negotiator Richard Ravitch (behind Usery) and players negotiator Donald Fehr.

other attempts to settle the dispute have failed or contract expiration is pending. An FMCS mediator is not empowered to force parties, like the baseball players association and the baseball owners, to reach an agreement, but he or she can use persuasion and other means of diplomacy to help them reach their own resolution of differences. Finally, a fact worth noting was the amendment in 1974 to extend coverage to the health-care industry. This health-care amendment now affords Taft–Hartley coverage to profit and nonprofit hospitals, as well as "special provisions for the health care industry, both profit and nonprofit, as to bargaining notice requirements and the right to picket or strike."[17]

The Labor and Management Reporting and Disclosure Act of 1959

Landrum–Griffin Act Also known as the Labor and Management Reporting and Disclosure Act, this legislation protected union members from possible wrongdoing on the part of their unions. Its thrust was to require all unions to disclose their financial statements.

The last major piece of federal labor law passed in the U.S. was the Labor and Management Reporting and Disclosure Act, commonly referred to as the **Landrum–Griffin Act.** Public outcry over misuse of union funds and corruption in the labor movement resulted in the passage of the Labor and Management Reporting and Disclosure Act in 1959. The thrust of the act is to monitor internal union activity by making officials and those affiliated with unions (e.g., union members, trustees, etc.) accountable for union funds, elections, and other business and representational matters. Restrictions are also placed on trusteeships imposed by national or international unions; and conduct during a union election is regulated. Much of this act, like the subsequent 1988 Department of Justice intervention into the Teamsters Union, is part of an ongoing effort to prevent corrupt practices and to keep organized crime from gaining control of the labor movement. The mechanisms used to achieve this goal are requirements for annual filing by unions as organizations and by individuals employed by unions, reports regarding administrative matters to the Department of Labor—reports such as their "adoption of constitutions and by-laws, administrative policies, and finances."[18] This information, filed under forms L-M 2 or L-M 3[19] with the Department of Labor, is available to the public. Furthermore, Landrum–Griffin included a provision that allowed all members of a union to vote irrespective of their race, sex, national origin, and so forth. This provision gave union members certain rights that would not be available to the general public for another five years until the passage of the Civil Rights Act of 1964. Landrum–Griffin also required that all who voted on union matters would do so in a secret ballot, especially when the vote concerned the election of union officers.

Other Pertinent Labor Legislation

While the Labor and Management Reporting and Disclosure Act was the last major private sector labor law passed in the United States to date, there are some other items that are pertinent to our discussion. Specifically, these are Executive Orders 10988 and 11491; the Racketeer Influenced and Corruption Organizations Act of 1970; and the Civil Service Reform Act of 1978.

Executive Order 10988 Affirmed the right of federal employees to join unions and granted restricted bargaining rights to these employees.

Executive Orders 10988 and 11491 Both of these executive orders deal specifically with labor legislation in the federal sector.[20] In 1962, President Kennedy issued **Executive Order 10988,** which permitted, for the first time, federal government employees the right to join unions. The order required agency heads to bargain in good faith, defined unfair labor practices, and specified the code of conduct to which labor organizations in the public sector must adhere. Strikes, however, were prohibited.[21]

While this executive order was effective in granting organizing rights to federal employees, areas for improvement were identified. This was especially true regarding the need for a centralized agency to oversee federal labor relations activities. To address these deficiencies, President Richard Nixon issued **Executive Order 11491** in 1969. The objectives of this executive order were to make federal labor relations more like those in the private sector, and to standardize procedures among federal agencies. This order gave the assistant secretary of labor the authority to determine appropriate bargaining units, oversee recognition procedures, rule on unfair labor practices, and enforce standards of conduct on labor relations. It also established the Federal Labor Relations Council (FLRC) to supervise the implementation of Executive Order 11491 provisions, handle appeals from decisions of the assistant secretary of labor, and to rule on questionable issues.

Both of these executive orders served a vital purpose in promoting federal sector unionization. However, if a subsequent administration ever decided not to permit federal sector unionization, a president would only have had to revoke a prior executive order. To eliminate this possibility, and to remove federal sector labor relations from direct control of a president, Congress passed the Civil Service Reform Act.

Racketeering Influenced and Corrupt Organizations Act (RICO) of 1970 Although this act has far-reaching tentacles, the Racketeering Influenced and Corrupt Organization Act (RICO) serves a vital purpose in labor relations. RICO's primary emphasis with respect to labor unions is to eliminate any influence exerted on unions by members of organized crime.[22] That is, it is a violation of RICO if "payments or loans are made to employee representatives, labor organizations, or officers and employees of labor organizations,"[23] where such action occurs in the form of "bribery, kickbacks, or extortion."[24] Over the past decade, RICO has been used to oust a number of labor officials in the Teamsters union who were alleged to have organized crime ties.[25]

Civil Service Reform Act of 1978 Title VII of the **Civil Service Reform Act** established the Federal Labor Relations Authority (FLRA) as an independent agency within the executive branch to carry out the major functions previously performed by the FLRC. The FLRA was given the authority to decide, subject to external review by courts and administrative bodies,[26] union election and unfair labor practice disputes, appeals from arbitration awards, and to provide leadership in establishing policies and guidance. An additional feature of this act is a broad-scope grievance procedure that can be limited only by the negotiators. Under Executive Order 11491, binding arbitration had been optional. While the Civil Service Reform Act of 1978 contains many provisions similar to those of the Wagner Act, two important differences exist. First, in the private sector, the scope of bargaining includes wages and benefits, and mandatory subjects of bargaining. In the federal sector, wages and benefits are not negotiable—they are set by Congress. Additionally, the Reform Act prohibits negotiations over union security arrangements.

The Structure of the Union Hierarchy

Have you ever given much thought to how organized labor in the United States is structured? Or what roles the AFL–CIO plays in labor–management relationships? Do you know what relationship exists between the AFL–CIO and its affili-

●

Executive Order 11491 Designed to make federal labor relations more like those in the private sector. Also established the Federal Labor Relations Council.

Civil Service Reform Act Replaced Executive Order 11491 as the basic law governing labor relations for federal employees.

ates? Are you aware that although most unions are affiliated with the AFL–CIO, some are not? Finding answers to questions such as these is the focus of this section on union structures.[27]

The best example of the structure of labor organizations in the United States is that of the AFL–CIO.[28] While the AFL–CIO represents the majority of all labor unions, some unions have decided not to affiliate. However, during the 1980s, some of the biggest unions—the United Auto Workers and the United Mine Workers—returned to the fold, leaving very few unions outside. Figure 17-2 represents an organizational structure of labor unions in the United States. It appears that the AFL–CIO is the governing body. Reporting to the AFL–CIO are the international or national unions, which direct the activities of their respective local unions. However, the structure is not a true picture of union power. Let's take a closer look at these parts and discuss the roles of each.

AFL–CIO The American Federation of Labor and the Congress of Industrial Organizations.

The AFL–CIO

The **AFL–CIO** is a governing body to unions that decide to affiliate with the Federation. The AFL–CIO has no authority over the national unions per se, ex-

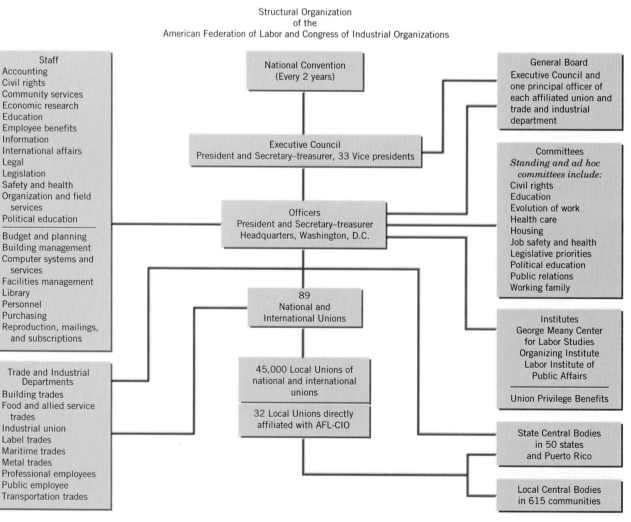

Figure 17-2
Structure of the AFL–CIO

cept for the authority the national unions have given it,[29] and that national and international unions must abide by the AFL–CIO constitution. The AFL–CIO is more involved in the areas of political lobbying, educational, research, and information management. Through the lobbying efforts of the AFL–CIO, major issues affecting workers, and society in general, are brought before the U.S. Congress and the working public.[30] For example, the AFL–CIO has always lobbied for worker protection issues such as OSHA laws, ERISA, health care, and child care. More recently, unions are lobbying lawmakers over the use of cheap labor—using prisoners to perform selected work activities at a fraction of what state's would have to pay if they hired actual employees.[31]

The AFL–CIO performs another vital function; that is, to police the activities of affiliated unions. Through the executive council, rules governing appropriate union conduct are established. For instance, unions affiliated with the AFL–CIO agree to a "no-raiding" pact, meaning that one union will not try to raid another affiliated union and steal its members. Additionally, the AFL–CIO serves as the mediator in jurisdictional disputes between national unions. It also serves as "watchdog" to ensure that union financial practices are appropriately handled.

The AFL–CIO also serves as the educational body for its affiliates. Its various departments collect and disseminate economic data and collective-bargaining information to national or local unions on activities that may directly affect them. Much of this information is obtained through standing committees, whose purpose is to obtain information in such areas as civil rights, economic policy, research, safety, and occupational health. These committees also collect information regarding labor issues from unions worldwide (such as imports, pay levels, working conditions, benefits, and female workers' needs). The AFL–CIO's focus is not just the United States—it also has a global perspective. Accordingly, the AFL–CIO serves a vital purpose in information processing for labor organizations. The AFL–CIO also serves as the public relations component of labor organizations.[32] Involved in community and societal issues (such as housing, the homeless, minimum wage, equal rights), the AFL–CIO tries to present a positive image of organized labor to the general public.

AFL–CIO Governance   The main governing body overseeing affiliated union activities is the AFL–CIO Executive Council. Composed of the president and the secretary of the AFL–CIO and thirty-three vice-presidents (generally presidents of national/international unions), this council has the responsibility to "propose and evaluate legislation of interest to the labor movement, and safeguarding the Federation from corrupt or communist influence."[33] Meeting at least three times a year, in between the Federation's biennial convention, the executive council handles most of the policy formulation for affiliated national unions. Additionally, this council is also responsible for:

1. Investigating and conducting hearings on malfeasance or maladministration charges against a council member and recommending appropriate action
2. Removing from office (by two-thirds vote) any council member found to be a follower or a member of a subversive organization
3. Assisting unions in organizing activities and chartering new national and international unions
4. Adjudicating jurisdictional disputes[34]

Joining the AFL–CIO   What advantages are there to joining the AFL–CIO? Since the AFL–CIO has no authority to force unions to affiliate, it must be offering something to the national and local unions for them to agree to a per capita tax of 19 cents per month, per member. Let's see what advantages there are.

As previously mentioned, one of the most important reasons for affiliating with the AFL–CIO is the "no-raiding" agreement. An affiliated union has some AFL–CIO constitutional backing that other affiliated unions will not intervene or disrupt their union efforts. This "frees the union from fighting sister unions . . . and the time and money conserved in this way can be used either to organize the unorganized or be devoted to other union programs."[35]

The national or local union receives various services from the Federation.[36] These services revolve around the political lobbying efforts, assistance in contract negotiation matters, educational programs, and research and information efforts. Affiliating with the AFL–CIO, then, provides benefits for both groups. The Federation becomes larger, increasing its voice on labor matters, and the national or local union is provided an array of services. That, we believe, is the premise of the AFL–CIO: to promote and assist the labor movement. It cannot be done alone, however. This is where the national unions take over, handling the day-to-day operations of a union.

National Unions

National/International Union
A federation of local unions

The governance of unions generates from the activities and chartering body policies of the **national or international union,**[37] which is a "federation of local unions."[38] These unions operate under the direction of a national union president and the executive committee (usually the secretary, treasurer, and vice-presidents), who set its policies to govern the activities of its locals at the union's convention. At these conventions, delegates, usually elected from the local unions in proportion to the size of the local's membership, convene to decide on various policy issues such as establishing the parent union's constitution, the amount of dues each member will pay, and the election of officers. At these conventions, usually held biannually, national union policies are created, reaffirmed, revised, or dropped.

The national union, however, has other roles in the labor relations process. The national union is instrumental in organizing workers. Through its organizing efforts, additional union locals may be added, or expansion of organized workers may be sought. The national union also serves as the liaison to its locals, providing economic data, collective-bargaining information, advice, and other services regarding labor–management relationships. It typically has a regional vice-president who is responsible for serving and facilitating the actions of the local unions. This is especially true during contract negotiations when a vice-president of the national union may assist the local union in preparing for negotiations, bargaining with management, and implementing and administering the contract.[39]

To a large extent, the national union serves a purpose similar to the AFL–CIO when providing services to its locals. More concerned with labor matters that directly affect their industry or trade, these unions support the efforts and the daily administration of the local unions. This is done through lobbying, supporting trade bills, and other special interests.

Local union Provides the grass roots support for union members in day-to-day labor–management relations.

The Local Union

The heart of day-to-day activities in labor–management relations exists at the **local union** level. It is at this level that workers have their greatest association with the union. No matter what the affiliation with a national union or the

AFL–CIO, the local union provides the grass-roots support for the workers. Local unions operate as any other business. They are typically guided by a president, a secretary–treasurer, and an executive board (all elected representatives), to serve and meet the needs of the rank and file.[40] It is this "executive committee's" responsibility to ensure that the day-to-day operations are handled effectively and efficiently. This means that it is the responsibility of the local union to collect dues and forward the per capita rate to the national union, and to work with local management in negotiating, implementing, and administering the contract. In other words, its primary purpose is to represent the workers effectively.

In its responsibilities, two major purposes arise. These purposes revolve around contract negotiation and handling grievances. The local union, with assistance from the national union, conducts the collective-bargaining sessions with management. It is the locals' responsibility to be aware of, and to try to achieve in negotiations, the desired needs of each member. This means that the local union must be well-informed of its members' expectations—information that can be obtained in various ways, but particularly through membership meetings. After negotiations have been completed, it is the responsibility of the local officers to present the "package" to the rank-and-file members for their ratification.

As part of the contract administration phase of a labor–management relationship, the local union's representative—usually the shop steward—is responsible for ensuring that the contract is being followed correctly. Any deviations from the contract's language, or problems arising from its implementation, will result in a grievance being filed. The local union is responsible for processing the grievance and ensuring that it is adjudicated appropriately.

How Are Employees Unionized?

Unions just don't appear overnight. Rather, they are voted in after an often lengthy, and in many cases, hard-fought process with management. Let's look at this process, called the organizing campaign. Figure 17-3 contains a simple model of how the process typically flows in the private sector.

Efforts to organize a group of employees may begin by employee representatives requesting a union to visit the employees' organization and solicit members, or the union itself might initiate a membership drive. Either way, as established by the NLRB, the union must secure signed **authorization cards** from at least 30 percent of the employees it wishes to represent. Employees who sign the cards indicate that they wish the particular union to be their representative in negotiating with the employer.

Although a minimum of 30 percent of the potential union members must sign the authorization card prior to an election, unions are seldom interested in bringing to vote situations in which they merely meet the NLRB minimum. Why? The answer is simply a matter of mathematics and business: To become the certified bargaining unit, the union must be accepted by a majority of those eligible voting workers.[41] Acceptance in this case is determined by a secret-ballot election. This election held by the NLRB, called a **representation certification (RC),** can occur only once in a twelve-month period; thus, the more signatures on the authorization cards, the greater the chances for a victory. How great? Research into union authorization card signatures suggests the following: When more than 75 percent of the eligible workers sign the authorization card,

Unionization in the United States is a "big business." Although its structure is hierarchical, for most union members, the union is their local. It is here that all the day-to-day activities of union matters occur.

Authorization Card A card signed by prospective union members indicating that they are interested in having a union election held at their work site.

Representation Certification The election process whereby union members vote in a union as their representative.

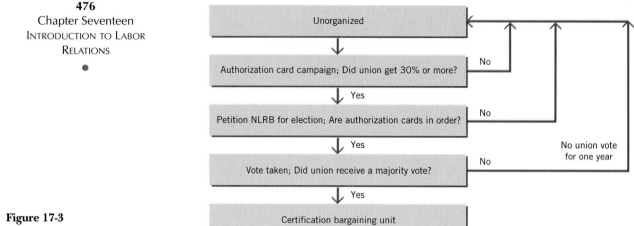

Figure 17-3
Union Organizing Process

the union has a 60 percent chance of winning the election; when the signatures total between 60–75 percent, the chances of winning drop to 50–50. And when the minimum is achieved (30 percent), unions have only an 8 percent chance of winning a certification election.[42]

Why the significant drop in numbers? Even when a sizable proportion of the workers sign authorization cards, the victory is by no means guaranteed. Management will not be passive during the organization drive; in fact, the management of most organizations can be expected to resist unions (see "Ethical Decisions in HRM"). Although there are laws governing what management can and cannot do, management undoubtedly will use a variety of tactics to protect its interest. During its "Stay Nonunion" campaign, it will attempt to persuade the potential members to vote no. Union organizers realize that some initial signers might be persuaded to vote no, and thus unions usually require a much higher percentage of authorization cards so they can increase their odds of obtaining a majority.

When that majority vote is received, the NLRB certifies the union and recognizes it as the exclusive bargaining unit. Irrespective of whether the individual in the certified bargaining union voted for or against the union, each worker is covered by the negotiated contract and must abide by its governance. Once a union has been certified, is it there for life? Certainly not. On some occasions, union members may become so dissatisfied with the union's actions in representing them that they may want to turn to another union or return to their nonunion status. In either case, the rank-and-file members petition the NLRB to conduct a **representation decertification (RD).** Once again, if a majority of the members vote the union out, it is gone. However, once the election has been held, no other action can occur for another twelve-month period. This grace period protects the employer from employees decertifying one union today and certifying another tomorrow.

Finally, and even more rare than an RD, is a representation decertification, or RM, initiated by management. The guidelines for the RM are the same as for the RD, except that it is the employer who is leading the drive. Although RDs and RMs are ways of decertifying unions, it should be pointed out that most labor agreements bar the use of either decertification election during the term of the contract. In fact, the NLRB only handled 40 decertification elections in 1991, compared to over 1,300 RCs.[43]

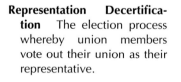

Representation Decertification The election process whereby union members vote out their union as their representative.

Ethical Decisions in HRM:

Antiunion Organizing Strategies

You recognize that your employees are not happy over the recent events in your organization. You've had to make significant personnel cuts, restructured the reporting relationships due to the elimination of several offices, and have announced that pay increases will not be forthcoming this year. You know there have been rumblings among the crowd, but you never expected it to lead to a union organizing drive. After all, you've had a respectful relationship with your employees over the past several years. Yet, late this morning, you noticed union literature on your parking lot. You also have witnessed something "hush-hush" going on between employees. In fact, one of your supervisors has mentioned that he overheard several workers talking about joining a union. Not wanting to take any chances, you contact your labor attorney, who suggests that you take some immediate steps.

First of all, you begin to send information to employees about all the good things you have done, and how you value their input. You prefer to solve problems one-on-one rather than through a third party. You even indicate that you feel the worst is behind you, but can't make absolute promises. Unfortunately, these actions appear to be having little effect on the union activity around your facility.

You call a meeting of all employees late one afternoon. You explain to them that although it is their right to pursue a union, you feel that it is only right for you to speak your mind. You explain that when a union organizes employees, there is historically an increase in administrative costs incurred by the company. In the financial shape your organization is in, if you were to incur more costs, it might create significant financial hardships. Thus, you tell them that if they unionize, and costs go up, you will have no other choice than to close the business and move to another state where costs won't be so high.

In the meantime, you have hired consultants to guide you on avoiding being unionized. You are more than willing to spend several tens of thousands of dollars to remain nonunion—even though it's an expense you prefer not to incur. By and large, it looks as if your investment paid off. When the election was finally held, 73 percent of those voting voted to remain nonunion.

You've successfully defended your "turf." But at what expense? You pressed hard to save the company from being unionized, spending a lot of money, and leaving the impression that you would close down the facility if the union election ultimately added to your administrative costs. Were your union avoidance tactics legal? Absolutely! But were they ethical and in the best interest of the company, or the employees? What's your opinion?

Organizing drives may be unsuccessful, but when they do achieve their goal to become the exclusive bargaining agent, the next step is to negotiate the contract. We'll look at the specific issues surrounding contract negotiations in our next chapter on collective bargaining.

Critical Issues for Unions Today

As the percentage of the work force that is unionized declines, a number of questions arise. Why are unions losing about half of their representation elections? What is management doing to weaken union's power in the United States? Is public sector unionization different than in the private sector? And where are unions likely to focus their attention in the next decade? In this section, we'll look at these issues.

Union Avoidance

As we stated a few paragraphs ago, management is unlikely to give up running the ship without a fight simply because a union organizing campaign is underway. However, its fighting strategies have changed. Let's review the old methods and the new antiunion tactics.

A popular long-term tactic of management has been to support lobbying efforts for state legislation that prohibits requiring union membership as a condition of employment. Management has a vested interest in supporting right-to-work laws. Remember from our discussion earlier on labor laws, under right-to-work legislation, unionization is solely a matter of individual choice. Consequently, employees cannot be forced to join a union if they want to work for an employer, even though employees at that location are unionized. As a result, where right-to-work laws exist, it is more difficult for unions to survive.

This approach is unrealistic, however, for many small organizations can muster little political power. Moreover, when confronted with the fact that an organizing drive is currently underway, the management in a small or large firm must make an immediate response. Management response tends to take the form of a counter-campaign to argue the benefits of maintaining a nonunion environment. Management frequently emphasizes what it has done in the past for its employees, the value of the individual ethic and the individual freedoms that workers relinquish when they become part of a collective-bargaining unit, and the costs of unionization.

Management's counter-campaign must be carefully planned and implemented, however. The information given workers must be factual and non-threatening, and management must be careful not to engage in illegal practices. These include physically interfering with, threatening, or engaging in violent behavior toward organizers; interfering with the employees involved in the organizing drive; disciplining or discharging employees for any pro-union activities; or promising to provide or withhold future benefits contingent on the employees' decision regarding unionization.

Backing right-to-work legislation and counter-campaign, while not obsolete, are giving way to new techniques. To meet the challenge of more sophisticated union-organizing efforts, some companies have been engaging in two major activities: remaining nonunion through expensive antiunion education campaigns (**union avoidance**), or **union busting.**

Many companies wishing to remain nonunion are engaging in activities that inform employees that joining a union is not worthwhile. Through educational

Union Avoidance A company tactic of providing to employees those things unions would provide without employees having to join the union.

Union Busting A company tactic designed to eliminate the union that represents the company's employees.

programs, these companies have tried to avoid having the campaign begin. To do so, they are implementing in their organizations sound employee relations programs that are designed to provide benefits similar to those that unions would provide, yet without the fees associated with joining the union. These companies also have elaborate complaint procedures designed to permit the employee to settle disputes. Therefore, employee relations programs are designed to correct the discretionary decisions of employers toward their workers. Companies are also using audiovisual devices to spread management's belief that if workers were knowledgeable about unions—understanding the issues and voting on these facts rather than emotions—unions would never win an election.

Other companies currently operating with a unionized group of employees have taken a different approach. Programs to educate workers about why they should not join a union may be moot; instead, these companies have implemented a major after-the-fact effort—union busting. Union busting is becoming a profitable venture for some individuals. Armed with a variety of tactics, these consultants are working with companies and developing alternatives to reduce the costs associated with unions. Some are running strong decertification campaigns or taking short-term losses in a lockout for future gains. Others are proclaiming that if the company does not regain more control, it will close down the plant and move. Although statistics are not readily available regarding how many companies do shut down to eliminate their union, many companies have migrated to the South or have moved entire operations out of the United States. Moving to an area that is traditionally antiunion, where the labor costs are cheaper, coupled with the fact that expenditures for capital improvements at an existing plant approximate the costs of building a new plant, are all inducements for a company to move.

Union Membership: Where Have the Members Gone?

The birth of unionization in the United States can be traced back to the late 1700s. Although there was labor strife for about 200 years, it was not until the passage of the Wagner Act in 1935 that we began to witness significant union gains. In fact, by the early 1940s, union membership in the United States reached its pinnacle of approximately 36 percent of the work force.[44] Since that time, however, there's been nothing more than a steady decline (see Figure 17-4). What accounted for this phenomenon? There is no single answer to this question. However, major contributing factors can be identified.

In the early to mid-1970s, many unionized workers, especially in the private sector, were able to join the ranks of the middle class as a result of their unions'

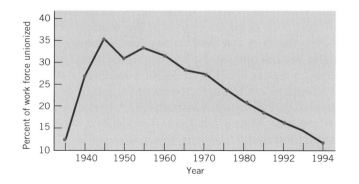

Figure 17-4
Trends in Union Membership

success at the bargaining table. This often meant that they were more concerned with taxes than with ideological and social issues or with support for legislation that favored the union movement. Furthermore, the private-sector labor movement had difficulty accepting into its ranks public and federal sector workers, women, African Americans, and the rising tide of immigrants.

The 1970s was also the decade in which predictions about the post-industrial age came to pass and manufacturing was replaced by service as the dominant industry in the American economy. As a consequence, the most rapid growth in employment was in wholesale and retail trade, service industries including high technology, and white-collar jobs. These are areas where unions either had not previously focused organizing efforts or were largely unsuccessful for a variety of reasons.

Double-digit inflation, beginning in the mid-1970s, was also a factor. High rates of inflation resulted in the first massive layoffs in both the private and public sectors, which radically diminished the financial resources of numerous unions to represent members and to engage in organizing and political activities. Additionally, the emergence of global competition caught much of American business by surprise. The primary response was to try to restore their financial positions by demanding concessions from workers (concession bargaining) and/or by reducing the work force. Both of these responses have had an enormous effect on the unions at the workplace. Fueled by these pressures, the latter half of the 1970s ushered in the strongest antiunion movement since the post–World War II era. And "outsourcing"[45] of production and assembly operations to foreign countries such as the Pacific Rim, Mexico, Brazil, Hong Kong, Taiwan, and parts of Africa was another means that originated in the late 1970s.

The 1980s and early 1990s witnessed an even more dramatic decline in union membership and power. Massive layoffs had ripped through the ranks of such unions as the United Automobile Workers (UAW), the United Steelworkers of America (USWA), the United Mine Workers (UMW), the Rubber Workers, and the Communications Workers, so that their numbers were significantly less than at the beginning of the decade. The cumulative effects of factors identified in the 1970s had even harsher consequences during the next fifteen years. Union busting and avoidance were no longer sideline issues for management consultants, but were a thriving and lucrative enterprise in their own right—attracting some of the best and brightest graduates of business and law schools. Worker replacement became management's "ace in the hole." Management simply hired new workers to replace those on strike, thus eliminating their union "problem." The 1980s also witnessed a legislative sentiment that began to turn against unions. In such an environment, the role of the strike also took on new meaning. The transition began in 1981, when nationwide attention focused on President Ronald Reagan's firing of illegally striking air-traffic controllers. Important here was the message this action sent to employers across the country: The strike is no longer a union weapon, but rather a management weapon to push workers out of their jobs in an effort to bust the union and/or to gain concessions from workers that they might not otherwise have given.[46]

The courts also became involved in the antiunion sentiment. In 1984, for example, the Supreme Court decision in ***NLRB* v. *Bildisco & Bildisco***[47] upheld the premise that a company could file for bankruptcy as a means of unilaterally declaring the labor contract as unduly burdensome. A year earlier, Frank Lorenzo had already proven this point when Texas Air declared bankruptcy and voided its union contracts. Subsequent to the Bildisco decision, Congress passed the Bankruptcy Amendments and the Federal Judgeships Act, which was intended to limit the use of a claim of bankruptcy to negate a collective bargaining agree-

NLRB* v. *Bildisco & Bildisco
Upheld the premise that a company could file for bankruptcy to have a labor contract nullified.

ment. According to this act, a company has the burden of proving that it meets specified requirements in order to set aside a bona fide labor agreement.[48]

The picture for unions in the remaining years of the 1990s appears just as bleak. Union avoidance and busting, delayering of corporate America, de-jobbed organizations, technology advancements, the contingent work force, replacement workers, and the like, are all contributing to a continual decline in membership. From its heyday of almost 36 percent in the early 1940s, to its current 11 percent in 1995, unions appear not to be the force they once were. But don't count unions down and out. Unions are changing some of their organizing tactics and public sentiment might be changing to support and sympathize with union causes. Unions have also posted some major victories, like reversing Nynex plans to lay off more than 22,000 workers.[49] And, if more proof is needed, one can look at unions' success in the public sector.

Public-Sector Unionization

Unionizing government employees, either in the federal sector, or in state, county, and municipal jurisdictions, has proven to be very lucrative for unions.[50] Significant gains have been made in these sectors, as unions have increased membership from 11 percent in 1970 to 38 percent in 1993.[51]

But labor relations in the government sector is not like its counterpart in the private sector.[52] For example, in the federal sector, wages are nonnegotiable. Likewise, compulsory membership in unions is prohibited. At the state, county, and local levels, laws must be passed to grant employees in any jurisdiction the right to unionize—and more importantly, the right to strike. Yet, probably the most notable difference lies in determining "who's the boss."

In a private company, management is the employer. This, however, is not the case in government sectors. Instead, a president, a governor, county executive, etc., is responsible for the government's budget. These are elected officials, who have fiduciary responsibilities to their citizenry. Who, then, "owns" the government? The people. Accordingly, unionized employees in the public sector are actually negotiating against themselves as taxpayers. And even if some agreement is reached, the negotiated contract cannot be binding, even though the unions members support it, until some legislative body has approved it.

Finally, because these negotiations are a concern to the general public, citizens have the right to know what is going on. This is handled through what are called **sunshine laws**.[53] The intent of these laws is to require the parties in public-sector labor relations to make public their negotiations; that is, contract negotiations are open to the public. This freedom of information is based on the premise that the public-sector negotiations directly affect all taxpayers, and thus, they should have direct information regarding what is occurring. However, while information is important, sunshine laws have been questioned by labor relations personnel. Their contention is, for those who do not understand what happens in negotiations, what the public may see or hear during open negotiations may ultimately differ from the final contract. As such, the public may gain a false sense of negotiation outcomes.

Unionizing the Nontraditional Employee

The strength of unionization in years past resided in the manufacturing industries of the U.S. economy. Steel, tires, automobiles, and transportation were major industries that dominated every aspect of American life—and the world. In each of these industries, there was a common element. That thread was the

Sunshine Laws Laws that exist in some states that mandate that labor–management negotiations be open to the public.

presence of unions. Over the past few decades, however, the United States has changed gears. While once a manufacturing giant, the United States has become a service economy. Unfortunately for unions, the service sector has not been one of their targeted areas for organizing employees. But that, too, is changing, as survival for unions depends on their reaching out, and fulfilling the needs of the nontraditional employee. Who are these groups? Nontraditional employees could be classified an anyone who is not in the manufacturing and related industries. Such people include government workers, nurses, secretaries, professional and technical employees, and even some management members.[54] Let's demonstrate this growth by looking at one of these groups of service workers—health-care professionals.

Union activities in the health-care field could logically be argued as nothing new for unions. After all, many a hospital's maintenance staffs have been associated with unions of employee associations for many years. What's different, however, is that unions are not confining their organizing efforts simply to these workers. Rather, they are focusing their sights on nurses, administrative employees, lab techs, and even those working in private doctor's offices.[55] In fact, from about 1989 through 1992, over 4,200 RC elections were held in an attempt to unionize these workers. That's about one-third of all NLRB elections held in that time period. And unions, like the Teamsters, won about 55 percent of these elections—much better than the success ratio of "winning" in the private sector as a whole.[56] Consequently, unions are tasting some success!

As the world of work continues to radically evolve, it is safe to assume that unions will target an even broader group of employees. The same things that unions "sold" fifty years ago to get people interested in the union cause—wages, benefits, job security, and having a say in how employees are treated at work—are the same things that concern employees as we move toward the year 2000.[57] Restructuring, delayering, and the de-jobbing of corporate America has forced affected workers to pay closer attention to what the unions promise. For the health-care professionals who voted to be represented by unions, this has resulted in more job security, and wages and benefits 10 to 15 percent above their nonunion counterparts.[58]

Is history repeating itself? Only time will tell. But remember, the decline in union membership, especially in the traditional industries in the 1970s—was brought about, in part, by people achieving their middle-class status. As organizational changes threaten this social class rank, there is every reason to believe that workers will present a unified, mutual front to the employer.[59] In some cases, that is best achieved through union activities.

International Labor Relations

Labor relations practices, and the percent of the work force unionized, are different in every country (see Table 17-2). Nowhere is employee representation exactly like that in the United States. In almost every case, the relationships among management, employees, and unions (or other administrative bodies) are the result of long histories. The business approach to unionism, or emphasizing economic objectives, is uniquely American. In Europe, Latin America, and elsewhere, unions have often evolved out of a class struggle, resulting in labor as a political party. The Japanese Confederation of Shipbuilding and Engineering Workers' Union only recently began dropping its "class struggle" rhetoric and slogans to pursue a "partnership" with management.[60] The basic difference in perspective sometimes makes it difficult for U.S. expatriates to un-

Country	Percent of Employees Unionized
Sweden	81%
Great Britain	39%
Italy	34%
Germany	32%
Japan	26%
Spain	11%
United States	11%
France	10%

Source: "European News in Brief," *Facts on File* (Chicago:
Rand McNally Corporation, 1993), p. 672.

derstand how the labor relations process works because even the same term
may have very different meanings. For example, in the United States, "collective
bargaining" implies negotiations between a labor union and management. In
Sweden and Germany, it refers to negotiations between the employers' organization and a trade union for the entire industry.[61] Furthermore, arbitration in
the United States usually refers to the settlement of individual contractual disputes, while in Australia arbitration is part of the contract bargaining process.

Not only does each country have a different history of unionism, each government has its own view of its role in the labor relations process. This role is
often reflected in the types and nature of the regulations in force. While the
U.S. government generally takes a "hands-off" approach toward intervention in
labor–management matters, the Australian government, to which the labor
movement has very strong ties, is inclined to be more involved. Thus, not only
must the multinational corporate industrial relations office be familiar with the
separate laws of each country, it also must be familiar with the environment in
which those statutes are implemented. Understanding international labor relations is vital to an organization's strategic planning. Unions affect wage levels,
which in turn affect competitiveness in both labor and product markets. Unions
and labor laws may limit employment-level flexibility through security clauses
that tightly control layoffs and terminations (or redundancies). This is especially true in such countries as England, France, Germany, Japan, and Australia,
where various laws place severe restrictions on employers.

Differing Perspectives Toward Labor Relations

If labor relations can affect the strategic planning initiatives of an organization, it is necessary to consider the issue of headquarters' involvement in host-
country international union relations. The organization must assess if the labor
relations function should be controlled globally from the parent country, or if it
would be more advantageous for each host country to administer its own operation. There is no simple means of making this assessment; frequently, the decision reflects the relationship of the product market at home to that of the overseas product market. For instance, when domestic sales are larger than those

overseas, the organization is more likely to regard the foreign office as an extension of the domestic operations. This is true for many U.S. multinational organizations because the home market is so vast. Thus, American firms have been more inclined to keep labor relations centrally located at corporate headquarters. Many European countries, by contrast, have small home markets with comparatively larger international operations; thus, they are more inclined to adapt to host-country standards and have the labor relations function decentralized.

Another divergence among multinational companies in their labor relations is the national attitude toward unions. Generally, American multinational corporations view unions negatively at home and try to avoid unionization of the work force. Europeans, on the other hand, have had greater experience with unions, are accustomed to a larger proportion of the work force being unionized, and are more accepting of the unionization of their own workers. In Japan, as in other parts of Asia, unions are often closely identified with an organization and may be more loyal to the enterprise's goals than is the case in the United States where unions demand worker/member loyalty. This may explain the extreme lengths to which Japanese auto manufacturers go in selecting plant sites in the United States, trying to avoid unionization of their American work forces.[62]

The European Community

The new European Community brings together a dozen or more individual labor relations systems. For both the member nations and other countries doing business in Europe, like the United States and Japan, it is important to understand the dynamics of what will necessarily be a dramatically changing labor environment.[63]

Legislation about workers' rights is continually developing,[64] which has far-ranging implications for all employers. While the French and Germans lean toward strong worker representation in labor policy, reflecting their cultural histories, the United Kingdom and Denmark oppose them. Many basic questions

Unionization is not limited to the United States. It is worldwide. Workers in other countries also have to fight for better wages, benefits, and working conditions. Here, these Russian coal miners are just a few 60 million union members who have been confronting Russian management to look for better ways to deal with the troubles confronting the Russian economy.

remain to be answered with the implementation of the free trade of labor across national boundaries. For example, with the increase in production that accompanies the opening of this market, workers and their union representatives are going to want their fair share. And what is this fair share? For starters, European unions want a maternity package that provides 80 percent of salary for a fourteen-week period. They are also seeking premium pay for night work, full benefits for workers who are employed more than eight hours a week, participation on companies' boards of directors, and an increase in the minimum wage level to two-thirds of each country's average manufacturing wage.[65] Some of these inducements will be difficult to obtain, but companies doing business overseas must be aware of what is happening in pending labor legislation, and fully understand and comply with the host country's laws and customs.

Study Tools and Applications

Summary

This summary relates to the Learning Objectives provided on p. 463.
After having read this chapter, you should know:

1. A union is an organization of workers, acting collectively, seeking to promote and protect their mutual interests through collective bargaining.
2. The main thrust of the Clayton Act was to limit the use of injunctions against union activity, especially when such activity supported union representation elections.
3. The Norris–LaGuardia Act of 1932 limited the use of injunctions in labor disputes. This resulted in the lessening of the court's role in labor–management relations. This act also made yellow-dog contracts unenforceable.
4. The Wagner (National Labor Relations) Act of 1935; the Taft–Hartley (Labor–Management Relations) Act of 1947; and the Landrum–Griffin (Labor and Management Reporting and Disclosure) Act of 1959 represent the most direct legislation affecting collective bargaining. The Wagner Act gave unions the freedom to exist and identified employer unfair labor practices. Taft–Hartley balanced the power between unions and management by identifying union unfair labor practices. Landrum–Griffin required unions to disclose their financial records in an effort to stymie organized crime efforts to control unions.
5. Executive Orders 10988 and 11491 paved the way for labor relations to exist in the federal sector. Additionally, Executive Order 11491 made federal labor relations similar to its private sector counterpart. The Civil Service Reform Act of 1978 removed federal sector labor relations from under the jurisdiction of the president and established a forum for its continued operation.
6. The structure of the AFL–CIO and its affiliated unions consists of various hierarchical relationships. The AFL–CIO Executive Council is the governing body of the AFL–CIO. The individuals on this council comprise the national headquarters. Next in the structure are the national unions, followed by their local unions. In the AFL–CIO structure, various service departments and committees exist under the direction of the executive council.
7. The main incentives for affiliating with the AFL–CIO revolve around the AFL–CIO's "no raiding" agreement; its political lobbying efforts; assistance in contract negotiation matters; educational programs; and information and research efforts.
8. The union-organizing process officially begins with the completion of an authorization. If the required percentage of potential union members show their intent to

vote on a union by signing the authorization card, the NLRB will hold an election. If 50 percent plus one of those voting vote for the union, then the union is certified to be the bargaining unit.

9. Union busting refers to a tactic and practice by companies to eliminate their unions, thus reducing the costs associated with a unionized work force.

10. Sunshine laws require parties in the public sector to make their collective bargaining negotiations open to the public.

Key Terms

AFL–CIO
authorization card
Civil Service Reform Act
Clayton Act
Executive Order 10988
Executive Order 11491
Federal Mediation and
   Conciliation Service (FMCS)
Landrum–Griffin Act
local union
National Labor Relations Board (NLRB)
national/international union

NLRB v. Bildisco & Bildisco
Norris–LaGuardia Act
Railway Labor Act
representation certification (RC)
representation decertification (RD)
sunshine laws
Taft–Hartley Act
union
union avoidance
union busting
Wagner Act
yellow-dog contracts

EXPERIENTIAL EXERCISE:

Conflict Resolution

Introduction

A great deal of human activity in business situations is concerned with resolving conflicts. Individuals or groups have different needs, preferences, and priorities; somehow, these conflicting preferences, and priorities must be resolved if individuals or groups are going to work together. Negotiation is one major process parties use to resolve their conflicts and manage disputes.

Procedure

Step 1: 15–20 MINUTES

Count off the class in groups of four. Two students will pair together to represent Campus Travel Agency, and two students will pair together to represent Midwest Airlines. Each pair should read its own role information provided by the instructor. Once each has read the information, the two should work together to understand the information. They should try to set a negotiating goal (the deal they would like to achieve) and a "bottom line" (a minimally acceptable deal) as a team. Midwest Airlines should prepare to make the first offer on ticket price.

Step 2: 15–20 MINUTES

After pairs are prepared to negotiate, they should meet with their opponent(s). Each pair or foursome should attempt to negotiate an agreement that specifies:

- The number of tickets to be sold
- The percentage of commission that will be paid to Campus Travel Agency
- Any other elements to the agreement.

You are NOT REQUIRED to agree. If you believe the other side is being unfair or unreasonable, you can take your business elsewhere. The instructor will signal when time is finished. The Campus Travel representative(s) should be prepared to report to the class on the outcome and the process of their negotiations. If no deal was achieved, please report the last offers on the table before negotiations ended, and reasons why negotiations broke down.

Step 3: 30 MINUTES

The instructor will ask for and record the results of the negotiations from each pair or foursome. The instructor will also ask for comments about the process of negotiation in each group, and the strategy and tactics used by various negotiators. Comparisons will be made, and the instructor will use these data to highlight the dynamics of the negotiation process.

Discussion Questions

1. What was the outcome that you negotiated in this situation? How did you feel about this outcome as you were agreeing to it?
2. How does your settlement compare to the other pairs or groups in the room? How do you feel about this settlement now that you have had a chance to compare it to what others did?
3. How does your outcome compare to the goal you set before negotiations began? Did you achieve your goal? Why or why not?
4. What strategy or tactics did you attempt to use to achieve your outcome? Did they work?
5. What strategy or tactics did your opponent(s) try? Did they work?

Source: Based on "Negotiation and Conflict," in Roy J. Lewicki, Donald D. Bowen, Douglas T. Hall, and Francine S. Hall, *Experiences in Management and Organizational Behavior* (New York: John Wiley, 1988), pp. 100–02. Used with permission.

CASE APPLICATION:
Organizing Attempts by the Service Employees Union

Every year, the Service Employees Union sets its agenda for organizing campaigns, in an effort to increase its membership and promote union philosophies in areas where unionization is weak. Their goal over the past several years has been to unionize workers in smaller companies in South Carolina, a state that has traditionally been pro-management.[66] Why smaller companies? Simply, the Service Employees Union has found that HRM activities in many of these companies has been ineffective—if they exist at all. As a result, many employee complaints have arisen, making the "benefits" unions offer appear attractive.

Similar to their larger counterparts, these smaller companies, too, are fighting to remain nonunion. For example, under no circumstances will the employer allow union organizers on company property. Although a current employee may discuss unionization during his or her own free time (like lunch), no disruption of the work routine may occur. Furthermore, any union literature may be rightfully banned from the work site, unless there are special locations where employees can post personal notices. No employer, regardless of size, has to roll over in the organizing process.

Ironically, although several barriers are erected to stymie union organizing, unions like the Service Employees Union are enjoying success in South Carolina. They are winning more than 60 percent of the elections held, 150 percent of the national average!

Questions

1. Why do you believe the courts, and employers, do not permit union organizing activities on company property? Wouldn't it make more sense to have the "campaign" in an open forum, rather than out on the street where activities are "unknown" to management? Explain.
2. How much "freedom" should be given to an employee who is pro-union to discuss union activities and distribute union literature on his or her own time on the job? If this person worked the 7–3 shift, would you give her that same freedom if she wanted to come in and talk to employees on the 11–7 shift? Explain.
3. The success rate in South Carolina has been startling in these smaller businesses. What factors can you identify that might be attributing to this success?

Testing Your Understanding

1. How do activities differ for human resource professionals in an organization that is unionized, and one that is not?
   a. Where a union exists, human resource professionals' responsibilities often consist mainly of following procedures and policies laid out in the labor contract. In a nonunion setting, human resource professionals are involved in a range of activities from planning through implementation of procedures and policies.
   b. In a union setting, human resource professionals spend most of their time in deciding wage rates. Where a union does not represent workers, human resource professionals are involved in a range of activities from planning through implementation of the whole array of human resource procedures and policies.
   c. Where a union represents workers, human resource professionals have setting and monitoring the hours of work as their primary responsibility. Where they don't, human resource professionals are involved in a range of activities from planning through implementation of the whole array of human resource procedures and policies.
   d. In a union setting, human resource professionals are responsible only for selecting and monitoring employee benefits packages, primarily health-care options. In a nonunion setting, human resource professionals are involved in a range of activities from planning through implementation of the whole array of human resource procedures and policies.
   e. There is no difference between the two.
2. What was the outcome of the Clayton Act?
   a. Injunctions became easier for management to obtain.
   b. Injunctions became more difficult for management to obtain.
   c. Strikes became easier to organize.
   d. Strikes became more difficult to organize.
   e. Unions could publicly recruit new members.
3. Which of the following statements is true regarding the Norris–LaGuardia Act and the National Industrial Recovery Act?
   a. Norris–LaGuardia was passed two years after the National Industrial Recovery Act.
   b. Both laws were declared unconstitutional.
   c. Union representatives were chosen under Norris–LaGuardia. Yellow-dog contracts were declared illegal by the National Industrial Recovery Act.
   d. Norris–LaGuardia dealt with the Teamsters. National Industrial Recovery Act dealt with federal union employees.
   e. Neither act had an enforcement mechanism.
4. The Wagner Act required employers to bargain in good faith over mandatory bargaining issues of all of the following except
   a. wages.   b. working hours.
   c. medical benefits.   d. terms of work.
   e. conditions of work.
5. Provisions of the Taft–Hartley Act include all of the following except
   a. management must bargain in good faith.
   b. unions must bargain in good faith.
   c. closed shops were declared illegal.
   d. unions could not obtain compensation for services not performed.
   e. the president of the United States can issue an eighty-day cooling off period if national security is involved.
6. All of the following are accurate comparisons of the Civil Service Reform Act and the Wagner Act except
   a. Wagner Act covers private sector employees. Civil Service Reform Act covers public sector employees.
   b. wages can be bargained for under the Wagner Act.

Wages are excluded from bargaining under the Civil Service Reform Act.

   c. both laws provide for binding arbitration.

   d. benefits can be bargained for under the Wagner Act. Benefits are set by Congress for federal employees.

   e. the Wagner Act prohibits negotiations over compulsory union membership arrangements. Civil Service Reform Act does not prohibit negotiations over these.

7. The AFL–CIO is responsible for all of the following except
   a. handling most of the policy formulation for affiliated national unions.
   b. investigating and conducting hearings on malfeasance changes against a council member and recommending appropriate action.
   c. removing from office any council member found to be a follower or a member of a subversive organization.
   d. conducting elections for national unions.
   e. adjudicating jurisdictional disputes.

8. Compare national unions to the AFL–CIO.
   a. National unions are larger than the AFL–CIO.
   b. National unions are an alternative structure to the AFL–CIO.
   c. National unions are more concerned with labor matters that directly affect their industry or trade. AFL–CIO is more concerned with general worker welfare. The AFL–CIO is a national union.
   e. The AFL–CIO is made up of two national unions.

9. Local union responsibilities include all of the following except
   a. collecting dues.
   b. working with local management in contract negotiations.
   c. processing any grievance that is filed.
   d. ensuring that the contract is being followed correctly.
   e. recruiting members from other local unions.

10. Erin has hired a group of consultants to educate her union workers about the folly of remaining union. This group points out loss of global competitiveness, lower market share, even the possibility of bankruptcy if the employees continue to work with the union organization. What is going on?
   a. union busting
   b. union avoidance
   c. right-to-work lobbying
   d. participative work structures
   e. union educational seminar

11. What effect do sunshine laws have on labor–management relations?
   a. All labor relations contract negotiations, public and private sector, are required to be open to the public.
   b. Sunshine laws are based on the premise that taxpayers have a right to know how their money is being spent.
   c. Sunshine laws assist in getting negotiations completed more quickly because the public is aware of the events occurring in negotiations.
   d. Sunshine laws adversely effect negotiations in that negotiations must stop periodically to allow for reporters to interview the negotiators.
   e. Sunshine laws permit unions to exist in the public sector.

12. Why are union activities important to the rest of work force?
   a. Unions affect important sectors of the U.S. economy.
   b. They are not important to the rest of the work force.
   c. Unions are instrumental in achieving successful globalization.
   d. Unions lead the way in empowering the work force.
   e. Unions are the one of the most innovative forces in the U.S. economy.

13. Why was the Sherman Antitrust Act applicable to unions?
   a. Unions are specifically mentioned in the law.
   b. Union activity was considered to be anticompetitive and was ruled to be in restraint of trade.
   c. Concession bargain was monopolistic.
   d. Managers were prohibited from discouraging union meetings.
   e. The act was not applicable to unions.

14. The initial impetus for widespread collective bargaining in the United States came from
   a. Taft–Hartley Act.
   b. Landrum–Griffin Act.
   c. Clayton Act.
   d. Norris–LaGuardia Act.
   e. Railway Labor Act.

15. Provisions of the Landrum–Griffin Act include all of the following except
   a. secret ballots were used for union elections.
   b. union officials were made accountable for union funds.
   c. management was restrained from filing injunctions.
   d. restrictions were placed on trusteeships.
   e. conduct during elections was regulated.

16. All of the following were provisions of Executive Order 10988 except
   a. federal employees could join unions.
   b. agency heads were required to bargain in good faith.
   c. unfair labor practices were defined.
   d. federal employees could strike.
   e. a labor organization code of conduct was specified.

Chapter Eighteen

COLLECTIVE BARGAINING

LEARNING OBJECTIVES

AFTER READING THIS CHAPTER, YOU WILL BE ABLE TO:

1. Identify the objectives of collective bargaining.
2. Describe the components of collective bargaining.
3. Identify the steps in the collective bargaining process.
4. Describe the role of a grievance procedure in collective bargaining.
5. Explain the various types of union security arrangements.
6. Describe how power flows in organized labor.
7. Discuss what is meant by the term *economic strike*.
8. Identify the various impasse resolution techniques.
9. Discuss the four-quadrant diagram of labor–management relationships.

One of the fundamental issues in labor–management relationships is that both sides will come to the bargaining table and negotiate. In fact, both the Wagner and the Taft–Hartley Acts mandate this, as these laws require both unions and management to negotiate in good faith. Good-faith bargaining requires both sides to willingly work toward a settlement. That is, their efforts must be viewed as having a positive influence on the process—toward the ultimate goal of reaching an agreement. But good-faith bargaining does not guarantee that this agreement will be reached. On the contrary, serious disagreements do arise at times, resulting in negotiations breaking off. That's all part of the process—and it's precisely what occurred between the Major League Players Association and the baseball owners.[1]

It's hard to imagine that a major labor dispute could arise between such groups. Baseball, like other professional sports, almost appears outside the realm of traditional labor–management relations. Baseball players earned a minimum of $109,000, and the players wanted that to increase to $200,000. Yet, there are very few players at the minimum level. In fact, the average salary for ball players in 1995 was just over 1 million, far above the $20,000-plus salary for the average U.S. worker.[2] And that's been a fourfold increase in average salary over the past ten years. The owners wanted a salary cap—a ceiling on the amount teams could spend on player personnel. But the players were adamant: They would not play under a salary cap arrangement! Consequently, negotiations reached a stalemate. Were the players at fault for negotiations breaking down? Not necessarily, for in every negotiation there are two side to every issue.

For about a decade, many of the baseball owners have enjoyed windfall profits. Increased attendance and ticket revenues at major league games, product licensing fees, and expansion franchising fees have made the owners part of a unique group. Revenues in 1993, for instance, although down from the previous year, approached the $2 billion mark. But this money is not evenly distributed among the twenty-eight major league teams. The big-market franchises, like those in New York, Atlanta, and Los Angeles, generate more television revenues than those in smaller markets like San Diego and Milwaukee. Thus, there's an inequity among club owners that allows the richer clubs to spend significantly more to buy better talent. Accordingly, the real issue is one between the owners, not the players. But as the chief negotiator for the union, Donald Fehr states, "The smaller-market guys need money and the larger ones won't pay, so they want us [players] to solve their problem."[3]

Trying to point fingers at the responsible party for the deadlock in negotiations was difficult, and a matter of perspective. Nonetheless, reality was that such events happen. And although the baseball players and owners have had some sort of work stoppage each of their last eight negotiations, never before had one progressed to the magnitude of the strike of 1994. For on August 12, baseball stopped—and the season was over. What two World Wars, the Great

Scenes like this sell-out crowd at Jacobs Field in Cleveland suddenly disappeared in mid-August 1994. Record attendance at games, and challenges to some key baseball records all went unfulfilled as an impasse in negotiations between the Major League Players' Association and the Baseball Owners brought a premature end to the 1994 season. Not even World War II could do what this strike did—cause the cancellation of the World Series—the first time for that in ninety years.

Depression, and civil unrest couldn't do, a baseball strike did—for the first time in ninety years, the World Series was cancelled. The owners threatened to run the 1995 season with replacement players and the players threatened to conduct picket lines, possibly with hired picketers. Ultimately, the strike ended without a final resolution, and players showed up at training camp for a shortened season. Unfortunately, everyone lost—the players, the owners, and the fans!

Introduction

Literally hundreds of thousands of managers direct the activities of unionized employees who work under a collective agreement. There are more than 130,000 union contracts with firms; in total, these contracts cover more than 14 million workers.[4] When the tens of thousands of smaller negotiations and non-industrial contracts are added to these figures, we can see that for a large segment of managers, HRM practices are determined substantially by the results of collective bargaining.

The term **collective bargaining** typically refers to the negotiation, administration, and interpretation of a written agreement between two parties that covers a specific period of time. This agreement, or *contract*, lays out in specific terms the conditions of employment; that is, what is expected of employees and what limits there are in management's authority. In the following discussion, we will take a somewhat larger perspective—we will also consider the organizing, certification, and preparation efforts that precede actual negotiation.

Most of us only hear or read about collective bargaining when a contract is about to expire or when negotiations break down. When a major trucking contract is about to expire, we may be aware that collective bargaining exists in the transportation industry. Similarly, teachers' strikes in New Orleans, workers striking General Motors at the Buick Plant in Flint, Michigan,[5] or hockey players striking against the hockey clubs remind us that organized labor deals with management collectively. In fact, collective-bargaining agreements cover about half of all state and local government employees and one-ninth of employees in the private sector. The wages, hours, and working conditions of these unionized employees are negotiated for periods of usually two or three years at a time. Only when these contracts expire and management and the union are unable to agree on a new contract are most of us aware that collective bargaining is a very important part of HRM.

Collective Bargaining The negotiation, administration, and interpretation of a written agreement between two parties, at least one of which represents a group that is acting collectively, that covers a specific period of time.

The Objective and Scope of Collective Bargaining

The objective of collective bargaining is to agree on an acceptable contract—acceptable to management, union representatives, and the union membership. But what is covered in this contract? The final agreement will reflect the problems of the particular workplace and industry in which the contract is negotiated. The agreement may be very vague or highly specific. It may cover the obvious or what may appear to be ridiculous or irrelevant issues:

> Some maritime agreements specify the quality of meals and even the number of bars of soap, towels, and sheets that management is to furnish the crew. Such provisions are natural subjects for negotiation, since they are vital to the men at sea, but they would make no sense in a normal manufacturing agreement . . . Detailed procedures respecting control over hiring are central to collective bargaining in industries with casual employment, where employees shift continually from one employer to another, as in construction or stevedoring; but in factory and office employment, new hiring typically is left to the discretion of management.[6]

What is important on one job may therefore have no bearing on another. This fact will definitely be reflected in the demands placed by the union on management and in the subject and terms of the agreement finally negotiated.

Irrespective of the specific issues contained in various contracts, four issues appear consistently throughout all labor contracts. Three of the four are mandatory bargaining issues, which means that management must be willing to negotiate with the union. These mandatory issues were defined by the Wagner Act as wages, hours, and terms and conditions of employment. The fourth issue covered in almost all labor contracts is the grievance procedure, which is designed to permit the adjudication of complaints (see the "Contract Administration" section of this chapter). But before we progress further into collective bargaining, let's inspect our cast of characters.

Collective-Bargaining Participants

Collective bargaining was described as an activity that takes place between two parties. In this context, the two parties are management and labor. But who represents management and labor? Given our previous discussion in Chapter 17, would it be erroneous to add a third party—government?

Management's representation in collective-bargaining talks tends to depend on the size of the organization. In a small firm, for instance, bargaining is probably done by the president. Since small firms frequently have no specialist who deals only with HRM issues, the president of the company often handles this. In larger organizations, there is usually a sophisticated HRM department with full-time industrial relations experts. In such cases, we can expect management to be represented by the senior manager for industrial relations, corporate executives, and company lawyers—with support provided by legal and economic specialists in wage and salary administration, labor law, benefits, and so forth.

On the union side, we typically expect to see a bargaining team made up of an officer of the local union, local shop stewards, and some representation from the international/national union.[7] Again, as with management, representation is modified to reflect the size of the bargaining unit. If negotiations involve a contract that will cover 50,000 employees at company locations throughout the United States, the team will be dominated by international/national union officers, with a strong supporting cast of economic and legal experts employed by the union. In a small firm or for local negotiations covering special issues at the plant level for a nationwide organization, bargaining representatives for the union might be the local officers and a few specially elected committee members.

Watching over these two sides is a third party—government. In addition to providing the rules under which management and labor bargain, government provides a watchful eye on the two parties to ensure the rules are followed, and it stands ready to intervene if an agreement on acceptable terms cannot be reached, or if the impasse undermines the nation's well-being.

Are there any more participants? No, for the most part, with one exception— financial institutions.[8] Most people are unaware of the presence of the financial institutions' role in collective bargaining. Although not directly involved in negotiations, these "banks" set limits on the cost of the contract. Exceeding that amount may cause the banks to call in the loans that had been made to the company. This results in placing a ceiling on what management can spend.

While we can show that there are more groups involved in collective bargaining, our discussion will focus on labor and management. After all, it is the labor and management teams that buckle down and hammer out the contract.

The Collective-Bargaining Process

Let's now consider the actual collective-bargaining process. Figure 18-1 contains a simple model of how the process typically flows in the private sector—which includes preparing to negotiate, actual negotiations, and administering the contract after it has been ratified.

Preparing to Negotiate

Once a union has been certified as the bargaining unit (see Chapter 17), both union and management begin the ongoing activity of preparing for negotiations. We refer to this as an ongoing activity because ideally it should begin as soon as the previous contract is agreed upon or union certification is achieved. Realistically, it probably begins anywhere from one to six months before the current contract expires. We can consider the preparation for negotiation as composed of three activities: fact gathering, goal setting, and strategy development. Since we are interested in the role of collective bargaining in HRM, we will focus on the process from management's perspective.

Information is acquired from both internal and external sources. Internal data include grievance and accident records; employee performance reports; overtime figures; and reports on transfers, turnover, and absenteeism. External information should include statistics on the current economy, both at local and national levels; economic forecasts for the short and intermediate terms; copies of recently negotiated contracts by the adversary union to determine what issues the union considers important; data on the communities in which the company operates—cost of living; changes in cost of living, terms of recently negotiated labor contracts, and statistics on the labor market; and industry labor statistics to see what terms other organizations, employing similar types of personnel, are negotiating.

This information tells management where it is, what similar organizations are doing, and what it can anticipate from the economy in the near term. These

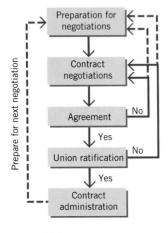

Figure 18-1
The Collective-Bargaining
Process

data are then used to determine what management can expect to achieve in the negotiation. What can it expect the union to ask for? What is management prepared to concede?

With homework done, information in hand, and tentative goals established, management must put together the most difficult part of the bargaining preparation activities—a strategy for dealing with the union's demands (see Table 18-1). This includes assessing the union's power and specific tactics. But not all unions bargain from equal power bases. The labor market, economic conditions, rates of inflation, and recent contract settlements all affect the degree of union influence. Management's ability to tolerate a strike is also crucial. If demand for the company's product or service has been high, management may be reluctant to absorb a strike, even one of short duration. On the other hand, if business has been slow, management may be considerably less willing to concede to union demands and may be prepared to accept a lengthy strike. That is precisely what Caterpillar faced as it "forced" a lengthy strike with the United Automobile Workers representing thousands of its workers.[9] And it worked so well that John Deere is employing the same strategy in its negotiations with the UAW, too.[10] Consequently, variations in power factors will affect the tactics used in bargaining.

Negotiating at the Bargaining Table

Negotiation customarily begins with the union delivering to management a long list of demands. By presenting extreme demands, the union creates significant room for trading in later stages of the negotiation; it also disguises the union's real position, leaving management to determine which demands are adamantly sought, which are moderately sought, and which the union is prepared to quickly abandon. Examples of recent demands made by unions in negotiations include an immediate increase in the hourly wage, special adjustments for skilled workers, cost-of-living adjustments, early retirement, free dental care, free psychiatric care, improved quality of work life, increased relief time off the assembly line, more paid holidays, extended vacations, a shorter workweek, and a guaranteed annual wage.

TABLE 18-1   Bargaining Strategies

In most negotiations, there are two distinct strategies either the union or management can employ. These are called distributive bargaining and integrative bargaining.

Distributive Bargaining: A competitive, confrontational, win–lose strategy. Distributive bargaining occurs when one side wants to achieve some contract provision that the other side is opposed to. For instance, if management wants mandatory overtime, and the union does not—instead preferring to have more workers hired—negotiations will continue until one side prevails. That is, there will either be mandatory overtime (management wins) or there won't (union wins).

Integrative Bargaining: A cooperative strategy in which a common goal is the focus of attention. Integrative bargaining occurs when both the union and management must work together to solve a mutual problem. For instance, to remain competitive and secure jobs, both sides agree to relax some work rules and permit the automation of the production operations. Some workers will be trained on the new equipment, and those displaced by the technological improvements will be retrained to fill labor shortages elsewhere in the production process.

A long list of demands often fulfills the internal political needs of the union. By seeming to back numerous wishes of the union's members, union administrators appear to be satisfying the needs of the many factions within the membership. In reality, however, these demands will be scaled down or abandoned if the union's negotiators believe it is expedient to do so. Not surprisingly, management's initial response is usually just as extreme—that is, management counters by offering little more (or even nothing more) than the terms of the previous contract. It is not unusual for management to begin by proposing a reduction in benefits and demanding that the union reduce or eliminate some of their work rules, such as job transfer or outsourcing work.

These initial proposals are then considered by each party. This is a time of exploration—each trying to clarify the other's proposals and to marshal arguments against them. As should be expected, political activity tends to accelerate as each group plays out various roles. Management may say: "If we concede to the union's demands, we'll be bankrupt within six months"; union representatives may argue, "Company profits are at an all-time high, and our previous settlement has been eaten away by inflation. We must not only achieve a large raise to cover the next two years, but we must also be compensated for the loss in buying power during the past two years."

While both management and union representatives publicly accentuate their differences, the real negotiations go on behind closed doors. Each party tries to assess the relative priorities of the other's demands, and each begins to combine proposals into viable packages. What takes place, then, is the attempt to get management's highest offer to approximate the lowest demands that the union is willing to accept. Hence, negotiation is a form of compromise. When an oral agreement is achieved, it is converted into a written contract. Negotiation finally concludes with the union representatives submitting the contract for ratification or approval from rank and file members.

Irrespective of how negotiations proceed, there are several issues that are specific to each group. For management, we refer to these as management rights; for the union, union security arrangements.

Management Rights   Under national labor laws, management and the union must negotiate over wages, hours, and terms and conditions of employment. Although this covers a wide array of topics, everything outside of these mandatory items is considered **management rights.**

Management Rights Items that are not part of contract negotiations, such as how to run the company, or how much to charge for products.

Even though a unionized work force may exist, management still retains its right to run the business. This means that management is not responsible for negotiating over such items as products to produce and sell, selling prices, the size of its work force, or the location of operations. Needless to say, it is in management's best interest to have as many of the issues that affect them labeled as management rights. In that manner, they reserve the right to make unilateral decisions about those issues without having to consult or negotiate with the union. Unions, on the other hand, desire to achieve a position where more and more is open to negotiations.

Just because something is a management right does not mean that it can never be part of negotiations. If management desires, it may take something that is rightfully theirs and place it into negotiations. When, and if that occurs, it is then removed from the "management right" category, and will remain so until subsequent negotiations remove it from the contract. It is important to note, however, that under no circumstances is management required to discuss such issues with the union. Furthermore, management cannot be found "guilty" of negotiating in bad faith for failing to entertain discussions on management rights issues.

Union Security Clauses When one considers the importance of security arrangements to unions—importance brought about in terms of numbers and guaranteed income—it is no wonder that such emphasis is placed on achieving a **union security arrangement** that best suits their goals. Such arrangements range from compulsory membership in the union to giving employees the freedom in choosing to join the union.[11] The various types of union security arrangements—the union shop, the agency shop, and the right-to-work shop, as well as some special provisions under the realm of union security arrangements—are discussed below and summarized in Table 18-2.

The most powerful relationship legally available (except in right-to-work states) to a union is a **union shop.** This arrangement stipulates that employers, while free to hire whomever they choose, may retain only union members. That is, all employees hired into positions covered under the terms of a collective-bargaining agreement must, after a specified probationary period of typically thirty to sixty days, join the union or forfeit their jobs.[12]

An agreement that requires nonunion employees to pay the union a sum of

Union Security Arrangements Labor contract provisions designed to attract and retain dues paying union members.

Union Shop Employers can hire nonunion workers, but they must become dues-paying members within a prescribed period of time.

TABLE 18-2 Union Security and Related Provisions

Union Shop	The strongest of the union security arrangements. Union shops make union membership compulsory. After a given period of time, typically 30 days, a new employee must join the union, or be terminated. A union shop guarantees the union that dues paying members will become part of the union. In a right-to-work state, union shops are illegal.
Agency Shop	The second strongest union security arrangement, the agency shop, gives workers the option of joining the union or not. As such, membership is not compulsory. However, because the "gains" that are made at negotiations will benefit those not joining the union, all workers in the unit must pay union dues. However, Supreme Court decisions dictate that those individuals not members of the union, who still pay dues, have the right to have their monies used solely for collective-bargaining purposes. Like the union shop, the agency shop, too, is illegal in a right-to-work state.
Open Shop	The weakest form of a union security arrangement is the open shop. In an open shop, workers are free to join a union. If they do, they must stay in the union for the duration of the contract—and pay their dues. Those who do not wish to join the union are not required to do so—and thus pay no dues. In an open-shop arrangement, there is an escape clause at the expiration (typically two weeks) in which an individual may "quit" the union. The open shop is based on the premise of freedom of choice, and is the only union security arrangement permitted under right-to-work legislation.
Maintenance of Membership	Because unions need to be able to administer their operations, in an open shop, once someone joins the union, they must maintain their union affiliation, and pay their dues, for the duration of the contract. At the end of the contract, an escape period exists in which those desiring to leave the union may do so.
Dues Checkoff	Dues checkoff involves the employer deducting union dues directly from a union member's paycheck. Under this provision, the employer collects the union dues and forwards a check to the union treasurer. Generally management does not charge an administrative fee for this service.

Agency Shop A type of union security arrangement whereby employees must pay union dues to the certified bargaining unit even if they choose not to join the union.

Open Shop Employees are free to choose whether or not to join the union, and those who do not are not required to pay union dues.

Dues Checkoff Employer withholding of union dues from union members' paychecks.

Contract Administration Implementing, interpreting, and monitoring the negotiated agreement between labor and management.

money equal to union fees and dues as a condition of continuing employment is referred to as an **agency shop.** This arrangement was designed as a compromise between the union's desire to eliminate the "free rider" and management's desire to make union membership voluntary. In such a case, if for whatever reason workers decide not to join the union (e.g., religious beliefs, values, etc.), they still must pay dues. Because workers will receive the benefits negotiated by the union, they must pay their fair share. However, a 1988 Supreme Court ruling upheld union members' claims that although they are forced to pay union dues, those dues must be specifically used for collective bargaining purposes only—not for political lobbying.[13] Additionally, in early 1992, President George Bush extended the same rights to federal-sector employees when he signed into law Executive Order 12800.[14]

The least desirable form of union security, from a union perspective, is the **open shop.** This is an arrangement in which joining a union is totally voluntary. Those who do not join are not required to pay union dues or any associated fees. For workers who do join, there is typically a maintenance of membership clause in the existing contract that dictates certain provisions. Specifically, a maintenance of membership agreement states that should employees join the union, they are compelled to remain in the union for the duration of the existing contract. When the contract expires, most maintenance of membership agreements provide an escape clause—a short interval of time, usually ten days to two weeks—in which employees may choose to withdraw their membership from the union without penalty.

A provision that often exists in union security arrangements is a process called the **dues checkoff.** A dues checkoff occurs when the employer withholds union dues from the members' paychecks. Similar to other pay withholdings, the employer collects the dues money and sends it to the union. There are a number of reasons why employers provide this service, and a reason why the union would permit them to do so. Collecting dues takes time, so a dues checkoff reduces the "downtime" by eliminating the need for the shop steward to go around to collect dues. Furthermore, recognizing that union dues are the primary source of income for the union, having knowledge of how much money there is in the union treasury can provide management with some insight as to whether or not a union is financially strong enough to endure a strike. The Major League Baseball Players' strike fund, for example, exceeded $175 million, allowing players to receive some compensation while on strike.[15] Giving these facts, why would a union agree to such a procedure? Simply, the answer lies in guaranteed revenues! By letting management deduct dues from a member's paycheck, the union is assured of receiving their monies. Excuses from members that they don't have their money, or will pay next week, are eliminated!

Contract Administration

Once a contract is agreed upon and ratified, it must be administered. In terms of **contract administration,** four stages must be carried out. These are: (1) getting the information agreed to out to all union members and management personnel; (2) implementing the contract; (3) interpreting the contract and grievance resolution; and (4) monitoring activities during the contract period.[16]

Information Dissemination In terms of providing information to all concerned, both parties must ensure that changes in contract language are spelled out. For example, the most obvious would be hourly rate changes; HRM must make sure its payroll system is adjusted to the new rates as set in the contract.

HRM *Skills*

Handling a Grievence

1. **Listen to the grievance being filed by an employee.** Although you may feel that the complaint has little merit, or become defensive because it is something directed at you, listen attentively to what the employee says. Ask questions, where necessary, to ensure you fully understand what the employee is grieving.

2. **Investigate the complaint.** Complaints may come in two forms—those that are based in fact, and those that are based in opinion and perceptions. Fully investigate the complaint. This means checking all relevant contract language concerning the issue, and interviewing others who may shed light on the subject. If you are unsure about the contract language, or what you uncover, seek assistance from someone in the labor relations department.

3. **Provide a response to the employee.** After you've fully investigated, and understood the complaint, render your decision. You are either going to find the complaint valid or without merit. If it is a valid complaint, communicate in writing to the employee (and the union) what steps you will take to correct the situation. Remember, too, your labor contract may specify a time frame in which this decision must be given.

4. **Document all activities.** You're not dealing with something here that can be taken lightly. Instead, you're dealing with something that has a legal basis. As such, you must keep meticulous records of what transpired during your part of the process. Every activity of your investigation—from reviewing relevant contract language to interviews with key people—should be documented to show the thorough nature of what you did. If your decision is appealed to a higher level, you'll have accurate data on the steps you took.

5. **Expect the grievance to go to the next step.** The grievance process itself is designed to give the union several avenues to redress its complaint. Just because you found no merit to the complaint, does not mean the union will ultimately accept your decision. Instead, it is likely to appeal it to the next step in the grievance process. That's its right! Accordingly, this adds support for proper documentation of your activities.

Source: Adapted from Stephen P. Robbins, *Supervision Today* (Englewood Cliffs, N.J.: Prentice-Hall, 1995), p. 534–35.

But it goes beyond just pay: Changes in work rules, hours, and the like must be communicated. If both sides agree to mandatory overtime, something that was not in existence before, all must be informed of how it will work.

Neither the union nor the company can simply hand a copy of the contract to each organization member and expect it to be understood. It will be necessary to hold meetings to explain the new terms of the agreement.

Implementing the Contract During this stage of contract administration, the agreement both sides reached is implemented. All communicated changes now take effect, and both sides are expected to comply with the contract terms. One concept to recognize during this phase is something called *management rights.* Typically, management is guaranteed the right to allocate organizational resources in the most efficient manner; to create reasonable rules; to hire, promote, transfer, and discharge employees; to determine work methods and assign work; to create, eliminate, and classify jobs; to lay off employees when necessary; to close or relocate facilities with a sixty-day notice; to institute technological changes, and so forth. Of course, good HRM practices suggest that whether the contract requires it or not, management would be wise to notify the union of major decisions that will influence its membership.

Grievance Procedures and Arbitration   Probably the most important element of contract administration relates to spelling out a procedure for handling contractual disputes.[17] Almost all collective-bargaining agreements contain formal procedures to be used in resolving grievances of the interpretation and application of the contract (see "HRM Skills"). These contracts have provisions for resolving specific, formally initiated grievances by employees concerning dissatisfaction with job-related issues.[18]

Grievance Procedures A complaint-resolving process contained in union contracts.

Grievance procedures are typically designed to resolve grievances as quickly as possible and at the lowest level possible in the organization (see Figure 18-2). The first step almost always has the employee attempt to resolve the grievance with his or her immediate supervisor.[19] If it cannot be resolved at this stage, it is typically discussed with the union steward and the supervisor. Failure at this stage usually brings in the individuals from the organization's industrial relations department and the chief union steward. If the grievance still cannot be resolved, the complaint passes to the facilities' manager, who discusses it typically with the union grievance committee. Unsuccessful efforts at this level give way to the organization's senior management and typically a representative from the national union. Finally, if those efforts are unsuccessful in resolving the grievance, the final step is for it to go to arbitration—called **grievance (rights) arbitration.**

Grievance (Rights) Arbitration Specialized steps followed for handling contractual disputes arising from a collective-bargaining agreement.

In practice, we find that 98 percent of all collective-bargaining agreements provide for grievance (rights) arbitration as the final step to an impasse.[20] Of course, in small organizations these five steps described tend to be condensed,

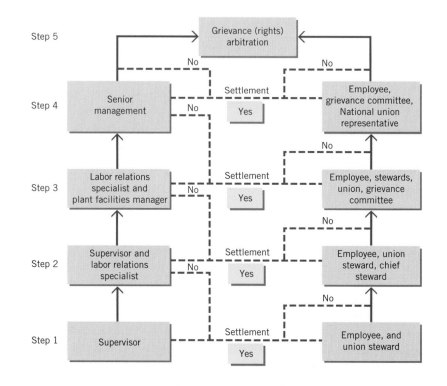

Figure 18-2
A Sample Grievance Process

possibly moving from discussing the grievance with the union steward to taking the grievance directly to the organization's senior executive or owner, and then to arbitration, if necessary.

Monitoring In our discussion of preparation for negotiations, we stated that both company and union need to gather various data. One of the most bountiful data bases for both sides is information kept on a current contract. By monitoring activities, company and union can assess how effective the current contract was, when problem areas or conflicts arose, and what changes might need to be made in subsequent negotiations.

When Agreement Cannot Be Reached

Although the goal of contract negotiations is to achieve an agreement that is acceptable to all concerned parties, sometimes that goal is not achieved. Negotiations do break down, and an impasse occurs. Sometimes these events are triggered by internal issues in the union, the desire to strike against the company, the company's desire to lock out the union, or its knowledge that striking workers can be replaced. Let's explore some of these areas.

Where the Power Lies

In the last chapter, we introduced you to the structure of organized labor in the United States. While that structure represents the overall framework of the union hierarchy, our discussion only briefly addressed the power the local union wields. We would like to take a closer look at local union power and show how it compares to the power of management.

The local union serves as the cornerstone of labor organizations. At the local level, decisions are made regarding which representatives are sent to the national convention, how governance will be established, and whether a contract is to be ratified. The local union holds much of the decision-making power in the union. While not always used to its fullest extent, the local union has, through the union hierarchy, a definite impact on all union activities, including the AFL–CIO.

Figure 18-3 is a graphic representation of the power flow in the labor hierarchy. The power flow for these labor organizations is considered to be "bottom–up"—that is, the power unions have in operating their own organization flows in an upward direction. This means that those at the lowest level in the hierarchy, the locals, generate the power in the union and charge higher levels in

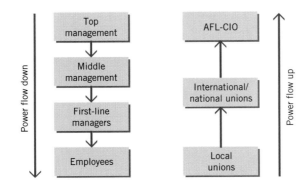

Figure 18-3
Power Flows: Organized Labor
v. Management

the organization (the national union and the AFL–CIO) to carry out their mission. In a sense, the union hierarchy is an inverted pyramid, with the bulk of power resting with the majority of the people, instead of a chosen few. Accordingly, decisions made at the national or, in some cases, at the AFL–CIO level, must reflect the wishes of those in charge. Failure to do so can result in turmoil, or at worst, organizational chaos.

The concept of workers having the power is completely opposite of that in companies. Traditional organization structures of companies follow many of the classic management principles. These principles require the establishment of clear hierarchical relationships and commensurate authority. In contrasting the labor and management structures, it is apparent that in one case the majority is supposed to rule (union), whereas in the other (management) the minority makes the decisions.[21] For the most part, these structures serve their respective organizations well. In unions, it is necessary for the expectations of all members to be heard, and accordingly they must afford all members the opportunity to voice their concerns. In management, running an efficient and effective organization requires clear direction, clear lines of authority and accountability, and good communication flows.

If these particular structures appear appropriate for their respective organizations, why the need to discuss them? Because the balance of power shifts when the employee population of an organization—who typically have no say in activities affecting their work lives—are also unionized. Instead of lacking a voice, these workers have greater power to deal with management over their concerns. In the majority of cases, this relationship with management does not cause a major problem. In situations where a major problem does exist, the power of the two groups often does not mesh, resulting in an impasse.

The critical element of differing structures and power bases can manifest itself during contract negotiations. When one looks at the composition of the negotiating teams from both sides, a fundamental question arises: If both sides are working together to reach a mutual agreement, why do some contracts fail to be ratified? The explanation may revolve around the cast of characters in these negotiations,[22] and their power and authority to "sign" the contract. For all intents and purposes, those involved appear to be the appropriate individuals. However, one element is missing: From management's perspective, the chief negotiator in the private sector generally has the authority to "bind" the company to the agreements reached.

Throughout the negotiations, when the management's spokesperson agrees to any provision of the contract, that mutually agreed-on issue becomes part of the new contract. The union's chief representative serves the will of the members at negotiations. This spokespersons attempts to achieve those gains that the rank and file have charged their leader to obtain. Yet when all is done and the two chief spokespersons appear to have a mutually agreeable contract, it cannot be accepted as a legal document and implemented. In this situation, the tentative contract must be submitted to the rank and file for their approval. If ratification, or rank-and-file approval, is achieved, only then is the contract legal. However, if the rank and file dispose of the contract or any of its terms, it sends notice to the chief spokesperson that negotiations are not over, and must resume.

Strikes versus Lockouts

There are only two possible preliminary outcomes from negotiations. First, and obviously preferable, is agreement. The other alternative, when no viable solution can be found to the parties' differences, is a strike or a lockout.

●

These striking workers are picketing the General Motors plant in Flint, Michigan. At issue is work overload. Through restructuring and delayering efforts, these transmission workers cannot keep up with production demands. To show their dissatisfaction with how negotiations have proceeded on resolving this issue, over 11,500 workers walked-out of this Buick City plant.

There are several types of strikes. The most relevant to contract negotiations is the economic strike. An **economic strike** occurs when the two parties cannot reach a satisfactory agreement before the contract expires. When that deadline passes, the union leadership will typically instruct its members not to work—thus leaving their jobs.[23] Although under today's legal climate, replacement workers can be hired, no disciplinary action can be taken against workers who participate in economic strike activities.

Another form of strike is the **wildcat strike.** A wildcat strike generally occurs when workers walk off the job because of something management has done. For example, if a union employee is disciplined for failure to call in sick according to provisions of the contract, fellow union members may walk off the job to demonstrate their dissatisfaction with management action. It is important to note that these strikes happen while a contract is in force—an agreement that usually prohibits such union activity. Consequently, wildcat strikers can be severely disciplined or terminated.

In the past, the most powerful weapon unions in the private sector had was the economic strike. By striking, the union was, in essence, withholding labor from the employer, thus causing the employer financial hardships. Today, however, the strike weapon is questioned.[24] For instance, the United States lost approximately 1.6 million workdays to strike activity in 1993.[25] Strikes are not only expensive, but public sentiment supporting their use by unions is not very strong. And management hasn't been sitting by idly, for today it is more inclined to replace striking workers.[26] Although strikes fell to a near record low in 1993,[27] worker dissatification over downsizing, pay cut, and the like may increase strike activity during the later half of the 1990s.[28]

In contemporary times, we have also witnessed an increase in management's use of the lockout. A **lockout,** as the name implies, occurs when the organization denies unionized workers access to their jobs during an impasse. A lockout, in some cases, is management's predecessor to hiring replacement workers (see "Ethical Decisions in HRM"). In others, it's management's effort to protect their facilities and machinery, and other employees at the work site.

In either case, the strategy is the same. Both sides are attempting to apply economic pressure to their "opponent" in an effort to sway negotiations in their

Economic Strike An impasse that results from labor and management's ability to agree on the wages, hours, terms, and conditions of a "new" contract.

Wildcat Strike An unauthorized and illegal strike that occurs during the terms of an existing contract.

Lockout A situation in labor–management negotiations whereby management prevents union members from returning to work

Ethical Decisions in HRM:

The Striker Replacement Dilemma

Inherent in collective-bargaining negotiations is an opportunity for either side to generate a power base that may sway negotiations in their favor. For example, when labor shortages exist, or when inventories are in short supply, a strike by the union could have serious ramifications for the company. Likewise, when the situation is reversed, management has the upper hand, and could easily lock out the union to achieve its negotiation's goals. In fact, both the Wagner and Taft–Hartley Acts saw to it that the playing field was to be as fair as possible, by requiring both sides to negotiate in good faith, and permit impasses if they should be warranted.

For decades, this scenario played itself out over and over again. Timing of a contract's expiration proved critical for both sides. For example, in the coal industry, having a contract expire just before the winter months—when coal is needed in greater supply for heating and electricity—worked to the union's advantage, unless the coal companies stockpiled enough coal to carry them through a lengthy winter strike. This game, although serious to both sides, never appeared to be anything more than bargaining strategies; one that could show how serious both sides were. And even though a Supreme Court case from 1938, *NLRB* v. *MacKay Radio,* gave employers the right to hire replacement workers for those engaged in an economic strike, seldom was that used. In fact, often to settle a strike, and for the organization to get back its skilled work force, one stipulation would be that all replacement workers be "let go."

But in the early 1980s, that began to change. When President Ronald Reagan fired striking air-traffic controllers and hired their replacements, businesses began to realize the weapon they had at their disposal. As their union-busting attempts materialized, some organizations, like Caterpillar, the National Football League, and John Deere, realized that using replacement workers could be to their advantage. The union members either came back to work on management's terms, or they simply lost their jobs. Period.

Undoubtedly, in any strike situation, management has the right to keep its doors open, and to keep producing what it sells. Often that may mean using supervisory personnel in place of striking workers, or in some cases, bringing in replacements. But does a law that permits replacement workers undermine the intent of national labor law? Does it create an unfair advantage for management in that it could play hardball just to break the union? Should a striker replacement bill (which would prevent permanent replacement workers from being hired) be passed? Should striking workers' jobs be protected while they exercise their rights under the Wagner Act? What's your opinion?

direction. And when they work, negotiations are said to reach an **impasse.** When that happens, impasse resolution techniques are designed to help.

Impasse Resolution Techniques

When labor and management cannot reach a satisfactory agreement themselves, they may need the assistance of an objective third-party individual. This assistance comes in the form of conciliation and mediation, fact-finding, or interest arbitration.

Conciliation and mediation are two very closely related impasse resolution techniques. Both are techniques whereby a neutral third party attempts to get labor and management to resolve their differences. Under conciliation, however, the role of the third party is to keep the negotiations ongoing. In other words, this individual is a go-between—advocating a voluntary means through which both sides can continue negotiating. Mediation, on the other hand, goes one step further. The mediator attempts to pull together the common ground that exists, and make settlement recommendations for overcoming the barriers that exist between the two sides. A mediator's suggestions, however, are only advisory. That means that the suggestions are not binding on either party. That is why the Federal Mediation and Conciliation Service (FMCS) could not step in and settle the baseball strike. The FMCS representatives could only attempt to keep the two sides meeting, and searching for a possible solution.

Fact-finding is a technique whereby a neutral third-party individual conducts a hearing to gather evidence from both labor and management. The fact-finder then renders a decision as to how he or she views an appropriate settlement. Similar to mediation, the fact-finder's recommendations are only suggestions—they, too, are not binding on either party.

The final impasse resolution technique is called **interest arbitration.** Under interest arbitration, generally a panel of three individuals—one neutral and one each from the union and management—hears testimony from both sides. After the hearing, the panel renders a decision on how to settle the current contract negotiation dispute. If all three members of the panel are unanimous in their decision, that decision may be binding on both parties. Interest arbitration is found more frequently in public-sector collective bargaining; its use in private-sector labor disputes is rare.

The Changing Labor–Management Environment—Are They Becoming More Cooperative?

Several years ago, two researchers described the relationship that existed between unions and management over the decades.[29] They classified the relationship as one that has four distinct quadrants through which the two groups pass (see Figure 18-4). Initially the authors identified a period during which relations between labor and management were classified as **confrontational.** In this quadrant, the two groups opposed one another. The actions of the two were characterized as a "we–they" syndrome. Any gains "we" made came at the expense of "them." Collective bargaining strategies for this phase, then, became a win–lose proposition (distributive bargaining), and lead to such confrontational issues as strikes and lockouts.

As this relationship matured, the groups moved into what was called the **cooperation stage** (integrative bargaining). While the "we–they" syndrome still dominated, reality set in; that is, faced with global competition, changing tech-

Impasse A situation where labor and management cannot reach a satisfactory agreement.

Fact-finder A neutral third-party individual who conducts a hearing to gather evidence and testimony from the parties regarding the differences between them.

Interest Arbitration An impasse resolution technique used to settle contract negotiation disputes.

Confrontational Stage A labor–management relationship characterized as fighting one another.

Cooperation Stage A labor–management relationship characterized as working together on a few specific issues.

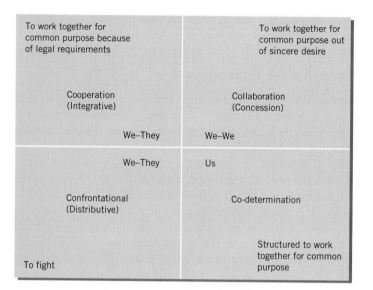

Figure 18-4
Labor–Management
Relationships

nology, and the like, the two groups cooperated with each other to fend off additional problems. For example, while automation has never been a friend to organized labor, unions have had to accept some of it to ensure competitiveness in the workplace. Without such cooperation, survival might have been threatened.

The third phase has been called the **collaboration stage.** Characterized as the "we–we" syndrome, this relationship was built to achieve gains for all concerned. For example, during the early to mid-1980s, unions made significant wage and benefit concessions in an effort to salvage floundering operations. In return for concessions, companies were to provide unions with more input in the decision-making process and other areas once reserved as "management rights." Although continuing debate exists on the success of concession bargaining and changes in management practice, the fact remains that for the first time in U.S. labor history, the two groups begin to think as "one."[30]

The final stage of labor–management relationships is called the **co-determination stage.** In this phase, management and unions act as one unit—or exhibit an "us" syndrome. Although prevalent in some European unions where the company is run by a board of directors comprised of union members, management personnel, and government representatives, this relationship has never materialized in the United States. Whether it could work, given U.S. society and the foundation on which it is built, is beyond the scope of this text.

Although there have been many recent instances of a retrogression toward the confrontational stage, especially with the extensive interest in using striker replacements, we must recognize that continued emphasis on the "we–they" syndrome serves little long-term purpose. Instead, we need to look at instances where cooperation abounds and at the benefits that may be derived from it. For instance, the agreement between General Motors and the UAW at its Saturn plant in Spring Hill, Tennessee, is one example of how progress can be made in the spirit of cooperation.[31] Workers at the Saturn plant are paid a salary rather than the customary hourly rate. Furthermore, union members sit on various decision-making management committees and are protected from any layoffs due to economic downturns.[32] In return, workers are cross-trained in an effort to enhance quality and productivity.

The basis of this Saturn project rests on the concepts of employee involve-

Collaboration Stage A labor–management relationship characterized as working together for a common cause.

Co-determination Stage A labor–management relationship characterized as separate but equal.

Are we returning to days of old in labor-management relationships? Rather than cooperating with one another, labor and management groups, such as the UAW and John Deere, are once again "confronting" each other. Deere management has witnessed the "hardball" tactics used by Caterpillar in their negotiations with the UAW in an effort to get them to accept company demands. As such, Deere is following suit. Although this might work for the Caterpillars and the Deeres of the U.S., is it in the best interest of long-term labor management relationships? Common sense says no, but only time will tell!

ment—employee decision making, teamwork, and collaboration. These concepts were evident when the company and the union delayed their plans to implement a plan to tie 20 percent of workers' pay to the quality and productivity goals set.[33] Even though tying one's wages to productivity has been challenged by unions, such provisions may be warranted for companies to remain competitive in a global marketplace.

Collaborative events such as those at Saturn are not isolated phenomena. Similar efforts have been witnessed in the airlines industry with U.S. Air's efforts to cut labor costs by giving unionized employees equity in the business. Likewise, the United Steelworkers' joint venture with an investment group to resurrect two previously idle Bethlehem Steel plants while giving workers one-fourth ownership reveals that confrontation needn't be the standard protocol![34]

Study Tools and Applications

Summary

This summary relates to the Learning Objectives provided on p. 490.
After reading this chapter, you should know:
1. The objective of collective bargaining is to agree on a contract that is acceptable to management, union representatives, and the union membership.
2. Collective bargaining typically refers to the negotiation, administration, and interpretation of a written agreement between two parties that covers a specific period of time.
3. The collective-bargaining process is comprised of the following steps: preparation for negotiation, negotiation, and contract administration.

4. The role of the grievance procedure is to provide a formal mechanism in labor contracts for resolving issues over the interpretation and application of a contract.
5. The various union security arrangements are the closed shop (made illegal by the Taft–Hartley Act); the union shop, which requires compulsory union membership; the agency shop, which requires compulsory union dues; and the open shop, which enforces workers' freedom of choice to select union membership or not.
6. Power, in organized labor, flows from the bottom to the top; that is, the power vested in labor organizations is at the local union level and flows upward to national unions and the AFL–CIO.
7. An economic strike occurs when labor and management fail to reach an agreement on a new contract, and the old contract expires. Although workers can be replaced during an economic strike, when these workers return to work, they cannot be disciplined for participating in strike activities.
8. The most popular impasse resolution techniques include mediation (a neutral third party informally attempts to get the parties to reach an agreement); fact-finding (a neutral third party conducts a hearing to gather evidence from both sides); and interest arbitration (a panel of individuals hears testimony from both sides and renders a decision).
9. The four-quadrant diagram depicting labor–management relationships consists of confrontation, cooperation, collaboration, and co-determination.

Key Terms

agency shop	grievance (rights) arbitration
co-determination stage	impasse
collaboration stage	integrative bargaining
collective bargaining	interest arbitration
confrontational stage	lockout
contract administration	management rights
cooperation stage	open shop
distributive bargaining	union shop
dues checkoff	union security arrangements
economic strike	wildcat strike
fact-finding	

EXPERIENTIAL EXERCISE:

Third-Party Conflict Resolution

Purpose

1. To understand the criteria that third parties use when they intervene and attempt to resolve others' conflicts.
2. To practice mediation skills as a mechanism for resolving conflict between others.

Introduction

In addition to being involved in their own conflicts, managers are often called upon to intervene and to settle conflicts between other people. The two activities in this section are designed to explore how third parties may enter conflicts for the purpose of resolving them, and to practice one very effective approach to intervention. In the first activity, you will read about a manager who has a problem deciding how to intervene in a dispute.

Procedure

Step 1: Individually, read the following scenario.

THE SEATCOR MANUFACTURING COMPANY

You are senior vice-president of operations and chief operating officer of Seatcor, a major producer of office furniture. Joe Gibbons, your subordinate, is vice-president and general manager of your largest desk-assembly plant. Joe has been with Seatcor for thirty-eight years and is two years away from retirement. He worked his way up through the ranks to his current position and has successfully operated his division for five years with a marginally competent staff. You are a long-standing personal friend of Joe's and respect him a great deal. However, you have always had an uneasy feeling that Joe has surrounded himself with minimally competent people by his own choice. In some ways, you think he is threatened by talented assistants.

Last week you were having lunch with Charles Stewart, assistant vice-president and Joe's second-in-command. Upon your questioning, it became clear that he and Joe were engaged in a debilitating feud. Charles was hired last year, largely at your insistence. You had been concerned for some time about who was going to replace Joe when he retired, especially given the lack of really capable managerial talent on Joe's staff. Thus, you prodded Joe to hire your preferred candidate—Charles Stewart. Charles is relatively young, 39, extremely tenacious and bright, and a well-trained business school graduate. From all reports he is doing a good job in his new position.

Your concern centers around a topic that arose at the end of your lunch. Charles indicated Joe Gibbons is in the process of completing a five-year plan for his plant. This plan is to serve as the basis for several major plant reinvestment and reorganization decisions that would be proposed to senior management. According to Charles, Joe Gibbons has not included Charles in the planning process at all. You had to leave lunch quickly and were unable to get much more information from Charles. However, he did admit that he was extremely disturbed by this exclusion and that his distress was influencing his work and probably his relationship with Joe.

You consider this a very serious problem. Charles will probably have to live with the results of any major decisions about the plant. More important, Joe's support is essential if Charles is to properly grow into his present and/or future job. Joe, on the other hand, runs a good ship and you do not want to upset him or undermine his authority. Moreover, you know Joe has good judgment; thus, he might have a good reason for what he is doing.

Step 2

Decide for yourself how you would proceed to handle this issue. (Hint: Assume you were the senior vice-president of operations. Exactly what would you do in this situation regarding the conflict between Joe and Charles? Also, why would you take this action—i.e., what are your primary objectives by intervening in this way?

Step 3

In groups of three to five students, compare your individual responses to Step 2, and develop a group response to the scenario.

Step 4

Each group will present its solution to the rest of the class.

Step 5

Answer the following questions: How much agreement was there within the class about the way that the senior vice-president should approach the problem? How did this compare with your own preferred strategy?

Source: Based on "Third Party Conflict Resolution" in Roy J. Lewicki, Donald D. Bowen, Douglas T. Hall, and Francine S. Hall, *Experiences in Management and Organizational Behavior* (New York: John Wiley, 1988), pp. 107–10. Used with permission.

CASE APPLICATION:

Caterpillar and the UAW

Caterpillar, manufacturers of large earth-moving equipment, faced a long-term strike when it broke off negotiations with the United Automobile Workers (UAW), which represented its unionized work force. Yet Caterpillar did not appear to be overly concerned about a strike; in fact, top management viewed the strike as being advantageous to the company. That was because the construction industry had been in a deep recession, and the company had plenty of inventory to carry it through a long strike.[35] Don Fites, CEO of Caterpillar, Inc., also viewed the strike as a means of reducing the size of Caterpillar's work force.[36] Furthermore, those striking workers who stayed off the job would just be replaced, because the law permitted the company to permanently replace their striking employees.

Initially, in a situation like this, emotions on both sides run high. Yet, from the union standpoint, something went amiss in these negotiations. Union members began crossing the picket line, going back to work without a contract. The bottom line for many of those who crossed the picket line was simple: If they didn't go back, Caterpillar would permanently replace them on the job. Faced with this dilemma, the UAW agreed that as many of its members as the company wanted would return to work if the company would stop hiring replacements. As a result, about 12,000 workers returned to their jobs, ending almost a six-month walk-out.

Caterpillar used their threats and advantages to get the UAW to accept terms that were more favorable to the company, including elimination of certain job classifications and plant modernization.[37] In fact, this is the first time since 1948 that Caterpillar's workers have worked without a contract. Wages, job security, and health insurance are still points of contention between the two groups, but there appears to be little movement. After all, the company knows that it can, and will, replace these workers if they go out again. Maybe that's why the standard uniform of Caterpillar workers is a bright red shirt with white lettering, boldly demanding "Permanently Replace Fites."[38]

Questions

1. Describe the relationship at Caterpillar in terms of the four quadrant diagram found in Figure 18-4. In what category would you place this relationship? Explain.
2. Is the threat of striker replacements dismantling years of cooperation between unions and management? Explain your position.
3. Why do you think the unionized workers at Caterpillar would work without a contract? Do you think that this may ultimately be a ploy to finally bust the UAW at Caterpillar? Discuss.

How well did you fulfill the learning objectives?

1. Issues that appear consistently throughout labor contracts are all of the following except
   a. wages.
   b. hours.
   c. grievance procedure.
   d. terms and conditions of employment.
   e. technology transfer.

2. Government is involved in labor negotiations in all of the following ways except
   a. to intervene if an impasse undermines the nation's well-being.
   b. to provide financial backing for the negotiators.
   c. to provide the rules under which labor and management bargain.
   d. to provide a watchful eye on the two parties to make sure the rules are followed.
   e. to intervene if an agreement on acceptable terms cannot be reached.

3. Management should gather all of the following internal information before collective bargaining negotiation except
   a. grievance and accident records.
   b. employee performance reports.
   c. cost-of-living changes.
   d. transfer, absenteeism, and turnover information.
   e. overtime figures.

4. Union contract negotiation
   a. is the attempt to get management's highest offer to approximate the lowest demands that the union is willing to accept.
   b. is conducted in public.
   c. begins with a written formal agreement and proceeds to verbal discussions of final details.
   d. is increasingly accompanied by union strikes.
   e. is most successful when a lockout results.

5. The concept of management rights typically includes all of the following except
   a. to create, eliminate, and classify jobs.
   b. to relocate facilities as needed with no advance warnings.
   c. to hire, promote, and transfer employees.
   d. to allocate organizational resources in the most efficient manner.
   e. to create reasonable rules.

6. Marti works for a company that has a union. She has refused, on religious grounds, to join the union. She must choose between forfeiting her job or paying a sum of money equal to union dues to the union to continue her employment. Marti works in a(n)
   a. closed shop.
   b. union shop.
   c. agency shop.
   d. open shop.
   e. right-to-work shop.

7. A professional sports players' union has been trying to negotiate a new contract with the team owners through most of the off-season. Preseason play is scheduled to begin next week. The parties have agreed to have a panel of three individuals—a player, an owner, and a neutral third party—hear testimony and render a decision about how to settle the contract dispute. If the three panel members agree, the decision will be binding on the players and the owners. What kind of impasse resolution technique is being used?
   a. lockout
   b. grievance arbitration
   c. fact-finding
   d. interest arbitration
   e. mediation

8. A city high school teachers' union has refused so far to sign a new three-year contract. The wages, vacations, and retirement plans are acceptable, but the teachers are holding out for approval to purchase, at school expense, and to carry with them into the classroom, semi-automatic weapons. The superintendent of schools is adamant about the effectiveness of new metal detectors in reducing student weapons, and says that such weapons must be paid for by the teachers themselves. School is supposed to start in two weeks, and so far, the only impasse resolution attempted was when the chief of police tried, informally, to get the teachers and the superintendent to resolve their differences by jointly purchasing used weapons from the police department, at cost. What technique was being used?
   a. lockout
   b. grievance arbitration
   c. fact-finding
   d. interest arbitration
   e. mediation

9. Which of the following statements is true regarding the power structures in unions and traditional bureaucratic organizations?
   a. Power flow is top down in unions. Power flow is bottom up in traditional bureaucratic organizations.
   b. Power in the union rests in the AFL–CIO governing body. Power in traditional bureaucratic organizations rests in the employees.
   c. With majority rule in the unions, all workers are given the opportunity to express their opinions. With minority rule in traditional bureaucratic organizations, effective and efficient performance requires clear direction and clear hierarchical lines of accountability and authority.
   d. Classic management principles consistently explain the power structures in both unions and traditional bureaucratic organizations.
   e. Classic management principles are not applicable to the power structures of either unions or traditional bureaucratic organizations.

511

10. Why are union contracts not ratified by union members after they have been negotiated?
   a. The negotiation process is considered binding on union members.
   b. The union representative doesn't carry the authority of all the union members to the bargaining table.
   c. Management participation is not considered binding during the negotiation process.
   d. Usually, arbitrators have to become involved in the negotiation process.
   e. Usually, grievances have to be handled during the negotiation process.

11. Collective bargaining for Berkeley Local 43202 traditionally proceeds from the mentality that the union and management are necessary partners in the success of the business. For example, two union members sit on the board of directors and strategic planning includes union members. The union does not strike. In fact, the union helps the company support lobbying efforts on behalf of the industry. What kind of relationship is evident in this union?
   a. confrontational   b. cooperation
   c. collaboration   d. co-determination
   e. co-dependency

12. Collective bargaining for Buffalo Local 131 traditionally proceeds from the mentality that although the union and management generally have opposing interests, the union must make some concessions to management, in the name of progress, to survive. For example, last year they agreed to change from typewriters to word processors because the work rate was so low that the firm was no longer competitive. What kind of relationship is evident in this union?
   a. confrontational   b. cooperation
   c. collaboration   d. co-determination
   e. co-dependency

13. A union security arrangement is
   a. a means to ensure some consistency in income.
   b. a way to keep the press out of union negotiation meetings.
   c. designed to prevent access of organized crime to union files.
   d. a cooperative venture between workers and managers.
   e. part of the health and safety provisions in most new union contracts.

14. John was hired last week as a fry cook at a fast-food restaurant. After he successfully completes his thirty-day probationary period, he must either join the union or forfeit his job. John is working in a(n)
   a. closed shop.   b. union shop.
   c. agency shop.   e. right-to-work shop.
   d. open shop.

15. Collective bargaining for Bristol Local 7 traditionally proceeds from the mentality that the union and management have to work on the same side. For example, when the company had to cut its operating costs by 40 percent a few years ago, the union took a hefty pay cut and gave up substantial benefits for a period of time to help with the cost containment measures. What kind of relationship is evident in this union?
   a. confrontational   b. cooperation
   c. collaboration   d. co-determination
   e. co-dependency

16. Mike works in a florist shop that has a union, although he has chosen not to join it. His job is not contingent on union membership. Mike works in a(n)
   a. closed shop.   b. union shop.
   c. agency shop.   d. open shop.
   e. right-to-work shop.

17. Workers in an automotive plant are threatening to burn the plant. Their union contract calls for 12 percent pay raises each year for the three years of the contract. However, for the last two years management has given them only 2 percent a year increases, citing disastrous sales and earnings figures and potential bankruptcy as the reason. Last week, one of the union members read an article in a business weekly that announced the quarterly earnings for the firm: "10th Straight Record-Setting Quarter" read the headline. The article went on to announce a doubling of executive salaries, for the third time in two years. The union steward has suggested that, before burning the buildings, they let a third party try to resolve the wage dispute under terms of the existing contract. The issue completed its way through the grievance process of the company this morning. What kind of impasse resolution technique is being used?
   a. lockout   b. grievance arbitration
   c. fact-finding   d. interest arbitration
   e. mediation

18. A secretaries' union has been trying to negotiate a new contract with management for ninety days. The old contract expires in two weeks. To resolve the contract negotiation disputes, a third party has been hired to gather evidence from both the secretaries and the managers and present the findings to both parties. The recommendation will not be binding on either party. What kind of impasse resolution technique is being used?
   a. lockout   b. grievance arbitration
   c. fact-finding   d. interest arbitration
   e. mediation

Appendix A:

MAKING A GOOD FIRST IMPRESSION — WRITING YOUR RESUME

One of the most trying and stressful situations that individuals face occurs when they begin the process of applying for a job. This is in part because there are no specific guidelines to follow to ensure success. However, we can offer some tips that could increase your chances of finding employment. Even though getting to the interview stage is a goal we all desire when we seek employment, obtaining that opportunity is not easy. As a rough guideline, expect the following:

100 targeted resumes, lead to
10 job interviews, which lead to
1 job offer.

Now, don't hold us to these numbers; they are merely a rule of thumb. The point, though, is that competition for jobs is fierce. Even so, there are things you can do to help increase your odds. After you have given some thought to your employment goals (e.g., what type of work you want to do—sales, HRM, accounting), start your job hunt early. Give yourself at least seven to nine months' lead time; that is, if you are looking for a job after graduation (May), you should begin your job search sometime around September of your senior year. You may not need the entire time, but you don't want to wait until March to begin, either.

How is starting early helpful? In two ways: First, it shows that you are taking an interest and that you are planning. You are not waiting until the last minute to begin, and this reflects favorably on a candidate. Second, this period coincides with companies' recruiting cycles. If you wait until March to start, some job openings may have already been filled. For specific information regarding the company recruiting cycles in your area, visit your career development center, which should be able to give you helpful information.

Our discussion so far has centered on getting to the interview. But let's digress for a moment. Before you go to an interview, you should have some information that reflects positively on your strengths. This information is circulated in a resume.

No matter who you are or where you are in your career, you will need a current resume. Your resume is typically the only information source that a recruiter will use in determining whether to grant you an interview. Therefore, it must be a sales tool; it must give accurate information that supports your candidacy, highlights your strengths, and differentiates you from others. Identifying these strengths can take a long time, but you must give them much thought and express them in ways that speak well of you. The information in the resume must also be listed in a way that is easy to read. An example of the type of information that should be included is shown in Figure A-1. It is important to pinpoint a few key themes regarding resumes that may seem like common sense. First of all, your resume must be printed on a quality printer. The style of font should be easy to read (e.g., Courier type font). Avoid any style that may be

Figure A-1
Sample Resume

CONFIDENTIAL RESUME OF:	CHRIS CONNOLLY
	21 Main Street
	Anywhere, USA 10001
	682-555-0028 (residence)
	682-555-8000 (work)

CAREER OBJECTIVE: Challenging opportunity to combine multidisciplinary skills of finance and management in a dynamic international environment.

EDUCATION: State University
B.S., Business Administration, May 1996.

EXPERIENCE:
5/94 to present   Westinghouse Electronics
Financial Analyst Assistant
Primary Functions
Responsible for developing monthly financial statements, analyzing payroll data, and reconciling corporate bank statements. Serving as finance department liaison to the HRM Compensation Committee.

8/92 to 5/94   Anywhere Recreation Council
Program Leader
Primary Functions:
Responsible for designing, planning, implementing, and evaluating recreational programs for teens aged 12–14. Responsible for a budget of $4,000. Three assistant staff members supervised.

SPECIAL SKILLS: Fluent in Spanish and Japanese; Computer-literate in word processing, database management, and spreadsheet applications.

SERVICE ACTIVITIES: President, Student Government Association; Student Representative, Faculty Senate; Hugger, Special Olympics.

REFERENCES: Furnished on request.

Figure A-2
Sample Resume with a Font Change

515

Appendix A:
Making a Good First
Impression—Writing Your
Resume
●

Confidential *Resume of:*	*Chris Connolly* *21 Main Street* *Anywhere, USA 10001* *682-555-0028 (residence)* *682-555-8000 (work)*
Career Objective:	*Challenging opportunity to combine multidisciplinary skills of finance and management in a dynamic international environment.*
Education:	*State University* *B.S., Business Administration, May 1996.*
Experience: *5/94 to present*	*Westinghouse Electronics* *Financial Analyst Assistant* *Primary Functions* *Responsible for developing monthly financial statements, analyzing payroll data, and reconciling corporate bank statements. Serving as finance department liaison to the HRM Compensation Committee.*
8/92 to 5/94	*Anywhere Recreation Council* *Program Leader* *Primary Functions:* *Responsible for designing, planning, implementing, and evaluating recreational programs for teens aged 12–14. Responsible for a budget of $4,000. Three assistant staff members supervised.*
Special Skills:	*Fluent in Spanish and Japanese; computer-literate in word processing, database management, and spreadsheet applications.*
Service Activities:	*President, Student Government Association; Student Representative, Faculty Senate; Hugger, Special Olympics.*
References:	*Furnished on request.*

hard on the eyes, such as a script or italics font. Look at the resume in Figure A-2. It contains exactly the same information as Figure A-1, but what a difference! A recruiter who must review two hundred resumes a day is not going to strain to read the script type; valuable information may not come across. So, use an easy-to-read font and make the recruiter's job easier.

It is also important to note that some companies today are using computer scanners to make the first pass through resumes. In a matter of moments, computers can be programmed to scan each resume for specific information like key job elements, experience, work history, education, or technical expertise.[1] The use of scanners, then, has created two important aspects for resume writing.[2] The computer matches key words in a job description. Thus, in creating a resume, typical job description phraseology should be used. Additionally (and this goes back to the issue of font type), the font used should be easily read by the scanner. If it can't, your resume may be put in the rejection file.

Your resume should be copied on good-quality paper (no off-the-wall colors—use standard white or cream). There are many definitions of good-quality paper, but you can't go wrong with a 20-bond-weight paper that has some cotton content (about 20 percent). Don't send standard duplicating paper—it looks as if you are mass-mailing resumes. (You probably are mass-mailing resumes—especially if you follow the "100 resumes" rule of thumb—but don't make it obvious.) To get your resume in order, typed, and copied on good-quality paper, you should expect to spend about $40 (excluding envelope and postage costs). Typing costs about $4 per page, and the paper (including copying) will cost about $20. The cost might seem an expense you would rather not incur, but remember that your competition is probably doing it—if you have to spend a few dollars to make a few copies, consider it a wise investment.

The last point on resumes, one that shouldn't have to be mentioned, relates to proofreading. Because the resume is the only representation of you the recruiter has, a sloppy resume can be deadly. If it contains misspelled words or is grammatically incorrect, your chances for an interview will be significantly reduced. Proofread your resume, and if possible, let others proofread it, too.

In addition to your resume, you need a cover letter. Your cover letter should contain information that tells the recruiter why you should be considered for the job. The cover letter should not be an "oversell" letter, but one that highlights your greatest strengths and indicates how these strengths can be useful to the company. Your cover letter should also contain some information citing why the organization getting your resume is of interest to you. Cover letters must be tailored to the organization; letters should be originals, not copies of a "To Whom It May Concern." One of the biggest turnoffs a recruiter may experience in reviewing resumes is the "To Whom It May Concern" letter. This tells the recruiter that you are on a fishing expedition and are sending out hundreds of resumes. This situation does not help your job hunting. A much greater impact is made when you write to a specific person. You might not have the recruiter's name and title, but with some work you can get it. Use whatever resources you can. Telephone the company in question and ask for it; most receptionists in human resources will give out the recruiter's name and title. If you just can't get a name, go to the library and locate a copy of the *Standard and Poor's Register Manual,* which lists the names and titles of companies' officers. If everything else fails, send your resume to one of the officers, preferably the officer in charge of HRM or administration, or to the president. This is much better than "To Whom It May Concern."

We won't belabor the point about typing and proofreading the cover letter except to say that it also must be impeccable. Finally, sign each letter individually. A real signature has a better effect than a duplicated one.

Appendix B:

THE CRITICAL MEETING — IMPROVING INTERVIEW SKILLS

If you are fortunate to have made it through the initial screening process, chances are good that you may be called in for an interview. Although you may be excited, some caution is in order. Remember that interviews play a critical role in determining whether you will get the job. Up to now, all the recruiter has seen is your well-polished resume. In the following paragraphs, we'd like to offer some suggestions on how to increase your chances of making it through the interview. Although we'll address the initial interview with the recruiter, realize that multiple interviews are the norm rather than the exception; that is, getting through the recruiter is only stage one of an interview. Should you meet the recruiter's expectations, you can expect to be interviewed by at least two other people. These individuals are the manager of the area in which you will work and typically the senior management official in the division. Although this final interview is mostly protocol, keep in mind that no final decision will be made unless you get passing grades from all who interview you. Let's look at some ways of achieving that goal.

First of all, do some homework. If you haven't already done so in your search of whom to send resumes, go to your library and get as much information as possible on the organization. Don't fall into the trap one applicant did when he didn't even know what IBM stood for. Gather as much data as possible, so you sound like you know a bit about the company. This will be time well spent, as it creates a perception of you as an individual who is taking charge. Many an interviewer may look at you favorably if you have read about a recent company venture in such publications as *Business Week, Fortune,* or *The Wall Street Journal.* In fact, the job you may be interviewing for may be directly related to that venture. So, go to the interview prepared!

517

The night before the interview, get a good night's rest. Eat a good breakfast to build your energy level, as the day's events will be grueling. As you prepare for the interview, keep in mind that your appearance is going to be the first impression you make. Dress appropriately. Even though appearance is not supposed to enter into the hiring decision, it does make an impression. In fact, one study suggests that 80 percent of the interviewer's perception of you in the interview comes from his or her initial perception of you, based primarily on your appearance and body language.[1] Therefore, dress appropriately and be meticulous in your attire.

Arrive at the interview location early. We don't mean two hours early, but about thirty minutes ahead of your scheduled interview. It is better for you to wait than to have to contend with something unexpected, like a traffic jam, that could make you late. Arriving early also gives you an opportunity to survey the office environment and possibly gather some clues about the organization. For instance, if the atmosphere is friendly and cheerful, this may indicate that the organization puts considerable emphasis on employee satisfaction. Again, any "hint" you can pick up to increase your chances, you should use. As you meet the recruiter, give him or her a firm handshake. Make good eye contact, and maintain it throughout the interview. Remember, your body language may be giving away secrets about you that you don't want an interviewer to pick up. Sit erect and maintain good posture.

At this point, you are probably as nervous as you have ever been. While this is natural, try your best to relax. Recruiters know you'll be anxious, and a good one will try to put you at ease. Being prepared for an interview can also help build confidence and reduce the nervousness. You can start building that confidence by reviewing a set of questions most frequently asked by interviewers. You can obtain a copy of these typically through the career development office of your college. More important, however, since you may be asked these questions, you should begin to develop responses to them. But let's add a word of caution here. The best advice we can give is to be yourself. Don't go into an interview with a prepared text and recite it from memory; have an idea of what you would like to say, but don't rely on verbatim responses. They will only frustrate you when you lose your place and may ultimately make you look foolish.

You should try to go through several "practice" interviews if possible. Universities often have career days on campus, when recruiters from companies are on-site to interview students. Take advantage of them. Even if the job does not fit what you want, the process will at least serve to help you become more skilled at dealing with interviews. You can also practice with family, friends, career counselors, student groups to which you belong, or your faculty advisor.

There's another issue that should be considered with respect to interviewing. You must be prepared to deal with the stress, or pressure interview, and interviews in which potentially discriminatory questions are asked.[2] The point of these tactics is to "see how you react when you're pressured and to test your professionalism and confidence."[3] These questions may appear rude, or even demeaning. But remember, they are designed to "rattle" you.[4] If you lose control, chances of a job offer are slim!

When the interview ends, thank the interviewer for his or her time, and for giving you this opportunity to talk about your qualifications. But don't think that "selling" yourself has stopped there. As soon as you get home, type a thank-you letter and send it to the recruiter. You'd be amazed at how many people fail to do this! This little act of courtesy carries a big impact—use it to your advantage. Then sit back and wait to see what happens.

We have tried to convey our experience with this process in the hope that it will help you in your interview. It takes long and hard work to get a job. But you needn't do it alone. Visit your school's career placement office, whose professionals can help you work through all aspects of the selection process and give you a lot of supporting information. Consider getting a job your job! It's not an easy task, but it will be time well spent if you achieve your ultimate goal—employment.

Appendix C:

KEEPING ABREAST IN THE FIELD: RESEARCH IN HRM

Among practicing managers, the term *research* frequently carries the connotation of academic "mumbo jumbo" or irrelevant findings that have little generalizability to practice. While this may sometimes be true, it need not be so. The research process and the findings it generates can provide valuable information to a manager. When we use the term *research*, we mean a systematic, goal-oriented investigation of facts that seeks to establish a relationship between two or more phenomena. Most of the conclusions presented throughout this book are based on systematic, goal-oriented research. For instance, in our discussion on selection, we presented the assessment center as an effective procedure for identifying high performers. This statement is not based on casual observation or intuition, but rather on a number of research studies, the results of which led us to our conclusion.

Research, however, is not the sole province of scientists and academicians. Keeping up-to-date in one's field is becoming a necessity. To that end, every effective manager should consider research—particularly human resources research—a mandatory and ongoing part of the job.

Why Research in HRM?

Research can lead to an increased understanding of and improvement in HRM practices. The following is a small sample of topics that can be better understood through HRM research.

Work-force diversity
The contingent work force
Wage surveys
Effectiveness of various recruitment sources
International HRM

Test validation
Health and wellness programs
Effectiveness of training efforts
Supervisor's effectiveness survey
Development of weighted application blanks
Recent community labor settlements
Recent industry labor settlements
Recent labor settlements negotiated by our union
Workplace Violence
Health Insurance Reform

This list suggests that HRM research can provide insights for managers as they attempt to increase employee productivity and satisfaction while reducing absence and turnover. For instance, research findings make managers aware of changes. The department manager who annually surveys her employees' attitudes about their work, her supervisory practices, and the organization in general will develop long-term data allowing her to assess changes in her employees' perception of the organization's climate. Research can also identify potential problem areas. If our department manager notes an unexpected drop in her employees' satisfaction with a certain element of their work, she can take rapid action to correct it, preferably before it leads to resignations, increased absenteeism, shoddy workmanship, or some similarly undesirable outcome.

Managers derive other positive benefits from engaging in research. Managers who keep current with what other managers are doing, and with the latest HRM concepts and practices, increase the probability that they will be more effective. In fact, engaging in some type of research into what is happening in the HRM discipline can be viewed as necessary for one's survival as a manager over the long term. Research also can help managers determine the success of programs—such as training and development programs—for which they bear responsibility. For example, research can help determine whether a program's benefits exceed its costs.

We should also remember that some of the research findings presented in a book such as this are not generalizable to all situations. Research studies on the motivation needs of unionized automobile workers in Detroit, for example, may have little practical application to someone managing a group of nonunionized civil engineers working for the New Hampshire Department of Highways. Therefore, a manager should understand the appropriate methodology or approach for engaging in primary research. Such research can provide answers to the unique issues and problems that managers face in their specific environment.

Secondary Sources: Where to Look It Up

As we have noted, a manager's long-term survival may depend on staying current. We propose, therefore, that every manager should aim, at a minimum, to keep abreast in the field. What sources should a manager look to in order to keep up with the latest findings in HRM? The answer to that question depends on the level of sophistication desired. Research journals are directed to different audiences. Some journals assume the reader has a solid background in statistics and research methodology; their articles contain more details but are more difficult to read. Other journals are meant to be read quickly; their articles are condensed and simplified. The type of journal you read depends on what you are looking for.

The following two lists cover the major sources in HRM. We have separated the more academic or rigorous sources from the nontechnical (those focusing on translating the academic research into practical application).

Technical Journals	Nontechnical Journals
Academy of Management Journal	*Academy of Management Review*
Behavioral Science	*Across the Board*
Human Relations	*Arbitration Journal*
Human Organization	*Business Horizons*
Industrial Relations	*Entrepreneur*
Industrial and Labor Relations Review	*Inc.*
Journal of Social Psychology	*Industry Week*
Journal of Industrial Relations	*HRMagazine*
Journal of Organizational Psychology	*Training*
Journal of Vocational Behavior	*Training and Development Journal*
Journal of Business Research	*Working Woman*
Journal of Human Resources	
Journal of Applied Behavioral Science	
Journal of Applied Psychology	
Organizational Behavior and Human Decision Processes	
Personnel Psychology	
Psychological Bulletin	

In addition to the journals we have listed, other secondary sources include books, government publications, and research reports from organizations such as the American Management Association, Society for Human Resources Management, American Society for Training and Development, The Bureau of National Affairs, Commerce Clearing House, and the National Conference Board.

Answers to Testing Your Understanding

The answers to the questions posed, and the location of where the correct response can be found, are presented below.

Chapter 1
1. b p. 4
2. d p. 4
3. e p. 8
4. d p. 8
5. a p. 11
6. b p. 12
7. a p. 15
8. c p. 15
9. b p. 15
10. a p. 16
11. c p. 18
12. a p. 19
13. d p. 23
14. d p. 24
15. d p. 3
16. a p. 15
17. b p. 17
18. a p. 19

Chapter 2
1. e p. 33
2. b p. 35
3. b p. 56
4. e p. 33
5. c p. 35
6. d p. 38
7. c p. 35
8. a p. 36
9. e p. 36
10. d p. 39
11. c p. 42
12. e p. 42
13. b p. 45
14. d p. 48

Chapter 3
1. b p. 66
2. c p. 66
3. a p. 67
4. a p. 68
5. c p. 68
6. b p. 68
7. b p. 71
8. d p. 72
9. c p. 73
10. d p. 75
11. c p. 76

Chapter 4
1. c p. 96
2. a p. 97
3. d p. 97
4. a p. 98
5. b p. 98
6. d p. 98
7. b p. 99
8. a p. 99
9. c p. 104
10. d p. 110

Chapter 5
1. c p. 128
2. d p. 135
3. d p. 128
4. a p. 130
5. d p. 136
6. b p. 137
7. c p. 138
8. c p. 139
9. b p. 142
10. d p. 142
11. e p. 143
12. d p. 149

Chapter 6
1. d p. 159
2. d p. 158
3. e p. 160
4. c p. 166
5. a p. 168
6. e p. 170
7. b p. 160
8. b p. 161
9. a p. 172
10. a p. 178
11. d p. 179
12. b p. 181
13. d p. 158
14. c p. 177

Chapter 7
1. d p. 191
2. b p. 192
3. b p. 195
4. a p. 197
5. d p. 195
6. c p. 197
7. e p. 201
8. c p. 205
9. a p. 206
10. e p. 207
11. c p. 208
12. d p. 208
13. b p. 191
14. c p. 191

Chapter 8
1. c p. 219
2. b p. 217
3. a p. 220
4. c p. 218
5. d p. 218
6. b p. 222
7. d p. 224
8. c p. 228
9. a p. 230
10. e p. 231
11. b p. 218
12. e p. 224
13. d p. 224

Chapter 9
1. b p. 237
2. d p. 238
3. c p. 239
4. d p. 240
5. d p. 242
6. c p. 244
7. a p. 252
8. b p. 248
9. a p. 248
10. d p. 249
11. c p. 251
12. d p. 259
13. a p. 255
14. c p. 256

Chapter 10
1. e p. 266
2. c p. 267
3. a p. 269
4. d p. 268
5. c p. 268
6. d p. 273
7. c p. 276
8. a p. 277
9. b p. 277
10. a p. 278
11. d p. 282
12 c p. 278
13. d p. 281
14. a p. 267

Chapter 11
1. a p. 296
2. e p. 296
3. b p. 297
4. e p. 298
5. b p. 300

6. c p. 301
7. a p. 304
8. b p. 308
9. b p. 309
10. e p. 311
11. e p. 296
12. b p. 297
13. c p. 300
14. c p. 297
15. b p. 297

Chapter 12
1. e p. 321
2. c p. 322
3. b p. 329
4. e p. 333
5. c p. 334
6. a p. 336
7. e p. 338
8. d p. 340
9. a p. 341
10. b p. 344
11. c p. 322
12. a p. 323
13. b p. 328
14. e p. 333
15. d p. 334

Chapter 13
1. e p. 352
2. c p. 353
3. d p. 354
4. c p. 355
5. d p. 361
6. a p. 366
7. b p. 366
8. a p. 368
9. c p. 369
10. b p. 371
11. d p. 374
12. a p. 374
13. e p. 354
14. a p. 354
15. d p. 355
16. b p. 375

Chapter 14
1. c p. 382
2. c p. 395
3. b p. 387
4. a p. 393
5. b p. 395
6. c p. 398

7. d   p. 398
8. b   p. 399
9. d   p. 401
10. a   p. 404

Chapter 15
1. d   p. 414
2. c   p. 417
3. e   p. 417
4. b   p. 421
5. a   p. 422
6. e   p. 425
7. d   p. 431
8. b   p. 434
9. a   p. 426
10. b   p. 417
11. a   p. 421
12. c   p. 424

Chapter 16
1. a   p. 445
2. c   p. 446
3. d   p. 447
4. a   p. 447

5. b   p. 448
6. d   p. 450
7. c   p. 455
8. a   p. 458
9. b   p. 459
10. e   p. 445
11. b   p. 446
12. a   p. 448
13. b   p. 447
14. d   p. 448

Chapter 17
1. a   p. 465
2. b   p. 466
3. e   p. 467
4. c   p. 468
5. a   p. 469
6. e   p. 471
7. d   p. 473
8. c   p. 474
9. e   p. 475
10. a   p. 478
11. b   p. 481
12. a   p. 465

13. b   p. 466
14. e   p. 467
15. c   p. 470
16. d   p. 470

Chapter 18
1. e   p. 493
2. b   p. 494
3. c   p. 494
4. a   p. 495
5. b   p. 496
6. c   p. 497
7. d   p. 505
8. e   p. 505
9. c   p. 501
10. b   p. 502
11. d   p. 506
12. b   p. 505
13. a   p. 497
14. b   p. 497
15. c   p. 506
16. d   p. 497
17. b   p. 500
18. c   p. 505

Chapter 1

1. Based on *Summarized Results of HRI's 1994 Annual Survey of Issues Impacting Human Resources Management* (St. Petersburg, Fla.: Human Resource Institute, 1994); and Commerce Clearing House, Human Resources Management, *Ideas and Trends* (May 25, 1994), p. 85.
2. Benjamin Schneder, "The People Make the Place," *Personnel Psychology,* Vol. 40, No. 3 (Autumn 1987), p. 437.
3. For a comprehensive overview of Management, see Stephen P. Robbins and David A. De Cenzo, *Fundamentals of Management* (Englewood Cliffs, N.J.: Prentice Hall, 1995), Ch. 1. It is also worth noting that changes in the world of work reveal that these work functions may no longer be just the purview of managers, but instead, be part of every worker's job responsibility.
4. While no specific date is identified regarding the "birth" of personnel departments, the generally accepted inception of personnel was in the early 1900s in the BF Goodrich Company.
5. They were seen as performing relatively unimportant activities. In fact, the personnel department was often seen as an "employee graveyard"—a place to send employees who were past their prime and couldn't do much damage.
6. See, for example, Augustine A. Lado, and Mary C. Wilson, "Human Resource Systems and Sustained Competitive Advantage: A Competency-Based Perspective," *Academy of Management Review,* Vol. 19, No. 4 (1994), pp. 699–727.
7. Jeffrey Pfeffer, "Producing Sustainable Competitive Advantage Through the Effective Management of People," *Academy of Management Executive,* Vol. 9, No. 1 (1995), p. 55.
8. David Guest, "Personnel and HRM: Can You Tell the Difference?" *Personnel Management* (January 1989), pp. 48–51.
9. Ibid., p. 49.
10. Barbara Presley Noble, "Retooling the 'People Skills' of Corporate America, *The New York Times* (May 22, 1994), p. F–7; and Linda Thornburg, "Moving HR to the Head Table," *HRMagazine* (August 1994), pp. 50–52.
11. Although there has been much criticism of the Hawthorne studies regarding the conclusions they drew, this has in no way diminished the significance of opinions they represent in the development of the field of HRM.
12. Of course we recognize that staffing, as other HRM activities, are continuous, and all occur simultaneously. However, for the sake of explanation, we present each function as a linear process.
13. See for example, Richard Henderson, *Compensation Management: Rewarding Performance,* 7th ed. (Englewood Cliffs, N.J.: Prentice-Hall, 1995).
14. Brian O'Reilly, "The New Deal: What Companies and Employees Owe One Another," *Fortune* (June 13, 1994), pp. 44–52; and Stanley J. Modic, "Is Anyone Loyal Anymore?" *Industry Week* (September 7, 1987), p. 75.
15. As we will show in Chapter 5, during a period of downsizing, employment may also be the department handling the layoffs.
16. See, for example, Nicholas J. Mathys, "Strategic Downsizing: Human Resource Planning Approaches," *Human Resource Planning* (February 1993), p. 71–86.
17. It should be noted that compensation and benefits may be, in fact, two separate departments. However, for reading flow, we will consider the department as a combined, singular unit.
18. Perquisites, or perks, are special offerings accorded to senior managers in an attempt to attract and retain the best managers possible. We will take a closer look at perks in Chapter 13, "Rewards and Compensation."
19. A strategic business unit, or market-driven unit, refers to a situation whereby these units operate as independent entities in an organization with their own set of strategies and mission.

20. Commerce Clearing House, *Human Resources Management: Ideas and Trends* (August 31, 1994), p. 141. This number represents an 11 percent increase over 1992.

21. Nicholas J. Mathys, "Strategic Downsizing: Human Resource Planning Approaches," *Human Resource Planning* (February 1993), p. 83.

22. *The Small Business Alliance Quarterly* (Winter 1990), pp. 6–7.

23. See for example, Commerce Clearing House, Human Resources Management, *1992 SHRM/CCH Survey* (1992), pp. 1–12.

24. The idea for this exercise was derived from Barbara K. Goza, "Graffiti Needs Assessment: Involving Students in the First Class Session," *Journal of Management Education,* Vol. 17, No. 1 [(February 1993), pp. 99-106.] Your authors first used a version of this exercise in their text, *Fundamentals of Management* (Englewood Cliffs, N.J.: Prentice-Hall, 1994), p. 22.

25. Based on the Associated Press article, Robert Naylor, Jr., "Companies Huge and Small Are Cited for Helping Mom," *The Baltimore Sun* (September 14, 1994), pp. D1-2; and Milton Moskowitz and Carol Townsend, "100 Best Companies for Working Mothers: 9th Annual Survey," *Working Mother* (October 1994), pp. 24–68. *Working Mother* evaluates companies on the "basis of pay levels, career opportunities for working moms, child-care assistance, family-friendly benefits (defined as benefits for part-timers, job sharing, and variable work hours).

Chapter 2

1. Mark Henricks, "Quantum Leap," *Entrepreneur* (October 1994), pp. 50, 52.

2. Ibid., p. 52.

3. William H. Wagel, "On the Horizon: HR in the 1990s," *Personnel* (January 1990), p. 6.

4. A multinational corporation is an organization that has significant operations in two or more countries. A transnational corporation is one that maintains significant operations in two or more countries simultaneously, and gives each the decision-making authority to operate in the local country.

5. Because of the global nature of work, it is important for students to be bilingual. In terms of gaining employment, those who speak more than one language will have an advantage in the job market.

6. "How America Will Change over the Next 30 Years," *Fortune* (April 23, 1990), p. 167.

7. For a more comprehensive coverage of cultural dimension, see Geert Hofstede, *Cultural Consequences: International Differences in Work-Related Values* (Beverly Hills, Calif.: Sage Publications, 1980).

8. Wagel, p. 17.

9. Stephanie Overman, "Managing the Diverse Work Force," *HRMagazine* (April 1991), p. 31.

10. Bruce W. Nolan, "Racism," *Time* (August 12, 1991), pp. 36–38.

11. *HRMagazine* (January 1991), pp. 40–41.

12. Ibid., p. 40.

13. William H. Wagel, *Personnel* (January 1990), p. 12.

14. "Riding the Tide of Change," *The Wyatt Communicator* (Winter 1991), p. 11.

15. Ibid.

16. Ann Crittenden, "Where Workforce 2000 Went Wrong," *Working Woman* (August 1994), p. 18.

17. The baby-boom generation refers to those individuals born between 1946 and 1964.

18. Sharon Nelton, "Winning with Diversity," *Nation's Business* (September 12, 1992), p. 18.

19. The Hudson Institute, *Workforce 2000: Work and Workers for the 21st Century* (Indianapolis, Ind.: The Hudson Institute, 1987).

20. Ann Crittenden, "Where Workforce 2000 Went Wrong," p. 18.

21. Betty Holcomb, "No, We're Not Going Home Again," *Working Mother* (November

1994), p. 28. See also, James Aley, "Men Ditch the Labor Market," *Fortune* (August 22, 1994), p. 24.

22. Faye Rice, "How to Make Diversity Pay," *Fortune* (August 8, 1994), p. 79.

23. For a good review of family-friendly companies, see Milton Moskowitz and Carol Townsend, "100 Best Companies for Working Mothers," *Working Mother* (October 1994), pp. 21–68.

24. Sue Shellenbarger, "Flexible Workers Come Under the Umbrella of Family Programs," *The Wall Street Journal* (February 8, 1995), p. B–1.

25. Adapted from C.M. Solomon, "Managing the Baby Busters," *Personnel Journal* (March 1992), p. 56.

26. Ibid.

27. See, for example, Suneel Ratan, "Why Busters Hate Boomers," *Fortune* (October 4, 1993), pp. 56–70.

28. Linda Thornburg, "The Age Wave Hits: What Older Workers Want and Need," *HRMagazine* (February 1995), pp. 43–44.

29. Charles E. Cohen, "Managing Older Workers," *Working Woman* (November 1994), pp. 61–62.

30. "Office Hours," *Fortune* (November 5, 1990), p. 184.

31. The Wyatt Communicator, p. 11.

32. Jane A. Sasseen, Robert Neff, Shekar Hattangadi, and Silvia Sansoni, "The Winds of Change Blow Everywhere," *Business Week* (October 17, 1994), p. 93.

33. Commerce Clearing House, "Employers to Bear Burden of Adult Literacy," *Human Resources Management: Ideas and Trends* (November 10, 1993), p. 182.

34. Commerce Clearing House, "AMA Surveys: Drug Testing, Basic Skills, and AIDS Policy Benchmarks," *Human Resources Management: Ideas and Trends* (June 8, 1994), p. 97.

35. Robbins, *Management*, p. 370.

36. "Employee Literacy," *Inc.* (August 1992), p. 81.

37. Ibid.

38. Blue Wooldridge and Jennifer Wester, "The Turbulent Environment of Public Personnel Administration: Responding to the Challenge of the Changing Workplace of the Twenty-First Century," *Public Personnel Management,* Vol. 20, No. 2 (Summer 1991), p. 213.

39. *Fortune* (April 23, 1990), p. 176.

40. Ibid; see also, Louis S. Richman, "The New Work Force Builds Itself," *Fortune* (June 27, 1994), p. 68–69.

41. Although this trend continues, there is a good counterpoint to this activity in Edmund Faltermayer, "Is This Layoff Necessary?" *Fortune* (June 1, 1992), pp. 71–86.

42. "Downsizing—The Toll Keeps Going Up," *U.S. News and World Report* (September 6, 1993), p. 16.

43. Brenton S. Schlender, "Japan's White Collar Blues," *Fortune* (March 12, 1994), pp. 97–104.

44. Joann S. Lublin, "Don't Stop Cutting Staff, Study Suggests," *The Wall Street Journal* (September 27, 1994), p. B–1.

45. We recognize that this number is not an accurate cost savings. In addition, one would have to add in the costs of employee benefits saved and subtract out any monies used to "buy people out." The $35 million figure is for illustration purposes only.

46. Anne B. Fisher, "Welcome to the Age of Overwork," *Fortune* (November 30, 1992), p. 64.

47. See Marjorie Armstrong-Stassen and Janina C. Latack, "Coping with Work-Force Reduction: The Effect of Layoff Exposure on Survivors' Reactions," in Jerry L. Wall and Lawrence R. Jauch, eds., *Academy of Management Best Papers Proceedings 1992,* Las Vegas (August 9–12, 1992), pp. 207–12. See also Terence Krell and Robert S. Spich, "A Tentative Model of Lame Duck Situations in Organizations," *Proceedings of the 1992 Conference of the Midwest Society for Human Resources/Industrial Relations* (March 25–27, 1992), pp. 161–75.

48. See, for example, Joann S. Lublin, "The Layoff Industry Learns that the Ax Can Be a Real Grind," *The Wall Street Journal* (November 28, 1994), pp. A–1; A–8.

49. Ibid.; and "A Comeback for Middle Managers," *Fortune* (October 17, 1994), p. 32.

50. Alan C. Fenwick, "Five Easy Lessons: A Primer for Starting a Total Quality Management Program," *Quality Progress,* Vol. 24, No. 12 (December 1991), p. 63.

51. Albert M. Koller, Jr., "TQM: Understanding the Barrier of `Total Quality Management,'" *Manage,* Vol. 42, No. 4 (May 1991), p. 15.

52. Fenwick, p. 63.

53. David Greising, "Quality: How to Make It Pay," *Business Week* (August 8, 1994), pp. 53–59.

54. For an in-depth, theoretical review of TQM, and related topics, see the special issue of the *Academy of Management Journal* (July 1994), pp. 390–584.

55. See W. Edwards Deming, *Quality Productivity and Competitive Position* (Cambridge, Mass.: MIT Center for Advanced Engineering Study, 1982).

56. See W. Edwards Deming, "Improvement of Quality and Productivity Through Actions of Management," *National Productivity Review* (Winter 1981), pp. 12–22.

57. See, for example, Brian M. Cook, "Quality: The Pioneers Survey the Landscape," *Industry Week* (October 21, 1991), pp. 68–73.

58. Ibid., p. 70.

59. Ibid.; see also Fenwick, p. 64; and David Hughes, "Motorola Nears Quality Benchmark after 12-Year Evolutionary Effort," *Aviation Week and Space Technology* (December 9, 1990), p. 64.

60. Fred R. Bleakley, "How an Outdated Plant Was Made New," *The Wall Street Journal* (October 21, 1994), pp. B–1; B–10.

61. Carla C. Carter, "Seven Basic Quality Tools," *HRMagazine* (January 1992), p. 81.

62. See, for example, Amit Majumdar, Megan Smolenyak, and Nancy Yenche, "Planting the Seeds of TQM," *National Productivity Review* (Autumn 1991), p. 492.

63. Frederick F. Reichheld and W. Earl Sasser, Jr., "Zero Defections: Quality Comes to Services," *Harvard Business Review* (September–October 1990), p. 105.

64. John Case, "The Change Masters," *Inc.* (March 1992), p. 60.

65. Adapted from ibid., p. 61.

66. See Morton Bahr, "Labor and Management . . . Working Together on Quality," *Journal for Quality and Participation,* Vol. 14, No. 3 (June 1991), pp. 14–17.

67. See, for example, Jay Mathews and Peter Katel, "The Cost of Quality," *Newsweek* (September 7, 1992), pp. 48–49.

68. Edward E. Lawler III, "Total Quality Management and Employee Involvement: Are They Compatible?" *Academy of Management Executive* Vol. 8, No. 1 (1994), pp. 68–76; and Richard Blackman and Benson Rosen, "Total Quality and Human Resources Management: Lessons Learned from Baldrige Award-Winning Companies," *Academy of Management Executive,* Vol. 7, No. 3 (1993), pp. 49–66.

69. Sandra E. O'Connell, "Reengineering: Ways to Do It with Technology," *HRMagazine* (November 1994), p. 40.

70. See, for example, John Byrne, "Reengineering: What Happened?" *Business Week* (January 30, 1995), p. 16; Benjamin F. Ball, "For ECR to Work, Some Comfortable Practices Must Go," *Advertising Age* (June 6, 1994), p. 28; and Jane A. Sasseen, Robert Neff, Shekar Hattangadi, and Silvia Sansoni, "The Winds of Change Blow Everywhere," *Business Week* (October 17, 1994), pp. 92–94.

71. Nancy K. Austin, "What's Missing from Corporate Cure-Alls," *Working Woman* (September 1994), pp. 16–19.

72. Ibid.

73. John A. Byrne, p. 16.

74. Sandra E. O'Connell, p. 40.

75. John A. Byrne, p. 16.

76. The following story is based on the story of Thermos, appearing in Brian Dumaine, "Payoff from the New Management" (December 13, 1993), pp. 103–4.

77. Thomas A. Stewart, "Reengineering: The Hot New Managing Tool," *Fortune* (August 23, 1993), p. 41.

78. Ibid.

79. Julie Connelly, "Have We Become Mad Dogs in the Office?" *Fortune* (November 28, 1994), p. 197.

80. See for example, Debra Phillips, "The New Service Boom," *Entrepreneur* (August 1994), pp. 134–140.

81. Ann Crittenden, "Temporary," *Working Woman* (February 1994), p. 32.

82. Jaclyn Fierman, "The Contingency Work Force," *Fortune* (January 24, 1994), p. 32; "BOOM TIMES for Temporary Help Aren't Temporary, Experts Agree," *The Wall Street Journal* (October 25, 1994), p. A–1; and Janet Novack, "Is Lean, Mean?," *Forbes* (August 15, 1994), p. 88.

83. Beth Rogers, "Temporary Help Industry Evolving as It Grows," *HR News* (January 1995), p. 4.

84. See for instance, Audrey Freedman, "Human Resources Forecast 1995: Contingent Workers," *HRMagazine Supplement* (1994), p. 13–14.

85. Maggie Mahar, "Part-time: By Choice or By Chance," *Working Woman* (October 1993), p. 20.

86. Ann Crittenden, "Temporary," p. 32.

87. Jaclyn Fierman, "The Contingency Work Force," p. 33.

88. Keith H. Hammonds, Kevin Kelly, and Karen Thurston, "The New World of Work," *Business Week* (October 17, 1994), p. 85.

89. Ann Crittenden, "Temporary," p. 33.

90. Ibid.

91. "Contracting Out White-Collar Jobs Continues to Gain Steam," *The Wall Street Journal* (September 20, 1994), p. A–1.

92. Ani Hadjian, "Hiring Temps Full-Time May Get the IRS On Your Tail," *Fortune* (January 24, 1994), p. 34.

93. For example, see Robert McGarvey, "Temporary Solution," *Entrepreneur* (August 1994), pp. 68–72.

94. See, for example, Leon Rubis, "Benefits Boost Appeal of Temporary Work," *HRMagazine* (January 1995), pp. 54–58; and Anne Murphy, "Do-It-Yourself Job Creation," *Inc.* (January 1994), pp. 36–50.

95. Michael P. Cronin, "The Benefits of Part-Time Work," *Inc.* (December 1994), p. 127.

96. Based on Sue Shellenbarger, "Refusing In-Home Work Costs Him His Job," *The Wall Street Journal* (April 8, 1994), p. B–1.

97. Commerce Clearing House, "Work at Home Increasingly Appealing to Employers, But Legal Pitfalls Abound," *Human Resources Management: Ideas and Trends* (February 16, 1994), pp. 25–26.

98. Ibid.

99. Thomas Roberts, "Who Are the High-Tech Home Workers?" *Inc. Technology* (1994), p. 31.

100. Ibid.

101. Commerce Clearing House, "Work at Home Increasingly Appealing to Employers, But Legal Pitfalls Abound," *Human Resources Management: Ideas and Trends* (February 16, 1994), pp. 25–26.

102. For a comprehensive overview of empowering employees, see Jay A. Conger and Rabindra N. Kanungo, "The Empowerment Process: Integrating Theory and Practice," *Academy of Management Review*, Vol. 13, No. 3 (July 1988), pp. 471–82.

103. See, for example, Jeffrey Pfeffer, "Producing Sustainable Competitive Advantage Through the Effective Management of People," *Academy of Management Executive*, Vol. 9, No. 1 (1995), pp. 55–72.

104. Keith H. Hammond, Kevin Kelly, and Karen Thurston, "The New World of Work," *Business Week* (October 17, 1994), p. 81.

105. See, for example, Jon L. Pierce, Stephen A. Rubenfeld, and Susan Morgan, "Employee Ownership: A Conceptual Model of Process and Effects," *The Academy of Management Review*, Vol. 16, No. 1 (January 1991), pp. 121–44.

106. Ibid, pp. 136–37; and Brian O'Reilly, "The New Deal: What Companies and Employees Owe One Another," *Fortune* (June 13, 1994), p. 44.

107. This case adapted from Stephanie Overman, "No-Frills HR at Nucor," *HRMagazine* (July 1994), pp. 56–60.

Chapter 3

1. Based on the articles by Jolie Solomon and Susan Miller, "Here or Harasser?" *Newsweek* (September 12, 1994), pp. 48–50; Seema Nayyar and Susan Miller, "Making It Easier to Strike Back," *Newsweek* (September 12, 1994), p. 50; and "Jury Finds Firm Knew of Lawyer's Harassment," *News Wire Reports: In the Nation, The Baltimore Sun* (August 28, 1994), p. 21A; and Commerce Clearing House, Human Resources Management, "7 Million Award Says Take Prevention Seriously," *Ideas and Trends* (September 14, 1994), p. 149.

2. "Jury Finds Firm Knew of Lawyer's Harassment," p. 21A.

3. Commerce Clearing House, *Human Resources Management: Ideas and Trends* (November 14, 1994), p. 149.

4. Ibid.; and Seema Nayyar and Susan Miller, p. 50. It should be noted, however, that in response to the jury's award to Rena Weeks, the Chairman of Baker and McKenzie's Executive Committee wrote a response claiming the law firm did not neglect its responsibility to handle this matter, and will appeal the award (see Commerce Clearing House [September 14, 1994, p. 156]).

5. See, for instance, Frederick R. Lynch and William R. Beer, "You Ain't the Right Color, Pal," *Policy Review* (Winter 1990), p. 64.

6. Cases filed under this act could be heard by a jury. Such opportunity was unavailable under the Civil Rights Act of 1964.

7. Under the Civil Rights Act of 1964, the only remedy is back pay.

8. *Patterson* v. *McLean Credit Union,* 87, U.S. Supreme Court 107 (1989).

9. 1981 Guidebook to Fair Employment Practices (Chicago: Commerce Clearing House, 1980), p. 16.

10. Ibid.

11. Another stipulation is receiving $50,000 or more of government monies. Thus, a two-person operation that has a government contract for more than $50,000 is bound by Title VII.

12. *Washington Metropolitan Police Department* v. *Davis,* 422 U.S. Supreme Court, 229 (1976).

13. R. Roosevelt Thomas, Jr., "From Affirmative Action to Affirming Diversity," *Harvard Business Review* (March–April 1990), p. 107.

14. Adverse impact refers to an employment practice that results in a disparate selection, promotion, or firing of a class of protected group members, whereas adverse treatment affects one or more individuals. See also Commerce Clearing House, *Human Resources Management; Ideas and Trends* (May 12, 1993), p. 64.

15. Jeffrey H. Greenhaus, Saroj Parasuraman, and Wayne M. Wormley, "Effects of Race on Organizational Experiences, Job Performance Evaluations, and Career Outcomes," *Academy of Management Journal,* Vol. 33, No. 1 (1990), pp. 64–86.

16. AEDA is afforded to all individuals age 40 and older who are employed in organizations with twenty or more employees. See, for example, David Israel and Stephen P. Beiser, "Are Age Discrimination Releases Enforceable?" *HRMagazine* (August 1990), p. 80.

17. Executive and high policy-making employees of an organization may still be required to retire. Three conditions must be met, however. These are that they are at least 65 years of age, will receive a pension from the organization of at least $44,000, and have been in this executive or high policy-making position for the previous two years. See, American Association of Retired People, *Age Discrimination in the Job* (Washington, D.C.: AARP, 1992), p. 10.

18. Mollie H. Bowers and David A. De Cenzo, *Essentials of Labor Relations* (Englewood Cliffs, N.J.: Prentice-Hall, 1992), p. 31.

19. The age 60 issue is currently being debated. Questions on who medical research was conducted on (e.g., private pilots, not commercial ones, etc.) have raised many questions. However, at this time, mandatory retirement for pilots attaining age 60 still is in force.

20. Katherine Bishop, "Pan Am to Pay Retired Pilots in Age Bias Suit," *The New York Times,* (February 4, 1988), p. A18.

21. See *Price* v. *Maryland Casualty Co.,* 561 F.2d 609, 612 (C.A. 5th Cir., 1977), and Helen Creighton, J.D., R.N., "Age Discrimination," *Nursing Management,* Vol. 20, No. 2 (February 1989), pp. 21–22.

22. Israel and Beiser, p. 81.

23. Adapted from Niki Scott, "Promotion Can't Be Denied Because of Pregnancy," *Universal Press Syndicate,* reprinted in *The Baltimore Sun* (August 12, 1990), p. M–5.

24. This will obviously vary within companies. Additionally, extended periods can be obtained by the workers using entitled sick and vacation benefits. See David A. De Cenzo and Stephen J. Holoviak, *Employee Benefits* (Englewood Cliffs, N.J.: Prentice-Hall, 1991), p. 30.

25. Lisa J. Raines and Stephen P. Push, "Protecting Pregnant Workers," *Harvard Business Review* (May–June 1986), p. 26.

26. Betty Southard Murphy, Wayne E. Barlow, and D. Diane Hatch, contributing editors, "Supreme Court to Decide Fetal Protection Conflict," *Personnel Journal* (May 1990), p. 12.

27. Stephen Wermeil, "Justices Bar Fetal Protection Policies," *The Wall Street Journal* (March 21, 1991), p. 81.

28. Ibid.

29. It should be pointed out that the Rehabilitation Act of 1973 applied only to federal contractors. The Americans with Disabilities Act covers a broader range of organizations.

30. Commerce Clearing House, "Can Physical Appearance Be a Disability?" *Human Resources Management; Idea and Trends* (March 31, 1994), p. 60.

31. This act defines a disability as any condition that curtails one or more major life activities for an individual.

32. Francine S. Hall and Elizabeth L. Hall, "The ADA: Going Beyond the Law," *Academy of Management Executive,* Vol. 8, No. 1 (1994), pp. 17–32.

33. "President Signs Disabilities Act into Law," *Human Resources Management: Ideas and Trends,* No. 227 (Chicago: Commerce Clearing House, August 8, 1990), p. 133.

34. Ibid.

35. Thomas J. Flygare, "Supreme Court Holds that Contagious Diseases Are Handicaps," *Phi Delta Kappa,* Vol. 68 (May 1987), p. 705.

36. Those states were Connecticut, New Jersey, Maine, Minnesota, Oklahoma, Oregon, Rhode Island, Tennessee, Vermont, Washington, West Virginia, and Wisconsin. See "Family Leave," *Human Resources Management: Ideas and Trends,* No. 225 (July 11, 1990), p. 115.

37. Under certain circumstances, and in compliance with company policy, the employee or the employer may substitute paid personal leave or accrued vacation time for the unpaid leave. The paid leave portion of the act, however, has several limitations and qualifiers.

38. Maggie Jones, "Giving Family Leave a Checkup," *Working Woman* (November 1993), p. 17.

39. Ibid.

40. "Family Leave Compliance Is Falling Short," *The Wall Street Journal* (March 16, 1993), p. A-1; and Francine G. Hermelin, "How Well Is Family Leave Really Working?" *Working Woman* (September 1994), p. 9.

41. Maggie Jones, p. 17.

42. Ibid.

43. Adapted from David A. De Cenzo and Stephen J. Holoviak, contributing editors, "Civil Rights Bill of 1990 Clears House of Representatives," *Audio Human Resources Report,* Vol. 1., No. 10 (November 1990), p. 8.

44. For example, with 15–100 employees, the maximum damage award is $50,000; 101–200 employees, $100,000; 201–500 employees, $200,000; and more than 500 employees, $300,000. From "The New Civil Rights Act," *Inc.* (August 1992), p. 81.

45. Gary Dessler, *Personnel/Human Resources Management,* 5th ed. (Englewood Cliffs, N.J.: Prentice-Hall, 1991), pp. 45–46.

46. *Federal Register,* p. 38, 290.

47. We must note here that the 4/5ths rule, as established, does not recognize specific individual's requirements: That is, a minority could be any group. For example, when airlines hired only females as flight attendants, males were the minority.

48. *Connecticut* v. *Teal,* U.S. Supreme Court 102, Docket No. 2525 (1982).

49. *McDonnell-Douglas Corp.* v. *Green,* 411 U.S. 792, 80 (U.S. 1973).

50. Such a case is frequently referred to as a prima facia case. In such a situation, there is enough evidence to support the charge, and will be considered sufficient evidence unless refuted by the organization.

51. *McDonnell-Douglas Corp.* v. *Green,* and Helen Creighton, "Age Discrimination," *Nursing Management* (February 1989), p. 21.

52. Susan Pouncey, "Airlines Aren't Sexy Anymore, but They Still Fly," *The New York Times* (March 10, 1987), p. B–8.

53. Reasonable accommodation here is a difficult area not to support. If through the use of personal leave an individual can be accommodated, then no BFOQ exists. Also, the courts may view how an enterprise treats traditional Christian holidays in viewing reasonable accommodation.

54. See James G. Frierson, "Religion in the Work Place," *Personnel Journal,* Vol. 7, No. 7 (July 1988), pp. 60–67.

55. A disparate impact occurs when an HRM practice eliminates a group of individuals from job considerations. Disparate treatment exists when an HRM practice eliminates an individual from employment consideration.

56. *Albemarle Paper Company* v. *Moody,* 422 U.S. Supreme Court (U.S. 1975).

57. *Wards Cove Packing Co., Inc.,* v. *Atonio,* U.S. Supreme Court, Docket No. 87–1387, June 5, 1989.

58. "The Blow to Affirmative Action May Not Hurt That Much," *Business Week* (July 3, 1989), p. 61.

59. Ibid., p. 62.

60. Adapted from Claudia H. Deutsch, "Don't Forget about the White Males," *The New York Times* (December 8, 1991), section 3, p. 29.

61. Ibid.

62. *Regents of the University of California* v. *Bakke,* 438 U.S. 265 (1978).

63. Kenneth L. Sovereign, *Personnel Law,* 2d ed. (Englewood Cliffs, N.J.: Prentice-Hall, 1989), p. 106.

64. *Firefighters Local 1784* v. *Stotts,* 467, Supreme Court 561 (1984).

65. *Wyant* v. *Jackson Board of Education,* 106, Supreme Court 842 (1986).

66. Rochelle Sharpe, "Blacks, Hispanics Had Greater Loss of Jobs in Last Recession, GAO Finds," *The Wall Street Journal* (September 19, 1994), p. A–2.

67. It is important to note that individuals are not required to file charges against the organization through the EEOC. They may, at their discretion, use a state agency (like a Human Rights Commission) or proceed on their own. However, the outcomes of these other avenues are not binding to the EEOC. Additionally, charges may be filed by the individual, his or her representative (e.g., union), or the EEOC itself.

68. In *EEOC* v. *Commercial Office Products,* U.S. Supreme Court Docket No. 86–1696 (1988), the Court ruled that if a work sharing arrangement exists between the EEOC and a state or local agency, then the time limit increases to 300 days. See also "EEOC Charges," *Human Resources Management: Ideas and Trends,* No. 171 (June 15, 1988), p. 93.

69. Adapted from the 1981 Guidebook to Fair Employment Practices, pp. 123–61; and unpublished manuscript by Stanley Mazaroff, Esquire, "A Management Guide to Responding to a Charge of Discrimination Filed with the EEOC,: (Baltimore, Md.: Venable, Baetjer, and Howard, Attorneys-at-Law, 1994), p. 1.

70. See, for example, Commerce Clearing House, "An Interview with Attorney Irving M. Miller," *Human Resources Management: Ideas and Trends,* No. 135 (January 23, 1987), p. 15.

71. Under Section 503 of the Vocational Rehabilitation Act, those organizations that have a contract or subcontract in the amount of $2,500 must have affirmative action plans to hire the disabled. For the Vietnam Veterans Readjustment Act, the amount is $10,000.

72. Anne B. Fisher, "Sexual Harassment, What to Do," *Fortune* (August 23, 1993), pp. 84–88.

73. Koen, Jr., p. 88.

74. "U.S. Leads Way in Sex Harassment Laws, Study Says," *The Evening Sun* (November 30, 1992) pp. A-1, A-7.

75. Susan Webb, *The Webb Report: A Newsletter on Sexual Harassment* (Seattle, Wash.: Premier Publishing, Ltd., January 1994), pp. 4–7; and (April 1994), pp. 2–5.

76. While the male gender was referred to here, it is important to note that sexual harassment may involve either sex sexually harassing another, or the same sex harassing another individual.

77. See for example, Ellen Joan Pollock, "Clinton Asks for Ruling on Immunity in Effort to Derail Paula Jones Suit," *The Wall Street Journal* (June 28, 1994), p. A–20.

78. Alice Steinbach, "D.C.'s Undead," *The Baltimore Sun* (August 22, 1994), pp. 1D; 8D.

79. Elizabeth Kadetsky, "Million-Dollar Man," *Working Woman* (October 1993), pp. 45–53.

80. See, for example, Jacqueline F. Strayer and Sandra E. Rapoport, "Sexual Harassment: Limiting Corporate Liability," *Personnel* (April 1986), pp. 30–31.

81. Commerce Clearing House, *Human Resources Management: Idea and Trends* (November 23, 1993), p. 189.

82. *Meritor Savings Bank* v. *Vinson*, U.S. Supreme Court 106, Docket No. 2399 (1986).

83. Clifford M. Koen, Jr., "Sexual Harassment Claims Stem from a Hostile Work Environment," *Personnel Journal* (August 1990), p. 89.

84. Ibid. See also L. A. Winokur, "Harassment of Workers by 'Third Parties' Can Lead into Maze of Legal, Moral Issues," *The Wall Street Journal* (October 26, 1992), p. B–1. Also, if an organization investigates the matter and takes immediate action, they may be held not liable for the action.

85. Elizabeth Rudolph and Paul Van Osdol, "A Set-Back for Pin-Ups At Work," *Newsweek* (February 4, 1991), p. 41.

86. Commerce Clearing House, *Human Resources Management: Ideas and Trends* (March 5, 1992), p. 39.

87. Fisher, p. 88

88. It should be noted here that under the Title VII and the Civil Rights Act of 1991, the maximum award that can be given, under the Federal Act, is $300,000. However, many cases are tried under State Laws which permit unlimited punitive damages, such at the $7.1 million Rena Weeks received in her trial based on California statutes.

89. Commerce Clearing House, *Human Resources Management: Ideas and Trends* (November 23, 1993), p. 185.

90. Don Mayer and Kenneth M. York, "In Search of the Reasonable Person Standard After *Harris* v. *Forklift Systems:* Use of Surveys to Determine Contemporary Community Standards," *Academy of Management Best Paper Proceedings*, Dorothy P. Moore, ed. (August 8–17, 1994), pp. 254–58.

91. Commerce Clearing House, *Human Resources Management: Ideas and Trends* (September 14, 1994), p. 156.

92. Mayer and York, p. 254.

93. Ibid.

94. Ellen E. Schultz and Junda Woo, "The Bedroom Ploy: Plaintiffs' Sex Lives Are Being Laid Bare in Harassment Cases," *The Wall Street Journal* (September 19, 1994), pp. A–1; A–9.

95. See Robert S. Smith, "Comparable Worth: Limited Coverage and the Exacerbation of Inequality," *Industrial and Labor Relations Review*, Vol. 41, No. 2 (January 1988), pp. 227–39, and Jonathan Tompkins, "Comparable Worth and Job Evaluation Validity," *Public Administration Review* (May–June 1987), pp. 254–58.

96. "Oles Envelope Settles Sexual Bias," *The Baltimore Sun* (July 23, 1993), p. 11–D.

97. "Throwing Stones at the Glass Ceiling," *Business Week* (August 19, 1991), p. 29.

98. Cari M. Dominguez, "A Crack in the Glass Ceiling," *HRMagazine* (December 1990), p. 65.

99. See, for example, "The Glass Ceiling Initiative," *Human Resources Management: Ideas and Trends,* No. 230 (September 5, 1990), pp. 161–67.

100. Commerce Clearing House, *Human Resources Management: Idea and Trends* (October 13, 1993), p. 161.

101. Ibid., p. 162.

102. Gary N. Powell and D. Anthony Butterfield, "Investigating the 'Glass Ceiling' Phenomenon: An Empirical Study of Actual Promotions to Top Management," *Academy of Management Journal,* Vol. 37, No. 1 (1994), pp. 68–86.

103. Erick Schonfeld, "A Fissure in the Glass Ceiling," *Fortune* (September 5, 1994), p. 15.

104. Elyse Mall, "Why Getting Ahead Is (Still) Tougher for Women," *Working Woman* (July 1994), p. 11.

105. Ruth Marcus, "Do U.S. Anti-Bias Laws Stop at Water's Edge?" *The Washington Post* (January 21, 1991), p. A4.

106. This case is based on the *EEOC* v. *ARAMCO, Facts on File,* Vol. 51, No. 2627 (March 28, 1991), pp. 236–37.

Chapter 4

1. This opening vignette, and quotes, come from Michael James, "Mechanic Fired for Refusing to Break Law Wins $176,000, *"The Baltimore Sun* (August 14, 1994), p. B–1.

2. George D. Webster, "Privacy in the Work Place," *Association Management,* Vol. 43, No. 4 (November 1990), pp. 36–37.

3. See, for example, Stephanie Overman, "A Delicate Balance Protects Everyone's Rights," *HRMagazine,* Vol. 35, No. 1 (November 1990), pp. 36–37.

4. Wayne F. Casio, *Applied Psychology in Personnel Management,* 4th ed. (Englewood Cliffs, N.J.: Prentice Hall, 1991), p. 37.

5. See, for example, Commerce Clearing House, *Government Implementation for the Drug-Free Workplace Act of 1988, Part 2* (Chicago: Commerce Clearing House, Inc., 1990), p. 17.

6. Public Law 100-347.

7. This act applies to all private sector organizations except those organizations the secretary of labor deems too small (e.g., family-owned businesses).

8. See, for example, Lois R. Wise and Steven J. Charuat, "Polygraph Testing in the Public Sector: The Status of State Legislation," *Public Personnel Management,* Vol. 19, No. 4 (Winter 1990), pp. 381–90.

9. However, in cases when they are job-related (requiring someone who has fiduciary responsibilities in an organization), they may be used.

10. Commerce Clearing House, "Polygraph Testing," *Human Resource Management: Ideas and Trends,* No. 173 (July 12, 1988), p. 105.

11. Gabriella Stern and Jeffrey A. Tannenbaum, "GM Plans to Sell Car Rental Unit to Buyout Firm," *The Wall Street Journal* (September 23, 1994), p. A–3.

12. Of course, GM could do just that; if it did, however, it would be in violation of WARN, and subjected to the penalties imposed under the act.

13. Worker Adjustment and Retraining Notification Act, Public Law 100-379.

14. Commerce Clearing House, "Plant Closing," *Human Resources Management: Ideas and Trends,* No. 175 (August 9, 1988), p. 129.

15. Fair Lanes was able to keep operating by filing for Chapter 11 (bankruptcy) status. See "Jay Hancock, "Fair Lanes Emerges from Bankruptcy," *The Baltimore Sun* (September 21, 1994), p. 8–C.

16. Donald M. Smith, "Workplace Drug Abuse: It's Deadly, It's Costly, It's Preventable," *National Petroleum News,* Vol. 83, No. 2 (February 1991), p. 28.

17. Kimberly A. Weber and Robin E. Shea, "Drug Testing: The Necessary Evil," *Bobbin,* Vol. 32, No. 12 (August 1991), p. 98.

18. Jim Carraher, "Progress Report: Drug Tests," *Security,* Vol. 28, No. 10 (October 1991), p. 40. See also Joseph G. Rosse, Deborah F. Crown, and Howard D. Feldman, "Alter-

native Solutions to the Workplace Drug Problem," *Journal of Employment Counseling,* Vol. 27 (June 1990), p. 60.

19. Commerce Clearing House, "Drug Testing, Basic Skills and AIDS Policy Benchmarks," *Human Resources Management: Ideas and Trends* (June 8, 1994), p. 97.

20. "And Whose Syringe Might This Be?" *Inc.* (August 1994), p. 104.

21. It is important to note that drug testing may be constrained by collective bargaining agreements, or state laws. See, Erica Gordon Sorohan, "Making Decisions About Drug Testing," *Training and Development* (May 1994), pp. 111–17.

22. "Motorola Aims High, So Motorolans Won't Be Getting High," *The Wall Street Journal* (June 26, 1990), p. A–19.

23. "Narc in a Can," *Executive Female* (November–December 1990), p. 24; and Edward J. Miller, "Investing in a Drug Free Workplace," *HRMagazine*, Vol. 36, No. 5 (May 1991), p. 48.

24. "Motorola Aims High, So Motorolans Won't Be Getting High," p. A19.

25. Ibid., and "Narc in a Can," p. 24.

26. Leslee Jaquette, "Red Lion Pleased with Drug-Testing Program," *Hotel and Motel Management,* Vol. 206, No. 3 (February 25, 1991), p. 3.

27. Commerce Clearing House, "The ADA Changes the Rules," *Human Resources Management: Ideas and Trends* (July 11, 1994), p. 111.

28. "Urine Tests Can Be Misleading," *USA Today* (February 1987), p. 13.

29. Joseph G. Rosse, et al., p. 62.

30. Dianna L. Stone and Debra A. Kotch, "Individuals' Attitudes Toward Organizational Drug Testing Policies and Practices," *Journal of Applied Psychology,* Vol. 74, No. 3 (1989), p. 521.

31. Ibid., and Michael R. Carroll and Christina Heavrin, "Before You Drug Test," *HRMagazine* (June 1990), p. 64.

32. See, for example, Kevin R. Murphy, George C. Thornton III, and Kristin Prue, "Influence of Job Characteristics on the Acceptability of Employee Drug Testing," *Journal of Applied Psychology,* Vol. 76, No. 3 (1991), pp. 447–53.

33. This question comes from an article citing actual questions on an honesty test. See Michael P. Cronin, "This Is a Test," *Inc.* (August 1993), p. 67.

34. Stephen Bennett, "Employee Testing: Truth or Consequence," *Progressive Grocer* (October 1990), p. 51.

35. Ibid.

36. Casio, p. 268.

37. Ed Bean, "More Firms Use Attitude Tests to Keep Thieves Off the Payroll," *The Wall Street Journal* (February 27, 1987), p. A–19.

38. Ibid.

39. Matthew Budman, "The Honest Business," *Across the Board* (November/December 1993), pp. 34–37.

40. See for example, H. John Bernardin and Donna K. Cooke, "Validity of an Honesty Test in Predicting Theft Among Convenience Store Employees," *Academy of Management Journal,* Vol. 38, No. 5 (1993), pp. 1097–108.

41. Ibid.

42. Casio, p. 268.

43. See for instance, Jolie Solomon and Daniel McGinn, "Scratches in the Teflon," *Newsweek* (October 3, 1994), pp. 50–52; and Terence P. Pare, "Jack Welch's Nightmare on Wall Street," *Fortune* (September 5, 1994), pp. 40–48.

44. Commerce Clearing House, "Whistleblower Can Sue for Emotional Distress, Supreme Court Rules," *Human Resources Management: Ideas and Trends,* No. 223 (June 13, 1990), pp. 97–98.

45. Ibid.

46. Kenneth L. Sovereign, *Personnel Law,* 3rd ed. (Englewood Cliffs, N.J.: Prentice-Hall, 1994), p. 177.

47. Timothy R. Barnett and Daniel S. Cochran, "Making Room for the Whistleblower," *HRMagazine* (January 1991), p. 58.

48. See, for example, Michael F. Rosenblum, "Security v. Privacy: An Emerging Employ-

ment Dilemma," *Employee Relations Law Journal,* Vol. 17, No. 1 (Summer 1991), pp. 81–101.

49. Adapted from Glenn Rifkin, "Do Employees Have a Right to Electronic Privacy?" *The New York Times* (December 8, 1991), sections 3–8.

50. Lee Smith, "What the Boss Knows About You," *Fortune* (August 9, 1993), p. 89.

51. Ibid.

52. See, for example, William L. Kandel, "Employee Dishonesty and Workplace Security: Precautions Against Prevention," *Employer Relations Law Journal,* Vol. 16, No. 2 (Autumn 1990), pp. 217–31.

53. Ellen Rapp, "Legislating Love," *Working Woman* (February 1992), p. 61.

54. Anne B. Fisher, "Getting Comfortable with Couples in the Workplace," *Fortune* (October 3, 1994), pp. 139–44.

55. Ibid., p. 142.

56. See, for example, Jonathan A. Segal, "A Need Not to Know," *HRMagazine,* Vol. 36, No. 10 (October 1991), pp. 85–90.

57. See Jennifer J. Koch, "Wells Fargo's and IBM's HIV Positive Policies Help Protect Employee Rights," *Personnel Journal,* Vol. 69, No. 4 (April 1990), pp. 40–51.

58. Ibid.

59. See, for example, Jack Hayes, "Cracker Barrel Comes Under Fire for Ousting Gays," *Nation's Restaurant News,* Vol. 25 (March 4, 1991), p. 1.

60. Commerce Clearing House, "Bills Banning Sexual Orientation Bias Introduced," *Human Resources Management: Ideas and Trends* (July 20, 1994), p. 117; and "Employment Rights for Gays Sought," *The Baltimore Sun* (June 24, 1994), p. A–3.

61. Ibid.

62. *Payne* v. *Western and Atlantic Railroad Co.,* 812 Tenn. 507 (1884). See also Marie Leonard, "Challenges to the Termination-at-Will Doctrine," *Personnel Administrator* (February 1983), p. 49. (Quoted from Lawrence E. Blades, *Columbia Law Review,* 67 [1967], 1405.)

63. Jane Easter Bahls, "Playing with Fire," *Entrepreneur* (October 1994), p. 66.

64. Commerce Clearing House, "Future of Employment-at-Will Uncertain, But Risk of Wrongful Discharge Suits Can Be Curtailed Now," *Human Resources Management: Ideas and Trends* (July 20, 1994), p. 119.

65. "Wrongful Discharge," *The Wall Street Journal* (September 10, 1991), p. A–1.

66. Commerce Clearing House, *Topical Law Reports* (Chicago: Commerce Clearing House, 1989), p. 2773.

67. Michael J. Lotito, Esq., "State by State, the Rules of the Employment Relationship Are Changing," Commerce Clearing House, *Human Resources Management: Ideas and Trends,* No. 226 (July 25, 1990), p. 126.

68. Adapted from Carroll R. Daugherty, *Enterprise Wire Co.* 46 LA 359 (1966).

69. See for example, Kenneth L. Sovereign, *Personnel Law,* 3rd ed. (Englewood Cliffs, N.J.: Prentice Hall, 1994), p. 178.

70. *Toussaint* v. *Blue Cross and Blue Shield of Michigan,* 408 Michigan, 529, 292 N.W. 2d 880 (1980).

71. Sovereign, p. 180.

72. Ibid.

73. Ibid., p. 179.

74. Ibid.

75. *Fortune* v. *National Cash Register,* 364 373 Massachusetts 91, 36 N.E. 2d 1251 (1977).

76. Lotito, p. 126.

77. "Wrongful Discharge," *The Wall Street Journal* (September 10, 1991), p. A–1.

78. "It's Getting Harder to Pass Out Pink Slips," *Business Week* (March 28, 1988), p. 68.

79. Wallace Wohlking, "Effective Discipline in Employee Relations," *Personnel Journal* (September 1975), pp. 491–92.

80. Martin Levy, "Discipline for Professional Employees," *Personnel Journal* (December 1990), pp. 27–28.

81. James G. Frierson, "How to Fire without Getting Burned," *Personnel* (September, 1990), p. 46.

82. Walter Kiechel, "How to Discipline in the Modern Age," *Fortune* (May 7, 1990), pp. 179–80.

83. It is true that two other disciplinary actions may be used—pay cuts or demotion—but they are rare. See for example, John P. Kohl and David B. Stephens, "Is Demotion a Four Letter Word?" *Business Horizons* (March–April 1990), p. 75.

84. Chimezie A. B. Osigweh Yg, and William R. Hutchinson, "To Punish or Not to Punish? Managing Human Resources Through Positive Discipline," *Employee Relations* (March 1990), pp. 27–32.

85. Chimezie A. B. Osigweh Yg, and William R. Hutchinson, "Positive Discipline," *Human Resource Management* (Fall 1989), p. 367.

86. Sue Shellenbarger, "Mom Questions Authority and Gets Fired," *The Wall Street Journal* (September 21, 1994), p. B–1.

Chapter 5

1. This opening vignette is based on the article by Alex Taylor III, "GM's $11,000,000,000 Turnaround," *Fortune* (October 17, 1994), pp. 54–74.

2. See, for example, Max Messmer, "Strategic Staffing for the 90s," *Personnel Journal* (October 1990), p. 92.

3. Martin J. Plevel, Sandy Nells, Fred Lane, and Randall S. Schuler, "AT&T Global Business Communications Systems: Linking HR with Business Strategy," *Organizational Dynamics* (1994), pp. 59–71. See also, Randall S. Schuler, "Strategic Human Resources Management: Linking the People with the Strategic Needs of the Business," *Organizational Dynamics* (1992), pp. 18–32.

4. Messmer, p. 96.

5. As one reviewer correctly pointed out, strategic planning cannot be oversimplified to a two-page discussion. We agree, but believe that a quick overview is in order. However, with respect to the strategic nature of business, we recommend for a comprehensive review of strategic planning: James Brian Quinn, Henry Mintzberg, and Robert M. James, *The Strategic Process* (Englewood Cliffs, N.J.: Prentice-Hall, 1988).

6. Goals that are established are a function of a number of factors. Such issues as the economy, government influences, market maturity, technological advances, company image, and location will factor into the analysis. See, for example, Henry J. Sredl and William J. Rothwell, *Professional Training Roles and Competencies,* vol. 1 (Maine: HRD Press, 1987), p. 154.

7. Todd S. Nelson, "Continental Banks on New Hiring Plan," *Personnel Journal* (November 1990), p. 95.

8. Ibid., p. 95.

9. Joan E. Goodman, "Does Your HRS Speak English?" *Personnel Journal* (March 1990), p. 81.

10. See, for example, John Spirig, "HRIS," *Employment Relations Today,* Vol. 16, No. 54 (Winter 1989/1990), pp. 347–50.

11. Stephen G. Perry, "The PC-Based HRIS," *Personnel Administrator* (February 1988), p. 60.

12. Even with fourth-generation languages, some glitches still exist. For example, generating reports still require knowledge of computer "lingo."

13. Jeffrey Knapp, "Trends in HR Management Systems," *Personnel* (April 1990), pp. 56–57. See also John P. Polard, "HRIS: Time Is of the Essence," *Personnel Journal* (November 1990), pp. 42–43.

14. Ibid., pp. 60–61.

15. See for example, Laurie M. Grossman, "Coke's Move to Retain Goizueta Spotlights a Succession Problem," *The Wall Street Journal* (May 13, 1994), p. A–1; and "Naming of Ivester as President Deemed Good Move for Coca-Cola," *The Baltimore Sun* (July 25, 1994), p. 11–C.

16. Michael Meyer, Charles Fleming, Stryker McGuire, and Daniel McGinn, "Looking for Mr. Right," *Newsweek* (August 1, 1994), pp. 40–42.

17. See for example, Michael Meyer, Stryker McQuire, Charles Fleming, Mark Millen,

Andrew Murr, and Daniel McGuire, "Of Mice and Men," *Newsweek* (September 5, 1994), pp. 41–47; and "Disney Studios Chief Abruptly Resigns," *The Baltimore Sun* (August 25, 1994), p. 9D; 12D.

18. Brian Henson, "Setting the Stage," *Inc.* (June 1994), pp. 23–24.

19. Commerce Clearing House, "Sabbaticals: a Good Investment for McDonald's," *Human Resources Management: Ideas and Trends* (May 11, 1994), pp. 77, 84.

20. Richard Henderson, *Compensation Management: Rewarding Performance*, 6th ed. (Englewood Cliffs, N.J.: Prentice Hall, 1994), p. 137.

21. Sidney A. Fine, Functional Job Analysis Scales: A Desk Aid, No. 7 (Kalamazoo, Mich.: WE Upjohn Institute for Employment Research, 1973).

22. Henderson, p. 168.

23. See Wayne Casio, *Applied Psychology in Personnel Management*, 4th ed. (Englewood Cliffs, N.J.: Prentice Hall, 1991), p. 207; see also Stephanie K. Butler and Robert J. Harvey, "A Comparison of Holistic Verses Decomposed Rating of Position Analysis Questionnaire Work Dimensions," *Personnel Psychology*, Vol. 41, No. 4 (Winter 1988), pp. 761–71.

24. See, for example, Louis S. Richman, "America's Tough New Job Market," *Fortune* (February 24, 1992), pp. 52–61.

25. See for example, John A. Byrne, "Why Downsizing Looks Different These Days," *Business Week* (October 19, 1994), p. 43.

26. Company and data taken from: "Taking an Ax to Allied," *Business Week* (November 4, 1991), p. 70; Donna Milbank, "Goodyear Plans to Further Cut Its Work Force," *The Wall Street Journal* (March 14, 1991), p. A–4; Neil Templin, "Ford to End Some Benefits to Executives, Cut Payroll," *The Wall Street Journal* (March 1, 1991), p. A–1; Laurie M. Grossman, "Pepsi to Take $62.3 Million in Change While Cutting 1,800 Jobs at Frito-Lay," *The Wall Street Journal* (September 17, 1991), p. A–4; Paul B. Carroll, "IBM Plans $3 Billion Charge and About 20,000 Jobs Cut," *The Wall Street Journal* (November 27, 1991), p. A–3.

27. John E. Gutknecht and J. Bernard Keys, "Mergers, Acquisitions, and Takeovers: Maintaining Morale of Survivors and Protecting Employees," *Academy of Management Executive*, Vol. 7, No. 3 (1993), p. 26.

28. John A. Byrne, p. 43.

29. Ibid.

30. This section is drawn from William Bridges, "The End of the Job," *Fortune* (September 19, 1994), pp. 62–74.

31. See John E. Gutknecht and J. Bernard Keys, pp. 26–35.

32. John A. Byrne, "Why Downsizing Looks Different These Days," *Business Week* (October 10, 1994), p. 43.

33. William Bridges, p. 72.

34. See, for example, Richard L. Bunning, "The Dynamics of Downsizing," *Personnel Journal* (September 1990), pp. 69–75.

35. Story adapted from Michael A. Verspej, "The New Workweek," *Industry Week* (November 6, 1989), p. 14.

36. Ibid.; see also Alan Deutschman, "Pioneers of New Balance," *Fortune* (May 20, 1991), p. 50.

37. Sharon Nelton, "A Flexible Style of Management," *Nation's Business* (December 1993), pp. 24–31; and Amy Saltzman, "Family Friendliness," *U.S. News and World Report* (February 22, 1993), pp. 59–66.

38. Jaclyn Fierman, "Are Companies Less Family-Friendly?" *Fortune* (March 21, 1994), pp. 64–67.

39. Bunning, p. 73.

40. Ibid.; see also Elaine M. Duffy, Richard M. O'Brien, William P. Brittian, and Stephen Cuthrell, "Behavioral Outplacement: A Shorter, Sweeter Approach," *Personnel* (March 1988), pp. 28–33.

41. Bunning, p. 73; see also Robert Volino, "Beyond Outplacement," *Information Week* (February 18, 1991), p. 24.

42. "Most Employers Laud `Outplacement' Firms, but Few Demur," *The Wall Street Journal* (October 1, 1991), p. A–1.

43. Case based on information provided in Michael Meyer, Stryker McQuire, Charles Fleming, Mark Millen, Andrew Murr, and Daniel McGuire, "Of Mice and Men," *Newsweek* (September 5, 1994), pp. 41–47; and "Disney Studios Chief Abruptly Resigns," *The Baltimore Sun* (August 25, 1994), p. 9D; 12D.

Chapter 6

1. Nancy Hass, and Seema Nayyar, "Squares Need Not Apply," *Newsweek* (June 27, 1994), p. 44.
2. Jim Castelli, "Finding the Right Fit," *HRMagazine* (September 1990), pp. 38–39.
3. Joseph Pereira and Joann S. Lublin, "A New CEO for Cherry Garcia's Creators," *The Wall Street Journal* (February 2, 1995), p. B–1.
4. Justin Martin, "One Company's Hiring Binge," *Fortune* (February 7, 1994), p. 14.
5. See, for example, Brian Dumaine, "Is Big Still Good?" *Fortune* (April 20, 1992), pp. 56–60; and "Rent-A-Center's Rapid Growth Challenges Human Resources to Recruit and Retain," *Chain Store Age Executive,* Vol. 667, No. 11 (November 1991), p. 6.
6. Andrew S. Bargerstock and Gerald Swanson, "Four Ways to Build Cooperative Recruitment Alliances," *HRMagazine* (March 1991), p. 49.
7. Ibid., pp. 50–51.
8. Linda B. Robin, "Recruitment: Troubleshooting Recruitment Problems," *Personnel Journal* (September 1988), p. 94.
9. See, for example, Stephen J. Holoviak and David A. De Cenzo, contributing eds., "Service Industry Seeks Summer Help," *Audio Human Resource Report,* Vol. 1, No. 9 (October 1990), p. 5.
10. See, for example, Clyde J. Scott, "Recruitment: Employing a Private Employment Firm," *Personnel Journal* (September 1989), pp. 78–83.
11. See, for example, "The New Headhunters," *Business Week* (February 6, 1988), pp. 64–71.
12. Ibid.
13. Laura M. Graves, "College Recruitment: Removing Personal Bias from Selection Devices," *Personnel* (March 1989), p. 48.
14. John Ross, "Effective Ways to Hire Contingent Personnel," *HRMagazine* (February 1991), pp. 52–53.
15. Ibid., p. 53. See also Steve Bergsman, "Setting Up a Temporary Shop," *HRMagazine* (February 1990), pp. 46–49.
16. "The Temporary Help Business," *The Wall Street Journal* (February 25, 1992), p. A–1.
17. See, for example, American Association of Retired Persons, *How to Recruit Older Workers* (Washington, D.C.: American Association of Retired Persons, 1993).
18. Lee Phillion and John R. Brugger, "Encore! Retirees Give Top Performance as Temporaries," *HRMagazine* (October 1994), pp. 74–77.
19. Reasons cited by the American Association of Retired Persons include the need to make money, to get health insurance coverage, to develop skills, to use their time more productively, to feel useful, to make new friends, to provide some structure to their daily lives, or to have a sense of achievement. See *How to Recruit Older Workers,* p. 27.
20. American Association of Retired Persons and the Society for Human Resource Management, *The Older Workforce: Recruitment and Retention* (Washington, D.C.: American Association of Retired Persons, 1993), p. 1.
21. Susan Greco, "Recruiting the Newly Retired," *Inc.* (August 1993), p. 23.
22. Caution is warranted regarding for whom an individual works. Generally, the employee is the responsibility of the leasing company. But under certain circumstances, like long-term duration of the lease, the acquiring organization may be the employer of record, with the leasing company handling a variety of HRM associated paperwork. See Jane Easter Bahls, "Employees for Rent," *Nation's Business* (June 1991), p. 36.
23. Bargerstock and Swanson, p. 50.
24. This story was influenced by an example in Arthur Sloan, *Personnel: Managing Human Resources* (Englewood Cliffs, N.J.: Prentice-Hall, 1983), p. 127.

25. See *Albermarle Paper Company* reference in Chapter 3.

26. See, for example, E. James Randall and Cindy H. Randall, "Review of Salesperson Selection Techniques and Criteria: A Managerial Approach," *International Journal of Research in Marketing,* Vol. 7, No. 2 (December 1990), pp. 81–95.

27. Ronald Henkoff, "Finding, Training, and Keeping the Best Service Workers," *Fortune* (October 3, 1994), p. 118.

28. See, for example, "What Personnel Offices Really Stress in Hiring," *The Wall Street Journal* (March 6, 1991), p. A–1.

29. "Responsible Background," ad in *HRMagazine* (February 1991), p. 50.

30. Adapted from Micelle Singletary, "Reference Gives Needed Wariness," *The Baltimore Sun* (October 28, 1991), pp. E1; E8; Commerce Clearing House, "Reference Checks/Lawsuits," *Human Resources Management: Ideas and Trends* (February 7, 1990), pp. 24–25; and "Management," *R&D Magazine* (April 1990), p. 95.

31. See, for example, Joyce Lain Kennedy and Dr. Darryl Laramore, *Career Book* (Lincolnwood, Ill.: National Textbook Company, 1988), Section 6; John L. Holland, *Making Vocational Choices: A Theory of Vocational Personalities and Work Environments,* 2nd ed. (Englewood Cliffs, N.J.: Prentice Hall, 1985); John L. Holland, Gary D. Gottfredson, and Deborah Kimili Ogwawa, *Dictionary of Holland Occupational Codes: A Comprehensive Cross-Index of Holland's RIASEC Codes with 12,000 DOT Occupations* (Palo Alto, Calif.: Consulting Psychologists Press, Inc., 1982).

32. See David E. Bowen, Gerald E. Ledford, Jr., and Barry R. Nathan, "Hiring for the Organization, Not the Job," *Academy of Management Executive,* Vol. 5, No. 4 (November 1991), pp. 35–51.

33. See, for example, Sara L. Rynes, Robert D. Bretz, and Barry Gerhart, "The Importance of Recruitment in Job Choice: A Different Way of Looking," *Personnel Psychology,* Vol. 44, No. 3 (Autumn 1991), pp. 487–521.

34. See, for example, Charles A. O'Reilly III, David I. Caldwell, and Richard Mirable, "A Profile Comparison Approach to Person v. Job Fit: More Than a Mirage," in Jerry L. Wall and Lawrence R. Jauch, eds., *Academy of Management Best Papers Proceedings 1992, Las Vegas* (August 9–12, 1992), pp. 237–42.

35. See, for example, Thomas F. Casey, "Making the Most of a Selection Interview," *Personnel* (September 1990), pp. 41–43.

36. See, for example, Wayne Casio, *Applied Psychology in Personnel Management* (Englewood Cliffs, N.J.: Prentice-Hall, 1991), pp. 151–54.

37. See, for example, Richard Kern, "IQ Tests for Salesmen Make a Comeback," *Sales and Marketing* (April 1988), pp. 42–46.

38. A limitation of concurrent validity is the possibility of restricting the range of scores in testing current employees. This occurs because current employees may have been in the upper range of applicants. Those not hired were undesirable for some reason. Therefore, these scores theoretically should represent only the top portion of previous applicant scores.

39. A specific correlation coefficient for validation purposes is nearly impossible to pinpoint. There are many variables that will enter into the picture, such as the sample size, the power of the test, and what is measured. However, for EEO purposes, correlation coefficients must be indicative of a situation where the results are predictive of performance that is greater than one where chance alone dictated the outcomes.

40. Cut scores are determined through a set of mathematical formulas—namely, a regression analysis and the equation of a line. We refer you to any good introductory statistics text for a reminder of how these formulas operate.

41. Frank L. Schmidt and John E. Hunter, "Developing a General Solution to the Problem of Validity Generalization," *Journal of Applied Psychology,* Vol. 62, No. 5 (October 1977), pp. 529–39.

42. Lauress L. Wise, Jeffrey McHenry, and John P. Campbell, "Identifying Optimal Predictor Composites and Testing for Generalizability Across Jobs and Performance Factors," *Personnel Psychology,* Vol. 43, No. 2 (Summer 1990), pp. 355–66.

43. Frank L. Schmidt, Kenneth Pearlman, John E. Hunter, and Hannah Rothstein Hirsh, "Forty Questions About Validity Generalization and Meta-Analysis," *Personnel Psychology,* Vol. 38, No. 4 (Winter 1985), pp. 697–822.

44. This exercise was directly influenced by and adapted from Richard W. Beatty and Craig Eric Schneier, *Personnel Administration*. Reprinted with permission of Addison-Wesley Publishing Company, 1981.

45. Case scenario is adapted from "When in Japan Recruit as the Japanese Do," *Business Week* (June 24, 1991), p. 64.

Chapter 7

1. "Best Practices: Hiring," *Inc.,* (March 1994), p. 10.

2. Ibid.

3. Wayne F. Casio, *Applied Psychology in Personnel Management* (Englewood Cliffs, N.J.: Prentice-Hall, 1991), p. 265. See also Edson G. Hammer and Lawrence S. Kleinman, "Getting to Know You," *Personnel Administration,* Vol. 33 (May 1988), pp. 86–92.

4. Wayne Casio, p. 265. see also Edson G. Hammer and Lawrence S. Kleinman, pp. 86–92.

5. See, for example, Brooks Mitchell, "Bio Data: Using Employment Applications to Screen New Hires," *Cornell Hotel and Restaurant Administration Quarterly,* Vol. 29, No. 4 (February 1989), pp. 56–61.

6. See, for example, M. C. Smith, J. M. Smith, and D. I. George, "Improving Access through a Software Design for the Weighted Application Form," *Journal of Occupational Psychology,* Vol. 61, No. 3 (September 1988), pp. 257–64.

7. Mitchell, p. 58. The seven items were not specifically identified so that the competitive edge the hotel had in hiring practices would not be weakened.

8. Jack J. Kramer and Jane Close Conoley, supplement to *The Tenth Mental Measurements Yearbook* (Lincoln, Neb.: Buros Institute of Mental Measurements, 1990).

9. John B. Miner, *Industrial Psychology* (New York: McGraw-Hill, 1992).

10. See, for example, Walter C. Borman and Glenn L. Hallman, "Observation Accuracy for Assessors of Work Sample Performance: Consistency Across Task and Individual Differences Correlates," *Journal of Applied Psychology,* Vol. 76, No. 4 (February 1991), p. 11. See also Ivan T. Robertson and Sylvia Downs, "Work Sample Tests of Trainability: A Meta Analysis," *Journal of Applied Psychology,* Vol. 74, No. 3 (June 1989), pp. 402–10.

11. See, for example, Cynthia D. Fisher, Lyle F. Schoenfeldt, and James B. Shaw, *Human Resource Management* (Boston: Houghton Mifflin, 1990), p. 264.

12. See, for example, Jeffrey R. Schneider and Neil Schmitt, "An Executive Approach to Understanding Assessment Center Dimension and Exercise Constructs," *Journal of Applied Psychology,* Vol. 77, No. 1 (February 1992), pp. 32–35.

13. Craig Russell, "Selecting Top Corporate Leaders: An Example of Biographical Information," *Journal of Management,* Vol. 16, No. 1 (March 1990), p. 74.

14. George Munchos III and Barbara McArthur, "Revisiting the Historical Use of Assessment Centers in Management Selection and Development," *Journal of Management Development,* Vol. 10, No. 1 (1991), p. 5.

15. Interview with George Shaffer, AT&T Assessment Director, March 12, 1992. Cost figures are not released according to company policy regarding proprietary information.

16. See, for example, Victor Dulewicz, "Improving Assessment Centers," *Personnel Management,* Vol. 23, No. 6 (June 1991), pp. 50–55.

17. See David L. Kurtz, C. Patrick Flecnor, Louis E. Boon, and Virginia M. Rider, "CEOs: A Handwriting Analysis," *Business Horizons,* Vol. 32, No. 1 (January–February 1989), pp. 41–43.

18. Ibid., p. 41.

19. Alan Fowler, "An Even-Handed Approach to Graphology," *Personnel Management,* Vol. 23, No. 3 (March 1991), pp. 40–43. See also "Graphology: The Power of the Written Word," *Economist,* Vol. 2315, No. 7659 (June 11, 1990), p. 97.

20. David Nye, "Son of the Polygraph," *Across the Board,* Vol. 26, No. 6 (June 1989), p. 20.

21. John F. Steiner, "Honesty Testing," *Business Forum,* Vol. 15, No. 2 (Spring 1990), p. 31.

22. See Rom Zemke, "Do Honesty Tests Tell the Truth?" *Training*, Vol. 27, No. 10 (October 1990), pp. 75–81. Also see Robin Inwald, "Those Little White Lies of Honesty Vendors," *Personnel*, Vol. 67, No. 6 (June 1990), p. 52.

23. Jerry Beilinson, "Applicant Screening Methods: Under Surveillance," *Personnel*, Vol. 67, No. 12 (December 1990), p. 3.

24. See Zemke, p. 75.

25. Linda D. McGill, "Psychological Tests in the Workplace: Should Your Company Use Them?" *Employee Relations Today*, Vol. 17, No. 3 (Autumn 1990), p. 227.

26. See also John W. Jones, Philip Ash, and Catalina Coto, "Employment Privacy Rights and Pre-Employment Honesty Tests," *Employee Relations Law Journal*, Vol. 15, No. 4 (Spring 1990), pp. 561–75.

27. Steven D. Maurer and Thomas W. Lee, "Toward a Resolution of Contrast Error in the Employment Interview: A Test of the Situational Interview," *Academy of Management Best Papers Proceedings*, Dorothy P. Moore, ed. (August 14-17, 1994), pp. 132–36.

28. Vignettes based on Tom Washington, "Selling Yourself in Job Interviews," *National Business Employment Weekly* (Spring/Summer 1993), p. 30.

29. For a discussion on fit and its appropriateness to the interviewing process, see "The Right Fit," *Small Business Reports* (April 1993), p. 28.

30. See, for example, A.I. Huffcutt and W. Arthur, Jr., "Hunter and Hunter (1984) Revisited: Interview Validity for Entry-Level Jobs," *Journal of Applied Psychology* (April 1994), pp. 184–90; M.A. McDaniel, D.L. Whetzel, F.L. Schmidt, and S.D. Maurer, "The Validity of Employment Interviews: A Comprehensive Review and Meta-Analysis," *Journal of Applied Psychology* (August 1994), p. 599–616; and Herbert George Baker and Morris S. Spier, "The Employment Interview: Guaranteed Improvement in Reliability," *Public Personnel Management* (Spring 1990), pp. 85–87.

31. Robert C. Dipboye, *Selection Interviews: Process Perspectives* (Cincinnati: Southwestern Publishing Co., 1992), pp. 6–9.

32. Adapted from Baker and Spier, p. 87; and Dipboye, Chapter 1.

33. Edward C. Webster, *Decision Making in the Employment Interview* (Montreal: Industrial Relations Center, McGill University, 1964).

34. Dipboye, p. 8; and Baker and Spier, p. 87.

35. For a more detailed discussion of impression management, see Amy L. Kristof and Cynthia Kay Stevens, "Applicant Impression Management Tactics: Effects on Interviewer Evaluations and Interview Outcomes," *Academy of Management Best Papers Proceedings*, Dorothy P. Moore, ed. (August 14–17, 1994), pp. 127–31.

36. Reported in Robert E. Carlson, Paul W. Thayer, Eugene C. Mayfield, and Donald A. Peterson, "Improvements in the Selection Interview," *Personnel Journal* (April 1971), p. 272.

37. Dipboye, p. 201.

38. Michael P. Cronin, "Try Taping Those Interviews," *Inc.* (September 1994), p. 120.

39. See, for example, Wayne F. Casio, *Applied Psychology in Personnel Management*, 4th ed. (Englewood Cliffs, N.J.: Prentice-Hall, 1991), p. 271.

40. Ibid.

41. See, for example, Casio, p. 273; A. Phillips and R.L. Dipboye, "Correlation Tests of Predictions from a Process Model of the Interview," *Journal of Applied Psychology*, Vol. 74 (1989), pp. 41–52; M. Ronald Buckley and Robert W. Edner, "B.M. Springbett and the Notion of the `Snap Decision' in the Interview," *Journal of Management*, Vol. 14, No. 1 (March 1988), pp. 59–67.

42. See, for example, Dipboye, pp. 39–45.

43. Michael W. Mercer, "Turnover: Reducing the Costs," *Personnel*, Vol. 65, No. 12 (December 1988), p. 36.

44. See, for example, Bruce M. Meglino, Angelo S. DeNisi, Stuart A. Youngblood, and Kevin J. Williams, "Effects of Realistic Job Previews," *Journal of Applied Psychology*, Vol. 79, No. 2 (May 1988), pp. 259–66.

45. Bruce M. Meglino and Angelo S. DeNisi, "Realistic Job Previews: Some Thoughts on Their More Effective Use in Managing the Flow of Human Resources," *Human Resources Planning*, Vol. 10, No. 3 (Fall 1987), p. 157.

46. Ibid.

47. See, for example, Robert J. Vanderberg and Vida Scarpello, "The Matching Model: An Examination of the Processes Underlying Realistic Previews," *Journal of Applied Psychology,* Vol. 75, No. 1 (February 1990), pp. 60–67.

48. Stories adapted from "Revenge of the Fired," *Newsweek* (February 11, 1987), pp. 46–47.

49. Ibid.

50. See, for example, Gregory Service, "Keeping Out of Court," *Security Management Supplement* (July 1990), p. 11A.

51. See, for example, Michael A. McDaniel, "Biographical Constructs for Predicting Employee Suitability," *Journal of Applied Psychology,* Vol. 74, No. 6 (December 1989), pp. 964–70; and Michael Tadman, "The Past Predicts the Future," *Security Management,* Vol. 33, No. 7 (July 1989), pp. 57–61.

52. Commerce Clearing House, *Human Resources Management: Ideas and Trends* (May 17, 1992), p. 85.

53. Norman D. Bates, "Understanding the Liability of Negligent Hiring," *Security Management Supplement* (July 1990), p. 7A.

54. William T. Hill, "Getting Help from the Outside," *Security Management Supplement* (July 1990), p. 15A.

55. Ibid.

56. Commerce Clearing House, pp. 439–40.

57. William R. Coradetti, "Teamwork Takes Time and a Lot of Energy," *HRMagazine* (June 1994), p. 74; and Brian Dumaine, "Who Needs a Boss?" *Fortune* (May 7, 1990), p. 52–62.

58. Dale E. Yeatts, Martha Hipskind, and Debra Barnes, "Lessons Learned from Self-Managed Work Teams," *Business Horizons* (July/August 1994), p. 11–18.

59. "How to Form Hiring Teams," *Personnel Journal* (August 1994), p. 14–17.

60. See for example, Alexander Mikalachki, "Creating a Winning Team," *Business Quarterly* (Summer 1994), pp. 14–22.

61. "How to Form Hiring Teams," p. 14.

62. Based on Roy J. Lewicki, Donald D. Bowen, Douglas T. Hall, and Francine S. Hall, *Experiences in Management and Organization Behavior,* third ed (New York, NY: John Wiley & Sons, Inc., 1988), pp. 268–70. Used with permission.

63. This case is based on the article, Michael P. Cronin and Stephanie Gruner, "Hiring: The Devil You Know?" *Inc.* (April 1994), p. 109.

Chapter 8

1. This opening vignette is based on Carol S. Klein and Jeff Taylor, "Employee Orientation Is an Ongoing Process at the DuPont Merck Pharmaceutical Company." *Personnel Journal* (May 1994), p. 67.

2. See, for example, Zandy B. Leibowitz, Nancy K. Schlossberg, and Jane E. Shore, "Stopping the Revolving Door," *Training and Development Journal,* Vol. 45, No. 2 (February 1991), pp. 43–50.

3. Ibid.

4. See, for example, Jitendra M. Mishra and Pam Strait, "Employee Orientation: The Key to Lasting and Productive Results, "*Health Care Supervisor*" (March 1993), pp. 19–29; Henry L. Tosi, *Organizational Behavior and Management: A Contingency Approach* (Boston, Mass.: PWS Kent Publishing, 1990), pp. 233–35; also John Van Maanen, "People Processing: Strategies of Organizational Socialization," in Henry L. Tosi's *Organizational Behavior and Management: A Contingency Approach,* pp. 65–66.

5. See for instance, R. L. Falcione and C. E. Wilson, "Socialization Process in Organizations," in G. M. Goldhar and G. A. Barnett (eds.) *Handbook of Organizational Communication* (Norwood, N.J.: Ablex Publishing, 1988), pp. 151–70; N. J. Allen and J.P. Meyer, "Organizational Socialization Tactics: A Longitudinal Analysis of Links to Newcomers' Commitment and Role Orientation," *Academy of Management Journal* (December 1990), pp. 847–58; V. D. Miller and F. M. Jablin, "Information Seeking During Organizational Entry: Influences, Tactics, and a Model of Process," *Academy of Management Review* (January 1991), pp. 92–120; and J. A. Chatam, "Matching Peo-

ple and Organizations: Selection and Socialization in Public Accounting Firms," *Administrative Science Quarterly* (September 1991), pp. 459–84.

6. Shirley A. Hopkins and Willie E. Hopkins, "Organizational Productivity 2000: A Work Force Perspective," *SAM Advanced Management Journal* (Autumn 1991), pp. 44–48.

7. See, for example, Timothy J. Fogarty, "Organizational Socialization in Accounting Firms: A Theoretical Framework and Agenda for Future Research," *Accounting, Organizations, and Society* (February 1992), p. 129–50.

8. Coy A. Jones and William R. Crandall, "Determining the Source of Voluntary Employee Turnover," *SAM Advanced Management Journal* (March 22, 1991), p. 16.

9. John Van Maanen, and Edgar H. Schein, "Career Development," in J. Richard Hackman and J. Lloyd Suttle (eds.), *Improving Life at Work* (Santa Monica, Cal.: Goodyear, 1977), pp. 58–62. See also J. P. Wanous, A. E. Reichers, and S. D. Malik, "Organizational Socialization and Group Development," *Academy of Management Review*, Vol. 9 (1992), pp. 670–83.

10. D. C. Feldman, "The Multiple Socialization of Organization Members," *Academy of Management Review* (April 1981), p. 310.

11. For a thorough discussion of these issues, see Jennifer A. Chatman, "Matching People and Organizations: Selection and Socialization in Public Accounting Firms," *Administrative Science Quarterly* (September 1991), pp. 459–85.

12. For example, see Lisa K. Gundry, "Fitting Into Technical Organizations: The Socialization of Newcomer Engineers," *IEEE Transactions of Engineering Management* (November 1993), p. 335.

13. For an interesting viewpoint on selection fit and socialization, see Isaiah O. Ugboro, "Loyalty, Value Congruency, and Affective Organizational Commitment: An Empirical Study," *Mid-American Journal of Business* (Fall 1993), pp. 29–37.

14. Ibid., p. 59.

15. Rabindra N. Kanungo and Jay A. Conger, "Promoting Altruism as a Corporate Goal," *Executive* (August 1993), pp. 37–48; Elizabeth Wolfe Morrison, "Longitudinal Study of the Effects of Information Seeking on Newcomer Socialization," *Journal of Applied Psychology* (April 1993), pp. 173–83; and Laurie K. Lewis and David R. Seinbold, "Innovation Modification During Intraorganizational Adoption, *Academy of Management Review* (April 1993), pp. 322–54.

16. Karen Bridges, Gail Hawkins, and Keli Elledge, "From New Recruit to Team Members," *Training and Development* (August 1993), pp. 55–59.

17. Cheri Ostroff and Steve W. J. Kozlowski, "Organizational Socialization as a Learning Process: The Role of Information Acquisition," *Personnel Psychology* (Winter 1992), pp. 849–74.

18. Tayla N. Bauer, and Stephen G. Green, "Effect of Newcomer Involvement in Work-Related Activities: A Longitudinal Study of Socialization," *Journal of Applied Psychology* (April 1994), pp. 211–23.

19. See, for example, H. Eugene Baker III and Daniel C. Feldman, "Linking Organizational Socialization Tactics with Corporate Human Resource Management Strategies," *Human Resource Management Review*, Vol. 1, No. 3 (Fall 1991), pp. 193–202.

20. John Van Maanen and Edgar H. Schein, "Toward a Theory of Organizational Socialization," in *Research in Organizational Behavior*, ed. Barry M. Staw (Greenwich, Conn.: JAI Press, 1979), p. 210. See also "New Employee Orientation: Ensuring A Smooth Transition," *Small Business Report*, Vol. 13, No. 7 (July 1988), pp. 40–43.

21. Van Maanen, pp. 80–81.

22. See Thomas J. Peters and Robert H. Waterman, *In Search of Excellence: Lessons from America's Best Run Companies* (New York: Harper & Row, 1982).

23. Adapted from Richard F. Federico, "Six Ways to Solve the Orientation Blues," *HRMagazine*, Vol. 36, No. 5 (May 1991), p. 69.

24. Andre Nelson, "New Employee Orientation: Are They Really Worthwhile?" *Supervision*, Vol. 51, No. 11 (November 1990), p. 6.

25. J. P. McCarthy, "Focus from the Start," *HRMagazine* (September 1992), pp. 77–83.

26. M. Michael Markowich and Jo Anna Farber, "If Your Employees Were the Customers," *Personnel Administrator*, Vol. 34, No. 9 (September 1989), p. 70.

27. Ibid., p. 71.

28. Allan Halcrow, "A Day in the Life of Levi Strauss," *Personnel Journal*, Vol. 67, No. 11 (November 1988), p. 14.

29. See, for example, Joseph F. McKenna, "Training: Welcome Aboard," *Industry Week*, Vol. 238, No. 21 (November 6, 1989), pp. 31–38.

30. Jeff Brechlin and Allison Rossett, "Orienting New Employees," *Training*, Vol. 28, No. 4 (April 1991), pp. 45–51.

31. See Marsha Kurman, "Customer Relations: The Personnel Angle," *Personnel*, Vol. 64, No. 9 (September 1987), pp. 38–40.

32. Linda J. Bennett, "Why Benefits Communications Is Your Business," *Supervisory Management* (June 1993), p. 10.

33. Federico.

34. Debra R. Comer, "Peers as Providers," *Personnel Administrator*, Vol. 34, No. 5 (May 1989), p. 84.

35. John Kane and Tony Wallace, "Developing Supervision," *Personnel Management*, Vol. 23, No. 10 (October 1991), p. 46.

36. Case based on information contained in Ronald Henkoff, "Finding, Training, and Keeping the Best Service Workers," *Fortune* (October 3, 1994), pp. 110–16.

Chapter 9

1. Michael P. Cronin, "Training: Asking Workers What They Want," *Inc.* (August 1994), p. 103.

2. Ronald Henkoff, "Companies that Train Best," *Fortune* (March 22, 1993), p. 62; and Commerce Clearing House, "Quality Challenge for HR: Linking Training to Quality Program Goals," *1994 SHRM/CCH Survey* (June 22, 1994), p. 1.

3. See, for example, Richard G. Zalman, "The Basics of In-House Skills Training," *HRMagazine* (February 1991), pp. 74–78.

4. David E. Bartz, David R. Schwandt, and Larry W. Hillman, "Difference Between 'T' and 'D,'" *Personnel Administrator* (June 1989), p. 164.

5. Ibid. A case can also be built that development can also occur for a current job, where, for example, a new skill is required because one will have greater responsibility. Nonetheless, we will differentiate these two primarily by time frames.

6. See Marilyn B. Gilbert and Thomas F. Gilbert, "What Skinner Gave Us," *Training*, Vol. 28, No. 9 (September 1991), pp. 42–48; see also B. F. Skinner, *Beyond Freedom and Dignity* (New York: Knopf, 1971).

7. See Stephen P. Robbins, *Organizational Behavior: Concepts, Controversy, and Applications*, 6th ed. (Englewood Cliffs, N.J.: Prentice-Hall, 1993), pp. 111–12.

8. See, for example, J. Stewart Black and Mark E. Mendenhall, "The U-Curve Adjustment Hypothesis Revisited: A Review and Theoretical Framework," *Journal of International Business Studies*, Vol. 22, No. 2 (2nd Quarter, 1991), pp. 225–47; Linda Klebe Trevino and Stuart A. Youngblood, "Bad Apples in Bad Barrels: A Causal Analysis of Ethical Decision-Making Behavior," *Journal of Applied Psychology*, Vol. 75, No. 4 (August 1990), pp. 378–85; see also Albert Bandura, *Social Learning Theory* (Englewood Cliffs, N.J.: Prentice-Hall, 1977).

9. See, for example, Howard J. Klein, "An Integrated Control Theory Model of Work Motivation," *Academy of Management Review*, Vol. 14, No. 2 (April 1989), pp. 150–72.

10. Commerce Clearing House, "Interview with George Odiorne," *Human Resource Management: Ideas and Trends*, No. 165 (March 22, 1988), p. 45.

11. Commerce Clearing House, "Training and Retention Programs," Topical Law Reports: *Human Resources Management Personnel Practices/Communication* (January 1990), p. 555.

12. Beth Rogers, "The Making of a Highly Skilled Worker," *HRMagazine* (July 1994), p. 62.

13. Leslie A. Bryan, Jr., "An Ounce of Prevention for Workplace Accidents," *Training and Development Journal*, Vol. 44, No. 7 (July 1990), p. 101.

14. William J. Rothwell and H. C. Kazanas, "Planned OJT Is Productive OJT," *Training and Development Journal*, Vol. 44, No. 10 (October 1990), pp. 53–56.

15. Ibid., p. 55, and Bryan, Jr., p. 102.

16. Richard P. Lookatch, "How to Talk to a Talking Head," *Training and Development Journal,* Vol. 44, No. 9 (September 1990), pp. 63–65.

17. See Jo McHale and David Flegg, "Training Extra: Screentest," *Personnel Management,* Vol. 23, No. 6 (June 1991), p. 69; Patricia A. Galagan, "IBM Faces the Future Again," *Training and Development Journal,* Vol. 44, No. 3 (March 1990), p. 36; and Bob Filipczak, "Leaders of the Pack," *Training,* Vol. 26, No. 12 (December 1989), p. 49.

18. Chris Lee, "Who Gets Trained in What," *Training,* Vol. 28, No. 10 (October 1991), p. 57.

19. William W. Lee, "Bridging the Gap with IVD," *Training and Development Journal,* Vol. 44, No. 3 (March 1990), p. 64.

20. See, for example, Gene Bylinsky, "The Marvels of Virtual Reality," *Fortune* (June 3, 1991), p. 138.

21. Bob Filipczak, "Distance Teamwork," *Training* (April 1994), p. 71; and Randall Johnson, "Alternative Methods: Technology, Good Client Relations Help Training to Thrive," *Training* (July 1992), p. B–05.

22. Ibid.

23. Jane Pickard, "Training on Another Plane," *Personnel Management* (August 1992), pp. 45–47.

24. See for example, Michael Emery, and Margaret Schubert, "A Trainer's Guide to Videoconferencing," *Training* (June 1993), pp. 59–64; and Bob Filipczak, "Distance Teamwork," *Training* (April 1994), p. 71.

25. See, for example, "Survival Training for Employees," *ABC World News Tonight/American Agenda* (July 21, 1993).

26. Commerce Clearing House, "Should Your Company Encourage Mentoring?" *Human Resources Management: Ideas and Trends* (July 20, 1994), p. 122.

27. Sue Shellenbarger, "Corporate America Grooms Women Execs," *Working Woman* (October 1993), pp. 13–14.

28. See, for example, James A. Wilson and Nancy S. Elman, "Organizational Benefits of Mentoring," *Academy of Management Executive,* Vol. 4, No. 4 (November 1990), pp. 88–94.

29. Ibid.

30. Sue Shellenbarger, p. 13.

31. Michelle Neely Martinez, *HRMagazine,* Vol. 36, No. 6 (June 1991), p. 46.

32. George F. Dreher and Ronald A. Ash, "A Comparative Study of Mentoring Among Men and Women in Managerial Professional, and Technical Positions," *Journal of Applied Psychology,* Vol. 75, No. 5 (October 1990), pp. 539–46.

33. For an excellent discussion of these issues, see William Whitely, Thomas W. Dougherty, and George F. Dreher, "Relationship of Career Mentoring and Socioeconomic Origin to Managers' and Professionals' Early Career Progress," *Academy of Management Journal,* Vol. 34, No. 5 (June 1991), pp. 331–51.

34. Daniel B. Turban and Thomas W. Dougherty, "Protégé Personality, Mentoring, and Career Success," in Jerry L. Wall and Lawrence R. Jauch (eds.) *Academy of Management Best Papers Proceedings 1992,* Las Vegas, Nevada (August 9–12, 1992), p. 419.

35. For a discussion of mentoring and minorities, see David A. Thomas, "The Impact of Race on Managers' Experiences of Developmental Relationships: An Intra-Organizational Study," *Journal of Organizational Behavior,* Vol. 11, No. 6 (November 1990), pp. 479–92. For an opposing view of mentoring and women/race issues, see Belle Rose Ragins, and Terri A. Scandura, "Gender and the Termination of Mentoring Relationships, *Academy of Management Best Papers Proceedings,* Dorothy P. Moore, ed., (August 14–17, 1994), pp. 361–65.

36. Michael D. Esposito, "Affirmative Action and the Staffing Demands of the 1990s," *Journal of Compensation and Benefits,* Vol. 6, No. 4 (January–February 1991), p. 41.

37. Cheryl McCortie, "Mentoring Young Achievers," *Black Enterprise,* Vol. 21, No. 11 (June 1991), p. 336.

38. See, for example, Stephen C. Bushardt, Cherie Elaine Fretwell, and B. J. Holdnak, "The Mentor/Protégé Relationship: A Biological Perspective," *Human Relations,* Vol. 44, No. 6 (June 1991), pp. 619–39.

39. See for example, Belle Rose Ragins and Terri A. Scandura, "Gender Differences in Expected Outcomes of Mentoring Relationships," *Academy of Management Journal* (1994), pp. 957–71.

40. John Lorinc, "The Mentor Gap—Older Men Guiding Younger Women: The Perils and Payoffs," *Canadian Business,* Vol. 63, No. 9 (September 1990), p. 93.

41. See Ronald J. Burke and Carol A. McKeen, "Mentoring in Organizations: Implications for Women," *Journal of Business Ethics,* Vol. 9, No. 4 (April–May 1990), pp. 317–32.

42. "Mentoring Programs Face Hard Times in the `90s," *The Wall Street Journal* (March 24, 1992), p. A–1.

43. Jerry Wisinski, "A Logical Approach to a Difficult Employee," *HR Focus* (January 1992), p. 9.

44. Ibid.

45. Gerald D. Cook, "Employee Counseling Session," *Supervision* (August 1989), p. 3.

46. See James Greiff, "When an Employee's Performance Slumps," *Nation's Business* (January 1989), pp. 44–45.

47. Kurt Lewin, *Field Theory in Social Science* (New York: Harper & Row, 1951).

48. R. Wayne Pace, Phillip C. Smith, and Gordon E. Mills, *Human Resource Development* (Englewood Cliffs, N.J.: Prentice-Hall, 1991), p. 131.

49. Ibid.

50. Thomas A. Stewart, "Reengineering: The Hot New Managing Tool," *Fortune* (August 23, 1994\3), pp. 41–48.

51. See Scott Kerr, "Managing Change Successfully," *Leadership and Organization Development Journal,* Vol. 12, No. 1 (January 1991), p. 2.

52. E. J. Muller, "How to Be an Agent of Change," *Distribution,* Vol. 90, No. 13 (1991), p. 24.

53. Ibid., p. 26.

54. See William Weitzel and Ellen Johnson, "Reversing the Downward Spiral: Lesson from W. T. Grant and Sears Roebuck," *Academy of Management Review,* Vol. 5, No. 3 (August 1991), pp. 7–22; Alan L. Wilgus, "Forging Change in Spite of Adversity," *Personnel Journal,* Vol. 70, No. 9 (September 1991), pp. 60–67; and Kevin Doyle, "The Many Behind the Men in Blue," *Incentive,* Vol. 165, No. 11 (November 1991), pp. 39–45.

55. Jacquelyn S. DeMatteo, Gregory H. Dobbins, and Kyle M. Lundby, "The Effects of Accountability on Training Effectiveness," *Academy of Management Best Papers Proceedings,* Dorothy P. Moore, ed. (August 4–17, 1994), p. 122; and Ronald Henkoff, "Companies that Train Best," p. 62.

56. Ronald Henkoff, "Companies that Train Best," p. 62.

57. See, for example, Joseph W. Weiss and Stanley Bloom, "Managing in China: Expatriate Experiences in Training," *Business Horizons,* Vol. 33, No. 3 (May–June 1990), pp. 23–29.

58. S. Ronen, "Training the International Assignee," in I.L. Goldstein & Associates (eds.), *Training and Development in Organizations* (San Francisco: Jossey-Bass, 1989), pp. 417–53.

59. From an undated Bristol-Myers handout.

60. G. Oddou, teaching note in "The Overseas Assignment: A Practical Look," *International Human Resource Management,* M. Mendenhall and G. Oddou (Boston: PWS-Kent Publishing, 1991), pp. 259–69.

61. Adapted from Myrna Hellerman, "Giving Executives a Field Day," *Working Woman* (March 1992), pp. 37–40.

Chapter 10

1. Based in part, on the article by Patricia Sellers, "Don't Call Me Slacker," *Fortune* (December 12, 1994), pp. 181–82.

2. Ibid., p. 181.

3. Douglas T. Hall, *Careers in Organizations* (Santa Monica, Calif.: Goodyear Publishing, 1976); and J. Van Maanen and E.H. Schein, "Career Development," in J.R. Hack-

man and J. L. Suttle (eds.), *Improving Life at Work: Behavioral Sciences Approaches to Organizational Change* (Santa Monica, Calif.: Goodyear Publishing, 1977), pp. 341–55.

4. Jeffrey H. Greenhaus, *Career Management* (New York: Dryden Press, 1987), p. 6.

5. See, for instance, E. P. Cook, "1991 Annual Review: Practice and Research in Career Counseling and Development, 1990," *Career Development Quarterly* (February 1991), pp. 99–131.

6. Justin Martin, "Employees Are Fighting Back," *Fortune* (August 8, 1994), p. 12.

7. See M. Koden and J. B. Rousener, *Workforce America: Managing Employee Diversity as a Vital Resource* (Homewood, Ill.: Irwin Publishing, 1991).

8. D. Yankelovich and J. Immerwahl, "The Emergence of Expressivism Will Revolutionize the Contract Between Workers and Employers," *Personnel Administrator* (December 1983), pp. 34–39, 114.

9. See B. B. Grossman and R. J. Blitzer, "Choreographing Careers," *Training and Development* (November 1991), pp. 68–89; R. Chanick, "Career Growth for Baby Boomers," *Personnel Journal* (January 1992), pp. 40–44.

10. Van Maanen and Schein.

11. Ibid.

12. Hall.

13. Van Maanen and Schein.

14. See M. London and S. A. Stumpf, *Managing Careers* (Reading, Mass.: Addison Wesley, 1982); and A. S. Miner, "Organizational Evolution and the Social Ecology of Jobs," *American Sociological Review* (Fall 1991), pp. 772–85.

15. Cook, p. 99.

16. Greenhaus, p. 6.

17. See, for example, Donald E. Super, *The Psychology of Careers* (New York: Harper & Row, 1957); Edgar Schein, *Career Dynamics: Matching Individual and Organizational Needs* (Reading, Mass.: Addison Wesley, 1978); and Daniel J. Levinson, C. N. Darrow, E. B. Klein, M. H. Levinson, and B. McKee, *A Man's Life* (New York: Knopf, 1978).

18. Jaclyn Fierman, "Beating the MidLife Career Crisis," *Fortune* (September 6, 1993), p. 51.

19. Frederic M. Hudson, "When Careers Turn Stale," *Next* (Lakewood, Calif.: American Association of Retired Persons, 1994), p. 3.

20. Adele Scheele, "Moving Over Instead of Up, *Working Woman* (November 1993), pp. 75–76.

21. "Kay Whitmore's New Sense of Mission," *Business Week* (September 26, 1994), p. 8.

22. D. E. Super, "A Life-span Life Space Approach to Career Development," *Journal of Vocational Behavior,* Vol. 16 (Spring 1980), pp. 282–98. See also E. P. Cook, pp. 99–131, and M. Arthur, *Career Theory Handbook* (Englewood Cliffs, N.J.: Prentice-Hall, 1991). See also Louis S. Richman, "The New Worker Elite," *Fortune* (August 22, 1994), pp. 56–66.

23. John Holland, *Making Vocational Choices,* 2d ed. (Englewood Cliffs, N.J.: Prentice-Hall, 1985).

24. Cheryl Granrose and James Portwood, "Matching Individual Career Plans and Organizational Career Plans and Organizational Career Management," *Academy of Management Journal,* Vol. 30, No. 4 (1987), pp. 699–720.

25. Trudy L. Somers, "A Study of Stress in Work–Family Relationships and Roles," working paper, Towson State University, 1992; and C. A. Higgins, L. E. Duxburey, and R. H. Irving, "Work–Family Conflict in the Dual-Career Family," *Organizational Behavior and Human Decision Processes* (January 1992), pp. 51–75.

26. N. Gupta and G. D. Jenkins, Jr., "Dual Career Couples: Stress, Stressors, Strains, and Strategies," in T. A. Beehr and R. S. Bhagat (eds.), *Human Stress and Cognition in Organizations: An Integrated Perspective* (New York: John Wiley, 1985), pp. 141–75; and Higgins, Duxburey, and Irving, pp. 51–75.

27. See, for example, Susan Caminiti, "What Happens to Laid-Off Managers," *Fortune* (June 13, 1994), pp. 68–78.

28. H. P. Weisman and M. S. Leibman, "Corporate Scale Down, What Comes Next?" *HRMagazine* (August 1991), pp. 33–37. See also L. M. Laarman, "Cut Compensation Costs to Avoid Layoffs," *Employment Relations Today* (February 1991), pp. 137–42.

29. Hal Lancaster, "Managing Your Career: You, and Only You, Must Stay in Charge of Your Employability," *The Wall Street Journal* (November 15, 1994), p. B-1.

30. "Do It Yourself: Even Employers that Provide Career Help Urge Self-Reliance," *The Wall Street Journal* (March 3, 1992), p. A-1.

31. D. E. Berlow and D. T. Hall, "The Socialization of Managers: Effects of Expectations on Performance," *Administrative Science Quarterly*, 11 (1966), pp. 207-23; and D.W. Bray, R.J. Campbell, and D.L. Grant, *Formative Years in Business: A Long-Term AT & T Study on Managerial Lives* (New York: John Wiley, 1974).

32. A. Cohen, "Career Stage as a Moderator of the Relationship Between Organizational Commitment and Its Outcomes: A Meta Analysis," *Journal of Vocational Psychology* (March 1991), pp. 253-68; see also T. W. Lee, S. J. Ashford, J. P. Walsh, and R. T. Mow-day, "Commitment Propensity, Organizational Commitment and Voluntary Turnover: A Longitudinal Study of Organizational Entry Processes," *Journal of Management* (January 1991), pp. 15-32.

33. "Career Counseling: Is It Making a Comeback?" *The Wall Street Journal* (March 3, 1992), p. A-1.

34. Ibid., pp. 85-86; and J. P. Galassi, R. K. Croce, G. A. Martin, R. M. James, Jr., and R. L. Wallace, "Client Preferences and Anticipations in Career Counseling: A Preliminary Investigation," *Journal of Counseling Psychology* (January 1992), pp. 46-55.

35. James W. Walker, "Let's Get Realistic About Career Paths," *Human Resource Management* (Fall 1976), p. 6. For additional information on this issue, see F. Blau and M. Ferber, "Career Plans and Expectations of Young Women and Men," *Journal of Human Resources*, Vol. 26, No. 4 (April 1991), pp. 581-607.

36. "Career Counseling: Is It Making A Comeback?" *The Wall Street Journal* (March 3, 1992), p. A-1.

37. M. Knowles, *Andragogy in Action* (San Francisco: Jossey-Bass), 1984.

38. The three-step process in competency-based training includes an evaluation step to determine beginning skill levels, a training event to present only the skills which were assessed as deficient, and a validation or post-training evaluation step.

39. H. G. Kaufman, *Obsolescence and Professional Career Development* (New York: AMACOM, 1974); and J. R. DeLuca, "Strategic Career Management in Non-Growing Volatile Business Environments," *Human Resource Planning* (January 1988), pp. 49-61; B. Nussbaum, "A Career Survival Kit," *Business Week* (October 7, 1991), pp. 98-104; and A. Gates, "Career Management: Hell No! I Won't Plateau," *Working Woman* (October 1990), pp. 100-05.

40. R. E. Hill, and Trudy L. Somers, *The Transformation from Technical Professional to Technical Manager: Special Career Managerial Concerns* (Ann Arbor, Mich.: The Industrial Development Dominion), 1988.

41. See, Kathy Kolbe, "Avoiding a Mentor Mismatch, *Working Woman* (October 1994), pp. 66-69.

42. Kathleen O'Brien, "Grooming Women for the Top," *Working Woman* (July 1994), pp. 23-24.

43. For another view of mentoring and careers, see Hal Lancaster, "Managing Your Career: A Good Executive Is a Matter of Nature, Not Nurture, *The Wall Street Journal* (November 1, 1994), p. B-1.

44. This categorization comes from G.A. Ford and Gordon L. Lippitt, *A Life Planning Workbook for Guidance in Planning and Personal Goal Setting* (Fairfax, Va.: NTL Learning Resources Corporation, 1972).

45. This case is an elaboration of an article by Raju Narisetti, "Managing Your Career: Shoved Down a Rung? It's Time to Find Another Ladder," *The Wall Street Journal* (September 28, 1994), p. B-1.

Chapter 11

1. Based on the story, "Motivation the Old-Fashioned Way," *Inc.* (November 1994), p. 134.

2. Ibid.

3. See, for example, Victor H. Vroom, *Work and Motivation* (New York: John Wiley, 1964).

4. Raju Narisetti, "Managing Your Career: Shoved Down a Rung? It's Time to Find Another Ladder," *The Wall Street Journal* (September 28, 1994), p. B–1.

5. Our model is based on the expectancy theory of motivation as developed by Victor Vroom. For a complete review of expectancy theory, see Victor Vroom, *Work and Motivation* (New York: John Wiley, 1964).

6. Abraham Maslow's motivation theory is called "the hierarchy of needs." See Abraham Maslow, *Motivation and Personality* (New York: Harper & Row, 1954).

7. Douglas McGregor's motivation theory is called "Theory X; Theory Y." See Douglas McGregor, *The Human Side of Enterprise* (New York: McGraw-Hill, 1960).

8. Frederick Herzberg's motivation theory is called "the motivation-hygiene theory." See Frederick Herzberg, *Work and the Nature of Man* (New York: World Publishing, 1966).

9. David McClelland's motivation theory is called "the achievement, affiliation and power motives theory." See David C. McClelland, *The Achieving Society* (New York: Van Nostrand Reinhold, 1961).

10. J. Stacey Adams's motivation theory is called "equity theory." See J. Stacey Adams, "Inequity in Social Exchanges," in Leonard Berkowitz (ed.), *Advances in Experimental Social Psychology,* Vol. 2 (New York: Academic Press, 1965), pp. 267–300.

11. Vroom.

12. See, for example, Kenneth A. Kovach, "What Motivates Employees? Workers and Supervisors Give Different Answers," *Business Horizons* (September–October 1987), pp. 58–65.

13. See, "What Do Workers Want?" *Inc.,* (June 1994), p. 12; Commerce Clearing House, "Employers: Employees Want Personal Satisfaction," *Human Resources Management: Ideas and Trends* (November 10, 1993), p. 181; and Nancy K. Austin, "Motivating Employees Without Pay or Promotion," *Working Woman* (November 1994), pp. 17–18.

14. The model of motivation we present for HRM is directly influenced by two of the more contemporary theories of motivation—equity theory and expectancy theory.

15. Phaedra Hise, "The Camera Doesn't Lie," *Inc.* (October 1993), p. 35.

16. Christopher Caggiano, "The Profit Promoting Daily Scorecard," *Inc.* (May 1994), pp. 101–03.

17. Timothy D. Schellhardt, "Eager to Boost Morale: Just Spin the Wheel," *The Wall Street Journal* (September 19, 1990), p. B–1.

18. See, for example, "Motivating Employees," *Personnel Report for the Executive* (New York: Research Institute of America, January 15, 1987), pp. 1–2.

19. See, for example, David A. De Cenzo and Stephen J. Holoviak, *Employee Benefits* (Englewood Cliffs, N.J.: Prentice-Hall, 1990), Chapter 11.

20. Kenneth M. Dawson and Sheryl N. Dawson, "How to Motivate Your Employees," *HRMagazine* (April 1990), p. 79.

21. J. Richard Hackman and Greg R. Oldham, "Development of the Job Diagnostic Survey," *Journal of Applied Psychology* (April 1975), pp. 159–70.

22. See, for example, Shaul Fox and Gerald Feldman, "Attention State and Critical Psychological States as Mediators Return Job Dimension and Job Outcomes," *Human Relations,* Vol. 41, No. 3 (March 1988), pp. 229–45.

23. J. Richard Hackman, "Work Design," in *Improving Life at Work,* J.R. Hackman and J.L. Suttle (eds.) (Santa Monica, Calif.: Goodyear, 1977), p. 129.

24. J. Barton Cunningham and Ted Eberle, "A Guide to Job Enrichment and Redesign," *Personnel,* Vol. 67, No. 2 (February 1990), p. 57.

25. Adapted from Brian Dumaine, "Unleash Workers and Cut Costs," *Fortune* (May 18, 1992), p. 88.

26. See, for example, "Job Characteristics Theory of Work Redesign," in John B. Miner, *Theories of Organizational Behavior* (Hinsdale, Ill.: Dryden Press, 1980), pp. 231–66; B. T. Loher, R. A. Noe, N. L. Moeller, and M. P. Fitzgerald, "A Meta-analysis of the Relation of Job Characteristics to Job Satisfaction," *Journal of Applied Psychology* (May 1985), pp. 280–89; and M. G. Evans, and D. A. Ondrack, "The Motivational Poten-

tial of Jobs: Is a Multiplicative Model Really Necessary?" in S. L. McShane (ed.), *Organization Behavior*, ASAC Conference Proceedings, Vol. 9, Part 5, Halifax, Nova Scotia (1988), pp. 31–39. It is important to note, however, that while these studies generally support the JCM, there still exists some debate about the dimensions used, and the duplicity of some of the dimensions. For an overview of that debate, see Y. Fried and G. R. Ferris, "The Dimensionality of Job Characteristics: Some Neglected Issues," *Journal of Applied Psychology* (August 1986), pp. 419–26.

27. Hackman, pp. 132–33.

28. See, for example, Cunningham and Eberle, p. 57.

29. See, for example, Norm Alster, "What Flexible Workers Can Do," *Fortune* (February 13, 1989), pp. 62–66.

30. See Stephen J. Havolic, "Quality of Work Life and Human Resource Outcomes," *Industrial Relations* (Fall 1991), pp. 469–79.

31. Mitchell W. Fields and James W. Thacker, "Influence on Quality of Work Life on Company and Union Commitment," *Academy of Management Journal* (June 1992), p. 448.

32. Robert A. MacDicken, "Managing the Plateaued Employee," *Association Management*, Vol. 43, No. 7 (July 1991), p. 37.

33. Timothy D. Schellhardt, "Few Employers Give Job Rotation a Whirl," *The Wall Street Journal* (July 21, 1992), p. B–1.

34. For an interesting view on work and home, see Michael P. Cronin, "The Return of Happy Hour, *Inc.* (December 1993), p. 165.

35. See Deutschman, pp. 50–55.

36. Verespej, p. 12.

37. David A. Ralston, "How Flextime Eases Work/Family Tension," *Personnel* (August 1990), pp. 45–48.

38. Helen Paris, "Balancing Work and Family Responsibilities: Canadian Employer and Employee Viewpoints," *Human Resource Planning*, Vol. 13, No. 2 (February 1990), p. 153.

39. Julie Cohen Mason, "Flexing More than Muscle: Employees Want Time on Their Side," *Management Review* (March 1992), pp. 7–8.

40. Ibid., p. 8.

41. Adapted from Jeff Davidson, "Motivation Employees," *Restaurant Business* (May 20, 1990), p. 61.

42. Charles Jaffe, "Management by Fun," *Nation's Business,* Vol. 78, No. 1 (January 1990), pp. 58–60.

43. See for example, Louis S. Richman, "The New Worker Elite," *Fortune* (August 22, 1994), pp. 56–66; and Ronald Henkoff, "Finding, Training, and Keeping the Best Service Workers," *Fortune* (October 3, 1994), pp. 110–22.

44. Louis S. Richman, "The New Worker Elite," *Fortune* (August 22, 1994), pp. 64–66.

45. Based on Jerald Greenberg, "Employee Theft as a Reaction to Under Payment Inequity: The Hidden Cost of Pay Cuts," *Journal of Applied Psychology,* Vol. 75, No. 5 (October 1990), pp. 561–68.

Chapter 12

1. This is an account of an event that has occurred in a fictitious company. Its sole purpose is to demonstrate the difficulties that can arise when performance evaluations are mishandled.

2. Danielle R. McDonald, "Performance Review Designed by Secretaries for Secretaries," *Journal of Compensation and Benefits,* Vol. 7, No. 7 (November/December 1991), pp. 36–38.

3. Ibid.

4. See, for example, Joseph P. McCarthy, "A New Focus On Achievement," *Personnel Journal,* Vol. 70, No. 2 (February 1991), pp. 74–76.

5. Mike Deblieux, "Performance Reviews Support Quest for Quality," *H.R. Focus,* Vol. 68, No. 11 (November 1991), pp. 3–4.

6. See, for example, Jeffrey A. Bradt, "Pay for Impact," *Personnel Journal,* Vol. 70, No. 5 (May 1991), pp. 76–79; and Kathleen A. Guinn and Roberta J. Corona, "Putting a Price on Performance," *Personnel Journal,* Vol. 70, No. 5 (May 1991), pp. 72–77.

7. James M. Jenks, "Do Your Performance Appraisals Boost Productivity?" *Management Review,* Vol. 80, No. 6 (June 1991), p. 45.

8. See Sandra O'Neal and Madonna Palladino, "Revamp Ineffective Performance Management," *Personnel Journal* (February 1992), pp. 93–102.

9. We would like to recognize Dr. Peter F. Norlin, an organizational consultant specializing in performance management systems, for providing the framework terminology for the purposes, who is served, and inherent difficulties.

10. Robert J. Sahl, Ph.D., "Design Effective Performance Appraisals," *Personnel Journal* (October 1990), pp. 56–57.

11. See Stuart Feldman, "Amoco Keeps Its Employees in the Big Picture," *Personnel* (June 1991), p. 24.

12. Mary Mavis, "Painless Performance Evaluations," *Training and Development* (October 1994), P. 40; and Herbert H. Meyer, "A Solution to the Performance Appraisal Feedback Enigma," *Academy of Management Executive* (February 1991), p. 68.

13. For a discussion on perception differences, see Kenneth P. Carron, Robert L. Cardy, and Gregory H. Dobbins, "Performance Appraisals as Effective Management or Deadly Management Disease: Two Initial Empirical Investigations," *Group and Organizational Studies* (June 1991), pp. 143–59.

14. See, for example, Maria Castanda and Afsaneh Nahavandi, "Link of Manager Behavior to Supervisory Performance Rating and Subordinate Satisfaction," *Group and Organizational Studies* (December 1991), pp. 357–66.

15. Ibid.

16. See Gary English, "Tuning Up for Performance Management," *Training and Development Journal* (April 1991), pp. 56–60.

17. Donald W. Myers, Wallace R. Johnston, and C. Glenn Pearce, "The Role of Human Interaction Theory in Developing Models of Performance Appraisal Feedback," *SAM Advanced Management Journal* (Summer 1991), p. 28.

18. See Barry R. Nathan, Allan M. Mohrman, Jr., and John Milliman, "Interpersonal Relations as a Context for the Effects of Appraisal Interviews on Performance and Satisfaction: A Longitudinal Study," *Academy of Management Journal* (June 1991), pp. 352–63.

19. Robert J. Nobile, "The Law of Performance Appraisals," *Personnel* (January 1991), p. 7.

20. Larry L. Axline, "Ethical Considerations of Performance Appraisals," *Management Review* (March 1994), p. 62.

21. See David C. Martin and Kathy M. Bartol, "The Legal Ramifications of Performance Appraisal: An Update," *Employee Relations Law Review* (Autumn 1991), pp. 257–86.

22. Richard Henderson, *Compensation Management: Rewarding Performance,* 6th ed. (Englewood Cliffs, N.J.: Prentice-Hall, 1994), p. 433.

23. Ahron Tziner and Richard Kopelman, "Effects of Rating Format on Goal-Setting: A Field Experiment," *Journal of Applied Psychology* (May 1988), p. 323.

24. See, for example, Dennis M. Daley, "Great Expectations, or a Tale of Two Systems: Employee Attitudes Toward Graphic Rating Scales and MBO-Based Performance Appraisal," *Public Administration Quarterly* (Summer 1991), pp. 188–201.

25. Richard Henderson, *Compensation Management: Rewarding Performance,* 6th ed. (Englewood Cliffs, N.J.: Prentice-Hall, 1994), p. 433.

26. Mary L. Tenopyr, "Artificial Reliability of Forced-Choice Scales," *Journal of Applied Psychology* (November 1988), pp. 749–51.

27. See Kevin R. Murphy, "Criterion Issues in Performance Appraisal Research: Behavioral Accuracy Versus Classification Accuracy," *Organizational Behavior and Human Decision Processes* (October 1991), pp. 45–50.

28. H. John Bernardin and Richard W. Beatty, *Performance Appraisal: Assessing Human Behavior at Work* (Boston: Kent Publishing, 1984), p. 86.

29. See, for example, Kevin R. Murphy and Virginia A. Pardaffy, "Bias in Behaviorally

Anchored Rating Scales: Global or Scale Specific," *Journal of Applied Psychology* (April 1989), pp. 343–46. See also Michael J. Piotrowski, Janet L. Barnes-Farrell, and Francine H. Esris, "Behaviorally Anchored Bias: A Replication and Extension of Murphy and Constans," J*ournal of Applied Psychology* (October 1988), pp. 827–28.

30. Ibid.

31. For an overview of MBO, see Peter F. Drucker, *The Practice of Management* (New York: Harper & Row, 1954).

32. Henderson, p. 428–29.

33. See for example, William H. Bommer, Jonathan L. Johnson, and Gregory A. Rich, "An Extension of Heneman's Meta-Analysis of Objective and Subjective Measures of Performance," *Academy of Management Best Papers Proceedings,* Dorothy P. Moore (ed.), (August 14–17, 1994), pp. 112–16.

34. Bernardin and Beatty, p. 140.

35. Ibid., p. 270.

36. Ibid., p. 139.

37. David Kipnis, Karl Price, Stuart Schmidt, and Christopher Stitt, "Why Do I Like Thee: Is It Your Performance or My Orders?" *Journal of Applied Psychology* (June 1981), pp. 324–28.

38. Ibid.

39. See, for example, Sandy J. Wayne and K. Michele Kacmar, "The Effects of Impressive Management on the Performance Appraisal Process," *Organization Behavior and Human Decision Processes* (February 1991), pp. 70–88.

40. See, for example, Bernardin and Beatty, pp. 271–76.

41. An assumption has been made here. That is, these raters have specific performance knowledge of the employee. Otherwise, more information may not be more accurate information. For example, if the raters are from various levels in the organization's hierarchy, these individuals may not have an accurate picture of the employee's performance; thus, quality of information may decrease.

42. See, for example, Hannah R. Rothstein, "Interrater Reliability of Job Performance Ratings: Growth to Asymptote Level with Increasing Opportunity to Observe," *Journal of Applied Psychology* (June 1990), pp. 322–27; see also Mary D. Zalesny, "Rater Confidence and Social Influence in Performance Appraisals," *Journal of Applied Psychology* (June 1990), pp. 274–89.

43. Ted H. Shore, Lynn McFarlane, and George C. Thornton III, "Construct Validity of Self- and Peer Evaluations of Performance Dimensions in an Assessment Center," *Journal of Applied Psychology* (February 1992), pp. 42–54.

44. Carol A. Norman and Robert A. Zamacki, "Team Appraisals—Team Approach," *Personnel Journal* (September 1991), p. 101.

45. Catherine M. Petrini, "Upside-Down Performance Appraisals," *Training and Development Journal* (July 1991), pp. 15–22.

46. See for example, Martin L. Ramsey and Howard Lehto, "The Power of Peer Review," *Training and Development* (July 1994), pp. 38–41.

47. See Jiing-Lib Farh, Albert A. Cannella, and Arthur G. Bedian, "Peer Ratings: The Impact of Purpose on Rating Quality Acceptance," *Group and Organization Studies* (December 1991), pp. 367–86.

48. Marilyn Moats Kennedy, "Where Teams Drop the Ball," *Across the Board* (September 1993), p. 9.

49. Irene H. Buhalo, "You Sign My Report Card—I'll Sign Yours," *Personnel* (May 1991), p. 23.

50. Jerry Baumgartner, "Give It to Me Straight," *Training and Development* (July 1994), pp. 49–51.

51. John F. Milliman, Robert A. Zawacki, Carol Norman, Lynda Powell, and Jay Kirksey, "Companies Evaluate Employees from All Perspectives," *Personnel Journal* (November 1994), p. 99.

52. John F. Milliman, Robert A. Zawacki, Carol Norman, Lynda Powell, and Jay Kirksey, "Companies Evaluate Employees from All Perspectives," *Personnel Journal* (November 1994), pp. 99–104.

53. "Companies Where Employees Rate Executives," *Fortune* (December 27, 1993), p. 128.

54. Brian O'Reilly, "360 Feedback Can Change Your Life," *Fortune* (October 17, 1994), p. 96.

55. Ibid.

56. See for example, Dianne Nilsen, "Self-Observer Rating Discrepancies: Once an Overrater, Always an Overrater," *Human Resource Management* (Fall 1993), pp. 265–82; Walter W. Turnow, "Perceptions or Reality: Is Multi-Perspective Measurement a Means or an End?" *Human Resource Management* (Fall 1993), pp. 221–30; Manuel London and Richard W. Beatty, "360-Degree Feedback as a Competitive Advantage," *Human Resource Management* (Fall 1993), pp. 353–73; and Robert E. Kaplan, "360-Degree Feedback PLUS: Boosting the Power of Co-Worker Rating for Executives," *Human Resource Management* (Fall 1993), pp. 299–315.

57. W. C. Borman, "The Rating of Individuals in Organizations: An Alternative Approach," *Organizational Behavior and Human Performance* (August 1974), pp. 105–24.

58. Beverly Dugan, "Effects of Assessor Training on Information Use," *Journal of Applied Psychology* (November 1988), pp. 743–48; and Clinton O. Longenecker, Dennis A. Gioia, and Henry P. Sims, Jr., "Behind the Mask: The Politics of Employee Appraisal," *Academy of Management Executive* (August 1987), p. 191.

59. Charles Lee, "Poor Performance Appraisals Do More Harm than Good," *Personnel Journal* (September 1989), p. 91.

60. Ibid.

61. See Peter J. Dowling, Randall S. Schuler, and Denice E. Welch, *International Dimensions of Human Resource Management,* 2d ed. (Belmont, Calif.: Wadsworth, 1994), pp. 103–20; and G. Oddou and M. Mendenhall, "Expatriate Performance Appraisal: Problems and Solutions," in M. Mendenhall and G. Oddiou, eds., *International Human Resource Management* (Boston: PWS Kent Publishing, 1991), pp. 364–74.

62. G. Oddou and M. Mendenhall, "Expatriate Performance Appraisal: Problems and Solutions," in M. Mendenhall and G. Oddiou, eds., *International Human Resource Management* (Boston: PWS Kent Publishing, 1991), pp. 366.

63. J. S. Solomon, "Employee Relations Soviet Style," *Personnel Administrator,* Vol. 30, No. 10 (October 1985), pp. 79–86.

64. Dowling, Schuler, and Welch, pp. 113–15; and Oddiou and Mendenhall, pp. 372–74.

65. Ibid.

66. Case adapted from Brian O'Reilly, "360-Feedback Can Change Your Life," *Fortune* (October 17, 1994), p. 100.

Chapter 13

1. Adapted from Michael P. Cronin, "Bottom-Up Bonuses," *Inc.* (January 1994), p. 97.

2. Susan Sonnesyn Brooks, "Noncash Ways to Compensate Employees," *HRMagazine* (April 1994), p. 43.

3. Stephenie Overman, "How Hot Is Your Reward System?" *HRMagazine* (November 1994), p. 51.

4. Clifford J. Mottaz, "Determinants of Organizational Commitment," *Human Relations* (June 1988), pp. 467–82.

5. Philip A. Rudolph and Brian H. Kleiner, "The Art of Motivating Employees," *Journal of Managerial Psychology* (May 1989), pp. i–iv.

6. Jim Braham, "A Rewarding Place to Work," *Industry Week* (September 18, 1989), p. 15.

7. Nancy Folbre, "Sexual Orientation Showing Up in Paychecks," *Working Woman* (January 1995), p. 15.

8. "The Pay Gap Narrows, But," *Fortune* (September 19, 1994), p. 32.

9. Judith M. Collins and Paul M. Muchinsky, "An Assessment of the Construct Validity of Three Job Evaluation Methods: A Field Experiment," *Academy of Management Journal,* Vol. 36, No. 4 (1993), p. 895.

10. "Pay Equity," *Executive Female* (March–April 1991), p. 9.

11. Ibid.

12. Richard Henderson, *Compensation Management: Rewarding Performance,* 6th ed. (Englewood Cliffs, N.J.: Prentice-Hall, 1994), p. 223.

13. Ibid.

14. Ibid.

15. John D. McMullen and Cynthia G. Brondi, "Job Evaluation Generate the Numbers," *Personnel Journal* (November 1986), p. 62.

16. See, for example, Henderson, p. 266.

17. David W. Bedler, *Compensation Administration* (Englewood Cliffs, N.J.: Prentice-Hall, 1974), p. 157.

18. Richard D. Arvey, "Sex Bias in Job Evaluation Procedures," *Personnel Psychology* (Summer 1986), pp. 316–18.

19. For a thorough mathematical discussion of various methods of determining the pay structure, see Henderson, Chapter 11, "Design a Base Pay Structure."

20. Henderson, pp. 315–16.

21. Jack C. O'Brien and Robert A. Zawacki, "Salary Surveys: Are They Worth the Effort?" *Personnel* (October 1985), pp. 70–73.

22. Margaret Dyekman, "Take the Mystery Out of Salary Surveys," *Personnel Journal* (June 1990), p. 105.

23. See, for example, Rosabeth Moss Kanter, "The Attack on Pay," *Harvard Business Review* (March–April 1987), pp. 60–67.

24. Earl Ingram II, "Compensation: The Advantage of Knowledge-Based Pay," *Personnel Journal* (April 1990), p. 138.

25. Stephen H. Applebaum and Barbara T. Shapiro, "Pay for Performance: Implementation of Individual and Group Plans," *Journal of Management Development* (July 1991) pp. 30–40.

26. Joseph Spiers, "Wages Are Starting to Inch Up," *Fortune* (June 1, 1992), p. 17.

27. Luis R. Gomez-Mejia and David B. Balkin, "Effectiveness of Individual and Aggregate Compensation Strategies," *Industrial Relations* (1989), pp. 431–45.

28. L. Kate Beatty, "Pay and Benefits Break Away from Tradition," *HRMagazine* (November 1994), p. 64.

29. Jaclyn Fierman, "The Perilous New World of Fair Pay," *Fortune* (June 13, 1994), p. 63.

30. Ibid., p. 20.

31. Hoyt Doyel and Thomas Riley, "Incentive Plans," *Management Review* (March 1987), pp. 36–37; and K. Dow Scott, Steven E. Markham, and Richard W. Robers, "Compensation," *Personnel Journal* (September 1987), pp. 114–15.

32. Howard Gleckman, Sandra Atchison, Tim Smart, and John A. Byrne, "Bonus Pay: Buzzword or Bonanza?" *Business Week* (November 14, 1994), p. 62.

33. Thomas B. Wilson, "Group Incentives: Are You Ready?" *Journal of Compensation and Benefits* (November 1990), pp. 25–29.

34. Commerce Clearing House, *Human Resource Management: Ideas and Trends* (May 17, 1990), p. 84.

35. Harold Stieglitz, "The Kaiser Steel Union Sharing Plan," *National Industrial Conference Board Studies in Personnel Policy Number 187* (New York, 1963).

36. Henderson, p. 461.

37. Ibid., p. 462

38. Ibid., pp. 455–58.

39. Ibid., p. 457; and Charles R. Gowen III, "Gainsharing Programs: An Overview of History and Research," *Journal of Organizational Behavior Management* (1990), pp. 77–99.

40. Roget T. Kaufman, "The Effects of IMPROSHARE on Productivity," *Industrial and Labor Relations Review* (January 1992), p. 311.

41. Ibid.

42. Ibid., pp. 319–22.

43. Based on Nancy J. Perry, "Talk About Pay for Performance," *Fortune* (May 4, 1992), p. 77.

44. See John Greenwald, "Workers: Rules and Rewards," *Time* (April 15, 1991), pp. 42–43.

45. Spragins, p. 79.

46. Towers Perrin, "Competency-Based Pay: Paying People, Not Jobs," presented at *The National Conference on Using Competency-Based Tools and Applications to Drive Organizational Performance* (Boston, Mass.: November 2–4, 1994), p. 8.

47. Marc E. Lattoni, and Andree Mercier, "Developing Competency-Based Organizations and Pay Systems," "Focus: A Review of Human Resource Management Issues in Canada" (Calgary, Canada: Towers Perrin, Summer 1994), p. 18.

48. Ibid., pp. 1–4.

49. Sandra O'Neal, "Competencies: The DNA of the Corporation," *ACA Journal* (Winter 1993/94), pp. 6–12.

50. Lattoni and Mercier, p. 7.

51. "Compensation: Sales Managers as Team Players," *Inc.* (August 1994), p. 102.

52. Howard Gleckman, Sandra Atchison, Tim Smart, and John A. Byrne, "Bonus Pay: Buzzword or Bonanza?" *Business Week* (November 14, 1994), pp. 62–64.

53. T. M. Wellborne and L. R. Gomez-Mejia, "Team Incentives in the Work Place," in L. Berger (ed.) *Handbook of Wage and Salary Administration* (New York: McGraw-Hill, 1991), pp. 236–47.

54. Henderson, p. 407.

55. See Stephen P. Robbins, and David A. De Cenzo, *Fundamentals of Management* (Englewood Cliffs, N.J.: Prentice-Hall, 1995), p. 262.

56. Brian Dumaine, "A Knockout Year," *Fortune* (July 25, 1994), p. 94.

57. John A. Byrne, and Lori Bongiorno, "CEO PAY: Ready for Take-off: Is Anybody Worth This Much?" *Business Week* (April 24, 1995), p. 88.

58. Steve Kichen, "Who Needs a High Salary?" *Forbes* (November 7, 1994), p. 256.

59. Ibid.

60. John A. Byrne, Lori Bongiorno, and Ronald Grover, "That Eye Popping Executive Pay: Is Anybody Worth This Much?" *Business Week* (April 25, 1994), pp. 55.

61. Rob Norton, "Making Sense of the Boss's Pay," *Fortune* (October 3, 1994), p. 36.

62. Jill Andresky Frazer, "Beyond the 401(K)," *Inc.* (July 1991), pp. 103–04.

63. Byrne, Bongiorno, and Grover, pp. 53–54.

64. Ibid.

65. Mark D. Fefer, "Your CEO Will Get Paid," *Fortune* (October 3, 1994), p. 18.

66. Ibid. Under IRS regulations, beginning in 1994, annual salaries paid to a company's five top officers in a publicly held firm are not tax deductible if the salaries are over $1 million. Most companies have simply ignored this new ruling, while others are deferring the excess income for these executives until retirement.

67. Current tax laws require tax to be paid on that amount of premium paid on life insurance over $50,000. Furthermore, Section 89 of the IRS Tax Code requires that those perks offered to the higher paid employees, that are not given to the average employee, to be considered taxable income to the recipient.

68. See, for example, Felix Kessler, "Executive Perks Under Fire," *Fortune* (July 22, 1985), pp. 29–30.

69. "Housing Assistance Gain as an Employee Benefit," *The Wall Street Journal* (September 24, 1991), p. A–1.

70. Ibid.

71. For further reading on international compensation, see Peter J. Dowling, Randall S. Schuler, and Denice E. Welch, *International Dimensions of Human Resource Management,* 2nd ed, Belmont, Calif.: Wadsworth, 1994), Chapter 6.

72. Anne V. Corey, "Ensuring Strength in Each Country: A Challenge for Corporate HQ Global HR Executives," *Human Resource Planning*, Vol. 14, No. 1 (1991), pp. 1–8.

73. Calvin Reynolds, "Compensation of Overseas Personnel," in *Handbook of Human Resources Administration*, 2d ed., Joseph J. Famularo, (ed.) (New York: McGraw-Hill, 1986), pp. 56–2, 56–3.

74. "I'll Take Manhattan," *Fortune* (May 1991), p. 120.

75. U.S. Department of State, *Indexes of Living Costs Abroad, Quarters, Allowances, and Hardship Differentials* (Washington, D.C.: Bureau of Labor Statistics, published quarterly).

76. Story based on Ellyn E. Spragins (ed.) "The Elements of Surprise," *Inc.* (July 1991), p. 79.

Chapter 14

1. Richard Lacayo, "Take This Job and Shove It," *Time* (December 13, 1993), p. 44; and Charles McCoy, "Texas County Reverses Course on Apple Plant," *The Wall Street Journal* (December 8, 1993), p. B–1.

2. For a more thorough coverage of this material, see David A. De Cenzo and Stephen J. Holoviak, *Employee Benefits* (Englewood Cliffs, N.J.: Prentice-Hall, 1991).

3. Frederick Herzberg, *Work and the Nature of Man* (New York: World, 1966).

4. *Employee Benefits Journal*, Vol. 12, No. 2 (June 1987), p. 38.

5. Commerce Clearing House, "Employees' Benefit Costs Averaged 40.2% of Payroll in 1992," *Human Resources Management: Ideas and Trends* (March 3, 1994), p. 36.

6. Ibid.

7. This assumes that the insurance policy is part of a group term plan. Should it be a single policy, other than term insurance, or if the plan discriminates in favor of the more highly paid employees, then the entire benefit would be taxable.

8. As discussed in Chapter 3, government regulations had a major impact on the increases in employee benefits. It is equally important to note that management practices and labor unions also have affected benefit offerings.

9. Social Security here refers to FICA taxes, for Old Age, Survivors, and Disability Insurance (OASDI).

10. U.S. Bureau of the Census, *Statistical Abstracts of the United States: 1990* (Washington, D.C.: Government Printing Office, 1990), p. 358.

11. Ibid., p. 356.

12. This $4,681.80 represents what both the employee and the employer will pay in Social Security taxes, for a total of $9,363.60.

13. Based on the passage of the Omnibus Budget Reconciliation Act of 1993, the 1.45% Medicare portion will no longer have a salary cap. That means that beginning in 1994, both the employee and the employer will have to pay the 1.45% on every dollar earned. Commerce Clearing House, "New Tax Law Will Require Review of Many HR Policies and Benefit Programs," *Human Resources Management: Ideas and Trends* (August 18, 1993), pp. 129–30.

14. For 1995, employees between the ages of 65 and 70 may earn a maximum of $11,280. For every dollar above this amount, they lose $1 for every $3 earned. For individuals under age 65, the maximum they can earn is $8,160. They lose $1 for every $2 they earn over this limit.

15. Richard I. Henderson, *Compensation Management: Rewarding Performance*, 6th ed. (Englewood Cliffs, N.J.: Prentice-Hall, 1994), p. 87.

16. Ibid.

17. Ibid., p. 88. Wage bases for unemployment insurance vary. A number of states follow the federal $7,000 base, while others vary to a maximum of $22,700 in Hawaii. See Henderson, p. 88.

18. In 1992, President George Bush signed into law a bill extending the unemployment coverage from 26 weeks to 39 weeks for those experiencing long durations of unemployment brought about by the recession in the early 1990s. This extension expired July 4, 1992. However, on July 2, 1992, President Bush again extended the coverage for an additional 20 or 26 weeks, depending on the unemployment rates in each state. This extension expired on March 6, 1993. Those who exhausted the original 39 weeks, however, were not eligible for this extended coverage.

19. Although unemployment benefits are federally mandated, that does not mean that problems will not occur. Because of the tremendous layoffs occurring in the latter part of 1990 and early 1991, a number of states had depleted their unemployment funds. Accordingly, in such states as Connecticut, Massachusetts, Ohio, Michigan, Arkansas, West Virginia, and Missouri, their rates charged to employers increased (*The Wall Street Journal*, January 16, 1991, p. B–1).

20. Mark D. Fefer, "Taking Control of Your Workers' Comp Costs," *Fortune* (October 3, 1994), pp. 131–36.

21. Lenore Schiff, "Is Health Care a Job Killer," *Fortune* (April 6, 1992), p. 30.

22. "Business Health Care Spending Up," *The Baltimore Sun,* January 10, 1991, p. B–9.

23. Health care cost increases, while averaging up to 15% per year in the early 1990s, have slowed in their rate of growth. That is, although health care costs continue to increase, they are doing so at a much slower pace.

24. Edmund Faltermayer, "Health Reform: Let's Do It Right," *Fortune* (October 18, 1993), pp. 54–56.

25. Point-of-service or network plans are often a variation of preferred provider organizations. The main distinction typically lies in the degree of choice permitted. For example, under a preferred provider, any physician who participates can be seen by a subscriber. In a point-of-service (POS) or network, the possible physicians may be more limited. Although there are some constraints placed on choosing a physician, they are not as great as those imposed by an HMO.

26. While Blue Cross and Blue Shield is the most widely known organization for traditional insurance, it is not the only one. Companies like Mutual of Omaha, New York Life, and Aetna, other commercial insurance companies all offer health-care coverage that models the BC/BS plan.

27. Jerry S. Rosenbloom and G. Victor Hallman, *Employee Benefit Planning,* 3d ed. (Englewood Cliffs, N.J.: Prentice-Hall, 1991), p. 80.

28. It is important to understand the difference between two terms that are widely used in Blue Shield contracts. These are non-pars and participating physicians. A non-par, or nonparticipating physician, will not accept Blue Shield payments as payment in full for services rendered. This means that any costs incurred above the repayment schedule set by the health insurer are the responsibility of the patient. Participating physicians, as the term implies, agree to accept Blue Shield payments as payments in full for services rendered.

29. Rosenbloom and Hallman, p. 85.

30. Stuart Gannes, "Strong Medicine for Health Bills," *Fortune* (April 13, 1987), p. 71.

31. Main, p. 92.

32. Kenneth S. Abromowitz, "End of Fee for Service," *Employee Benefit Plan Review,* Vol. 40, No. 9 (March 1986), p. 32.

33. "Preferred Provider Organizations: The Newest Form of Health Care Delivery," *Small Business Report* (March 1987), p. 20.

34. Rosenbloom and Hallman, p. 90.

35. It also should be noted that in some self-funding cases, organizations seek assistance from another company commonly referred to as a "Third Party Administrator (TPA)." The TPA's role is simply to process the health-care forms.

36. For employees who have been terminated or whose hours have been reduced, their coverage is for a period of 18 months (possibly extended to 29 months if qualifying dependents are covered). See Robert M. McCaffery, *Employee Benefit Programs: A Total Compensation Perspective,* 2d ed. (Boston, Mass.: PWS-Kent Publishing, 1992), p. 96.

37. Leslie Wayne, "Pension Changes Raising Concerns," *New York Times* (August 29, 1994), pp. A–1; D–3.

38. Rodney N. Mara, "Communication of Benefits," in *Employee Benefits Handbook,* Fred K. Foulkes (ed.), (Boston, Mass.: Warren, Gorham, and Lamont, 1982), p. 6–2.

39. The Tax Reform Act of 1986 modified vesting rights, now requiring full vesting after five years, partial vesting after three years, and seven-year full vesting with plan years beginning after December 1, 1988. Those companies with a retirement plan year prior to that date were not required to go to the new lower vesting rules until December 1, 1989. It is also important to note, as will be discussed later in the chapter, that any monies contributed by employees toward their retirement are 100 percent vested immediately.

40. Portability of pension rights is a complex issue that goes beyond the scope of this book. However, depending on the company, employees may receive a permanent right to their monies, receiving a pension from the organization at retirement age, or be given a check that allows them to reinvest those monies on their own.

41. Cindy Skrzycki, "Agency Returns Pension Liabilities to LTV," *The Washington Post* (September 23, 1987), p. D–1.

42. "Forewarning Rule", *The Wall Street Journal* (June 2, 1992), p. A–1.

43. Robert M. McCaffery, *Employee Benefit Programs: A Total Compensation Perspective* (Boston, Mass.: PWS-Kent Publishing, 1992), pp. 234, 246–47.

44. See, for instance, "Tell Employees: Summary Plan Descriptions," *Employee Benefit Plan Review* (May 1991), pp. 23–26.

45. "Company Keeps Costs Steady while Long Service Employees Get Protection Through Floor Plan," *Employee Benefit Plan Review*, Vol. 42, No. 1 (July 1987), pp. 76–78.

46. McCaffery, p. 131.

47. Ibid., p. 142.

48. Profit-sharing plans require that there be profits before a contribution can be made. When there are no profits for the period, no contributions need to be made. The only partial exception is that contributions can be made in a year in which there are no profits if there are accumulated profits from prior years. However, should this occur, further restrictions apply.

49. Most companies offering matching contribution features to their 401(k) programs limit the amount of their contribution. Typically, their matching amount is set as one-half of the amount the employee contributes, with a 3 percent maximum. Thus, an employee setting aside 4 percent of his or her salary will have a 2 percent match, with up to 3 percent for a 6 percent deduction.

50. Anita Bruzzese, "Workers Getting More Say in When, How They Take Time Off," *Carroll County Times* (July 23, 1993), p. B–5; and "Vacations Are Shorter in the U.S. and Japan than in Europe," *The Wall Street Journal* (June 2, 1992), p. A–1.

51. Bill Leonard, "The Employee's Favorite, The Employer's Quandary," *HRMagazine* (November 1994), p. 53.

52. Anita Bruzzese, "Workers Getting More Say in When, How They Take Time Off," *Carroll County Times* (July 23, 1993), p. B–5.

53. Rosenbloom and Hallman, p. 208.

54. Short-term disability programs may be provided through commercial carriers or through self-funding arrangements. The more popular of the two is purchased coverage.

55. Before we proceed, an important piece of federal legislation warrants mentioning. Based on the 1978 Pregnancy Disability Act, employers that offer short-term disability insurance to its employees must include pregnancy as part of the policy's coverage. This means that in whatever capacity employers "cover" other disabilities like an extended illness, the coverage for disability due to pregnancy must be the same (see Chapter 3).

56. The number of sick days offered to employees generally varies according to their position in the organization and their length of service. Many organizations require a waiting period, approximately six months, before sick leave kicks in.

57. Other employers are simply doing away with sick leave and are adding the time to vacation or personal days.

58. Commerce Clearing House, *Compensation* (May 1988), p. 2699–97.

59. Ibid.

60. The reason for the 70 to 80 percent of replacement income stems from the tax-free nature of some payments. (Payments from an employer LTD are generally taxable; the amount received from LTD based on employee paid premiums is not taxable income.) If long-term payments were not reduced, it is conceivable that an employee re-ceiving LTD and government disability payments could have a greater income than when the employee was working. This logic defeats the purpose of the program.

61. Rosenbloom and Hallman, p. 222.

62. Some disability plans pay benefits for different periods if the disability is due to illness rather than injury.

63. Depending on company policy, there may be a time lag before a new employee's insurance policy takes effect. Waiting periods, when used, typically last about

six months. Additionally, eligibility periods may be waived for management personnel.

64. Commerce Clearing House, *Compensation* (August 1990), p. 2651.

65. Ibid, p. 2605–03.

66. For a thorough discussion of flexible benefits, the advantages and disadvantages, see De Cenzo and Holoviak, *Employee Benefits*, Chapter 11.

67. Main, p. 94.

68. Ibid.

69. Richard E. Johnson, "Flexible Benefit Plans, *Employee Benefits Journal*, Vol. 11, No. 3 (September 1986), pp. 3–6.

70. Johnson, p. 4.

71. Ibid, p. 4.

72. McCaffery, p. 197.

73. Adverse selection in flexible benefits refers to a situation where those in greatest need of a particular benefit choose that benefit more often than the average employee. For instance, an employee with a ratable medical condition, say high blood pressure, is more likely to select the company's life insurance policy, because it is cheaper than what that individual could afford on his or her own. Healthier individuals, on the other hand, may find it less expensive to purchase their own policies directly through an agent. Accordingly, if only those with greater risk select a benefit, costs to the company will increase.

74. Linda M. Laarman, "The Facts About Domestic-Partner Benefits," *Employment Relations Today* (Summer 1992), p. 247; and D.J. Jefferson, "Family Matters: Gay Employees Win Benefits for Partners at More Corporations," *The Wall Street Journal* (March 8, 1994), pp. A–1; A–6.

75. See for example, D.J. Jefferson, "Family Matters: Gay Employees Win Benefits for Partners at More Corporations," *The Wall Street Journal* (March 8, 1994), pp. A–1; A–6.; Judy Greenwald, "San Diego Offers Domestic Partner Benefits," *Business Insurance* (June 13, 1994), p. 6; and Luis R. Gomez-Mejia, David Balkin, and Robert L. Cardy, *Managing Human Resources* (Englewood Cliffs, N.J.: Prentice-Hall, 1995), p. 443.

76. Ibid.

77. David Stipp, "Lotus Extends Company Benefits to Cover Domestic Partners of Homosexual Staff," *The Wall Street Journal* (September 9, 1991), p. B–6.

78. Ibid. However, previous court rulings have upheld a self-insured employer's right to reduce the lifetime limit provided to employees with AIDS; see Commerce Clearing House, *Human Resource Management: Ideas and Trends* (Issue No. 290, December 9, 1992), p. 198.

79. Ibid.

80. McCaffery, p. 98.

81. Ibid.

82. Jeremy Main, "The Battle Over Benefits," *Fortune* (December 16, 1991), p. 92.

83. Ibid.

84. See, for example, Lynn K. Saubert, Beverly L. Little, and Philip L. Little, "A Strategic HRM View of Benefits for Retirees," *Proceedings of the 30th Annual Meeting Southeastern Chapter The Institute of Management Sciences*, Robert T. Sumichrast, ed. (Myrtle Beach, S.C.: October 6–7, 1994), pp. 289–92.

85. Commerce Clearing House, "DuPont Revamps Its Health Plan to Rein in Costs," *Human Resources Management: Ideas and Trends* (January 5, 1994), p. 1–2.

86. B.P. Noble, "Making a Case for Family Friendly Programs, *The New York Times* (May 2, 1993), p. F–25.

87. See for example, Shirley Hand and Robert A. Zawacki, "Family-Friendly Benefits: More than a Frill, *HRMagazine* (October 1994), pp. 79–84; and Sharon Nelton, "A Flexible Style of Management, *Nation's Business* (December 1993), pp. 24–31.

88. Shirley Hand and Robert A. Zawacki, "Family-Friendly Benefits: More than a Frill, *HRMagazine* (October 1994), pp. 82–83.

89. Sue Shellenbarger, "A Tangible Commitment to Work–Family Issues, *The Wall Street Journal* (September 21, 1994), p. B–1.

90. We group these two issues together because of similarity. Their only difference lies in the age of the individual. Obviously, child care deals with the young, and elder care deals with caring for one's elderly dependents (e.g., parents).

91. Richard Levine, "Childcare: Inching Up the Corporate Agenda," *Management Review,* Vol. 78, No. 1 (January 1989), pp. 43–47.

92. Douglas J. Petersen and Douglas Massengill, "Childcare Programs Benefit Employers, Too," *Personnel* (May 1988), pp. 58–62.

93. "Companies Team Up to Improve Quality of Their Employees' Child-care Choices," *The Wall Street Journal* (October 17, 1991), p. B–1; see also Susan Gordon, "Helping Corporations Care," *Working Woman* (January 1993), p. 30.

94. Jaclyn Fierman, "Are Companies Less Family-Friendly?" *Fortune* (March 21, 1994), pp. 64–67.

95. Based on Michael P. Cronin, "Benefits: Taking Care of Sick Kids," *Inc.* (August 1993), p. 27.

Chapter 15

1. Anastasia Toufexis, "Workers Who Fight Firing with Fire," *Time* (April 25, 1994), p. 35; and *L.A. Times* (April 9, 1994), p. A–31.

2. U.S. Department of Commerce, Bureau of the Census, *Statistical Abstracts of the United States: 1991* (Washington, D.C.: Government Printing Office, 1994), p. 434.

3. In the case of the Supreme Court case of *Whirlpool Corporation* v. *Marshall* [445 U.S. 1(1980)], employees may refuse to work if they perceive doing so can cause serious injury. This case has weakened termination for insubordination when the refusal stems from a safety or health issue. This refusal was further clarified in *Gateway Coal* v. *the United Mine Workers* [94 S. Ct. 641(1981)], where a three-part test was developed. This was where (1) the refusal is reasonable; (2) the employee was unsuccessful in getting the problem fixed; and (3) normal organizational channels to address the problem haven't worked.

4. Horace A. Thompson III, "Negotiate with the Inspectors—Then Let Them In," *Human Resources Management: Ideas and Trends* (Chicago: Commerce Clearing House, April 18, 1990), p. 72.

5. Jerome Mansfield, "OSHA Rule 1910.120: A Rule to Live By," *Professional Safety* (May 1990), p. 38.

6. Ibid., pp. 39–40.

7. *Marshall* v. *Barlow, Inc.,* 436 U.S., 307 (1978).

8. Thompson III, p. 72.

9. Peter J. Sheridan, "How to Handle An OSHA Inspection," *Occupational Hazards* (September 1991), p. 132.

10. Adapted from Myron I. Peskin and Francis J. McGrath, "Industrial Safety: Who Is Responsible and Who Benefits?" *Business Horizons* (May–June 1992), p. 62.

11. Vic H. Henry, "Make Sure You Know Your Legal Rights When OSHA Arrives at Your Facility," *Occupational Health and Safety* (January 1992), p. 18.

12. State of Maryland, *Occupational Safety and Health Regulations* (Baltimore, Md.: Division of Labor and Industry, 1993), pp. 25–39,; and U.S. Department of Labor, Occupational Safety and Health Administration, *All About OSHA* (Washington, D.C.: Government Printing Office, 1985).

13. The material in this section is adapted from U.S. Department of Labor, Bureau of Labor Statistics, *A Brief Guide to Recordkeeping Requirements for Occupational Injuries and Illnesses* (Washington, D.C.: Government Printing Office, June 1986), pp. 1–19.

14. Ibid., p. 3.

15. Ibid., p. 9.

16. Ibid., p. 12.

17. Ibid., p. 15.

18. Ibid.

19. The number 3,600,000 is determined as follows: 1800 employees, working 40 hour weeks, for 50 weeks a year [1800 × 40 × 50].

20. *Statistical Abstract of the United States* (1994), p. 434.

21. Ibid, p. 437.

22. See Stephen C. Yohay, "Safety and Health Regulation Intensified," *Employee Relations Law Journal* (Autumn 1991), pp. 323–34; and "OSHA Trends," *Human Resources Management: Ideas and Trends* (Chicago: Commerce Clearing House, Inc., January 23, 1991), p. 14. For willful violation the minimum penalty is $5,000; other fines levied for violations other than willful and repetitive carry with them a $7,000 maximum.

23. John W. Ruser and Robert S. Smith, "Reestimating OSHA's Effects: Has the Data Changed?" *Journal of Human Resources* (Spring 1991), p. 212; see also Bradlee Thompson, "OSHA Bounces Back," *Training* (January 1991), pp. 45–53.

24. Colleen Johnson, "Concern over Safety Shows up on Companies' Bottom Line; Directory of Safety Consultants," *Business Insurance* (September 10, 1990), p. 36.

25. Susan B. Garland, "A New Chief Has OSHA Growling Again," *Business Week: Industrial/Technology Edition* (August 20, 1990), p. 57; and Robert Reid, "OSHA Warns Industry: Big Fines Are Here to Stay," *Occupational Hazards* (May 1988), p. 87.

26. Jonathan Tasini, "A Death at Work Can Put the Boss in Jail," *Business Week* (March 2, 1987), p. 38.

27. Stephen G. Minter, "Courts Give Criminal Prosecution a Green Light," *Occupational Hazards* (December 1989), p. 41.

28. Howard Banks, "The Agenda for Labor Law Reform," *Forbes* (January 16, 1995), p. 37.

29. Gregg Labar, "OSHA in 1992: Standards Are Job One," *Occupational Hazards* (December 1991), p. 31.

30. Rhonda West and Art Durity, "Does My Company Need to Worry about AIDS?" *Personnel* (April 1991), p. 5.

31. "Procedures for Bloodborne Disease Standards Outlined," *Human Resource Management: Ideas and Trends* (Chicago: Commerce Clearing House, Inc., April 15, 1992), p. 62.

32. Gregg Labar, "OSHA in 1992: Standards Are Job One," *Occupational Hazards* (December 1991), p. 31.

33. See, for example, Matthew M. Carmel and Michael F. Dolan, "An Introduction to Employee Right-to-Know Laws," *Personnel Journal* (September 1984), pp. 117–21.

34. "Hazard Communication Standard," *Human Resources Management: Ideas and Trends* (Chicago: Commerce Clearing House, Inc., March 7, 1990), p. 45.

35. Ibid.

36. Neville C. Tompkins, "Labor-Supported Committees Advocate Workers Right to Understand an MSDS," *Occupational Health and Safety* (July 1991), p. 23.

37. Ibid.

38. Garland, p. 57.

39. *Statistical Abstracts of the United States* (1991), p. 368.

40. Mark D. Fefer, "What to Do About Worker's Comp," *Fortune* (June 29, 1992), p. 80.

41. "Falling Behind: The U.S. Is Losing the Job Safety War to Japan, Too," *The Wall Street Journal* (May 16, 1992), p. A–1.

42. See Peskin and McGrath, pp. 66–69.

43. Ibid.

44. Ibid., p. 67.

45. Toufexis, pp. 35–36.

46. Douglas Harbrecht, "Talk About Murder, Inc.," *Business Week* (July 11, 1994), p. 8.

47. Ibid.; and Tom Dunkel, "Danger Zone," *Working Woman* (August 1994), pp. 39–40.

48. "Vehicle Accidents, Homicide Led 1993 Workplace Deaths," *HR News* (September 1994), p. 3.

49. Brett Pulley, "Crime Becomes Occupational Hazard of Deliverers," *The Wall Street Journal* (March 7, 1994), p. B–1; and John D. Thompson, "Employers Should Take Measures to Minimize Potential for Workplace Violence," *Commerce Clearing House: Ideas and Trends* (December 20, 1993), pp. 201–03; 208.

50. John D. Thompson, "Employers Should Take Measures to Minimize Potential for

Workplace Violence," *Commerce Clearing House: Ideas and Trends* (December 20, 1993), pp. 201–03; 208.

51. Ibid.

52. See, for example, Commerce Clearing House, "Workplace Violence: Strategies Start with Awareness," *Human Resources Management: Ideas and Trends* (July 11, 1994), p. 109.

53. Kathleen Menda, "Defusing Workplace Violence," *HRMagazine* (October 1994), p. 113.

54. Harbrecht, p. 8.

55. Faye Rice, "Do You Work in a Sick Building," *Fortune* (July 2, 1990), p. 88.

56. Ibid.

57. See for example, Stephanie Barlow, "Up In Smoke," *Entrepreneur* (August 1994), pp. 126–31.

58. Ibid., p. 130.

59. Jim Collison, "Work Place Smoking Policies: Questions and Answers," *Personnel Journal* (April 1988), p. 80.

60. Ibid.

61. Rudy M. Yandrick, "More Smokers Prohibit Smoking," *HRMagazine* (July 1994), pp. 68–69.

62. Ibid., p. 71.

63. See, for example, Frank Swoboda, "U.S. Acts to Reduce Repetitive Motion Injuries," *Washington Post* (August 31, 1990), p. A–4.

64. Michael A. Verespej, "Ergonomics: Taming the Repetitive Motion Monster," *Industry Week* (October 7, 1991), p. 26.

65. Linda Thornburg, "Workplace Ergonomics Makes Economic Sense," *HRMagazine* (October 1994), pp. 58–60.

66. J. A. Savage, "Stuck Between a VDT and a Hard Place," *Computerworld* (May 13, 1991), p. 63.

67. Ibid.

68. Ibid.

69. Adapted from Randall S. Schuler, "Definition and Conceptualization of Stress in Organizations," *Organizational Behavior and Human Performance* (April 1980), p. 189.

70. Ibid., p. 191.

71. "Workplace Stress Is Rampant, Especially with the Recession," *The Wall Street Journal* (May 5, 1992), p. A–1.

72. This information is adapted from a newswire report by Mari Yamaguchi as cited in "Stress in Japanese Business," *Audio Human Resource Report,* Vol. 2, No. 2 (March 1991), pp. 6–7.

73. Randall S. Schuler, pp. 200–05. See also Kenneth E. Hart, "Introducing Stress and Stress Management to Managers," *Journal of Managerial Psychology* (February 1990), pp. 9–16.

74. Nick Mykodym and Katie George, "Stress Busting on the Job," *Personnel* (July 1989), p. 56.

75. Ibid., p. 293.

76. Ibid.; see also Patti Watts, "Are Your Employees Burnout Proof?" *Personnel* (September 1990), pp. 12–14; and Philip J. Dewe, "Applying the Concepts of Appraisal to Work Stresses: Some Explanatory Analysis," *Human Relations* (February 1992), pp. 114–115.

77. Donald F. Parker and Thomas A. DeCotiis, "Organizational Determinants of Job Stress," *Organizational Behavior and Human Performance,* 32 (1983), p. 166.

78. Whiton Stuart Paine, *Job Stress and Burnout* (Beverly Hills, Calif.: Sage, 1982), p. 19.

79. Stuart Feldman, "Today's EAPs Make the Grade," *Personnel* (February 1991), p. 3.

80. Kevin J. Williams and George M. Alliger, "Role Stressors, Mood Spillover, and Perceptions of Work-Family Conflict in Employed Parents," *Academy of Management Journal,* Vol. 37, No. 4 (1994), p. 837.

81. Ibid.

82. Valla Howell, "The Groggy Beginnings of EAPs," *JEMS* (November 1988), p. 43.

83. Ibid.

84. Employee rights legislation mandates that any activity in an EAP remains confidential. This means records of who is visiting the EAP, the problems, and intervention, must be maintained separately from other personnel records. See Robert J. Noble, "Matter of Confidentiality," *Personnel* (February 1991), p. 11.

85. Feldman, p. 3.

86. See George Nicholas, "How to Make Employee Assistance Programs More Productive," *Supervision* (July 1991), pp. 3–6; and "EAPs to the Rescue," *Employee Benefit Plan Review* (February 1991), pp. 26–27.

87. "EAPs Evolve to Health Plan Gatekeeper," *Employee Benefit Plan Review* (February 1992), p. 18.

88. Edward Stetzer, "Bringing Sanity to Mental Health Costs," *Business and Health* (February 1992), p. 72.

89. See Meg Bryant, "Testing EAPs for Coordination," *Business and Health* (August 1991), pp. 20–24.

90. Diane Kirrane, "EAPs: Dawning of a New Age," *HRMagazine* (January 1990), pp. 30–34.

91. Deborah Shalowitz, "Employee Assistance Plan Trends," *Business Insurance* (June 24, 1991), p. 24.

92. Michael M. Harris and Mary L. Fennell, "Perceptions of an Employee Assistance Program and Employees' Willingness to Participate," *Journal of Applied Behavioral Science,* Vol. 24, No. 4 (1988), p. 423.

93. See for instance, Joan Hamilton, "Can Company Counselors Help You Cope?" *Business Week* (November 14, 1994), p. 141.

94. Shari Caudron, "The Wellness Payoff," *Personnel Journal* (July 1990), p. 55.

95. Stephanie L. Hyland, "Health Care Benefits Show Cost-Containment Strategies," *Monthly Labor Review* (February 1992), p. 42.

96. Therese R. Welter, "Wellness Programs: Not a Cure-All," *Industry Week* (February 15, 1988), p. 42.

97. Harry Harrington, "Retiree Wellness Plan Cuts Health Costs," *Personnel Journal* (August 1990), p. 60.

98. Leah Ingram, "Many Healthy Returns," *Entrepreneur* (September 1994), p. 84.

99. Caudron, p. 56.

100. Ibid.

101. John E. Riedel and Andrea Frank, "Corporate Health Promotion: Marketing Studies Show Who Buys and Who Succeeds," *Employee Benefits Journal,* Vol. 15, No. 2 (June 1990), p. 29.

102. See Kenneth J. Smith, George S. Everly, Jr., and G. Timothy Haight, "An Empirical Analysis of the Impact of a Corporate Health Promotion Intervention on Reported Sick Leave Absenteeism," *Benefits Quarterly,* Vol. 6, No. 1 (1990), pp. 37–45.

103. James W. Busbin and David P. Campbell, "Employee Wellness Programs: A Strategy for Increasing Participation," *Journal of Health Care Marketing,* Vol. 10, No. 4 (December 1990), p. 22.

104. Adapted from Caudron, pp. 57–58.

105. David E. Upton, "When Health Is Money," *Northwest Airlines World Traveler* (May 1992), p. 34.

106. Lucia Landon, "Pump Up Your Employees," *HRMagazine* (May 1990), p. 35.

107. Ibid., p. 46.

108. See Faye Rice, "How Execs Get Fit," *Fortune* (October 22, 1990), pp. 144–52.

109. U.S. Department of State, *Traveler's Telephone Advisory Line* (January 12, 1990 and February 27, 1990).

110. Osha Gray Davidson, "It's Still 1911 in America's Rural Sweatshops," *The Baltimore Sun* (September 7, 1991), p. A–7.

111. "Victims of Poultry-Plant Fire to Get $16.1 Million," *The New York Times* (November 11, 1992), p. A–40.

112. *The Baltimore Sun* (September 15, 1992), p. A–3; and "Factory Owner Is Given Prison for Fatal Blaze," *The New York Times* (September 15, 1992), pp. A–8, A–20.

1. Donna Fenn, "Communication: Tell It Like It Was," *Inc.* (January 1995), p. 95.

2. Mary V. Williams, "Managing Work-Place Diversity: The Wave of the '90s," *Communication World* (January 1990), p. 16.

3. See "Tell Employees: Summary Plan Descriptions," *Employee Benefit Plan Review* (May 1991), pp. 23–26.

4. William Briggs, "Taking Control after a Crisis," *HRMagazine* (March 1990), p. 60.

5. Thomas A. Stewart, "The Search for the Organization of Tomorrow," *Fortune* (May 18, 1992), pp. 91–92.

6. Edward E. Lawler III and Susan A. Mohrman, "With HR Help, All Managers Can Practice High Involvement Management," *Personnel* (April 1989), pp. 26–31.

7. Elizabeth Coleman, "Communication: A Precursor for the New Industrial Environment," *Work and People* (March 1991), pp. 17–21.

8. Richard G. Charlton, "The Decade of the Employee," *Public Relations Journal* (January 1990), p. 26.

9. Ibid.

10. Julie Foehrenback and Steve Goldfarb, "Employee Communication in the '90s: Great(er) Expectation," *Communication World* (May–June 1990), pp. 101–06.

11. Alvie L. Smith, "Bridging the Gap between Employees and Management," *Public Relations Journal* (November 1990), p. 20.

12. Jerry Beilinson, "Communicating Bad News," *Personnel* (January 1991), p. 15.

13. Leslie Lamkin and Emily W. Carmain, "Crisis in Communications at Georgia Power," *Personnel Journal* (January 1991), p. 35.

14. Ibid., p. 36.

15. See Brad Whitworth, "Proof at Last," *Communication World* (December 1990), pp. 28–31.

16. Commerce Clearing House, "Challenger Meets Employee Communication Challenge with Merit Plan," *Human Resources Management: Ideas and Trends* (April 13, 1994), p. 61.

17. James V. O'Connor, "Building Internal Communications," *Public Relations Journal* (June 1990), p. 29.

18. See Pamela K. Cook, "Employee Communications in the United States: What Works, and Why," *Benefits and Compensation International* (June 1991), pp. 2–5.

19. Adapted from David K. Lindo, "They're Supposed to Know," *Supervisor* (March 1992), pp. 14–17.

20. Walter H. Read, "Gathering Opinion On-Line," *HRMagazine* (January 1991), pp. 51–52.

21. David N. Bateman, "Communications," *Human Resource Management: Ideas and Trends* (Chicago: Commerce Clearing House, Inc., July 26, 1988), p. 128.

22. Smith.

23. Bateman.

24. McKeand, p.26.

25. Bateman.

26. Whitworth, p. 28.

27. Randal G. Hesser, *Nation's Business* (December 1989), p. 50.

28. Roderick Wilkinson, "All-Purpose Employee Handbook," *Supervision* (January 1992), p. 5.

29. Lori Block, "Texas Utility Effort Shines among Benefit Handbooks," *Business Insurance* (November 18, 1991), p. 63.

30. Ibid.

31. Commerce Clearing House, "Handbooks: Should Your Business Have One?" in *Topical Law Reports* (Chicago: Commerce Clearing House, Inc., May 1989), p. 5406.

32. See, for example, Robert J. Nobile, "Leaving No Doubt About Employee Leaves," *Personnel* (May 1990), pp. 54–60.

33. Ibid.

34. Ibid.

35. Paula Cohen and Robert J. Nobile, "Confessions of a Handbook Writer, Say It Legally," *Personnel* (May 1991), p. 9.

36. See Randall G. Hesser, "Watch Your Language," *Small Business Reports* (July 1991), pp. 45–49.

37. See Cohen and Nobile; Elliot H. Shaller, "Avoiding the Pitfalls in Hiring, Firing," *Nation's Business* (February 1991), pp. 51–54; and Pamela R. Johnson and Susan Gardner, "Legal Pitfalls of Employee Handbooks," *Advanced Management Journal* (Spring 1989), pp. 42–46.

38. Wilkinson.

39. Marilyn Melia, "Mergers, New Laws Spur Rewrites of Employee Handbooks," *Savings Institutions* (April 1992), p. 47.

40. See Bruce G. Posner, "The Best Little Handbook in Texas," *Inc.* (February 1989), pp. 84–88.

41. Ibid., p. 6.

42. Cohen and Nobile.

43. This format is adapted from the compilation of data presented in Commerce Clearing House, "What Should Be in the Handbook?" *Topical Law Reports* (Chicago: Commerce Clearing House, Inc., October 1990), pp. 5451–76.

44. See Linda Lee Brubaker, "Six Secrets for a Great Employee Newsletter," *Management Review* (January 1990), pp. 47–50.

45. Art Durity, "Confessions of a Newsletter Editor," *Personnel* (May 1991), p. 7; see also Brubaker.

46. Suellyn McMillian, "Squelching the Rumor Mill," *Personnel Journal* (October 1991), pp. 95–101.

47. See, for example, Jay Merchant, "Interactive Employee Communication: The Technology of the Nineties Is Here," *Topics in Total Compensation* (Summer 1989), pp. 339–46.

48. Karen Matthes, "Corporate Television Catches Employees' Eyes," *Personnel* (May 1991), p. 3.

49. Jennifer J. Laabs, "Oliver: A Twist on Communications," *Personnel Journal* (September 1991), p. 79.

50. Ibid.

51. Ibid., p. 81.

52. See, for example, Peter D. Bergh, "Ten Steps for Communicating Flex Benefits," *HRMagazine* (April 1991), p. 47.

53. Gayle Potter, "Personalized Benefits Statements," *HRMagazine* (May 1991), p. 23.

54. Ibid., p. 25.

55. Denis Detzel, "Their Employees Tend to Report that Management Listens to 'Problems and Complaints,'" in *Human Resources Management: Ideas and Trends* (Chicago: Commerce Clearing House, Inc., February 21, 1990), p. 39.

56. Ibid.

57. See, for example, Pamela Bloch-Flynn and Kenneth Vlach, "Employee Awareness Paves the Way for Quality," *HRMagazine* (July 1994), p. 78.

58. Ibid.

59. Adapted from Patrick J. McKeand, "GM Division Builds a Classic System to Share Internal Information," *Public Relations Journal* (November 1990), pp. 24–26.

60. Ibid., p. 24.

Chapter 17

1. Clifford Oviatt, Jr., "Courts Find Room for Labor-Employer Communication," *HR News* (December 1994), p. 10.

2. Janet Novack, "The Agenda for Labor Law Reform," *Forbes* (January 16, 1995), p. 37.

3. Clifford Oviatt, Jr., "Courts find Room for Labor-Employer Communication," *HR News* (December 1994), p. 10.

4. "Why Labor Keeps Losing," *Fortune* (July 11, 1994), p. 178.

5. For a comprehensive review of labor laws, see Bruce Feldacker, *Labor Law Guide to Labor Law*, 3d ed. (Englewood Cliffs, N.J.: Prentice-Hall, 1990).

6. Commerce Clearing House, *Labor Law Course*, 24th ed. (Chicago: Commerce Clearing House, Inc., 1979), p. 7141.

7. As a result of *Duplex Printing* v. *Dearing* (254 U.S. 443, 1921), the Clayton Act affirmed labor unions as legal entities, but did not give them the right to restrain trade through their concerted action.

8. The Railway Labor Act created the National Mediation Board, which works on matters of recognition, dispute resolution, and unfair labor practices in the railroad and airline industries only. The National Railroad Adjustment Board was also part of the Railway Labor Act, and this body arbitrated disputes between railroads and unions.

9. See "Lawmakers Attack the Railway Labor Act, but Change Isn't Likely," *The Wall Street Journal* (June 30, 1992), p. A–1.

10. Ibid.; "National Rail Bargaining May Be Doomed in the Future," *The Wall Street Journal* (June 30, 1992), p. A–1; and James Harney and Judi Hasson, "Rail Strike Puts Nation in 'State of Crisis,'" *USA Today* (June 25, 1992), p. A–1.

11. *Schechter Corporation* v. *United States*, 295 U.S. 495 (1935).

12. Commerce Clearing House, p. 1521.

13. As passed in 1947, the NLRB administrative body originally consisted of three members. It was expanded to five members with the passage of Taft–Hartley in 1947.

14. Commerce Clearing House, p. 1521.

15. A secondary boycott occurs when a union strikes against Employer A (a primary and legal strike), and then strikes and pickets against Employer B (an employer against which the union has no complaint) because of a relationship that exists between Employers A and B, such as Employer B handling goods made by Employer A. See Commerce Clearing House, Labor Law Course, p. 1524.

16. Commerce Clearing House, Labor Law Course, p. 7054.

17. Bruce Feldacker, *Labor Law Guide to Labor Law*, 3d ed., p. 5. For a more in-depth look at unionization in the hospital sector, see Edmund R. Becker and Jonathon S. Rakich, "Hospital Union Election Activity, 1974–1975," in *Health Care Financing*, Vol. 9, No. 3 (Spring 1988), pp. 59–66.

18. Commerce Clearing House, p. 1524.

19. L-M 2 reports are required of unions that have revenues of $100,000 or more. L-M 3 reports are required of unions that have less than $100,000 in revenues.

20. It must be noted that when one discusses government labor relations, two categories emerge. One is the federal sector, the other the public sector. In a brief discussion of government labor relations, the focus is on the federal sector due to its federal legislation. However, one must realize that state or municipal statutes do define practices for labor–management relationships for state, county, and municipal workers (typically police officers, fire fighters, and teachers). Because these laws differ in the many jurisdictions, it goes beyond the scope of this text to attempt to clarify each jurisdiction's laws.

21. Although government employees often face a no-strike clause, with the exception of the Air Traffic Controllers case, such restrictions are generally ineffective. Working to rules, "blue flues" and recorded sanitation, nursing, and teacher strikes across this country support the contention that a no-strike clause is weak.

22. *United States Code Annotated*, Title 18, Section 1961 (St. Paul, Minn.: West Publishing, 1984), p. 6.

23. Ibid., p. 228.

24. *United States Code Annotated*, Title 29, Section 186 (St. Paul, Minn.: West Publishing, 1978), p. 17.

25. See, for example, "The Liberation of the Teamsters," *National Review* (March 30, 1992), p. 35; and "Breaking the Teamsters," *Newsweek* (June 22, 1987), p. 43.

26. Only pure grievance awards can be solely determined by the FLRA. See Joseph R. Gordon and Joyce M. Najita, "Judicial Response to Public-Sector Arbitration," in Aaron et al., op. cit., p. 247.

27. This section was adapted from Bowers and De Cenzo, Chapter 3.

28. It is important to note that the AFL–CIO itself is not a labor union, but rather an affiliation of the international/national unions.

29. It must be noted, however, that the AFL–CIO has the authority to suspend or expel international/national unions from the Federation.

30. In addition to national efforts, issues affecting workers are also brought before state and local levels.

31. David R. Sanders, "Unions Labor Over Prisoner Right-to-Work Issue," *Insight on the News* (September 19, 1994), p. 17.

32. To eliminate any misunderstanding, we must also state that individual unions may also do public relations work.

33. U.S. Department of Labor, Bureau of Labor Statistics, *Directory of National Unions and Employee Associations* (Washington, D.C.: Government Printing Office, 1980), p. 1.

34. Ibid.

35. Arthur A. Sloane and Fred Witney, *Labor Relations,* 4th ed. (Englewood Cliffs, N.J.: Prentice-Hall, 1981), p. 145.

36. Services offered to national or local unions are an important feature of affiliation with the AFL–CIO. This is especially true for the "poorer" unions.

37. It should be noted, however, that independent locals can form and affiliate directly with the AFL–CIO.

38. Edwin F. Beal and James P. Begin, *The Practice of Collective Bargaining* (Homewood, Ill.: Richard D. Irwin, 1982), p. 107.

39. National and local unions are not always in agreement. In fact, with respect to an issue of control, instances were witnessed in the 1980s where local unions such as the Steelworkers accepted the contract terms that were unacceptable to the national union.

40. Negotiation committees and shop stewards oversee the collective bargaining process (i.e., negotiation, administration). Some overlap between the former and the executive committee may exist.

41. Elections may not be the only means of unionizing. In cases where a company has refused to recognize a union because of a past unfair labor practice, the NLRB may certify a union without a vote.

42. Jim Wimberly, "Union Elections," Commerce Clearing House, *Human Resources Management: Ideas and Trends* (February 15, 1990), p. 35.

43. Clyde Scott, and Christopher M. Lowery, "Union Election Activity in the Health Care Industry," *Health Care Management Review* (Winter 1994), p. 25.

44. "Why Labor Keeps Losing," *Fortune* (July 11, 1994), p. 178.

45. Outsourcing refers to a situation where work is taken away from unionized workers in a company and given to nonunionized employees in a separate location.

46. "Why Labor Keeps Losing," *Fortune* (July 11, 1994), p. 178; and John David, "U.S. Labor Movement Cornered," *The Charleston Gazette* (June 21, 1989), p. 6–A. It is also interesting to point out that President Clinton lifted the ban on hiring air traffic controllers who had been fired by President Reagan. Any air traffic controller fired by Reagan was not eligible to work again for the Federal Aviation Administration—the agency that hires air controllers. The removal of the ban came on August 12, 1993.

47. 464 US 513, 115 LRRM 2805 (1984).

48. Stephen D. Gordon, Timothy P. O'Reilly, and Harold J. Datz (editors in chief), *The Developing Labor Law: The Board, the Courts, and the National Labor Relations Act,* 2d ed., Fourth Supplement (1982–87) (Washington, D.C.: The Bureau of National Affairs, Inc., 1988, pp. 628–29).

49. George J. Church, "Unions Arise—With New Tricks," *Time* (June 13, 1994).

50. See for example, Leo Troy, "Why Labor Unions Are Declining," *Journal of Commerce and Commercial* (August 1994), p. 6A; and S. Overman, "The Union Pitch Has Changed," *HRMagazine* (December 1991), pp. 44–46.

51. Janet Novack, "An Agency Out of Step with the Times," *Forbes* (January 16, 1995), p. 37.

52. Adapted from Molly H. Bowers and David A. De Cenzo, *Essentials of Labor Relations* (Englewood Cliffs, N.J.: Prentice-Hall, 1992), pp. 138–44.

53. Sunshine laws exist in eleven states: Alaska, California, Delaware, Florida, Idaho, Iowa, Minnesota, Texas, Ohio, Vermont, and Wisconsin. In addition, Indiana, Kansas, Maryland, Montana, and Tennessee have laws regarding openness of the collective bargaining process. From B.V.H. Schneider, "Public Sector Labor Legislation—An Evolutionary Analysis," p. 219.

54. "Why White-Collar Staff Join Unions," *IRS Employment Trends* (August 1994), pp. 2–3.

55. See, for example, Clyde Scott and Christopher M. Lowery, "Union Election Activity in the Health Care Industry," *Health Care Management Review* (Winter 1994), pp. 18–28.

56. Ibid.

57. *IRS Employment Trends,* p. 3

58. Clyde Scott and Christopher M. Lowery, "Union Election Activity in the Health Care Industry," *Health Care Management Review* (Winter 1994), p. 22.

59. *IRS Employment Trends,* p. 3

60. "Japan Report," *The Wall Street Journal* (April 23, 1991), p. A–1.

61. See, for example, Peter J. Dowling and Randall S. Schuler, *International Dimensions of Human Resource Management* (Boston: PWS-Kent Publishing, 1990), pp. 138–57.

62. See Robert E. Cole and Donald R. Deskins, Jr., "Racial Factors in Site Location and Employment Patterns of Japanese Auto Firms in America," *California Management Review* (1988), pp. 9–22.

63. See, for example, Peter Dowling, Randall S. Schuler, and Denice E. Welch, *International Dimensions of Human Resource Management,* 2d ed. (Belmont, Calif. Wadsworth, 1994), pp. 201–03.

64. Brooks Tigner, "The Looming Crunch," in M. Mendenhall and G. Oddou, eds., *Readings and Cases in International Human Resource Management* (Boston: PWS-Kent Publishing, 1991), pp. 412–17.

65. "Workers Want Their Piece of Europe Inc.," *Business Week* (October 29, 1990), p. 46.

66. This case is fictitious case designed for classroom purposes only. It does not accurately reflect the operations of the Service Employees Union. However, some details presented were from actual events, and can be found in Mary Helen Yaroborough, "Unions Are Targeting Pro-Management States," *HRFocus* (April 1994), pp. 1, 4; and William E. Lissy, "Access of Non-Employee Union Organizers to Employers' Property," *Supervision* (October 1992), pp. 19–20.

Chapter 18

1. Opening vignette based on Ronald Grover, Aaron Bernstein, and Zachary Schiller, "Ste-e-e-rike?" *Business Week* (August 15, 1994), pp. 26–28; Aaron Bernstein and David Griesing, "Baseball's Strike Talk Turns Serious," *Business Week* (June 27, 1994), p. 34; and Aaron Bernstein, "Are Baseball's Players Getting Caught in a Rundown?" *Business Week* (September 26, 1994), p. 58.

2. "Salary Survey," *The Baltimore Sun* (April 30, 1995), p. 110; and Aaron Bernstein and David Griesing, "Baseball's Strike Talk Turns Serious," *Business Week* (June 27, 1994), p. 34.

3. Ibid.

4. American Federation of Labor—Congress of Industrial Organizations, *This Is the AFL–CIO* (Washington, D.C.: AFL–CIO, 1991), p. 2.

5. "Rumble in Buick City," *Business Week* (October 10, 1994), p. 42.

6. D.C. Bok and J.T. Dunlop, "Collective Bargaining in the United States: An Overview," in W. Clay Hammer and Frank L. Schmidt (eds.), *Contemporary Problems in Personnel* (Chicago: St. Clair Press, 1977), p. 383.

7. An international union, in this context, refers to a national union in the United States that has local unions in Canada.

8. If we take into account public-sector collective bargaining, then we have another exception—the public. The tax-paying voting public can influence elected officials to act in certain ways during negotiations.

9. Alison Rogers, "Now Playing in Peoria," *Fortune* (July 12, 1993), p. 11; and "Caterpil-

lar Strike," *USA Today* (June 22, 1994), p. B–1. Also, the official name of the UAW is the United Automobile, Aerospace, and Agriculture workers union.

10. Kevin Kelly, "Why the Talks at Deere Hit Bedrock," *Business Week* (October 31, 1994), p. 48.

11. Readers should recognize that although the closed shop (compulsory union membership before one is hired) was declared illegal by the Taft–Hartley Act, a modified form still exists today. That quasi-closed shop arrangement is called the hiring hall, and is found predominantly in the construction and printing industries. However, a hiring hall is not a form of union security because it must assist all members despite their union affiliation. Additionally, the hiring hall must establish procedures for referrals that are nondiscriminatory. See Bruce Feldecker, *Labor Guide to Labor Law*, 3d ed. (Englewood Cliffs, N.J.: Prentice-Hall, 1990), pp. 319–23.

12. There are, however, exceptions to this in the construction industry.

13. *Communication Workers of America* v. *Beck*, U.S. Supreme Court, 109LC (1988).

14. Commerce Clearing House, *Human Resources Management: Ideas and Trends* (April 29, 1992), p. 70.

15. Aaron Bernstein and David Griesing, "Baseball's Strike Talk Turns Serious," *Business Week* (June 27, 1994), p. 34.

16. Mollie H. Bowers and David A. De Cenzo, *Essentials of Labor Relations* (Englewood Cliffs, N.J.: Prentice-Hall, 1992), p. 101.

17. For a thorough explanation of the grievance procedure, see ibid., pp. 109–14.

18. Michael R. Carroll and Christina Heavrin, *Collective Bargaining and Labor Relations* (New York: Merrill/MacMillan Publishing, 1991), pp. 310–11.

19. Adapted from Stephen P. Robbins, *Supervision Today* (Englewood Cliffs, N.J.: Prentice-Hall, 1995), p. 533.

20. Ibid., p. 316.

21. One must be aware, however, that in some organizations where participative management styles exist, the minority does not make the decisions.

22. Other factors can affect a settlement, such as political infighting, unreasonable legislation, efforts to bust the union, and so on.

23. To be accurate, a strike vote is generally held at the local union level in which the members authorize their union leadership to call the strike.

24. See Jim Stern, "Unions Rethinking Role of the Strike," *Washington Post* (March 18, 1990), p. H–3.

25. "Unions Arise—With New Tricks," *Time* (June 13, 1994), p. 56.

26. "The Strike Weapon Remains Highly Troublesome for Unions," *The Wall Street Journal* (February 26, 1991), p. A–1.

27. U.S. Bureau of the Census, *Statistical Abstract of the U.S.: 1994,* 114th ed. (Washington, D.C.: Government Printing Office, 1994), p. 438; "Unions and Strikers: A Huge Non-problem," *Fortune* (May 31, 1994), pp. 175–76; and "Unions Arise—With New Tricks," p. 56.

28. "Unions Arise—With New Tricks," p. 56.

29. Eugene C. Hagburg and Marvin J. Levine, *Labor Relations: An Integrative Perspective* (St. Paul, Minn.: West Publishing, 1978), p. 8.

30. See, for example, Peter Nulty, "Look What the Unions Want Now," *Fortune* (February 8, 1993), pp. 128–35.

31. See, for example, Ross Laver, "Joining Hands," *MacLeans* (April 15, 1991), p. 46.

32. "GM's New Saturn Pact Blazes Trail," *Facts on File*, Vol. 45, No. 2332 (August 2, 1985), pp. 570–71.

33. David Woodruff, "At Saturn, What Workers Want Is . . . Fewer Defects," *Business Week* (December 2, 1991), p. 117.

34. Keith L. Alexander, "USAirs's Flight Plan Leaves Little Room to Maneuver," *Business Week* (October 17, 1994), p. 48; and Keith L. Alexander and Stephen Baker, "If You Can't Beat 'Em, Buy 'Em," *Business Week* (October 24, 1994), pp. 79–81.

35. Robert C. Rose, Alex Kotlowitz, and Dana Milbank, "Caterpillar Says that Some Strikers May Not Be Allowed to Return to Work," *The Wall Street Journal* (April 16, 1992), p. A–3.

36. Andrew Kupfer, "Caterpillar's Union Fallout," *Fortune* (May 18, 1992), p. 16.

37. K. Kelly, "CAT May Be Trying to Bulldoze the Immovable," *Business Week* (December 2, 1991), p. 116; see also Robert C. Rose and Alex Kotlowitz, "Strife Between UAW and Caterpillar Blights Promising Labor Idea," *The Wall Street Journal* (November 23, 1992), p. A–1.

38. Alison Rogers, "Now Playing in Peoria," *Fortune* (July 12, 1993), p. 11.

Appendix A

1. See, for example, Julia Lawlor, "Scanning Resumes: The Impersonal Touch," *USA Today* (October 7, 1991), p. 7B.

2. Terry Mullins, "How to Land a Job," *Psychology Today* (September/October 1994), pp. 12–13.

Appendix B

1. Kirsten Schabacker, "Tips on Making a Great First Impression," *Working Woman* (February 1992), p. 55.

2. See Jundra Woo, "Job Interviews Pose Risk to Employers," *The Wall Street Journal* (March 11, 1992), p. B1; and Joann Keyton and Jeffrey K. Springston, "What Did You Ask Me?" *National Business Employment Weekly* (Spring 1991), p. 32.

3. Stephen M. Pollan and Mark Levine, "How to Ace a Tough Interview," *Working Woman* (July 1994), p. 49.

4. Ibid.

Glossary

(Number in parentheses indicates chapter in which term first appeared)

Absolute Standards (12) Measuring an employee's performance against some established standards.

Accept Errors (6) Accepting candidates who would later prove to be poor performers.

Adjective Rating Scales (12) A performance appraisal method that lists a number of traits and a range of performance for each.

Adverse (Disparate) Impact (3) A consequence of an employment practice that results in a greater rejection rate for a minority group than it does for the majority group in the occupation.

Adverse (Disparate) Treatment (3) An employment situation where protected group members receive different treatment than other employees in matters like performance evaluations, promotions, etc.

Adverse Selection (14) A situation in flexible benefits administration where those in greatest need of a particular benefit choose that benefit more often than the average employee.

Advertisements (6) Materials communicating to the general public that a position in a company is open.

Affirmative Action (3) A practice in organizations that goes beyond discontinuance of discriminatory practices, including actively seeking, hiring, and promoting minority group members and women.

AFL–CIO (17) The American Federation of Labor and the Congress of Industrial Organizations.

Age Discrimination in Employment Act (3) Passed in 1967 and amended in 1978 and 1986, this act prohibits arbitrary age discrimination, particularly among those over age 40.

Agency Shop (18) A type of union security arrangement whereby employees must pay union dues to the certified bargaining unit even if they choose not to join the union.

Albermarle Paper Company v. *Moody* (3) Supreme Court case that clarified the requirements for using and validating tests in selection processes.

Americans with Disabilities Act of 1990 (3) Extends EEO coverage to include most forms of disability, requires employers to make reasonable accommodations, and eliminates post-job-offer medical exams.

Apathy (11) Significant dysfunction tension resulting in no effort being made.

Application Form (6) Company-specific employment forms used to generate specific information the company wants.

Apprenticeship (9) A time—typically two to five years—when an individual is considered to be training to learn a skill.

Assessment Centers (7) A facility where performance simulation tests are administered. These are made up of a series of exercises and are used for selection, development, and performance appraisals.

Attitude Survey (9) Questionnaires used to elicit responses from employees regarding how they feel about their jobs, work groups, supervisors, and the organization.

Attribution Theory (12) A theory of performance evaluation based on the perception of who is in control of an employee's performance.

Attrition (5) A process whereby the jobs of incumbents who leave for any reason will not be filled.

Authorization Card (17) A card signed by prospective union members indicating that they are interested in having a union election held at their work site.

Autonomy (11) The freedom and independence involved in doing one's job.

Baby Boomers (2) Those individuals born between 1946 and 1964.

Baby Busters (2) Those individuals born in 1965 and years after. Often referred to as "generation Xers."

Background Investigation (6) The process of verifying information job candidates provide.

Behavioral Symptoms (15) Symptoms of stress characterized by decreased productivity, increased absenteeism and turnover, and increased smoking and alcohol/substance consumption.

Behaviorally Anchored Rating Scales (BARS) (12) A performance appraisal technique that generates critical incidents and develops behavioral dimensions of performance. The evaluator appraises behaviors rather than traits.

Blind-box Ad (6) An advertisement in which there is no identification of the advertising organization.

Blue Cross (14) A health insurer concerned with the hospital side of health insurance.

Blue Shield (14) A health insurer concerned with the provider side of health insurance.

Broad-banding (13) Paying employees at preset levels based on the level of competencies they possess.

Bulletin Board (16) A means a company uses to post information of interest to its employees.

Burnout (15) Chronic and long-term stress.

Career (10) The sequence of positions that a person has held over his or her life.

Career Counseling (10) Assisting employees in setting directions and identifying areas of professional growth.

Career Development (10) A process designed to assist workers in managing their careers.

Career Stages (10) An individual's career moves through five stages: exploration, establishment, mid-career, late-career, and decline.

Central Tendency (12) The tendency of a rater to give average ratings.

Change Agent (9) Individuals responsible for fostering the change effort, and assisting employees in adapting to the changes.

Checklist Appraisal (12) A performance appraisal type in which a rater checks off those attributes of an employee that apply.

Civil Rights Act of 1866 (3) Federal law that prohibited discrimination based on race.

Civil Service Reform Act (17) Replaced Executive Order 11491 as the basic law governing labor relations for federal employees.

Civil Rights Acts of 1991 (3) Employment discrimination law that nullified selected Supreme Court decisions. Reinstated burden of proof by the employer, and allowed for punitive and compensatory damage through jury trials.

Classification Method (13) Method of job evaluation that focuses on creating common job grades based on skills, knowledge, and abilities.

Clayton Act (17) Labor legislation that attempted to limit the use of injunctions against union activities.

Co-determination Stage (18) A labor–management relationship characterized as separate but equal.

Coaching (9) A development activity in which a manager takes an active role in guiding another manager.

Collaboration Stage (18) A labor–management relationship characterized as working together for a common cause.

Collective Bargaining (18) The negotiation, administration, and interpretation of a written agreement between two parties, at least one of which represents a group that is acting collectively, that covers a specific period of time.

College Placements (6) An external search process focusing recruiting efforts on a college campus.

Communication (16) The transference of meaning and understanding.

Communications Programs (1) HRM programs designed to provide information to employees.

Company Newsletter (16) A means of providing information for employees in a specific recurring periodical.

Company-wide Meetings (16) Frequently held meetings used to inform employees of various company issues.

Comparable Worth (3) Equal pay for similar jobs, jobs similar in skills, responsibility, working conditions, and effort.

Compensation Administration (13) The process of managing a company's compensation program.

Competency-based Compensation Programs (13) Organizational pay system that rewards skills, knowledge, and behaviors.

Complaint Procedure (16) A formalized procedure in an organization through which an employee seeks resolution of a work problem.

Comprehensive Interviews (6) A selection device in which in-depth information about a candidate can be obtained.

Comprehensive Selection (6) Applying all steps in the selection process before rendering a decision about a job candidate.

Concurrent Validity (6) Validating tests by using current employees as the study group.

Confrontational Stage (18) A labor–management relationship characterized as fighting one another.

Consolidated Omnibus Budget Reconciliation Act (14) Provides for the continuation of employee benefits for a period up to three years after an employee leaves a job.

Constraints on Recruiting Efforts (6) Factors that can affect maximizing outcomes in recruiting.

Construct Validity (6) The degree to which a particular trait is related to successful performance on the job (e.g., IQ tests).

Content Validity (6) The degree to which the content of the test, as a sample, represents all the situations that could have been included (e.g., a typing test for a clerk typist).

Contingent Work Force (2) The part-time, temporary, and contract workers used by organizations to fill peak staffing needs, or perform work unable to be done by core employees.

Continuous Process Improvement (2) A total quality management concept whereby workers continue toward 100 percent effectiveness on the job.

Contract Administration (18) Implementing, interpreting, and monitoring the negotiated agreement between labor and management.

Controlling (1) A management function concerned with monitoring activities.

Cooperation Stage (18) A labor–management relationship characterized as working together on a few specific issues.

Core employees (2) An organization's full time employee population.

Core-plus Plans (14) A flexible benefits program whereby employees are provided core benefit coverage, and then are permitted to buy additional benefits from a menu.

Correlation Coefficients (6) A statistical procedure showing the strength of the relationship between one's test score and job performance.

Cost/Benefit Analysis (9) Evaluating an activity where costs are known, but where the standard by which these costs must be measured is ambiguous.

Criterion-related Validity (6) The degree to which a particular selection device accurately predicts the important elements of work behavior (e.g., the relationship between a test score and job performance).

Critical Incident Appraisal (12) A performance appraisal method that focuses on the key behaviors that make the difference between doing a job effectively or ineffectively.

Culture (8) The rules, jargon, customs, and other traditions that clarify acceptable and unacceptable behavior in an organization.

Cultural Environments (2) The attitudes and perspectives shared by individuals from specific countries that shape their behavior and how they view the world.

Cumulative Trauma Disorder (15) An occupational injury that occurs from repetitively performing similar physical movements.

Cut Score (6) A point at which applicants scoring below that point are rejected.

Decentralized Work Sites (2) Work sites that exist away from an organization's facilities.

Decline Phase (10) The final stage in one's career, usually marked by retirement.

Defined Benefit A type of retirement program whereby a retiring employee receives a fixed amount of retirement income based on some average earnings over a period of time.

Defined Contribution Plans (14) A retirement plan whereby an employer only agrees to contribute to employees' retirement funds. The amount contributed is not fixed.

Delegation (2) A management activity in which activities are assigned to individuals at lower levels in the organization.

Deprivation (11) A state of having an unfulfilled need.

Diary Method (5) A job analysis method requiring job incumbents to record their daily activities.

Dictionary of Occupational Titles (5) A government publication that lists more than 30,000 jobs.

Differential Validity (6) A special type of validation whereby a cut score is lower due to bias in the test.

Discipline (4) A condition in the organization when employees conduct themselves in accordance with the organization's rules and standards of acceptable behavior.

Dismissal (4) A disciplinary action that results in the termination of an employee.

Distributive Bargaining (18) A competitive, confrontational bargaining strategy.

Documentation (12) Used as a record of the performance appraisal process outcomes.

Downsizing (2) An activity in an organization aimed at creating greater efficiency by eliminating certain jobs.

Drug Testing (4) The process of testing applicants/employees to determine if they are using illicit drugs.

Drug-free Workplace Act (4) Requires specific government related groups to ensure that their workplace is drug free.

Dual-career Couples (10) A situation in which both husband and wife have distinct careers outside the home.

Dues Checkoff (18) Employer withholding of union dues from union members' paychecks.

Dysfunctional Tension (18) Tension that leads to negative stress.

E-mail (16) An electronic device that allows for messages to be left for another party.

Early Retirement (5) A downsizing effort whereby employees close to retirement are given some incentive to leave the company earlier than expected.

Economic Strike (18) An impasse that results from labor and management's ability to agree on the wages, hours, terms, and conditions of a "new" contract.

Effort (11) Outward action of individuals directed toward some goal.

Effort–performance Relationship (11) The likelihood that putting forth the effort will lead to successful performance on the job.

Electronic Media (16) Any technological device that enhances communications.

Employee Assistance Programs(EAPS) (15) Specific programs designed to help employees with personal problems.

Employee Benefits (14) Membership-based, nonfinancial rewards offered to attract and keep employees.

Employee Counseling (9) A process whereby employees are guided in overcoming performance problems.

Employee Development (16) Future-oriented training, focusing on the personal growth of the employee.

Employee Handbook (16) A booklet describing the important aspects of employment an employee needs to know.

Employee Leasing (6) Hiring "temporary" employees for long periods of time.

Employee Monitoring (4) An activity whereby the company is able to keep informed of its employees' activities.

Employee Referrals (6) A recommendation from a current employee regarding a job applicant.

Employee Retirement Income Security Act (14) Law passed in 1974 designed to protect employee retirement benefits.

Employee Rights (4) A collective term dealing with varied employee protection practices in an organization.

Employee Training (9) Present-oriented training, focusing on individuals' current jobs.

Employment Legislation (1) Laws that directly affect the hiring, firing, and promotion of individuals.

Employment Tests (7) Any selection examination that is designed to determine if an applicant is qualified for the job.

Employment-at-Will (4) Nineteenth-century common law that permitted employers to discipline or discharge employees at their discretion.

Empowering (2) Affording employees more delegation, participative management, work teams, goal setting, and training.

Encounter Stage (8) The socialization stage where individuals confront the possible dichotomy between their organizational expectations and reality.

Environmental Influences (1) Those factors outside the organization that directly affect HRM operations.

Equal Employment Opportunity Commission (3) The arm of the federal government empowered to handle discrimination in employment cases.

Equal Pay Act (13) Passed in 1963, this act requires equal pay for equal work.

Ergonomics (15) The process of matching the work environment to the individual.

Essay Appraisal (12) A performance appraisal method whereby an appraiser writes a narrative about the employee.

Establishment Phase (10) A career stage in which one begins to search for work. It includes getting one's first job.

Ethics (4) Going beyond the law in employment decisions designed to protect employee rights and dignity.

Executive Order 10988 (17) Affirmed the right of federal employees to join unions and granted restricted bargaining rights to these employees.

Executive Order 11491 (17) Designed to make federal labor relations more like those in the private sector. Also established the Federal Labor Relations Council.

Expatriates (6) Individuals who work in a country in which they are not citizens of that country.

Exploration Phase (10) A career stage that usually ends in one's mid-twenties as one makes the transition from school to work.

External Dimension (10) The objective progression of steps through a given occupation.

Extinction (9) The elimination of any reinforcement that maintains behavior.

Extrinsic Rewards (13) Rewards one gets from the employer, usually money, a promotion, or benefits.

Fact-finder (18) A neutral third-party individual who conducts a hearing to gather evidence and testimony from the parties regarding the differences between them.

Factor Comparison Method (13) A method of job analysis in which job factors are compared to determine the worth of the job.

Fair Credit Reporting Act (4) Requires an employer to notify job candidates of its intent to check into their credit.

Fair Labor Standards Act (13) Passed in 1938, this act established laws outlining minimum wage, overtime pay, and maximum hour requirements for most U.S. workers.

Family and Medical Leave Act (3) Federal legislation that provides employees up to twelve weeks of unpaid leave each year to care for family members, or for their own medical reasons.

Family-Friendly Benefits (14) Flexible benefits that are supportive of caring for one's family.

Family-Friendly Organization (5) Organizations that provide benefits that support employees' caring for their families.

Federal Mediation and Conciliation Service (17) A government agency that assists labor and management in settling their disputes.

Feedback (11) Knowledge of results.

Flexible Benefits (14) A benefits program in which employees are permitted to pick benefits that most meet their needs.

Flexible Spending Accounts (14) Special benefits accounts that allow the employee to set aside money on a pretax basis to pay for certain benefits.

Flextime (11) A scheduling system in which employees are required to work a number of hours per week but are free, within limits, to vary the hours of work.

Forced-choice Appraisal (12) A type of performance appraisal method in which the rater must choose between two specific statements about an employee's work behavior.

4/5ths Rule (3) A rough indicator of discrimination, this rule requires that the number of minority members that a company hires must be at least 80 percent of the majority members in the population hired.

401(k)s (14) Tax code section that permits employees to set aside a part of their salary for retirement on a pretax basis.

Functional Tension (11) Positive tension that creates the energy for an individual to act.

Glass Ceiling (3) The invisible barrier that blocks females and minorities from ascending into upper levels of an organization.

Global Village (2) The production and marketing of goods and services worldwide.

Golden Parachute (13) A protection plan for executives in the event that they are severed from the organization.

Graphology (13) Handwriting analysis.

Grievance (Rights) Arbitration (18) Specialized steps followed for handling contractual disputes arising from a collective-bargaining agreement.

Grievance Procedures (18) A complaint-resolving process contained in union contracts.

Griggs v. Duke Power (3) Landmark Supreme Court decision stating that tests must fairly measure the knowledge or skills required for a job.

Group Interview Method (5) Meeting with a number of

employees to collectively determine what their jobs entail.

Group Order Ranking (12) A relative standard of performance characterized as placing employees into a particular classification, such as the "top one-fifth."

Halo Error (12) The tendency to let our assessment of an individual on one trait influence our evaluation of that person on other specific traits.

Hawthorne Studies (1) A series of studies that provided new insights into group behavior.

Hazard Communication Standard (15) Requires organizations to communicate to its employees hazardous chemicals they may encounter on the job, and how to deal with them safely.

Health Insurance (14) An employee benefit designed to provide coverage in the event of an injury or illness.

Health Maintenance Act (14) Established the requirement that companies offering traditional health insurance to its employees must also offer alternative healthcare options.

Health Maintenance Organization (14) Provide comprehensive health services for a flat fee.

Holland Vocational Preferences (10) An individual occupational personality as it relates to vocational themes.

Honesty Tests (4) A specialized paper-and-pencil test designed to assess one's honesty.

Host-country national (6) Hiring a citizen from the host country to perform certain jobs in the global village.

Hot-stove Rule (4) Discipline should be immediate, provide ample warning, be consistent, and be impersonal.

Human Resource Management System (5) A computerized system that assists in the processing of HRM information.

Human Resource Inventory (5) Describes the skills that are available within the organization.

Imminent Danger (15) A condition where an accident is about to occur.

Impasse (18) A situation where labor and management cannot reach a satisfactory agreement.

Implied Employment Contract (4) Any organizational guarantee or promises about job security.

Impression Management (7) Influencing performance evaluations by portraying an image that is desired by the appraiser.

IMPROSHARE (13) A special type of incentive plan using a specific mathematical formula for determining employee bonuses.

Incident Rate (15) Number of injuries, illnesses, or lost workdays as it relates to a common base of 100 full-time employees.

Independent Contractors (6) Temporary employees offering specialized services to an organization.

Individual Interview Method (5) Meeting with an employee to determine what his or her job entails.

Individual Needs (11) A basic want or desire.

Individual Performance–Organizational Goal Relationship (11) The likelihood that successful performance on the job will lead to the attainment of organizational goals.

Individual Ranking (12) Ranking employees' performance from highest to lowest.

Initial Screening (6) The first step in the selection process whereby inquiries about a job are screened.

Integrative Bargaining (18) A cooperative strategy in which a common goal is the focus of negotiations.

Interactive Videos (9) Videos that permit the user to make changes/selections.

Interest Arbitration (18) An impasse resolution technique used to settle contract negotiation disputes.

Internal Search (6) A promotion-from-within concept.

Interview (7) A selection method that involves a face-to-face meeting with the candidate.

Intrinsic Rewards (13) Rewards one receives from the job itself, such as pride in one's work, a feeling of accomplishment, or being part of a team.

Job Analysis (5) Provides information about jobs currently being done and the knowledge, skills, and abilities that individuals need to perform the jobs adequately.

Job Characteristics Model (11) A framework for analyzing and designing jobs. JCM identifies five primary job characteristics and their interrelationship.

Job Description (5) A written statement of what the jobholder does, how it is done, and why it is done.

Job Enrichment (11) The process of expanding the depth of the job by allowing employees to do more planning and controlling of their work.

Job Evaluation (5) Specifies the relative value of each job in the organization.

Job Instruction Training (9) A systematic approach to on-the-job training consisting of four basic steps.

Job Rotation (9) Moving employees horizontally or vertically to expand their skills, knowledge, or abilities.

Job Specifications (5) Statements indicating the minimal acceptable qualifications incumbents must possess to successfully perform the essential elements of their jobs.

Jungian Personality Typology (10) Four dimensions of personality matched to work environments.

Karoshi (15) A Japanese term meaning death from overworking.

Labor and Management Reporting and Disclosure Act (17) (See Landrum–Griffin Act.)

Labor–Management Relations Act (17) Also known as the Taft–Hartley Act, it constrained the powers of unions.

Landrum–Griffin Act (17) Also known as the Labor and Management Reporting and Disclosure Act, this legislation protected union members from possible wrongdoing on the part of their unions. Its thrust was to require all unions to disclose their financial statements.

Late-career Phase (10) A career stage in which individuals are no longer learning about their jobs, nor is it expected that they should be trying to outdo levels of performance from previous years.

Layoffs (5)   Removing workers from an organization on a temporary or permanent basis.

Leading (1)   A management function concerned with directing the work of others.

Learning Curve (9)   Depicts the rate of learning.

Legally Required Benefits (14)   Employee benefits that are required by law.

Legislating Love (4)   Company guidelines on how personal relationships may exist at work.

Leniency Error (12)   A means by which performance appraisal can be distorted by evaluating employees against one's own value system.

Local union (17)   Provides the grass-roots support for union members in day-to-day labor–management relations.

Lockout (18)   A situation in labor–management negotiations whereby management prevents union members from returning to work.

Management (1)   The process of efficiently getting activities completed with and through other people.

Management by Objectives (MBO) (12)   A performance appraisal method that includes mutual objective setting and evaluation based on the attainment of the specific objectives.

Management Rights (18)   Items that are not part of contract negotiations, such as how to run the company, or how much to charge for products.

Management Thought (1)   Early theories of management that promoted today's HRM operations.

Marshall v. *Barlow, Inc.* (15)   Supreme Court case that stated an employer could refuse an OSHA inspection unless OSHA had a search warrant to enter the premises.

Mature Workers (2)   Those workers born before 1946.

McDonnell-Douglas Corp. v. Green (3)   A four-part test used to determine if discrimination has occurred.

Medical/Physical Examination (6)   An examination indicating an applicant is physically fit for essential job performance.

Membership-based Rewards (13)   Rewards that go to all employees regardless of performance.

Mentoring or Coaching (9)   Actively guiding another individual.

Merit Pay (13)   An increase on one's pay, usually given on an annual basis.

Metamorphosis Stage (8)   The socialization stage whereby the new employee must work out any inconsistencies discovered during the encounter stage.

Mid-career Phase (10)   A career stage marked by a continuous improvement in performance, leveling off in performance, or the beginning of deterioration of performance.

Mission Statement (5)   The reason an organization is in business.

Modular Plans (14)   A flexible benefit system whereby employees choose a pre-designed package of benefits.

Motivating Potential Score (11)   A predictive index suggesting the motivation potential of a job.

Motivation (11)   The willingness to do something, conditioned by the action's ability to satisfy some need.

National Institute for Occupational Safety and Health (NIOSH) (15)   The government agency that researches and sets OSHA standards.

National Labor Relations Board (17)   Established to administer and interpret the Wagner Act, the NLRB has primary responsibility for conducting union representation elections.

National/International Union (17)   A federation of local unions.

National Labor Relations Act (17)   Legislation giving employees the right to form and join unions and to engage in collective bargaining. (Also known as the Wagner Act.)

Negative Reinforcement (9)   An unpleasant reward.

NLRB v. *Bildisco & Bildisco* (17)   Upheld the premise that a company could file for bankruptcy to have a labor contract nullified.

Norms (8)   Tells group members what they ought or ought not do in certain circumstances.

Norris–LaGuardia Act (17)   Labor law act that set the stage for permitting individuals full freedom to designate a representative of their choosing to negotiate terms and conditions of employment.

Observation Method (5)   A job analysis technique in which data are gathered by watching employees work.

Occupational Safety and Health Act (15)   Set standards to ensure safe and healthful working conditions and provided stiff penalties for violators.

Office of Federal Contract Compliance Programs (3) The government office that administers the provisions of Executive Order 11246.

Omnibus Budget Reconciliation Act of 1990 (15)   Law that increased OSHA penalties from $10,000 to $70,000 for a severe, willful, and repetitive OSHA violation.

Open Shop (18)   Employees are free to choose whether or not to join the union, and those who do not are not required to pay union dues.

Operant Conditioning (9)   A type of conditioning in which behavior leads to a reward or prevents punishment.

Organizational Development (9)   The part of HRM that deals with facilitating systemwide change in the organization.

Organizational Goals (11)   Meeting company objectives.

Organizational Goal–Individual Goal Relationship (11)   The expectation that achieving organizational goals will lead to the attainment of individual goals.

Organizing (1)   A management function that deals with what jobs are to be done, by whom, where decisions are to be made, and the grouping of employees.

Orientation (8)   The activities involved in introducing new employees to the organization and their work units.

Outdoor Training (9)   Specialized training that occurs outdoors that focuses on building self-confidence and teamwork.

Outplacement (5)   A process whereby an organization assists employees, especially those being severed from the organization, in obtaining employment.

Paired Comparison (12)   Ranking individuals' performance by counting the number of times any one individual is the preferred member when compared with all other employees.

Participative Management (2)   A management concept giving employees more control over the day-to-day activities on their job.

Pay-for-performance (11)   Rewarding employees based on their performance.

Peer Evaluations (12)   A performance evaluation situation in which coworkers provide input into the employee's performance.

Peer Orientation (8)   Coworker assistance in orienting new employees.

Pension Benefit Guaranty Corporation (14)   The organization that lays claim to corporate assets to pay or fund inadequate pension programs.

Performance (11)   Effective and efficient work, which also considers personnel data such as measures of accidents, turnover, absence, and tardiness.

Performance Appraisal Process (12)   A formal process in an organization whereby each employee is evaluated to determine how he or she is performing.

Performance-based Rewards (13)   Rewards exemplified by the use of commissions, piecework pay plans, incentive systems, group bonuses, or other forms of merit pay.

Performance Simulation Tests (7)   Work sampling and assessment centers focusing on actual job activities.

Perquisites (13)   Attractive benefits, over and above a regular salary, granted to executives ("perks").

Physiological Symptoms (15)   Characteristics of stress that manifest themselves as increased heart and breathing rates, higher blood pressure, and headaches.

Piecework Plans (13)   A compensation plan whereby employees are typically paid for the number of units they actually produce.

Planning (1)   A management function focusing on setting organizational goals and objectives.

Plant Closing Bill (4)   Also known as WARN, requires employers to give sixty days' advanced notice of pending plant closings or major layoff.

Plant-wide Incentives (13)   An incentive system that rewards all members of the plant based on how well the entire group performed.

Plateauing (10)   A condition of stagnating in one's current job.

Point Method (13)   Breaking down jobs based on identifiable criteria and the degree to which these criteria exist on the job.

Polygraph Protection Act (4)   Prohibits the use of lie detectors in screening all job applicants. Often referred to as a "lie-detector" test.

Position Analysis Questionnaire (5)   A job analysis technique that rates jobs on 194 elements in six activity categories.

Positive Reinforcement (9)   Providing a pleasant response to an individual's actions.

Post-Training Performance Method (9)   Evaluating training programs based on how well employees can perform their jobs after they have received the training.

Pre–Post-Training Performance Method (9)   Evaluating training programs based the difference in performance before and after one receives training.

Pre–Post-Training Performance with Control Group (9)   Evaluating training by comparing pre- and post-training results with individuals who did not receive the training.

Prearrival Stage (8)   The socialization process stage that recognizes individuals arrive in an organization with a set of organizational values, attitudes, and expectations.

Predictive Validity (6)   Validating tests by using prospective applicants as the study group.

Preferred Provider Organizations (14)   Organization that requires using specific physicians and health-care facilities to contain the rising costs of health care.

Pregnancy Discrimination Act (3)   Law prohibiting discrimination based on pregnancy.

Privacy Act (4)   Requires federal government agencies to make available information in an individual's personnel file.

Professional Organizations (6)   A source of job applicants where placement facilities at regional conferences and national conferences usually occur.

Programmed Instruction (9)   Material is learned in a highly organized, logical sequence, that requires the individual to respond.

Protected Group Member (3)   Any individual who is afforded protection under employment discrimination laws.

Psychological Symptoms (15)   Characteristics of stress that manifest themselves as tension, anxiety, irritability, boredom, and procrastination.

Public Policy Violation (4)   Prohibiting the termination of an employee for refusing to obey an order the employee considered illegal.

Punishment (9)   Penalizing an employee for undesirable behaviors.

Railway Labor Act (17)   Provided the initial impetus to widespread collective bargaining.

Ranking Method (13)   Rating employees from highest to lowest.

Realistic Job Preview (7)   A selection device that allows job candidates to learn negative as well as positive information about the job and organization.

Reduced Work Hours (5) A downsizing concept whereby employees work fewer than forty hours and are paid accordingly.

Reengineering (2) Radical, quantum change in an organization.

Reject Errors (6) Rejecting candidates who would later perform successfully.

Relative Standards (12) Evaluating an employee's performance by comparing the employee with other employees.

Reliability (6) A selection device's consistency of measurement.

Repetitive Motion Disorder (15) Injuries sustained by continuous and repetitive movements of the hand.

Replacement Charts (5) HRM organizational charts indicating positions that may become vacant in the near future and the individuals who may fill the vacancy.

Representation Certification (17) The election process whereby union members vote in a union as their representative.

Representation Decertification (17) The election process whereby union members vote out their union as their representative.

Restricted Policy (3) An HRM policy that results in the exclusion of a class of individuals.

Reverse Discrimination (3) A claim made by white males that minority candidates are given preferential treatment in employment decisions.

Rightsizing (5) Linking employee needs to organizational strategy.

Roles (8) Behaviors that job incumbents are expected to display.

Scanlon Plan (13) An organization-wide incentive program focusing on cooperation between management and employees through sharing problems, goals, and ideas.

Scientific Management (1) A set of principles designed to enhance worker productivity.

Selection Process (6) The process of selecting the best candidate for the job.

Sexual Harassment (3) Anything of a sexual nature where it results in a condition of employment, an employment consequence, or creates a hostile or offensive environment.

Shared Services (1) Sharing HRM activities among geographically dispersed divisions.

Sick Building (15) An unhealthy work environment.

Similarity Error (12) Evaluating employees based on the way an evaluator perceives himself or herself.

Simulations (9) Any artificial environment that attempts to closely mirror an actual condition.

Situational Interview (7) Structured interview where questions relate directly to actual work activities.

Skill Deficiencies (2) The lacking of basic abilities to perform many of today's jobs.

Skill Variety (11) A situation in which jobs require a number of skills.

Smoke-free Environment (15) A work environment where smoking is significantly reduced or eliminated.

Smoke-Free Policies (15) Organization policies that reduce or prohibit smoking on company premises.

Social Security (14) Retirement, disability, and survivor benefits, paid by the government to aged, former members of the labor force, the disabled, or their survivors.

Social Learning Theory (9) Theory of learning that views learning occurring through observation and direct experience.

Socialization (8) A process of adaption that takes place as individuals attempt to learn the values and norms of work roles.

Span of Control (2) The number of employees a supervisor can effectively and efficiently direct.

Strategic Goals (5) Organization-wide goals setting direction for the next five to twenty years.

Strategic Human Resource Planning (5) The process of linking human resource planning efforts to the company's strategic direction.

Stress (15) A dynamic condition in which an individual is confronted with an opportunity, constraint, or demand related to what he or she desires and for which the outcome is perceived to be both uncertain and important.

Stress Interview (7) An interview designed to see how the applicants handle themselves under pressure.

Stressors (15) Something that causes stress in an individual.

Structured Interviews (7) An interview in which there are fixed questions that are presented to every applicant.

Structured Questionaire Method (5) A specifically designed questionaire on which employees rate tasks they perform on their jobs.

Succession Planning (5) An executive inventory report indicating which individuals are ready to move into higher positions in the company.

Suggestion Program (16) A process whereby employees have the opportunity to tell management how they perceive the organization is doing.

Summary Plan Description (14) An ERISA requirement of explaining to employees their pension program and rights.

Sunshine Laws (17) Laws that exist in some states that mandate that labor–management negotiations be open to the public.

Suspension (4) A period of time off from work as a result of a disciplinary process.

Taft–Hartley Act (17) See Labor–Management Relations Act.

Task Identity (11) A situation in which a worker completes all phases of a job.

Task Significance (11) A situation in which the employee has a substantial impact on the lives of other employees.

Team-Based Rewards (13)   Rewards based on how well the team performed.

Technical Conference Method (5)   A job analysis technique that involves extensive input from the employee's supervisor.

Temporary Employees (6)   Employees hired for a limited time to perform a specific job.

360-Degree Appraisal (12)   Performance appraisal process in which supervisors, peers, employees, customers, and the like evaluate the individual.

Title VII (3)   The most prominent piece of legislation regarding HRM, it states that it is illegal to discriminate against individuals based on race, religion, color, sex, or national origin.

Total Quality Management (2)   A continuous process improvement.

Transactional Analysis (9)   An approach for defining and analyzing communication interactions between people and a theory of personality.

Unemployment Compensation (14)   Program designed to provide employees with some income continuation during periods of involuntary unemployment.

Union (17)   Organization of workers, acting collectively, seeking to protect and promote their mutual interests through collective bargaining.

Union Avoidance (17)   A company tactic of providing to employees those things unions would provide without employees having to join the union.

Union Busting (17)   A company tactic designed to eliminate the union that represents the company's employees.

Union Security Arrangements (18)   Labor contract provisions designed to attract and retain dues-paying union members.

Union Shop (18)   Employers can hire nonunion workers, but they must become dues-paying members within a prescribed period of time.

Upward Appraisals (12)   An employee appraisal process whereby employees evaluate their supervisors.

Validity (6)   The proven relationship of a selection device to some relevant criterion.

Validity Generalization (6)   Statistically corrected test that is valid across many job categories.

Values (6)   Basic convictions about what is right or wrong, good or bad, desirable or not.

Vesting Rights (9)   The permanent right to pension benefits.

Virtual Reality (9)   A process whereby the work environment is simulated by sending messages to the brain.

Vocational Rehabilitation Act (3)   This act extended to the physically and mentally disabled the same protection afforded racial minorities and women.

Wage Curve (13)   The result of the plotting of points of established pay grades against wage base rates to identify the general pattern of wages and find individuals whose wages are out of line.

Wage Structure (13)   A pay scale showing ranges of pay within each grade.

Wage Surveys (13)   Used to gather factual data on pay practices among firms and companies within specific communities.

Wagner Act (17)   Also known as the National Labor Relations Act of 1935, this act gave employees the legitimate right to form and join unions and to engage in collective bargaining.

Walk-ins (6)   Unsolicited applicants.

Weighted Application Form (7)   A special type of application form where relevant applicant information is used to determine the likelihood of job success.

Wellness Program (15)   Organizational programs designed to keep employees healthy.

Whistle-blowing (4)   A situation in which an employee notifies authorities of wrongdoing in an organization.

Wildcat Strike (18)   An unauthorized and illegal strike that occurs during the terms of an existing contract.

Work-Force Diversity (2)   The varied personal characteristics that make the work force heterogeneous.

Work Sampling (7)   A selection device requiring the job applicant to actually perform a small segment of the job.

Work Sharing (7)   A work concept whereby two or more individuals share one full-time job with the remaining time spent on individual pursuits.

Work Teams (2)   Formal work groups made up of interdependent individuals who are responsible for attainment of a specific goal.

Worker Adjustment and Retraining Notification Act (4)   Federal law requiring employers to give sixty days' notice of pending plant closing or major layoff.

Workers' Compensation (14)   Payment to workers or their heirs for death or permanent or total disability that resulted from job-related activities.

Workplace Security (4)   A situation in which employers protect their property and trade business.

Written Tests (4)   An organizational selection tool designed to indicate whether an applicant will be successful on the job if hired.

Written Verbal Warning (7)   The first formal step in the disciplinary process.

Written Warning (4)   First formal step of the disciplinary process.

Yellow-dog Contract (17)   An agreement whereby employees state that they are not now, nor will they be in the future, union members.

Name Index

(Notations following names in the format [e.g. E2n17] indicate endnote page number 2, footnote 17. All others indicate text page reference.)

Organization Index

Subject Index

Photo Credits